**Current approaches
to religion in ancient Greece**
Papers presented at a symposium
at the Swedish Institute at Athens,
17–19 April 2008

Matthew Haysom & Jenny Wallensten (eds)

SKRIFTER UTGIVNA AV SVENSKA INSTITUTET I ATHEN, 8°, 21
ACTA INSTITUTI ATHENIENSIS REGNI SUECIAE, SERIES IN 8°, 21

Current approaches to religion in ancient Greece

Papers presented
at a symposium at the
Swedish Institute at Athens,
17–19 April 2008

Edited by Matthew Haysom
& Jenny Wallensten

STOCKHOLM 2011

SECRETARY'S ADDRESS:
Department of Archaeology and Ancient History
Box 626
SE-751 26 Uppsala, Sweden

EDITOR:
Dr Jenni Hjohlman, Stockholm
E-mail: jenni.hjohlman@antiken.su.se

DISTRIBUTOR:
eddy.se ab
Box 1310
SE-621 24 Visby, Sweden

For general information, see www.ecsi.se.
For prices, orders and delivery, see http://ecsi.bokorder.se

Published with the aid and of a grant from the The Royal Swedish Academy of Letters, History and Antiquities
The English text was revised by Dr Jonathan Tomlinson, Athens

ABSTRACT
In recent years Greek religion has emerged as one of the main topics for the study of ancient Greek society as a whole. This flourishing interest is certainly due to the recognition of the centrality of religion to Greek culture: religious beliefs and practices were connected to almost every aspect of the Greek world. This volume brings together fourteen contributions from a group of upcoming international scholars, presented at a conference held in the Swedish Institute at Athens and the British School at Athens in 2008. The papers take a wide range of approaches: archaeological, epigraphic, iconographical, philological and historical. They demonstrate the diversity of the subject, covering such issues as nineteenth-century historiography, cult epithets, the pantheon, regionalism, *polis* religion, the performance of ritual, the use of music in ritual, the accessibility of sacred space, and the visual aspects of dedications. The contributions bring new theoretical perspectives, seek to better understand ritual, and highlight the variety of Greek religion.

ISSN 0081-9921
ISBN 978-91-7916-059-3
© Svenska Institutet i Athen
Typeset in Sweden 2011 by eddy.se ab
Printed in Sweden 2011 by Elanders, Sverige AB, Vällingby

Table of contents

Preface

The organization of the symposium *Current Approaches to Religion in Ancient Greece* and the publication of the present symposium proceedings would not have been possible without the kind support and assistance of many individuals and institutions. We warmly thank Vetenskapsrådet (The Swedish Research Council), Kungliga Vitterhetsakademien (The Royal Swedish Academy of Letters, History and Antiquities) with Enbom's Donation Fund, and Föreningen Svenska Atheninstitutets vänner (The Association of the Friends of the Swedish Institute at Athens) for their generous financial support. The staff of the Swedish Institute at Athens and of the British School at Athens offered invaluable help; we would especially like to offer our gratitude to Mrs Bodil Nordström-Karydaki of the Swedish Institute, who kindly shared her experience during all stages of the planning, organization and realization of the symposium. We are furthermore most grateful to Professor Robert Parker, Oxford University, and Professor Catherine Morgan, Director of the British School at Athens, who provided an excellent framework for the event, the former through the stimulating Opening Lecture and the latter through her thoughtfully presented Closing Remarks.

We also wish to thank the authors for their important scientific contributions to the present volume and for their patience with the editorial process. Finally, we deeply thank Dr Maria Mili for inspirational discussions and endless assistance during the work with the final publication.

MATTHEW HAYSOM & JENNY WALLENSTEN
Cambridge & Athens, 2011

Introduction

In making general statements about a discipline one will necessarily stray from characterization to caricature. But it is not too much of a simplification to say that, in spite of a long recognition that religion impacted on all aspects of life, the study of ancient Greek religion has in the past tended to be heavily focused on the study of rituals or the study of gods. In both cases the goal of research swung between the discovery of the origin and interpretation of the function of the rituals or gods in question. Whether the end result was put in terms of structurally opposed pairs or primitive agricultural concerns, approaches to Greek religion shared a feeling that scholarship should take the form of puzzle solving. The common aim often seemed to be to arrive at meanings or truths that were in a sense hidden, obvious neither to a casual observer nor, in many cases, to the ancient Greeks themselves. This puzzle solving aspect of Greek religion studies also led to a tendency to search for single answers and monolithic underlying truths. It would be understandable, even today, for a non-specialist to view the study of Greek religion as consisting of confusing assemblages of divine epithets or detailed mythical and ritual variations selectively assembled to arrive at single core meanings.

For some time, however, the study of religion has been moving away from any such caricature. The field is now extremely diverse and the long acknowledgement of the pervasiveness of religion is better ingrained than ever before. Scholars are increasingly conscious of the lack of a clear division between the spheres of religion and politics, of most social groups being also worshiping groups, of the ritual contexts in which poetry was delivered, or of the sanctuary derivation of much of the material of traditional Classical Archaeology, to name but a few examples. Perhaps as a result, the study of religion has become more prominent in the broader field of Classical Studies.

The long series of conferences, seminars and publications on religious subjects which have appeared in the *Acta Instituti Atheniensis Regni Sueciae*, organized under the aegis of Robin Hägg and his various collaborators, have played an important role in the positive trends that the study of Greek religion has witnessed over the last decades. It was our, perhaps hubristic, aim to revive this tradition of conferences which led to the book in your hands. The lively intellectual environment in Athens, with its constant stream of young scholars coming through the Greek universities and the various foreign schools, encouraged us to make this first symposium as broad as possible and focused on the work of academics in the early stages of their careers. We were aware that breadth would bring with it the danger of disconnection. As an antidote, in our original planning for the symposium we laid out a series of themes which we hoped would help unify the widely ranging papers and provide connections that would facilitate discussion. This list necessarily curtailed, somewhat, the range of the symposium and it is due to it that some important subjects are missing from this volume. Most notable by their absence are studies of economy and cult, studies of magic and sectarian cults, and studies of the religious landscape. This is not because we believe these areas are unimportant or unconnected but simply because it was unrealistic to cover everything and we were more interested, in this first symposium, in looking at novel trends within the more traditional concerns of religious studies: festivals, gods and sanctuaries. Academics, like any group of independent and creative people, are impossible to direct. It comes as no surprise that the themes appearing in this book do not perfectly align with those we originally set out.

Some themes fell by the wayside, others receded into the background, while still others became more prominent than we would have imagined. But we think that the end result is a more honest and in some ways a more interesting reflection of current trends.

The concerns of several of the papers can be seen to be closely aligned with broader trends in Classical Studies as a whole. Michael Konaris' paper on Karl Otfried Müller's views on Apollo, for example, is part of that burgeoning interest in detailed historiography and reception studies that has appeared in recent years. Such studies are important, not only for the general history of the western intellectual tradition, but also for our assessment of new ideas and interpretations. As Konaris' paper shows, debates such as that between the primacy of myth and the primacy of ritual in interpretation can have long and convoluted histories and an appreciation of the historiography of even such commonly accepted ideas as the equation of Apollo with harmony, tranquillity and brightness can shed new light and raise important doubts. Athena Kavoulaki's paper, on the other hand, belongs in the context of the high critical awareness of the problem of emic and etic, ancient and modern categories that marks much of the best in modern research. She demonstrates how a close reading of the ancient uses and contexts of even familiar terms and categories can give new insights into their meaning and significance. The influence of the recent emphasis on breaking interdisciplinary boundaries can be seen in almost all the papers. Matthew Haysom, for example, crosses the gulf between prehistory and history in his attempt to recast the kinds of question that are asked about the long term development of religion between the Bronze Age and the Classical period on Crete. An openness to theoretical debate in the social sciences beyond the traditional neighbours of Classical Studies, and a willingness to mobilize these debates for the understanding of Classical material, is perhaps one of the most distinctive trends of recent years. This openness is visible in many of the papers. Oliver Pilz explores the limitations of various discussions of ritual through Greek examples and mobilizes performance theory as a tool with which to understand Greek festivals. Petra Pakkanen uses a range of theoretical approaches to religion to explore the interplay along the axis between public and private, sacred and secular, and individual and corporate in her interpretation of some of the activities occurring at the sanctuary of Poseidon at Kalaureia. Katerina Kolotourou, meanwhile, takes the insights of musicology to give new perspectives on the use of percussion in ritual. She demonstrates its importance, ever-presence and variety and shows the relationships between the experience of percussion, its symbolism and cosmological significance. The result moves far away from the simple equation of percussion and ecstasy in Greek cult that one so often sees.

As might be expected of a conference organized in Athens, with its bustling archaeological community, the archaeological object sat at the centre of many of the papers but an intriguingly diverse set of approaches were taken to it. Nassos Papalexandrou's approach to objects addresses the question of historically contingent visuality in the setting of early Greece. He mobilizes literary sources to understand the ancient responses to material culture and through this he illuminates the religious experience of viewing votives in sanctuaries. Christina Mitsopoulou takes a contextual approach to the understanding of a particular type of cult vase. She builds an interpretation of it based on its discovery in a limited number of sanctuaries and on its associations in a range of iconography. Her study demonstrates how this kind of contextually based study can add new dimensions even to such well studied rites as the cult at Eleusis. Clarisse Prêtre, on the other hand, underlines the importance of reading epigraphic documents in their archaeological context. She shows once again the necessity of bridging the gap between words and objects, a theoretical *sine qua non* that yet has to become commonplace in practice.

One of the most influential models of recent years in the study of Greek religion has been the *polis* religion model as outlined by Christiane Sourvinou-Inwood. Its effect can be felt through several of the papers. Petra Pakkanen, for example, is inspired by the debates circulating this model in her discussion of public and private concerns in the phenomena of *asylia*, and group dining on Poros. Matthew Haysom sees the details of *polis* religion as a particularly Greek phenomenon, the appearance of which across a regionally fragmented Aegean requires explanation. Alexander Herda explores the articulation of the *polis* through the twin cults of Apollo Delphinios and Apollo Didymeus, investigating the ritual complex of the festival and its relationships to the groups involved, to the topography of the city and to colonization.

Three of our papers dealt with the problem of the Greek gods and how we should understand them within a pantheon and a politi-cally fragmented world. As one can appreciate from Michael Konaris' paper this is the foundational debate of Greek religious studies. Maria Mili, inspired by Sourvinou-Inwood's emphasis on the local basis of Greek religion and, therefore, the locally differentiated nature of divine personalities, explores through literary, archaeological and epigraphic evidence the cult of Apollo Kerdoos, a cult so far attested only in Thessalian *poleis*. She untangles the complex of relationships between epithet and function and situates these within the local milieu. Jenny Wallensten contributes to our understanding of the dynamics of a pantheon by exploring the phenomenon of the pairing of gods in cult, something generally explained in terms of function. Through her study of the inscribed dedications—one of our most direct sources for the worshippers—she investigates the degree to which mythological relations or cult functions led to the pairing of Apollo and Artemis.

Probably the biggest single theme to emerge from the symposium is an emphasis on the moment, the experience of the participant in cult. Nassos Papalexandrou's paper, for example, shows how a consideration of the worshipper's experience of viewing objects can shed new light on such important themes as the explosion in imagery at the end of the Iron Age and the question of the Orientalizing period. Ioannis Mylonopoulos struggles with the only partially preserved evidence for barriers in temples. He emphasizes their importance for the perception, and thus the understanding, of the symbolic meanings within temples. He explores and interweaves cultic, aesthetic and practical considerations in the explanation of this phenomenon, drawing out questions of accessibility and the everyday versus the festival use of temples. Michael Scott's paper dealing with inscribed inventory lists also tackles questions of functionality versus symbolism, accessibility and viewing. His concentration is on how the lists would have or were aiming to be perceived. He shows that there could be multiple facets to their use, allowing, for example, views of treasures in otherwise inaccessible parts of the sanctuary or being used by communities to cement their relationship to the sanctuary and to define themselves in opposition to others. In his application of performance theory to his case study of the Oschophoria festival Oliver Pilz emphasizes the ritual as re-enactment, the personal experience of the participants and their identification with mythic protagonists over previous interpretations, which see the festival as an agricultural or initiation rite. Indeed, if there is something that ties all the papers together it is the feeling that the truths of ancient Greek religion are more immediate than are portrayed in some of the traditional approaches to the subject. The various approaches contained in this volume all point to the need for investigating perceptions, attitudes, actions and interrelations of the worshippers rather than forgotten origins or underlying structures. This is, perhaps, a reflection of an appreciation that Greek religion did not exist as a set of core constants separate from the worshippers but only existed within their minds as a set of messily diverse but interrelating conceptions and perceptions. It is this immediacy, this concentration on the worshipper and on their social and mental world that may be the distinctive mark of modern studies in religion.

MATTHEW HAYSOM & JENNY WALLENSTEN
Cambridge & Athens, 2011

MICHAEL KONARIS

Apollo in nineteenth-century scholarship
THE CASE OF KARL OTFRIED MÜLLER

Abstract

Dionysos has been at the centre of attention in modern scholarship. For the greater part of the nineteenth century, by contrast, the focus of scholarly attention was largely directed towards Apollo. This paper examines a seminal treatment of Apollo in nineteenth-century scholarship, namely K.O. Müller's theory of a Dorian Apollo as it appears in his *Die Dorier* (1824) against the cultural and religious background of the period. It investigates what was at stake in the debate over the origins and nature of Apollo between K.O. Müller and fellow scholars of his like Creuzer. It further assesses the impact of K.O. Müller's portrayal of Apollo on later scholarship including the part it played in inducing a reaction in favour of Dionysos towards the end of the nineteenth century.

Dionysos has attracted unrivalled attention in the scholarship of the twentieth and twenty-first centuries.[1] For the greater part of the nineteenth century, by contrast, the focus of scholarly attention was largely claimed by another god, Apollo.[2] K.O. Müller (1797–1840) played an instrumental role in bringing about this era of Apolline pre-eminence. In his *Die Dorier* (1824) he gave powerful expression to a Winckelmannian view of Apollo as god of tranquillity, clarity and harmony which would captivate scholars for decades until the resurgence in the foreground of his brother and *Gegenbild*, Dionysos, towards the end of the nineteenth century.

"Historien et critique, géographe et ethnographe, archéologue et mythologue, éditeur et professeur", Müller was, in the words of his French translator K. Hillebrand, "le plus universel des philologues allemands" of the first half of the nineteenth century.[3] In the field of Greek religion Müller stands out as the leading exponent of the "historical-critical" approach, which through his followers, H.D. Müller (1819–1893) and E. Curtius (1814–1896), reached into the 1890s. The historical-critical approach was based on the premise that the Greek pantheon had been the end-product of a long process of historical development. Looking back at the course of the discipline from the vantage-point of 1894 Curtius maintained that the historical perspective of Müller formed part of a broader trend in the first decades of the nineteenth century according to which, the objects of historical study should

---

[1]   Henrichs 1984, 240; Bremmer 1994, 19.
[2]   For a history of the modern fascination with Apollo since the Renaissance, see Heissmeyer 1967. For Winckelmann's adoration of Apollo Belvedere, see also Reschke 2009. Another favourite god in the 19th century was Zeus, see Konaris, forthcoming.

[3]   Hillebrand 1866, xxvii. For biographical information on K.O. Müller, see E. Müller 1847. For a groundbreaking analysis of Müller's work and its reception, see Calder & Schlesier 1998.

be approached in terms of their historical development. He cited Müller and Niebuhr as its two main representatives in Greek and Roman historiography respectively.[4] In particular, Müller regarded Greek polytheism as the historical result of the gradual unification of the worships of the various Greek communities and, especially, of the Greek tribes. In his view, its apparent uniformity was to be attributed to the later impact of sanctuaries of Panhellenic influence like Delphi and of epic poetry.[5] As a consequence, Müller placed emphasis on the examination of Greek tribal worships. According to Dilthey, the notion of a tribal approach to Greek history was not original to Müller.[6] However, it was with his work that the tribal divisions of the Greeks came to the foreground in Greek historiography.[7]

Müller intended to write a comprehensive history of Greece, the *Geschichten Hellenischer Stämme und Städte*. This ambitious project in the event remained incomplete. Müller did produce, however, such studies as on the Minyans of Orchomenos (1820) and on the Dorians. The latter consisted of a broad examination of Dorian history ranging from the areas of political institutions and law to art to religion.

In his account of Dorian religion Müller accorded a central place to Apollo.[8] At the beginning of his treatment of Apollo Müller set out to refute the view that Apollo had been a god of the indigenous Pelasgian population of Greece or that his worship had been introduced to Greece from the East, as had been argued, for example, by Creuzer in his *Symbolik und Mythologie der alten Völker, besonders der Griechen* (1810–1812). Müller maintained that the dominant position of Apollo in all Do-

rian areas and the allegedly Dorian origins of every major institution of his worship conclusively established that he had been a genuinely Greek god and, in particular, by origin Dorian. According to Müller, Apollo's worship had spread into the Greek world with the expansion of Dorian settlements.[9]

Müller's claim that Apollo had by origin been a Greek god may be seen as representative of the broader thrust in his work in support of the "national autonomy" of Greek culture. From the realm of religion to the sciences and the arts, he mounted a sustained attack against a conventional view in earlier historiography, namely that the younger civilization of Greece had been largely derivative from the older civilizations of the Near East.[10] In *Black Athena* Bernal argued that this subversion of historiographical orthodoxy should be understood in terms of rampant racism against the peoples of Asia and Africa.[11] In her article 'Proof and persuasion in *Black Athena*: the case of K.O. Müller' Blok maintained that Bernal failed to demonstrate that Müller had been motivated by racism.[12] An examination of the grounds on which Müller defended the "national autonomy" of Greek religion can contribute evidence to the issue.

Müller reacted to the view that Greek myths and worships derived virtually in their entirety from the East, a view in currency in the mythological writings of the early nineteenth century.[13] According to Müller, Greek religion was to be studied primarily in the context of Greek geography and history. In taking this approach, he appears to have been under the influence of the Herderian notion that each *Volk* tended to develop their own distinct culture in

---

[4] Curtius 1894, iii–iv. On Niebuhr and Müller, see Walther 1998.
[5] K.O. Müller 1825, 241.
[6] Dilthey 1898, 19.
[7] See Wilamowitz-Moellendorff 1921, 57–58.
[8] K.O. Müller 1824, 199.

[9] K.O. Müller 1824, 199–201.
[10] See his letter to Böckh of 28 March 1819 in Böckh 1883, 33.
[11] Bernal 1987, 2, 33.
[12] Blok 1996, 707, 713, 715–717.
[13] K.O. Müller 1840a, 98; H.D. Müller 1857, 116.

relation to their geographic and climatic conditions mediated by his teacher at Berlin, K.F. Solger (1780–1819).[14] Müller asserted that in objecting to theories which derived Greek religion from the East his purpose was not to dismiss the question of foreign influences on Greek religion altogether; but rather to transpose it from the level of speculation to the level of proof and, conversely, to point to the significance of studying Greek myths and worships in their local contexts.[15] Müller's correspondence casts further light on the grounds of his opposition to the derivation of Greek religion from abroad and, especially, from Egypt. In a letter of 1831 he maintained by way of comment on the work of Champollion that recent discoveries made the Egyptian pantheon appear more dissimilar to the Greek than previously thought.[16]

However, in his early "Ueber den angeblich ägyptischen Ursprung der griechischen Kunst" (1820) Müller also characterized the Egyptians as weak and cowardly and asserted that the Greeks were superior to them in intellectual power as nobler races tended to be.[17] It is significant that Müller's case for the defence of the autonomy of Greek culture against earlier paradigms of derivation from the East was largely presented in methodological terms. However, at least in his "Ueber den angeblich ägyptischen Ursprung der griechischen Kunst" a racist attitude comes to the fore.

In his account of Apollo Müller further argued emphatically against what had become a prevalent view in the scholarship of the period, namely the ancient view that Apollo

had been a sun-god.[18] In a diptych devoted to an examination of Müller's intellectual and scholarly profile Blok has suggested that the question of Müller's position in the context of contemporary scholarship and especially in the context of the debate between "rationalist" and "romantic" scholars surrounding Creuzer's *Symbolik* should be revisited. In her view, there has been a tendency to overestimate Müller's links to the rationalist approach of J.H. Voss (1751–1826) and C.A. Lobeck (1781–1860) and, conversely, his distance from the romantic scholarship of Creuzer. Blok has argued that Müller had been strongly influenced by mystic and romantic elements in German Pietism that "prevented his unambiguous siding with rationalism" and that "his views belonged as much to 'romantisch-theologische Spekulation' as to 'rationale Wissenschaft'".[19] She has further maintained that there were substantial similarities between Creuzer and Müller such as in terms of their views on the origin of the religious feeling and their romantic receptivity to the experience of nature.[20]

I would like to suggest that Müller's opposition to the interpretation of Apollo as a sun-god in addition to his opposition to the theory that Apollo had been of Eastern origins provides a means of situating him against the background of the scholarship of the period. In a letter to L. Schorn, Müller stated that in disputing that Apollo was a sun-god, he was reacting, in particular, against Creuzer's account of Apollo.[21] In his *Symbolik* the latter had advanced the view that the worship of Apollo had

---

[14] Gruppe 1921, 153. On Herder's influence on Müller, see also Feldman & Richardson 1972, 416 and Hall 1997, 7–8.
[15] K.O. Müller 1840a, 98.
[16] Letter to P.W. Forchhammer of 9 June 1831, n. 116, in Reiter 1950, 153–154. On Müller's interest in Egyptian religion, see Blok 1996, 705–706.
[17] K.O. Müller 1820, 536. Contrast Blok 1996, 718–719.

[18] K.O. Müller 1824, vol. II, 284–290.
[19] Blok 1998, 57–59, 94, "Müller's mythopoetic soul was still too mystical for the current 'wissenschaftliche' philology" (Blok 1998, 94). The ambivalence surrounding Müller's position is drawn attention to in the title of Calder & Schlesier 1998, *Zwischen Rationalismus und Romantik: Karl Otfried Müller und die antike Kultur*.
[20] Blok 1994, 37, 41–42; Blok 1998, 84, 93.
[21] K.O. Müller to L. Schorn, letter of mid January 1821, n. 13, in Reiter 1910, 344. Contrast Solomon

its origins in Asian fire- and sun-worship.[22] In this context it should be noted that Voss as well had launched an attack on Heyne's portrayal of Apollo as a sun-god and that Creuzer had challenged him into a debate regarding the solar nature of Apollo.[23] The clash over the interpretation of Apollo between Müller and Creuzer can be seen as a continuation of the clash between Voss and Heyne and Creuzer and is indicative of broad differences in their conception of Greek religion and their attitudes towards nature-worship and mysticism.[24]

Müller's argumentation against the view that Apollo was a sun-god suggests a prioritization of evidence from cult over myth. Thus he asserted that there were no signs of what he regarded as hallmark traits of the worship of nature gods in the worship of Apollo, namely a worship of powers of procreation. He stressed that, in contrast to nature gods, Apollo was not conceived as an offspring-producing god but rather as an unmarried youth. In his view, the stories about Apollo's paramours and progeny were confined to literature and had no bearing on the conception of him in cult.[25] In addition, Müller argued that Apollo's association with agriculture was fundamentally to be understood in the light of his function as an apotropaic god rather than in solar terms, as a reflection of the importance of the sun for the growth of vegetation. Müller maintained further that the worship of Helios as attested in places such as Corinth, Attica or Rhodes bore essentially no relation to the worship of Apollo. His conclusion was that Apollo came to be identified with the sun only when philosophers started to reinterpret the gods of traditional religion in terms of natural elements.[26]

Müller's view that Apollo was not by origin a sun-god constitutes the most conspicuous example of his broader thesis that the Olympian gods of the historical period were not, or had ceased to be, nature gods and were rather to be seen as ideal representations of human characteristics and activities.[27]

It should be emphasized that Müller's opposition to the interpretation of Apollo as a sun-god and to the interpretation of the Olympian gods as nature gods more broadly ranged beyond the level of methodological objections. This manner of interpretation of the Greek gods conflicted with his idealized conception of the Greeks and especially of the Dorians.[28] In Müller's writings the Dorians appear as a people outstanding for their heroism and their devotion to clarity, beauty and harmony in all aspects of life even in the field of battle.[29] His portrayal of the Dorians, and not least the celebration of their warlike *ethos*, has given rise to the suggestion that he viewed them as "the Prussians of antiquity".[30] As for Voss, for Müller the worship of nature gods as typically encountered in the religions of "Oriental" peoples like the Syrians involved emotions of joy and sorrow of cataclysmic intensity that ultimately produced a dampening effect on the mind and mysticism.[31] Müller's attitude to-

---

1994, xi, who associates Müller's criticism of the solar interpretation of Apollo with Louis XIV, the Sun King.

[22] Creuzer 1811, vol. II, 132–133, 152–155.

[23] Voss 1794, vol. II, 331–334; Voss 1824, 17.

[24] At the same time it should be observed that Müller also expressed scathing disapproval of "rationalist" approaches to Greek religion: letter to Elvers of 7 July 1830 in Kern 1936, 123–124. See also n. 37.

[25] K.O. Müller 1824, vol. II, 290.

[26] K.O. Müller 1824, vol. II, 286–288.

[27] K.O. Müller 1838, 237.

[28] Compare "Dorians sound more like self-respecting Teutons than Greek pagans. Sunlit nature-worship could never, he [Müller] believed, have led to their manly achievements" and "Müller cannot stomach the notion that his clean-living and soldierly Dorians were simply worshipping an elemental or generative force of nature" (Birch 1989, 115–116).

[29] K.O. Müller 1820, 533.

[30] Momigliano 1984, 899. See also Will 1956, 11–12.

[31] K.O. Müller 1841, 21–22; K.O. Müller 1824, vol. II, 409–410. On Müller's association of the worship of nature deities with mysticism and orgiasm, see Schlesier 1998, 404–406.

wards mysticism varies in his writings. In *Die Dorier* he associated mysticism with the notion of the incomprehensibility of God, with a lack of formal clarity and with states of mental and emotional excitement that bordered on morbidity. As such, he regarded it as unbefitting of the Dorians.[32] Accordingly, Müller stressed that mysticism was alien to the worship of Apollo. In his eyes, in contrast to the mystical worships of nature gods, Apollo's worship displayed a tendency to brightness and clarity and an abhorrence of formlessness. Epitomizing the best aspects of Dorian culture it promoted tranquillity and harmony.[33] The representation of the god in art attested further to these core Apolline qualities.[34] Müller maintained that, to the extent that elements of emotional instability and excess manifested themselves in Greek religion, these had no place in Apolline worship but were chiefly associated with the worship of Dionysos. In contrast to Apollo, Müller regarded the latter as a nature god of Thracian origins.[35]

Müller's emphatic dissociation of Apolline worship from mysticism should be seen against the background of the negative connotations that mysticism came to acquire in German classical scholarship with the discrediting of

Creuzer's *Symbolik*. In his *Antisymbolik* (1824) Voss attacked Creuzer's work in the name of the rational Protestantism of the Enlightenment, portraying it as a specimen of a growing epidemic of papal mysticism.[36] Müller himself in his first year at Göttingen had had to be cautious lest he was considered by the rationalist circles prevalent there as a promoter of superstition or mysticism because he did not adhere to their view that the religions of antiquity were devoid of any genuine religious content and were to be seen in terms of priestly deception.[37] It would appear that rationalist German scholars like Voss and G. Hermann (1772–1848) tended to level the term "mystic" as a reproach against scholars whose views of Greek religion did not conform with their own. In his *Philologie, Histoire, Philosophie de l'Histoire* Bravo cites a revealing letter of Müller's teacher, A. Böckh (1785–1867). In a letter of 1825 Böckh stated that the followers of Hermann detected mysticism everywhere and were keen on promoting enlightenment.[38] Müller's celebration of the moderation and clarity of Apolline worship and, by the same token, his stress on its anti-mystical character can, therefore, be seen in terms of a response to the allegations of Creuzerian mysticism that threatened to surround him at the beginning of his career.

In spite of Müller's reputation, key aspects of his portrayal of Apollo failed to gain broader acceptance in nineteenth-century scholarship. The theory that Apollo had been by origin a Dorian god was rejected even by scholars who placed themselves in his tradition like Curtius.[39] In addition, the interpretation of Apollo as a sun-god, without necessarily having the associations with mysticism it had had for Voss and Müller, remained predominant in nineteenth-century

---

[32] K.O. Müller 1824, vol. II, 284, 406, 409–410. Compare K.O. Müller 1840b, 290.
[33] K.O. Müller 1824, vol. II, 341, 343; K.O. Müller 1824, vol. IV, 399.
[34] K.O. Müller 1824, vol. II, 356.
[35] K.O. Müller 1824, vol. II, 290. For an analysis of Müller's view of Dionysos, see Schlesier 1998. In particular for the contrast between Apollo and Dionysos and the broader contrast between Olympian and Chthonian gods and its significance in Müller's work, see Schlesier 1998, 400–401 and Schlesier 1994, 23. See also Baeumer 1977, 146. The notion of a sharp contrast between the two gods was by no means uncontested in the scholarship of the period, perhaps most powerfully by Preller 1854, 172. For an examination of the relationship between Apollo and Dionysos in nineteenth-century scholarship before Nietzsche, see Vogel 1966, 67; Baeumer 1977, 146–153; Losemann 1998, 320–321.

[36] Voss 1824, 383.
[37] Letter n. 39 in Kern & Kern 1908, 54–55.
[38] Bravo 1968, 85–86.
[39] The hypothesis of a Dorian Apollo has been revived by Burkert 1975.

scholarship. In 1873 W.H. Roscher (1845–1923) could assert that it was a generally accepted hypothesis.[40] As late as 1907 Farnell claimed that "the solar theory, which ruled so much of the nineteenth-century speculation on ancient polytheism, still dazzles many people's eyes".[41]

However, this should not obscure the historical significance of Müller's account of Apollo. The vocabulary of tranquillity, brightness, simplicity and harmony recurring in it reproduced the Winckelmannian conception of Greek culture and resonated with the values of *Moralprotestantismus* with its emphasis on emotional restraint and anti-mystical ethos.[42] Largely because of the writings of Müller, the interest in the figure of Osiris-Bacchus visible in the works of the late eighteenth and the early nineteenth century such as C. Dupuis' *Origine de tous les cultes* (1795) and Creuzer's *Symbolik* would give way for much of the remainder of the nineteenth century to a focus on Apollo.[43]

Heir to Müller's Apollo was arguably the Apollo of Curtius, a student and successor of Müller at Göttingen. Curtius deviated from his teacher in holding that the origins of Apollo went back to the Near East. However, he placed the greatest emphasis on the development of his worship in Greece in the Archaic and Classical periods. In his eyes, it marked one of the most important moments in the history of Greek cul-

ture. In his *Griechische Geschichte* (vol. 1, 1857) he celebrated, in particular, Apollo at Delphi as the most sublime figure of the Greek pantheon.[44] Curtius portrayed Apollo, the son and prophet of Zeus, in Christianizing terms as a force standing for order and monotheism within Greek polytheism.[45] He maintained further that with Apollo's purification of Orestes a world of higher harmony and mercy was established. In his eyes, Delphi exercised a pervasive, beneficial influence over every aspect of Greek culture, promoting the ideals of moderation, restraint of sensuality, clarity and sobriety prescribed by the Pythian god.[46] This portrayal of Apollo in what would become one of the most widely-read histories of Greece in the German-speaking world in the course of the second half of the nineteenth century can be seen as symbolic of an era's conception of Greek religion, even of Greek culture as a whole. To Curtius himself the Greeks were, revealingly, the *apollonian people*.[47]

In a letter to Nietzsche of 1871 the young Rohde would dismissively refer to Curtius' Apollo as the "enlightened Apollo of Göttingen". In his view, the latter stood for a superficial, rationalistic understanding of Greek culture that failed to do justice to its complexity. Rohde would argue for the need to recognize the importance of Dionysos as well.[48] Through the writings of Nietzsche, Rohde himself and Harrison a reaction would eventually set in whereby Dionysos would replace Apollo in the foreground of scholarship and a new vision of Greece emphasizing ecstasy and irrationality over order and clarity would establish itself. Yet if Müller's and Curtius' conception of Apollo,

---

[40] Roscher 1873, 16. For Roscher's account of Apollo see Versnel 1985–1986 and Konaris 2010, 483–487.
[41] Farnell 1907, 136. For restatements of the case for a solar Apollo in twentieth-century scholarship, see Boyancé 1966 and Moreau 1996.
[42] Hermelink 1951, 341; Nipperdey 1988, 77. For Müller as being in the idealizing tradition of German classicism, see also Bleicken 1989, 109.
[43] For the alternating interest between Apollo and Dionysos in the 19th century, see Aurnhammer & Pittrof 2002. See also Konaris forthcoming. According to Andler, Müller's account of Apollo influenced Nietzsche's portrayal of Apollo in *Die Geburt der Tragödie*: Andler 1934, vol. II, 244–253. However, it should be noted that in *Die Geburt der Tragödie* Apollo appears as a sun-god: Nietzsche 1872, 27.

[44] Curtius 1857, 47–48.
[45] Curtius 1857, 400. Compare Curtius 1882, 3.
[46] Curtius 1857, 48, 400–401.
[47] Curtius 1856, 3.
[48] Quoted in Crusius 1902, 55. Rohde appears slightly unfair to Curtius in that the latter had attached importance to the rapprochement between Apollo and Dionysos at Delphi: Curtius 1857, 446–447.

and with it their conception of Greek religion, was subjected to a powerful challenge and dethroned, it was not eclipsed. Its impact reached deep into the twentieth century resonating in the work of Farnell, of Wilamowitz and arguably even of Nilsson.[49]

MICHAEL KONARIS
m.konaris@gmail.com

---

[49]   In his account of Apollo in *The cults of the Greek states* Farnell stated that "currents of mystic speculation, coming partly from the East, and bringing new problems concerning the providence of the world and the destiny of the soul, scarcely touched and in no way transformed the personality of Apollo. A Panhellenic god, he survived almost down to the close of paganism as a brilliant and clearly-outlined figure of the genuinely national religion" (Farnell 1907, 98). The dissociation of Apollo from "Oriental" mysticism, the notion that his was a "brilliant and clearly-outlined" conception and that he belonged to the "genuinely national religion", all these points appear to be in the tradition of Müller's portrayal of Apollo. In his 1908 lecture on Apollo, Wilamowitz objected to the view that Apollo was a solar god, dissociated Apollo from mysticism, placed emphasis on the importance of Delphi and famously suggested that Apollo had been of Lycian origins: Wilamowitz-Moellendorff 1908, 28, 31–32, 36, 42. In these respects Wilamowitz's account of Apollo is reminiscent of Curtius'. However, for Wilamowitz Apollo was not typical of Greek religion: see Fowler 2009, 188–193. Nilsson's closing paragraph on Apollo in his *Geschichte der griechischen Religion* also recalls Curtius: "so ist Apollon zum dem griechischsten aller Götter geworden, dem lichtstrahlenden und hehren Jüngling, dem Beschützer ... des Masses und der sinnvollen Ordnung. Die Veredelung des alten kleinasiatischen Gottes und seine Erhebung zum Ausdruck des echten Griechentums ist eine der grössten Geistestaten des griechischen Volkes" (Nilsson 1955, 564).

Bibliography

Andler 1934   C. Andler, *Nietzsche, sa vie et sa pensée* vol. II, Paris 1934.

Aurnhammer & Pittrof 2002   *"Mehr Dionysos als Apoll". Antiklassizistische Antike-Rezeption um 1900*, eds. A. Aurnhammer & T. Pittrof, Frankfurt am Main 2002.

Baeumer 1977   M.L. Baeumer, 'Das moderne Phänomen des Dionysischen und seine "Entdeckung" durch Nietzsche', *Nietzsche Studien* 6, 1977, 123–153.

Bernal 1987   M. Bernal, *Black Athena. The Afroasiatic roots of Classical civilization*, London 1987.

Birch 1989   D. Birch, '"The Sun is God": Ruskin's solar mythology', in *The sun is god: painting, literature and mythology in the 19th century*, ed. J.B. Bullen, Oxford 1989, 109–123.

Bleicken 1989   J. Bleicken, 'Die Herausbildung der alten Geschichte in Göttingen: von Heyne bis Busolt', in *Die klassische Altertumswissenschaft an der Georg-August-Universität Göttingen*, ed. C.J. Classen, Göttingen 1989, 98–127.

Blok 1994   J.H. Blok, 'Quests for a scientific mythology. F. Creuzer and K.O. Müller on history and myth', in *Proof and persuasion in history* (= *History and Theory*, theme issue, 33) 1994, 26–52.

Blok 1996   J.H. Blok, 'Proof and persuasion in *Black Athena*: The case of K.O. Müller', *Journal of the history of ideas* 57, 1996, 705–724.

Blok 1998   J.H. Blok, '"Romantische Poesie, Naturphilosophie, Construktion der Geschichte": K.O. Müller's understanding of history and myth', in Calder & Schlesier 1998, 55–97.

Böckh 1883   A. Böckh, *Briefwechsel zwischen August Böckh und Karl Otfried Müller*, Leipzig 1883.

Boyancé 1966   P. Boyancé, 'L' Apollon solaire', in *Mélanges d'archéologie, d'épigraphie et d'histoire offerts à Jérôme Carcopino*, ed. J. Carcopino, Paris 1966, 149–170.

Bravo 1968   B. Bravo, *Philologie, Histoire, Philosophie de l'Histoire*, Wroclaw 1968.

Bremmer 1994   J.N. Bremmer, *Greek religion*, Oxford 1994.

Burkert 1975   W. Burkert, 'Apellai und Apollon', *RhM* 118, 1975, 1–21.

Calder & Schlesier 1998   *Zwischen Rationalismus und Romantik: Karl Otfried Müller und die antike Kultur*, eds. W.M. Calder III & R. Schlesier, Hildesheim 1998.

Christ 1999   K. Christ, *Hellas: Griechische Geschichte und deutsche Geschichtswissenschaft*, München 1999.

Creuzer 1811   G.F. Creuzer, *Symbolik und Mythologie der alten Völker, besonders der Griechen* vol. II, Leipzig 1811.

Crusius 1902   O. Crusius, *Erwin Rohde: ein biographischer Versuch*, Tübingen & Leipzig 1902.

Curtius 1856   E. Curtius, 'Der Wettkampf' (1856), in E. Curtius, *Göttinger Festreden*, Berlin 1864, 1–22.

Curtius 1857   E. Curtius, *Griechische Geschichte* vol. I, Berlin 1857.

Curtius 1882   E. Curtius, 'Die Hellenen und das Volk Israel', in *Alterthum und Gegenwart. Gesammelte Reden und Vorträge* vol. II, Berlin 1882, 1–14.

Curtius 1894   E. Curtius, *Gesammelte Abhandlungen* II, Berlin 1894.

Dilthey 1898   K. Dilthey, *Otfried Müller*, Göttingen 1898.

Farnell 1907   L.R. Farnell, *The cults of the Greek states* vol. IV, Oxford 1907.

Feldman & Richardson 1972   *The rise of modern mythology 1680–1860*, eds. B. Feldman & R.D. Richardson, Bloomington 1972.

Fowler 2009   R.L. Fowler, 'Blood for the ghosts: Wilamowitz in Oxford', *Syllecta Classica* 20, 2009, 171–213.

Gruppe 1921   O. Gruppe, *Geschichte der klassischen Mythologie und Religionsgeschichte während des Mittelalters im Abendland und während der Neuzeit*, Leipzig 1921.

Hall 1997   J. Hall, *Ethnic identity in Greek antiquity*, Cambridge 1997.

Heissmeyer 1967   A. Heissmeyer, *Apoll und der Apollonkult seit der Renaissance*, Tübingen 1967.

Henrichs 1984   A. Henrichs, 'Loss of self, violence, suffering: the modern view of Dionysus from Nietzsche to Girard', *HSCP* 88, 1984, 205–240.

Hermelink 1951   H. Hermelink, *Das Christentum in der Menschengeschichte* vol. I, Tübingen & Stuttgart 1951.

Hillebrand 1886 — K. Hillebrand, *Histoire de la literature grecque jusqu' à Alexandre le grand par Otfried Müller*, Paris 1866.

Kern & Kern 1908 — O. Kern & E. Kern, *Carl Otfried Müller: Lebensbild in Briefen an seine Eltern mit dem Tagebuch seiner italienisch-griechischen Reise*, Berlin 1908.

Kern 1936 — O. Kern, *Briefwechsel von Carl Otfried Müller*, Göttingen 1936.

Konaris 2010 — M. Konaris, 'The Greek gods in late nineteenth- and early twentieth-century German and British scholarship', in *The Gods of Ancient Greece. Identities and Transformations*, eds. J.N. Bremmer & A. Erskine, Edinburgh 2010, 483–503.

Konaris forthcoming — M. Konaris, 'Dionysos in nine-teenth-century scholarship', in *A different god? Dionysos and ancient polytheism*, ed. R. Schlesier, forthcoming.

Losemann 1998 — V. Losemann, '*Die Dorier* im Deutschland der dreissiger und vierziger Jahre', in Calder & Schlesier 1998, 313–348.

Momigliano 1984 — A. Momigliano, 'Premesse per una discussione su K.O. Mül-ler', *AnnPisa* 14, no. 3, 1984, 895–909.

Moreau 1996 — A. Moreau, 'Quant Apollo devint soleil', in *Les Astres* vol. I, eds. B. Bakhouche, A. Moreau & J-C. Turpin, Montpellier 1996, 11–35.

E. Müller 1847 — E. Müller, 'Biographische Erinnerungen an Karl Otfried Müller', in K.O. Müller 1847, vol. I, VII–LXXVI.

H.D. Müller 1857 — H.D. Müller, *Mythologie der Griechischen Stämme, Erster Theil*, Göttingen 1857.

K.O. Müller 1820 — K.O. Müller, 'Ueber den ange-blich ägyptischen Ursprung der griechischen Kunst' (1820), in K.O. Müller 1848, vol. II, 523–537.

K.O. Müller 1824 — K.O. Müller, *Geschichten Helle-nischer Stämme und Städte. Die Dorier* vols. II, IV, Breslau 1824.

K.O. Müller 1825 — K.O. Müller, *Prolegomena zu einer wissenschaftlichen Mytho-logie*, Göttingen 1825.

K.O. Müller 1838 — K.O. Müller, 'Pallas Athene', in K.O. Müller 1848, vol. II, 134–242.

K.O. Müller 1840a — K.O. Müller, review of Preller's *Demeter und Persephone: ein Cyclus mythologischer Untersuch-ungen* (1840), in K.O. Müller 1848, vol. II, 89–99.

K.O. Müller 1840b — K.O. Müller, 'Eleusinien' (1840), in K.O. Müller 1848, vol. II, 242–311.

K.O. Müller 1841 — K.O. Müller, *Geschichte der Griechischen Literatur* vol. I, Breslau 1841.

K.O. Müller 1847–1848 — K.O. Müller, *Kleine deutsche Schriften über Religion, Kunst, Sprache und Literatur, Leben und Geschichte des Alterthums* vols. I & II, Breslau 1847–1848.

Nietzsche 1872 — F. Nietzsche, *Die Geburt der Tragödie aus dem Geiste der Musik*, Leipzig 1872.

Nilsson 1955 — M.P. Nilsson, *Geschichte der Griechischen Religion* vol. I, München 1955².

Nipperdey 1988 — T. Nipperdey, *Religion im Umbruch*, München 1988.

Preller 1854   L. Preller, *Griechische Mytholo-gie* vol. I, Leipzig 1854.

Reiter 1910   S. Reiter, 'Briefwechsel zwischen Karl Otfried Müller und Ludwig Schorn', in *Neue Jahrbücher für das Klassische Altertum, Geschichte und Deutsche Literatur und für Pädagogik* 26, 1910, 340–360.

Reiter 1950   S. Reiter, *Carl Otfried Müller: Briefe aus einem Gelehrtenleben 1797–1840* vol. I, Berlin 1950.

Reschke 2009   R. Reschke, 'Die Erfindung eines Gottes aus dem Geist der Aufklärung. Johann Joachim Winckelmanns „Apollon im Belvedere"', in *Die Antike der Moderne*, ed. V. Elm, Hannover 2009, 309–341.

Roscher 1873   W.H. Roscher, *Studien zur vergleichenden Mythologie der Griechen und Römer* vol. I. *Apollon und Mars*, Leipzig 1873.

Schlesier 1994   R. Schlesier, *Kulte, Mythen und Gelehrte. Anthropologie der Antike seit 1800*, Frankfurt am Main 1994.

Schlesier 1998   R. Schlesier, ,,Dieser mystische Gott". Dionysos im Spiegel von Karl Otfried Müllers Religions-theorie', in Calder & Schlesier 1998, 397–421.

Solomon 1994   J. Solomon, 'Introduction', in *Apollo. Origins and influences*, ed. J. Solomon, Tucson, Ariz. 1994, ix–xii.

Versnel 1985–1986   H.S. Versnel, 'Apollo and Mars one hundred years after Roscher', in *Visible religion* 4–5, 1985–1986, 134–167.

Vogel 1966   M. Vogel, *Apollinisch und Dionysisch*, Regensburg 1966.

Voss 1794   J.H. Voss, *Mythologische Briefe* vol. II, Königsberg 1794.

Voss 1824   J.H. Voss, *Anti-Symbolik*, Stuttgart 1824.

Wilamowitz-Moellendorff 1908   U. von Wilamowitz-Moellendorff, 'Apollo', in *Oxford lectures on classical subjects 1909–1920*, Oxford 1924, 27–45.

Wilamowitz-Moellendorff 1921   U. von Wilamowitz-Moellendorff, *Geschichte der Philologie*, Leipzig & Berlin 1921.

Will 1956   E. Will, *Doriens et Ioniens*, Paris 1956.

JENNY WALLENSTEN

Apollo and Artemis

FAMILY TIES IN GREEK DEDICATORY LANGUAGE?

Abstract*

Among the multitude of divine beings that surrounded the Greek worshippers, the twelve Olympian gods
were connected by especially close family ties: many
of them were as close as siblings. But of these twelve,
only two are consistently characterized as brother and
sister: Apollo and Artemis. Myths and iconography illustrate the strong family ties and undisputed loyalty
between Apollo and Artemis, not least when defend-
ing their mother Leto's honour and safety. This paper
examines *if*, and in that case *how*, and perhaps *why*, this
mythological complicity between brother and sister is
expressed in worship, as visible through dedicatory language, i.e. as found in inscribed dedications. The study
is based on 127 dedications where Apollo and Artemis
together are approached as recipient deities, either just
the two of them, or in the company of other gods. The
dossier includes inscriptions dating from the Archaic
period to the first century AD. They stem from the entire Greek world, with a strong concentration in Delos.

Introduction

Today's domestic relationship patterns, featuring families filled with half brothers, stepmoth-
ers, ex-husbands, etc., might be complicated
enough. But such modern families are nothing compared to the genealogy of the Greek
gods: the deities of Greek mythology were all
more-or-less related, in various intricate ways.
Furthermore, among the multitude of divine
beings that surrounded the Greek worshippers,
the mighty Olympian gods were connected
by especially close family ties—many of them
were even full siblings. Interestingly enough,
however, of these twelve deities only two are
consistently characterized as brother and sister:
Apollo and Artemis. The story of their birth
is well known. After long and painful wander-
ings, their pregnant mother Leto found refuge
in Delos where she could finally give birth. The
Homeric hymn to Apollo treats (logically) only
the arrival of Apollo, but other sources add that
Artemis was born first and immediately rose to
the occasion as she assisted her mother in de-
livering her brother Apollo.[1] Then, as soon as
the two could string their bows, their exploits
became legendary, often illustrating a fierce
loyalty towards Leto and each other. According to some of our sources, as a first joint action, Apollo and Artemis slew Python, since
the monster had menaced Leto relentlessly

* I would like to thank Maria Mili and Matthew
Haysom who read and and gave valuable comments on
various versions of this paper. I am also grateful to the
participants in the Current Approaches symposium, as
well as the anonymous reviewer of the present volume.
Their questions and observations were very helpful.

---

[1] Dasen adds that according to Servius, this episode
explains why pregnant women called upon a virgin goddess for protection (Dasen 2005, 63).

during her pregnancy.[2] But the two most famous stories are of course those about the giant
Tityos and the Theban Queen Niobe. Tityos
assaulted Leto as she was travelling to Delphi,
and his subsequent death by the arrows of the
twins is a relatively frequent motif in early vase
painting.[3] (The continuation of the story is
perhaps better known: as further punishment,
Tityos was subsequently condemned to endless
suffering in Tartaros, where he was tied down,
unable to defend himself against the vultures
that kept pecking at his ever-regenerating liv-
er.) And in an even better known story, Niobe
suffers the fate of seeing her children, all twelve
or fourteen of them, being picked off one by
one; the girls by the shots of Artemis and the
boys by those of Apollo.[4] Other images of the
ancient world also clearly underline Apollo
and Artemis' special relationship. Iconography
often expresses this simply through physical
proximity: the twins fight side by side in the
Gigantomachies, for example, or simply stand
or sit next to each other in more peaceful surroundings. As Zeus and Hera physically belong
next to each other, or Demeter and Kore, so do
Apollo and Artemis.

Thus, reading the ancient texts and studying the ancient images, the family ties between
Apollo and Artemis are well articulated. The
present paper examines *if*, and in that case *how*,
and perhaps *why*, this mythological complicity
between brother and sister is expressed in worship as visible through dedicatory language, i.e.
as found in inscribed dedications.

The material

I have identified and based this part of the
study on 127 dedications where Apollo and
Artemis together are the recipient deities: either just the two of them, or in the company of
other gods.[5] The dossier includes inscriptions
dating from the Archaic period to the first
century AD, where I have intentionally drawn
the line to limit the investigation. The dedications in question stem from the entire Greek
world, with a strong concentration (as perhaps
expected) in Delos. Of these 127 dedications,
Apollo and Artemis are the sole recipient deities in only 26 instances.[6] In the other dedications, they are teamed with a variety of deities. In an Attic dedication datable to shortly
after 400 BC, Apollo with the epithet Pythios,
and Artemis Lochia are approached between
Hestia, Kephissos, Leto, Eileithyia, Acheloos,
Kallirhoe, the Geraistan Nymphs of Birth and
Rhapso.[7] In first-century Delos, Apollo and
Artemis are joined once by Dionysos, Leto and
the Charites, and once, in an undated inscription, by Asklepios, Hygieia, Leto, and—for the
dedicator to be on the safe side—all *synbomoi*
and *synnaooi* divinities that might otherwise
take offence.[8] Zeus Megistos, Apollo Bathy-

---

2   Paus. 2.7.6.
3   See for example Paus. 3.15.18, 10.11.1. See Fontenrose 1974, 23, n. 15 for further references.
4   See for example Hom. *Il.* 24.602; Diod. 4.74.3. According to some accounts two children were spared:
Paus. 2.21.9; Apollod., *Bibl.* 3.46.

5   I have used only "direct" dedications, i.e., only
the dedications themselves and not other mentions of
dedications, such as in inventories, etc. A survey of this
material has however convinced me that their inclusion
would not change the result of the present study.
6   *IG* II² 3725; *IG* II² 4726; *IG* II² 4854; *SEG* 24 620;
Meletemata 11 K3 (*SEG* 42 586); *IGBulg* I² 33; *ID* 55;
IG XI 4 1134; *IG* XI 4 1343; *IG* XII 3 268; *IG* XII 3
269; *IG* XII 3 270; *IG* XII 3 271; *IStratonikeia* 502;
IDidyma 17; *IDidyma* 104aII; *IDidyma* 105; *IDidyma*
106; *IDidyma* 107; *Milet* II 3, 400; Lolling 1884, 25;
Mendel 1912–1914, Nr. 854; Petzl & Wagner 1976,
213; Papachristodoulou 1989, 168,4 (*IG* XII 1 733+);
Susini 1955, 341–343; *SEG* 9 102. I have counted
among these inscriptions one that includes Demos
among the recipient deities (*Milet* II 3 400).
7   *IG* II² 4547.
8   *ID* 1873; *ID* 2387. In the latter inscription, Artemis carries the epithet Agrotera.

limenites and Artemis received a *charisterion* from two Romans, dedicating in the Kyzikene in the first century BC.[9] An administrator in Egyptian Koptos dedicated in the third century BC to Apollo Hylates, Artemis Phosphoros, Artemis Enodia, Leto Euteknos and Herakles Kallinikos, whereas a former priest in Lindos honoured Athena Lindia, Zeus Polieus, Apollo Pythios, Poseidon Hippios, Artemis en Kekoia and Dionysos.[10] In Epirote Ambrakia, around 200 BC, a *prytanis* and his *symprytaneis* presented a dedication to Hestia, Zeus Prytaneus, Aphrodite, Apollo and Artemis.[11] However, when joined by other gods, Apollo and Artemis are most frequently associated with their mother Leto. The Delian triad are the sole protagonists of the vast majority of the studied group of inscriptions: 94 of the 127.

The dedicators present in the material are predominantly men; they stand behind 68 of the inscriptions with identifiable dedicants.[12] Another large share was presented by more-or-less official groupings such as "The Athenians who live in Delos", "Those who sail to Delos", various *demoi*, etc., providing 41 examples.[13] Conversely, magistrates' dedications are rare in this group. Only two possible examples can be put forward, one from a *prytanis* and his colleagues, and perhaps the aforementioned administrator of Koptos should count as a magistrate.[14] There are 18 examples of women dedicating to Artemis and Apollo, but they appear almost exclusively in the context of joint dedications: women seem to have approached

Apollo and Artemis in the company of their husbands or brothers. I have identified only two cases of women dedicating on their own, a Kleopatra (an unidentified princess of the name) erecting the statue of an Athenian in the Delian sanctuary, and a woman in Cyrene presenting the statue of a man, most likely her husband, to the twins.[15] Of the total of 127 inscriptions, 17 were made by unknown dedicators.

The image presented here is heavily skewed by the Delian provenance of such a large part of the material. If one looks at either only the inscriptions of Delos, or the remaining dedications, the picture painted appears to change somewhat in regard to dedications made by groupings of merchants, ship-owners etc. In Delos only, men dominate the scene (with 41 male dedicants, including 9 presented in the company of women and one with a group), closely followed by official or semi-official groupings (35), and women dedicating as part of family groupings (9), apart from the single exception of a royal female dedicator. The non-Delian material features 27 male dedicators, whereas associations or political bodies stand behind six dedications, and family groups involving both men and women can be identified in seven instances.[16]

---

9 *SEG* 15 767.
10 Bernand 1984, no. 47=*OGI* 53; *ILindos* II 159.
11 *SEG* 42 543bis.
12 This includes dedications where men dedicate together with women (16 inscriptions), or magistrates (2 inscriptions), as well as one instance where one named man (a priest) dedicates together with a group (*IG* XI 4 1343).
13 This includes the above mentioned inscription combining a man and a group (*IG* XI 4 1343).
14 *SEG* 42 543bis; Bernand 1984, no. 47.

15 *ID* 1537; *SEG* 9 102.
16 A summary of the dedicators present in the material gives the following table. M = Male; F = Female; G = Group; Mag = Magistrate; ? = Unknown. Parenthetical numbers indicate exclusively male or female dedicators, i.e., without dedications made jointly by men and women or other groups.

All dedicators	Delos excepted	In Delos only
M: 68 (49)	M: 27 (18)	M: 41 (31)
· M & G: 1		M & G: 1
M & F: 16	M & F: 7	M & F: 9
G: 40	G: 6	G: 35 (34)
F: 18 (2)	F: 8 (1)	F:10 (1)
?: 17	?: 6	?: 11
Mag.: 2	Mag.: 2	

If?

After this brief presentation of the material, let us consider the questions, starting with the *if*: if the mythological conception of Apollo and Artemis—as brother and sister—was expressed through dedicatory language. This may at first seem to be a question with the obvious answer *yes*. The fact that they are never explicitly referred to as siblings is not necessarily a problem; it could be explained by the economical epigraphic preference for not wasting space by stating the obvious. However, the scarcity of their exclusive joint worship visible through dedications makes our *if* a valid question. But how are we to tell if Apollo and Artemis are conceived as brother and sister in dedicatory language, when they are not explicitly said to be so? The answer is to be found in the context of dedications where other deities are present.

As previously mentioned, the Delian triad are the sole protagonists of the vast majority of the studied group of inscriptions: 94 of the 127. It is hard to escape the conclusion that the consistent combination of Artemis and Apollo with their mother Leto indicates that they are understood specifically as siblings at least in these dedications. Almost all of the Apollo-Artemis-Leto dedications come from Delos, 82 of the 94 collected examples. But the joint worship of the three was not, of course, restricted to this island: in the studied material a dossier of ten dedications comes from the Euboian cities Tamynai, Eretria and Amarynthos, moreover, one example has been identified in Lykian Xanthos, and a final one comes from Kydonia in Crete.[17]

But this still leaves us with the dedications to Apollo and Artemis in the company of other gods—not only Leto—and dedications to Apollo and Artemis alone. We have seven examples of the first category.[18] Examining this material, firstly it is significant that Leto is present in four of these, her name inscribed next to that of her children (and once with the epithet *Euteknos*). This again articulates the family relations between the twins: Leto again becomes a mythological marker that turns the gods specifically into brother and sister. As regards the remaining inscriptions of this group, those to the twins alone but in the company of other gods, it is noteworthy that the names of the siblings are separated in only one case. Artemis and Apollo otherwise seem intentionally to be placed together: their unity is not split by the names of other gods. Thus, visually, in the epigraphic layout, the two are to be read as a unity. They are paired between or after their fellow gods, as, for example between Dionysos and the Charites, or after Hestia, Zeus and Aphrodite.[19] A corpus of seven dedications might seem small, but I believe that this can be corroborated by the context of other epigraphic material, such as oaths and sacrifical calendars, where Apollo and Artemis also appear side by side in instances when they are both mentioned.

How?

Summing up the study of the previous section, the answer to the question *if* the ties between Apollo and Artemis as brother and sister is expressed in dedicatory language appears to be *yes*, and definitely so when their mother is present. But whereas the addition of Leto persistently points to their siblingship, the pairing of only Apollo and Artemis, either alone or with other gods, could in theory be ascribed to some function they have in common, and

---

[17]   *IG* XII 9 97–99, 140–143, 276–278; *TAM* II 266; van Effenterre *et al.* 1993.

[18]   *IG* II² 4547; *ID* 1873; *ID* 2387; *SEG* 15 767; Bernand 1984, no. 47; *ILindos* II 159; *SEG* 42 543bis.
[19]   *ID* 1873; *SEG* 42 543bis.

not to ideas of family ties. What we can see in the inscriptions where Leto is not included is simply a *belonging together*, an affinity that without the provision of further details is impossible to ascribe to either family or function. This brings us further in our quest, to questions of *how*, both how the established siblingship is understood, and in the more anonymous cases, how the belonging, the pairing, of Apollo and Artemis functions.

Could an examination of the epithets used for the two give us further information in these matters? Either Apollo or Artemis is presented with a byname in 24 inscriptions.[20] We can see that Leto is present in only four of these, and in three of these cases, epithets appear when Artemis and Apollo are part of a larger group of recipient deities. It is furthermore immediately striking that it is rare for Apollo and Artemis to be called by the same epithets, which would otherwise have provided a convenient way of answering the question of how they were understood as a couple. The two occasions on which they are given matching epithets are the following: in an undated inscription from Attica, the epithet Delphinios/Delphinia is used, and the twins are once approached as Epekooi in Thrace.[21] Unfortunately, these particular epithets do not reveal much of the character of their carriers. The latter byname, Epekooi, says nothing in particular: that the gods listened reveals nothing about their specific powers. Delphinios and Delphinia gods appear to have cared for the youth of Attica, and so in this case we perhaps get a glimpse at the reason for this Attic dedication. The dedicated object, the statue of a priestess, was however presented by her husband, not by a mother or father, and thus the interpretation is not clear-cut.

In the remaining dedications featuring epithets, either Apollo and Artemis are invoked by different names, or only one of the gods, usually Apollo, receives an epithet. In Athens, Apollo Patroos and Apollo Smintheus seem joined to an Artemis with no epithet, as do Apollo Komaios in Philippi, and Apollo Erethimios in Ialysos.[22] When both gods receive (different) epithets, these are primarily broad cult names: Apollo Pythios together with Artemis Hegemone, Apollo Pythios with Artemis Soteira, and Apollo Didymeus with Artemis Pythia. A possible exception is the combination of Apollo Epekoos and Artemis Diktynna, where Artemis' characterization is more specifically defined than Apollo's, and, conversely, Apollo Pylaios combined with Artemis Soteira. Some recurring pairings can be found, such as Apollo Pythios and Artemis Soteira from the island of Anaphe, and of course Apollo Didymeus and Artemis Pythia in Didyma. Otherwise the epithets present in the examined material give the impression that they rather separate than bring the two gods together. Instead of creating matching deities, the epithets define one god as different from the other. This is, I suggest, a clue to the interpretation. By inversion, the separating epithets tell us something about the cases when unspecified Apollo and Artemis receive worship.

There are cases when gods in combination more-or-less become each other's epithets. The examples Hermes and Herakles, and Hermes and Aphrodite, could be put forward. When Hermes and Herakles work together, they are rarely given an extra name, because no epithets are needed to understand that a dedication to this pair was most likely intended for the gods of the gymnasion. The same could be said for

---

[20]   See Appendix 2.

[21]   *IG* II² 3725; *IGBulg* I² 33. Mention can also be made of the inscription *St. Pontica* III 146a. The publication does not give a date, but the name of the dedicator indicates a date in the Severan period, thus too late for inclusion in the present study.

[22]   *IG* II² 4726; *IG* II² 4854; *SEG* 24 620; Papachristodoulou 1989, 168,4.

Hermes and Aphrodite. In the dedicatory dossier of the Greek world, this combination of gods is closely connected with the religious acts of magistrates.[23] Among the extant examples where Hermes and Aphrodite are paired, the gods are provided with epithets in a single joint votive inscription, when the *eisagogeis* of Samos dedicated specifically to Hermes Eisagogeus and Aphrodite Synarchis.[24] In the other cases, the combination of the gods works as an epithet, or to put it in another way, the gods become epithets of each other, and from their pairing we get a clue to the reason behind the dedication. The epithets of Hermes Eisagogeus and Aphrodite Synarchis only specify the general character of magistrates' deities that is inherent in the combination Hermes-Aphrodite. Separating epithets are needed precisely because the divinities take on a specific meaning when worshipped together, so epithets are needed when this meaning changes for some reason.[25] This is perhaps corroborated by a comparison with iconographical representations of the twins. Carpenter has shown that, in Archaic vase painting, the artists, while often picturing "the terrible twins" Apollo and Artemis together, sometimes chose to highlight Artemis by giving her attributes that distinguish and separate her from her brother.[26]

To arrive at an understanding of a combination of deities, a profile of the dedicators is necessary. To continue with our previous examples, ephebes dedicating to Hermes and Herakles in the gymnasion, and magistrates honouring Hermes and Aphrodite in their office space, give us an idea of the character of the recipient deities. Unfortunately, in the case of Apollo and Artemis, our sources are meagre. No specific, unambiguous profile can be ascribed to the dedicators. The examined inscriptions predominantly come from votive bases. It is however tempting to attach a certain significance to dedications made in a family context: parents presenting statues of their children, and vice versa. 36 dedications can be said to belong to this category. This is also the category where we find women worshippers. 17 of the 18 dedications where female dedicators are present belong to this group, with the exception of the princess Kleopatra, who dedicated the statue of a man who does not appear to be a relative. But apart from this example, and from a Karian inscription where a husband and wife dedicate a piece of wooded land to the divine twins, all the objects presented by female dedicators to Apollo and Artemis (often in the company of Leto), were sculptures of relatives. Is it possible that Apollo and Artemis had connotations of care of family? Mythology presents the twins as always prepared to help each other, no matter the danger of the situation. They steadily stand united and they become positively ferocious when the safety or the honour of their mother Leto is at stake. This mythological setting would indeed fit an understanding of Apollo and Artemis as family providers. Dasen's conclusions about the competences held by twins in mythology are of interest in this context: one of their prime capacities is to promote fertility and health. Dasen argues that as a couple, Apollo and Artemis, specifically, watch over human and animal fecundity and care of the growth of the young.[27]

---

[23]   See Wallensten 2003, 137–138.

[24]   Schede 1912, 216–17, no. 17. It is noteworthy that in the Parian inscription *IG* XII 5 220, a dedication to Aphrodite, Zeus, Hermes and Artemis, Zeus and Artemis are epithet-clad, whereas Aphrodite and Hermes are not. They define each other.

[25]   See Wallensten, forthcoming.

[26]   Carpenter 1994, 71.

[27]   Dasen 2005, 164. It should however be pointed out that besides the statues of family members, there is likewise a strong presence of the presentation of honorary statues erected for more official reasons, and again, we should be aware that the dominance of the Delian material muddles any attempt at explanation. A sound second step will be to study the present material in the

Another aspect of how Apollo and Artemis were conceived in dedicatory language also deserves a brief comment: it is what could be called the ranking of the gods. Which of the two takes first place in the inscriptions? Assuming that the first name is considered as the most important, is there a fixed hierarchy? At a first glance it appears that Apollo is doubtless the god who is thought worthy of first mention, in spite of his sister's primogeniture. However, as one leaves the Delian context, it becomes clear that the situation changes according to the locality. For example, Artemis is mentioned first in Euboian dedications, no matter the *polis* (there is one exception where Leto is ranked first).[28] Leto herself takes precedence in Xanthos in Lycia: she is mentioned first in her own surroundings, with her offspring following in her wake.[29] Suggestions of causes more specific than local preferences have also been put forward for the extant variations. Artemis is actually mentioned first twice at Delos, and apropos of *ID* 1575 it has been suggested that Artemis is accentuated because of the honorand of the statue, a young girl. It has also been put forward, however, that the order was an error made by the editor.[30] Unfortunately the piece has since gone missing, and the sequence of deities cannot be verified. The other Delian instance of Artemis getting priority is the dedication of the statue of a son, and not a daughter, which caused the editor to comment that the order of the divinities was bizarre.[31] Be that as it may, in the light of examples from outside Delos, we can conclude that it is not necessarily a mere error when the triad

is variously presented. Through manipulation of the placing within the couple or the trio, a kind of votive emphasis could be placed on one of the deities.

Why?

Having established that we can see that Apollo and Artemis are articulated as brother and sister in the dedicatory material, and after an exploration of possible ways in which this was expressed, we are closing in on the *why*. Why should the mythological complicity between brother and sister be expressed in dedicatory language? To some scholars, the obvious answer to this would simply be *why not*? But if I specify my *why* into why the mythological complicity between brother and sister should be expressed specifically through Apollo and Artemis, a more nuanced response appears.

It is of significance that Apollo and Artemis were not only brother and sister, but also twins, a phenomenon towards which Greek society held an ambivalent attitude. In the ancient medical writings there were two main trends concerning multiple births. The Hippocratic writers thought twins to be the result of an ideal conception: a two-for-the-price-of-one phenomenon that occurred only under the most favourable of circumstances. Aristotle, on the other hand, argued that a double progeny was not normal, but caused by some unnatural excess and often associated with some kind of monstrosity.[32] Our divine twins could surely not be used to corroborate Aristotle's opinions. They were, in the words of the *Homeric Hymn to Apollo*, "glorious children" and Hesiod hails them as "the loveliest brood of all the Ouranians".[33] Leaving the physical and moving to the psychological, we do not find any trace

---

light of separate dedications to Apollo and Artemis respectively, something which unfortunately lies outside the scope of the current paper.
[28] *IG* XII 9 97–99, 140–142, 276–278. Leto first: *IG* XII 9 143.
[29] *TAM* II 266.
[30] *ID* 1575.
[31] *IG* XI 4 1186.

[32] Dasen 2005, 22.
[33] *Hymn. Hom. Ap.*16; Hes. *Theog.* 923.

of strained relations between Leto's children, although relations between twins are often especially sensitive, certainly in cultures where the firstborn automatically takes centre stage. Instead, Apollo and Artemis form the prime example of what Dasen, in a study of twins in ancient Greece and Rome, calls a model fraternal couple. Reminiscent of the two camps among the medical writers, Dasen identifies two kinds of stories that explore twinship. One kind serves to illustrate the uncanny and abnormal regarding their birth: as friends or foes, they threaten society by their daring behaviour and turn to horrors like murder or incest. The other kind of account presents twins that form the epitome of brotherly/sisterly love. Sometimes identical, sometimes complementary, these siblings are bound by unbreakable family ties.[34]

In ancient Greek society, sibling rivalry was surely as common a phenomenon as it is today. Plutarch comments on the matter and concludes that enmity between brothers may arise from rivalry for parents' affection, differences in ability or achievement, competition for honours or office, at the instigation of wives and other intimates, because of the roles of younger or older child, or simply through childhood squabbles.[35] Bremmer, in a recent study focusing on the relationship between brothers, singles out inheritance issues, and rivalry between legitimate and illegitimate sons or between a younger and an older brother, as common factors that created family tensions.[36] Surely, because of such strain, cordiality and loyalty between siblings was a widely held ideal,[37] an ideal that the combination Apollo-Artemis, of all the Olympian brothers and sisters, fully embody. Apollo and Artemis, as the Olympian sibling couple *par excellence*, avoid the kinds of rivalries that Plutarch and Brem-

mer list, to a large extent because they are more than siblings, i.e., twins. On a mythological level, they of course belong to Dasen's category of twins as the role model of fraternal relations, a harmonious co-dependence created not only through a sharing, but also through a division, of competences. Avoiding rivalries, each twin develops his or her own specialty. In our case we could perhaps mention the areas of the hunt and musicianship, working according to a principle which Dasen refers to as "equality in difference".[38] Bremmer notes other mythological instances where brotherly competition is avoided through split interests: whereas Castor was a tamer of horses, Polydeukes was a good boxer, for example.[39]

Although twins in some cultures can symbolize rivalry, for our investigation we can note that the Greek mythological ideal of twin solidarity seems to match Athenian law court rhetoric, from which it is indicated that twins were supposed to be *extra* loyal to their other half. Judging by these sources, twins appear to have been considered intensified siblings, and thus a suitable symbol for fraternal or sororal affection. Furthermore, in the case of twins, the question of younger or older is perhaps of less importance, especially when the pair consists of sister and brother. This is generally a crucial point; Apollo and Artemis' union is a case of one male and one female sibling, and thereby many spheres of competition simply cease to exist.

This paper has sprung from an inscription that I happened to notice while searching for something completely different: from a dedication where a father presents a thank-offering

---

[34] Dasen 2005, 164.
[35] Golden 1990, 118; Plut. *Mor.* 478A–492D.
[36] Bremmer 2008, 57–72.
[37] Bremmer 2008, 59–62.

[38] Dasen 2005, 104.
[39] Bremmer 2008, 67–68. He furthermore points to similar modern strategies to avoid sibling strife: "Like the Berbers, the Sarakatsani tried to discourage rivalry between brothers by encouraging them to pursue different vocations: for example, by making one a muleteer and the other a cheese-maker." (68).

to Aphrodite for the benefit of his two daughters Artemò and Apollonia. I would like to think that Apollonios' choice of names for his daughters in fact illustrates, with epigraphic eloquence, all the main points of my paper. Yes, Apollo and Artemis were approached as siblings, they cared especially for the family and its younger members and symbolized in this case sisterly love. But this, unfortunately, would surely be to read too much between the lines.

JENNY WALLENSTEN
Swedish Institute at Athens
jenny.wallensten@sia.gr

Appendix 1: Dedications to Apollo and Artemis

ND = No date   M = Male dedicator   F = Female dedicator   G = Group dedicator
Mag = Magistrate dedicator

	Location	Other gods	Date	Reference	Dedicator	Inscribed object
1	Attica		ND	IG II² 3725	M	?
2	Attica	Hestia, Kiphissos, (Apollo Pythios), Leto, (Artemis Lochia), Eileithyia, Acheloos, Kallirhoe, Gerastian Nymphs of Birth, Rhapso	P. post 400 BC	IG II² 4547	?	Altar
3	Attica		1st cent. AD?	IG II² 4726	?	?
4	Attica		ND	IG II² 4854	?	?
5	Macedonia		350–300 BC–17AD	SEG 24 620	M	Base
6	Macedonia		c. 100 BC	Meletemata 11 K3; SEG 42 586	?	Stele
7	Thrace and Moesia Inferior, Ekrene		ND	IGBulg I² 33	M	Stele
8	Delos		ND	ID 55	M	Plaque
9	Delos	(Apollo, Artemis), Leto	180–145 BC	ID 1525	M	Base
10	Delos	(Apollo, Artemis), Leto	145–116 BC	ID 1527	M	?
11	Delos	(Apollo, Artemis), Leto	P. post 127 BC	ID 1528	G	Base
12	Delos	(Apollo, Artemis), Leto	145–116 BC	ID 1529	G	Base
13	Delos	(Apollo, Artemis), Leto	End 2nd cent. BC	ID 1530	M	Base
14	Delos	(Apollo, Artemis), Leto	116–80 BC	ID 1535	M	?
15	Delos	(Apollo, Artemis), Leto	2nd Athenian period	ID 1537	F	Base
16	Delos	(Apollo, Artemis), Leto	129–117 BC	ID 1547	M	Base
17	Delos	(Apollo, Artemis), Leto	129–117 BC	ID 1548	M	Base
18	Delos	(Apollo, Artemis), Leto	96–94 BC	ID 1553	M	?
19	Delos	(Apollo, Artemis), Leto	160/159–139/138 BC	ID 1554	M	?
20	Delos	(Apollo, Artemis), Leto	149–120 BC	ID 1559	M	Part of base

21	Delos	(Artemis, Apollo), Leto	138–134 BC	*ID* 1575	G	Plaque of bronze
22	Delos	(Apollo, Artemis), Leto	Ante 27 BC	*ID* 1588	G	?
23	Delos	(Apollo, Artemis), Leto	Ante 27 BC	*ID* 1589	M	Base
24	Delos	(Apollo, Artemis), Leto	21–12 BC	*ID* 1592	G	Base
25	Delos	(Apollo, Artemis), Leto	ND	*ID* 1608	G	Base
26	Delos	(Apollo, Artemis), Leto	*c.* 68 BC	*ID* 1621	G	Fragments of plaque
27	Delos	(Apollo, Artemis), Leto	1st cent. BC	*ID* 1624bis	G	?
28	Delos	(Apollo, Artemis), Leto	Before beg. 1st cent. AD	*ID* 1625	G	Base
29	Delos	(Apollo, Artemis), Leto	Beginning 1st cent. AD	*ID* 1626	G	Base
30	Delos	(Apollo, Artemis), Leto	*c.* 61 AD	*ID* 1629	G	Base
31	Delos	(Apollo, Artemis), Leto	ND	*ID* 1630	G	Base
32	Delos	(Apollo, Artemis), Leto	ND	*ID* 1631	G	Base
33	Delos	(Apollo, Artemis), Leto	ND	*ID* 1633	G	Fragment of base
34	Delos	(Apollo, Artemis), Leto	ND	*ID* 1635	G	?
35	Delos	(Apollo, Artemis), Leto	Post 65 BC	*ID* 1641	G	Base
36	Delos	(Apollo, Artemis), Leto	"Relatively low date"	*ID* 1642	G	Base
37	Delos	(Apollo, Artemis), Leto	112/111 BC	*ID* 1653	G	Base
38	Delos	(Apollo, Artemis), Leto	96/95 BC	*ID* 1657	G	Base
39	Delos	(Apollo, Artemis), Leto	94/93 BC	*ID* 1658	G	Base
40	Delos	(Apollo, Artemis), Leto	85–78 BC	*ID* 1659	G	Base
41	Delos	(Apollo, Artemis), Leto	85–78 BC	*ID* 1660	G	Base
42	Delos	(Apollo, Artemis), Leto	*c.* 70 BC	*ID* 1661	G	Pedestal
43	Delos	(Apollo, Artemis), Leto	ND ("late letters")	*ID* 1665	G	?
44	Delos	(Apollo, Artemis), Leto	Mid 2nd cent. BC	*ID* 1666	G	Base
45	Delos	(Apollo, Artemis), Leto	ND	*ID* 1682	G	Base

46	Delos	(Apollo, Artemis), Leto	P. post 97 BC	*ID* 1700	G	Base
47	Delos	(Apollo, Artemis), Leto	99–89 BC	*ID* 1701	G	Plaque
48	Delos	(Apollo, Artemis), Leto	ND	*ID* 1705	G	Base
49	Delos	(Apollo, Artemis), Leto	ND	*ID* 1706	G	Part of base
50	Delos	(Apollo, Artemis), Leto	Beg. 1st cent. BC	*ID* 1725	G	Base
51	Delos	(Apollo, Artemis), Leto	End 2nd/beg. 1st cent. BC	*ID* 1729	G	Orthostate of base
52	Delos	(Apollo, Artemis), Leto	150–100 BC	*ID* 1830	M & F	Block
53	Delos	(Apollo, Artemis), Leto	134 BC?	*ID* 1842	M	Base
54	Delos	(Apollo, Artemis), Leto	End 1st cent. BC	*ID* 1854	M	Base and statue
55	Delos	(Artemis, Apollo), Leto	125–100 BC	*ID* 1868	M	Plinth
56	Delos	(Apollo, Artemis), Leto x 3	120–110 BC	*ID* 1869	M & F	Plaque from exedra
57	Delos	(Apollo, Artemis), Leto	Beg. 1st cent. BC	*ID* 1870	M	Base
58	Delos	(Apollo, Artemis), Leto	Beg. 1st cent. BC	*ID* 1871	M & F	Base
59	Delos	(Apollo, Artemis), Leto	101–99 BC	*ID* 1872	M & F	Base
60	Delos	Dionysos, (Apollo, Artemis), Leto, Charites	*c.* 89/88 BC	*ID* 1873	?	Fragment
61	Delos	(Apollo, Artemis), Leto	*c.* 130 BC	*ID* 1875	M & F	Base
62	Delos	(Apollo, Artemis), Leto	*c.* mid 1st cent. BC	*ID* 1876	M	Base
63	Delos	(Apollo, Artemis), Leto x 3	125–100 BC	*ID* 1964	M	Fragments of exedra
64	Delos	(Apollo, Artemis), Leto	ND	*ID* 1965	M	Fragments of exedra
65	Delos	(Apollo, Artemis), Leto x 2	ND	*ID* 1967	M	Parts of exedra
66	Delos	(Apollo, Artemis), Leto x 3	ND	*ID* 1968	M	Parts of exedra
67	Delos	(Apollo, Artemis), Leto	127/126 BC?	*ID* 1972	M & F	Fragment of base
68	Delos	(Apollo, Artemis), Leto	ND	*ID* 1973	M	Base
69	Delos	(Apollo, Artemis), Leto	P. post 148/147 BC	*ID* 1979	M & F	Base

70	Delos	(Apollo, Artemis), Leto	ND	*ID* 1984	M	Pedestal
71	Delos	(Apollo, Artemis), Leto	ND	*ID* 1993	M	Base
72	Delos	(Apollo, Artemis), Leto	2–1st cent. BC	*ID* 1994	M	Base
73	Delos	(Apollo, Artemis), Leto	ND	*ID* 1995	M	Block
74	Delos	(Apollo, Artemis), Leto	ND	*ID* 2003	?	Block
75	Delos	(Apollo, Artemis), Leto	ND	*ID* 2005	M	Pedestal
76	Delos	(Apollo, Artemis), Leto	*c.* 94 BC	*ID* 2006	M & F	Base
77	Delos	(Apollo, Artemis), Leto	ND	*ID* 2008	M	?
78	Delos	(Apollo, Artemis), Leto	ND	*ID* 2010	M	Fragment of base
79	Delos	(Apollo, Artemis), Leto	Beg. 1st cent. BC?	*ID* 2012	M	Base
80	Delos	(Apollo, Artemis), Leto	ND	*ID* 2015	?	Plaque, from base
81	Delos	(Apollo, Artemis), Leto	ND	*ID* 2020	?	Base
82	Delos	(Apollo, Artemis), Leto	150–100 BC	*ID* 2335	M	Base
83	Delos	(Apollo, Artemis), Leto	ND	*ID* 2336	?	Fragment of pedestal
84	Delos	(Apollo, Artemis), Leto	ND	*ID* 2337	?	Fragment (of base?)
85	Delos	(Apollo, Artemis), Leto	ND	*ID* 2338	?	?
86	Delos	(Apollo, Artemis), Leto	ND	*ID* 2339	?	?
87	Delos	(Apollo, Artemis), Leto	ND	*ID* 2340	?	?
88	Delos	(Apollo, Artemis), Leto	ND	*ID* 2341	?	Base
89	Delos	Asklepios, Hygieia, (Apollo), Leto (Artemis Agrotera), *synbomoi, synnaoi*	ND	*ID* 2387	M	Block
90	Delos		3rd cent. BC	*IG* XI 4 1134	G	?
91	Delos	(Phoibos), Leto, (Artemis)	3rd cent. BC	*IG* XI 4 1163	?	?
92	Delos	(Artemis, Apollo), Leto	Beg. 2nd cent. BC?	*IG* XI 4 1186	M & F	Base
93	Delos		End 3rd cent. BC	*IG* XI 4 1343	M & G	?

94	Delos	(Apollo, Artemis), Leto	P. post 2nd cent. BC, or 1st cent. BC (*SEG*)	*SEG* 23 494	G	Base
95	Anaphe		ND	*IG* XII 3 268	M	Base and statue
96	Anaphe		ND	*IG* XII 3 269	M & F	Base
97	Anaphe		ND	*IG* XII 3 270	G	
98	Anaphe		2nd–1st cent. BC	*IG* XII 3 271	M	Base
99	Euboia, Tamynai	(Artemis, Apollo), Leto	ND	*IG* XII 9 97	M & F	Base
100	Euboia, Tamynai	(Artemis, Apollo), Leto	Late 2nd cent. BC	*IG* XII 9 98	M & F	Base
101	Euboia, Tamynai	(Artemis, Apollo), Leto	ND	*IG* XII 9 99	G	Base
102	Euboia, Amaryn-thos	(Artemis, Apollo), Leto	Mid 2nd cent. BC	*IG* XII 9 140	M & F	Base
103	Euboia, Amaryn-thos	(Artemis, Apollo), Leto	Early 1st cent. BC	*IG* XII 9 141	M & F?	Base (or *mensa sacra*)
104	Euboia, Amaryn-thos	(Artemis, Apollo), Leto x 2	ND	*IG* XII 9 142	M and ?	Base
105	Euboia, Amaryn-thos	Leto (Artemis, Apollo)	ND	*IG* XII 9 143	?	*Mensa sacra*
106	Euboia, Eretria	(Artemis, Apollo), Leto	200–150 BC	*IG* XII 9 276	G	?
107	Euboia, Eretria	(Artemis, Apollo), Leto	Late 2nd cent. BC	*IG* XII 9 277	G	Base
108	Euboia, Eretria	(Artemis, Apollo), Leto	2nd cent. BC?	*IG* XII 9 278	G	Base
109	Karia, Lagina		*c.* 350 BC	*IStratonikeia* 502	M & F	Stele
110	Ionia, Didyma		Archaic, post 550 BC	*IDidyma* 17	?	Base
111	Ionia, Didyma		3rd–2nd cent. BC	*IDidyma* 104aII	M	Votive column
112	Ionia, Didyma		50–1 BC	*IDidyma* 105	M	(Fragments of) perirrhan-terion
113	Ionia, Didyma		50–1 BC	*IDidyma* 106	M	(Fragments of) perirrhan-terion
114	Ionia, Didyma		Early Imperial	*IDidyma* 107	G	Base
115	Ionia, Miletos	(Apollo, Artemis), Demos	100–50 BC	*Milet* II 3, 400	M	Altar

116	Mysia, Kyzikene	Zeus Megistos, (Apollo Bathyli-menites, Artemis)	1st cent. BC	*SEG* 15 767 *Hellenica* X, 125–127	M	Stele
117	Mysia, Kyzikene		ND	Lolling 1884, 25, no 2=*CIG* 3699	M	?
118	Mysia, Mi-letoupolis		1st BC?	Mendel 1912–1914, Nr. 854=Joubin 1896, no. 116	M & F (?)	Stele
119	Lykia, Xanthos	Leto, (Apollo, Artemis)	P. post 197 BC	*TAM* II 266	M	Building (door)
120	Comma-gene		69–38 BC	Petzl & Wagner 1976, 213	M	Stele
121	Egypt	(Apollo Hylates, Ar-temis Phosphoros, Artemis Enodia), Leto Euteknos, Herakles Kallinikos	*c.* 246 BC	*OGI* 53=Ber-nand 1984, 47=*SB* 5 8857	M, mag (?)	Base
122	Do-decanese, Lindos	Athena Lindia, Zeus Polieus, (Apollo Pythios), Poseidon Hip-pios, (Artemis en Kekoia), Dionysos	192–191 BC	*ILindos* II 159	M	Base
123	Dodeca-nese, Rhodes, Ialysos		200–150 BC	*IG* XII,1 733; Papachristodou-lou 1989, 168, 4	M	Omphalos
124	Megiste		3rd–2nd BC	Susini 1955, 341–343	M	*Agalmata*
125	Epeiros	Hestia, Zeus Pry-taneus, Aphrodite, (Apollo, Artemis)	*c.* 200 BC	*SEG* 42 543bis	Mag	Block
126	Crete	(Apollo, Artemis), Leto	400–350 BC	*SEG* 33, 735,1; v. Effenterre *et al.* 1993, 405–419	M	Base
127	Cyrene		2nd–1st BC	*SEG* 9, 102; *AA* 44, 1929, 404	F	*Tabula*

Appendix 2: Epithets of Apollo and Artemis

APOLLO	ARTEMIS	REFERENCE
Delphinios	Delphinia	*IG* II² 3725
Pythios	Lochia	*IG* II² 4547
Patroos		*IG* II² 4726
Smintheus		*IG* II² 4854
Komaios		*SEG* 24:620
Pythios	Hegemone	*Meletemata* 11 K3; *SEG* 42.586
Epekoos	Epekoos (Epekooi)	*IGBulg* I² 33
	Agrotera	*ID* 2387
Pythios	Soteira	*IG* XII 3 268
Pythios	Soteira	*IG* XII 3 269
Pythios	Soteira	*IG* XII 3 270
Pythios	Soteira	*IG* XII 3 271
Didymeus	Pythia	*IDidyma* 104aII
Didymeus	Pythia	*IDidyma* 105
Didymeus	Pythia	*IDidyma* 106
Didymeus	Pythia	*IDidyma* 107
Didymeus	Pythia	*Milet* II 3, 400
Bathylimenites		*Hellenica* X, 125–127
Prokentis		Mendel 1912–1914, Nr. 854
Epekoos	Diktynna	Petzl & Wagner 1976, 213
Hylates	Phosphoros, Enodia	*OGI* 53
Pythios	H en Kekoia	*ILindos* II 159
Erethimios		*IG* XII,1 733; Papachristodoulou 1989, 168, 4
Pylaios	Soteira	Susini 1955, 341–343

Bibliography

Bernand 1984   A. Bernand, *Les portes du désert: recueil des inscriptions grecques d'Antinooupolis, Tentyris, Koptos, Apollonopolis Parva et Apollonopolis Magna*, Paris 1984.

Bremmer 2008   J.N. Bremmer, *Greek religion and culture, the Bible and the ancient Near East*, Leiden 2008.

Carpenter 1994   T.H. Carpenter, 'The terrible twins in sixth-century Attic art', in *Apollo: Origins and influences*, ed. J. Solomon, Tucson 1994, 61–81.

Dasen 2005   V. Dasen, *Jumeaux, jumelles dans l'antiquité grecque et romaine*, Kilchberg 2005.

van Effenterre et al. 1993   H. v. Effenterre, A.-M. Liesenfelt & I. Papaoikonomou, 'Base inscrite de Kydonia', *BCH* 107, 1993, 405–419.

Fontenrose 1974   J. Fontenrose, *Python. A study of Delphic myth and its origins*, New York 1974.

Golden 1990   M. Golden, *Children and childhood in Classical Athens*, Baltimore 1990.

Hellenica X   L. Robert, *Recueil d'épigraphie, de numismatique et d'antiquités grecques* vol. 10, Paris 1955.

ILindos II   Ch. Blinkenberg, *Lindos: Fouilles et recherches 1902–1914* II. *Inscriptions* 2, Nos. 282–710, Berlin 1941.

Joubin 1896   A. Joubin, *Sculptures grecques et romaines et byzantine*, Constantinople 1896.

Lolling 1884   H.G. Lolling, 'Inschriften aus der Küstenstädte des Hellespontos und der Propontis', *AM* 9, 1884, 15–35.

Meletemata 11   M.B. Hatzopoulos & L.D. Loukopoulou, *Recherches sur les marches orientales des Temenides: (Anthemonte–Kalindoia)* (Meletemata, 11), Athens 1992–1996.

Mendel 1912–1914   G. Mendel, *Catalogue des sculptures grecques, romaines et byzantines*, Istanbul 1912–1914.

Milet II 3   A. von Gerkan, *Ergebnisse der Ausgrabungen und Untersuchungen seit dem Jahre 1899* Bd II:3. *Die Stadtmauern, mit epigraphischem Beitrag von A. Rehm*, Berlin 1935.

OGI   W. Dittenberger, *Orientis Graeci Inscriptiones Selectae*, Leipzig 1903–1905.

Papachristodoulou 1989   I. Papachristodoulou, *Hoi archaioi rodiakoi demoi. Historike episkopese: He Ialysia*, Athens 1989.

Petzl & Wagner 1976   G. Petzl & J. Wagner, 'Eine neue Temenos-Stele des Königs Antiochos I. von Kommagene', *ZPE* 20, 1976, 201–223.

SB   *Sammelbuch griechischer Urkunden aus Ägypten*, eds. F. Preisigke *et al.*, Wiesbaden 1915–1993.

Schede 1912   M. Schede, 'Mitteilungen aus Samos', *AM* 37, 1912, 199–218.

St. Pontica III   J.G.C. Anderson, F. Cumont & H. Grégoire, *Studia Pontica* III. *Recueil des inscriptions grecques et latines du Pont et de l'Arménie* fasc. 1, Bruxelles 1910.

Susini 1955   G. Susini, 'Iscrizioni greche di Megiste e della Licia nel Museo di Mitilene', *ASAA* 30–32 (N.S. 14–16), 1952–1954 (pr. 1955), 341–353.

Wallensten 2003   J. Wallensten, *ΑΦΡΟΔΙΤΗΙ ΑΝΕΘΗΚΕΝ ΑΡΞΑΣ. A study of dedications to Aphrodite from Greek magistrates*, diss. Lund University, Lund 2003.

Wallensten forthcoming   J. Wallensten, 'Two studies in dedicatory language', forthcoming.

MARIA MILI

Apollo Kerdoos

A CONNIVING APOLLO IN THESSALY?

Abstract*

It is now well established that divine personalities should be studied on a regional as well as a Panhellenic level. This paper explores the cult of Apollo Kerdoos—an epithet that is associated with Apollo only in Thessaly. After discussing the evidence for the cult of the god and the various potential roles of the cult it examines the degree to which the epithet can be related to particular aspects of Thessalian society.

There are two phenomena that make a study of the cult of Apollo Kerdoos (or Kerdoios)[1] particularly interesting. The first is that his cult has thus far been attested only in one area, Thessaly. The epithet is found in several inscriptions from cities in the North of Thessaly. Apollo is only once called Kerdoos outside Thessaly, in Lykophron's *Alexandra*, where the epithet is used to describe the god at Delphi, and it might well be significant that, throughout the centuries, Thessaly had a close relationship with the Delphic sanctuary.[2]

The other interesting phenomenon is the nature of the epithet of the god. The cult ti-

tle Kerdoos comes from the word *kerdos* and means the one who brings profits. All gods were supposed to bring gifts to their worshippers, and perhaps some will be inclined to interpret the epithet Kerdoos along such lines: Apollo Kerdoos was Apollo the gift-giver.[3] Gift and profit, however, is not the same thing: we can generally say that while gift emphasizes the reciprocal element in an exchange, profit makes the relation seem unequal. Many literary sources show that the Greeks were actually troubled by the difference between them. Cozzo, in a study of the various words with the root κερδ-, has argued that in the Homeric epics *kerdea* were skills characterizing warriors and traders that allowed them to gain at the expense of others. When brought into the *polis*, *kerdea* could be destabilizing forces. In several other later sources *kerdos* denoted personal profit, often material, acquired through guile and trickery, and sometimes to the detriment of the communal interest.[4] In Pindar's poetry, Kurke notes, profit is generally presented as evil and corrupting; when *kerdos* is used in the context of aris-

---

* Alina Hatzispyrou, Matthew Haysom, Vicky Panoutsakopoulou, Robert Parker and Jenny Wallensten have heard, read and commented on various drafts of this paper. I am very grateful to all of them.

[1] Both forms of the epithet are attested in the Thessalian inscriptions.

[2] Lycoph. *Alex*. 207.

[3] See for instance Jaillard 2007, 95, who mentions the epithet Kerdoos together with epithets such as Megalodorotatos.

[4] Cozzo 1988, who also notes that the connection with trickery is less common after Homer. Roisman 1990, argues that all adjectival uses of κερδ- words include the meaning of skill and trickiness.

tocratic *megaloprepeia*, however, it can acquire positive connotations.[5] Cozzo has also argued that in the fifth and especially the fourth century, and due to the expansion of small-scale retail trade, the associations between *kerdos* and exploitation were dispelled.[6] The word *kerdos* then, although in general negative, could have different meanings and connotations at different times and in different contexts. How should we understand the epithet when used with Apollo?

Other than with Apollo, the epithet Kerdoos (or similar kinds of epithets formed from the word *kerdos*) is, in literary sources, most often connected with Hermes.[7] And in most books on Greek religion the epithet is considered a very appropriate one: Hermes was, after all, the protector of trade, the god of *metis* (cunning intelligence) *par excellence*, and the patron of thieves.[8] If we look at the very few other instances of *kerdos*-related epithets,[9] then the epithet *Kerdeie* is found once, in Herodas' Seventh *Mimiambus*, as an epithet of Peitho. The context is again that of trade. The goddess is invoked, together with Hermes *Kerdeon*, by a hero-shoemaker, who is also, it is noteworthy,

called Kerdon.[10] There is also a single epigraphic attestation of an Artemis *Kerdoia*.[11] Artemis and Apollo often shared cult titles and, presumably, functions, and since the inscription was found at Thessalian Larisa, we should seek to understand this cult in the context of the Thessalian cult of Apollo Kerdoos. Finally, Pindar in a much-discussed passage attributes the epithet *Philokerdes* to the Muse who inspires him.[12] Was Apollo Kerdoos, as his half brother was, a god connected with trade and other material transactions? Understanding the nature and functions, the "essence", of a god has been at the heart of studies of Greek religion for many years. Apollo is a god who is really difficult to pin down; he has been described as the god of light, as the upholder of the moral order, as a fundamentally agricultural divinity, as the god of young men, or in a more abstract way, as the power of creation.[13] In none of these portraits is there much space left for an Apollo the god of trade. Farnell, for instance, argued that his cult title Kerdoos might allude to "the god whose revenues are swelled by the transmission of first fruits", associating thus the Thessalian cult with other known cults of Apollo in the Greek world, where he was worshipped as *Dekatephoros*.[14] In doing so, however, he essentially dismissed all the connotations of the word *kerdos*.

In the works of a few scholars Apollo is allowed a share in the domain of trade, and some-

---

[5]   Kurke 1991, 225–239. See also von Reden 1995, 61–67, who describes *kerdos* as the ability to gain power over people by means of trickery, and argues that it did not always have negative connotations.
[6]   Cozzo 1988, 82–92.
[7]   Alkiphron 3.47; Heliod. *Aeth*. 6.7; Lucian *Tim*. 41; Plut. *Mor*. 472b. Hermes is also called *Kerdeon* in Herod. 7.74 and *Kerdemporos* in *Hymn. Orph*. 28.6. A Hermes called *Kerdon* was represented twice on a mosaic found at the "roadside house" at Cilicia dated to the second century AD (Russel 1987, 26–28, no. 2; *SEG* 37 1266). See also Hicks 1887, 409–433, esp. 415, who argues that the *kerdemporoi* dedicating in the second century AD at Thasos had as patron god Hermes *Kerdemporos*. The dedication, however, was made to Athena and Herakles.
[8]   See for instance Farnell 1896–1909, vol. 5, 23, n. 37.
[9]   Apart from the cases discussed here see also Vollmer 1836, 1045, who lists *Kerdoos* as an epithet of Herakles, but does not give any reference. I have not managed to confirm his assertion.

[10]   Cunningham 1971, 184, n. 74, comments on the similarity between the name of the hero and the divinities he invokes. For a discussion of various aspects of the phenomenon, see Wallensten 2008.
[11]   Rakatsanis & Tziaphalias 1997, 28, pl. 15 (unpublished).
[12]   Pind. *Isthm*. 2.6. For the passage, see for instance Woodbury 1968.
[13]   Apart from the works cited below, see Nilsson 1955, 529ff., and Konaris in this volume for a review of nineteenth-century approaches to Apollo. On morality and Apollo, see also Davies 1997, 43–64.
[14]   Farnell 1896–1909, vol. 4, 104 (followed by Axenidis 1949, 169). See also Gruppe 1906, 1233, n. 6.

times actually a quite large one. Wilamowitz considered it as a shared function between Hermes and Apollo.[15] While for him this was a function Apollo acquired as he came into Greece from the pre-existing cult of Hermes (and perhaps only in Thessaly?), in other later works Apollo's connection with exchange in general, or with trade more specifically, seems to be considered an established function of the god. Bruit Zaidman and Schmitt Pantel, for instance, building on the work of Dumézil, believe that the "articulate voice of Apollo … manifested itself in all three levels, as prayer and oracle, as battle cry, and as everyday economic intercourse among men".[16] But it should be noted that for these scholars the involvement of Apollo in commerce comes indirectly, because of the communication necessary for any economic activity to take place.[17] Conversely, for Silver, who specifically refers to the cult of Apollo Kerdoos in this way, the connection with trade is part and parcel of Apollo's persona.[18] He puts forward two further pieces of evidence. Firstly, the use of the sanctuary of Apollo at Delos as a bank, and an inscription referring to the tax paid by the *naukleroi* (shipowners) and perhaps the *emporoi* to Apollo Delios (?) at Athens. The use of the sanctuary at Delos as a bank is an example of a function connected with sanctuaries and not the god.[19] As for the tax paid, if it was indeed paid to Apollo Delios,[20] one may wonder whether this was related to his supposed function as a protector of trade, or to his well-established function as a protector of seafaring.[21] There is a passage, though, which clearly connects Apollo with exchange. A fragment of Theophrastos tells us that at Ainos one had to sacrifice to Apollo Epikomaios after the purchase of immovable property.[22] Apollo Epikomaios, Apollo who oversees the village, is involved here principally because the transaction had to become known to the local community.[23] But in this case it would be artificial to draw too strict a distinction between the motive behind the sacrifice and the function of the god as revealed by the epithet.

A more profitable approach might be to turn to the small number of sources that connect Apollo and the concept of *kerdos*. The *Homeric Hymn to Hermes* associates Apollo more prominently with the world of exchange and *kerdos* than any other source. The hymn deals with the division of the *timai* between the two divine brothers. And although cunning Hermes does his best to ensure his profit, he soon finds out, in his first encounter with his half brother, that Apollo too is *polymechanos*,[24] and that he too likes his profit (… *kerdaleon per' eonta*).[25] But we struggle to describe in neat structuralist terms how the profits of Apollo might have differed from those of Hermes.[26] Apollo is often

---

[15] Wilamowitz-Moellendorff 1931, 328.
[16] Bruit Zaidman & Schmitt Pantel 1992, 194, referring to the work of Dumézil 1982.
[17] Dumézil 1982, 17 writes: "… d'où que vienne cette nourriture, qu'elle résulte du travail pastoral ou agricole, du commerce ou de l'industrie, un minimum de communication, d'information de demandes et de réponses, donc de parole est en effet nécessaire pour la produire".
[18] Silver 1992, 161.
[19] For the use of various sanctuaries as banks, see Bogaert 1968, 279–304; see also the works cited in Bremmer 1999, 32.
[20] *IG* I³ 130. The name and epithet of the god have been restored: Lewis 1960, 190–194. See the doubts

and alternative restoration by Mattingly 1990, 112–113; Matthaiou 2000–2003.
[21] Apollo and seafaring: Farnell 1896–1909, vol. 4, 145; Detienne 1998, 138ff.; Graf 1979, 5.
[22] Fortenbauch *et al.* 1992, Fr. 650 (=Stob. *Flor.* 44.22).
[23] For the debate on whether the epithets Komaios and Epikomaios for Apollo are to be connected with the word *kome*, or with *komos*, see Graf 1985, 185–188; Detienne 2003, 69; Koukouli-Xrysanthaki 2009.
[24] *Hymn. Hom. Merc.* 319.
[25] *Hymn. Hom. Merc.* 495.
[26] In a non-structuralist approach N.O. Brown (1947, 95ff.) has seen the opposition expressed in the *Homeric Hymn to Hermes* as one between Hermes the god of the nouveau riches of the Archaic age, and Apollo the god of the old aristocracy. Shall we, then, distinguish

not included among the gods who possess *metis*.[27] As for Apollo's wealth, it is argued, it seems to come not through exchange but through the accumulation and storing of riches in his sanctuaries. Apollo is described as a greedy god, and it is his greediness that puts him in opposition with the Hermaic world of exchange.[28] But it is not only the *Homeric Hymn to Hermes*, where the god acquires the lyre in exchange for his cattle, which shows Apollo engaged in exchange. Tradition had it that Apollo acquired his two most sacred places, Delphi and Delos, by exchanging them with Poseidon for Kalaureia and Tainaron.[29] Indeed, one may wonder if this was why Poseidon received at Delphi the strange epithet *Amoibeus*.[30]

None of the scholars who have discussed Apollo Kerdoos have looked at the Thessalian context and the actual evidence for his cult; but Apollo Kerdoos was worshipped in a certain society by particular worshippers and with particular rituals, all of which will have shaped to a certain extent the understanding of his cult. Some thirty years ago Christiane Sourvinou-Inwood argued for the need to study divine personalities also at a local level: Greek gods did not have exactly the same functions everywhere in the Greek world. In some places a god's powers could be circumscribed, his functions being taken over by other deities of the pantheon, or conversely a certain divinity could receive particular emphasis, and come to acquire functions he or she did not normally possess elsewhere.[31] This raises the question of the unity of the divine figure, the degree to which local divine personalities could diverge from their Panhellenic norm. Apollo in particular has been considered as the most "Greek" of all deities: his main two cult centres, Delphi and Delos attracted a Panhellenic clientele and exercised throughout Greek history a strong influence on local cults.[32]

The cult of Apollo Kerdoos in Thessaly

Let us begin the discussion with the place and role of trade in Thessalian society. Thessalian cities were ruled by more-or-less exclusive oligarchies dominated by a landed aristocracy. There is some evidence that, as in other oligarchic states, trade was looked down upon. Aristotle mentions that Thessalian cities had an

---

between Hermes the god of small-scale traders, and Apollo the aristocratic god of ship-owners? Kurke (1999, 72–75) argues for a distinction between professional trade, which was scorned, and occasional, non-professional trade which was acceptable. Contra: Moreno 2007, 225ff.

[27] Detienne & Vernant (1974, 263, 266–267) do not include Apollo among the gods who possess *metis*. See also Corsano 1988, 111–112, for Apollo using the *metis* of other gods. Strauss Clay (1989, 135, 140) notes that Apollo too is *polymechanos*.

[28] Detienne 1998, 178 for the "avidité apollinienne". The theme is taken and explored in relation to Hermes by Jaillard (2007, 95 and 150, n. 78), where he refers to the evidence for Apollo Kerdoos in Thessaly but does not comment on the cult. Strauss Clay (1989, 85) also comments on the unnatural wealth of Delos and Delphi. In this respect the fact that at Ainos Apollo Epikomaios is involved in the transaction of immovable property could become meaningful: perhaps we could think in terms of an opposition between Hermes/movable property versus Apollo/storage and immovable property?

[29] Strab. 8.6.14; Paus. 2.33.2; 10.5.3; Schol. Aesch. *Eum*. 27; Schol. Ap. Rhod. 3.1242; Callim. (F593 Pfeiffer); *Suda* s.v. ἀνεῖλεν. On the myth, see Sourvinou-Inwood 1987, esp. 231–232.

[30] Lycoph. *Alex*. 617. Farnell (1896–1909, vol. 4, 27) argues that the title is scarcely to be explained by the legend that he gave up his Delphic inheritance to Apollo. But see Detienne 1998, 166, n. 220, who associates the epithet with this tradition. For ἀμείβω and related words: Scheid-Tissinier 1994, 37–40.

---

[31] Sourvinou-Inwood 1978.

[32] Sourvinou-Inwood herself (1978, 102) argues that "... in some cases, as in that of Apollo, the Panhellenic dimension is particularly strong, due to the special circumstances of its diffusion".

agora, the so-called free agora (*eleuthere agora*), into which no trader was allowed entrance unless summoned by the archons.[33] We have to assume that whatever commercial activities took place in Thessalian cities would have been hosted elsewhere, in a separate "trade agora". The attitude of the Thessalians towards trade has implications, of course, for our understanding of the cult of Apollo Kerdoos. Several scholars believe that the sanctuary of the god at Larisa was located in the agora of the city, but they do not take into consideration the distinction made by Aristotle between the "free" and the trade agora. We thus read that the sanctuary of the god was in the free agora, and that the god had a trade function.[34]

Let me first review the evidence for the suggested location of the sanctuary in the free agora at Larisa. The sanctuary of Apollo Kerdoos at Larisa was the main place of publication of civic decrees (occasionally copies were also set up in the sanctuary of Athena Polias on the acropolis), and several scholars believe that such an important *polis* sanctuary must have been located in the "free agora" of the city.[35] Rescue excavations at the modern square of Tachydromeiou have revealed architectural remains, such as Doric columns, parts of a *geison* and an *epistylion*, all of which seem to date from the fourth century onwards.[36] The degree of monumentalization that went into the area, its central location and its proximity to the acro-

polis (as well as its use in modern times as the main square of Larisa) have suggested to several scholars that this might have been the location of the free agora of Larisa. Furthermore, the discovery of two fragmentary decrees in the area, it has been argued, could indicate that this was also the location of the sanctuary of Apollo Kerdoos.[37] The suggestion is plausible, but still far from proved: other parts of the city than the agora could be monumentalized and decrees could be set up in any important sanctuary in the city, not only in those in the agora. And in any case, according to the reports, it seems that the decrees were found in secondary use and, thus, one is free to assume that they might have come from anywhere in the city.[38]

Also involved in the discussion of the location of the sanctuary of Apollo Kerdoos at Larisa is a Hellenistic inscription.[39] The inscription records the decision of the city of Larisa to enrol new citizens following the orders of Philip V. Initially, we are told, the city followed the orders of the king. Two stone stelai with the names of those who had been given citizenship were set up in the sanctuaries of Athena Polias and Apollo Kerdoos. But then, we are told, some names were erased, because, for reasons left unexplained, it was deemed that they did not deserve citizenship. The king then wrote back to the *tagoi* of the city demanding that these names be included on the stele and that he would hear the cases concerning them when he returned from campaign. The city then decided that a catalogue with the names of those not yet accepted as citizens (a *leukoma*) should be set up at the so-called *limen*, while two copies of the decree with the names

---

[33] Arist. *Pol.* 7.1331a. Martin (1951, 283–308, esp. 296) believes that the banning of commercial activities from the agora was a common feature of oligarchic cities.
[34] Cf. Helly 1987, 157, n. 78, who accepts that the epithet Kerdoos is related with trade and attempts to explain it by reference to the supposed function of the city as a boundary market in the pre-Archaic period.
[35] Decrees set up in the sanctuary of Apollo Kerdoos include *IG* IX 2 512, 517, 521, add. 205; Béquignon 1935, 55–64; Tziaphalias 1984, 229–230, no. 121; Gallis 1977; Cabanes & Andreou 1985; *IG* VII 4131; Malay & Ricl 2009.
[36] Verdelis 1955, 147–150; *AD* 31 (1976) *Chron.*, 176; *AD* 34 (1979) *Chron.*, 215–219.

[37] Verdelis 1955, 146–147 (= McDevitt 1970, 45, nos. 331–332). Tziaphalias 1994; Rakatsanis & Tziaphalias 1997, 20.
[38] Verdelis 1955, 147. At Scotussa the *Kerdoion* was not in the agora, but somewhere close to the city walls: Missailidou-Despotidou 1993, A. 73–74.
[39] *IG* IX 2 517. See also Austin 1981, 117, no. 60.

of those accepted as citizens would be set up at the sanctuaries of Apollo Kerdoos and Athena Polias. Several scholars have assumed that both the *leukoma* and a copy of the decree were set up in the sanctuary of the god which was in the *limen*.[40] The main reason behind this assertion was the belief that the sanctuary of Apollo Kerdoos in Larisa was located in the free agora and that the free agora and the *limen* were the same, because a gloss of Hesychius tells us that the Thessalians' name for the agora was *limen*.[41] But the evidence of the inscription does not allow us to establish any relation between the *limen* and the sanctuary of Apollo Kerdoos, which are mentioned at a few lines distance from one another.

Our first problem, with regard to this inscription, is to establish to what precisely the term *limen* refers. For a variety of reasons I believe that it is far more likely that the word *limen* was used in Thessaly for the trade agora than for the "free" agora. First, the term means port, and the association between ports and trading areas is well established.[42] It has been shown that other words used mainly for sea trade, such as *emporos*, could also be used for overland trade.[43] Moreover, the fact that the names of the non-citizens were set up in the *li-men* accords extremely well with this interpretation; just as labourers and traders, i.e. non-citizens, were excluded from the free agora, so were the names of those not deemed worthy of citizenship. The fact that different kinds of documents are to be set up in the sanctuary of Kerdoos (those accepted as citizens) and in the area of the *limen* (those not accepted) is very significant, since it clearly establishes the sanctuary of Kerdoos as quite distinct from and opposed to the *limen*—the trade agora. Not only, then, does there seem to be no connection between Apollo Kerdoos and trade, the two in fact appear in this context placed in strong opposition to one another. Whether the sanctuary of the god was actually in the free agora or not is not for our purposes very important to decide.

All the other evidence we have for the cult of the god is in the form of dedicatory inscriptions. There are three inscribed dedications made to Apollo Kerdoos, two of which were offered by men, while the third was offered in favour of a man. In all cases the offering seems to have been quite an expensive one, and there is some evidence that the dedicants may actually have belonged to the highest levels of society, to what we may call the Thessalian nobility. A statue base found at Larisa and dated to the third century BC preserves, in the form of a dedicatory epigram composed by a certain Herakleidas from Tralleis, the offering of two brothers, Simias and Eukratidas: "... there is not for us as much enjoyment of our wealth as all time will recognise our piety".[44] The names of the two brothers sound aristocratic (we know of similar names belonging to members of the aristocratic family of the Aleuads), and their dedication, a statue, was certainly not a negligible offering. The second dedication, found at

---

[40] See for instance Axenidis 1949, 168. Tziaphalias (1994, 159) believes that the *limen* was a specific part of the agora, or the name of a building in it.

[41] Some independent evidence for a connection between the *limen* of Thessalian cities and sanctuaries of Apollo might be furnished by the cult title Panlimnios attested for Apollo at Gonnoi (*AD* 29 [1974] *Chron.* 571; Kontogiannis 2000). Shall we perhaps explain it as Apollo of all *limens*, instead of Apollo of all lakes? But, a lake seems to have existed nearby, there is some other evidence for a sanctuary of Apollo in that area, and Kontogiannis argues that the dedication may have been made by fishermen. Garcia Ramón (2004, 242) follows a rather different line of argument, taking the *limen* to be, among other things, also a place of reunion.

[42] Martin 1951, 284.

[43] Knorringa 1926, 44. Note the use of the word *enlimena*, which means tax collected from harbours (Thiel 1924, 62–67), in a fragmentary decree from inland

Western Thessaly (Helly 1993). Perhaps the word was here used metaphorically to denote a land tax.

[44] *IG* IX 2 637. For Herakleidas: Bouvier 1979, 258.

Vlachogianni (perhaps the ancient city of Erei-kinion), northwest of Larisa, and dated to the second century BC, recorded the dedication by Politas and Ptolema of a statue of their son.[45] The reason behind the dedication is not stated, but it is a plausible conjecture that the dedication was made after the young boy had served in a ritual office in honour of the god, perhaps, judging from the third dedication, which we will discuss below, as a *daphnephoros*.

The third dedication, dating to the third century, was found at Tyrnavo, a few kilometres northwest of Larisa.[46] The site has been identified by some with ancient Phalanna (others prefer to place Phalanna at nearby Tatar Magoula).[47] Be that as it may, the inscription might not have come from the area, as there is some evidence that several other inscriptions found at Tyrnavo were transferred there from Larisa.[48] It was inscribed on a stone base and was offered by a man called Sousipatros Polemarchidaios. Sousipatros called himself a *thytas*, and he also recorded that he had served as a *hieromnemon* and as a *daphnephoros*. *Thytas*, the sacrificer, or something like that, comes from the verb *thyo* and was obviously a ritual office (for which see more below). *Hieromne-*

mon was the name of local Thessalian officials, about whose functions we know little, but also, as is well known, the name of the representatives of the various *ethne* in the Delphic amphictyony.[49] And *daphnephoros* was a ritual office connected with the cult of Apollo.

The *daphnephoria*, the carrying of the sacred laurel was a rite celebrated in honour of Apollo seemingly in various areas of central Greece. A famous *daphnephoria* took place at Delphi; it was part of the festival Stepteria which was celebrated every nine years and it involved the carrying of the sacred laurel from Tempe to Delphi.[50] A rite of *daphnephoria* was also part of the cult of Apollo Ismenios at Thebes and possibly, it has recently been argued, of other Boiotian cults of Apollo.[51] Both at Delphi and Thebes, where we have more information about the rite, a young boy belonging to one of the best families of the city played a prominent role in the ritual. He was accompanied by other *paides eugeneis* at Delphi, or by a chorus of *parthenoi* at Thebes. Sousipatros, to judge by the various offices he had held, must have belonged to a good Thessalian family. In his dedication he seems to have commemo-

[45]   Woodward 1910, 154, no. 6 (= McDevitt 1970, 139, no. 116). For the identification of Vlachogianni with ancient Erikeinion, see Stählin 1924, 28; Rakatsanis & Tziaphalias 2004, 99–100, who do not, however, mention the dedication to Kerdoos. Lucas (1995) locates at Vlachogianni ancient Mylai.

[46]   *IG* IX 2 1234 (first century BC); Helly 1987, 141, n. 34, for a date in the third century and for the possibility that it was transferred from Larisa.

[47]   Ancient remains have been found both at Kastri Tyrnavou and at Tatar Magoula, and there is a disagreement concerning which are impressive enough to be identified with that of a city: Stählin 1924, 30 located Phalanna at Kastri. He is followed by Tziaphalias 2000, 100. Contra: Helly 1999, 112–113, argues that a central place was located at Tatar Magoula, not at Kastri. But he identifies it with Kondaia and he places Phalanna instead at Damasi.

[48]   Of problematic origin are also *IG* IX 2 1034, 1227 and 1233.

[49]   For the local *hieromnemones* see Axenidis 1949, 129–130, who suggests that they were important officials, responsible for the sacred money and property. Note also the mention of *hieromnemones* in Helly 1970, esp. 276–277, 283 (and the reservations of Salviat and Vatin 1971, esp. 34). There is a problem concerning the *hieromnemones* mentioned as partakers of the oath, together with various other Thessalian federal officials, in the fourth-century treaty with Athens (*IG* II² 116, 175): Hatzopoulos (1996, 288) argues that these were not the representatives at the Delphic amphictyony, but representatives of the local communities vis-à-vis the ethnos. What the relationship between all these different levels of *hieromnemones* might have been is a problem.

[50]   Farnell 1896–1909, vol. 4, 293–295; Jeanmaire 1939, 387–411; Brelich 1969, 387–438; Burkert 1983, 127–130.

[51]   Brelich 1969, 413–419; Schachter 1981, i. 83–85; Calame 2001, 59–63; Kurke 2007; Kowalzig 2007, 371–382.

rated the various stages of his ritual career: he must have been a *daphnephoros* at a young age, *hieromnemon* certainly at a later one, and the language of the inscription seems to describe him as being a *thytas* now. All three were possibly connected with the cult of Apollo, even if not necessarily, as the case of *hieromnemon* most clearly indicates, with the cult of Apollo Kerdoos.[52] On the other hand, the fact that the dedication at Chyretiai was made for a young boy adds some strength to the suggestion that a rite of *daphnephoria* was performed in honour of Apollo Kerdoos.[53]

Men, and young men in particular, appear from the evidence discussed above to have had a prominent role in the cult of Apollo Kerdoos. This observation squares well with the belief that Apollo in general was a god closely connected with boys and young men.[54] We could seek to understand the cult title Kerdoos in this light. It has been noted above that the word *kerdos* had connotations of guile and trickery, and in discussions of initiatory cults guile and trickery are considered a common feature.[55] It is worth pointing out also here, that for some scholars the rite of the *daphnephoria*, in which young people had a prominent role, was, or had elements of, an initiatory rite, marking the

passage into adulthood.[56] Is, then, Apollo Kerdoos the conniving Apollo who brings gains through guile and trickery, a deity similar to Athena Apatouria, the goddess who presided over Athenian phratries, her own name deriving, for the ancients at least, from the word *apate*, that is deception?[57] The problem is that this explanation restricts the meaning of Kerdoos only to one of its connotations, and accounts for it by reference to a particular age group. But Sousipatros dedicated to the god years after he had served as *daphnephoros*, also associating with the god the other ritual roles he had assumed in his lifetime.

Sousipatros also called himself a *thytas*. Berthiaume has discussed the literary and epigraphic evidence for the word, which seems to have been used in various contexts, where it is not clear exactly what it denoted.[58] Clearly in the Thessalian context the office of *thytas* must have been an important one, since Sousipatros, as we saw, had also held other very prestigious offices. Berthiaume noted that in several cases the word was used for a diviner, who practised divination through sacrifice, a possibility that we can hardly prove in the Thessalian case but that is, I think, worth entertaining a little further. We may recall here that the scholiast of Lykophron's *Alexandra* explained the epithet Kerdoos in relation to Apollo's oracular activity: he was the god who brought gains to those who consulted him. Furthermore, it has recently been argued that daphnephoric rituals had in Boiotia (but perhaps behind them, the

---

52 The connection for instance between the cult of Kerdoos and *daphnephoria* depends on whether this was the cult at Larisa or not.

53 I cannot discuss here what the relationship between these local daphnephoric rituals and the Stepteria might have been. See for instance Rakatsanis & Tziaphalias 1997, 22, who suggest that the Delphic *theoria* stopped at the Larisean Kerdoion.

54 Burkert 1975, 1–21; Graf 1979; Jameson 1980, 213–236; Versnel 1993, 314ff.; Parker 2005, 393, 436–437.

55 The bibliography on initiatory cults is large and continually increasing. For the theme of guile and trickery, see the classic discussion by Vidal-Naquet 1986, 106–128. For a critical discussion of the problems of using the category for classifying and understanding Greek rituals, see more recently Parker 2005, 209–210.

56 Brelich 1969, 387–438; Kurke (2007) accepts that the Boiotian rite had initiatory elements but argues that the cult represented symbolically all aspects of the Theban population.

57 See in general Lambert 1993, 143ff. In Athens the patron of the festival was Athena Phratria but the epithet Apatouria for the goddess is attested at Troizen: Paus. 2.33.1 and Lambert 1993, 147, n. 26, for other gods with a similar epithet.

58 Berthiaume 1982, 20–21 and n. 27 for the Thessalian inscription.

argument goes, there was a common Thessalo-Boiotian tradition), a close connection with oracular cults.[59]

Conclusions

In the preceding discussion we have explored various aspects of the cult of Apollo Kerdoos. We have seen that his cult was an important *polis* cult: at Larisa the sanctuary of the god was the most common place to publish public decrees, the *epiphanestatos topos* of the city. His worshippers accordingly included some of the most privileged members of society, and in his cult, part of which was perhaps a rite of *daphnephoria*, young aristocratic boys played a prominent role. Finally, there is some slight evidence that his cult might have had oracular functions. We have explored how the epithet Kerdoos might have been understood in relation to some of these functions: Apollo a god of guile and trickery as the patron of Thessalian ephebes, or Apollo who brought gains through his ambiguous oracles. Neither of these interpretations seem to me to be very satisfactory, as they explain the epithet only by reference to isolated aspects of the cult, and aspects which are in any case speculative.

Something else that emerged from this study is there are recurring links between the Thessalian cult of Apollo Kerdoos and the Delphic cult of the god. The rite of *daphnephoria* which might have united both cults, the fact that Sousipatros commemorated his service as

a *hieromnemon* (if of course he was the Thessalian representative at Delphi) at the sanctuary of Apollo Kerdoos, and the fact that the only literary attestation of Apollo Kerdoos refers to the Pythian Apollo, indicate that there was a perceived relation between the two cults. It is, I think, a plausible suggestion that the Thessalians would at some level have understood the cult of Apollo Kerdoos in relation to Delphi. This is hardly surprising given the close connections between Thessaly and Delphi, and there is evidence, which I cannot discuss here, that myth and ritual also helped link other Thessalian cults of Apollo with the Delphic cult. We have seen at the beginning of this paper that a group of myths centred on the Panhellenic sanctuaries of Apollo implicated the god in the world of exchange and *kerdos*, and it is a likely conjecture that the epithet Kerdoos, which Lykophron also attributed to the Pythian Apollo, was understood in reference to these stories.

If Panhellenic myth and the radiant figure of Apollo Pythios helped shape the Thessalians' perception of the local cult of Apollo Kerdoos, we also have to allow that a parallel and more "local" understanding of the god might also have been at work. In order to understand how the Thessalians might have made sense of the epithet Kerdoos we have to examine how *kerdos* in its various possible connotations (that is personal profit, often material, and which involved trickery) might have been perceived in Thessalian society. The evidence for the cult of Apollo Kerdoos in Thessaly shows that we have to understand the word *kerdos* and the epithet Kerdoos not in the context of the world of trade, but in the context of an aristocratic society. Xenophon in the *Anabasis* gives us one of the rare portraits of a Thessalian individual: Menon, a typical Thessalian aristocrat who came from a rich and well-known family from Pharsalos. It is interesting to read the traits which Xenophon ascribes to Menon. He describes him as a man who only cared for profit

---

[59] Kowalzig 2007, 371–382. I am not convinced, though, by Kowalzig's arguments that the Theban daphnephoric rite was a late sixth- or early fifth-century addition to the cult. She does not discuss the cult of Apollo Daphnephoros at Eretria, archaeological evidence for which goes back to the Geometric period. Unless we explained away this case, by arguing that the rite was a later addition in this cult too, then daphnephoric rites seem to be attested at an early time in a wide area, which would include Thebes.

(*kerdainei*), and who thought that the best way to achieve his aims was through guile and trickery and deception.[60]

This is not the place to go into details about what Thessalian society might have been like; attention should be drawn to some of its fundamental characteristics. The co-existence of various power groups which could often act independently and even in opposition to each other is an element of Thessalian society that has troubled scholars.[61] In histories of the area we often hear of the various Thessalian cities, such as Pharsalos, Pherai and Larisa. But together with the *poleis* we frequently hear of other groups cutting across the cities, such as the nobility, the cavalry class, the so-called Thessalian masses and the *penestai*, the serf population of Thessaly. We even see powerful individuals, such as Menon, who in 476 sent a force of his own *penestai* to assist Kimon at Eion, acting on their own with no apparent constraint either from the city or from the ethnos.[62] The wealth of the various illustrious Thessalian families was proverbial. It is important also to remember that Thessaly was a cavalry society. According to some ancient sources the proportion of hoplites to cavalrymen in Thessaly was 2:1, in comparison with other states where the proportion was usually 5:1, or even 10:1.[63] While the implications of hoplite warfare and hoplite ideology for society at large have been belaboured, those of cavalry warfare have not

received as much attention.[64] In hoplite warfare discipline was important, and *arete* was described as the will and power to remain in one's rank and resist the enemy without fleeing. Brave was the man who went against his enemy face to face. On the contrary, ambush and ruse are considered to have been the mainstays of cavalry warfare. Manoeuvring, leaving the field of battle to make another sudden attack were characteristics of cavalry operations.[65]

Thessalian society, we have to concede, allowed for the individual to excel, to distinguish himself. Inequality does not seem to have been deemed inappropriate, in need of concealment. On the contrary the wealthy, powerful individual was at the heart of Thessalian society. In one line, Pindar praises the blessed happiness of Thessaly's nobility and of Thessaly itself: the fortune of the Thessalian elite families was portrayed and perceived to some level to have been interdependent with the fortune and plenitude of Thessaly at large.[66] What seems to have eased the passage from one to the other was the idea of *megaloprepeia*, of making one's wealth, one's *kerdos* public.[67] It is, I think, this image of a wealthy Thessaly relying on the profit of its rich noblemen that the cult of Apollo Kerdoos celebrated.

This paper has struggled with the problem of the relationship between local and Panhellenic divine personalities, starting with the question of the degree to which the local persona of a god could differ from the Panhellenic one. We have seen that the cult of Apollo Kerdoos in Thessaly in general followed broader Greek patterns of Apollo worship: he appeared as a god of men and young men, worshipped

---

[60] Xen. *An*. 2.6.21–29. For Menon and his career, see Morisson 1942; T.S. Brown 1986.

[61] Here I can only refer the reader to some standard works: Meyer 1909; Westlake 1935; Sordi 1958; Larsen 1968, 12–26; Gehrke 1985, 184–197. Helly's radical re-evaluation of Thessalian society (Helly 1995) remains controversial.

[62] Dem. 13.23; Dem. 23.199. On this passage and its implications for the existence of so-called "private armies", see Helly 1995, 303–312 (who argues that Menon was acting in an official context, as representative of the Thessalian ethnos) and the response by Ducat 1997, 186–187.

[63] Arist. Fr. 498 (Rose); Xen. *Hell*. 6.1.8.

[64] See for instance Detienne 1968; Raaflaub 1997.

[65] For the difference between hoplite and cavalry warfare, see Spence 1993, 164–172. Eur. *Phoen*. 1407–1413 for the so-called "Thessalian feint".

[66] Pind. *Pyth*. 10.2–3.

[67] The hospitality and *megaloprepeia* of the Thessalians was also proverbial; cf. Xen. *Hell*. 6.1.3.

with daphnephoric rituals which are well attested in general, and may have had oracular
functions; and his characteristic local cult title
Kerdoos could be understood by reference to
his Pythian cult. Even if the Thessalian Apollo
Kerdoos does not look out of place from the
Panhellenic perspective, this should not lead
us to doubt the existence of a regional divine
personality. There might not have been strong
oppositions and divergences of functions, but
Apollo Kerdoos was perceived both through
Panhellenic and local Thessalian lenses. There
was, it has been argued, a constant co-existence
and interplay of Panhellenic and regional perceptions of the divine.

MARIA MILI
Department of Archeology and Ancient History
Lund University
milimaria3@gmail.com

Bibliography

Austin 1981   M.M. Austin, *The Hellenistic
               world from Alexander to the
               Roman conquest*, Cambridge
               1981.

Axenidis   Th. Axenidis, *Η Πελασγίς
1949   Λάρισα και η αρχαία Θεσσαλία.
               Β΄ Οι μακεδονικοί και ρωμαϊκοί
               χρόνοι*, Athens 1949.

Béquignon   Y. Béquignon, 'Etudes Thessa-
1935   liennes VII', *BCH* 59, 1935,
               36–77.

Berthiaume   G. Berthiaume, *Les rôles du
1982   mágeiros. Étude sur la bouche-
               rie, la cuisine et le sacrifice dans
               la Grèce ancienne*, Leiden 1982.

Bogaert 1968   R. Bogaert, *Banques et ban-
               quiers dans les cités grecques*,
               Leiden 1968.

Bouvier 1979   H. Bouvier, 'Poètes et prosa-
               teurs de Thessalie dans les
               inscriptions', in *La Thessalie.
               Actes de la table ronde 21–24
               Juillet 1975*, ed. B. Helly,
               Lyon 1979, 257–264.

Brelich 1969   A. Brelich, *Paides e parthenoi*,
               Roma 1969.

Bremmer   J.N. Bremmer, *Greek religion*,
1999   Cambridge 1999².

N.O. Brown   N.O. Brown, *Hermes the thief.
1947   The evolution of a myth*,
               New York 1947.

T.S. Brown   T.S. Brown, 'Menon of
1986   Thessaly', *Historia* 35, 1986,
               387–404.

Bruit   L. Bruit Zaidman & P. Sch-
Zaidman   mitt Pantel, *Religion in the
& Schmitt   ancient Greek city*, Cambridge
Pantel 1992   1992.

Burkert 1975   W. Burkert, 'Apellai und Apol-
               lon', *RhM* 118, 1975, 1–21.

Burkert 1983   W. Burkert, *Homo Necans. The
               anthropology of ancient Greek
               sacrificial ritual and myth*,
               Berkeley 1983.

Cabanes   P. Cabanes & J. Andreou,
& Andreou   'Le reglement frontalier entre
1985   les cités d'Ambrakie et de
               Charadros', *BCH* 109, 1985,
               499–544.

Calame 2001   C. Calame, *Choruses of young
               women in ancient Greece*,
               Maryland 2001.

Corsano   M. Corsano, *Themis. La norma
1988   e l'oracolo nella Grecia Antica*,
               Lecce 1988.

Cozzo 1988   A. Cozzo, *Kerdos. Semantica,
               ideologia e società nella Grecia
               antica*, Roma 1988.

Cunningham   I.C. Cunningham, *Herodas
1971   Mimiambi*, Oxford 1971.

Davies 1997 J.K. Davies, 'The moral dimensions of Pythian Apollo', in *What is a god? Studies in the nature of Greek divinity*, ed. A.B. Lloyd, London 1997, 43–64.

Detienne 1968 M. Detienne, 'La phalange: problèmes et controverses', in *Problèmes de la guerre en Grèce ancienne*, ed. J-.P. Vernant, Paris 1968, 119–142.

Detienne 1998 M. Detienne, *Apollon. Le couteau à la main*, Paris 1998.

Detienne 2003 M. Detienne, 'Misogynous Hestia, or the city in its autonomy', in M. Detienne, *The writing of Orpheus. Greek myth in cultural context*, Baltimore, Md 2003, 59–69.

Detienne & Vernant 1974 M. Detienne & J.-P. Vernant, *Les Ruses de l'intelligence. La Mètis des Grecs*, Paris 1974.

Ducat 1997 J. Ducat, 'Bruno Helly et les pénestes', *Topoi* 7, 1997, 183–189.

Dumézil 1982 G. Dumézil, *Apollon sonore et autres essais*, Paris 1982.

Farnell 1896–1909 L.R. Farnell, *The cults of the Greek states* (5 vols), Oxford 1896–1909.

Fortenbauch et al. 1992 W.W. Fortenbauch *et al.*, *Theophrastus of Eresus. Sources for his life, writings, thought and influence* vol. II, Brill 1992.

Gallis 1977 K. Gallis, 'Χρυσόγονος εξ Εδέσης. Λαρισαϊκόν τιμητικόν ψήφισμα', in *Archaia Makedonia* 2, 1977, 33–43.

Garcia Ramón 2004 J.L. Garcia Ramón, 'Del trabajo en una gramática del Tesalo: para una valoración lingüística de las glosas', in *Dialetti, dilettismi, generi letterari e funzioni sociali. Atti del V Congresso Internazionale di Linguistica Greca*, ed. G. Roccas, Milano 2004, 235–264.

Gehrke 1984 H. Gehrke, *Stasis. Untersuchungen zu der inneren Kriegen in den griechischen Staaten des 5. und 4. Jahrhunderts v. Chr.*, München 1985.

Graf 1979 F. Graf, 'Apollon Delphinios', *MusHelv* 36, 1979, 2–22.

Graf 1985 F. Graf, *Nordionische Kulte*, Roma 1985.

Gruppe 1906 O. Gruppe, *Griechische Mythologie und Religionsgeschichte*, München 1906.

Hatzopoulos 1996 M. Hatzopoulos, *Macedonian institutions under the kings* (Meletemata, 22) Athens 1996.

Helly 1970 B. Helly, 'À Larisa. Bouleversements et remise en ordre de sanctuaires', *Mnemosyne* 23, 1970, 249–296.

Helly 1987 B. Helly, 'Le "Dotion Pedion", Lakéreia et les origines de Larisa', *JSav*, 1987, 127–158.

Helly 1993 B. Helly, 'Accord de sympolitie entre Gomphoi et Thamiai (Ithômé)', in *Dialectologica Graeca. Actas del II coloquio international de dialegtologia Griega*, eds. E. Crespo, J.L. Garcia-Ramón & A. Striano, Madrid 1993, 167–200.

Helly 1995 B. Helly, *L'état Thessalien. Aleuas le Roux, les tetrads et lestagoi*, Lyon 1995.

Helly 1999 B. Helly, 'Modèle de l'archéologie des cités à l'archéologie du paysage', in *Territoires de cités grecques. Actes de la table ronde internationale 31 Octobre–3*

Novembre 1991 (BCH, Suppl. 34), ed. M. Brunet, Athens 1999, 99–124.

Hicks 1887   E.L. Hicks, 'Inscriptions from Thasos', *JHS* 8, 1887, 409–433.

Jaillard 2007   D. Jaillard, *Configurations d'Hermès. Une 'théogonie hermaique'* (Kernos, Suppl. 17), Liège 2007.

Jameson 1980   M. Jameson, 'Apollo Lykeios in Athens', *Archaiognosia* 1, 1980, 213–236.

Jeanmaire 1939   H. Jeanmaire, *Couroi et courètes*, Lille 1939.

Knorringa 1926   H. Knorringa, *Emporos. Data on trade and trader in Greek literature from Homer to Alexander*, Amsterdam 1926.

Kontogiannis 2000   A. Kontogiannis, 'Ἀπόλλωνι Αἰσωνίῳ (αναθηματικές επιγραφές από τους Γόννους)', in *Το έργο των εφορειών αρχαιοτήτων και νεοτέρων μνημείων του ΥΠ.ΠΟ στη Θεσσαλία και στην ευρύτερη περιοχή της*, Volos 2000, 125–143.

Koukouli-Chrysanthaki 2009   Ch. Koukouli-Chrysanthaki, 'Ἀπόλλων Κωμαῖος στους Φιλίππους', in *Κερμάτια Φιλίας. Τιμητικός τόμος για τον Ιω. Τσουράτσογλου. Επιγραφική–Αρχαιολογία–Varia* vols 1–2, Athens 2009, 481–503.

Kowalzig 2007   B. Kowalzig, *Singing for the gods. Performances of myth and ritual in Archaic and Classical Greece*, Oxford 2007.

Kurke 1991   L. Kurke, *The traffic in praise. Pindar and the poetics of social economy*, Cornell 1991.

Kurke 1999   L. Kurke, *Coins, bodies, games and gold. The politics of meaning in Archaic Greece*, Princeton 1999.

Kurke 2007   L. Kurke, 'Visualizing the choral: Epichoric poetry, ritual and elite negotiation in fifth-century Thebes', in *Visualizing the tragic. Drama and ritual in Greek art and literature*, eds. C. Kraus, S. Goldhill, H.P. Foley & J. Elsner, Oxford 2007, 63–101.

Lambert 1993   S.D. Lambert, *The phratries of Attica*, Michigan 1993.

Larsen 1968   J.A.O. Larsen, *Greek federal states. Their institutions and history*, Oxford 1968.

Lewis 1960   D.M. Lewis, 'Apollo Delios', *BSA* 55, 1960, 190–194.

Lucas 1995   G. Lucas, 'A propos d'Èreikinion, cité Perrhèbe', *ZPE* 105, 1995, 105–130.

Malay & Ricl 2009   H. Malay & M. Ricl, 'Two new Hellenstic decrees from Aigai in Aiolis', *EA* 42, 2009, 39–47.

Martin 1951   R. Martin, *Recherches sur l'agora grecque*, Paris 1951.

Matthaiou 2000–2003   A. Matthaiou, 'Εἰς IG I³ 130', *Horos* 14–16, 2000–2003, 45–49.

Mattingly 1990   H.B. Mattingly, 'Some fifth-century Attic epigraphic hands', *ZPE* 83, 1990, 110–122.

McDevitt 1970   A.S. McDevitt, *Inscriptions from Thessaly*, Hildesheim 1970.

Meyer 1909   E. Meyer, *Theopomps Hellenika*, Halle 1909.

Missailidou-Despotidou 1993
V. Missailidou-Despotidou, 'A Hellenistic inscription from Scotoussa 1993 (Thessaly) and the fortifications of the city', *BSA* 88, 1993, 187–217.

Moreno 2007
A. Moreno, *Feeding the democracy. The Athenian grain supply in the fifth and fourth centuries B.C.*, Oxford 2007.

Morisson 1942
J.S. Morisson, 'Meno of Pharsalus, Polycrates, and Ismenias', *CQ* 36, 1942, 57–78.

Nilsson 1955
M. Nilsson, *Geschichte der griechischen Religion* I, München 1955².

Parker 2005
R. Parker, *Polytheism and society at Athens*, Oxford 2005.

Raaflaub 1997
K.A. Raaflaub, 'Soldiers, citizens and the evolution of the early Greek polis', in *The development of the polis in Archaic Greece*, eds. L.G. Mitchell & P.J. Rhodes, London 1997, 49–59.

Rakatsanis & Tziaphalias 1997
K. Rakatsanis & A. Tziaphalias, *Λατρείες και ιερά στην αρχαία Θεσσαλία. Α΄ Πελασγιώτις*, Ioannina 1997.

Rakatsanis & Tziaphalias 2004
K. Rakatsanis & A. Tziaphalias, *Λατρείες και ιερά στην αρχαία Θεσσαλία. Β΄ Περραιβία*, Ioannina 2004.

von Reden 1995
S. von Reden, *Exchange in ancient Greece*, London 1995.

Roisman 1990
H.M. Roisman, 'Kerdion in the Ilias: Profit and trickiness', *TAPA* 120, 1990, 23–35.

Russel 1987
J. Russel, *The mosaic inscriptions from Anemurium*, Wien 1987.

Salviat & Vatin 1971
F. Salviat & C. Vatin, 'Inventaire de terrains sacrés à Larisa', in *Inscriptions de Grèce central*, Paris 1971, 9–34.

Schachter 1981
A. Schachter, *The cults of Boiotia*, London 1981.

Scheid-Tissinier 1994
E. Scheid-Tissinier, *Les usages de don chez Homère. Vocabulaire et pratiques*, Nancy 1994.

Silver 1992
M. Silver, *Taking ancient mythology economically*, Leiden 1992.

Sordi 1958
M. Sordi, *La Lega Tessala fino as Alessandro Magno*, Roma 1958.

Sourvinou-Inwood 1978
C. Sourvinou-Inwood, 'Persephone and Aphrodite at Locri: A model for personality definitions in Greek religion', *JHS* 48, 1978, 101–121.

Sourvinou-Inwood 1987
C. Sourvinou-Inwood, 'Myth as history: The previous owners of the Delphic oracle', in *Interpretations of Greek mythology*, ed. J. Bremmer, London 1987, 215–241.

Spence 1993
I.G. Spence, *The cavalry of Classical Greece*, Oxford 1993.

Stählin 1924
F. Stählin, *Das hellenische Thessalien*, Stuttgart 1924.

Strauss Clay 1989
J. Strauss Clay, *The politics of Olympus*, Princeton 1989.

Thiel 1924
J.H. Thiel, 'Zu altgriechischen Gebühren', *Klio* 20, 1924, 54–67.

Tziaphalias 1984
A. Tziaphalias, 'Ανέκδοτες θεσσαλικές επιγραφές', *Θεσσαλικό Ημερολόγιο* 7, 1984, 193–234.

Tziaphalias 1994
A. Tziaphalias, 'Δεκαπέντε χρόνια ανασκαφών στην αρχαία Λάρισα', in *Θεσσαλία. Δεκαπέντε χρόνια αρχαιολογικής έρευνας 1975–1990. Αποτελέσματα*

και προοπτικές, Athens 1994, 153–178.

Tziaphalias 2000   A. Tziaphalias, 'Τἀυτιση του αρχαίου Μόψιου', in *Το έργο των εφορειών αρχαιοτήτων και νεοτέρων μνημείων του ΥΠ.ΠΟ στη Θεσσαλία και στην ευρύτερη περιοχή της*, Volos 2000, 97–101.

Verdelis 1955   N.M. Verdelis, 'Ανασκαφή Λαρίσης', *PAE,* 1955, 147–150.

Versnel 1993   H.S. Versnel, 'Apollo and Mars. One hundred years after Roscher', in H.S. Versnel, *Inconsistencies in Greek and Roman religion* 2. *Transition and reversal in Greek myth and ritual*, Leiden 1993, 290–334.

Vidal-Naquet 1986   P. Vidal-Naquet, *The black hunter*, Baltimore 1986.

Vollmer 1836   W. Vollmer, *Wörterbuch der Mythologie aller Nationen*, Stuttgart 1836.

Wallensten 2008   J. Wallensten, 'Personal protection and tailor-made deities: The use of individual epithets', *Kernos* 21, 2008, 81–95.

Westlake 1935   H.D. Westlake, *Thessaly in the fourth century B.C.*, London 1935.

Wilamowitz-Moellendorff 1931   U. von Wilamowitz-Moellendorff, *Der Glaube der Hellenen*, Berlin 1931.

Woodbury 1968   L. Woodbury, 'Pindar and the mercenary muse: *Isthm*. 2.1–13', *TAPA* 99, 1968, 527–542.

Woodward 1910   A.M. Woodward, 'Greek inscriptions from Thessaly', *AnnLiv* 3, 1910, 145–160.

ALEXANDER HERDA

How to run a state cult

THE ORGANIZATION OF THE CULT OF APOLLO DELPHINIOS IN MILETOS

Abstract*

The cult of Apollo Delphinios was the main state cult of Ionian Miletos, from the seventh century BC until Late Antiquity. His cult association, the so-called Molpoi, controlled access to citizenship. Their executive board formed the governing body of the *prytaneis* and supplied the *aisymnetes-stephanephoros*, the eponymous magistrate. At the beginning of every new year, the rituals of the city's most important festival of Apollo Delphinios, including officers' oaths, sacrifices, dining, competitions, and citizen initiations were performed. The sanctuary of Apollo, the Delphinion, incorporated the prytaneion of Miletos. It thus functioned not only as a religious, but also as a political centre of the polis, a role that is emphasized by its position in the agora. The ritualization of public space, signifying the firm bond between religion and politics, manifests itself in the New Year procession to the extra-urban sanctuary of Apollo in Didyma. This "bipolarity" of the Milesian Apollo cult can also be detected in Miletos' colonial enterprises, sanctioned by the oracle of Apollo Didymeus Milesios.

Introduction

The cult of Apollo Delphinios was the main state cult of ancient Miletos. Though his sanctuary, the Delphinion, was excavated at the beginning of the twentieth century,[1] the cult itself was never subjected to a comprehensive historical treatment.[2] It was only in 1979 that Fritz Graf showed, in a comparative study, the syncretistic origin of the widespread cult of Apollo Delphinios.[3] It combined the late Bronze Age god Delphinios with the "Greek", "Doric", Apollo in Submycenaean or Protogeometric times. Graf—as well as some of his forerunners—clearly demonstrates the political importance of that cult in some Greek *polis*-

stimulating conference, as well as to the Swedish Institute and the British School at Athens for being such perfect hosts. These were wonderful days in springtime Athens. For improving my English I would like to thank Emily Collinson in Los Angeles and Alexandra Villing in London. My research on the cult of Apollo Delphinios and on his sanctuary in Miletos is made possible by generous grants from the Deutsche Forschungsgemeinschaft (Bonn), the Gerda Henkel Stiftung (Düsseldorf), and the Harvard Foundation, Center for Hellenic Studies (Washington DC). The fieldwork in Miletos is supported by the Miletos excavation and its director Volkmar von Graeve. Finally, I am most indebted to Fritz Graf, who has supported this project from its earliest stages on in a highly unselfish and helpful manner. I am grateful for his critical advice as well as his fundamental contributions to the study of Greek religion in general and to the study of Apollo Delphinios in particular, providing many vital insights and good ideas.

[1]   *Milet* I 3.
[2]   Older treatments of the cult are Aly 1911 and Bourboulis 1949.
[3]   Graf 1979.

*   Let me express here my special thanks to Jenny Wallensten and Matthew Haysom for organizing this

states, in which government, citizenship, time reckoning, and male initiation were organized.[4]

This is not the place to discuss the complicated origin of Apollo Delphinios. I would just like to stress that the Doric offspring, even the Greekness of Apollo, has been a matter of dispute since the nineteenth century, and today there is increasing support for his origin being from western Asia Minor (cf. Apollon as Λυκηγενής, "Lycian-born", in Homer *Iliad* 4.101, 119; and the homonymous Trojan god Appaliunaš in the famous Hittite Alakšandu-treaty), as is also the case with Delphinios who shows connections not only with Bronze Age Crete—via Athens and Attica[5]—but also with the Hittite god Telipinu.[6]

The following will summarize some results of my ongoing studies on the epigraphical and archaeological testimonia for this cult and its religious and political context in Miletos, where it can best be analysed.[7]

The article is divided into four parts: first I deal with the most important inscription concerning the cult of Apollo Delphinios, the so-called Molpoi decree; second, I examine the appearance of the Apollo Delphinios sanctuary and try to reconstruct its various functions; third, I explore the close relationship between religion and politics as it is manifested in the treatment of ritual space in Miletos and beyond; finally, in the fourth section, I reveal the importance of the specific complementary pair of Apollo Delphinios and Apollo Didymeus for Milesian colonization in Archaic times.

The Molpoi decree and its meaning

We start with the most important epigraphical source, the famous Molpoi decree, named after the cult association of Apollo Delphinios (*Fig. 1*, Appendix).[8] It was found in 1903 in the Delphinion. Only one year later Ulrich von Wilamowitz-Moellendorff published it with an extensive commentary.[9] Following this *editio princeps* the inscription has again and again attracted epigraphists, ancient historians and historians of Greek religion. Surprisingly enough, before 2006 this interest never resulted in a complete and satisfactory commentary.[10]

Palaeographically the inscription has to be dated around 200 BC.[11] The text itself goes back to Late Archaic times. There are some later additions, the earliest of which dates to the year 476/75 BC. The whole text was then redacted in the year 447/46 BC (cf. Appendix).[12]

---

[4] The political role of the Molpoi was recognized by A. Rehm in *Milet* I 3, 283f.; Wilamowitz-Moellendorff 1914, 76–79; cf. also Luria 1928, 113–136; Luria 1963; De Sanctis 1930; Poland 1935, 511–513. Ehrhardt 1988, 143 follows Graf 1979. The political role was dismissed by Robertson 1987, esp. 357, 359; Gorman 2001, 176–186; and most recently Grieb 2008, 199–262, but see Parker 2008, 178.

[5] Bourboulis 1949, 45 stresses Delphinios' origin from Attica and an "old Ionian religious stratum". Graf (1979, 20) thinks of a Mycenaean Delphinios cult which survived the early Iron Age migrations in the remote areas of eastern Attica, Euboia and Crete, from where it spread again in the Ionian and Doric regions after being merged with the "Doric" Apollo.

[6] Herda 2008, 15, 51–53, 55, 61; *idem* 2009, 85–89, with nn. 329–350.

[7] Cf. Herda 2005; *idem* 2006a; *idem* 2008.

[8] *Milet* I 3, 277–284, no. 133; Herda 2006a, figs. 1–4.

[9] Wilamowitz-Moellendorff 1904.

[10] Older commentaries which attempted to provide at least an overview: Danielsson 1914; Vollgraff 1918; Poland 1935; see now Herda 2006a.

[11] Herda 2006a, 16–17, n. 51. I see a connection between issuing the inscription and the reorganization of the Didymeia as a Panhellenic festival: Herda 2006a, 16, 317–318, 427 (shortly before 206/5 BC); Rigsby 2010, 157 (first held in 215 BC). For the letter forms see Herda 2006a, figs. 1–3.

[12] On the dating of the text and its changes, see Herda 2006a, 15–20, 425–427, table 1. According to the argumentation of Cavaignac 1924, 285–317 and esp. 311–314, the dates for the eponymous *aisymnetai-stephanephoroi* Philtes (l. 1) and Charopinos (l. 40f.) have to be lowered by three years to 447/46 (Philtes) and 476/75 BC (Charopinos) respectively; cf. P. Herr-

Fig. 1. Molpoi decree, Pergamon-museum Berlin (photo S. Gräbener, Berlin).

A new analysis of this text leads to a reconstruction of the Milesian New Year festival in Archaic and later times.[13] This festival was especially devoted to Apollo Delphinios and Apollo Didymeus.

One part took place in the town of Miletos itself between the seventh and tenth day of the spring month Taureon.[14] Taureon, which fell at a similar time to our April/May, was the first month of the Milesian year cycle, at least from early Archaic times onwards. This is attested by the fifth-century BC so-called calendar-graffito from Olbie Polis, a Milesian colony in the Black Sea region. The inscription gives the complete number and order of the Milesian months which formed the prototype for the calendar of the colony, founded around the

middle of the sixth century BC on the site of an older emporion.[15]

Of primary importance were the different participants in the four-day festival in the Delphinion, which is simply called "festival of Apollo Delphinios" (ἑορτὴ Ἀπόλλωνος Δελφιν[ίο) in a Late Archaic sacrificial calendar, written on the walls of the Milesian Delphinion.[16]

The most important of these is the *aisymnetes-stephanephoros*, who was at the same time chairman of Apollo Delphinios' cult association of the Molpoi and eponymous highest magistrate. As all other higher magistrates, the *aisymnetes-stephanephoros* was solemnly introduced into his office during the festival. There were, therefore, always two *aisymnetai-stephanephoroi* present: the outgoing and the incoming. The Molpoi decree makes a clear distinction between the use of the term *aisymnetes* and *stephanephoros*: *aisymnetes* is always used in the singular and designates the "new" (νέος, compare line 10) or "leaving" (ἐξιών, compare lines 12 and 17) one involved in ritual actions, while *stephanephoroi* is always in the plural and designates both *aisymnetai*, the "leaving" and the

---

mann in *Milet* VI 1, 166, n. 122; Herda 2005, 260, n. 87; Rhodes 2006, 116. Misleading is: Slawisch 2009, 29–34, who doubts the dating of the text without any convincing arguments.

[13]   Herda 2006a *passim*. Despite the reservations of some about the concept of New Year festivals in Greece (cf. Parker 2005, 194, 201–202; *idem* 2008, 179) and my interpretation of the Molpoi decree as regulation for (part of) the Milesian New Year festival (Parker 2008, 179; Chaniotis 2010, 377), I prefer to retain it. There might not be a Greek term for "Happy New Year" in the sense of one single point in time, but the change from one year to the other was definitely marked by religious festivals and other rituals in a "festival cycle": for example the relighting of the altars (see below), the exchange of the *eponymoi* and other magistrates, the integration of citizen groups, etc. Parker 2005, 211, rightly stresses the aspect of renewal (he proposes the term "festivals of renewal" instead of "New Year festival"). This topic calls for more study; see Graf 2000, 869–873, esp. 871–873; Herda 2006a, 460f. For a possible New Year festival in honour of Apollo in Ithaka, compare Homer, *Od.* 19.306–307, 20.156, 276–278; cf. Hölscher 1990, 251–258; Herda 2006a, 176–178. The most complete analysis of New Year festivals in Greek culture is the comparative work of Auffarth 1991 (I thank the anonymous reviewer of this article for directing me to this important book).

[14]   On the festival in Miletos itself, see Herda 2006a, 38–167, 237–249. Only the first day (seventh of Taureon) was called Hebdomaia ("festival of the seventh day"): Herda 2006a, 38–44, 247.

[15]   *SEG* 30 977; Dubois 1996, 160–164, no. 99; Onyshkevych 1998, 11–69, figs. 1, 2–6; Herda 2006a, 38, 524, fig. 7. This graffito ended the long discussion about whether the Milesian year began in the month of Taureon or Boedromion: cf. Ehrhardt 1988, 120–122; Onyshkevych 1998, 24–27, fig. 1.9; Herda 2006a, 38. Additional evidence is supplied by the so-called Olbian Louterion graffito (*SEG* 30 980) which suggests Taureon as an intercalary month of the Olbian calendar. As a rule the intercalary month is the initial month of the year in a Greek city: Onyskhevych 1998, 25–27, 227–242, figs. 1.14–15. Taureon is named after the festival of the Taureia for Poseidon Taureos, the former main god of the "Ionians": Herda 2009, 40–41, n. 88. On the foundation of Olbie Polis around 550 BC, see Herda 2008, 32 with nn. 139 & 141.

[16]   *Milet* I 3, 162–166, n. 31a, ll. 12–13; Herda 2006a, 247–249, 428; *idem* 2008, 18–20. On the reconstruction of the calendar inscription see also: Herda 2005, 265–272, figs. 21–24; see below nn. 81–83.

"new" one involved in ritual actions (compare lines 9, 14f., 15f., 18, 23, 33, 35, 38, 40f., 42).[17]

It is clear from the ritual activity that the *aisymnetai-stephanephoroi* had to perform all actions of cult as "masters of the public sacrifices". This means they had to sacrifice to the gods in the name of the *polis*. But they were not priests of Apollo Delphinios. This again is evident through the Molpoi decree, where in lines 16 and 45 a "priest" (ἱέρεως) of Apollo Delphinios is mentioned besides the *aisymnetai-stephanephoroi*.[18]

The latter were assisted by the so-called *Onitadai*, who functioned as sacrificial butchers and cooks, or in ancient terminology, as *mageiroi*. One third of the Molpoi decree, lines 17–18 and 31–42, deals with the *Onitadai*: they provided the equipment for slaughtering the victims and preparing the meat; for example they had to supply fetters to bind the ani-mals, vessels made of pottery, bronze and iron, as well as the firewood and even the water for cooking. The *Onitadai* roasted the entrails on sticks, cooked the meat, and baked sacrificial cakes. Subsequently they distributed and served the portions to the participants.[19]

The *Onitadai* were a fictitious *genos*-like cult association of Herakles, that traced itself back not to an ὄνος, "donkey", as is often believed, but to Onites, a mythical son of Theban Herakles.[20] This makes sense: not only are the *Onitadai* specialists in sacrificing but Herakles, the hero, is himself an enthusiastic sacrificer. From Archaic times onwards the sacrificing Herakles, or sometimes just Herakles in the process of preparing sacrificial meat, is an iconographic *topos* in vase painting.[21] When Milesian local tradition puts forward that the Theban Herakles had built the ash altar of Apollo Didymeus, it actually tells us that Herakles himself was believed to be the first sacrificer in Didyma, the arrival point of the Milesian New Year procession.[22]

[17] On the two *aisymnetai-stephanephoroi* during the New Year festival cf. Herda 2006a, 58–61, 407–409, 428–429; idem 2008, 18–20. The title *aisymnetes*, "arbitrator" (the etymology is unclear, the word may be non-Greek, perhaps borrowed from western Asia Minor: Gorman 2001, 99, n. 23) may be the older one (seventh century BC; cf. Herda 2005, 289–290, n. 227; idem 2006a, 17–20, 407). The title *stephanephoros*, "wreath bearer", occurs first in the Late Archaic Molpoi decree, while the double title *aisymnetes-stephanephoros* seems to occur first in an inscription of the Milesian colony Olbie Polis in the second half of the fifth century BC: Herda 2006a, 61, n. 335, 408. In a singular honorary inscription from the Milesian *klerouchia* Aigiale on Amorgos (cf. Ehrhardt 1988, 28, 194 on the *klerouchia*), where the Molpoi are also attested (*IG* XII 7 418, ll. 4f. οἱ Μολ[ποί; first century BC), the *stephanephoros* title is replaced by the title *molparchon*: *IG* XII 7 415, l. 2 μολ[π]αρχήσας: Graf 1974, 209–215, esp. 211–212, n. 11; idem 1979, 3, n. 13; Ehrhardt 1988, 194, n. 1111. Therefore, it is clear that the *aisymnetes-stephanephoros* was the chairman of the Molpoi; compare also the heading of the *aisymnetes-stephanephoros* lists from Miletos, *Milet* I 3 122–123, 125–127: Οἵδε Μολπῶν ἠ(ι)σύμνησαν and *Milet* I 3 128: Στεφανηφόροι οἱ καὶ αἰσυμνῆται, where the title *aisymnetes* is equated with *stephanephoros*.
[18] Herda 2006a, 65–76. On the priest of Apollo Delphinios, cf. Herda 2006a, 101–103, 143–144.

[19] Herda 2006a, 124–138, 385–420, 433–434. A perfect illustration of their actions is provided by the frequently-discussed Late Archaic black-figured Ricci hydria from Caere in the Villa Giulia in Rome, attributed to an East Greek painter, maybe from north Ionian Klazomenai. The shoulder picture depicts a Dionysiac feast (the rural Dionysia?) with young *mageiroi* in action: Ricci 1946–48, 47–57, fig. 1, pls. 3–4; cf. Herda 2006a, 386–391, with further references in n. 2731. For good illustrations and commentary see also Durand 1979, 133–165, pls. I–IV.
[20] Herda 2006a, 126–133, 433. The *genos*-like organization of cult associations for Herakles seems to be typical: Herda 2006a, 130, n. 911. Herakles' Theban origin (cf. also Hom. *Il.* 19.98f.) may be explained by Boiotian groups of settlers participating in the so-called Ionian Migration to Asia Minor. They not only brought with them place names and personal names, but also cults: cf. Herda 2006a, 133; idem 2006b, 43–102, esp. 67–79; idem 2009, 60–67.
[21] Herda 2006a, 355, n. 2543.
[22] The altar's mythical age gave Pausanias (5.13.11) the opportunity to make a joke about the Milesians: despite its declared age the altar, which consisted of the blood of the sacrificial animals, remained modest

The high rank of the *Onitadai* in the hierarchy of religious matters becomes clear from their compensations from the public sacrifice: meat, the leftovers of the wine and the sacrificial cakes as well as all the skins. From this it can be deduced that they themselves were participants in the sacrificial meal in the Delphinion during the New Year festival as well as at Didyma.[23] It turns out that an originally "private", hereditary cult corporation is integrated into the cult of Apollo, institutionalized and controlled by the Milesian state.[24] The close relationship between Herakles and the *Onitadai* on the one hand and Apollo Delphinios on the other becomes more evident from the location of Herakles' cult at Miletos: the discovery of an Archaic *lex sacra* for Herakles in the Delphinion indicates that he was a θεός ἐντεμένιος, "god (venerated) within (the same) sanctuary" of Apollo Delphinios.[25]

I now come to the *Molpoi*, the cult association of Apollo Delphinios. Unlike the name *Onitadai* their name does not imply hereditary membership. Instead it can best be translated "singers and dancers" reflecting the importance of music in the cult of Apollo, especially the performance of the hymnic paian. They formed a corporation of so-called *orgeones* of Apollo Delphinios as they conducted the customary "rites" (l. 4, τὰ ὄργια) for the god.[26]

Their executive board, the five so-called *proshetairoi,* or "companions", were introduced by the new *aisymnetes-stephanephoros* in a special ritual on the eighth day of Taureon, the second day of the New Year festival. Unfortunately the relevant passage of the Molpoi decree, lines 6–8, is a little corrupt. We may suppose an oath ritual at the altar of Apollo Delphinios, which involved the handing over of raw entrails and which ended in a sacrificial meal with wine and singing of paians.[27]

The *proshetairoi* formed the staff of the *prytaneis,* who dined around the sacred hearth of the *polis* together with the *aisymnetes-stephanephoros* in charge as executive *prytanis.* All six together constituted the government of oligarchic Miletos.[28] In the praescript of the Molpoi decree, lines 1–4, these six individuals

---

in size up to Pausanias' time. For the altar in Didyma, the so-called Rundbau in front of the temple, see Herda 2006a, 351–356; for Herakles in Didyma, see Herda forthcoming.

[23] On the parts of the sacrificial meal for the *Onitadai*, see Herda 2006a, 135–138, 385, 399–404, 411–414, 433f. Again the Ricci hydria delivers an illustration: in the right-hand corner of the scene the young "servants" serve themselves wine and meat; cf. Durand 1979, pl. IV; for the interpretation of the scene, see Herda 2006a, 378, n. 2734, 390, n. 2759, 400, n. 2837.

[24] For the interconnectedness of "public" and "private" cults in *polis* religion which often developed out of cults of smaller groups (families etc.), see Sourvinou-Inwood 1990, 295–322, esp. 312; *eadem* 1988, 259–274; Burkert 1995, 201–210, esp. 203–204; Aleshire 1994, 9–16. On *oikoi, gene,* local and private cult corporations in Athens, see Parker 1996, 284–342, appendices 2–4; *idem* 2005, esp. 9–115.

[25] Stele inscription with oracle of Apollo Didymeus concerning the Herakles cult: *Milet* I 3, 276–277, n. 132a–d; *Milet* VI 1, 167, no. 132; Herakles as *entemenios* of Apollo Delphinios: cf. Herda 2006a, 131, 161. For the rare term θεός ἐντεμένιος resp. θεοὶ ἐντεμένιοι, which is used to designate the cult companions of Apollo in the Delphinion, see Herda 2006a, 213–214, n. 1493. For the Milesian *isopoliteia* decree from Amyzon, mentioning the θεοὶ ἐντεμένιοι see now W. Günther in *Milet* VI 3, 30, no. 1050 l. 3 (third century BC); for the *lex sacra* found

in the theatre, probably from the Delphinion, where οἱ ἄλλοι θεοὶ ἐντεμένιοι are mentioned, see N. Ehrhardt in *Milet* VI 3, 135f., no. 1221, ll. 3f. (ca 300 BC).

[26] Herda 2006a, 31–37, 80–86, 178–179, 400–401, 430, 452; *idem* 2008, 16–17, 35–36, 52, n. 300, 54. For older literature on the Molpoi, see nn. 4, 10, add also Sommer 2006, 166–169. The modern confusion about the different groups mentioned together with the Molpoi in the Molpoi decree (*aisymnetes, stephanephoroi, proshetairoi, Onitadai, neoi* etc.) is great, see my exemplification in Herda 2006a, 86–90.

[27] Herda 2006a, 48–56. Compare the Milesian decree ordering an oath ritual to Apollo Didymeus and the Roman emperor for all magistrates entering or leaving their office: W. Günther in *Milet* VI 3, 26–27, no. 1044, pl. 6 (late first century BC/early first century AD).

[28] Herda 2005, 249–250; *idem* 2006a, 33, n. 143, 35, n. 153, 55, n. 290, 121, n. 838, 159, n. 1142, 429–430, 452.

are attributed to three of the six Archaic Milesian tribes, namely the Oinopes, Hoplethes and Boreis.[29] Therefore, only three tribes were in charge at the same time. They probably rotated every half a year or every year.[30]

Since it was the Molpoi and not the Milesian *demos* who decided the ὄργια, the "rites" of the Molpoi decree,[31] it is evident that in 447/6 BC, the year of the *aisymnetes* Philtes, son of Dionysios, Miletos was still ruled by the oligarchy of the Molpoi.[32] A democracy was only introduced after 445 BC with Athenian backing.[33]

The sacred hearth, the *Hestia Prytaneia*, was situated in the *Molpon*, the assembly hall of the Molpoi, which itself was part of the Delphinion and which had the function of the prytaneion, the seat of the government of ancient Miletos.[34] Here the "leaving" *aisymnetes* performed his farewell sacrifice to Hestia on the ninth day of Taureon, the third day of the New

Year festival, as described in lines 12–13 of the Molpoi decree.[35]

The name Μολπόν, a *hapax legomenon* mentioned three times in the Molpoi decree (lines 11f., 17, 20), can be best explained as contracted dialectal form for *Molpeion*, "House of the Molpoi".[36]

The closing ritual of the initiatory circle for the "new" young citizens of Miletos, the νεοί,[37] was the *Hamilleteria*, "the contests". They most likely formed part of a *pannychis*, a night-feast. This feast happened on the tenth of Taureon, the fourth day of the New Year festival, and it included, in all likelihood, a competition between three paian-choruses of the *neoi*, provided by every second of the six Milesian tribes. The two *aisymnetai-stephanephoroi* and the

---

29   The other three are: Argadeis, Aigikoreis and Geleontes. The four old "Ionian" tribes were the Argadeis, Geleontes, Aigikoreis and Hoplethes; specifically Milesian are the Boreis and Oinopes, see Ehrhardt 1988, 98; Gorman 2001, 38–40; Herda 2006a, 31, n. 133.

30   Herda 2006a, 31–33.

31   L. 4–6: ἔδοξε Μολποῖσιν τὰ ὄργια ἀναγράψαντας θεῖναι ἐς | τὸ ἱερὸν καὶ χρῆσθαι τούτοισιν, καὶ οὕτωι τάδε γραφθέντα ἐτέ-|θη; see Herda 2006a, 35–37. The equivalent formula ll. 40. 41 ἔαδε Μολποῖσιν is borrowed from early Archaic Cretan political language: Herda 2006a, 17, n. 54, 35, 404–407; below n. 140.

32   See Robertson 1987, 386–387, and Gorman 2001, 219, 221 (with the old dating 450/49 BC, but compare here n. 12) for an oligarchic constitution of Miletos. But both dismiss the political role of the board of the *proshetairoi* and the *aisymnetes*; cf. Herda, in preparation.

33   Robertson 1987; Cobet 1997, 249–284, esp. 264, n. 150; Gorman 2001, 235–236; Herda, in preparation.

34   For the *Molpon* as prytaneion, situated within the Delphinion, see Herda 2005, 263–273; *idem* 2006a, 78–79, 80–83, 138–150, 157–167. The *Molpon*-prytaneion has to be identified with the older south hall of the sanctuary: see below nn. 77–78.

35   Herda 2005, 249, n. 39–40; *idem* 2006a, 80–84; *idem* 2008, 17, 54. Hestia also "ruled" over the state funds, compare Molpoi decree l. 41 ἀπὸ Ἱστιήιων παρέχεν; cf. Herda 2006a, 136, n. 957–958, 410. On the transferring of the sacred fire from the hearth (= Hestia) of the *Molpon*-prytaneion to the *prytaneia* of the new Milesian colonies see below, nn. 138–139.

36   Herda 2006a, 78–80, n. 473: Μολπεῖον/Μολπήιον>Μολπέον>Μολπόν; followed now by Parker 2008, 180 and Gonzales 2008 but doubted by Chaniotis 2010, 378–379. Von Wilamowitz's emendation of ΜΟΛΠΟΝ (l. 20) and ΜΟΛΠΩΙ (l. 12. 17. 43) in the inscription to Μολπ<ῶ>ν and Μολπῶ<ν>, "(the house) of the Molpoi", is unnecessary. Other *hapax legomena* in the Molpoi decree are: ll. 25–27 Γυλλος/Γυλλοι (= sacred stone markers, cf. below n. 106), l. 30f. πάνθυον (ἔτος) (= "year of all offerings", cf. Herda 2006a, 318–319), l. 36 πλακόντινα (ἔλατρα) (= "flat" sacrificial cakes, cf. Herda 2006a, 146, n. 1027, 397–398, n. 2820), l. 33 φαλαγγτήρια (wooden blocks to chop the meat [?], cf. Herda 2006a, 136, n. 953, 238, 392).

37   The Late Archaic–Early Classical Molpoi decree preserves the earliest use of the age class term *neoi* in a Greek inscription. It becomes more frequent from the fourth century BC onwards: Herda 2006a, 94, n. 607, 203, n. 1414. The older term may have been *kouroi*, but *neoi* is used as early as Homer: Herda 2006a, 156, n. 1117. The age class system as part of the male initiation cycles (it may have been missing for females: Herda 2006a, 93, n. 600) is widespread in ancient Greek culture. Its similarity in "Ionic" and "Doric" city states may indicate a common origin and high age, probably going back to the late Bronze Age: Herda 2006a, 203, n. 1417.

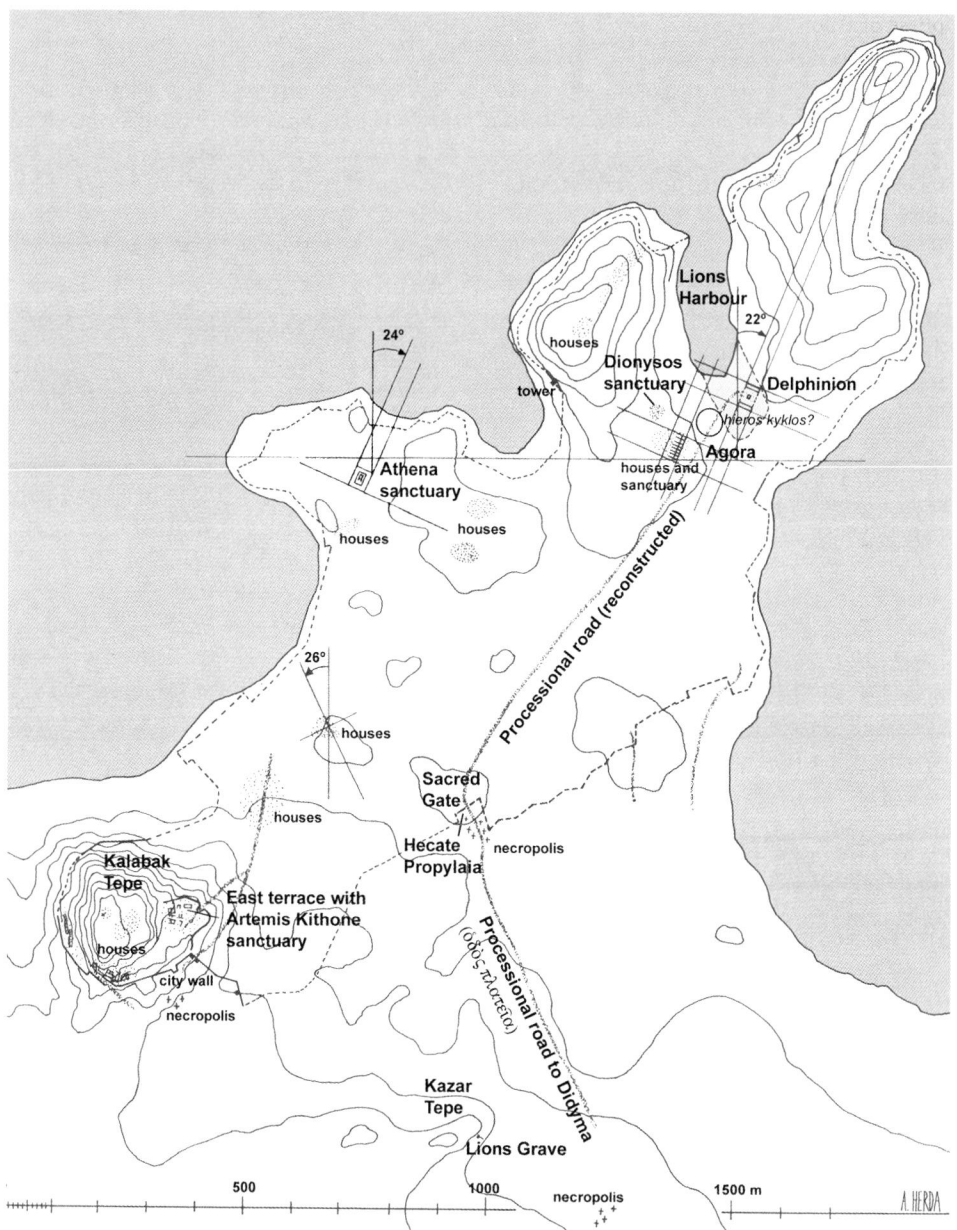

Fig. 2. Miletos, Late Archaic city, showing the position of the Delphinion, the agora and the assumed course of the New Year procession (light grey: artificial drainage area).

priest of Apollo Delphinios functioned most probably as *choregoi*, as "leaders of the (three) choruses".[38]

After the *pannychis* of the *Hamilleteria* the New Year festival moved in a procession to Didyma, where it culminated in the feasting for Apollo Didymeus which, in Hellenistic times, was called *Boiégia* or *Didymeia*.[39]

Not mentioned in the Molpoi decree but in inscriptions from Didyma, and depicted on reliefs and coins is the torch-race, the *lampas*, which was part of the Didymeia. This fire ritual is typical for the end of a New Year festival cycle, for example during the Hephaisteia on Lemnos or the Panathenaia in Athens.[40] It served the relighting of the altars, as is also indicated on the theatre-frieze from Miletos, where we see the burning ash altar of Apollo Didymeus between the racers.[41] Another comparison illustrating the inauguration aspect of fire rituals is the relighting of the ash altar in Olympia, which Pausanias explicitly equates with the altar of Apollo in Didyma, built by Herakles:[42] the victor in the first contest in Olympia, the stadion race, opened the sacrifices of the Olympic Games by lighting the ash altar of Zeus.[43]

The archaeology of the Delphinion in relation to its different functions

Let us now turn to the Delphinion, the sanctuary of Apollo Delphinios in Miletos (*Fig. 2*). It lay in the heart of the town, SE of the so-called Lions Harbour. The Late Archaic and Classical sanctuaries were the size of one *insula* within the street-*insula*-grid-plan of Miletos and consisted of two halls (*stoai*) to the north and south framing an open courtyard with altars and dedicatory monuments (*Fig. 3*).[44]

The diverse functions of this main sanctuary in Miletos are reflected in the rich epigraphical evidence. The finds from the Delphinion form the largest inscriptional corpus within the ancient city so far.[45] The sanctuary's impor-

---

[38] Herda 2006a, 48, 84–118. From around the middle of the fourth century BC onwards, under the influence of the "New Dithyramb movement", a professional solist (*kitharodos?*), called ᾠδός in the Molpoi decree l. 45, accompanied the *choregoi*: Herda 2006a, 420–424. For the "New Music" and one of its most influential front men, Timotheos of Miletos, see D'Angour 2006.

[39] For the procession: Herda 2006a, 167–186, 249–356, 371–385, 435–442, 447–461, figs. 9, 12–14, 16–22. For the Boiégia/Didymeia: Herda 2006a, 187–211, 317–319, 351, 441–442, 453–454.

[40] Cf. Burkert 1970, 1–16 (= Burkert 1990, 60–76); Graf 1985, 234–235; Parisiniou 2000, 36–44; Herda 2006a, 210, n. 1468.

[41] Herda 2006a, 205–211, fig. 11a (theatre-frieze from Miletos, late second century AD); Kekule von Stradonitz 1904, 786–801, esp. 800, with fig. (two Roman bronze coins of the time of Septimius Severus and Balbinus, Pupienus and Gordianus, ca AD 200 and 238). The contest is called λαμπὰς ἡ ἀπὸ βωμοῦ καὶ λαμπὰς ἡ πρὸς βωμοῦ in the inscriptions from Didyma.

[42] Paus. 5.13.11; cf. Herda 2006a, 131–132, 354–355.

[43] Philostr. *Gymn.* 5; Burkert 1985, 106, 130.

[44] See Herda 2005.

[45] The inscriptions are published by A. Rehm in *Milet* I 3 (nos. 31–186); see also with addenda and German translations: P. Hermann in *Milet* VI 1, 160–195. Additional later finds from inside and outside the Delphinion are: W. Günther in *Milet* VI 3, 6–7, no. 1026 (honorary decree, early third century BC), 14–15, no. 1032 (*isopoliteia* with Athens, late third century BC), 17–18, no. 1036 (honorary decree of Iasos (?) for a Milesian judge, first half of second century BC), 34–44, nos. 1055–1064 (citizen lists, third–second century BC), 40–44, nos. 1065–1070 (*proxenoi* lists, third–first century BC), 51, no. 1076 (letter of Caracalla?), 55, nos. 1080–1082 (honorary decrees, third century BC); N. Ehrhardt in *Milet* VI 3, 135f., no. 1221 (cf. Herda 2006a, 213: *lex sacra* for Apollo from the theatre, ca 300 BC). The latest finds are a fragmentary *aisymnetes* list (see below n. 65) and four Hellenistic wall blocks inscribed with citizen lists found reused in a basilica of the late sixth century AD. NE of Kalabak Tepe: Niewöhner 2008, 181–201, esp. 194f., fig. 17; Günther 2009, 167–170, no. 1 (*proxenoi* list, 274/73 BC); Günther 2009, 170–173, no. 2 (citizen list, ca 240 BC); Günther 2009, 173–177, no. 3 (citizen list, mid

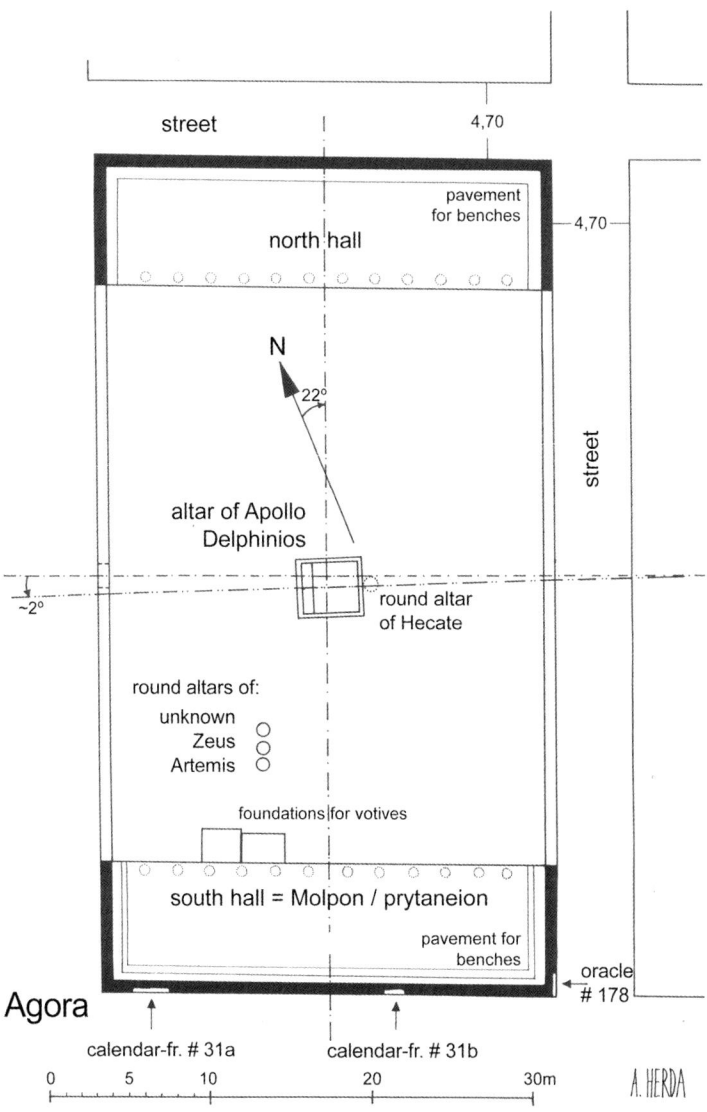

Fig. 3. Miletos, ground plan of the sanctuary of Apollo Delphinios (Delphinion) in Classical times.

tance as a place for the public display of inscriptions, on free-standing *stelai* and on the walls
of the *stoai*, is directly attested in the formula
ὁ ἐπιφανέστατος τόπος τῆς πόλεως, "the most
prominent place of town".[46] Despite this fact,
one should not confuse the Delphinion with
the city archives—as sometimes happens.[47]
These were at another—still unknown—place.[48]

A lot of other cults were also located here.
In the open space around the central altar of
Apollo Delphinios were five re-erected Archaic
round altars, four of them bearing inscriptions.
That for Hekate was placed on the eastern side
close to the Delphinios altar. According to the
Late Archaic inscription it was dedicated by
the *prytaneis* in office.[49]

Three other Archaic round altars with
Hellenistic dedicatory inscriptions for Zeus
Soter,[50] Artemis,[51] and a third unknown god
were positioned in a line several metres to the
south. Other inscriptions mention the cults of
Zeus Nosios, the "healer",[52] the Nabataean Zeus
Dushares,[53] Herakles,[54] Hestia of the *Molpon*,[55]
Hellenistic rulers (Seleukos I and Ptolemy
I),[56] (Artemis or Hekate?) Phosphoros,[57] and
later the Roman emperors.[58] The Delphinion is
therefore characterized as the leading religious

---

third century BC); Günther 2009, 177, no. 4 (citizen
list, third century BC); compare two other fragmentary *proxenoi* lists, found in 1918 and first published by
Günther 2009, 178–180, nos. 5–6 (ca 140 BC). Our
recent investigation within the Delphinion has yielded
additional material. Most noteworthy: a new fragment
of the Archaic sacrificial calendar, cf. below n. 83.

[46] Herda 2005, 247, with n. 30.

[47] See Th. Wiegand in *Milet* I 3, 408.

[48] For the archives of Miletos, called *archeion/archeia*,
basileion or *grammatophylakion* in the inscriptions, see
Herda 2006a, 233f., 434.

[49] Herda 2005, 261f., figs. 14, 17. On the dedicatory
inscription: G. Kawerau in *Milet* I 3, 153, fig. 41, 156,
fig. 45; A. Rehm in *Milet* I 3, 275f., no. 129, fig. 71; P.
Herrmann in *Milet* VI 1, 167, no. 129; Gorman 2001,
99f., 184; Herda 2005, 262, n. 93, 265, n. 102 (dating
to between 540 and 510 BC). The participle praesens
πρυτ[α]-|νεύοντες, ll. 4f., signifies that the *prytaneis* were
in office at the time when they dedicated the altar. The
number of the *prytaneis* originally named should have
been three or six (Gorman 2001, 100), but six seems
more likely in accordance with the prescript of the Molpoi decree, where five *prosthetairoi* and one *aisymnetes*
form a collegium of six individuals representing three
of the six old *phylai*, to be identified with the *prytaneis*
of Miletos: see n. 28. On the cult of Hekate in the Delphinion, see Herda 2006a, 282–289 397–399; here
below, nn. 69–72.

[50] G. Kawerau in *Milet* I 3, 154f., figs. 43f.; A. Rehm
in *Milet* I 3, 276, no. 130; on the cult see Gorman 2001,
174; Herda 2006a, 196, 212, 215. The cult of Zeus Soter in the Delphinion may go back to Archaic times, as
it is also attested in the Milesian colonies from at least
the fifth century BC onwards: Ehrhardt 1988, 156f.

[51] G. Kawerau in *Milet* I 3, 154f., figs. 43f; A. Rehm
in *Milet* I 3, 276 no. 131; most probably with the *epiklesis* Delphinia: Ehrhardt 1988, 148; Herda 2006a, 213,
with n. 1490; *idem* 2008, 16, n. 18.

[52] The cult is attested in two Archaic inscriptions: A.
Rehm in *Milet* I 3, 162–166, no. 31a, l. 9, 400f., no.
186, Abb. 98; cf. Herda 2006a, 211–217. The *epiklesis*-
form Νόσιος is an Ionic contraction of Νούσιος, and
is not to be confused with Νότιος, the "rain bringing"
Zeus: Herda 2006a, 216.

[53] Dedication of the Nabataean minister Syllaios for
king Obodas III (9 BC): A. Rehm & M. Lidzbarski in
Milet I 3, 387–389, no. 165, fig. 94; P. Herrmann in *Milet* VI 1, 195, no. 165; Healey 2001, 101, 179.

[54] See above n. 25.

[55] See above nn. 34f.

[56] For the statue of Seleukos I, see A. Rehm in *Milet*
I 3, 383f., no. 158, fig. 92; P. Herrmann in *Milet* VI 1,
194, no. 158; Herda 2005, 249, with n. 37. For the cult-
statue of Ptolemy I (A. Rehm in *Milet* I 7, 321, no. 244;
P. Herrmann in *Milet* VI 1, 202f. n. 244 pl. 17, 1) see
Herda 2005, 249, with n. 37; *idem* 2006a, 25, with n.
100; 214, n. 1493; *idem* 2008, 45, with n. 256.

[57] *Milet* I 3, 155f., fig. 45, 392, no. 172 (round altar,
early first century BC, found close to the western front
of the Delphinion); P. Herrmann in *Milet* VI 1, 195,
no. 172. The Phosphoros can be equated with Artemis
or more probably with Hekate: Herda 2006a, 282f.

[58] The emperor-cult can be deduced from a Neronian
lex sacra (*Milet* I 3, 284–286, no. 134 ll. 8–10; *Milet*
VI 1, 169, no. 134; see also the letter of Claudius to the
Dionysian *technitai*, written on a statue base, probably
for the emperor, *Milet* I 3, 381–383, no. 156; *Milet* VI
1, 194, no. 156; Herda 2005, 248 with n. 32).

centre, where "the other gods" were venerated "within the same temenos" as Apollo, called οἱ ἄλλοι θεοὶ ἐντεμένιοι in inscriptions.[59]

The political importance of the Delphinion is clear from some other facts. For example, the association of the Molpoi controlled access to citizenship in Miletos.[60] Under their auspices the initiation of the new young citizens, the *neoi*, during the New Year festival took place.[61] Another indication is the numerous copies of new citizens lists which were inscribed on the sanctuaries' walls in Hellenistic times.[62] The largest is from the year 229/8 BC, naming hundreds of Cretan immigrants.[63] The *prytaneis* as executive board of the Molpoi distributed (διαίρεσις) the immigrants to the Milesian tribes by casting lots (ἐπικλήρωσις). The procedure was controlled by the *demos* who also oversaw record-keeping in the city archives.[64]

Official time reckoning was also under the control of the Molpoi. Miletos named its years after the eponymous *aisymnetai-stephanephoroi*, who were introduced into their office every new year during the festival for Apollo Delphinios, as discussed above. Marble stelai with lists of four hundred names were preserved in the Delphinion, reaching back as far as 537/6

BC and forming the most complete of all Greek eponymic lists.[65]

Finally the *Molpon*, the clubhouse of the Molpoi, which functioned as the prytaneion and included the *hestia prytaneia*, or *koine hestia*, the sacred hearth of the city-state, was located in the Delphinion, as the Molpoi decree shows.[66] Hellenistic proxeny decrees and honorary decrees stipulating dining rights in the prytaneion of Miletos were therefore set up in the Delphinion,[67] and the Molpoi awarded the δίκη τῆς ξενίας, the privilege for diplomatic guests to dine in the prytaneion of Miletos.[68]

The fact that the Archaic altar of Hekate, which stood right beside the central altar of Apollo Delphinios, was dedicated by the Milesian *prytaneis* in office serves as an additional argument for the location of the prytaneion within the Delphinion.[69] Hekate appears here primarily as political goddess, not as a dark and secret "goddess of the outside" or god-

---

[59] See above, n. 25.
[60] The juridical process is called ἐμ Μολποῖς ἔνστασις (see *Milet* I 3, 284, 365). It is mentioned in some Milesian interstate decrees, for example that concerning Seleukia-Tralleis of 218/17 BC (*Milet* I 3, 318–324, no. 143, l. A 32; *Milet* VI 1, 176f., no. 143), the treaty with Mylasa of 215/14 BC (*Milet* I 3, 330–334, no. 146, l. A 42; *Milet* VI 1, 178–180, no. 146), and the treaty with Herakleia of 184–181 BC (*Milet* I 3, no. 150, l. 66; *Milet* VI 1, 185–189, no. 150, pl. 11).
[61] See above nn. 37f.
[62] *Milet* I 3, 166–220, nos. 33–93, 398–400, nos. 179–181, 183; *Milet* VI 1, 160–165, nos. 33–92, 195, nos. 180–181; for the new finds of lists, cf. above n. 45.
[63] The lists of Cretans: *Milet* I 3, 166–202, nos. 33–38, fig. 54, 56. cf. enclosure 404–406 no. 36aa; *Milet* VI 1, 160–163, nos. 33–38.
[64] For the procedure, see Günther 2009, 176.

[65] *Milet* I 3, 241–275, nos. 122–128; *Milet* VI 1, 166f., nos. 122–128, with corrections to dates; see above n. 12. The oldest known fragment of the list (fifth–fourth century BC) was found reused as a "pierre errante" in 1994 some 16 km northeast of Miletos in the village of Nalbantlar, 3 km east of Myous: Blümel 1995, 35–64, esp. 56–58, no. 26, pl. 13, 3; *SEG* 45 1620; *Milet* VI 3, 216f., no. 1360, pl. 34. For the Milesian eponymic lists as "the longest and most complete of all lists of eponymous officials on stone": Sherk 1990, 251.
[66] See above with nn. 32–36.
[67] Herda 2005, 250 with n. 44; *Milet* I 3, 312–316, no. 141, ll. 53f. (*sitesis* for *hieropoioi*, treaty with Kios, ca 230 BC; *Milet* VI 1, 175f., no. 141); *Milet* I 3, 318–324, no. 143, l. A 43 (sitesis for *presbeutai*, treaty with Seleukia-Tralleis, 218/17 BC; *Milet* VI 1, 176f., no. 143); *Milet* I 3, 324–326, no. 144, l. A 12 (*sitesis* for *presbeutai*, treaty with unknown city, end of third century BC; *Milet* VI 1, 177f., no. 144); *Milet* I 3, 330–334, no. 146, l. 55 (sitesis for *presbeutai*, treaty with Mylasa, 215/14 BC; *Milet* VI 1, 178–180, no. 146).
[68] *Milet* I 3, 284, 365. This is convincing since the prytaneion was at the same time the clubhouse of the Molpoi, the *Molpon*.
[69] See above n. 49.

dess of witchcraft:[70] in analogy to the situation described for Boiotia by Hesiod,[71] she is to be understood as a protectress of the political and judicial assemblies as well as of the competitions, for example the *Hamilleteria*, taking place in the Delphinion and the nearby agora of Miletos. As the Molpoi decree (l. 36f.) testifies, she received sacrifices on her altar during the New Year festival[72]. We may suppose that the two *aisymnetai-stephanephoroi* as executive *prytaneis* conducted the sacrifice for Hekate, as they also sacrificed to Apollo Delphinios.

As in Athens, "the path to political activity led, one might say, past several altars".[73] To those for Hestia, Apollo Delphinios and Hekate we may add the aforementioned Hellenistic altar for Hekate or Artemis Phosphoros in the Milesian Delphinion.[74] It is again in Athens that the *prytaneis* had to sacrifice to Artemis Phosphoros "before the assemblies".[75]

The two halls (*stoai*) which frame the Delphinion to the north and the south deliver the perfect setting for assembling and ritual dining: both possess 0.60 m deep benches running along the inner walls (*Fig. 3*).[76] But there is one feature of the southern hall that provides a strong argument for identifying this building with the Molpon-prytaneion:[77] the Early Classical rebuilding of the southern hall not only reused the foundation of the Late Archaic building that had been destroyed by the Persians in 494 BC, it also reused marble blocks of the older walls, some of them bearing Archaic inscriptions. They were visible, placed on the outer east and south sides of the new building, and formed a kind of memorial commemorating the Persian war and its tremendous destruction of flourishing Late Archaic Ionia,[78] comparable for example to the incorporation of elements from the old Athena temple and the so-called Ur-Parthenon within the Early Classical northern wall of the Athenian Acropolis.[79] The stone on the southeastern corner, for ex-

[70] First seen by Sourvinou-Inwood 1990, 309 ("civic aspect"). As protective "goddess of the outside" Hekate was, however, venerated as Hekate *Propylaia* at the gates of Miletos, where the New Year procession stopped for the first time: Herda 2006a, 282–285; see here *Figs. 2* and *6*. On the often suspected Karian origin of Hekate, see Herda 2009, 98 with n. 406.

[71] Hes. *Theog.* 404–452, esp. 430, 434–444 ("Hymn to Hekate"); see also West 1966, 45, 75, 276–290; Kolb 1981, 12, 58, 101; Kenzler 1999, 49f., 208. Kolb and Kenzler stress the chthonic aspect of the Hekate cult in connection with the agora: see Kolb 1981, 12, n. 31; Kenzler 1999, 50 with n. 18. Others, in contrast, stress her character as a protective as well as a purifying and atoning goddess of the moon and the light: see Roscher I 2 (1886–1890) 1885–1910, s.v. Hekate (M.H. Roscher), esp. 1891, 1895f.; but see also West 1966, 277. Martin 1951, 189 believed that Hesiod is referring to "une tradition locale (...) particulièrement fréquent en Béotie" without taking into account the Milesian cult.

[72] The modest sacrifice of cakes (ἔλατρα) to Hekate, which the Molpoi decree orders (l. 36 f.; see also Herda 2006a, 396–399), is typical for so-called Ἑκαταῖα, the monthly sacrifices for Hekate during the new moon (first day) and the full moon (fifteenth/ sixteenth day): Roscher I 2 (1886–1890) 1885–1910 s.v. Hekate (M.H. Roscher), esp. 1888f. But in Ionian Erythrai Hekate receives public sacrifices of lamb and piglet on the first and seventh and eighth day: Graf 1985, 257f. Correspondingly, not only cakes but also animal sacrifices for Hekate might have been included on the first day of the Milesian New Year festival, the day of the *Hebdomaia* (seventh of Taureon), as it is the case for Apollo, who also is offered cakes as well as animals: Herda 2006a, 397.

[73] Parker 2005, 404.

[74] Above n. 57.

[75] Parker 2005, 404f.

[76] Herda 2005, 263f. with nn. 100f. For ritual dining in a seated position in the *Molpon*-prytaneion of Miletos: Herda 2006a, 157–167; for seated dining in the *tholos-prytanikon* in the new agora of Athens cf. below n. 92.

[77] Herda 2005, 249f., 263–268, 272–278, 291.

[78] Herda 2005, 259–272, figs. 14, 20, 21f. In contrast, no Archaic inscriptions were found reused in the walls of the Early Classical northern hall of the Delphinion. However, our investigation of the eastern wall of the northern hall in 2010 detected at least the reuse of Archaic stone material.

[79] Herda 2005, 266, with n. 109. For Athens, where the memorialization was, of course, on a much grander scale, see also: Schneider & Höcker 2001, 104–107, figs. 117–118; Holtzmann 2003, 91–95, figs. 75–76.

ample, retained a copy of an oracle of Apollo Didymeus of about 530/20 BC. It is built into the wall standing upside down.[80]

Two other blocks on the south side, one of which is still *in situ* today, form part of a truly monumental inscription.[81] Four columns—ca 3.70 m high and ca 3.25 m broad, with letters of max. 3.5 cm—covered not only the whole eastern wall of the Archaic southern hall, but also extended to the right half of the south side. In total, the text had an area of approximately 42 to 49 m². The inscription is written in *boustrophedon* with letter cutting of exceptional quality.[82] It can be dated to ca 520/10 BC and forms the best-preserved early monumental state sacrificial calendar ever found in a Greek city.[83] It also gives an idea of how voluminous the sacrificial calendar of Athens must have been, which under Solon was written on the so-called *kyrbeis* in the Athenian prytaneion.[84]

The treatment of ritual space

The close relationship between religion and politics is also manifest in the treatment of ritual space—or, in other words, in the ritualization of public space: the Milesian New Year festival happened in the Delphinion as religio-political centre of the *polis*. It incorporated the *Molpon*-prytaneion of Miletos.

From the middle of the sixth century BC at the latest, the sanctuary was located directly north of the agora, as can be seen on a provisional reconstruction of the Late Archaic town map (*Fig. 2*). The sanctuary's construction was made possible by intentional drainage in the former marshy area of the southeastern corner of the Lions harbour embayment. It resulted in an enlargement of the city centre which itself formed part of a far-ranging, Late Archaic replanning of the northeastern parts of Miletos in the so-called Hippodamian orthogonal street-*insula*-grid-system.[85]

The joint positioning of the prytaneion as the religio-political centre and the agora has to be taken as a typical feature of Greek town planning since early Archaic times, as the examples of Athens and Dreros on Crete demonstrate.

In Athens the prytaneion with its "unmovable hearth", the ἑστία ἀκίνητος as it is called by Aelius Aristeides,[86] was until the end of antiquity situated somewhere at the edges of the so-called Older agora[87] or "agora of Kekrops",[88] named after the first king of Athens. According

---

[80]   *Milet* I 3, 397f., no. 178; *Milet* VI 1, 195, no. 178; Herda 2005, 265, fig. 20.

[81]   *Milet* I 3, 162–166, nos. 31a–b; cf. Herda 2005, 265–267, figs. 14, 21–22.

[82]   It was rightly compared with one of the finest Athenian inscriptions, the so-called Hekatompedon inscription which is to be dated some 30 years later: Rehm 1939, 217f., pl. 28. For the Hekatompedon inscription see Holtzmann 2003, 85–87, fig. 67.

[83]   Herda 2005, 268–272, fig. 24 (reconstruction); for the extension of the inscription see *ibid.* 271, n. 134. A third fragment of the calender was found in 1912: *Milet* I 3, 401–404, no. 31c, fig. 99; Herda 2005, 268–270, fig. 23. Three other small fragments were found outside the Delphinion between 1902 and 1911(?): *Milet* VI 3, 124f., no. 1215a–c, pl. 20. A seventh fragment, most probably the left lower corner of the first column of the inscription, was discovered in 2006 in the Delphinion. A revised edition and commentary of all fragments including the reconstruction of the inscription's display on the architecture of the Delphinion is in preparation.

[84]   Paus. 1.18.3; cf. Parker 1996, 43–55. Parker 1996, 43, n. 1 cites the earliest known monumental calendar of about 600 BC from the temple of Apollo in Corinth (see also Lupu 2005, 65f., figs. 1–2), and two fragments from Gortyn (*LSCG*, 247f., nos. 146f., fifth century BC), perhaps not belonging together and a little younger than the Milesian calendar.

[85]   Herda 2005, 272–279, figs. 25, 29; Müllenhoff, Herda & Brückner 2009, 97–110; Herda in preparation.

[86]   Ael. Arist., *Panath.* 30, with scholia; see also Miller 1978, 43, 174, no. 226, 180f., nos. 255–257.

[87]   *Lex. Harpokration* s.v. Πάνδημος Ἀφροδίτη quoting the second century BC Athenian historian Apollodoros (= *FGrH* 244 F 113).

[88]   Plut., *Cim.* 4, 481a = Melanthios fr. T 1b (Snell & Kannicht); see also Robertson 1998, 283–302, esp. 296.

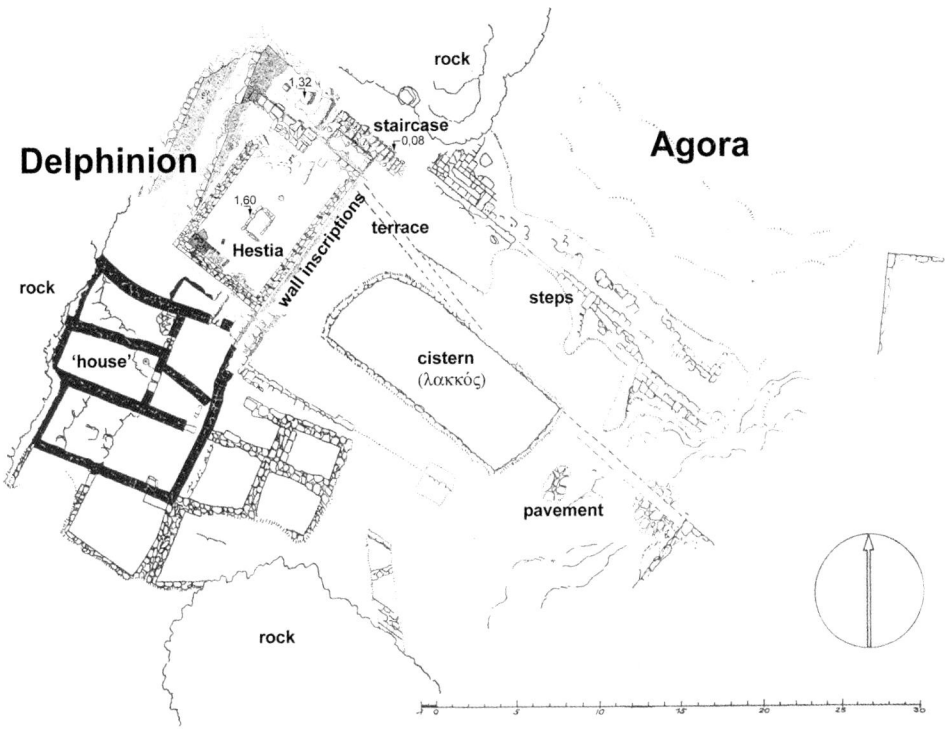

Fig. 4. Dreros/Crete, showing the position of the Delphinion near the agora (author after Marinatos 1936, 214–285, pl. 27 left and Demargne & Van Effenterre 1937, 5–32, pl. 1).

to the Athenian tradition preserved in Thukydides and Plutarch, Theseus had built the prytaneion when bringing together in a *synoikismos* the villages of Attica to form the Athenian state. The area of the "Older agora" and the prytaneion was called *asty* in Plutarch's time.[89] It was located at the eastern foot of the Acropolis, not far from the Aglaurion.[90] By contrast the "New agora" of democratic Athens was built east of Kolonos Agoraios in the so-called inner

Kerameikos, following the Kleisthenic reforms (508/7 BC).[91] Here we find the so-called *tholos*, a circular dining and assembly hall which was most likely built for the new committee of the *prytaneis*, introduced by Ephialtes in 462 BC. To distinguish it from the prytaneion on the old agora where dining at public expense is testified until the third century AD, the Athenians called the tholos the *prytanikon*.[92]

[89] Thuc. 2.15; Plut., *Thes.* 24.
[90] Herda 2005, 274f., fig. 26 with bibliography; see now Lippolis 2006, 37–62, figs. 8–10. The recently proposed localization of the prytaneion in the area of a Roman peristyle complex at the square of *Agias Aikaterinis* east of the choregic monument of Lysikrates is not convincing: Lippolis 2006, 52–55; contra Schmalz 2006, 33–81.

[91] Shear 1994, 225–248; Miller 1995, 201–242, esp. 224, followed by Papadopoulos 2003, 289–297, would like to lower the dating of the democratic agora in the Kerameikos to the time after the Persian destruction of Athens and the liberation in 480/79 BC.
[92] Miller 1978, 38–66, esp. 54 (*tholos*), 61 (*prytanikon*). Compare the honorary decree for Ulpius Eubiotus and his children of around 220 AD, where public meals in the *tholos* and the prytaneion are distinguished:

Fig. 5. Miletos, start of the New Year procession to Didyma in the second century AD, view from the north, hypothetical reconstruction (author, graphic design by S. Gräbener, Berlin, after a model of the city centre of Miletos in the Pergamonmuseum, Berlin).

In the small Cretan *polis* of Dreros we find the earliest close comparison to the situation in Miletos (*Fig. 4*). Here, the Delphinion, built ca 700 BC, is situated on a paved terrace above the SW corner of the agora. The one-room building incorporates an open, rectangular hearth, the sacred hestia, around which the *prytaneis*

sat dining with their guests.[93] The outer face of the eastern wall is covered with inscriptions that record some of the oldest known Greek laws, dated to the second half of the seventh century BC. This situation resembles the inscribed south hall of the Milesian Delphinion. In this way, Apollo Delphinios, the protector of the city, sanctioned the human laws and secured the stability of social relations.[94]

Oliver 1941, 125–141, no. 31, l. 15 σείτησιν τὴν ἐν τῇ θόλω καὶ πρυτανείω; cf. Wycherley 1957, 174, 184, no. 609. For the architecture of the *tholos-prytanikon* cf. Camp 1989, 77, 94–97, figs. 51–53, 66, 68, 71. Camp stresses (*ibid.* 94f.) that the Athenian *prytaneis* did not dine lying on couches (cf. the old reconstruction Miller 1978, 54ff., fig. 2), but sitting on benches which ran along the inner walls. The situation resembles the seated dining in the *Molpon*-prytaneion of Miletos: see above n. 76.

[93] Herda 2005, 276–278, fig. 28; for the identification of the "hearth temple" of Dreros with the Delphinion, see Demargne & Van Effenterre 1937, 29–31, fig. 17 (a Hellenistic inscription found in the cistern east of the temple, mentioning that Apollo Delphinios had sanctioned the construction of the cistern); Herda 2005, 277, n. 160; *idem* 2008, 18, n. 38, 54 n. 313.

[94] Herda 2005, 277f.; Hölkeskamp 2003, 99.

In Miletos as in other towns, the agora was surrounded by a number of public buildings together with the Delphinion in the north (*Fig. 2*). On the better-explored western side, for example, lay the sanctuary of Dionysos[95] and the sanctuary of another unknown, perhaps female deity,[96] as well as a building which has tentatively been called a prytaneion, though finds supporting this hypothesis are still missing.[97]

The vast rectangular open space of the agora not only served as an assembly place for the *demos*, but here too the choral competitions that formed part of the Dionysiac festivals may have taken place in a χορός, a dancing place, the forerunner of later theatre *orchestrai*. Earlier, Homer calls such places on *agorai*, where trials also took place, the ἱερὸς κύκλος, "holy circle".[98] Indeed, Miletos—as many other Greek cities—lacked a theatre until at least the late fourth century BC.[99] Besides the choral competitions for Dionysos, the dancing place in the agora may have also served as a perfect setting for the presumed paian choruses of the *neoi* during the *Hamilleteria* as part of the New Year festival for Apollo Delphinios.[100]

After finishing the *Hamilleteria* in the Delphinion, the whole population of Miletos assembled in the agora on the morning of the eleventh day of Taureon in order to form the state-procession to the extra-urban oracle sanctuary of Apollo at Didyma.[101] A reconstruction drawing (*Fig. 5*) may give an idea of how this might have looked in the late second century AD, when most of Miletos' city centre was filled with public buildings, orientating their splendid facades towards the open assembly space.[102]

The Molpoi decree extensively describes, in lines 18–20 and 23–31, the rituals which had to be carried out before and during the procession.[103] The procession's destination was Didyma (*Fig. 6*). There, the New Year festival ended with final sacrifices to Apollo Didymeus during the Boiégia/Didymeia festival, which also included competitions, such as the torch race mentioned above.[104] The sacrifices took place

---

[95] Müller-Wiener 1977–78, 94–103, fig. 1, addendum 1, W. Real, 2. *Ausgewählte Funde aus dem Dionysos-Tempel, ibid.* 105–116; Müller-Wiener 1979, 162–169, figs. 2–4; Müller-Wiener 1988, 279–290, figs. 22a–b; Hirsch 2001, 217–272, esp. 218–228, figs. 1–3; Herda in preparation.

[96] Finds of terracottae and the fragment of a *lex sacra* in the *insula* W of the Hellenistic *bouleuterion*: Wiegand 1901, 909f. (thought of a Demeter sanctuary); Mayer 1932, 1622–1655, esp. 1629f.; *Milet* VI 3, 126–128, no. 1217a, pl. 20 (*lex sacra*, early fifth century BC); Herda in preparation.

[97] The so-called Gneisgebäude ("Mica shist building") was named the prytaneion by A. v. Gerkan in *Milet* I 6, 30f., 89f. But his identification is hypothetical, as it rests only on the building's position close to the agora: Miller 1978, 231; Herda 2005, 272f.

[98] Hom. *Il.* 18.503–506 (*hieros kyklos*); *Od.* 8.260 (*choros*); see also Martin 1951, 39; Kolb 1981, 3f., 5–19; Kenzler 1999, 42–45, 53–59, 62, 64f., 99f., 243f., 306f. The term κύκλος is epigraphically attested for the agora of Erythrai in the early fifth century BC. Inside this *kyklos* was a sanctuary of Zeus Agoraios, where law inscriptions were installed: *IErythrai* 1, 22–32, no. 2 l. B 5–10 ἐς [τ]ὸγ κύκλ|ον στῆσ|αι τὸ Ζη|νὸς τὼγ|οραίο; cf. the commentary of Merkelbach *ibid.* 28; Martin 1951, 178; Kolb 1981, 13, n. 40; Graf 1985, 197–199. Compare also the "*kyklos* of the agora" in Eur. *Or.* 919 or the "round throne of the agora" in Soph. *OT.* 161: Kolb 1981, 11; Kenzler 1999, 210, 243.

[99] *Milet* IV 1, 35 with n. 41, fig. 8. An *orchestra* is archaeologically attested in the Classical *agorai* of Argos (T. Hölscher 1999, 39; Kenzler 1999, 216–218, fig. 17) and Corinth (Kenzler 1999, 213–216, figs. 14–16).

[100] See above with n. 38.

[101] For the date, see Herda 2006a, 167–170.

[102] Herda 2006a, fig. on cover (= *Fig. 5*). For the course of the procession inside the city, see *ibid.* 259f., figs. 12–14. Regarding the course in Archaic times, where we have only limited information about the settlement, see here *Fig. 2*, for Classical and later times (street-*insula*-grid-system) I prefer the reconstruction of A. v. Gerkan: Herda 2006a, fig. 14 (blue line), but note that geophysical survey has shown the shape of the *insula*e in the southern districts to be much longer: Herda 2005, 281–285, fig. 30; Weber 2007, 327–362, esp. 355–359, figs. 19f., Beilage 3.

[103] Herda 2006a, 167–186, 249–356, 371–385, 435–442, 447–461, figs. 9, 12–14, 16–22.

[104] See above nn. 40f.

in front of the oracle temple, on the ash altar built by Herakles.[105]

Before the procession started, two so-called *Gylloi* were positioned at the Holy Gates of Miletos, close to a shrine of the goddess Hekate Propylaia, and at the entrance to the oracle in Didyma. Being worshiped in a cult of their own, the *Gylloi* were wreathed and received a sponde of unmixed wine while a paian was sung for them. They functioned as deified sacred stone markers to signal the beginning and the end of the sacred road between city and sanctuary.[106]

In the course of the procession local Milesian gods and heroes were venerated at seven stations along the way, where the participants performed paians and sometimes additional sacrifices.[107]

The 18 km long processional road—as François de Polignac has named it—clearly formed the "cultic spine" of the Milesian *chora*, connecting its two religious poles, the Delphinion at the city's heart and Didyma in the middle of the *chora*.[108] It therefore expressed the city's claim upon its territory and the main extraurban sanctuary in Didyma, the oracle of Apollo Didymeus, run in Archaic times by the clan of the *Branchidai* and presumably Karian in origin.[109] In effect the procession helped to shape the identity and cohesion of the Milesian people.[110]

The Milesian state and its colonial activity in Archaic times

As can be demonstrated from the evidence of the Milesian colonies, especially Sinope, founded ca 630 BC, and Olbie Polis, founded ca 550 BC, and from fragments of local Milesian chronicles preserved in the late Hellenistic authors Konon and Nikolaos of Damascus,[111] the cult of Apollo Delphinios with its specific institutions was the main state cult in the mother city itself from the beginning of the seventh century BC at the latest. The procession to Didyma can equally be traced back to the late eighth or the beginning of the seventh century BC, which implies that there was already a firm connection between the city and

---

[105] For the Boiégia/Didymeia: Herda 2006a, 187–211, 317–319, 351, 441–442, 453–454. For the altar see above nn. 41–42.

[106] Molpoi decree ll. 25–27; cf. Herda 2006a, 249–259. The *Gylloi* are not images of Apollo (as most recently Gonzales 2008, 2), as they also feature as sacred stone markers during the processions for Dionysos: Haussoullier 1921, 99, n. 2; Herda 2006a, 250f. For their probable epichoric origin in Asia Minor: Herda 2009, 89 with n. 351.

[107] Herda 2006a, 259–350, 371–385, 438–441, figs. 9, 10, 12, 13–14, 17, 20–22 for the course of the procession and the seven stations (Hekate at the gates, Dynamis [personification of the power of the magistrates], Nymphs in the meadow, Hermes in the sanctuary of the river god Kelados, [Apollo?] Phylios [protector of the tribes], Apollo Keraiites, statues of Chares). Only one of them (no. 3, the sanctuary of the Nymphs, halfway, on the heights of the *Akron*) has been located so far: *ibid.* 293–302, fig. 16; cf. here *Fig. 6*. The statement of Lohmann 2006, 201–204, that the Archaic inscription mentioning the nymphs was not found in the sanctuary of the nymphs on the *Akron* is misleading, cf. Herda 2006a, 262, with n. 1862, 293f.; N. Ehrhardt in *Milet* VI 3, 186 f., no. 1298.

[108] de Polignac 1984, 48, with n. 11, 156 ("axes du territoire civique"; see also de Polignac 1995, 40, 154); Graf 1996, 55–65, esp. 60f. ("bipolarity"); T. Hölscher 1999, 74–83 ("sakrale Achsen"); cf. Herda 2006a, 1–5, 385 with n. 2719, 448 with n. 3179.

[109] On the Karian toponym Didyma and the possibly Karian origins of the *Branchidai* and the oracle: Herda 2008, 20–22; *idem* 2009, 87f., 96–101. On the Karian god *ntro- prnjida-*, mentioned in a Karian votive-inscription from Egypt (Naukratis?), who can be tentatively equated with "Apollo Branchideus", cf. Herda & Sauter 2009, 98–100.

[110] Herda 2006a, 447–457; *idem* 2008, 18–20.

[111] Konon: *FGrH* 26 F 44; Nikolaos: *FGrH* 90 F 52f.

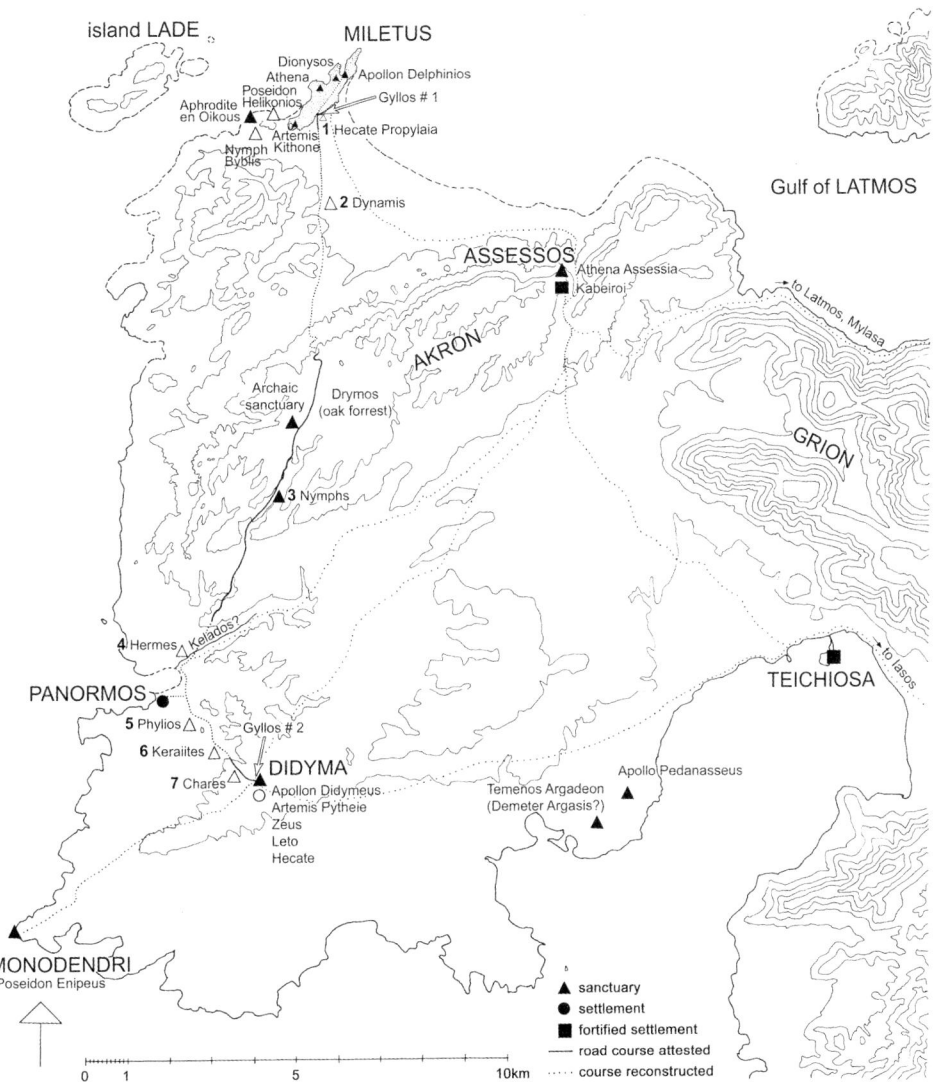

Fig. 6. Milesian peninsula, showing the main sanctuaries and the course of the procession from Miletos to Didyma (empty symbols: exact location unknown).

the extraurban oracle sanctuary of Apollo Didymeus at this early date.[112]

The functioning of the main cult pair of Apollo Delphinios and Apollo Didymeus, which has to be considered as specifically Milesian,[113] can be better understood by comparison with the situation in the *Homeric*

---

[112] Herda 2005, 246, 286–290; *idem* 2006a, 18–20, 173–178, 268–277, 447–453, 458; *idem* 2008, 14–24; *idem*, in preparation.

[113] See Herda 2008.

Fig. 7. Two Milesian bronze coins of the archiprytanis Tiberios Klaudios Damas for emperor Nero, on each reverse (left) the earliest known depiction of the cult statue of Apollo Delphinios, made and dedicated by the Milesian sculptor Demetrios, ca 100 BC. Above: Paris, Cabinet de France 1864, after Robert 1967, pl. 1, 9; below: ex SNG von Aulock 2103, after Burnett, Amandry & Ripollès 1992, pl. 117, no. 2712.

Hymn to Apollo, which can be dated to the seventh century BC. The hymn narrates that Apollo as a theriomorphic, dolphin-like god, jumps onto the ship of some seafaring Cretans from Knossos. He takes control of the ship, changes their route and leads them securely to a beach called Crisa, near Pytho, the later Delphi. Having landed on the beach he changes his appearance to a *kouros*, a young man, and orders them to found an altar and sanctuary to venerate him as Apollo Delphinios. Afterwards he leads them in a paian singing procession from Crisa to Pytho, where he installs them as the first administrators (ὀργίονες) of his newly-founded oracle.[114]

Irad Malkin has pointed out that in the story of the *Homeric Hymn* Apollo Delphinios has two main functions:[115] First, he is the protector of seafarers and ships (Νηοσσόος),

the god of the shores and beaches (Ἄκτιος, Ἀκταῖος) and the happy landing (Ἐμβάσιος).[116] Second, he is a god of colonization, as he leads the foundation of his sanctuary at the beach in Crisa. The altar of the sanctuary is the first fire of the colonists, the future sacred hearth in the Delphinion. Therefore Apollo himself is the founder, the *ktistes*, of the *polis* Crisa which controlled the oracle of Pytho from the beginning until around 600 BC. At that time Crisa was destroyed by the *amphyktiones* and a new city was founded in Pytho, the place of the oracle, which now received the name Delphi,[117]

---

[114] *Hymn. Hom. Ap.* 388–546; Herda 2006a, 35–37, 268–277; *idem* 2008, 51–57, 63f. The act of "choosing" the Cretans as *orgiones* explains the epiklesis *Epopsios*, "the one who chooses", with which Apollo labels himself (*Hymn. Hom. Ap.* 496): Herda 2008, 52 with n. 300.

[115] Malkin 2000, 69–77, esp. 71, 76f.

[116] The role of the *Homeric Hymn* as an early and important source to determine the character of Apollo Delphinios as a protector of seafaring was doubted by Graf 1979, 2–3, 5–7, 21 and Parker 2003,179.

[117] *Hymn. Hom. Ap.* 487–501; cf. Herda 2008, 52–54, with n. 311: Apollo Delphinios founds the *polis* Crisa, not the *polis* Delphi on the beach (so Malkin 2000, 71, 76f.). Crisa controlled the oracle in Pytho, before it was destroyed by the *amphyktiones* in the first Holy War ca 600 BC. See for example *Hymn. Hom. Ap.* 499–501, 511–524, where the procession from Crisa to Pytho after the sacrifices to Delphinios at the beach, led by the god himself, is described and ll. 440–447, where the Crisaean women and girls are assembled around the adyton of the oracle and the tripod votives in Pytho.

probably in remembrance of the cult of Apollo Delphinios in Crisa.[118]

The third function of Apollo Delphinios, which was determined by Fritz Graf in his comparative study of cults in different Greek *poleis*,[119] is directly connected with the second: as founder of the *polis* state and its sacred centre, Apollo Delphinios is the god of politics *per se*. Connected with this is his metamorphosis from a dolphin to a long-haired *kouros*:[120] being a *kouros* the god himself figures as a model for the initiation of the new citizens, the *neoi* or *kouroi*. Therefore Apollo is not the *arch-ephebos*,[121] but the *arch-kouros*, the one who at the same time "makes (male) youths grow" (κουρίζειν) in order to become new citizens and who protects this most important step in the life of young men.[122]

Indeed, the famous late Geometric cult statuette of Apollo, found in the Delphinion of Dreros, depicts a naked, long-haired young man,[123] as also many of the famous Greek dedicatory statues and statuettes of long-haired youths for Apollo may represent votives of grateful *kouroi* and their families for a successful initiation.[124] The late Hellenistic cult statue of the god in the Delphinion of Miletos, a dedication of the sculptor and *aisymnetes-stephanephoros* Demetrios (*Fig. 7*), still displays this iconographic chiffre, even though Apollo's posture—seated instead of standing and resting the right arm on the head—has become more comfortable.[125]

Let us now turn to the connection between the colonizing god Apollo Delphinios and the oracle-giving gods Apollo Pythios and Apollo Didymeus: as in Miletos, the Delphinion of the *polis* Crisa is connected to the oracle by a procession.[126] This not only signals the control of the *polis* over the oracle, it also demonstrates that both oracles had something to do with colonization: Pytho-Delphi and Didyma each protected and sanctioned Greek colonization in Archaic times. Pytho-Delphi not only sanctioned the Crisaean colonization of Metapontion in the mid-seventh century BC,[127] but as

---

Only after the fall of Crisa was the *polis* Delphi established at the site of the oracle in Pytho.

[118] Herda 2008, 53, n. 311.

[119] Graf 1979.

[120] *Hymn. Hom. Ap.* 440–451.

[121] The term was coined by Harrison 1927, 441; cf. Burkert 1975, 1–21, esp. 11, 18.

[122] Brelich 1969, 435f. The terms *epheboi* and *kouroi/neoi* are often confused in scholarship. Indeed, Apollo is not the god of the *epheboi* but of the *kouroi*. This is why Gorgos, the son of Asklepiades, offers his hair to Apollo Delphinios when becoming a *kouros* (*A. P.* 6. 278 = *Rhianos* fr. 68 Powell), and the *agelaioi*, the new citizens in Dreros (sometimes incorrectly equated with the *epheboi*), swear to Apollo Delphinios (*ICret* I IX 1, l. A 14; oath of the Drerian *agelaioi*, errected in the Delphinion): Herda 2005, 289, with n. 223; *idem* 2006, 45f. with n. 222, 94–96 with nn. 611–613, 624; *idem* 2008, 18f. with n. 38, 55f. with n. 326; 51 with n. 290. Therefore "the oddity (...) that the ephebes [in Athens, A.H.], who honour all the gods (so to speak), do not in fact honour Apollo Delphinios" (Parker 2005, 436) simply disappears.

[123] Herda 2005, 289 with nn. 222f.; fig. 31; *idem* 2008, 18f., n. 38, 23 with n. 77, 55 with n. 326.

[124] de Polignac 1984, 45; Bremmer 1994, 33; Herda 2008, 51 with n. 290f.

[125] The cult in Miletos lacked a cult statue until the local sculptor Demetrios, being *aisymnetes-stephanephoros* of Apollo Delphinios himself, dedicated his classicizing work of about 100 BC. It was exhibited in a round temple in the centre of the Delphinion, east of the altar (cf. here *Fig. 5*): Th. Wiegand in *Milet* I 3, 409–411, figs. 100f.; Thomas 1983, 124–133, pls. 27–30; 1988, 314–317, figs. 5–6; Herda 2005, 289 with n. 225; *idem* 2006, 213f., n. 1493; *idem* 2008, 17 with n. 29, fig. 2.

[126] See above n. 114.

[127] Metapontion in southern Italy (Lucania) is said to have been founded under the leadership of Daulios, tyrant of Crisa (Ephoros, *FGrH* 70 F 141 = Strab. 6.1.15). The involvement of Pytho-Delphi in the colonization may explain why Metapontion sent a θέρος χρυσοῦν, a "golden harvest", to Apollo in Delphi every year: Strab. 6.1.15 (Strabo gives instead the presumably later local Metapontian foundation myth, the "golden harvest" recalls the first "Pylian" settlers "who sailed from Troy with Nestor" and "prospered (such) from farming ... that they dedicated a golden harvest at Delphi"). This may be reflected in Metapontian silver staters issued from the mid-sixth century BC on-

a developing Panhellenic oracle centre it had, of course, a much wider circle of action than Didyma, which was especially connected to the activities of Miletos as a metropolis in the Propontic and Black Sea areas.[128]

The clearest evidence for the latter assumption is the copy—presumably private—of an oracle of Apollo Didymeus concerning the foundation of the Milesian Black Sea colony of Olbie Polis. It was found scratched on a bone plaque only 30 years ago on the island of Berezan and can be dated between 550 and 525 BC.[129] The identification as an oracle of Didymaean Apollo is attested by the dedication formula: the bone plaque is consecrated to Apollo Didymeus with the additional *epiklesis* "Milesios", "the Milesian".[130] The oracle text, written in prose, mentions four different Apollo cults linked to seven and multiples of seven, the holy number of Apollo, in ascending positions. Walter Burkert has convincingly argued that these

numbers symbolise years of rule, resulting in the number 7777, the "Great Year"—or to put it another way—eternity: 7 years of Apollo Lykeios, the "wolf" god, 70 years of Apollo Helios, the "lion" god, 700 years of Apollo Ietros, the "healer" god, and 7000 years of the "wise dolphin", Δελφὶς φρόνιμος, that is: Apollo Delphinios.[131]

It is again important to note the theriomorphic concept of Apollo Delphinios in Olbie Polis. This is also evident in the city's coinage, issued from the late sixth century BC onwards: the coins made of bronze have the shape of dolphins (*Fig. 8*).[132]

All in all, this colony is an exact copy of its mother city Miletos: we not only find the cult of Apollo Delphinios, the Molpoi, and the *aisymnetes-stephanephoros* as eponymous, but also the Delphinion incorporates the prytaneion and is situated at the northern side of the agora as in Miletos.[133] Again the potential ritualization of public, political space is evident.

A distribution chart of the Milesian cults of Apollo Delphinios and Apollo Didymeus clearly highlights Milesian colonizing activities (*Fig. 9*).[134] From the epigraphical and literary evidence in three to six cases—see the asterisks—the direct intervention of Didyma in the foundation of a colony is attested.[135] Some-

---

wards that display an ear of barley on both sides: *Kl. Pauly* 3, München 1975, 1260, s.v. Metapontum (G. Radke); Boardman 1988, 198, fig. 236. As can be gathered in addition fom Hdt. 4.15, Apollo led the *oikistes* (Daulios?) and his companions to Italy in the shape of a raven. Such theriomorphic epiphanies of protecting deities during colonization are typical also for Artemis Hegemone, compare the Ionian migration to Asia Minor, where she figures as a dog: Lib. 5.34; Herda 2008, 28f., n. 118, 52 with n. 295. Unfortunately no Delphian foundation oracle related to Crisa and Metapontion is preserved: see Malkin 1987, 24, 28. On the foundation myths and the archaeology of early Metapontion, see De Juliis 2001, 13–47.

[128] See Herda 2008, 24–31, 51–64 with further references.

[129] *SEG* 36 694; Herda 2006a, 272f., figs. 15a–f; *idem* 2008, 24f., 31–35, fig. 7.

[130] Ll. B 1–3: Ἀπόλλωνι | Διδυμ(εῖ) | Μιλησίωι. The combination of the epikleseis Milesios and Didymeus is also attested by graffiti naming Apollo Milesios and once Apollo Didymeus in the Archaic sanctuary of Apollo in Egyptian Naukratis. This sanctuary was a Milesian foundation of the late seventh century BC backed by the oracle in Didyma: Herda 2006a, 449f. with n. 3185; *idem* 2008, 24 with n. 87, 39 with n. 208, 59, 61.

[131] Burkert 1994, 49–60, esp. 56f. with n. 35; Herda 2006a, 272f.; *idem* 2008, 24f., 35 with n. 159.

[132] Herda 2006a, 273; *idem* 2008, 35 with nn. 160f. on the disputed dating and distribution of the dolphin- and arrowhead-shaped coins. The motif of an eagle grappling a dolphin on Classical coins, amphora- and tile-stamps as well as weights from the Milesian Black Sea colonies Sinope, Istria and Olbie Polis should not be interpreted as Zeus catching Delphinios. Instead it symbolizes an omen of Zeus: Hind 2007, 9–22, pl. 1f.

[133] Graf 1979, 6, 8f.; cf. Herda 2005, 275–276, fig. 27.

[134] For the following see Herda 2008, 24–45, 51–64, fig. 8.

[135] Epigraphically attested for Olbie Polis and most probably also for Phasis and the "special case" Naukratis (for Naukratis, which in its earlier phases was a Milesian *emporium*, not a colony, and Apollo Didymeus Milesios, see: Herda 2008, 39–50); literary sources ex-

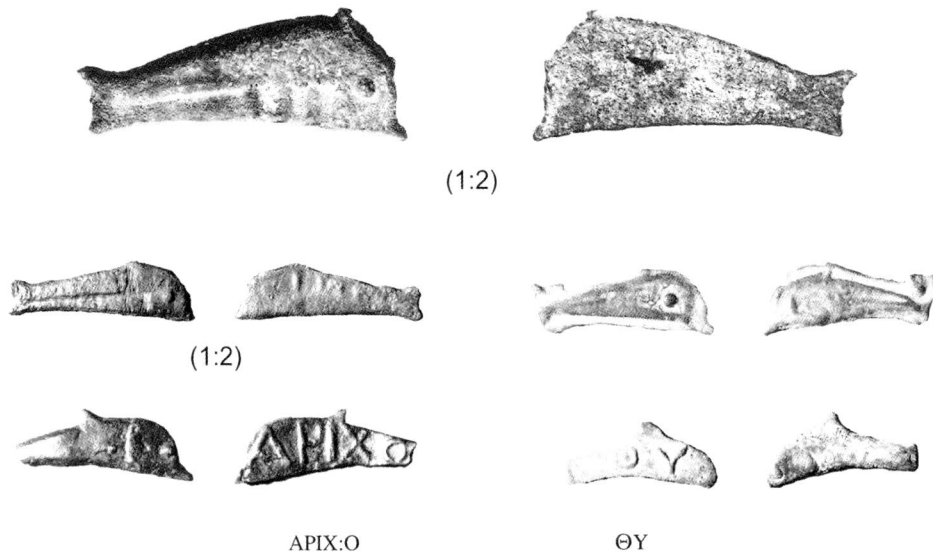

(1:2)

(1:2)

APIX:O   ΘY

Fig. 8. Olbie Polis/Black Sea, bronze weights and coinage in the shape of dolphins, representing Apollo Delphinios, ca 6th–4th century BC. After Stingl 2005, pl. 63, 1–5.

times the cult of Apollo Didymeus was transferred to the new colony,[136] but more often this happened with the cult of Apollo Delphinios.[137] We may suppose, then, that the cult was organised after the Milesian model, for which Olbie Polis again forms the clearest evidence.

The dolphin god figured as protector of the colonizing seafarers and as founder of the sacred hearths in the city centres of the new colonies. These hearths were lit with a flame stemming from the *koine hestia* in the *Molpon*-prytaneion of Miletos, which itself was an offspring of the ἑστία ἀκίνητος, the "unmovable hearth" in the prytaneion of the Ionian metropolis Athens, as we learn from Herodotos.[138] Again we de-

---

ist for Kyzikos, Apollonia at Rhyndakos and probably for Apollonia Pontike.

[136] Epigraphically attested for Olbie Polis, Phasis, Amisos and the special case Naukratis; literary sources exist for Trapezos and probably Sinope. Unrelated to the Archaic colonization of Miletos are the cults of Didymeus in Ekbatana/Persia, the "city of the Branchidai" near the river Oxos/Baktria-Sogdiana, the altars at the river Iaxartes near Alexandreia Eschate/Baktria-Sogdiana and in Medinet Habu near Thebes/Egypt: Herda 2008, 38, 58, 62 (Ekbatana); 37f., 58, 62 ("city of the Branchidai"; altars near Alexandreia Eschate); 38, 63 (Medinet Habu). For the religious act of transferring a cult, the so-called *aphidryma* or *aphidrysis*, see Malkin 1987, 9, 69–72, 119–122; *idem* 1991; Herda 2008, 33, 40.

[137] Epigraphically attested for Olbie Polis, Hermonassa and Odessos; indirectly conjectured with the help of theophoric personal names (Delphinios), or names connected to the cult association of the Molpoi (Molpagoras, Molpothemis, etc.) for Prokonessos, Kios, Apollonia Pontike, Pantikapaion, Nymphaion, Kepoi and Gorgippia. In Sinope we find the theophoric name

Delphinios as also a Molpagoras. Additionally the *aisymnetes-stephanephoros* was eponymous.

[138] Hdt. 1.146.2 uses the term "setting out from the prytaneion" (ἀπὸ τοῦ πρυτανηίου ... ὁρμηθέντες), which has the meaning of transferring the sacred fire from the hearth of the Athenian prytaneion: Malkin 1987, 117f., 121. For the role of the sacred hearth in colonization see *ibid.* 114–134. Malkin (*ibid.* 121) stresses that Hdt. 1.146.2 is the only case where the practice of transferring the sacred fire to a colony is related to a certain *polis* and its colony, namely Athens and Miletos, but that it was a common Greek practice. We may therefore take it to also be a regular ritual in Milesian

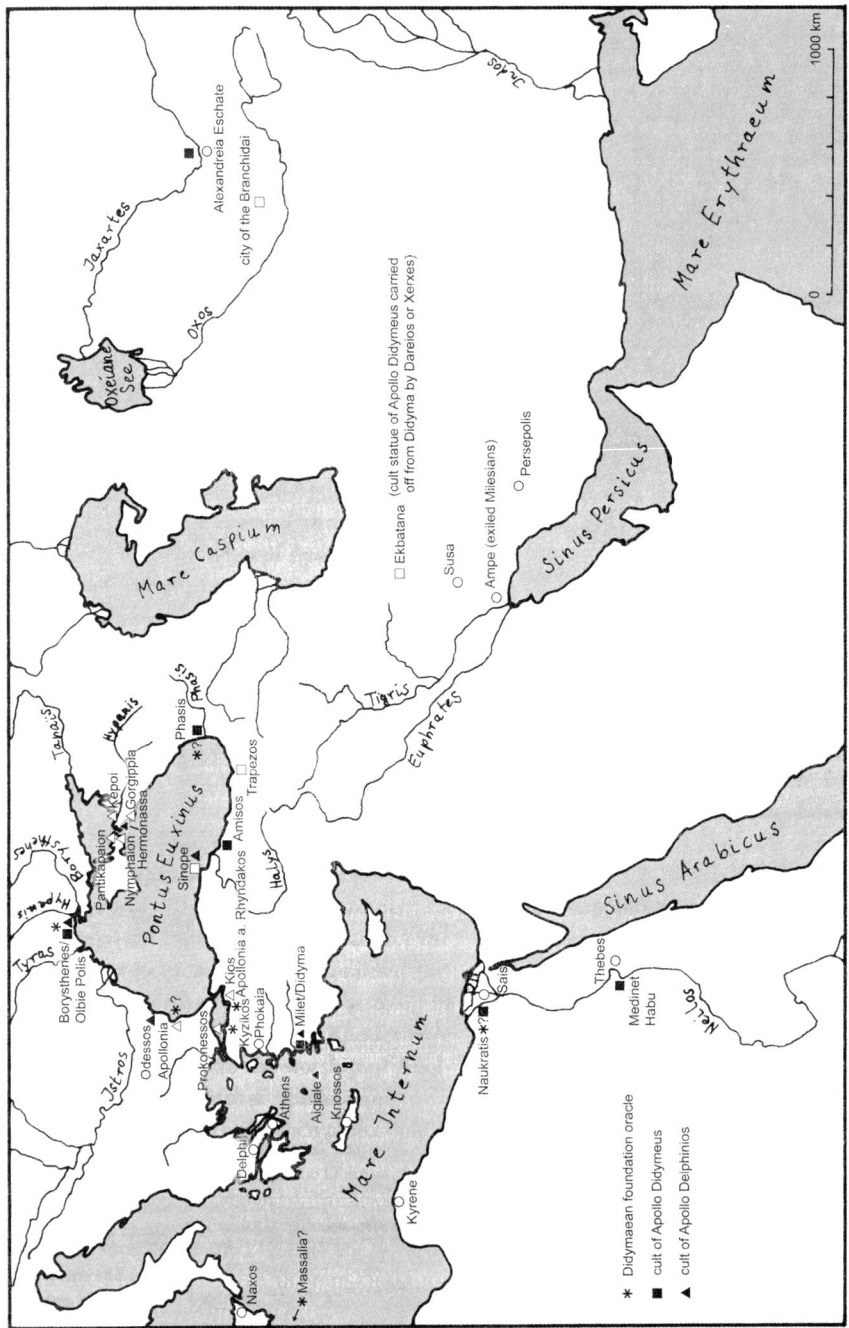

Fig. 9. Distribution of the Milesian cult of Apollo Delphinios, of the Didymaean cult of Apollo Didymeus, and of Didymaean foundation oracles (filled symbols: cult directly attested; empty symbols: cult indirectly attested).

tect a fire ritual as a "universal Greek religious custom".[139]

But Herodotos illuminates only one side of the Milesian foundation story: there was another one reaching further into the past. It dealt with the Bronze Age history of the city. Miletos was said to be a colony of Minoan Crete, the island from where the Delphic Apollo took his cult association.[140] Another fragmentary tradition, preserved in Kallimachos, told of Apollo, who in the shape of a dolphin—or riding on a dolphin, embarked from Delos, his birthplace, to Miletos. Here he landed at the suburb *Oikous* and continued to Didyma to found the oracle there.[141]

If we consider the *Homeric Hymn to Apollo*, we may reconstruct the complete story: Apollo Delphinios came from Crete via Delos, first to found Oikous-Miletos, and afterwards the oracle in Didyma. The procedure of founding Miletos may have taken place in the same manner as that of Crisa in the Apollo hymn: Apollo himself established his altar on the beach where he landed appearing as a dolphin (or dolphin rider).[142] The beach altar is that of Apollo Delphinios. Here the sacred hearth of the new city has to be located. This fits with the archaeologically detected situation of the Delphinion in Miletos: it is built on the drained shore of the Lions harbour embayment, on the beach so to speak, and it contained the *Hestia* in the *Molpon*-prytaneion.[143]

I would like to conclude by stating that Miletos not only successfully managed to run the main state cults of Apollo Delphinios and Didymeus but that it was also able to export them—individually or as the original couple— to many other places outside the Greek world, binding them closely to the mother city.

ALEXANDER HERDA
Institut für Klassische Archäologie
Universität Tübingen
alexander.herda@klassarch.uni-tuebingen.de

---

colonization, especially regarding the high percentage of Apollo Delphinios cults in the Milesian colonies. On Hdt. 1.146, cf. Herda 2006a, 159f.; *idem* 2008, 54; *idem* forthcoming.

[139] Malkin 1987, 122.

[140] Herodoros of Herakleia *FGrH* 31 F 45; Aristokritos of Miletos *FGrH* 493 F 1, F 3; Paus. 7.2.5 (Cretan Milatos as *heros ktistes*); Ephoros *FGrH* 70 F 127 (Cretan Sarpedon as founder); cf. Herda 2009, 67f. Is it by accident that the Molpoi decree uses an Archaic Cretan formular (l. 40 ἔαδε Μολποῖσιν; cf. Herda 2006a, 404–406; above n. 31) to label a decision of the Apollo Delphinios cult association of the Molpoi in 476/5 BC, or is it an intentional "Cretism"?

[141] Callim. *Branchos* fr. 229 ll. 12f. (Pfeiffer). On the foundation myths of Miletos and Didyma, see Herda forthcoming.

[142] The theriomorphic appearance of Apollo as a dolphin should be the older version of the myth: Herda 2005, 287, n. 212; *idem* 2008, 55f., n. 326. Note that Artemis Kithone Hegemone appears as a dog when leading the Ionian *heros ktistes* Neileos to found (the Ionian) Miletos: Herda 2008, 28f. with n. 118; 52 with n. 295.

[143] Herda 2005, 288–289; *idem* 2008, 54–55; see above n. 34–36.

Appendix: The Molpoi decree.
Text, translation and systematic overview

EDITIONS AND COMMENTARIES:

U. v. Wilamowitz, *Satzungen einer milesischen Sängergilde, SBBerlin* 1904, 619–640; *Sammlung der griechischen Dialektinschriften* III 2, eds. H. Collitz & F. Bechtel, Göttingen 1905, 627–632, no. 5495; A. Rehm in *Milet* I 3, 277–284, no. 133; *Sylloge Inscriptionum Graecarum*[3] I, eds. W. Dittenberger & F. Hiller von Gaertringen, Leipzig 1915, 69–72, no. 57; E. Schwyzer, *Dialectorum Graecarum exempla epigraphica potiora*, Leipzig 1923, 352–354, no. 726; F. Solmsen & E. Fraenkel, *Inscriptiones Graecae ad inlustrandas dialectos selectae*[4], Stuttgart 1930, 102–105, no. 58; *LSAM* 1955, 129–135, no. 50; Herda 2006a.

STONE AND LETTER CUTTING:

Cf. Herda 2006a, 21, 27–28, figs. 1–4: *stele*-like block made of bluish-white marble; height 2.54 m; width diminishes from bottom (1.28 m) to top (1.15 m), as does the thickness (0.27 m at the bottom; 0.14 m at the top); front smoothed for inscription; a 8 to 13 cm high band of rougher smoothing indicates a removed crowning profile; two clamp holes on the top and an *anathyrosis* (3 to 5 cm broad) on both sides indicate a secondary (?) fixation within or to a wall; upper half of back smoothed, lower half rough.

The 1.6–2.4 cm high lines are each framed by two incised lines; space between lines: 0.5–1.4 cm; between line 42 and 43: empty space of 5 cm; between line 44 and 45: empty space of 4 cm (cf. Herda 2006a, 414); between last line and bottom: empty space of 0.94 m; height of letters: 1.5–2.3 cm; for the letterforms see Herda 2006a, 513, fig. 1–3; for the dating see above n. 11.

The inscription is now on display in the permanent exhibition in Altes Museum, Berlin.

TEXT:

Cf. Herda 2006a, 9–12, but edited here with the *psilosis* of the East Ionian dialect, cf. ls. 11f. 17 κατόπερ and l. 38 ἀπ' ἱερήο.

Ἐπὶ Φιλτέω τὸ Διονυσίο Μολπῶν αἰσυμνῶντος· προσέταιροι ἦσαν Οἰνώ-
πων Ἀγαμήδης Ἀριστοκράτεος, Ὁπλήθων Λύκος Κλέαντος,
Βίων Ἀπολλοδώρο, Βωρ<έ>ων Κρηθεὺς Ἑρμώνακτος, Θράσων Ἀν-
τιλέοντος. ἔδοξε Μολποῖσιν τὰ ὄργια ἀναγράψαντας θεῖναι ἐς
5   τὸ ἱερὸν καὶ χρῆσθαι τούτοισιν, καὶ οὕτωι τάδε γραφθέντα ἐτέ-
θη. Ἑβδομαίοισι (...). τῆι ὀγδόωι ΑΠΟΛΕΙΚΑΙ τὰ ἱερὰ ἢ σπλάγχνα σπείσοσι Μολπῶν
αἰσυμνήτης. ὁ δὲ αἰσυμνήτης καὶ ὁ προσέταιρος προσαίρεται, ὅταν οἱ
κρητῆρες πάντες σπεσθέωσι καὶ παιωνίσωσιν. τῆι δὲ ἐνάτηι καὶ ἀπὸ
τῆς ὀσφύος καὶ τῆς πεμπάδος, ἣν ἴσχοσιν στεφανηφόροι,

10   τούτων προλαγχάνει τὰ ἰσξα ὁ νέος. ἄρχονται θύειν τὰ ἱερῆα
ΑΡΧΟ ἀπὸ τούτων Ἀπόλλωνι Δελφινίωι. καὶ κρητῆρες κιρνέαται κατόπερ ἐμ Μολπῶι καὶ παιὼν γίνεται. ὁ δὲ ἐξιὼν αἰσυμνήτης ἀπὸ τῶν ἡμίσε-
ων θύει Ἱστίηι ((καὶ κρητῆρας σπενδέτω αὐτὸς καὶ παιωνιζέτω)). τῆι δεκά-
τηι Ἀμιλλητήρια, καὶ δίδοται ἀπὸ Μολπῶν δύο ἱερήια τοῖσι στεφανηφό-
15   ροισιν τέλῃα, καὶ ἔρδεται Ἀπόλλωνι Δελφινίωι, καὶ ἀμιλλῶνται οἱ στεφανηφόροι οἵ τε νέοι καὶ ὁ ἱέρεω<ς>, καὶ οἶνον πίνοσι τὸμ Μολπῶν, καὶ κρητῆρες
σπένδονται κατόπερ ἐμ Μολπῶι. ὁ δὲ ἐξιὼν αἰσυμνήτης παρέχει ἅπερ ὁ
Ὀνιτάδης καὶ λαγχάνει ἅπερ ὁ Ὀνιτάδης. ὅταν στεφανηφόροι ἴωσιν ἐς
Δίδυμα, ἡ πόλις διδοῖ ἑκατόνβην τρία ἱερήια τέλεια· τούτων ἓν θῆλυ, ἓν
20   δὲ ἐνορχές. ἐς Μολπὸν ἡ πόλις διδοῖ Ταργηλίοισιν ἱερὸν τέλειον καὶ Μεταγει -
τνίοισιν ἱερὸν τέλειον, Ἑβδομαίοισι δὲ δύο τέλεια καὶ χὸν τὸμ παλαιὸν ὁ[ρ-]
τῆς ἑκάστης. Τούτοισιν τοῖσ’ ἱεροῖσιν ὁ βασιλεὺς παρίσταται, λαγχάνει δὲ
οὐδὲν πλῆον τῶν ἄλλων Μολπῶν. καὶ ἄρχονται οἱ στεφανηφόροι Ταυρεῶ-
νος θύειν Ἀπόλλωνι Δελφινίωι ἀπὸ τῶν ἀριστερῶν ἀπαρξάμενοι, καὶ κρητη-
25   ρίσας τέσσερας. καὶ Γυλλοὶ φέρονται δύο, καὶ τίθεται παρ’Ἑκάτην τὴν πρόσθεν
πυλέων ἐστεμμένος καὶ ἀκρήτω κατασπένδετε, ὁ δ’ ἕτερος ἐς Δίδυμα ἐπὶ
θύρας τίθεται. ταῦτα δὲ ποιήσαντες ἔρχονται τὴν ὁδὸν τὴν πλατεῖαν μέχρι
Ἄκρο, ἀπ’ Ἄκρο δὲ διὰ δρυμõ. καὶ παιωνίζεται πρῶτον παρ’Ἑκάτη τῆ πρόσθεν πυλέων, παρὰ Δυνάμει, εἴτεν ἐπὶ λειμῶνι ἐπ’ Ἄκρο παρὰ Νύμφαις’, εἴτεν παρ’Ἑρμῆ ἐν
30   Κελάδο, παρὰ Φυλίωι, κατὰ Κεραΐτην, παρὰ Χαρέω ἀνδριᾶσιν. ἔρδεται δὲ (((τῶι παν-
θύωι ἔτει))) παρὰ Κεραΐτηι δαρτόν, παρὰ Φυλίωι δὲ θύα θύεται (((παντ’ ἔτεα))). Ὀνιτά-
δηισι πάρεξις κεράμο, σιδήρο, χαλκõ, ξύλων, ὕδατος, κύκλων, δαΐδος, ριπῶν,
κρέα ἐπιδιαιρῆν, φαλαγκτηρίων, δεσμῶν τοῖσ’ ἱερηίοισιν. ((παρὰ στεφανηφόρος
λύχνον καὶ ἄλειφα)). ὄπ..τησις σπλάγχνων, κρεῶν ἕψησις, τῆς ὀσφύος καὶ
35   τῆς πεμπάδος, ἣν στεφανηφόροι ἴσχοσι, ἕψησις καὶ διαίρεσις, καὶ μοίρης λά-
ξις. ((ἐπιπέσσεν τὰ ἔλατρα ἐξ ἡμεδίμνο τωπόλλωνι πλακόντινα, τῆι Ἑκά-
τηι δὲ χωρίς)). Γίνεται Ὀνιτάδηισιν ἀπὸ Μολπῶν ὀσφύες πᾶσαι ἐκτὸς ὧν οἱ
στεφανηφόροι ἴσχοσιν, δέρματα πάντα, θυαλήματα τρία, ἀπ’ ἱερῆο ἑκάστο, ((? θύ-
ων τὰ περιγινόμενα, οἶνον τὸν ἐν τῶι κρητῆρι περιγινόμενον)), πεμπὰς τῆς ἡ-
40   μέρης. ((ὅτι δ’ ἂν τούτων μὴ ποιῶσιν Ὀνιτάδαι, ἔαδε Μολποῖσιν ἐπὶ Χαροπίνο στεφανηφόρος ἀπὸ Ἱστιήιων παρέχεν. ὅ τι δ’ ἂν Ὀνιτάδαι χρηΐζωσιν, ἔαδε Μολποῖ-
σι στεφανηφόροισιν ἐπιτετράφθαι)).
empty line
((((τῶι κήρυκι ἀτελείη ἐμ Μολπῶι πάντων καὶ λᾶξις σπλάγχνων ἀπὸ θυῶν ἑκασ-
τέων καὶ οἴνο φορὴ ἐς τὰ ψυκτήρια τέλεσι τοῖσ’ ἑωυτõ, ὁ δ’οἶνος ἀπὸ Μολπῶ<ν> γίνεται))).
empty line
45   ((((τῶι ὠιδῶι δεῖπνον παρέχει ὁ ἱέρ<ε>ως, ἄρισ.τον δὲ ὠισυμνήτης)))).

TRANSLATION:

Modified from Gorman 2001, 176–181. In angular brackets stand the line numbers and insertion dates. Single round brackets contain my own comments and explanations. Double and triple round brackets signify later insertions in the original text of the late sixth century BC. Double brackets mark insertions of the redaction by Philtes (447/46 BC) or before; triple brackets of the time between the Hellenistic redaction (ca 200 BC) and the redaction of Philtes (for an overview see Herda 2006a, 426f. table 1 but note the corrected absolute dates for Philtes and Charopinos, above, n. 12).

[1] When Philtes, the son of Dionysios, was *aisymnetes* (=*stephanephoros,* the chairman) (447/46 BC) of the Molpoi (cult association of Apollo Delphinios): companions (*proshetairoi*, the *prytaneis*) were from the (tribe) Oinopes, Agamedes, the son of Aristokrates, from the (tribe) Hoplethes, Lykos, the son of Kleas, Bion, the son of Apollodoros, and from the (tribe) Boreis, Kretheus, son of Hermonax, and Thrason, the son of Antileon. The Molpoi decided to place the engraved rites (*orgia*) in [5] the sanctuary (of Apollo Delphinios) and to act in accordance with them. And thus the following was engraved and placed:

At the (festival of the) Hebdomaia (...) (some text is missing). On the eighth day the (new) *aisymnetes* of the Molpoi provides (?) to the persons pouring libations (his new *proshetairoi*?) the holy parts (?) or the entrails. The (new) *aisymnetes* and the (new) *proshetairoi* (collective sing.) also drink (together), when all the kraters have been poured and they have chanted the paian. On the ninth day both from the haunch and the fifth part, which the (two, the old and the new) *stephanephoroi* receive, [10] the new (*aisymnetes-stephanephoros*) gets the equal share first. They begin to sacrifice the victims for Apollo Delphinios by starting to sacrifice from it (the equivalent portion of the new *aisymnetes-stephanephoros*). And the kraters are mixed just as it is common in the *Molpon* (the assembly hall of the Molpoi, the prytaneion of Miletos) and a paian is sung. And the *aisymnetes* leaving office sacrifices to Hestia from the halves ((([insertion late sixth–fifth century BC?:] and let him himself pour the libation from the kraters and sing the paian)). On the tenth day, there are the *Hamilleteria* ("contests"), and two full-grown victims are given from the Molpoi to the *stephanephoroi* [15] and sacrificed to Apollo Delphinios. And the (two, the old and the new) *stephanephoroi* as well as the *neoi* (young "new" citizens) and the priest (of Apollo Delphinios) compete, and they drink the wine of the Molpoi, and the libation is poured from the kraters just as it is common in the *Molpon*. The outgoing *aisymnetes* provides the things like the *Onitades* (collective sing. for *Onitadai*, cult association of Herakles and sacrificial butchers and cooks) does and takes for his portion just as the *Onitades* does.

When the (two, the old and the new) *stephanephoroi* go to Didyma, the city gives as a hekatomb three full-grown victims, one of which is to be female and another [20] uncastrated. And the city gives a full-grown victim to the *Molpon* at the Targelia (festival) and a full-grown victim at the Metageitnia (festival), at the Hebdomaia two full-grown and an old *chous* (measure of wine) at each festival. The king (*basileus*) is assisting at the (sacrifice of) these victims, and he receives no more than the other Molpoi.

And the (two, the old and the new) *stephanephoroi* begin in (the month of) Taureon to sacrifice to Apollo Delphinios offering the first fruits from the left parts and he (the new *aisymnetes-stephanephoros?*) pours libations from the four [25] kraters.

Two *Gylloi* (sacred stones) are brought, (one of which) is placed next to (the sanctuary of) Hekate before the Gates (of Miletos); wreathed and poured with unmixed (wine). The other is placed at the doors of Didyma. And after doing these things, they march the broad road as far as the *Akron* ("heights") and from the *Akron* through the woods. And paians are sung, first at Hekate before the Gates (of Miletos), then at (the sanctuary of) *Dynamis* ("power" of the Milesian magistrates?), then in the meadow on the *Akron* at the nymphs, then at the (statue of?) Hermes in (the sanctuary) of [30] Kelados (rivergod "Clamour"), at Phylios (Apollo the "tribesman"?), in the area of Keraïites (the "horned" one, another Apollo?), at the statues of Chares. ((([insertion around 200 BC:] In the "year of all offerings" [= at the Panhellenic Didymeia, every fifth year]))) a skinned (victim) is offered at Keraïites, at Phylios sacrificial cakes are offered ((([insertion around 200 BC:] every year.)))

The *Onitadai* have to provide (the equipment) of pottery, of iron, of bronze, of wood, of water, of round plates(?) (to serve), of chips of pinewood, and of wicker to cut the meat, of wooden blocks (to chop?), of fetters for the sacrificial animals. (([insertion late sixth–mid-fourth century BC:] At the *stephanephoroi*: lamp and oil.)), the roasting of the entrails, the boiling of the meat; of the haunch and [35] of the fifth part, which the *stephanephoroi* receive, the boiling, the cutting and the distribution of the portion. ((([insertion late sixth–mid-fourth century BC:] The flat *elatra* [sacrificial cakes] for Apollo are to be cooked from half a medimnos [ca 20.5 l] and [the ones] for Hekate separately.)) All the haunches go to the *Onitadai* from the Molpoi apart from those that the *stephanephoroi* receive, all skins, three *thyalemata* (prepared portions of meat for sacrifice?) from every victim, ((?[insertion early fifth century BC:]? the remaining *thya* [sacrificial cakes?], and the wine that is left in the krater)), a fifth (of the left meat) every [40] day. ((([insertion 476/75 BC:] In case the *Onitadai* do not do [supply] whatever of these things, the Molpoi decided in the year of [the *aisymnetes-stephanephoros*] Charopinos that the *stephanephoroi* should supply from the things of Hestia [the state funds]. And whatever the *Onitadai* are claiming, the Molpoi have decided to entrust it to the *stephanephoroi*.))

(((([insertion after 447/6–mid-fourth century BC:] For the herald an exemption from all expenses in the *Molpon*, and (the duty) of dividing the entrails of each of the sacrifices and the transport of the wine to the *psykter* (cooling device) at his own cost, but the wine is provided by the Molpoi.)))

[45] (((([insertion ca 400–300 BC:] And the priest [of Apollo Delphinios] provides the feast to the singer, and the *aisymnetes* provides the breakfast/lunch?.)))

SYSTEMATIC OVERVIEW:

lines

1–6	prescript: executive board of the Molpoi (cult association of Apollo Delphinios) with eponymous *aisymnetes-stephanephoros* Philtes (447/6 BC) and five *proshetairoi* (= *prytaneis*, oligarchic government of Miletos) sign responsible for the decree.
6–18	regulations for the festival of the Hebdomaia and the following three days in the Delphinion of Miletos (= "festival of Apollo Delphinios", Taureon seventh–tenth, including the *Hamilleteria* on the tenth).
18–20	supply (victims) by the *polis* for the procession to Didyma (Taureon tenth), given to the two *aisymnetai-stephanephoroi*.
20–22	insertion: supply by the *polis* for the *Molpon* (assembly hall of the Molpoi in the Delphinion, the prytaneion of Miletos) during certain Apollo festivals.
22–23	insertion: duties and rights of the *basileus* ("king") during certain Apollo festivals in the Delphinion.
23–25	insertion: primal offering (*aparché*) by the *aisymnetai-stephanephoroi* to Apollo Delphinios on Taureon seventh (= Hebdomaia, cf. lines 6.21f.).
25–27	placing of the two *Gylloi* at the gates of Miletos and Didyma (sacred boundary stones of the processional road).
27–31	regulations for the procession to Didyma (course, stations, sacrifices).
31–40	duties and rights of the *Onitadai* (sacrifical butchers and cooks) during the sacrifices in the Delphinion, in the course of the procession, and in Didyma.
40–42	addition under *aisymnetes* Charopinos (476/5 BC) concerning the duties and rights of the *Onitadai*.
43–44	addition (after 447/6 and before middle of fourth century BC): duties and rights of the *keryx* (herald) during the festivals in the Delphinion and the *Molpon*.
45	addition (fourth century–300 BC): rights of the *oidos* (= *kitharodos*).

Bibliography

Aleshire 1994   S.B. Aleshire, 'Towards a definition of "state cult" for ancient
Athens', in *Ancient Greek cult
practice from the epigraphical
evidence, Proceedings of the second
international seminar on ancient
Greek cult, organized by the
Swedish Institute at Athens,
22–24 November 1991*
(ActaAth-8°, 13), ed. R. Hägg,
Stockholm 1994, 9–16.

Aly 1911   W. Aly, 'Delphinios. Beiträge
zur Stadtgeschichte von Milet
und Athen', *Klio* 11, 1911,
1–25.

Auffarth 1991   C. Auffarth, *Der drohende Un-
tergang. 'Schöpfung' in Mythos
und Ritual im Alten Orient und
in Griechenland am Beispiel
der Odyssee und des Ezechielbu-
ches* (Religionsgeschichtliche
Versuche und Vorarbeiten, 39),
Berlin 1991.

Blümel 1995   W. Blümel, 'Inschriften aus
Karien I', *EpigAnat* 25, 1995,
35–64.

Boardman
1988   J. Boardman, *The Greeks overseas. The early colonies and
trade*, London 1988².

Bourboulis
1949   Ph.P. Bourboulis, *Apollo Delphinios*, Thessaloniki 1949.

Brelich 1969   A. Brelich, *Paides e parthenoi*,
Roma 1969.

Bremmer
1994   J. Bremmer, *Greek religion*,
Oxford 1994.

Burkert 1970   W. Burkert, 'Iason, Hypsipyle
and the New Fire at Lemnos.
A study in myth and ritual',
CQ 20, 1970, 1–16 (reprint in
W. Burkert, *Savage energies:
Lessons of myth and ritual in
ancient Greece*, Chicago 2001,
64–84).

Burkert 1975   W. Burkert, 'Apellai und Apollon', *RhM* 118, 1975, 1–21.

Burkert 1985   W. Burkert, *Greek religion*,
Cambridge, Mass. 1985.

Burkert 1990   W. Burkert, 'Neues Feuer auf
Lemnos', in *Wilder Ursprung.
Opferritual und Mythos bei den
Griechen*, Berlin 1990, 60–76.

Burkert 1994   W. Burkert, 'Olbia and Apollo
of Didyma: A new oracle text',
in *Apollo. Origins and influences*, ed. J. Solomon, Tucson &
London 1994, 49–60.

Burkert 1995   W. Burkert, 'Greek *poleis*
and civic cults: Some further
thoughts', in *Studies in the
ancient Greek polis. Papers from
the Copenhagen Polis Center* 2
(Historia Einzelschriften, 95),
eds. M.H. Hansen & K. Raaflaub, Stuttgart 1995, 201–210.

Burnett,
Amandry &
Ripollès 1992   A. Burnett, M. Amandry & P.P.
Ripollès, *Roman provincial
coinage* I. *From the death of Cesar
to the death of Vitellius (44BC–
AD 69)*, London & Paris 1992.

Camp 1989   J.M. Camp, *The Athenian
agora. Excavations in
the heart of Classical Athens*,
London 1989.

Cavaignac
1924   E. Cavaignac, 'Les dékarchies
de Lysandre', *RÉH* 90, 1924,
285–317.

Chaniotis
2010   A. Chaniotis, 'The Molpoi
inscription: ritual prescription
or riddle?', *Kernos* 23, 2010,
375–379.

Cobet 1997   J. Cobet, 'Die Mauern sind die Stadt. Zur Stadtbefestigung des antiken Milet', *AA* 1997, 249–284.

D'Angour 2006   A. D'Angour, 'The New Music —so what's new?', in *Rethinking revolutions through ancient Greece*, eds. S. Goldhill & R. Osborne, Cambridge 2006, 264–283.

Danielsson 1914   O.A. Danielsson, 'Zu der milesischen Molpeninschrift', *Eranos* 14, 1914, 1–20.

Demargne & Van Effenterre 1937   P. Demargne & E. Van Effenterre, 'Recherches à Dréros', *BCH* 61, 1937, 5–32.

Dubois 1996   L. Dubois, *Inscriptions grecques dialectales d'Olbia du Pont*, Genève 1996.

Durand 1979   J.-L. Durand, 'Bêtes grecques. Propositions pour une topologique des corps à manger', in *La cuisine de sacrifice en pays grec*, eds. M. Detienne & J.-P. Vernant, Paris 1979, 133–165.

Ehrhardt 1988   N. Ehrhardt, *Milet und seine Kolonien. Vergleichende Untersuchung der kultischen und politischen Einrichtungen*, diss. Hamburg, Frankfurt am Main 1988².

Gonzales 2008   M. Gonzales, Online Book Review of A. Herda, Der Apollon-Delphinios-Kult in Milet und die Neujahrsprozession nach Didyma. Ein neuer Kommentar der sog. Molpoi-Satzung, *AJA* 112, 3, 2008. http://www.ajaonline. org/sites/default/files/06_ Gonzales.pdf

Gorman 2001   V. Gorman, *Miletos, the ornament of Ionia. A history of the city to 400 BCE*, Ann Arbor 2001.

Graf 1974   F. Graf, 'Das Kollegium der Μολποί von Olbia', *MusHelv* 31, 1974, 209–215.

Graf 1979   F. Graf, 'Apollon Delphinios', *MusHelv* 36, 1979, 2–22.

Graft 1985   F. Graf, *Nordionische Kulte. Religionsgeschichtliche und epigraphische Untersuchungen zu den Kulten von Chios, Erythrai, Klazomenai und Phokaia* (Bibliotheca Helvetica Romana, 21), Roma 1985.

Graf 1996   F. Graf, 'Pompai in Greece. Some considerations about space and ritual in the Greek polis', in *The role of religion in the early Greek polis. Proceedings of the third international seminar on ancient Greek cult, Swedish Institute at Athens 1992* (ActaAth-8°, 14), ed. R. Hägg, Stockholm 1996, 55–65.

Graf 2000   F. Graf, 'Neujahrsfest III. Griechenland und Rom', *Der Neue Pauly* 8, 2000, 869–873.

Grieb 2008   V. Grieb, *Hellenistische Demokratie: Politische Organisation und Struktur in freien griechischen Poleis nach Alexander dem Großen* (Historia Einzelschriften, 199), Stuttgart 2008.

Günther 2009   W. Günther, 'Funde aus Milet XXV. Hellenistische Bürgerrechts- und Proxenielisten aus dem Delphinion und ihr Verbleib in byzantinischer Zeit', *AA* 2009, 167–185.

Harrison 1927
J. Harrison, *Themis: A study of the social origins of Greek religion*, Cambridge 1927[2].

Haussoullier 1921
B. Haussoullier, 'La Voie Sacrée de Milet à Didymes', *Cinquantenaire de l'École Pratique des Hautes Études*, Paris 1921, 85–101.

Healey 2001
J. Healey, *The religion of the Nabataeans*, Leiden 2001.

Herda 2005
A. Herda, 'Apollon Delphinios, das Prytaneion und die Agora von Milet', *AA* 2005, 243–294.

Herda 2006a
A. Herda, *Der Apollon-Delphinios-Kult in Milet und die Neujahrsprozession nach Didyma. Ein neuer Kommentar der sog. Molpoi-Satzung* (Milesische Forschungen, 4), Mainz 2006.

Herda 2006b
A. Herda, 'Panionion-Melia, Mykalessos-Mykale, Perseus und Medusa. Überlegungen zur Besiedlungsgeschichte der Mykale in der frühen Eisenzeit', *IstMitt* 56, 2006, 43–102.

Herda 2008
A. Herda, 'Apollon Delphinios Apollon Didymeus: Zwei Gesichter eines milesischen Gottes und ihr Bezug zur Kolonisation Milets in archaischer Zeit', in *Kult(ur)kontakte. Apollon in Myus, Milet/Didyma, Naukratis und auf Zypern. Akten der Table Ronde Mainz 11.–12. März 2004*, eds. R. Bol, U. Höckmann & P. Schollmeyer, Rahden-Westfalen 2008, 14–87.

Herda 2009
A. Herda, 'Karkiša-Karien und die sog. Ionische Migration', in *Die Karer und die Anderen, Internationales Kolloquium an der Freien Universität Berlin, 13. bis 15. Oktober 2005*, ed. F. Rumscheid, Bonn 2009, 27–108.

Herda & Sauter 2009
A. Herda & E. Sauter, 'Karerinnen und Karer in Milet: Zu einem spätklassischen Schüsselchen mit karischem Graffito aus Milet', *AA* 2009, 51–112.

Herda forthcoming
A. Herda, 'From Anax to Thales: The many founders of Miletos in Asia/Ionia', in *Foundation myths in dialogue. One-day round table, University of Cambridge, Faculty of Classics, Saturday 15th January 2011*, ed. N. Mac Sweeney, Cambridge forthcoming.

Herda in preparation
A. Herda, *Agora und Stadtplanung von Milet vor und nach den Perserkriegen*, in preparation for *Milesische Forschungen*.

Hind 2007
J.G.F. Hind, 'City heads/personifications and omens from Zeus (the coins of Sinope, Istria and Olbia in the V–IV centuries BC)', *NC* 167, 2007, 9–22.

Hirsch 2001
B. Hirsch, 'Orte des Dionysos – Kultplätze und ihre Funktion', *IstMitt* 51, 2001, 217–272.

Hölkeskamp 2003
K.-J. Hölkeskamp, 'Institutionalisierung durch Verortung. Die Entstehung der Öffentlichkeit im frühen Griechenland', in *Sinn (in) der Antike. Orientierungssysteme, Leitbilder und Wertkonzepte im Altertum*, eds. K.-J. Hölkeskamp, J. Rüsen, E. Stein-Hölkeskamp & H.Th. Grütter, Mainz 2003, 81–104.

T. Hölscher 1999
T. Hölscher, *Öffentliche Räume in frühen griechischen Städten*, Heidelberg 1999[2].

U. Hölscher 1990   U. Hölscher, *Die Odyssee. Epos zwischen Märchen und Roman*, München 1990³.

Holtzmann 2003   B. Holtzmann, *L'acropole d'Athènes. Monuments, cultes et histoire du sanctuaire d'Athèna Polias*, Paris 2003.

IErythrai 1   *Die Inschriften von Erythrai und Klazomenai 1 (Nr. 1–200)* (Inschriften griechischer Städte aus Kleinasien, 1), eds. H. Engelmann & R. Merkelbach, Bonn 1972.

De Juliis 2001   E.M. De Juliis, *Metaponto*, Bari 2001.

Kekule von Stradonitz 1904   R. Kekule von Stradonitz, 'Über den Apoll des Kanachos', *SBBerl* 1904, 786–801.

Kenzler 1999   U. Kenzler, *Studien zur Entwicklung und Struktur der griechischen Agora in archaischer und klassischer Zeit*, Frankfurt am Main 1999.

Kolb 1981   F. Kolb, *Agora und Theater, Volks- und Festversammlung* (AF, 9), Berlin 1981.

Lippolis 2006   E. Lippolis, 'Lo spazio per votare e altre note di topografia sulle *agorai* di Atene', *ASAtene* 84, 2006, 37–62.

Lohmann 2006   H. Lohmann, 'Zum Fundort der archaischen Nymphen-inschrift Milet VI/3, 1298', in *Maiandros. Festschrift für Volkmar von Graeve*, eds. R. Biering *et al.*, München 2006, 201–204.

LSAM   F. Sokolowski, *Lois sacrées de l'Asie Mineure*, Paris 1955.

LSCG   F. Sokolowski, *Lois sacrées des cités grecques*, Paris 1969.

Lupu 2005   E. Lupu, *Greek sacred law. A collection of new documents*, Leiden & Boston 2005.

Luria 1928   S. Luria, 'Ein milesischer Männerbund im Lichte ethnologischer Parallelen', *Philologus* 83, 1928, 113–136.

Luria 1963   S. Luria, 'Kureten, Molpen, Aisymneten', *Acta Antiqua Academiae Scientiarum Hungaricae* 11, 1963, 31–36.

Malkin 1987   I. Malkin, *Religion and colonization in ancient Greece*, Leiden 1987.

Malkin 1991   I. Malkin, 'What is an Aphidryma?', *ClAnt* 10, 1991, 77–96.

Malkin 2000   I. Malkin, 'La fondation d'une colonie apollinienne: Delphes et l'hymne homérique à Apollon', in *Delphes cent ans après la Grande Fouille. Essai de bilan*, *Actes du Colloque international, Athènes–Delphes, 17–20 septembre 1992* (BCH, Suppl. 36), ed. A. Jacquemin, Paris 2000, 69–77.

Marinatos 1936   S. Marinatos, 'Le temple geometrique de Dreros', *BCH* 60, 1936, 214–285.

Martin 1951   R. Martin, *Recherches sur l'agora grecque. Études d'histoire et d'architecture urbaines*, Paris 1951.

Mayer 1932   M. Mayer, 'Miletos', *RE* XV, 2 (1932), 1622–1655.

Milet I 3   G. Kawerau & A. Rehm, unter Mitwirkung von F. Freiherr Hiller von Gaertringen, Mark Lidzbarski, Th. Wiegand & E. Ziebarth, *Das Delphinion in Milet* (= *Milet* I 3), Berlin 1914.

Milet I 6 A. von Gerkan, *Der Nordmarkt und der Hafen an der Löwenbucht* (= *Milet* I 6), Berlin & Leipzig 1922.

Milet I 7 H. Knackfuss, *Der Südmarkt und die benachbarten Bauanlagen* (= *Milet* I 7), Berlin 1924.

Milet IV 1 F. Kraus, *Das Theater von Milet Teil 1. Das hellenistische Theater. Der römische Zuschauerbau* (= *Milet* IV 1), Berlin 1973.

Milet VI 1 *Die Inschriften von Milet* Teil 1 A. *Inschriften n. 187–406* von A. Rehm mit einem Beitrag von H. Dessau; B. *Nachträge und Übersetzungen zu den Inschriften n. 1–406* von P. Herrmann (= *Milet* VI 1), Berlin & New York 1996.

Milet VI 3 P. Herrmann, W. Günther & N. Ehrhardt, mit Beiträgen von D. Feissel und P. Weiss, *Die Inschriften von Milet* Teil 3. *Inschriften n. 1020–1580* (= *Milet* VI 3), Berlin & New York 2006.

Miller 1978 S. Miller, *The Prytaneion. Its function and architectural form*, Berkeley 1978.

Miller 1995 S. Miller, 'Architecture as evidence for the identity of the early polis', in *Sources for the ancient Greek city-state. Symposium, August 24–27, 1994* (Acts of the Copenhagen Polis Center, 2), ed. M.H. Hansen, København 1995, 201–242.

Müllenhoff, Herda & Brückner 2009 M. Müllenhoff, A. Herda & H. Brückner, 'Georchaeology in the City of Thales. Deciphering palaeogeographic changes in the agora area of Miletus', in *Mensch und Umwelt im Spiegel der Zeit. Aspekte geoarchäologischer Forschungen im östlichen Mittelmeergebiet*, eds. T. Mattern & A. Vött, Wiesbaden 2009, 97–110.

Müller-Wiener 1977–1978 W. Müller-Wiener, 'Milet 1973–1975. 1. Michaelskirche und Dionysostempel. Baubefunde und Phasengliederung', *IstMitt* 27–28, 1977–1978, 94–103.

Müller-Wiener 1979 W. Müller-Wiener, 'Milet 1977. 1. a) Untersuchungen im Dionysos-Heiligtum', *IstMitt* 29, 1979, 162–169.

Müller-Wiener 1988 W. Müller-Wiener, 'Untersuchungen im Bischofspalast in Milet (1977–1979)', *IstMitt* 38, 1988, 279–290.

Niewöhner 2008 Ph. Niewöhner, 'Sind die Mauern die Stadt? Vorbericht über die siedlungsgeschichtlichen Ergebnisse neuer Grabungen im spätantiken und byzantinischen Milet', *AA* 2008, 181–201.

Oliver 1941 J.H. Oliver, *The sacred Gerusia* (Hesperia, Suppl. 6), Athens 1941.

Onyshkevych 1998 L. Onyshkevych, *Archaic and Classical cult-related graffiti from the northern Black Sea region*, diss. University of Pennsylvania, 1998.

Papadopoulos 2003 J.K. Papadopoulos, *Ceramicus Redivivus. The early Iron Age Potter's field in the area of the Classical Athenian agora* (Hesperia, Suppl. 31), Athens 2003.

Parisiniou 2000 E. Parisiniou, *The light of the gods. The role of light in Archaic and Classical Greek cult*, London 2000.

Parker 1996   R. Parker, *Athenian religion. A history*, Oxford 1996.

Parker 2003   R. Parker, 'The problem of the Greek cult epithet', *OpAth* 28, 2003, 173–183.

Parker 2005   R. Parker, *Polytheism and society at Athens*, Oxford 2005.

Parker 2008   R. Parker, 'Review of Alexander Herda, Der Apollon-Delphinios-Kult in Milet und die Neujahrsprozession nach Didyma. Ein neuer Kommentar der sog. Molpoi-Satzung', *CR* 58, 2008, 178–180.

Poland 1935   F. Poland, Μολποί, *RE* Suppl. VI, 1935, 509–520.

de Polignac 1984   F. de Polignac, *La naissance de la cité grecque. Cultes, espace et société VIIIᵉ–VIIᵉ siècles avant J.-C.*, Paris 1984.

de Polignac 1995   F. de Polignac, *Cults, territory and the origins of the Greek city state*, Chicago, London 1995.

Rehm 1939   A. Rehm, 'Die Inschriften', in *Handbuch der Archäologie*, ed. W. Otto, München 1939, 132–238.

Rhodes 2006   P.J. Rhodes, 'Milesian stephanephoroi: Applying Cavaignac correctly', *ZPE* 157, 2006, 116.

Ricci 1946–1948   G. Ricci, 'Una hydria da Caere', *ASAtene* 24–26, 1946–1948, 47–57.

Rigsby 2010   K.J. Rigsby, 'Cos and the Milesian Didymeia', *ZPE* 175, 2010, 155–157.

Robert 1967   L. Robert, *Monnaies grecques. Types, légendes magistrats monétaires et géographie*, Genève & Paris 1967.

Robertson 1987   N. Robertson, 'Government and society at Miletos, 525–442 B.C.', *Phoenix* 41, 1987, 356–398.

Robertson 1998   N. Robertson, 'The city center of Archaic Athens', *Hesperia* 67, 1998, 283–302.

De Sanctis 1930   G. De Sanctis, 'I Molpi di Mileto', in *Studi in onore di P. Bonfante nel 40 anno d'insegnamento* II, Milano 1930, 671–679. (Reprint in G. De Sanctis, *Scritti minori* 4, Roma 1976, 461–471.)

Schmalz 2006   G.C.R. Schmalz, 'The Athenian prytaneion discovered?', *Hesperia* 75, 2006, 33–81.

Schneider & Höcker 2001   L. Schneider & Ch. Höcker, *Die Akropolis von Athen*, Darmstadt 2001.

Shear 1994   T.S. Shear, 'ΙΣΟΝΟΜΟΣ Τ'ΑΘΗΝΑΣ ΕΠΟΙΗΣΑΤΗΝ: the Agora and the democracy', in *The archaeology of Athens and Attica under the democracy. Proceedings of an international conference at the American School of Classical Studies at Athens 1992*, eds. W.D.E. Coulson *et al.*, Athens 1994, 225–248.

Sherk 1990   R. Sherk, 'The eponymous officials of Greek cities: I', *ZPE* 83, 1990, 249–288.

Slawisch 2009   A. Slawisch, 'Epigraphy versus archaeology: Conflicting evidence for cult continuity in Ionia during the fifth century BC', in *Sacred landscape in Anatolia and neighboring regions*, eds. C. Gates, J. Morin & Th. Zimmermann (BAR-IS, 2034), Oxford 2009, 29–34.

Sommer 2006 S. Sommer, *Rom und die Ver-einigungen im südwestlichen Kleinasien (133 v. Chr.–284 n. Chr.)*, Hennef 2006.

Sourvinou-Inwood 1988 C. Sourvinou-Inwood, 'Further aspects of polis religion', *AION* 10, 1988, 259–274. (Reprinted in *Oxford readings in Greek religion*, ed. R. Buxton, Oxford 2000, 38–55.)

Sourvinou-Inwood 1990 C. Sourvinou-Inwood, 'What is polis religion?', in *The Greek city from Homer to Alexander*, eds. O. Murray & S. Price, Oxford 1990, 295–322. (Reprinted in *Oxford readings in Greek religion*, ed. R. Buxton, Oxford 2000, 13–37.)

Stingl 2005 T. Stingl, 'Frühe bronzene Geldformen im nordwestlichen Schwarzmeerraum', in *Bilder und Objekte als Träger kulturel-ler Identität und interkultureller Kommunikation im Schwarz-meergebiet. Kolloquium in Zschortau/Sachsen 13.–15. Februar 2003*, eds. F. Fless & M. Treister, Rahden-Westfalen 2005, 119–123.

Thomas 1983 E. Thomas, 'ΔΗΜΗΤΡΙΟΣ ΓΛΑΥΚΟΥ ΜΙΛΗΣΙΟΣ. Bemerkungen zur Person und zum Werk eines späthellenisti-schen Bildhauers', *IstMitt* 33, 1983, 124–133.

Thomas 1988 E. Thomas, 'Atimetos oder Demetrios—ein neronischer oder ein späthellenistischer Erzbildner?', in *Griechische und römische Statuetten und Groß-bronzen. Akten der 9. Interna-tionalen Tagung über antike Bronzen, Wien, 21.–25. April 1986*, eds. K. Gschwantler & A. Bernhard-Walcher, Wien 1988, 314–317.

Vollgraff 1918 W. Vollgraff, 'De lege collegii cantorum Milesiorum', *Mne-mosyne* 46, 1918, 415–427.

Weber 2007 B.F. Weber, 'Der Stadtplan von Milet', in *Frühes Ionien. Eine Bestandsaufnahme. Panionion-Symposion Güzelçamlı, 26. September–1. Oktober 1999*, eds. J. Cobet *et al.* (= *Milesische Forschungen* 5), Mainz 2007, 327–362.

West 1966 Hesiod, *Theogony*, ed. M.L. West, Oxford 1966.

Wiegand 1901 Th. Wiegand, 'Zweiter vorläu-figer Bericht über die von den Königlichen Museen begon-nenen Ausgrabungen in Milet', *SBBerlin* 1901, 903–913.

Wilamowitz-Moellendorff 1904 U. von Wilamowitz-Moellen-dorff, 'Satzungen einer milesi-schen Sängergilde', *SBBerl* 1904, 619–640.

Wilamowitz-Moellendorff 1914 U. von Wilamowitz-Moellen-dorff, Review of *Milet* I 3 in *GGA* 1914, 65–109.

Wycherley 1957 R.E. Wycherley, *Agora* III. *Literary and Epigraphical Testimonia*, Princeton, N.J. 1957.

MATTHEW HAYSOM

The strangeness of Crete

PROBLEMS FOR THE PROTOHISTORY OF GREEK RELIGION

Abstract*

Scholarship on Cretan religion has always emphasized the island's oddity. It emerges from the literature as a land of suckling and dying gods, prehistoric practices, and tribal initiation rites. This paper will explore the interlinked themes of strangeness and continuity on the island. After investigating how idiosyncratic Cretan religious practices really were, it will argue that the real surprise, given the island's development through prehistory, is not oddity or continuity but the degree to which it conformed to wider Greek norms.

Introduction

Reading any of the literature that covers Early Iron Age, Archaic or Classical Crete will soon leave one with the impression that the island was distinctly odd. Differences between Crete and the rest of the Greek world are constantly emphasized and this is particularly so in the sphere of religion. Scholars have long pointed to the failure of Cretans to take up elements of religious material culture or religious practice that are common elsewhere. Pointing, for ex-

ample, to the lack of cult at Prehistoric tombs, the lack of peripteral temples on the island, or the rarity of sculpture.[1] Concomitant with this, the Cretans' attachment to forms that are supposedly descended from antecedents in the Bronze Age is frequently highlighted—for example, in religious architecture, the well-known series of buildings with a hearth and/or benches which are usually identified as temples or, in iconography, the late appearance of seemingly divine females with upraised arms.[2]

Indeed, it is signs of supposed continuity from the Bronze Age that play the greatest part in making Crete seem strange. The presence of cult sites in caves, for example, is closely tied in the literature to the broader phenomenon of continuity at Bronze Age cult sites, which

---

* This paper was inspired by ongoing discussions with Maria Mili and James Whitley. I would like to thank them both for their extensive comments. I would like also to thank Robert Parker for his comments on this paper. All errors are, of course, my own.

[1] Lack of tomb cult: Coldstream 1976, 13–14; Snodgrass 1980, 39; Morris 1988, fig. 3; Whitley 1988, 174; lack of peripteral temples and small temples as a sign of continuity from the Bronze Age: Nilsson 1950, 453–456; Desborough 1972, 285; Gesell 1985, 57; Sporn 2002, 344–345; Prent 2005, 4; rarity of sculpture especially from the sixth and fifth centuries: Sporn 2002, 349–350; Whitley 2009a, 286.

[2] For the long and increasingly tangled discussion of bench and hearth temples: Gesell 1985, 57–59; Coldstream 2003, 263–264; Prent 2005, 188–200, 424–476 (for continuity see especially 468–470); Whitley 2009a, 279. For the late appearance of the Goddess with upraised arms: Coldstream 1984; Coldstream & Catling 1996, 155; Prent 2009.

Crete apparently displays to a greater extent than any other part of the Greek world.[3] Oddities in the Cretan pantheon, the worship of Eileithyia as an unusually prominent and distinct figure, or the existence of such singularly Cretan divinities, such as Diktynna, are regularly put down to continuity from the Bronze Age and tied to the high survival of apparently pre-Greek place, month and personal names all over the island and even the survival of a possibly pre-Greek language in the east of the island.[4]

An accompanying, not incompatible, though occasionally discordant, strand of scholarship associates some of the oddities in the island's religious practices with the island's supposedly conservative social structure—with its *syssiteia* and *agelai*—which have traditionally been thought to preserve the primitive tribal customs of migrating groups of Iron Age Dorians.[5]

It is the two themes that underlie both of these strands in the island's scholarship that I wish to explore and problematize in this paper: the strangeness of Crete and the continuity and conservatism of Crete.

How strange was Crete?

The first problem I want to raise is with establishing how strange Crete really was, and with establishing how significant were its oddities. In terms of religious architecture, for example,

the significance of the island's apparent resistance to the peripteral temple is hard to gauge. Stray finds, such as that of a metope depicting one of the labours of Herakles from Knossos, hint that we are missing some structures that are closer to the monumental Greek norm, and it is surely problematic that at several major cities later occupation has destroyed so much of what went before. At Knossos, for instance, the Roman foundations have destroyed the majority of the Greek town and sit directly above the Bronze Age levels.[6] Many Cycladic temples are not dissimilar from those known on Crete: small and non-peripteral.[7] Similarly, such supposedly distinctively Cretan elements in temple architecture as hearths and benches are known elsewhere.[8] Indeed, the building of peripteral temples around the Greek world is patchy, with notable concentrations in some areas and not in others. Patterns in monumental temple building have been explained in multiple ways, some of which have very little directly to do with the nature of religious belief or practice.[9] On Crete the more general simplicity in material culture in the sixth century—a boom period for temple building elsewhere—is surely relevant.[10] Moreover, Crete's earlier precocity in temple building should also be important. However, the Cretans failure to build peripteral temples is preceded by a failure to build temples of the long, thin or apsidal variety known so widely elsewhere[11]—a failure that must be

3   Willetts 1962, 141–147; Snodgrass 1971, 401; Desborough 1972, 284; Tyree 1974, 134–138; Burkert, 1985, 48; Morris 1998, 61–62; Prent 2005, 200–209, 554–610.
4   Diktynna: Nilsson 1955, 311; Sporn 2002, 323–325; Whitley 2009a, 277; Eileithyia: Sporn 2002, 329; on Cretan goddesses generally and their prehistoric origins see Willetts 1962, Chapter 6; Pre-Greek names and language: Willetts 1965, 34–35; Duhoux 1982.
5   Willetts 1955, *passim* but especially 17–20, 249–56; *idem* 1965, *passim* but especially 112–113; Malkin 1994, 44–45.

6   Metope: Benton 1937 (where the survival until 1934 of a Doric column at Knossos is also mentioned); on the evidence for the Greek town at Knossos: Coldstream 1991; *idem* 1999; *idem* 2000.
7   See for example Ohnesorg 2005.
8   Mazarakis-Ainian 1997; Gounaris 2005.
9   Snodgrass 1980, 149–151; *idem* 1986; Osborne 1996, 262–266; Whitley 2001, 223–230; Morgan 2003, 73–76.
10   On this poverty (sometimes referred to as a gap) see Huxley 1994; Morris 1998, 59–68, 74; Coldstream & Huxley 1999; Erickson 2002; Whitley 2009a.
11   Mazarakis-Ainian 1997.

just as significant as the lack of peripteral temples later, and a failure which is clearly related to the norms of domestic architecture on the island. The apsidal building is all but unknown on Crete.[12]

The significance of oddities in the Cretan pantheon is similarly hard to gauge and to quantify. Other regions of the Greek world have divinities, like Diktynna on Crete, that are unique to them, such as En(n)odia in Thessaly or the northeast Peloponnesian divinities Damia and Auxesia.[13] Considerable caution needs to be taken with extrapolating too much from the idea that divinities like Diktynna on Crete are Bronze Age hangovers. It is ironic that the Diktynnaion is most closely associated with Kydonia, a city whose non-Cretan roots and sense of identity were particularly strong—using the Aiginetan script and apparently minting *Aiginetan* coins.[14] Christiane Sourvinou-Inwood and Robert Parker have demonstrated in multiple works that differences between local pantheons were the Greek norm.[15] For every Cretan divinity like Hermes that we find in unusual circumstances[16] we find others—Apollo, Athena, Demeter—more or less where we

would expect them.[17] Regional distinctiveness exists in terms of what functions are stressed but this holds true of all regions of Greece.

Evidential problems naturally hamper our understanding of the peculiarities of the Cretan pantheon. For example, relatively few functional epithets are attested on the island, in comparison to some other regions.[18] But this may be as much a side effect of the island's odd epigraphic habit as a genuine reflection of divergent attitudes to the divine. Inscribed dedications are an important source for these epithets in other regions. But inscribed dedications are relatively rare on Crete, and the 125 or so examples are usually on small objects, pots, rings and so on, rather than on stelai, altars and sculpture as elsewhere.[19] Functional epithets, such as Xenios and Hetairaios for Zeus, are rather more commonly attested in the—obviously non-Cretan—literary sources for the island and interestingly those epithets that do appear on inscribed dedications tend to be topographic epithets from sanctuaries, such as that of Zeus Idaios, that drew people from a wide area.

To balance scholarly emphasis on those things that distinguish Crete from the rest of the Greek world it is worth highlighting some of the things Crete had in common with other places.

---

[12] The only example I know of is reported from the still unpublished Stratigraphic Museum Excavations at Knossos and is both early (dating to LH IIIC) and very large, Warren 1982–1983, 70–71, fig. 40.

[13] On En(n)odia, see Chrysostomou 1998; Mili 2005, 250–258, 281–292; on Damia and Auxesia, see Nilsson 1906, 413–417.

[14] For the Diktynnaion and Kydonia, Hdt. 3.59; Kydonian coinage, Stefanakis 1999, 257; Kydonian script, Jeffery 1990, 314.

[15] For two prime early examples, see: Sourvinou-Inwood 1978; Parker 1988.

[16] The interpretation of the worship of Hermes at Kato Syme as a god of initiation would put him in unusual circumstances (scholars usually place Apollo in this role). Hermes' widely-attested cult in the gymnasium, though it can of course be connected, is not really the same thing. On Hermes at Kato Syme, see Sporn 2002, 85–89 (with previous bibliography); on Hermes as a god of the gymnasium, see Parker 2005, 391 (note fn. 21).

---

[17] On Apollo, Athena and Demeter, see Sporn 2002, 321–322, 325–328. Sporn's characterization of the worship of Athena at extra-urban sanctuaries in Crete as odd (and connected to fertility) needs to be treated with some caution. Most of the cases she cites are of the goddess' worship in secondary settlements: a phenomenon that can be closely paralleled with the very common worship of Athena in Attic demes. On Athena in Attic demes, see Parker 1987, for a general critique of the use of urban vs. extra-urban as characterizations of divinities, see Polinskaya 2006.

[18] For Cretan epithets, see: Willetts 1962, chapters 9–14; Sporn 2002, tables 1–18; on the classification of epithets, see Parker 2003.

[19] Whitley 1997; *idem* 2006; Perlman 2002, 194–197, 218–225.

As with other aspects of material culture relating to religion it is possible to emphasize the oddity of the situation in Crete with regard to votives.[20] Together with such well-known phenomena as continuity in visible dedication on the island, and the early appearance of orientalizing motifs in Cretan votives, one could point to other, less widely acknowledged oddities such as the apparent scarcity of pins and fibulae, so prevalent as Iron Age dedications elsewhere, but reported from only thirteen sanctuaries on Crete and from only four (Psychro Cave, Idaian Cave, Tsoutsouros Cave and Kato Syme) in any quantity.[21] Or, one could point to odd elements in the iconography, the naked women, or women hitching up their skirts or the ithyphallic warriors.[22] At a later period, there is the already alluded to failure of the Cretans to take up the habit of sculptural dedications except in the cult of Asklepios.[23] But one should not let these idiosyncrasies detract too much from Crete's overall accordance with patterns of votive dedication through time attested elsewhere in the Greek world at least from the late ninth century onwards. There are perennial problems with the dating of some Cretan votive types, most importantly bronzes, but the pattern appears similar to elsewhere: an increase in particularly bronze dedication from the late ninth to the eighth centuries, followed by distinct changes in the seventh century on Crete—an increase in the range and frequency of terracotta dedications and perhaps a decline in metal dedications and/or a shift from large bronzes, such as tripods, to armour.[24]

Scholarship on patterns in votive dedication has focused on the social and political implications—the emergence of and competition between social groups. And in such a discussion regional and local differences are naturally emphasized as powerful interpretive tools. But it is important not to lose sight of the broader issue. What we are seeing is the crystallization of a very characteristic religious practice—not all human societies interact with their gods in this way—and one that is quite distinct from the more variegated depositional practices of the Bronze Age. Crete is fully integrated in this process, which, it is not too fantastical to suggest, represents the materialization of the *charis* relationship between men and gods that was so important to Greek religion.[25]

It is a truism that religion and society are always interdependent. The particulars of the way in which Greek religious practice was articulated through Greek society—participation in worship being through a complex set of nestled and overlapping groups or civic subdivisions (*gene, phylai,* phratries and so on), religious authority lying with the city, the lines between magistrate and priest being hazy (with the latter in many respects seeming like a specialized form of the former), in short that complex of features known as *polis* religion—are as defining a feature of Greek religion as the pantheon or as temple architecture.[26] It is because they are defining that it is a struggle to apply the *polis* religion model to other societies and even to other city-states such as ancient Rome.[27]

Again, lack of evidence hampers our understanding of the degree to which Crete con-

[20] For discussion of Cretan votives see Sporn 2002; 348–356; Prent 2005, 353–420.
[21] Prent 2005, 397–398.
[22] Women hitching up their skirts at Axos: Rizza 1967–1968, fig.12, no. 86; naked women at Gortyn: Rizza & Santa Maria Scinari 1968, pls. 12, 16, 22–24.
[23] Most of the sculptural dedications to Asklepios are from Lissos, Sporn 2002, 349.
[24] Prent 2005, 420–424. The classic statement of the general pattern is Snodgrass 1989–1990. Whitley has

pointed out to me that the precise pattern may differ on Crete, which seems to start and peak earlier than the mainland both in metal and terracotta dedication. Problems with dating and with regional patterns, not to mention site specific ones, are a problem on the mainland as they are on Crete.
[25] Parker 1998.
[26] Sourvinou-Inwood 2000a; *eadem* 2000b.
[27] Beard, North & Price 1998, 1–72; Bendlin 2000.

forms with the rest of Greece. Tribes are well attested on Crete doing in the political sphere exactly what we would expect them to be doing: ratifying decrees, having an oversight role in certain types of inheritance and supplying magistrates on a rotational basis.[28] *Gene* are less well attested, Aristotle tells us that the *kosmoi* were chosen from *gene*. Many people believe him, and the same may well have been true for priests.[29] One possible, albeit problematic, explanation for the reference to "whatsoever gods are without priests" in the late sixth-century Spensithios decree is that they are deities whose priesthoods stood temporarily empty because vagaries of heredity and lifecycle had left the gene supplying the priests without suitable candidates.[30] Phratries are unknown on Crete but the *hetaireiai*, those famous groups of men, dining in the *andreion*, with which so many of the literary testimonia for Crete are concerned, are usually seen as their equivalent—as male associations overseeing citizenship into which boys would be initiated. Many scholars have noted that the rite for introducing a son to the *hetaireiai* attested already in the early fifth century by the Gortyn code is very similar to that accompanying the introduction of sons

to phratries in Athens;[31] while the Zeus Hetairaios attested on Crete by Hesychios makes a tempting parallel for Zeus Phratrios in Attica.[32]

Unfortunately, our only detailed information on how participation in religion in Cretan cities might have been articulated through these groups comes from a rare sacrificial code dating to the fourth century and coming from Axos.[33] It outlines that one of the *kosmoi* is to conduct the sacrifice to Zeus Agoraios in front of the other *kosmoi* and the four tribes of the *polis*, and it goes on to record that portions of the meat are to be given to the *hetaireiai*. There are oddities here, the sacrifice being undertaken by a *kosmos* where elsewhere we might expect a priest, the *hetaireiai* as a, or as the, main forum in which the sacrifice was consumed. But in overall outline and in the prominence of the tribes it is just what we would expect of participation in a city festival in any Greek *polis*. However, care needs to be taken here, the Axos decree is relatively late and inscriptions like this are put up as a response to specific political circumstances—when something changes.[34] Nevertheless, the reference in the Spensithios decree to τὰ δαμόσια τά τε θήια καὶ τανθρώπινα, making the public or state domain up of a combination of those things that are for the gods and those things that are for men sounds like a pretty good formula for something like typical Greek *polis* religion on the island by the end of the sixth century.[35] Moreover, a fragmentary late-sixth-century decree from Eleutherna dealing with cult at a place called Dion Akron, which seemingly requires the priest there to remain sober, might nicely show the *polis* exer-

---

[28] Jeffery & Morpurgo-Davies 1970, 129; Jones 1987, 219–231.

[29] Arist. *Pol.* 2.7.5. Debate has circulated around the question of whether *kosmoi* were appointed according to *gene* (*pace* Aristotle) or according to tribe (*pace* Cretan inscriptions) something that would be a false dichotomy if *gene* were subgroups within tribes, Spyridakis 1969; Huxley 1971, 510–511; Perlman 1992, 195–196.

[30] Line 4 on side B, Jeffery & Morpurgo-Davies 1970, 141, suggest instead that this refers to new state cults that have not yet had alternative arrangements made for their priesthoods. But the logical conclusion of such an interpretation of the provision is that the *polis* is actually anticipating the introduction of a lot of new gods (since they are "whatsoever"—they cannot be named yet) and, therefore, an extraordinary, unprecedented, and to my mind unlikely, change in traditional religious practice.

[31] Willetts 1967, 23.

[32] Hesych. s.v. Ἑταιρείος.

[33] *LSCG*, 245–247, no. 145.

[34] But note the suggestion in *LSCG* that it looks like a copy of an earlier document.

[35] Side A line 4; for discussion of this phrase, see Jeffery & Morpurgo-Davies 1970, 131–132; Beattie 1975, 25–26.

cizing control over priests in a typically Greek manner.[36]

The limitations of the evidence mean that any portrait of religion on Crete will necessarily be a collage drawing evidence from sources that are rather too widely distributed through time and space for comfort. It is irresistible, for example, to equate many of the phenomena relating to the religion of Crete in Early Iron Age to Archaic period, from the iconography of bronze plaques like those found at Kato Syme Viannou, to the failure to adopt some of the more spectacular elements of Archaic religious material culture, to the social structures, the groups of dining aristocrats with their dour, conservative warrior traditions and homoerotic initiation rites, described in most detail by Ephoros (400–330 BC).[37] But if we do so we must at least acknowledge that by the fourth century, when Ephoros, Plato and Aristotle were actually describing these groups, the predominant votive type, as everywhere in the Greek world, were small terracottas, most often depicting women, and the Cretans were starting to take up sculptural dedication, at least in the case of the cult of Asklepios.[38]

Since whatever picture we paint of Cretan society is bound to be a collage, it is important to accept that the evidence can be combined in multiple ways. And it is certainly possible to combine the evidence in such a way as to minimize strangeness and to highlight the similarities between the island and other parts of the Greek world. This statement should not really be controversial since no one, to my knowledge, has actually expressed a problem with characterizing Cretan religion as fundamentally Greek.[39]

The surprise of the normal

But this is precisely the main point I want to make in this paper: given the development of Crete through prehistory the real surprise is not that Cretan religion is odd in comparison to other parts of Greece, but that it is so similar.

There are nearly always signs of contact and influence between the island and the rest of the Aegean from the Early Bronze Age onwards, and the island's material culture goes through periods of looking more and less distinct from that elsewhere. There are also very significant regional differences in the nature of contact with other parts of the Aegean through time, but I think it is fair to say that Crete pretty consistently follows a quite distinct trajectory throughout prehistory. A precocious start and early demise for its Bronze Age palatial civilization;[40] a transition from Bronze Age to Iron Age quite unlike that elsewhere;[41] a delayed and always partial adoption of mainland Iron Age styles in such things as pottery;[42] a quite distinct Iron Age settlement pattern with early nucleated settlements and early signs of town planning; a consistently idiosyncratic burial habit; a unique response to early contacts

---

[36] Lupu 2005, no. 22.
[37] Kato Syme plaques: Lembessi 1985, esp. 236–237; Ephoros is the source for the famous and evocative description of Classical Cretan social forms in Strab. 10.4.20–22.
[38] Terracottas: Sporn 2002, 352; perhaps the earliest sculptural dedication to Asklepios is a relief supposedly from Gortyn depicting the god, Hygieia and the Asklepiads dated to c. 400 BC, Sporn, 2002, 158, 350–351, pl. 28, no.1.

[39] For two more or less cautious expressions of the Greekness of Cretan religion as the end point for the development of Cretan religion through the Iron Age: D'Agata 2006; Whitley 2009a.
[40] Watrous 2001; Rehak & Younger 2001.
[41] Godart & Tzedakis 1991; papers in Driessen & Farnoux 1997 and D'Agata & Moody 2005.
[42] See, for example, Coldstream 2008, 234–235, 239, 241, 242–244, 251–254, 475–477. As a comparison, for objects originating overseas found on Crete (calculated as amounting to only about 3.5–5% of catalogued Iron Age artefacts from even Knossian cemeteries), see Jones 2000.

with the eastern Mediterranean.[43] Overall, Crete's early precocity in such things as temple building, the introduction of oriental styles, figurative scenes or sculptural decoration, followed by its apparent rejection of elaborate material culture at a point where elsewhere the Greek world was booming, has led some scholars to question whether Crete is an exception to the patterns of state or *polis* formation found elsewhere.[44]

Similarly, signs of continuity from the Bronze Age in cult place, iconography, and language, while they may appeal to the antiquarian in all of us, are hardly surprising given the more general continuity in the archaeology of the island. Perhaps the best way to gain an insight into the nature of continuity on the island in this period of transition from Bronze to Iron is through brief snapshots of three different regions. At Knossos, the only major break in occupation seems to be well before the end of the Bronze Age, towards the middle of the LM IIIB period when the Bronze Age town was abandoned—apparently peacefully. By the end of the LM IIIB period, around 1200 BC, a new settlement had formed on the west slopes of the former town. And from this period on, settlement around Knossos—largely based on burial and well material—seems more or less continuous.[45] In the south of the island, at Phaistos, the settlement survives all the way through the transition from the Bronze to the Iron Age while settlements around it disappear. By the Geometric period it had grown to contain sizeable stone-built houses and paved streets, it continued to grow in the seventh

century and survived until it was destroyed by Gortyn in the second century BC.[46]

The mountainous east of the island offers a third pattern of continuity—one of a shifting settlement pattern within a small area. For example, on the eastern arm of the Mirabello Bay between LM IIIB and LM IIIC the very small villages of the plain disappeared and new settlements formed on the hills and mountains to the east. These sites, while more defensible, were also strategically situated for access to water and to fertile plains and they were more populous. From the Late Geometric to Early Orientalizing periods one of these sites, Azoria, grows, while those around it shrink—the cemeteries of one of these other sites, Vronda, continue after the settlement itself is abandoned. This pattern has been very convincingly interpreted as a sign of synoicism on the emergent centre of Azoria.[47] Azoria itself survives until it is destroyed in the mid-fifth century and provides our most complete view of an Archaic Cretan city, complete with substantial houses; an enormous public building, which has got to be one of the island's better candidates for an *andreion*; and alongside it an Archaic shrine featuring the typical hearth and altar, which was itself close to the eroded remains of an earlier LM IIIC bench shrine containing a Goddess with upraised arms.[48]

This combination of idiosyncrasy and continuity in Crete's development from the Bronze Age through to the Classical period, then, means that signs of oddity or continuity in Cretan religion should be hardly remarkable. But they do make Crete's ultimate con-

---

[43] Whitley 1991, 186–189; Morris 1998, 59–68; Coldstream 2003, 46–48, 78–81, chapter 10, 366–370.

[44] See for example, Perlman 2000, 59; Whitley 2009a, 273.

[45] Coldstream 1991; *idem* 1999; *idem* 2000; Hatzaki 2005.

[46] Watrous & Hadzi-Vallianou 2004a; 2004b.

[47] Haggis 2001; *idem* 2005, 81–85.

[48] For the monumental building that seems to me to be at least as good a candidate for an *andreion* as the building the excavators have identified as such, see Haggis *et al.* 2007, 295–301; for the shrines, see the summary report of the 2006 season available on the project website at www.unc.edu/~dchaggis/.

formation with so many wider Greek norms highly problematic and, I would argue, more desperately in need of explanation than scholars have tended realise. Two elements of the wider scholarly debate have made this problem especially acute.

For Willetts, of course, the answer to why Crete was strange in some respects and not in others was easily answered by appeal to the Dorian invasion of the island. But almost everything relating to the idea of migrating Dorians has been called into question; including the key idea that all Doric dialects descended from a single proto-Doric ancestor originally spoken in west Greece, an idea that is fundamental to seeing them as a discrete migrating ethnic group. Rather, the suggestion has been made that since Doric dialects share no innovatory feature that is not also found in non-Doric dialects they might have evolved over time in close contact with both Doric and non-Doric dialects.[49] The observation has also been made that names, such as that of the Messana, reminiscent of those that later became attached to Dorian groups, are already attested in Linear B.[50] Meanwhile, Chadwick suggested long ago that there were already echoes of the Doric dialect in some Linear B tablets.[51] Archaeologically the Dorians are proving extremely elusive. And on Crete, even with the eye of faith, there is really no convincing archaeological sign of their arrival—so, if they did arrive, they are archaeologically invisible. These types of doubts seem to be leading an increasing number of scholars to regard them as a case of relatively late ethnogenesis. One does not need to go all this way to get a healthy dose of scepticism about the issue, and, once one starts doubting

the Dorian invasion, the easiest answer to the question of Cretan normality is removed.

At the same time a second type of healthy scepticism is affecting scholarship. The questioning of the written sources for early Archaic history and an emphasis on regional studies and local differences in archaeology is leading to the down dating of the emergence of many of the features that unified the Greeks. This, in turn, is a necessary side effect of the good archaeological practice of assuming in a "Dark Age" that things were small scale and isolated until it is proved otherwise. Some of the conformity of Crete with the wider Greek world in, for example, the pantheon does not really become explicit until at least the Archaic period. The appearance of a so-called sixth-century gap on Crete has naturally led scholars to ponder whether something momentous was happening at that time.[52] Could, then, a dramatic change bringing a more unusual Crete into line with the Greek norm be placed here? Evidence could be cited to support such a proposition—there is that reference to those "whatsoever gods are without priests" in the Spensithios decree, or the change in votive imagery on the acropolis at Gortyn from naked females to a panoply-wearing Athena.[53] Such an argument would fit in with similar arguments elsewhere, but in the case of Crete it is problematic. Although sixth-century Crete can no longer be said to have been isolated, it does seem, through its simplicity in material culture, to have been distinguishing itself and rejecting much that was doing the rounds elsewhere in the Greek world. The tenor of the momentous sixth-century changes seems to be taken as traditionalist, of old elites ossifying and isolating their society in response to the dangerous changes brought

---

[49] The linguistic debate is summarized in Hall 2002, 76–78.
[50] On the appearance of an ethnic Mezana/Messana (the local form of Messene) in Pylian Linear B, see Bennet 2007, 132–133.
[51] Chadwick 1976.

[52] For a couple of examples, see Coldstream 1991, 298; Morris 1998, 66–68; the most significant contribution to discussion of the sixth-century gap is Erickson 2002.
[53] Sporn 2002, 159–162; Prent 2005, 267–273.

about by increasing wealth and contact.[54] If all this is right—and the case for it is strong—is this really the time to place the revolutionary Hellenization of Cretan religion?

Conclusion

But if the Greekness of Cretan religion did not come about because of an invasion of Dorians and did not happen in a jolt at a late date, how did it happen? The importance of this question should not be underestimated. It is merely a local facet of a much larger question affecting the whole of Greek religion. Across the Greek world, whenever evidence becomes available, underlying regional dissimilarities is a great deal of commonality. Modern trends in scholarship have meant that any explanation of the commonalities of Greek religion tends to fall through the gap between the doubts over the naïve approaches of scholars like Willets, who took the Greeks' stories about their own past as historical, and the excitement over occasional spectacular cases of continuity at individual cult sites. Recent work on the period between the end of the Bronze Age and the Archaic period by scholars such as Prent has shown the artificial and sterile nature of the question of continuity.[55] The addressing of questions around the issue of the nature and development of the consistencies across Greek religion may be a much more profitable avenue for research to go down. Apart from anything else addressing such an issue plays to the strengths of archaeology, which is, on the whole, rather better at telling us about interactions between regions than it is at telling us about what people believed.

The point of this article has been to highlight that Crete makes an exceptionally good case study for addressing these questions. Not only is its oddity over the Bronze and Iron Ages as great or greater than that elsewhere, but the nature of its development in the Archaic and Classical period makes the straightforward placing of a congruence with the rest of Greece here, as modern approaches might be tempted to do, extremely problematic. This last can be seen as a sort of control, focusing attention on earlier periods.

The effect of statements about Bronze Age evidence by scholars such as Finley and Roussel has been a dislocation between the Bronze Age and the Classical periods,[56] a disconnect that is heightened and confirmed by the nature of much "Dark Age" scholarship. Whereas, once upon a time, a scholar like Nilsson might have considered it necessary to understand the Bronze Age in order to understand Greek religion, today the gulf that has opened up between historic and prehistoric means scholars of one period feel not only safe but even impelled to ignore the other. However, as this paper should have made obvious, the question of the place of Cretan religion in the wider Greek world cannot be answered through reference to any single period: whether that be the Bronze Age, Iron Age or Archaic period. The nature of the Cretan evidence, where in some respects we have rather better direct evidence for the religion of the island around 1350 BC than we do for 550 BC, should highlight to scholars the artificiality of divisions between prehistoric and historic periods. If the apparent Greekness of Cretan religion cannot be attributed to a single historical moment—whether that be an invasion of Dark Age Dorians or an emergent Archaic Panhellenism—then it must be attributed to a longer process; one that encompasses both the prehistoric and historic periods.

The investigation of this process, as well as taking a long view, must wrestle with a number

---

[54] Perlman 1992, 201–204; Davies 2005; Whitley 2009a, 291.
[55] For critique of the notion of continuity see Whitley 2009b.

[56] Roussel 1976; Finley 1978.

of methodological problems and assumptions that have been touched upon in this paper. The basic methodological problem arises because the Greekness of Cretan religion is primarily visible through written sources, culminating in the fourth century when inscriptions like the Axos decree allow us to see not only the pantheon but also the articulation of religion through social structures. But, as I have attempted to show, a minimalist alignment of the first appearance of similarity with the period in which it is first evinced is unlikely to be the true story. Solving this impasse requires an appreciation of the limitations of the archaeological and epigraphic evidence and the historical circumstances under which phenomena become manifest within this evidence. The basic assumption that needs to be tested is that there was a continuous movement towards similarity in religion across what was to become the Greek world. Moments where congruence is likely to have been intense have been identified, such as during the time that the centre and east of the island were administered in mainland Greek from Knossos. But the detailed analysis of the religion of these periods and, more so, their wider significance has barely begun. Other less recognized periods of potential congruence might be worth examining. What, for example, were the religious correlates of interregional influences in pottery visible in the Iron Age? How old are such interregional religious systems as amphictyonies? Are they old enough to interrelate with Iron Age *koine* visible in material culture? But it is also worth asking whether there were periods of divergence, out of step with a unidirectional movement towards similarity. Was, for example, the suggested rejection of mainland developments by sixth-century Crete accompanied by the rejection of developments in the religious sphere?

MATTHEW HAYSOM
Darwin College
Cambridge University
mh641@cam.ac.uk

Bibliography

Beard, North & Price 1998   M. Beard, J. North & S. Price, *Religions of Rome* I. *A history*, Cambridge 1998.

Beattie 1975   J.A. Beattie, 'Some notes on the Spensitheos decree', *Kadmos* 14, 1975, 8–47.

Bendlin 2000   A. Bendlin, 'Looking beyond the civic compromise: Religious pluralism in late republican Rome', in *Religion in Archaic and Republican Rome and Italy*, eds. E. Bispham & C. Smith, Edinburgh 2000, 115–135.

Bennet 2007   J. Bennet, 'The Linear B archives and the kingdom of Nestor', in *Sandy Pylos: An archaeological history from Nestor to Navarino*, eds. J.L. Davies & J. Bennet, Athens 2007[2].

Benton 1937   S. Benton, 'Herakles and Eurystheus at Knossos', *JHS* 57, 1937, 38–43.

Burkert 1985   W. Burkert, *Greek religion*, Oxford 1985.

Chadwick 1976   J. Chadwick, 'Who were the Dorians?', *PP* 31, 1976, 103–117.

Chrysostomou 1998   P. Chrysostomou, *Η Θεσσαλική Θεά Εν(ν)οδία ή Φεραία Θεά*, Athens 1998.

Coldstream 1976   J.N. Coldstream, 'Hero cults in the age of Homer', *JHS* 96, 1976, 8–17.

Coldstream 1984   J.N. Coldstream, 'A Protogeometric Nature Goddess from Knossos', *BICS* 31, 1984, 93–104.

Coldstream 1991   J.N. Coldstream, 'Knossos: An urban nucleus in the Dark Age?', in *La Transizione dal Miceneo all'Alto Arcaismo. Dal palazzo alla città. Atti del Convegno Internazionale Roma, 14–19 marzo 1988*, eds. D. Musti *et al.*, Roma 1991, 287–299.

Coldstream 1999   J.N. Coldstream, 'Knossos 1951–61: Classical and Hellenistic pottery from the town', *ABSA* 94, 1999, 321–351.

Coldstream 2000   J.N. Coldstream, 'Evans's Greek finds: The early Greek town of Knossos and its encroachment on the borders of the Minoan palace', *ABSA* 95, 2000, 259–299.

Coldstream 2003   J.N. Coldstream, *Geometric Greece*, London 2003².

Coldstream 2008   J.N. Coldstream, *Greek Geometric pottery: A survey of ten local styles*, London 2008².

Coldstream & Catling 1996   J.N. Coldstream & H.W. Catling, *Knossos North Cemetery: Early Greek tombs* (BSA, Suppl. 28), London 1996.

Coldstream & Huxley 1999   J.N. Coldstream & G.L. Huxley, 'Knossos: The Archaic gap', *ABSA* 94, 1999, 289–307.

D'Agata 2006   A.L. D'Agata, 'Cult activity on Crete in the Early Dark Age: Changes, continuities and the development of a "Greek" cult system', in *Ancient Greece: From the Mycenaean palaces to the age of Homer*, eds. S. Deger-Jalkotzy & I.S. Lemos, Edinburgh 2006, 397–416.

D'Agata & Moody 2005   A.L. D'Agata & J. Moody, *Ariadne's threads: Connections between Crete and the Greek mainland in Late Minoan III (LMIII A2 to LM IIIC)*, Athens 2005.

Davies 2005   J.K. Davies, 'Gortyn within the economy of Archaic and Classical Crete', in *La grande iscrizione di Gortyna: cento-venti anni dopo la scoperta*, eds. E. Greco & M. Lombardo, Athens 2005.

Desborough 1972   V.R.D'A. Desborough, *The Greek Dark Ages*, London 1972.

Driessen & Farnoux 1997   *La Crète mycénnienne* (BCH, Suppl. 30), eds. J. Driessen & A. Farnoux, Paris 1997.

Duhoux 1982   Y. Duhoux, *Les étéocrétois: les texts, la langue*, Amsterdam 1982.

Erickson 2002   B.L. Erickson, 'Aphrati and Kato Syme: Pottery, continuity and cult in Late Archaic and Classical Crete', *Hesperia* 71, 2002, 41–90.

Finley 1978   M.I. Finley, *The world of Odysseus*, New York 1978.

Gesell 1985   G.C. Gesell, *Town, palace and house cult in Minoan Crete* (SIMA, 67), Göteborg 1985.

Godart & Tzedakis 1991   L. Godart & Y. Tzedakis, 'La Crète du Minoen Récent IIIB à l'époque géométrique', in *La transizione dal Miceneo all'Alto Arcaismo. Dal palazzo alla città. Atti del convegno internazionale Roma, 14–19 marzo 1988*, eds. D. Musti *et al.*, Roma 1991, 187–198.

Gounaris 2005   A. Gounaris, 'Cult places in the Cyclades during the Protogeometric and Geometric periods: Their contribution in interpreting the rise of the Cycladic poleis', in *Architecture and Archaeology in the Cyclades*, eds. M. Yeroulanou & M. Stamatopoulou, Oxford 2005, 13–68.

Haggis 2001   D.C. Haggis, 'A Dark Age settlement system in East Crete and a reassessment of the definition of refuge settlements', in *Defensive settlements of the Aegean and the Eastern Mediterranean after c. 1200 BC*, eds. V. Karageorghis & C.E. Morris, Nicosia 2001, 41–57.

Haggis 2005   D. C. Haggis, *Kavousi I. The archaeological survey of the Kavousi region*, Philadelphia 2005.

Haggis et al. 2007   D.C. Haggis, M.S. Mook, R.D. Fitzsimons, C.M. Scarry & L.M. Snyder, 'Excavations at Azoria 2003–2004, Part 1. The Archaic civic complex', *Hesperia* 76, 2007, 243–321.

Hall 2002   J.M. Hall, *Hellenicity: Between ethnicity and culture*, Chicago 2002.

Hatzaki 2005   E. Hatzaki, 'Postpalatial Knossos: Town and cemeteries from LM IIIA2 to LM IIIC', in *Ariadne's threads: Connections between Crete and the Greek mainland in the Postpalatial Period (LM IIIA2 to SM)*, eds. A.L. D'Agata & J. Moody, Athens 2005, 65–95.

Huxley 1971   G.L. Huxley, 'Crete in Aristotle's *Politics*', *GRBS* 12, 1971, 505–515.

Huxley 1994   G.L. Huxley, 'On Knossos and her neighbours (7th century to mid 4th century B.C.)', in *Knossos, a labyrinth of history: Papers presented in honour of Sinclair Hood*, eds. D. Evely, H. Hughes-Brock & N. Momigliano, London 1994, 123–133.

Jeffery 1990   L.H. Jeffery, *The local scripts of Archaic Greece*, Oxford 1990.

Jeffery & Morpurgo-Davies 1970   L.H. Jeffery & A. Morpurgo-Davies, 'ΠΟΙΝΙΚΑΣΤΑΣ and ΠΟΙΝΙΚΑΖΕΝ: BM 1969.4-2.1, a new Archaic inscription from Crete', *Kadmos* 9, 1970, 118–154.

Jones 1987   N.F. Jones, *Public organization in ancient Greece*, Philadelphia 1987.

Jones 2000   D.W. Jones, *External relations of Early Iron Age Crete 1100–600 B.C.*, Pennsylvania 2000.

Lembessi 1985   A. Lembessi, Ιερό του Ερμή και της Αφροδίτης στη Σύμη Βιάννου I. Χάλκινα Κρητικά Τορεύματα, Athens 1985.

LSCG   F. Sokolowski, *Lois sacrées des cités grecques*, Paris 1969.

Lupu 2005   E. Lupu, *Greek sacred law: A collection of new documents*, Leiden 2005.

Malkin 1994   I. Malkin, *Myth and territory in the Spartan Mediterranean*, Cambridge 1994.

Mazarakis-Ainian 1997   A. Mazarakis-Ainian, *From rulers' dwellings to temples* (SIMA, 121), Jonsered 1997.

Mili 2005   M. Mili, *Studies in Thessalian religion*, diss. University of Oxford, Oxford 2005.

Morgan 2003   C. Morgan, *Early Greek states beyond the polis*, London 2003.

Morris 1988   I. Morris, 'Tomb cult and the Greek renaissance: The past in the present in the eighth century B.C.', *Antiquity* 62, 1988, 750–761.

Morris 1998   I. Morris, 'Archaeology and Archaic Greek history', in *Archaic Greece: New approaches and new evidence*, eds. N. Fischer & H. van Wees, London, 1998, 1–91.

Nilsson 1906 M.P. Nilsson, *Griechische Feste von religiöser Bedeutung mit Ausschluss der attischen*, Leipzig 1906.

Nilsson 1950 M.P. Nilsson, *Minoan-Mycenaean religion and its survival in the Greek religion*, Lund 1950.

Nilsson 1955 M.P. Nilsson, *Geschichte der griechischen Religion*, München 1955².

Ohnesorg 2005 A. Ohnesorg, 'Naxian and Parian architecture: General features and new discoveries', in *Architecture and archaeology of the Cyclades*, eds. M. Yeroulanou & M. Stamatopoulou, Oxford 2005, 135–152.

Osborne 1996 R. Osborne, *Greece in the making 1200–479 BC*, London 1996.

Parker 1987 R. Parker, 'Festivals of the Attic Demes', in *Gifts to the Gods. Proceedings of the Uppsala symposium 1985* (Boreas, 15), eds. T. Linders & G. Nordquist, Uppsala 1987, 137–147.

Parker 1988 R. Parker, 'Demeter, Dionysus and the Spartan pantheon', in *Early Greek cult practice. Proceedings of the fifth international symposium at the Swedish Institute at Athens, 26–29 June, 1986* (ActaAth-4°, 38), eds. R. Hägg, N. Marinatos & G. Nordquist, Stockholm 1988, 99–103.

Parker 1998 R. Parker, 'Pleasing thighs: Reciprocity in Greek religion', in *Reciprocity in Ancient Greece*, eds. C. Gill, N. Postlethwaite & R. Seaford, Oxford 1998, 105–125.

Parker 2003 R. Parker, 'The problem of the Greek cult epithet', *OpAth* 28, 2003, 173–183.

Parker 2005 R. Parker, *Polytheism and society at Athens*, Oxford 2005.

Perlman 1992 P. Perlman, 'One hundred-citied Crete and the Cretan ΠΟΛΙΤΕΙΑ', *CP* 87, 1992, 193–205.

Perlman 2000 P. Perlman, 'Gortyn. The first seven hundred years', in *Polis and politics: Studies in ancient Greek history*, eds. P. Flensted-Jensen, T.H. Nielsen & L. Rubinstein, København 2000.

Perlman 2002 P. Perlman, 'Gortyn. The first seven hundred years part II. The laws from the temple of Apollo Pythios', in *Even more studies in the ancient Greek polis*, ed. T.H. Nielsen, Stuttgart 2002, 187–227.

Polinskaya 2006 I. Polinskaya, 'Lack of boundaries, absence of oppositions: The city-countryside continuum of a Greek pantheon', in *City, countryside and the spatial organization of value in Classical antiquity*, eds. R.M. Rosen & I. Sluiter, Leiden 2006, 61–92.

Prent 2005 M. Prent, *Cretan sanctuaries and cults. Continuity and change from Late Minoan IIIC to the Archaic Period*, Leiden 2005.

Prent 2009 M. Prent, 'The survival of the goddess with upraised arms: Early Iron Age representations and contexts', in *Archaeologies of cult: Essays in honour of Geraldine C. Gesell* (Hesperia, Suppl. 42), eds. A.L. D'Agata & A. Van de Moortel, Athens 2009, 231–238.

Rehak & Younger 2001
P. Rehak & J.G. Younger, 'Neopalatial, Final Palatial and Postpalatial Crete', in *Aegean prehistory: A review*, ed. T. Cullen, Boston 2001, 383–473.

Rizza 1967–1968
G. Rizza, 'Le terrecotte di Axòs', *ASAtene* 65–66 (n.s. 29–30), 1967–1968, 211–302.

Rizza & Santa Maria Scinari 1968
G. Rizza & V. Santa Maria Scinari 1968, *Il Santuario sull Acropoli di Gortina*, Roma 1968.

Roussel 1976
D. Roussel, *Tribu et cité: études sur les groupes sociaux dans les cités grecques aux époques archaïque et classique*, Paris 1976.

Snodgrass 1971
A. Snodgrass, *The Dark Age of Greece*, Edinburgh 1971.

Snodgrass 1980
A. Snodgrass, *Archaic Greece*, London 1980.

Snodgrass 1986
A. Snodgrass, 'Interaction by design: the Greek city state', in *Peer polity interaction and socio-political change*, eds. C. Renfrew & J.F. Cherry, Cambridge 1986, 47–58.

Snodgrass 1989–1990
A. Snodgrass, 'The economics of dedication at Greek sanctuaries', in *Anathema: Atti del convegno internazionale: Regime della offerte e vita dei santuari nel mediterraneo antico* (ScAnt, 3–4), 1998–1990, 287–294.

Sourvinou-Inwood 1978
Ch. Sourvinou-Inwood, 'Persephone and Aphrodite at Locri: A model for personality definitions in Greek religion', *JHS* 98, 1978, 101–121.

Sourvinou-Inwood 2000a
Ch. Sourvinou-Inwood, 'What is polis religion?', in *Oxford readings in Greek religion*, ed. R. Buxton, Oxford 2000, 13–37.

Sourvinou-Inwood 2000b
Ch. Sourvinou-Inwood, 'Further aspects of polis religion,' in *Oxford readings in Greek religion*, ed. R. Buxton, Oxford 2000, 38–55.

Sporn 2002
K. Sporn, *Heiligtümer und Kulte Kretas in klassischer und hellenistischer Zeit*, Heidelberg 2002.

Spyridakis 1969
S. Spyridakis, 'Aristotle on the election of kosmoi', *PP* 24, 1969, 265–269.

Stefanakis 1999
M.I. Stefanakis, 'The introduction of coinage in Crete and the beginning of local minting', in *From Minoan farmers to Roman traders: Sidelights on the economy of ancient Crete*, ed. A. Chaniotis, Stuttgart 1999, 247–268.

Tyree 1974
E.L. Tyree, *Cretan sacred caves: Archaeological evidence*, diss. University of Missouri, 1974.

Warren 1982–1983
P.M. Warren, 'Knossos: Stratigraphical museum excavations, 1978–2. Part II', in *Archaeological Reports* 29, 1982–1983, 63–87.

Watrous 2001
L.V. Watrous, 'Crete from earliest prehistory through the Protopalatial period', in *Aegean prehistory: A review*, ed. T. Cullen, Boston 2001, 157–223.

Watrous & Hadzi-Vallianou 2004a
L.V. Watrous & D. Hadzi-Vallianou, 'Palatial rule and collapse (Middle Minoan IB–Late Minoan IIIB)', in *The plain of Phaistos. Cycles of social complexity in the Mesara region of Crete* (Monumenta Archaeologica, 23), eds. L.V. Watrous, D. Hadzi-Vallianou & H. Blitzer, Los Angeles 2004, 277–304.

Watrous & Hadzi-Vallianou 2004b L.V. Watrous & D. Hadzi-Vallianou, 'The polis of Phaistos: development and destruction (Late Minoan IIIC–Hellenistic)', in *The plain of Phaistos. Cycles of social complexity in the Mesara region of Crete* (Monumenta Archaeologica, 23), eds. L.V. Watrous, D. Hadzi-Vallianou & H. Blitzer, Los Angeles 2004, 307–338.

Whitley 1988 J. Whitley, 'Early states and hero cults: A reappraisal', *JHS* 108, 1988, 173–182.

Whitley 1991 J. Whitley, *Style and society in Dark Age Greece: The changing face of a preliterate society 1100–700 BC*, Cambridge 1991.

Whitley 1997 J. Whitley, 'Cretan laws and Cretan literacy', *AJA* 101, 1997, 635–661.

Whitley 2001 J. Whitley, *The archaeology of ancient Greece*, Cambridge 2001.

Whitley 2006 J. Whitley, 'Before the great code: Public inscriptions and material practice in archaic Crete', in *La grande iscrizione di Goryna: Centoventi anni dopo la scoperta*, eds. E. Greco & M. Lombard, Athens 2006, 41–56.

Whitley 2009a J. Whitley, 'Crete', in *A companion to Archaic Greece*, eds. K.A. Raaflaub & H. van Wees, Chichester 2009, 273–293.

Whitley 2009b J. Whitley, 'The chimera of continuity: What would "continuity of cult" actually demonstrate', in *Archaeologies of cult: Essays in honour of Geraldine C. Gesell* (Hesperia, Suppl. 42), eds. A.L. D'Agata & A. Van de Moortel, Athens 2009, 279–88.

Willetts 1955 R.F. Willetts, *Aristocratic society in ancient Crete*, London 1955.

Willetts 1962 R.F. Willetts, *Cretan cults and festivals*, London 1962.

Willetts 1965 R.F. Willetts, *Ancient Crete: A social history*, London 1965.

Willetts 1967 R.F. Willetts, *The law code of Gortyn* (Kadmos, Suppl. 1), Berlin 1967.

PETRA PAKKANEN

Polis within the *polis*

CROSSING THE BORDER OF OFFICIAL AND PRIVATE RELIGION AT THE SANCTUARY OF POSEIDON AT KALAUREIA ON POROS

Abstract

The first part of this article discusses general ideas about the way we conceptualize ancient Greek religion. In order to provide an insight into the picture of how ancient Greek religion has been framed within Classical scholarship, the historiography of ancient Greek religion is examined through two interrelated themes: first, the emergence of the so-called *polis*-model in interpretations of Greek religion, and second, the understanding of rationality in the opposition communal–private Greek religiosity. In the second part of the article these observations are contextualized to the study of the material related to religion and cult from the sanctuary of Poseidon at Kalaureia on the island of Poros. This discussion implies rethinking the division between public and private religious spheres in the study of ancient Greek religion on both a general and a particular level.

Introduction

The views on and interpretations of Greek religion presented in this paper are based on the material related to the cultic life of the sanctuary of Poseidon at Kalaureia on Poros. The sanctuary is located at the centre of the island of Kalaureia, the larger of the two islands that make up today's Poros in Greece, and is known as the place where Demosthenes took poison to kill himself.[1] In 1894 an archaeological investigation was undertaken for one season,[2] and fieldwork resumed in 1997.[3] An international team of researchers is currently working at the site and on the island carrying out a long-term investigation under the auspices of the Swedish Institute at Athens, funded by the Stiftelsen Riksbankens Jubileumsfond.[4] Kalaureian material related to cult represents here a particular, a case which reflects larger ideas and interpretative challenges in trying to understand Greek religion in general.[5] Because I attempt to pinpoint some more general ideas about the way we conceptualize religion, and particularly how ancient Greek religion has been framed within Classical scholarship, this paper is not only about the cults of Kalaureia. In the first part I shall look back to the tradition, and in the second focus these ideas on the study of the site of Kalaureia. For my contribution to the study of the particular, the cultic life at the Kalaureian sanctuary, methodological considerations have

---

[1]   See Plut., *Dem*. 29–30; Strab. 8.6.14, Paus. 1.8.2–3.

[2]   The results were published in Wide & Kjellberg 1894, 248–282.

[3]   For results, see excavation reports: Wells *et al*. 2003, 29–87; Wells *et al*. 2005, 127–215 and Wells *et al*. 2008, 31–129.

[4]   For further information about the project, see www.kalaureia.org.

[5]   The terms 'general' and 'particular' are used here in order to refer back to their philosophical role in Aristotelian and Kantian analyses on universality and specificity.

proved to be of importance because they also provide an insight into the general picture of the "historiography of ancient Greek religion".[6]

Methodological approach for studying Kalaureian religion: Hermeneutics

The process of formulating interpretative views of the cultic life of this particular site involves a rather complex cluster of ideas, the accumulation of which is a result of a long line of evolvement and modifications in how ancient Greek religion has generally and traditionally been conceptualized. This reflects as much our understanding of religion as a phenomenon as it does our understanding of Kalaureian cultic life. In our interpretative work we operate with the existing schemata about ancient Greek religion in general: our views are bound to the structure we impose on what usually is included in ancient Greek religion. Thus, awareness of the role of the tradition behind our current formulations may (and hopefully does) lead us to a dialogue between the tradition and the current situation, and this could change our readings of the past 'reality'. The two form a dialectic process. Even preliminary views about the material's cultic connections by archaeologists and specialists working at the site are very important as they have a lot to tell us about the framework within which our general as well as particular views of Greek cult operate. Preceding and current interpretative frameworks also have a role in the process by which archaeology formulates itself in the sanctuary context into 'archaeology of cult'. Yannis Hamilakis has emphasized that an archaeological record does not exist as such; instead, it is archaeology that produces the entity we call the archaeological record out of material fragments of the past: "Archaeology as a discipline, as a set of principles, devices, methods, and practices, creates its objects of study, out of existing and real, past material traces".[7] In our case this creation will be a depiction of the cultic life of the Kalaureian sanctuary. A methodological background for this type of investigation is to be found in hermeneutical tradition.

The study of (Classical) antiquity, or the 'science of Classical antiquity' (*klassische Altertumswissenschaft*), played a role in the emergence of hermeneutics as a method. Methodological hermeneutics was first analytically fulfilled in philological studies of Classical antiquity, and almost all hermeneuticists of the nineteenth century were scholars of Classical philology.[8] However, by the mid nineteenth century the term 'archaeological hermeneutics' was already being used within the discussion of the method of understanding, but it was still largely based on the notion of archaeological artefacts being the fine art and architecture of Classical antiquity, i.e. the 'monuments'.[9] It was only through the slow process of accepting all types of human artefacts into the category of 'archaeological objects' that new questions started emerging within hermeneutical discussion. H.-G. Gadamer's views are a good exam-

---

[6] I have presented preliminary outlines of the methodology for the study of Kalaureian cults in Pakkanen 2008b.

[7] Hamilakis 2007, 14.
[8] Seebohm 2004, 8–9, 50–51 (for the emergence of philological-historical hermeneutics, see 46–54); see also Sherratt 2006, 51–52, 56–58. The term hermeneutics was introduced by the Church Fathers and its praxis was bound to a tradition of an interpretation of the holy scriptures. Another scholarly tradition seeks to locate the origins of hermeneutics (as a method) in antiquity and trace back the etymology of the term to *hermeneia* (particularly in Aristotle), see Sherrat 2006, 23–29.
[9] In 1834 K. Levezow was the first author to write a treatise on archaeological hermeneutics (his doctoral thesis was entitled *Über archäologische Kritik und Hermeneutik*); see esp. Fuchs 1979, 202–204; Seebohm 2004, 86–87.

ple of this: as a professional classicist, he was interested in interpreting ancient Greek texts.[10] In his writings, the importance of tradition plays a crucial role. We relate to the matter in focus—in our case a conceptual formation of religion and cult—in a manner which is determined by an antecedent interpretative framework.[11] Understanding is not to be thought of so much as an action of one's subjectivity, but of placing oneself within the process of tradition in which past and present are constantly fused.[12] The present and its circumstantial perspective are not regarded as obstacles to knowing the past, but rather resources to draw from. The reason for this is that 'reconstructing' the past may involve and even require revision of existing views, even beliefs, about both the past and the present. Understanding is a process of transmission in which past and present are constantly mediated. Gadamer notes, therefore, that historical understanding is a dialectic of identity and difference, and it may even change us.[13] Similarly, J.N. Bremmer reminds us that the use of the terms 'religion', 'ritual' and 'sacred' for certain Greek ideas and practices reflects the observer's point of view, not that of the actor; the Greeks themselves did not even yet have a term for 'religion'.[14] In other words, it ought to include self-reflection. Taking into account the tradition and its varying standpoints may continuously change our own models of viewing and interpreting the past.

In practice, therefore, it is important to gain an idea of how religion and cultic activity is conceptualized among archaeologists and scholars of religion working on cult. These preliminary views stand for expectations about the nature of religion at a certain site; it is an initial set of definitions, a kind of prototypal core of the conception of religion within the scholarly community. Therefore, it reflects the prototypal senses that scholars regard as being included in "religion", of what it necessarily must entail.[15] The context in which we work, the sanctuary setting, may affect both the questions asked of the material and the answers we are predisposed to regard as reasonable and relevant.[16] The aim is to gain a general view of cultic activity through archaeological lenses and the premises by which the nature of primary material shapes it. Even though we are not on a paradigm-changing mission it is worth remembering T. Kuhn's reminder that "any study of paradigm-directed or paradigm-shattering research must begin by locating the responsible group or groups".[17] Analysis and examination of these views aim at providing a new definition and interpretation, perhaps even a concept of a particular Kalaureian religion which

---

[10] Gadamer's doctoral thesis in 1922 was on 'Nature and pleasure according to Plato's dialogues' and his Habilitation thesis in 1929 on 'The Interpretation of Plato's *Philebos*'; in the late 1920s Gadamer took a state examination in Classical philology (with an essay in Latin on Pindar). For Gadamer's lifelong passion particularly for the ancient Greeks, see e.g. Grondin 2003, esp. 109–127, 133–141.

[11] See e.g. DiCenso 1990, 79–80. Gadamer (1989, 185 and 197–200) discusses the nature of our understanding of historical realities and the definition of historical sources.

[12] Gadamer 1989, 260–263, 276–277, 290. Gadamer postulated the 'openness' of historical inquiry: access to history is necessarily interpretative since specific interpretations are not presumed to be objective but rather epistemological (not ontological); Gadamer terms this approach 'effective history' because it can be a process of cultivating an awareness of the ways in which understanding has been shaped by historical forces. See esp. DiCenso 1990, 79–83.

[13] Gadamer 1989, 185, 190–191. For a similar tone in more recent historiography, see Koselleck 2002, 48–50; also Callinicos 1995, 89–90.

[14] Bremmer 1998, 12, 15, 23–24, 31.

[15] I have called this starting point of conceptualization elsewhere a relative *a priori* approach which does not strive for a final definition of religion but firstly examines some commonly shared pre-understanding of the confines of the concept 'past religion'; see Pakkanen 2000–2001, 76–78 with references; also Comstock 1984, 499–517 and Lakoff 1987, 17–21, 312, 327.

[16] Cf. Trigger 1989, 379.

[17] Kuhn 1996, 179–180.

inevitably also reflects Greek religion at large, thus binding together both general and particular aspects of Greek religion. The sanctuary at Kalaureia potentially provides us with something specific with its cultic past, and, as a process of formulating and conceptualizing the nature of its cultic life, it also reflects the general view of ancient religion. This type of investigation is dialectic and hermeneutic.[18] In this article it is logical, therefore, to start from the general, proceed to the particular and turn back to the general at the end. The specific question here is located in the dichotomy of the private and communal understanding of ancient Greek religion.

Tradition and current standpoint: Models of defining Greek religion

When Greek religion is in focus it is almost always pointed out that "there is no religious sphere separate from that of politics and warfare or private life; instead, religion is embedded in all aspects of life, public and private".[19] Or: "The Greek city knows no separation between sacred and profane. Religion is present in all the levels of social life, and all collective practices have a religious dimension."[20] This

view in which Greek religion as a phenomenon is firmly embedded in the city-state has almost gained the role of a dominant paradigm. A structure of the *polis* has provided the framework for conceptualizing Greek religion. This agenda was put forward particularly (and influentially) by C. Sourvinou-Inwood who coined it, for example, in the following way: "in the Classical period *polis* religion encompassed, symbolically legitimated, and regulated all religious activity within the *polis*, not only the cults of the *polis* subdivisions such as the demes, but also cults which modern commentators are inclined to consider private, such as, for example, *oikos* cults."[21] It is worth taking a closer look at the reasons behind this clear emphasis on the communal understanding of ancient Greek religion, because *polis* has not always been the primary reference point in interpretations of Greek religion. For example, M.P. Nilsson, writing in the early 1940s, stressed the element of piety, personal and—as he called it—popular religion among the Greeks as a basis for understanding Greek religiosity. In the introduction to Nilsson's 1940 volume *Greek Folk Religion* (first published under the title *Greek Popular Religion*), A.D. Nock (writing in 1961) reminded us that "the hard core of Greek religion is to be found in its observances: these took their shape among men whose focus was *first* the heart and then the city-state".[22]

---

[18] Because in our archaeological interpretative work we are bound to operate with the terms and symbols learned through the community to which we belong, by investigating those very modes of thought we can still widen our conceptual perspectives. This is what, in the language of e.g. P. Ricœur's hermeneutic phenomenology, could be called simply "interpretation", i.e. deciphering multiple significances of "texts" (symbols) and their inherent meanings. See e.g. Ricœur 1974, 315–319 (for Ricœur's phenomenology of religion); Allen 1978, 238–241; also Hodder 1992 on contextual archaeology within an interpretative framework and on the role of hermeneutics within it.

[19] Price 1999, 3.

[20] Schmitt-Pantel 1990, 200 (with references).

[21] Sourvinou-Inwood 1990, 322. Similar views abound in the literature on Greek religion; see e.g. Bruit-Zaidman & Schmitt-Pantel 1992, 6: "(...) Greek religious beliefs and rituals were given their characteristic structure at the moment when one of the most distinctive forms of the Greek political organization was emerging—the *polis* or city"; P. Cartledge, translator of the English edition of this book (the 1992 edition), underlines the same: "... the proper context for evaluating Classical Greek religion is not the individual immortal soul but rather the city, the peculiar civic corporation that the Greeks labelled *polis*." ('Translator's introduction', xv).

[22] Nock 1961, vii (my italics). E.R. Dodds' seminal study *The Greeks and the irrational* from 1951 builds heavily on the same assumption.

When J.-P. Vernant noted, around the same time as Nock wrote his *Introduction* to Nilsson, that the elaboration of a new, abstract notion of the political in Greek life was superimposed on kinship, family solidarity and hierarchical relations of dependence moving all previously private *sacra* to an open and public place,[23] did he mean that the Greeks superimposed *polis* on various existing institutions, or is it the scholars who do so? Or both? Vernant saw public life as the pinnacle of understanding Greek culture, and an individual essentially and primarily as citizen. In his view, social and private life was brought to full public view, and in a way ceased to exist.[24] The idea is naturally similar to the '*polis*-model'. This tendency can also be seen in a clear social emphasis prominent in the archaeological study of ancient Greek religion which seems to value empiricism and interpret Greek religion primarily from a strong social point of view. In this social perspective religious belief loses its primary role. It should be noted that this trend is also embedded in the so-called social turn in the humanities which took place in the 1960s when it was fuelled by a renewed interest in the works of Marx, Weber and Durkheim. However, scholars who have recently expressed criticism towards the *polis*-model have mainly addressed problems such as the difficulties of covering local differences in cultic life, the model's inflexibility in offering a comprehensive framework for the study of Greek religion beyond the Classical period, etc.[25] Before elaborating on these questions I wish to further explore the tradition in religious studies which has affected and shaped our conceptualizations of ancient Greek religion towards the postulates of the *polis*-model.

Since E. Durkheim's theories on the origins of religion at the beginning of the 20th century, the social role of religion has been heavily emphasized.[26] The purpose of religion, and indeed the reason for its upsurge, is seen to be the promotion of social interaction and cohesion. In this view religious beliefs are regarded as synchronized with and founded upon the network of social relations in a given society. In the Durkheimian sociology of religion there is one supra-individual power on which everybody is dependent, and it is society itself.[27] It means a totality of the forms of social interaction in which the religious aspect predominates, or it pervades everything; "all that is social is religious: the two words are synonymous".[28] This view can be linked with the trend, particularly in British scholarship in religion, by the end of the 19th century: behaviour and action, i.e. ritual as a part of religion, gained prominence over belief and mythology. J. Bremmer traces this development back to the emergence of the use of the term 'ritual' in England around 1890 when W. Robertson Smith introduced it in his famous *Lectures on the Religion of the Semites* (1889). Robertson Smith writes: "The conclusion is that in the study of ancient religions we must begin, not with myth, but with ritual and traditional usage."[29]

Max Weber, too, emphasized the importance of society for religion, and his thinking continues to influence the way we approach ancient Greek religion even today.[30] Weber was

[23]   Vernant 1982, 54–55, 131.
[24]   Vernant 1982, esp. 130–131.
[25]   See Kindt 2009.

[26]   Durkheim's sociology of religion rejected earlier evolutionary theories of religion giving way to new points of view for looking at the phenomenon. For evolutionary theories of religion and the history of the science of religion or comparative religion, see esp. Sharpe 1994; Bellah 1964, 358; for the sociology of religion see Robertson 1969, 11–15.
[27]   See e.g. Durkheim 1912, esp. 493–500; also Durkheim 1969 (1912) in Robertson 1969, 49–54.
[28]   Durkheim 1984, 119. See also Murray 1990, 6.
[29]   Robertson Smith 2005, 18. See Bremmer 1998, 15–17, 19 who notes that Durkheim was explicitly influenced by Robertson Smith.
[30]   For Weber's method as a sociological historian or historical sociologist, see Nafissi 2005, esp. 120–122.

concerned with the rationalization of religious belief systems in a process in which consistency and rationality were achieved in relation to the contingencies and problems of social life. This was exemplified in his classic study on Protestantism and capitalism (1904/1905). He was interested in ancient society, and indeed wrote extensive treatises about it, in 1909[31] postulating his cyclical reading of ancient history which nevertheless exhibits an evolutionary contour in its developmental sequence containing 'stages' of evolution, particularly in the case of the city of Athens.[32] Even though Weber discussed a history of political economies, in the case of antiquity he nevertheless underlines the primacy of the political over other aspects of the society.[33] Weber's influential study *Religionssoziologie* was published in 1922, two years after his death. It is a key work that unlocks Weber's larger theoretical achievement. He studied how ideas shape human action, and developed a theory of religious change through the exploration of how religious practitioners come to develop comprehensive belief systems.[34] Weber saw this leading to class stratification which was intensified by the development of the city-state (*polis*). The exclusiveness of the *polis* from other communities is exemplified in its absolute opposition to the formation of a unified priesthood which would overarch the various groupings. Thus, the *polis* is a result of political particularism and remained essentially

a *personal* association of cultic brotherhoods around the civic god, and it was further organized internally into cultic associations of tribal, clan and domestic gods who were exclusive of one another with respect to their individual cults.[35] Weberian ideas may help us understand the dispute between models which emphasize the importance of communal or, alternatively, individual or private religious practices.

O. Murray sees two distinct readings in the tradition of theorizing on the Greek city: the Anglo-Saxon reading, which owes its process to Weber, and an alternative, holistic approach which is associated with the tradition of Durkheim. The former presents the Greek city as politically self-conscious, capable of separating out principles of state organizations and political discourse from general traditional spheres and skills of community life, like religious affairs. This led to a differentiation of activities and spheres within community life. According to Murray, in the latter, Durkheimian-influenced view there is no separation, as we have seen, between public and private activities, as the ancient city is to be understood in terms of the totality of forms of social interaction. In this model the collective consciousness was highly religious, as religion itself functioned as a factor both forming and claiming social cohesion.[36] Principally, therefore, and particularly with the role of religion in mind, the question is about rationality (conscious differentiation) *versus* religious (pervasiveness of religion). The 'holistic' model, in which religion is seen to infiltrate every section of social life and interaction, can be seen as primitivistic (though not as evolutionist) if it is contrasted, as Murray does, with the 'differentiation model' in which religion is regarded as a more separate sphere within communal activities. However, if the Greek city provided the fundamental framework in

---

[31] Weber studied the agrarian history of the ancient Greeks in his *Agrarverhältnisse im Altertum* (1909) and 'Die sozialen Gründe des Undergangs der antiken Kultur' (1896) which were both jointly published in an English edition *The Agrarian Sociology of Ancient Civilizations* (1976, 1998).

[32] For a detailed discussion, see esp. Nafissi 2005, esp. 95–120.

[33] Weber writes in *Agrarvelthältnisse* (1909, 358): "In antiquity, on the contrary, everything about *polis* from its foundation onwards was motivated by political forces." See also Nafissi 2005, 97–100.

[34] Weber 1993. See e.g. Swindler 1993, x–xiii.

[35] Weber 1993, 18, 50–51. Weber's italics.

[36] Murray 1990, 5–6.

which Greek religion operated and in which it was embedded by anchoring, legitimating, and mediating all religious activities,[37] our understanding of religion becomes a reflection of the *polis* and its institutions. Do the common divisions of Greek religious activities into individual, private, family, local or regional and civic, communal and official cults reflect our views of the Greek *polis* and its institutions rather than religion as a phenomenon and its belief system? Is political development within the *polis* thought of as rational, whereas religion and the pervasiveness of religiousness are irrational? Is there a bridge between the rational 'political animal' and the irrational *homo religiosus*? Thus, Durkheim's and Weber's theories of religion have come to represent the binary oppositions which continue to play a role in our views on religion today: Weber emphasized individual and internal meanings, whereas for Durkheim the only unit that really counted was collectivity.[38] In this sense Murray's categories do not necessarily cover the whole spectrum of interpretations, and therefore for my purposes naming them additionally 'individual' and 'collective' models is more helpful. Why have the collective/official and individual/private often been set in opposition?

Private life of *homo religiosus*– communal religion of *zoon politikon*

The private sphere is often connected with spontaneity: particularly in political theory it represents activities less organized than those of public life, in which acts are performed in the light of higher public knowledge.[39] Since antiquity, often influenced by Aristotle's views on a man as *zoon politikon*, questions have been asked as to whether, for example, the activities of voluntary associations should be considered public rather than private in nature. In other words, the public–private dichotomy has been subject to criticism.[40] After all, ancient Greek society has often been idealized as a system in which both the public and private dimension of life existed together, forming a harmonious whole. The *polis*-model of religion can be seen as one example: it offers a brilliant rationalizing frame to explain and understand ancient Greek religion. It provides a rational analogy within which religion and religious behaviour become explainable in parallel with the *polis*. A problem remains, however: how do we explain the gap between, on the one hand 'individual' or 'private', and on the other 'communal' or 'public' (i.e. *polis*) religion. It is easy to get the impression that the domain of a basic *homo religiosus*, an often irrationally, magically, even madly behaving human being, is his or her private religion. It is the sphere of *religiosity*, and in its excessive form it was already a target of sarcasm and mockery in ancient Athens. Regulated, rational, explainable religious behaviour, on the other hand, is seen to have taken place within the domain of official and communal, within the controlling framework of the *polis*. This is the sphere of *religion*. *Homo religiosus*

---

[37]   Sourvinou-Inwood 1990, 295–297.
[38]   See esp. Parkin 2002, 18–19. The author explains the reasons for Durkheim's rejection of individuality as a meaningful unit (19): in the course of their dealings with one another, individuals create a kind of synthesis or social compound, and this could resemble the way that the combination of certain chemicals produces an entirely new compound. It is this synthesis which is the very basis of social reality and hence the very object of inquiry, and since it cannot be reduced to its constituent parts, it cannot be accessible via mental or emotional stages of individual actors.

---

[39]   See e.g. Schwartz 1979, 245.
[40]   Schwartz 1979, 246, 250. One of the most obvious cases being Marxism.

does not fit easily with the rational political animal, and this controversy, I think, has led to a need to further categorize ancient Greek religion into domains which may be problematic. J.-P. Vernant exemplifies the situation in the following way: "We find a civic and political religion whose essential function is to integrate the individual who accomplishes the religious rites into the social groups to which he belongs [...] in order to elevate him to a higher sphere. [...] In contrast is a religion whose function is, to some extent, the opposite, and that can be seen as complementing the state religion. [...] This 'mystic' sense of religion, which differs so much from the communally shared Greek piety in its desire to escape, its cult of madness, *mania*, and its quest for individual salvation, manifests itself in social groups that are themselves peripheral to the city and its normal institutions".[41]

Theophrastos' description of a superstitious man (*Char.* 16) is often cited in introductions to Greek religion. It exemplifies the *homo religiosus* aspect of Greek religiousness and is also worth considering in relation to Kalaureian religion, discussed below:

> "Evidently superstition (*deisidaimonia*) would seem to be an abject fear of the supernatural.[42] The superstitious man typically tries to guard against pollution by constantly washing his hands and sprinkling himself from a sacred spring, and by chewing leaves of the sacred laurel; these precautions keep him busy all day ... He is also likely to keep purifying his house all the time, on the excuse that Hecate has come to haunt it. ... And in the case he accidentally notices somebody making a meal out of Hecate's garlic at the crossroads, he feels compelled to bathe; and after that he calls in priestesses to finish the purification by carrying herbs or a puppy around him."[43]

The superstitious man is a man whose life is permeated by religion: everything he does is a religious act. He is like Lucien Lévy-Bruhl's man with 'primitive mentality' who acts in a 'pre-logical' way. This anthropologist-philosopher who wrote extensively on "primitive mentality" in the first half of the 20th century,[44] states that among such peoples as the Arunta and the Bororo—the 'primitives'—participation is directly felt and therefore all life might be said to be religious, and yet we do not really find what we understand by 'religion'.[45] Here, participation[46] is an antithesis to categorization and, therefore, rationalizing about religion. In fact analytical distinctions are specified among

---

[41] Vernant 1990, 118–119.

[42] The word: Theophrastos was the first Greek writer to give the meaning 'superstitious' to *deisidaimonion*. The term *delia*, an abject fear regularly meant 'cowardice', but here Theophrastos renders its meaning as 'supernatural' in conjunction with *to daimonion*. See Anderson (1970, 69, n. 1), who remarks that "fear of evil spirits—not of the gods—furnishes the motivation for the superstitious man's action. He places his real trust not in religion but in magic. Presumably it was such behaviour that made *deisidaimonia* come to designate actual impiety as Christians used the term". In the early English translation of the text from the year 1698 the opening sentence of the *Deisidaimonia* reads: "We may define Superstition to be a timorous worshipping of the Deity".

[43] English translation by W. Anderson 1970.

[44] For Lévy-Bruhl's work on the subject, see esp. the first of his major works *Les fonctions mentales dans les sociétés inférieures* (1910) (published in English translation in 1926 under the somewhat misleading title *How natives think*); *La mentalité primitive* (1922), and *La mythologie primitive* (1935). Note that Lévy-Bruhl changed his views in the course of his career and was not later prepared to use without caution the terms mentioned; see Saler 1997, 46–49; Sharpe 1994, 190–192.

[45] Lévy-Bruhl 1910, esp. 76–83, 261, 301, 305. See also Saler 1997, 50–52.

[46] Participation here is a philosophical term denoting the *relation* which accounts for the togetherness of elements of diverse ontological type. See esp. Bigger 1968, 7. For Lévy-Bruhl, participation became an important concept since he claimed that participation was primary, in an experience it was first, before notification of elements between which one may see relations. See Saler 1997, 50–51.

elements, and this conceptual exercise is implicitly or explicitly related to ordering the somewhat chaotic field of activities which in this way obtains labels and specific characterizations. It may be that our need to categorize phenomena on the one hand, and our definition of the rational on the other, makes it difficult for us to place religion in the continuum between rational and irrational, since as a phenomenon it seems to include elements which defy rationality. And yet, when studying a religious system such as the Greek, when we do not know as much about the beliefs of past people as we do about the social setting of this belief-system, it is often easier to focus on the social aspect of religion. This is also reflected in the archaeological study of ancient religion, which tends to focus on ritual over religion: ritual is more concerned with action than beliefs in relation to material objects.[47] Religious beliefs and institutions become social facts, and the context of the belief-system becomes primary.[48] It seems that the object of the study through theories—like the *polis*-model—which hold that religion promotes social cohesion and solidarity, is not questioning or seeking reasons but looking for a functional explanation about the wholeness of society. This is why in our current view of ancient Greek religion there often seems to be in the background an irrationally behaving *homo religiosus* whose religion is left over and hence confined to quite ambiguous categories such as 'private cults', 'domestic cults' and 'religion of the individual'. In contrast, religious behaviour within the confines of the *polis* or the civic sphere can be analyzed and put on a par with political and historical phenomena or events.

It could be useful to regard rationality as intrinsic to holistic systems of beliefs and values, i.e. to view it in relation to a functioning cultural whole. This has, of course, been the starting point in (functionalist) anthropological study since Malinowski and other pioneers. It is noteworthy that holistic views make it possible to see rationality, including all religious behaviour, as a flexible strategy; for example, it may enable individuals or groups to transcend rules and thus refine or alter traditions by using culturally-defined situational logic.[49] Rationality can be related to the context of a culture, and, instead of analyzing meanings of rationality itself, the implicational meanings should be the focus of our attention.[50] In this respect we can consciously blur the gap between irrational *homo religiosus* and rational political animal and regard him/her as a single functioning whole whose religion was neither dominantly *polis*-religion nor isolated individual business. This has an inevitable effect on our conceptualization of ancient Greek religion: the borders between different religious activities are crossed over; *polis*-religion may appear within domains which are not traditional fields of the city-state, and within the arenas of traditional *polis* activities there may arise activities which stem from non-political spheres of life. Walter Burkert's analysis is one example of this kind of alternative interpretation. He writes about the controversy between the amorality of the Greek gods and the required civic reverence within the confines of religion in the Greek city-state. Since *polis*-religion was to secure morality and enforce the effectiveness of laws which were to guarantee good social conduct, the irrational element (which Burkert sees as necessary) was left to exist in religious rituals. In them, traces of amorality (violence, bloodshed, even madness) could manifest themselves

---

[47] See e.g. Insoll 2004b, 3 and 2007, 2 and also 2004a, 12 noting that ritual is often treated as the description for religion itself in archaeological parlance.
[48] Trigg 1998, 30–31.

[49] Cf. Buchowski 1997, 27; Jensen 1997, 19–21.
[50] Buchowski 1997, 37–40. Buchowski describes this method as "relativizing rationality historically within a cultural context". For the theme of rationality in relation to religion, see Trigg 1998, esp. 43–47.

regardless of society's attempts to restrict human 'beastlike' behaviour by creating a realm of solidarity through religious sanctification.[51] Thus, according to Burkert both individual and communal religious actions retained traces of the irrational. In some of his writings Burkert reduces these traces to biology, thus abandoning the discourse between rationality and irrationality almost altogether. Transmitting fear and attempts to overcome basic anxiety makes religion which "keeps to the tracks of biology".[52]

What does the sanctuary of Poseidon at Kalaureia have to tell us about its cultic life in the light of the speculations above on private and individual religion and about religion and rationality within existing models explaining ancient Greek religion?

Kalaureia and the *polis*-model: From amphictyony to *asylia* and ritual dining

Strabo (8.6.14) mentions that the Kalaureian sanctuary was an asylum sacred to Poseidon or an inviolable temple of Poseidon, who gained the island from Leto in exchange for Delos.[53]

Kalaureia appears also in Plutarch's list of inviolable temples attacked by the Cilician pirates (Plut., *Pomp*. 24.6). The best-known asylum seeker at Kalaureia is Demosthenes.[54] In fact, his reputation as the most famous *hiketes* of the Kalaureian sanctuary may have prompted, or at least increased, the reputation of Kalaureia as a known place of asylum.[55] Kalaureia was also the seat of an amphictyony, an association of neighbouring states to defend and maintain a common religious sanctuary or shrine in the name of shared common interest. Information about this is largely based again on Strab. 8.6.14, who informs us that the members of the Kalaureian amphictyony were Prasiai, Nauplia, Minyan Orchomenos, Athens, Aigina, Epidauros and Hermione. The date of origin of the Kalaureian amphictyony remains in dispute: it is either placed in the Mycenaean period, in the eighth century, or within the years between 680 and 650 BC.[56]

In the case of particularly Classical and post-Classical Kalaureia the two phenomena, *asylia* and amphictyony, might have been connected with each other: the analogy of Delos and Kalaureia may well have been based on the role of both as places of amphictyony, and known places of asylum, therefore providing a mythological reference point to connect the two. Referring to the (relatively late) year AD 22, Tacitus (*Ann*. 3.60–63) writes that the right to receive refugees was enjoyed only by

---

[51] Burkert 1985, 246–249.
[52] Burkert 1996, 19–23, 25, 30–33. In Burkert 1985 (218) he wrote: "The conglomerate of tradition which constitutes religion perhaps owes its particular form less to the cunning of reason than to the cunning of biology."
[53] The theme of the exchange of Delos and Kalaureia appears also in Callim., Frg. 593, Paus. 2.33.2 and Ephoros (*FGrH* 70f 150). For the oracular reply on Delos and Kalaureia, see Parke & Wormell 1956, 125–126, no. 314. For the term *asylia*, see e.g. Schlesinger 1933, 2–6, 28–38 who distinguishes two different types of *asyliai*: one concerning an individual ("personal *asylia*") and another connected with a place, such as a sanctuary (53–68); cf. Gauthier 1972, 209–230 who distinguishes a personal *asylia* (also as a social formulaic mode of behaviour), *asylia* granted to a community, and *asylia* of sanctuaries and villages consecrated to a divinity); see also Chaniotis 1996, 66. For Kalaureia as a "doubtful case" of declared inviolability, see Rigsby 1996, 90–91.

[54] See above, n. 1.
[55] Hjohlman in Penttinen & Mylona, forthcoming.
[56] A summary of the discussion is provided esp. by Kelly 1966, 113–115 (with references) who strongly supports the last possibility on the grounds of the archaeological material excavated by Wide and Kjellberg in 1894; for more recent studies, see Tausend 1992, 12–19; Schumacher 1993, 74–76; Mylonopoulos 2003, 427–431 (pointing out phases of increased importance of the amphictyony after the Late Geometric period); Figueira 2004, 622–623; Hjohlman in Penttinen & Mylona, forthcoming. The existence of the Kalaureian amphictyony during Hellenistic times can be attested on the grounds of an inscription, *IG* IV 842.

temples of special veneration, and it was a right formally granted by the king of the amphictyonic council. The two phenomena are political in many of their aspects,[57] and the connection of granting *asylia* to temples has been seen as evidence of a city's and its territory's neutrality, particularly during Hellenistic times when civic inviolability guaranteed immunity from war. Rigsby regards this as generally a tool of foreign relations, an affair of international relations among sovereign states.[58] Commercial interests may have had a role to play as well: asylum granted by the sanctuary guaranteed security for trade relations and revenues for the city (port taxes, for example), particularly as people from even distant places could meet during the festivals connected with these sanctuaries.[59] Whether for political, mercantile or religious reasons *asylia*-declarations of sanctuaries themselves in any case increased in number during the Hellenistic period.[60] In the case of Kalaureia we may ask here what was the role of the *polis* as regards the sanctuary's right of *asylia*, and what was its connection with religion and cultic life, and how can we discern

this in the archaeological material? Therefore, we should also look at the matter from the point of view of the *polis*-model in the study of Greek religion.

Kalaureia gained independence from Troizen in 323 BC after having been under Troizen's control during the fifth century and at times attacked and occupied by Athens during the Peloponnesian war.[61] The city of the Kalaureians is mentioned in the Hellenistic inscriptions from the sanctuary, thus confirming the sovereignty and existence of the *polis* of Kalaureia.[62] The sanctuary of Poseidon peaked during the Hellenistic period when a number of building programmes were carried out within the *temenos*. It is situated in a relatively isolated topographical position.[63] Apart from its remote geographical setting, suitable for asylum purposes, the sanctuary could have been associated with the sanctuary of Troizen specifically as a place of asylum: at least Demosthenes went first to Troizen on his flight from Athens, but fearing that Troizen was not safe enough he went over to Kalaureia.[64] In trying to understand the cultic life of the sanctuary its right for *asylia* appears more illuminating if

---

[57] The religious aspect of the amphictyony has been underlined by some scholars; see e.g. Tausend 1992, 19, 58–60, who regards the function of the league which Kalaureia led as purely religious and centred around the sanctuary of Poseidon, and Penrose Harland 1925, 166, 168 who claims that it was originally a purely religious association, and political as well as economic aspects developed later.
[58] Rigsby 1996, 4–5.
[59] Gauthier 1972, 227–228; Sinn 1996, 67–69 and Figueira 2004, 623 underline this aspect of asylum at sanctuaries with references to religious festivals on Delos termed a "kind of commercial affair" (*panegyris emporikon pragma*) by Strabo (10.5.4) and at Thermos as "a splendid fair and festival" by Polybius (5.8.5). See also Mylonopoulos 2003, 430–431 underlining the commercial aspect centred around the maritime role of Poseidon, which united the sanctuaries dependent on seafaring.
[60] Rigsby 1996, 3, who shows that the declarations of inviolability concentrate on a coherent historical period from 260 BC to the senatorial review of the status in AD 22–23.

[61] This is attested by the inscription *IG* IV 839. Thuc. 5.18.7 mentions Kalaureia in connection with the Peloponnesian War; see also Hjohlman in Penttinen & Mylona, forthcoming.
[62] *IG* IV 839 (4th cent. BC), ll. 4,7 and *IG* IV 848, l. 3 (197–159 BC); see Hjohlman in Penttinen & Mylona, forthcoming. Furthermore, *IG* IV 842, (second century BC) from Kalaureia has it on the last line (9) Ἀμφικτ[ύοσι]; see also Penrose Harland 1925, 161; Figueira 2004, 622; Hjohlman in Penttinen & Mylona, forthcoming.
[63] It has been noted that this is often the case with Poseidon sanctuaries: his sanctuaries are remarkably frequently located outside the city, and as such they stand in contrast particularly to those of Athena. See Schumacher 1993, 80–82.
[64] Dem. *Epist.* 2.20 in which he explains that "from Troizen I changed my residence and now have my quarters in the sanctuary of Poseidon in Kaulaureia ... from [where] I look across the sea every day to my native land ...".

seen in connection with its role as the seat of an amphictyony. It has been pointed out that as a phenomenon *asylia* has to be seen against the background of the absence of international civic law in the Greek world.[65] That is, reasons for it lie in the particularism of *poleis*, whose law, rules and regulations did not intersect even though supra- and intra-regional contacts certainly existed and were necessary. This was understandably also one of the reasons for the formation of amphictyonies, and in the case of Kalaureia the aims could have been mercantile as well as military.[66] Even though sanctuaries could also themselves declare *asyla* in order, for example, to seek protection against piracy, the amphictyony aspect also includes a function as a tool in organizing 'international' relations among sovereign states, as Rigsby interprets the role of amphictyony particularly in Hellenistic contexts. In the case of Kalaureia this indicates that even though its clear regional character and ambiguous status in relation to *polis*, the *asylia* and amphictyony functions made the sanctuary international and hence brought it beyond its local bounds, bringing an element of encounters of people and communities, a certain 'multiculturality' to the life of the sanctuary.

Both *asylia* and amphictyony can, therefore, be regarded in terms of political and cultural relations for which religion plays a sanctifying role. *Asylia*, however, could also have been an individual matter (Demosthenes certainly sought protection at Kalaureia as an individual regardless of his political motivations), and in these cases it becomes strongly linked with *hiketeia*, supplication.[67] This is an individual aspect of religion, and could be connected with expressing personal *pistis* within a fixed ritual in which a particular physical contact (with an altar, a statue of a deity, etc.) was of ritual significance. A *hiketes* is a person who approaches (a deity) as a suppliant, who by means of prayer and other ritual gestures establishes a physical contact with a representation of divinity, sacred ground, or altar.[68] As a social communication code the phenomenon is known in Homeric texts, drama and historical writing,[69] and it is suggested that within strictly religious contexts of the everyday it was mostly addressed to deities who were close to the common people and could be trusted to hear their invocations as helpers where aid was needed.[70] Thus, apart from the political and communal aspect of *asylia* it had, as a phenomenon, a personal aspect, and these two were fundamentally intertwined. In principle all the sanctuaries accommodated *hikesia* as they were themselves inviolable, properties of gods, but some of them were better suited or more reputable as particular asylum sanctuaries.[71] The sanctuary

---

[65] Schumacher 1993, 69 (with references); Sinn 1993, 90 stating that *asylia* provided a compensation for the lack of a law code common to all of the Greeks.
[66] Cf. Schumacher 1993, 75.
[67] For the concept, see esp. Gould 1973, 75ff.; Gould 2001, 76ff.; Freyburger 1988, 501–525; also Rigsby 1996, 10–11; Sinn 1993, 91; 1996, 68. Gould under-

lines the reciprocity of relations in the phenomenon which he regards as much a social as a religious institution permeating the modes of (reciprocal) social encounters of the Greeks (esp. 93–94), and sees physical contact with sacred objects and with parts of the body as essential in this behaviour.
[68] Gould 1973, 75–78, 94; Sinn 1993, 91; 1996, 68.
[69] The study of supplication has, in fact, concentrated on Homer and tragedy following Gould's seminal study (1973); see Crotty 1994 for supplication in Homer; Gödde 2000 for the phenomenon in drama, particularly in Aischylos; also Naiden 2002, 185–186, 189.
[70] van Straten 1974, 183–184; see also Motte 1986, 125.
[71] Generally every sanctuary was inviolable, and a personal inviolability could have been guaranteed by a sanctuary official to an individual. See e.g. Schlesinger 1933, 2, 52; Gauthier 1972, 226–227, 229; Chaniotis 1996, 66. *Hiketeria* denotes to the right to accept suppliants (Chaniotis 1996, 68 and n. 12) apart from meaning an olive branch held by the suppliants as markers of their condition, *LSJ*, s.v. ἱκετηρία. See also Gould 2001, 76ff. with comments on Burkert's ethological explanation of *hiketeia* and *hiketeria*. Chanio-

at Kalaureia was certainly one of those which could grant *asylia*. As it was not the easiest to reach, a *hiketes* had to make efforts to seek refuge there, particularly as there was a degree of reciprocity implied: it was not wholly guaranteed that *asylia* be granted to a *hiketes* as it depended on the decision made by a priest.[72] On the other hand, *asylia* not only protected individuals (by definition sanctuaries themselves were protected by *asylia*), but was also politically motivated, and as such could be used for more 'mundane' purposes, like protecting political or mercantile interests. A sanctuary on a summit generally served a wider audience than that of a *polis* due to its territorial inclusiveness.[73] These sanctuaries could have been associated with motion and encounters, people travelling through a mountain pass where frontier sanctuaries provided places of meeting.[74] This also means that the role of *polis* as an identifier of sanctuaries' character and role was less determinate than in cases where one *polis* was closely associated with its sanctuary. Moreover, the Kalaureian sanctuary peaked in the early Hellenistic period when new aspects such as interregional and international contacts began to infiltrate religion.[75] This could have resulted in various scenarios, both positive and negative. Tacitus (*Ann* 3.60–63) tells us of Tiberius' actions in investigating the demands of the provinces in AD 22. He mentions that "in the Greek cities license and impunity in establishing sanctuaries were on the increase. Temples were

thronged with the vilest of the slaves; the same refuge screened the debtor against his creditor, as well as men suspected of capital offences. No authority was strong enough to check the turbulence of a people which protected the crimes of men as much as the worship of the gods".[76] Though this quote describes a later period it nevertheless gives hints about the possible consequences of *asylia* as a provider of protection: unlimited application of the *asylia* as divine law could clash with profane law and the interests of secular authorities and institutions such as the city-state.[77] The anarchy at certain Greek sanctuaries in the Hellenistic era has been connected with the "degradation of religious sentiments" and increased use for political gain at the expense of accommodating people's religious needs.[78] This view of Hellenistic times is somewhat anachronistic, particularly when reflected in the interpretations of the concept of *asylia* itself. Rather than separating different *asyliai* and seeing them either as a *religious* institution protecting individuals or as a *political* institution protecting communities (sanctuaries, cities) and their interests, commercial as well as military, it is worth remembering that both these aspects were intermingled similarly, as private/individual religiousness and official/communal religion were interlinked. Thus, *asylia* and *polis* were naturally closely related,

---

tis 1996 (esp. 83–85) assumes that the efforts to limit automatic right for *asylia* to all increased in time from the Classical period onwards, and each individual case was submitted to a close examination by sacred and civil authorities.

[72] See e.g. Rigsby 1996, 10; Sinn 1993, 91–93. Chaniotis 1996, 70ff. elaborates the methods and cases for getting rid of suppliants and removing them from sanctuaries, also Gould 1973, 82–85.

[73] Langdon 2000, 462.

[74] Cole 2000, 467; Sinn 1996, 71.

[75] For the theme see Pakkanen 1996.

[76] Similar description also in Strab. 14.1.23. See also Chaniotis 1996, 69.

[77] See Chaniotis 1996, 69ff. for the inherent conflict between divine and secular authority.

[78] Gauthier 1972, 228–228 with well-grounded reservations. Chaniotis 1996, esp. 82, 84–86, regards changing attitudes to *asylia* from being regarded as an institution based on unlimited divine law to becoming dependent on considerations of moral and legal conditions as reflections on changes in attitudes to religious purity and *miasma*. A moral underlining of, for example, 'purity of heart' or the right state of mind of those visiting sanctuaries certainly starts appearing in inscriptions towards the latter part of the Hellenistic period; see e.g. *LSS* 108 (Rhodes, first century AD) and 118 (Cyrene, second century AD).

and *asylia* had both moral and political implications. At Kalaureia we have a potentially old
amphictyony, and a possibly increasing role
of *asylia* under the umbrella of amphictyony.
They guaranteed a framework for both individual and communal religious activities to be
carried out, but also provided a safe place for
mercantile and political encounters between
communities and individuals. What is, then,
the role of *polis* and how can it help us in understanding what went on at the sanctuary of
Kalaureia?

Reflecting earlier notions about the *polis*-
model, we can try to figure out a multi-layered
view in which a social and political framework,
which might as well be called a *polis*-frame,
existed on one level, but it was not necessarily the most determining factor on Kalaureia's
religious scene. It merely provided a confined
or safe space for the evolution of Kalaureian
cultic life, particularly in the name of the amphictyony and *asylia*. Within and beyond that
there were aspects of religion which developed
quite independently of *polis* intervention, or
even without its active participation. These
were, for example, largely *hiketeia* to a place
of asylum, which could have resulted in differing, even ambiguous and unofficial ritual
activities that took place in the sanctuary. One
example of this is dining, or ritual dining, in
its varying forms. It combines the sacral and
profane functions of the sanctuary, and in the
case of Kalaureia it leads us not only to think
about differences between communal and
individual religion, but also to consider the
interplay between official and private religion
and religiousness. Given that the sanctuary received visitors and seekers of asylum from far
away places, particularly during the Hellenistic
era, we may also assume an encounter between
various dietary and ritual customs. I shall now
look at an example provided by the material
evidence found at the site.

(RITUAL) DINING

Building D is situated on the southern edge of
the sanctuary close to its entrance. For a potential cult building it is unconventional in form,
consisting of a main building on the north side
and an open irregular courtyard on the southern side.[79] The finds from the construction fill,
datable to the last quarter of the fourth century
BC, give a *terminus post quem* for the construction of the new structure at the very end of the
fourth century BC.[80] Particularly the triangular area west of Building D has yielded material[81] which shows that dining was the main
activity here, especially in the Hellenistic period.[82] Hence the deposit, the material from
which will be briefly discussed here, is called
the 'dining deposit'. The aforementioned corner of the area produced a deposit containing
a huge number of potsherds, organic material,
bones of a large number of animals including
fish, molluscs, carbonized seeds and charcoal.[83]

---

[79] New extensive excavations of the area have been
carried out from 1997 to 2003; Wells *et al.* 2003 and
2005. The architecture of the building is currently being studied by Jari Pakkanen, for whose comments I am
grateful.

[80] Wells *et al.* 2003, 79–80.

[81] Some of the material was probably thrown over the
low southern wall of the triangle, though the majority
was found deposited within it; Penttinen in Wells *et al.*
2005, 166; Wells *et al.* 2008, 87 (*ibid.* 45: "A huge deposition of dining refuse was excavated outside the southwestern corner of the building."); also recent discussion
with A. Penttinen.

[82] For the Hellenistic finds, see Wells *et al.* 2005, 165–
166. Dining as a predominant activity within Building
D has also been attested for the Archaic period: Wells
et al. 2008, 78. It should be noted that continuity, even
relative continuity is, however, a different and meth-
odologically challenging question, see Pakkanen 2000–
2001, 74–81 for methodology for studying continuity
of cult.

[83] Animal remains discovered and studied from this
assemblage consist of several thousand bones, most of
them of medium and large mammals; there are also
more than fifteen hundred fish bones, a few from birds,
and about a dozen from small mammals. The deposit
also produced several seashells. The fish bone assem-

The deposition date was narrowed down to *c.* 165–160 BC based on pottery analysis.[84] The pottery is generally domestic in character and the vessels do not exhibit a great variety of shapes, although those for drinking, preparing and serving of food outnumber all other categories. The finds were almost consistently of Hellenistic date.[85] D. Mylona observes that the animal remains deposited in the triangular area west of Building D seem to have been rapidly accumulated and buried. The bones did not remain exposed, either to weathering or to scavengers. This is evidenced by their sharp breakage lines and the preservation of even the small, fragile fish elements. All the fish present in the assemblage, apart from the large migratory species, such as tuna, seem to have been brought onto the site and consumed whole. The pottery found in this deposit is also characterized by clean, unworn breaks, therefore it is well preserved within a relatively undisturbed deposit.[86] Thus, archaeologically speaking, the activity related to eating here seems to have been an individual occurrence; we are talking about a feast of massive proportions after which the activities within this particular area ceased altogether.[87]

A cistern was excavated in 2004 immediately to the north of the northwest corner of Building D.[88] It proved to be Archaic in date in terms of construction,[89] but yielded interesting remains which may be related to the finds from the dining deposit as they seem to have associations with eating and dining. This old cistern appears to have been filled with material, the largest accumulation of which is datable to the late Hellenistic period, to *c.* 50 BC.[90] The cistern is, in fact, one of the most enigmatic features of the Kalaureian site. Although the remains of organic material it produced are from the late Hellenistic period, not from the early phase of the period as in the case of the dining deposit, the two still share some analogous and rather unusual characteristics which have to do with eating and feasting. The deposit in the cistern can also be regarded as a single deposition.[91] It is worth underlining, however, that archaeologically the two deposits are separate features. The remains of dogs and snakes are a special characteristic of the late Hellenistic accumulation of the fill in the cistern: Mylona observes that among the identifiable bones two thirds are dog bones and they fall into two main groups, namely adults and newborns. Remains of at least eight adult dogs survive with all anatomical parts present, though not in the form of complete skeletons. Some of them bear disarticulation and skinning cut marks. There are remains of at least 26 puppies and they come in a variety of sizes; the remains of whole carcasses are preserved although in disarticulated form. Some of the adult dog bones are burnt. Mylona suggests that various adult dogs were eaten af-

---

blage from the dining deposit is particularly rich in variation and species: at least 18 different species of fish, probably more, seem to have been consumed there. See Wells *et al.* 2008, 45, 88 and Mylona in Penttinen & Mylona, forthcoming. All details of animal bone analysis have been kindly provided by Dimitra Mylona who is responsible for their study, analysis and interpretation. My thanks go to her.

[84] Wells *et al.* 2005, 169, 179, 182; Wells *et al.* 2008, 45.

[85] Wells *et al.* 2005, 169–178, fig. 47, Appendix 2 and catalogue of finds from the area D03 (the southwestern corner of the building).

[86] Mylona in Penttinen & Mylona, forthcoming.

[87] Wells *et al.* 2005, 166–168, 182; Wells *et al.* 2008, 48.

[88] Wells *et al.* 2005, 180; Wells *et al.* 2008, 36–38, 48, 64, 89–89. The finds from the cistern have not yet been published, though see Wells *et al.* 2008, 90. I am here, as in the case of the dining deposit, relying on information provided to me by Dimitra Mylona concerning the animal finds, and on personal communication with Arto Penttinen and Berit Wells concerning other archaeological features.

[89] Wells *et al.* 2005, 180.

[90] Wells *et al.* 2008, 37–38, 41 (fig. 14).

[91] Wells *et al.* 2008, 48.

ter they had been skinned in the vicinity of the cistern. Their preparation probably involved char-grilling portions of the meat. After the consumption of the meat and probably the temporary deposition of the bones in a hearth, the dog bones and possibly their skins were deposited in the cistern. The puppies might also have been cut into pieces, because they do not seem to have been char-grilled like the adults. Instead, they were either cooked in another manner (boiled, stewed), or left uncooked. The cistern deposit also produced a very large number of snake remains, some of large species over 1.5 metres long. It appears that various snakes were killed, cut into pieces and exposed to fire with their flesh still on. Mylona thinks it possible that the snake flesh was also consumed; she proposes a scenario in which an old cistern was filled up with soil and stones, and when the filling was almost complete a mass of animal remains was thrown in. In addition to dogs, puppies and snakes there were parts of two horses, a pig and a piglet, a cow, four sheep and goats, alongside birds, eggs, fish, frogs and a pile of sea-shells. On top of all this a number of complete or broken glass vessels were thrown into the cistern. Berit Wells has pointed out another possibility for the sequence of events: the material may have accumulated at another cult place elsewhere, and was finally thrown into the cistern at the sanctuary.[92]

I have interpreted this dining material elsewhere from an anthropological perspective considering the distinction between ritual and cult.[93] Here, instead, I would like to draw attention to the difficulty of trying to fit our material into the *polis*-centred view of religion. Namely, we are not looking at 'classical' Classical religion, but a local, regional and supra-regional setting during the Hellenistic period. It is clear that the *polis*-model does not suit this situation

very well. It does, however, lead us to ask questions which are important from the point of view of the changing role of *polis* and its relation to the sanctuary. Could the phenomenon of dining at the Kalaureian sanctuary have been linked with the sanctuary's *asylia* and, particularly, to *hiketeia*? And if so, what does it tell us about the encounter between official *polis*-religion and that of the private sphere?

It has been pointed out that certain pairs of Greek terms usually connected with religion may reveal quite different conceptions beneath their merely apparent similarity. For example, *hosia* was used for things that were sanctioned or permitted by divine law, and the word was, in fact, often associated with *dikaion*, sanctioned by human law; hence the expression *ta hosia kai ta dikaia*, 'things of divine and human ordinance'.[94] Thus the term derives its meaning from being opposed to *hieron* which as a term is closest in meaning to our understanding of 'sacred' or 'holy': normal days are *hosiai* in contrast to festival days, the permitted portion of sacrificial meat that was reserved for human consumption was *he hosie kre(a)on* (*Hymn. Hom. Merc.* 130). The term *hosion* signifies the condition of liberation from the sacred, i.e. being desacralized after sacralization, and therefore free of religious domain.[95] In connection with rights to enter sanctuary spaces *hosion* could signify that it is not religiously offensive for everyone to have free access to sacred space.[96] Similar semantic duplicity exists too, for example, in a pair of words such as *hagos*, 'to be revered, sacred', and *agos*, 'impurity' (defilement,

---

[92]   Wells, personal communication.
[93]   Pakkanen 2008a, 250–255; *eadem* 2008b.

[94]   Esp. Plat., *Resp.* 301d; *Leg.* 1.631b; *Grg.* 507b; *Euthphr.* 11e and 12a.
[95]   *Hosia* is discussed by esp. Jeanmaire 1945, 66–86 (for the double meaning, esp. 67–70, for *hosie kreaon*, 78–82); see also Burkert 1985, 269–270; Parker 1983, 338; Bruit-Zaidman & Schmitt-Pantel 1992, 9. Bremmer 1998, 28, 30 reminds us that the term does not mean 'profane', but rather non-holy behaviour.
[96]   Parker 1983, 338 (in connection with *hosion* in the Cyrenean cathartic law (see n. 103 below).

close in meaning to *miasma*).[97] Close interaction between 'sacred'—particularly in its more common forms *hagnos* or a newer counterpart *hagios*—and its opposites such as *agos* and *miasma*, implies that the purification of defilement was of immense importance in Greek religious thinking and was also manifested at a practical level in the demarcation of ritual and cult from profane. "Sacred and dangerous are close together", W. Burkert reminds us.[98] J. Bremmer suggests that this very combination of sanctity and purity led to the introduction of the word *hagios*, first attested by Simonides (frg. 519.9).[99] Thus, pollution may in fact conceal a positive religious quality within the framework of the ritual system and the prescriptions which govern the functioning of rituals.[100] If we suppose that the remains of the meal that took place in the triangular area just outside Building D, or those deposited in the cistern, are remains of a sacrificial meal, why were they thrown to the marginal space on the border between the sacred and profane? Might it be possible to construct a scenario in which our meal could have taken place within the confines of sacred space, *temenos* or *hieron*,[101] but as it was not a proper, regulated sacred meal, the remnants of

it had to be thrown away from the sacred place: deities could not get their share of an 'improper' meal and the purity of the place had to be restored, *agos* had to be driven out?[102] In order to restore sanctity, ritual repair had to take place to purify space which had been polluted in one way or another. We could also speculate on who the *deipnosophistai* (translated here as 'gastronomers') might have been. Could they have been people like Tacitus' robbers and criminals entering the sanctuary and putting on a massive meal, shaking up all the categories, carrying out a blasphemous and polluting act at the sanctuary comparable to the meals described by Demosthenes in his speech against Conon: a bunch of young men used to devour the foot set out for Hekate at the crossroads (*hekataia*), indulge in eating the testicles of the pigs which were sacrificed for purifying the space before the assembly convened?[103] This play with ideas would necessitate revisiting conceptions of purity and exclusions in the granting of *asylia*: the two seem to be interrelated, as the Greek moral code prohibited murderers and those accused of crime from setting foot in sanctuaries and

---

[97] E.g. Fehrle 1910, 45; Moulinier 1952, esp. 15–16 (denying the connection between the roots *ag-* and *hag-*); Vernant 1990, 121, 128, 135–138; Parker 1983, 5–6; Bremmer 1998, 28–29.

[98] Burkert 1985, 271; see also Pakkanen 2008a, 252–254. Mary Douglas was one of the first scholars to pay attention to the significant role of pollution in framing social structures and boundaries in terms of their inner danger in her well-known work *Purity and danger. An analysis of the concepts of pollution and taboo* (1966).

[99] Bremmer 1998, 29.

[100] Vernant 1990, 138; Bruit-Zaidman & Schmitt-Pantel 1992, 10.

[101] The term *hieron* was used for a sacred enclosure or place; the term *temenos* designates a 'piece of land marked off from common use and dedicated to a divinity', thus being 'place set aside' and deriving from the verb *temno* 'to cut off' (from the secular). See *LSJ*, s.v. ἱερός, τέμενος, τέμνω; also Bruit-Zaidman & Schmitt-Pantel 1992, 55; Pedley 2005, 29.

[102] *Agos elaunein*, cf. Thuc. 1.126.2 and 12; 1.127.1; 1.128.1–2; 2.13.1 where *agos* denotes 'curse'; also Soph., *OT* 971, 1246.

[103] Dem., 54.39. For *hekataia* see esp. Parker 1983, 30, 229; Johnston 1991, 219–220; Cole 2004, 47–48; Zografou 2005, 197–201, 205. Plut., *Mor.* 280B–C (*Quaest. Rom.* 68, 111) tells that dogs are carried out to Hekate with the other *katharsia* (purification refuse), and that puppies were used in cleansing rituals themselves (*periskylakismos*). A Hippocratic writer wrote about *katharmata* (used in healing purposes): "They bury some of them in the ground, they throw some into the sea, and others they carry off to the mountains where nobody can touch or tread on them" (Hippoc. *Morb. Sacr.*, 1.99–102). Johnston 1991, 221, following Parker 1983, reminds us that even though *katharmata* are sometimes identified with *hekataia*, they still should not be confused with *oksythymia*, polluted refuse from house purification rituals. Parker 1983, 30, suggests that the constituents of the 'meals' (*deipna*) were *magides*, puppies, and perhaps certain fish, and discusses the laws restricting where *katharmata* might be thrown out. See also Zografou 2005, 197.

sacred places.[104] Whether the moral code met the realities in which the sacred and secular encountered each other, as in the cases of administering sanctuaries, is questionable. Nevertheless, within the scheme of private–public religion it is possible to imagine that a syntagmatic occurrence of a spontaneous ritual act could have been carried out within the confines of regulated cultic life at Kalaureia. Unregulated, unofficially oriented ritual acts could have taken place within the confines of an established cult setting. Ritual purity had to be restored, however, after such an act. Sacralized items, such as components of (unregulated) meals had to be desacralized in order to maintain equilibrium and minimize the dangers entailed by crossing the borders, both symbolically and physically. Yet, this still does not transform these undertakings into purely secular activities, but rather shows us the reverse of the same ritual act. It just blurs most of the borders between communal, official and state-oriented and private, individual and pious Greek religion.

In this light we might reconsider our general premises for making a distinction between the public and private spheres of life. Aristotle contrasted the *polis* with the lesser forms of human association: man can individuate himself only within the political community under the umbrella of the *polis* institutions: public and private spheres are distinct, but the former is higher than the latter.[105] This legacy may have influenced the way we tend to regard official cultic activities tied to the *polis* as more important and indeed as providers of our frame of reference for interpreting ancient Greek religion. It seems that our modern understanding of religion has been driven outwards towards polity, state, nations and the complex we call 'culture'.[106] We hear of "religious refiguration of power politics", the proliferation of devotional organizations at the margins of state, etc. C. Geertz observed that "[particularly in the post-Wall world] the projection of religiously defined groupings and loyalties onto all aspects of collective life from the family and neighbourhood outward is, thus, a part of general movement ...".[107] Still, it would be possible to rethink the situation and regard the private sphere of religious life as deeply permeated into and intermingled with the public sphere; so much so that it is sometimes impossible to separate one from another, similarly as religion and *polis* have been seen as fundamentally interdependent in the study of Greek religion.

PETRA PAKKANEN
Swedish Institute at Athens
petra.pakkanen@sia.gr

---

[104] The sanctuaries had measures against convicts and criminals either lodging in them or seeking *asylia* in them. Plat., *Leg.* 9.871a and 874b and Arist., [*Ath. Pol.*] 57.4 state that an accused man is debarred from sacred places. This theme is, of course, well known in tragedy. See also Chaniotis 1996, 74. Two epigraphical examples may be mentioned here: 1) *LSS* 112: a second-century BC inscription from the sanctuary at Lato in Crete stating regulations regarding exclusion from the sanctuary for murderers and those guilty of violent attacks (entrance was also prohibited to dogs [IVB] due to a danger of bites which were regarded a cause for *miasma*); 2) an early Hellenistic cathartic law from Cyrene (*LSS* 115 = *SEG* 9 72; detailed discussion in Parker 1983, 332–351) lists a number of cases that cause impurity (disease, death, sexual contact with a woman in the daytime, contact with a corpse, presence in a house where a woman has been in labour or has miscarried etc.) and states rules for those entering the sanctuary for purification from *miasma*; part of the text concerns suppliants and their different status depending on whether they come from abroad, are initiated or non-initiated, or have committed murder (they are not allowed to enter the sanctuary).

---

[105] See e.g. Schwartz 1979, 253, 256, 262.
[106] Geertz 2000, 169–170.
[107] Geertz 2000, 176, also 184: "The movement of religious identities and religious issues toward the center of social, political, and even economic life may be widespread and growing, in both scale and significance."

Bibliography

Allen 1978 — D. Allen, *Structure and creativity in religion. Hermeneutics in Mircea Eliade's phenomenology and new directions* (Religion and Reason, 14), Haag, Paris & New York 1978.

Anderson 1970 — W. Anderson, *Theophrastus, The character sketches, translated with notes and introductory essays by W. Anderson,* Iowa 1970.

Bellah 1964 — R.N. Bellah, 'Religious evolution', *American Sociological Review* 29, 1964, 358–374.

Bigger 1968 — C.P. Bigger, *Participation. A platonic inquiry,* Baton Rouge 1968.

Buchowski 1997 — M. Buchowski, 'Anti anti-rationalism: Anthropology and the rationality of human acts', in *Rationality and the study of religion* (Acta Jutlandica, 72:1, Theology Series), eds. J.S. Jensen & L.H. Martin, Aarhus & Oxford 1997, 24–43.

Bruit-Zaidman & Schmitt-Pantel 1992 — L. Bruit-Zaidman & P. Schmitt-Pantel, *Religion in the ancient Greek city,* Cambridge 1992.

Bremmer 1998 — J.N. Bremmer, '"Religion", "ritual" and the opposition "sacred vs. profane". Notes towards a terminological genealogy', in *Ansichten griechisher Rituale. Geburtstags-Symposium für Walter Burkert, Castelen bei Basel 15. Bis 18. März 1996,* ed. F. Graf, Stuttgart & Leipzig 1998, 9–32.

Burkert 1985 — W. Burkert, *Greek religion. Archaic and Classical,* Cambridge, Mass. 1985.

Burkert 1996 — W. Burkert, *Creation of the sacred. Tracks of biology in early religions,* Cambridge, Mass. & London 1996.

Callinicos 1995 — A. Callinicos, *Theories and narratives. Reflections on the philosophy of history,* Durham 1995.

Chaniotis 1996 — A. Chaniotis, 'Conflicting authorities. *Asylia* between secular and divine law in the Classical and Hellenistic *poleis*', *Kernos* 9, 1996, 65–86.

Cole 2000 — S.G. Cole, 'Landscapes of Artemis', *CW* 93:5, 2000, 471–481.

Cole 2004 — S.G. Cole, *Landscapes, gender and ritual space. The ancient Greek experience,* Berkeley & Los Angeles 2004.

Comstock 1984 — W.R. Comstock, 'Toward open definitions of religion', *Journal of American Academy of Religion* 52(3), 1984, 499–517.

Crotty 1994 — K. Crotty, *The poetics of supplication. Homer's* Iliad *and* Odyssey, Ithaca 1994.

DiCenso 1990 — J. DiCenso, *Hermeneutics and the disclosure of truth. A study in the work of Heidegger, Gadamer and Ricoeur,* Charlottesville 1990.

Dodds 1951 — E.R. Dodds, *The Greeks and the irrational,* Berkeley & Los Angeles 1951.

Douglas 1966 — M. Douglas, *Purity and danger. An analysis of the concepts of pollution and taboo,* London 1966.

Durkheim 1912   E. Durkheim, *Les formes élémentaires de la vie réligieuse. Le système totémique en Australie* (Travaux de l'Année sociologique), Paris 1912.

Durkheim 1969   E. Durkheim, 'The social foundations of religion', in *Sociology of religion*, ed. R. Robertson, Harmondsworth 1969, 42–54.

Durkheim 1984   E. Durkheim, *The division of labour in society, with an introduction by L. Coser, translated by W.D. Halls*, London 1984.

Fehrle 1910   E. Fehrle, *Die kultische Keuschheit im Altertum* (Religionsgeschichtliche Versuche und Vorarbeiten, 6), Gießen 1910.

Figueira 2004   T.J. Figueira, 'The Saronic Gulf', in *An inventory of Archaic and Classical poleis*, eds. M.H. Hansen & T.H. Nielsen, Oxford & New York 2004, 620–623.

Freyburger 1988   G. Freyburger, 'Supplication grecque et supplication romaine', *Latomus* 47, 1988, 501–526.

Fuchs 1979   W. Fuchs, 'Fragen der archäologischen Hermeneutik in der ersten Hälfte des 19. Jahrhunderts', in *Philologie und Hermeneutik im 19. Jahrhundert. Zur Geschichte und Methodologie der Geisteswissenschaften*, eds. H. Flashar, K. Gründer & A. Horstmann, Göttingen 1979, 201–224.

Gadamer 1989   H.-G. Gadamer, *Truth and method*, London 1989[2].

Gauthier 1972   P. Gauthier, *Symbola. Les étrangers et la justice dans les cités grecques* (Annales de l'est, 42), Nancy 1972.

Geertz 2000   C. Geertz, *Available light. Anthropological reflections on philosophical topics*, Princeton, N.J. 2000.

Gödde 2000   S. Gödde, *Das Drama der Hikesie. Ritual und Rhetorik in Aischylos' 'Hiketiden'* (Orbis Antiquus, 35), Münster 2000.

Grondin 2003   J. Grondin, *Hans-Georg Gadamer. A biography*, New Haven & London 2003.

Gould 1973   J. Gould, 'Hiketeia', *JHS* 93, 1973, 74–103.

Gould 2001   J. Gould, 'Addendum (2000)' [to 'Hiketeia' 1973], in *Myth, ritual, memory, and exchange. Essays in Greek literature and culture*, ed. J. Gould, Oxford 2001, 74–77.

Hamilakis 2007   Y. Hamilakis, *The nation and its ruins. Antiquity, archaeology, and national imagination in Greece*, Oxford 2007.

Hodder 1992   I. Hodder, 'Interpretive archaeology and its role', in *Theory and practice in archaeology*, ed. I. Hodder, London & New York 1992, 183–200.

Insoll 2004a   T. Insoll, *Archaeology, ritual, religion*, London & New York 2004.

Insoll 2004b   T. Insoll, 'Are archaeologists afraid of gods? Some thoughts on archaeology and religion', in *Belief in the past. The proceedings of the 2002 Manchester conference on archaeology and religion* (BAR-IS, 1212), ed. T. Insoll, Oxford 2004, 1–6.

Insoll 2007 — T. Insoll, 'Introduction: The archaeology of world religion', in *Archaeology and world religion*, ed. T. Insoll, London & New York 2007, 1–32.

Jeanmaire 1945 — H. Jeanmaire, 'Le substantif *hosia* at sa signification comme terme technique dans le vocabulaire religieux', *RÉG* 58, 1945, 66–89.

Jensen 1997 — J.S. Jensen, 'Rationality and the study of religion: Introduction', in *Rationality and the study of religion* (Acta Jutlandica, 72:1, Theology Series), eds. J.S. Jensen & L.H. Martin, Aarhus & Oxford 1997, 9–23.

Johnston 1991 — S.I. Johnston, 'Crossroads', *ZPE* 88, 1991, 217–224.

Kelly 1966 — T. Kelly, 'The Calaurian amphictiony', *AJA* 70, 1966, 113–121.

Kindt 2009 — J. Kindt, 'Polis religion – A critical appreciation', *Kernos* 22, 2009, 9–34.

Koselleck 2002 — R. Koselleck, *The practice of conceptual history. Timing history, spacing concepts*, translated by T.S. Presner *et al.*, Stanford 2002.

Kuhn 1996 — T.S. Kuhn, *The structure of scientific revolutions*, Chicago & London 1996[3].

Langdon 2000 — M.K. Langdon, 'Mountains in Greek religion', *CW* 93:5, 2000, 461–470.

Lakoff 1987 — G. Lakoff, *Women, fire, and dangerous things. What categories reveal about the mind*, Chicago & London 1987.

Lévy-Bruhl 1910 — L. Lévy-Bruhl, *Les fonctions mentales dans les sociétés inférieures*, Paris 1910.

LSS — F. Sokolowski, *Lois sacrées des cités grecques. Supplément* (Travaux et mémoires des anciennes membres étrangers de l'école et divers savants, 11), Paris 1962.

Motte 1986 — A. Motte, 'L'expression du sacré dans la réligion grecque', in *L'Expression du sacré dans les grandes réligions* 3 (Homo Religiosus, 3), ed. J. Ries, Louvain-la-Neuve 1986, 109–256.

Moulinier 1952 — L. Moulinier, *Le pur et l'impur dans la pensée des grecs d'Homère à Aristote* (Études et commentaires, 12), Paris 1952.

Murray 1990 — O. Murray, 'Cities of reason', in *The Greek city from Homer to Alexander*, eds. O. Murray & S. Price, Oxford 1990, 1–25.

Mylonopoulos 2003 — J. Mylonopoulos, *Heiligtümer und Kulte des Poseidon auf der Peloponnes* (Kernos, Suppl. 13), Liège 2003.

Nafissi 2005 — M. Nafissi, *Ancient Athens & modern ideology. Value theory and evidence in historical sciences. Max Weber, Karl Polanyi & Moses Finley*, London 2005.

Naiden 2002 — F.S. Naiden, 'Review of S. Gödde, *Das Drama der Hikesie. Ritual und Rhetorik in Aischylos' "Hiketiden"* (Orbis Antiquus, 35), Münster (Aschendorff) 2000', *CP* 97:2, 2002, 185–189.

Nock 1961   A.D. Nock, 'Foreword', *Greek Folk Religion. With a foreword to the Torchbook edition by Arthur Darby Nock*, New York 1961, xiii–xvii.

Pakkanen 1996   P. Pakkanen, *Interpreting early Hellenistic religion. A study based on the mystery cult of Demeter and the cult of Isis* (Papers and Monographs of the Finnish Institute at Athens, 3), Helsinki 1996.

Pakkanen 2000–2001   P. Pakkanen, 'The relationship between continuity and change in Dark Age Greek religion. A methodological study', *OpAth* 25–26, 2000–2001, 71–88.

Pakkanen 2008a   P. Pakkanen, 'From *polis* to borders: Demarcation of social and ritual space in the sanctuary of Poseidon at Kalaureia, Greece', *Temenos. Nordic Journal of Comparative Religion* 44:2, 2008, 233–262.

Pakkanen 2008b   P. Pakkanen, 'Defining cult site. Theoretical observations on the nature of religion at the sanctuary of Kalaureia on Poros, Greece', *Anodos. Studies of the Ancient World* 6–7, 2006–2007 (2008), 343–345.

Parke & Wormell 1956   H.W. Parke & D.E.W. Wormell, *The Delphic oracle* 2. *The oracular responses*, Oxford 1956.

Parker 1983   R. Parker, *Miasma. Pollution and purification in early Greek religion*, Oxford 1983.

Parkin 2002   F. Parkin, *Max Weber*, revised edition, London & New York 2002².

Pedley 2005   J. Pedley, *Sanctuaries and the sacred in the ancient Greek world*, Cambridge 2005.

Penttinen & Mylona forthcoming   *Daily life and physical environment at the sanctuary of Poseidon at Kalaureia*, eds. A. Penttinen & D. Mylona, forthcoming in *ActaAth*.

Penrose Harland 1925   J. Penrose Harland, 'The Calaurian amphictyony', *AJA* 29:2, 1925, 160–171.

Price 1999   S. Price, *Religions of the ancient Greece*, Cambridge 1999.

Ricœur 1974   P. Ricœur, *The conflict of interpretations. Essays in hermeneutics*, ed. D. Ihde, Paris 1974.

Rigsby 1996   K.J. Rigsby, *Asylia. Territorial inviolability in the Hellenistic world*, Berkeley, Los Angeles & London 1996.

Robertson 1969   R. Robertson, 'Introduction', in *Sociology of religion*, ed. R. Robertson, Harmondsworth 1969, 11–16.

Robertson Smith 2005   W. Robertson Smith, *Lectures on the religion of the Semites, Elibron Classics replica edition of the 1894 edition*, London 2005³.

Saler 1997   B. Saler, 'Lévy-Bruhl, participation, and rationality', in *Rationality and the study of religion* (Acta Jutlandica, 72:1, Theology Series), eds. J.S. Jensen & L.H. Martin, Aarhus & Oxford 1997, 44–64.

Schlesinger 1933   E. Schlesinger, *Die griechische Asylie*, Gießen 1933.

Schmitt-Pantel 1990   P. Schmitt-Pantel, 'Collective activities and the political in the Greek city', in *The Greek city from Homer to Alexander*, eds. O. Murray & S. Price, Oxford 1990, 199–213.

Schumacher 1993   R.W.M. Schumacher, 'Three related sanctuaries of Poseidon: Geraistos, Kalaureia and Tainaron', in *Greek sanctuaries. New approaches*, eds. N. Marinatos & R. Hägg, London 1993, 62–87.

Schwartz 1979   N.L. Schwartz, 'Distinction between public and private life. Marx on the *zōon politikon*', *Political Theory* 7:2, 1979, 245–266.

Seebohm 2004   T.M. Seebohm, *Hermeneutics. Method and methodology* (Contributions to Phenomenology, 50), Dordrecht, Boston & London 2004.

Sharpe 1994   E.J. Sharpe, *Comparative religion. A history*, London 1994².

Sherratt 2006   Y. Sherratt, *Continental philosophy of social science. Hermeneutics, genealogy and critical theory from ancient Greece to the twenty-first century*, Cambridge 2006.

Sinn 1993   U. Sinn, 'Greek sanctuaries as places of refuge', in *Greek sanctuaries. New approaches*, eds. N. Marinatos & R. Hägg, London & New York 1993, 88–109.

Sinn 1996   U. Sinn, 'The influence of Greek sanctuaries on the consolidation of economic power', in *Religion and power in the ancient Greek world. Proceedings of the Uppsala Symposium 1993* (Boreas. Acta Universitatis Upsaliensis, 24), eds. P. Hellström & B. Alroth, Uppsala 1996, 67–74.

Sourvinou-Inwood 1990   C. Sourvinou-Inwood, 'What is *Polis* religion?', in *The Greek city from Homer to Alexander*, eds. O. Murray & S. Price, Oxford 1990, 295–232.

van Straten 1974   F.T. van Straten, 'Did the Greeks kneel before their gods?', *BABesch* 49, 1974, 159–189.

Swindler 1993   A. Swindler, 'Foreword', in M. Weber, *Religionssoziologie*, 1993⁴, ix–xvii.

Tausend 1992   K. Tausend, *Amphiktyonie und Symmachie. Formen zwischenstaatlicher Beziehungen im archaischen Griechenland* (Historia Einzelschriften, 74), Stuttgart 1992.

Trigg 1998   R. Trigg, *Rationality of religion. Does faith need reason?*, Oxford & Malden, Mass. 1998.

Trigger 1989   B.G. Trigger, *A history of archaeological thought*, Cambridge 1989.

Vernant 1982   J.-P. Vernant, *The origins of Greek thought*, Ithaca 1982.

Vernant 1990   J.-P. Vernant, *Myth and society in ancient Greece*, New York 1990.

Weber 1993 (1922)   M. Weber, *Religionssoziologie, 4th edition, revised by J. Winckelmann, Introduction by T. Parsons with a new Foreword by A. Swindler. English translation by E. Fischoff 1963², Boston 1993⁴.

Wells *et al.* 2003   B. Wells, A. Penttinen & M.-F. Billot, 'Investigations in the Sanctuary of Poseidon on Kalaureia, 1997–2001', *OpAth* 28, 2003, 29–87.

Wells *et al.* 2005   B. Wells, A. Penttinen, J. Hjohlman, E. Savini & K. Göransson, 'The Kalaureia Excavation Project: The 2003 season', *OpAth* 30, 2005, 127–215.

Wells *et al.* 2008   B. Wells, A. Penttinen, J. Hjohlman with contributions by K. Göransson, A. Karivieri & D. Trifirò, 'The Kalaureia Excavation Project: The 2004 and 2005 seasons', *OpAth* 31–32, 2006–2007, 31–129.

Wide & Kjellberg 1894   S. Wide & L. Kjellberg, 'Ausgrabungen auf Kalaureia', *AM* 19, 1894, 248–282.

Zografou 2005   A. Zografou, 'Élimination rituelle et sacrifice an Grèce ancienne', in *La cuisine et l'autel. Les sacrifices en questions dans les sociétés de la Méditerranée ancienne* (Bibliothèque de l'école des hautes études sciences religieuses, 124), eds. S. Georgoudi, S. & R. Koch Piettre & F. Schmidt, Turnhout 2005, 197–212.

ATHENA KAVOULAKI

Observations on the meaning and practice of Greek *pompe* (procession)

Abstract

Processions in the Greek world belong to a category of phenomena which are particularly complicated due to their broad distribution and occurrence and to the multiplicity and diversity of the sources. As a result, constant revision of terms and categories is necessary, since the complex material may yield better results under careful scrutiny and the application of different methods and approaches. The present discussion will approach the broad issue of processions from specific angles: it will focus on processions in the domain of the worship of gods (and heroes) in the context of the Archaic and Classical Greek *polis*, and will examine terminology and basic linguistic usage (generally and in the context of specific historical sources). The foregrounding of the interesting semantic facets of the related terms and their usage in the poetic, mythico-ritual context of Greek tragedy will be at the centre of the following discussion (with Aischylos' *Eumenides* as a primary example). As the analysis will point out, the related language seems to constitute a kind of filter through which the mythical patterns and historical practices may interact and associate.

Introduction

In recent times scholarship has become well aware of the fact that the analysis of ancient phenomena in and through modern terms involves considerable dangers of distortion, misunderstanding or oversight. For this reason the re-examination of terms and categories and the re-evaluation or renewal of methods and approaches are central issues of concern for the current study of antiquity. Such an attitude is all the more necessary when the phenomena under study seem to be particularly complicated due to their broad distribution and occurrence, and due to the multiplicity and diversity of the sources. Processions in the Greek world (by which I mean ritual[1] movements through space with a clear destination and a ritual purpose) certainly belong to this category, since they constitute a phenomenon with a remarkable distribution throughout Greek history and regions. Their presence seems to have characterized almost every communal ritual occasion; they were included in the programme of all major religious festivals[2] and they would form

---

[1] The term "ritual" can be conventionally used to describe a repetitive, differentiated, strategic action with a performative and "alerting" quality and with a compulsory nature for its practitioners, relating to the divine; on these aspects (from an anthropological perspective), see especially Bell 1992; cf. also Grimes 1982; Smith 1982; Parkin 1992. For useful definitions of ritual in works of classical scholars, see Burkert 1979, 35–52 and 1985, 23–34 (communicative aspect); Seaford 1994, xi–xix (social effects); Bremmer 1994, 38–39.

[2] In the cultic domain the presence of processional rituals was remarkable. More than 250 cases of periodic processions for gods and heroes seem to have been attested: see the long list in Bömer 1952; Pfuhl (1900) discusses 35 Athenian examples (excluding *theoriai*). See also the list in Parker 2005, 178, n. 2.

the basic part of all major *rites de passage* (such as funerals or weddings)[3]. Such a widespread phenomenon, attested through a variety of different sources, exemplifies a richness of forms and functions that can hardly be dealt with uniformly, if justice to distinct features is to be done. At the same time its analysis requires extensive treatment of individual features as well as of possible interrelations. In parallel to all this, constant revision of terms and categories is also necessary, since the complex material may yield better results under careful scrutiny and the application of different methods and approaches.

In accordance with these basic considerations, the present discussion will approach the broad issue of processions from specific angles: it will focus on cultic processions, i.e. processions in the domain of the worship of gods and heroes in the context of the Archaic and Classical Greek *polis*, and will examine terminology and basic linguistic usage, an aspect that figures less prominently in modern analyses.[4] Such an approach seems to be all the more necessary, since the basic term used in Greek to denote the category "procession" (i.e. the term πομπή) seems to differ—in its basic semantic core—from its standard modern renderings (procession, *Prozession*, *festlicher Zug*, etc.). The foregrounding of the interesting semantic facets of the related terms and their usage in the poetic, mythico-ritual context of Greek tragedy will be at the centre of the following discussion. The analysis will ultimately illuminate the issue of whether a rigid distinction between the technical and the non-technical use of the term *pompe* (a distinction which has been generally taken for granted) may be obtained or not. As the evidence seems to suggest, instead of being a barrier or a dividing line, the related language seems to constitute a kind of filter through which the mythical patterns and historical practices may interact and associate.

Analyzing terms and texts

The category "procession" normally refers to a spatially progressive, bipolar movement, which usually involves a plurality of people. In traditional societies (either ancient or modern) such movements take place on ritual occasions and are generally defined by tradition in the context of which their performance is compulsory. They are executed along a defined route (outside an agonistic temporal frame) and for a specific purpose, i.e. for reasons of performing a significant act (e.g. sacrifice) or of accomplishing a significant change at the end of the journey (e.g. entering into marital status). These basic characteristics differentiate a procession from other movements such as ordinary walking or the locally-fixed dance. At the same time these features constitute a generalized and non-culturally specific pattern, which is strongly evocative of the Greek processional pattern (featuring in numerous festivals throughout the Greek world, as mentioned above)[5] but also largely familiar across space and time. As such it has even been conjectured for Paleolithic times by the anthropologist and theatre expert R. Schechner. As he writes, "understood as a coherent system [processions] form

---

3 See for example Kavoulaki 1997 & 2005 (with earlier bibliography).
4 Such as—for example—Bömer 1952 (with earlier bibliography); Burkert 1985, 56–57, 99–101; Graf 1996; Seaford 1996; Kavoulaki 1999; True *et al.* 2005; Parker 2005, 162f., 178–180 (Parker is right to insist on the meaning of *pompai* as "escortings").

5 The example that almost automatically springs to mind is probably the Panathenaic procession (and the Parthenon frieze must have helped in this direction). For a less well-known but surely grand-scale processional pattern (amply documented both historically and archaeologically) outside Athens see the Apollo feast in Miletos, on which Herda in this volume and Herda 2006. See also the references in the preceding notes.

a bipolar model of the performances that took place in the ceremonial centers which arose at points where Paleolithic hunting bands, moving across the terrain on their seasonal treks, met", and he continues (*ibid.*), "in a procession the event moves along a prescribed path, spectators gather along the route, and at appointed places the procession halts and performances are played".[6]

As Schechner openly admits, his conjectures of Paleolithic performances are not totally theoretical constructs but intersect with ethnographic data from traditional communities and—he adds—"both bear on patterns within modern and postmodern societies".[7] From this broad anthropological perspective the processional pattern (in its basic and abstract form) seems to emerge as a universal (or almost universal) phenomenon,[8] a fact which may explain its amazing diffusion in human space and time. At the same time, however, numerous and multifarious re-workings and variations developed out of basic characteristics create a rich and complex picture not only among different cultures but even within the same culture.

Under these conditions, factors which may allow us to acquire a more culturally specific view of the phenomenon prove to be important and require particular emphasis and attention. Language is certainly basic among these factors, as it constitutes a primary means of articulating, defining and communicating experience in a particular cultural context.

In Archaic and Classical times and on a synchronic level, the Greek language system seems to have included two basic and recurrent terms

to refer to this important cultural category,[9] namely the terms πρόσοδος and πομπή. The latter of these terms may sound more familiar due to its diachronic presence in Greek as well as to its borrowing by the Latin (*pompa*) which allowed its survival in European languages in various derivative forms (e.g. English pompous, etc.).[10] On a synchronic level, however, both terms were valid to denote processional movements in a cultic context, and in some passages both appear as alternatives or in combination.[11]

---

[6] Schechner 1988, 158–159.
[7] Schechner 1988, 157.
[8] There are some tribes in which the concept of processions does not seem to exist (Kirschenblatt-Gimblett & McNamara 1985, 3), but the issue is contested; the problem may lie in our system of classification: Turnbull 1985.

[9] For other terms, less standard and more restricted in usage, see below.
[10] Chantraine 1968, s.v. πέμπω, "πομπή ... est passé avec cette valeur en latin, puis en français etc.".
[11] E.g. Pl. *Leg.* 796c: πᾶσι θεοῖς προσόδους τε καὶ πομπὰς ποιουμένους (an instance of rhetorical amplification apparently). In the famous lyric portrait that Aristophanes draws for Athens in the parodos of his *Clouds* (Ar. *Nub.* 299–313), πρόσοδοι μακάρων ἱερώταται ("most sacred processions for the gods", 308) constitute one of the markers of Athenian *eusebeia*. The common and wide usage of the term πρόσοδος is probably best witnessed in the survival of the word προσόδιον as the standard term for a song sung in sacred processions. Thus in Aristophanes' *Birds* the two words are used interchangeably: the priest is invited πέμψοντα τὴν πομπήν (Ar. *Av.* 849) and the chorus wholeheartedly wishes to take part, προσόδια μεγάλα σεμνὰ προσιέναι (853). Occasionally some other terms seem to crop up in the surviving texts, e.g. Hdt. 2.58: πανηγύριας δὲ ἄρα καὶ πομπὰς καὶ προσαγωγάς. Πανήγυρις is a collective term (comprising both procession and sacrifice), while προσαγωγή is obviously parallel to πρόσοδος; in this case the emphasis falls on leading or carrying (people, animals, objects, etc.) through the use of the verb ἄγω. It should be stressed that ἄγω is one of the *basic* terms to denote ritual movements in Greek (which has not, however, produced a standard noun comparable in frequency to πομπή); see e.g. phrases such as ἄγω ἑκατόμβην (Hdt. 4. 150), χοροὺς ἀνάγω (Thuc. 3. 104), πομπὴν ἄγω (Plut. *Lyc.* 30; cf. βοήγια in *Syll.*³ 577. 72), etc. Note also various derivatives and compounds of the verb ἄγω as part of procession-related vocabulary, such as the κλειδὸς πομπή or ἀγωγή in Lagina for Hekate, the εἰσαγωγή ἀπὸ τῆς ἐσχάρας, καταγώγια etc. Apart from the verbs πέμπω and ἄγω, there is also the verb φέρω which produces derivatives and compounds that are used in related contexts, e.g. θαλλοφόροι, ὑδριαφόροι, σκαφηφόροι (denoting duties performed in processions). Outside the context of divine worship there are

The two terms, however, are different morphologically and etymologically and constitute semantic variants of the same notion or category. In this respect the different semantic connotations of each term may disclose distinct and perhaps complementary aspects of the phenomenon (the processional activity) that were given due acknowledgment and expression.

As regards the term πρόσοδος (a compound derived from the preposition πρός meaning "towards" and the noun ὁδός, "route", "way"), the semasiological aspect that is highlighted is that of moving forward, of moving *towards* something. This element seems to be the distinctive feature of the term *prosodos*, as ancient lexicographers acknowledged. The Byzantine lexicon *Suda*, for example, glosses the term *prosodos* (sounding unfamiliar by that time) not simply through its synonym *pompai* but through the expression προσαγόμεναι πομπαί ("they called by this term [sc. πρόσοδος] the προσαγόμεναι πομπαί"),[12] i.e. the *pompai* that were carried along, that were on the move. The element, thus, "movement forward", "movement towards" seems to characterize particularly the Greek term *prosodos* and brings to the fore the targeted goal of the action which invests the whole procedure with meaning. The combination of the preposition πρός with the element ὁδός underlines the effort and the action of the human agent to reach a symbolic centre, a ritually significant point of arrival. In the context of cult (in which the term is used) *prosodos* seems to exemplify the turning towards the divine, the redirection of human action towards a different (from ordinary) centre.

The semantic emphasis on movement and direction apparent in the term *prosodos* seems to be prominent also in the modern English term "procession" (used indifferently for the translation of both terms, i.e. for both *pompe* and *prosodos*). Procession means literally a movement forward, as it ultimately stems from the Latin verb *procedo* "to go forward, to advance" (and the Latin noun *processio* means actually "advance"). The modern term "procession" seems thus to correspond more closely to the term *prosodos,* while *pompe* seems to have further connotations (which tend to be obliterated if the two terms are always equated in translation).

The term πομπή derives from the verb πέμπω and is a so-called *nomen actionis*, i.e. a noun which denotes the action signified by the verb, according to a pattern that can be discerned in such pairs of words as σπένδω-σπονδή, χέω-χοή, μέλπω-μολπή, τρέπω-τροπή etc.[13] According to the *LSJ*[9] (s.v.), the verb πέμπω means first of all "send" (used in a number of variations, e.g. send something, send forth or dismiss, send as a present, send up or produce) and secondly, "conduct", "escort". The two meanings are not unrelated. "Send" signifies "to cause to go", in other words to propel in a particular direction, to set something in motion with an aim, in order to reach a destination.[14] This aspect of ultimate goal or destination is highlighted in the use of send. The second meaning of πέμπω, "to conduct, to escort", brings to the fore the means by which this destination is reached, it particular-

---

also other related terms used for different types of processions, e.g. ἐκφορά (funeral procession), γάμος, ἔκδοσις or periphrastically ἄγω νύμφην/γυναῖκα (for wedding processions; cf. ἄγομαι γυναῖκα for getting married), etc.

[12] *Suda* s.v. προσόδια· ἀπὸ τῶν προσόδων. οὕτω δὲ ἔλεγον τὰς προσαγομένας τοῖς θεοῖς πομπάς.

[13] Risch 1974, 10. Schwyzer (1959, 422) classifies such nouns into the category "Wurzelnomen" but tentatively surmises that the *nomina agentis* may have preceded in formation the *nomina actionis*. The order of formation is usually taken to be the reverse; but the two are not always distinguishable; see Chantraine 1968 s.v. πέμπω; Frisk 1973 s.v. πέμπω.

[14] See *Oxford English Dictionary* (online) s.v. send; it is interesting that "send" etymologically goes back to the root of the old English word "sithe" meaning "path, way" (*ibid.*). Unfortunately the original (Indo-European or other) etymology and meaning of πέμπω are unknown (Chantraine 1968 s.v. πέμπω "il n'est pas possible de trouver une étymologie i.-e. plausible").

izes the meaning of direction by highlighting the mediation, the actual presence and accompaniment that leads to the destination. If πέμπω implies purposeful motion ("send"), it can also signify the means by which this purpose is fulfilled. This meaning of πέμπω as "escort, direct" is prominent when the verb is used in contexts of processional action. In such contexts πέμπω (which is a transitive verb, governing an accusative) recurrently takes as an object words which refer to offerings, symbols etc. taken along in processions (e.g. Hdt. 2.49: φαλλὸς Διονύσῳ πεμπόμενος, Thgn. 1.777: πέμπωσιν ἑκατόμβας, [Arist.] *Mir. ausc.* 844b: θυσία ... ἐν ᾗ πέμπουσιν αἶγα, Dem. 3.31.6: Βοηδρόμια πέμψωσιν (cf. Dion. Hal. *Dem.* 21.73: βοΐδια), Plut. *Ant.* 56. 9: βοῦν, Athen. 10. 84.24: βοῦν, Diod. 12.30.4: ἱερεῖα, Strab. 10.5.2: θεωροὺς καὶ θυσίας etc.; cf. Pind. fr. 193: ἑορτὰ βουπομπός). All these objects are not simply sent to their ultimate destination (although destination is the goal of the whole action) but are also accompanied, escorted and directed to this ultimate point.

Πομπή as a *nomen actionis* is formed from the root (πεμπ-/πομπ-) that is also found in the verb and thus expresses and concretizes the meaning of the verb (πέμπω); so it denotes "despatch" and "escort" in various contexts (e.g. Hom. *Il.* 3.116, 6.171, *Od.* 6.20; Aesch. *Ag.* 748; Pind. *Pyth.* 4.164; Thuc. 1.129; Eur. *IA* 651; Xen. *Mem.* 1.4.15 etc.) and relates to the term *prosodos* as regards the semantic aspect of goal or destination that is also prominent in the notions of sending and escorting. As *pompe* gradually appeared in contexts related to periodically repeated and traditionally sanctioned processional action, it acquired a more marked sense; it was not simply an ordinary escort but a *ritual*, solemn escort, a "procession" (in current, modern terms). It is important to underline that even in these "marked" contexts the semantic aspect "escort" is not neutralized or eliminated, despite the impression one may get from modern lexicographical and bibliographical sources which tend to present the two

meanings (and usages, i.e. "escort" and "procession") as distinct and apparently unrelated.[15] It is noteworthy, however, that on a synchronic level, the Archaic and Classical Greek language system contained and used concurrently (and complementarily) two ritual terms (i.e. *pompe* and *prosodos*) with slightly different semantic connotations (as noted above). *Prosodos* clearly emphasizes movement and route taken ("procession"); *pompe*, on the other hand, points at movement and goal but from the point of view of mediation, of conducting, of the route set out and led along. The particular semantic content that the term seems to carry is most likely retained, even when it is "technically" used: it is characteristic that in "technical" contexts πομπή often appears as an internal accusative of the verb πέμπειν which unambiguously signifies and highlights "escort" in such contexts (as noted above).[16] The phrase πέμπειν πομπήν became recurrent and was established as the technical term for conducting a procession (e.g. Hdt. 5.56; Thuc. 6.56; Ar. *Ach.* 248–49, *Av.* 849; Xen. *Eq. mag.* 2. 1 ; Arist. [*Ath. Pol.*] 57.1.6 ; Polyaenus *Strat.* 5.5.2 ; Aen. Tact. *Poliorc.* 17.5 ; Paus. 8.39.6, etc.). As an internal object of the verb from which it is directly derived, the noun πομπή obviously and unambiguously emphasizes the basic meaning of the verb that it complements. Such a structure leaves no doubt that the noun shares in the meaning of the verb when it appears in analogous contexts. Thus, the aspect "escort" is retained and not eliminated when *pompe* appears as a marked term in its technical, ritual usage.

---

[15] See e.g. *LSJ*⁹ s.v. πομπή; Bömer 1952, 1879–1882.

[16] Chantraine 1968 s.v. πέμπω (880) acknowledges the standard meaning of *pempo* as "despatch, escort", while underlining the particular, "narrow" sense of *pompe* (without commenting on the recurrent, technical use of the phrase πέμπειν πομπήν): "Πέμπω signifiant 'envoyer, accompagner', πομπή a pris le sens particulier et important de 'procession, défilé.'"

This conclusion reached on grammatical grounds may prove helpful for a better understanding of some historical sources which attest processional ceremonies. At the beginning of Plato's *Republic*, for example, we have an account (brief but still valuable) of the first public celebration (ἑορτή) in honour of Bendis,[17] an account which is presented as Socrates' personal experience (327a–b). As we are informed, the philosopher (along with many Athenians apparently) went down to Piraeus to attend the *heorte*. The location is justified since the temple of Bendis was in Piraeus.[18] Apparently the whole celebration would culminate with sacrifices at the temple of the Thracian goddess.[19] In the Platonic account, however, Socrates omits other details and focuses on his impression of the processional spectacle of the *heorte* which was apparently the highlight of the event.[20] The interesting feature in Socrates' description is his explicit reference not to one but to two *pompai*, one of the Thracians and one of the *epichorioi*. Since the *heorte* was a single event, which Socrates attended at the same venue and on the same day, the two *pompai* imply two distinct escortings, two group formations participating in the *heorte* and heading to the same destination (the temple of Bendis). There is no doubt that the Thracian cult and personnel were

given considerable public prestige through this ceremony: they were allowed to parade prominently and thus to mark the Attic land ritually (starting from the Prytaneion, as other sources attest,[21] a fact which underlines the acceptance of the cult by the *polis*). Nonetheless, at the crucial time of the festival the groups of adherents (to the cult of Bendis) formed two distinct escorting groups and thus the *epichorioi*, the local Athenian adherents (organized probably in a group of *orgeones*) were visibly distinct from— though together with—the foreign adherents.

A comparable arrangement of distinct escorts termed *pompai* during the same sacrificial event is also described by pseudo-Andokides in his narration of Alkibiades' notoriously provocative behaviour at Olympia ([Andoc.] 4.29). As the speaker of the oration notes with indignation, on the day of the great sacrifice[22] Alkibiades participated with an escorting group (*pompe*) decked with the *polis' pompeia* which he had appropriated;[23] he thus surpassed in grandeur the escorting group of the *polis* which also took part in the great event ("τὴν πομπὴν τὴν κοινὴν ὁρῶντες ὑστέραν οὖσαν τῆς Ἀλκιβιάδου τοῖς τούτου πομπείοις χρῆσθαι ἐνόμιζον ἡμᾶς", [Andoc.] 4.29.9–10; cf. Plut. *Alc.* 13.3). The broader frame of the major event allowed the formation of and accommodated units ar-

---

[17] The cult of Bendis seems to have been introduced in 429 BC (*IG* I[3] 136) but at the dramatic date of the *Republic* (410) the festival was first publicly organized: see Parker 1996, 170–175 for a succinct discussion of issues relating to the cult (with earlier bibliography). See also Pache 2001.

[18] And apparently constituted a well-known location: Xen. *Hell.* 2.4.11.

[19] Of which we hear in inscriptions such as *IG* II[2] 1496; Parker 1996, 173.

[20] Pl. *Resp.* 327a: "καὶ ἄμα τὴν ἑορτὴν βουλόμενος θεάσασθαι τίνα τρόπον ποιήσουσιν ἅτε νῦν πρῶτον ἄγοντες· καλὴ μὲν οὖν μοι καὶ ἡ τῶν ἐπιχωρίων πομπὴ ἔδοξε εἶναι, οὐ μέντοι ἧττον ἐφαίνετο πρέπειν ἣν οἱ Θρᾷκες ἔπεμπον. Προσευξάμενοι δὲ καὶ θεωρήσαντες ἀπῇμεν πρὸς τὸ ἄστυ". On Socrates' theoria here and its philosophical implications, see Nightingale 2005.

[21] *IG* II[2] 1283.

[22] By stating ἡ θυσία (τῇ προτεραίᾳ τῆς θυσίας) the text points at a well-known and distinctive event which must be the great hecatomb sacrifice to Zeus (and it is thus understood by historians, e.g. Miller [2003, 18], who also offers a reconstruction of the festival [9–40, and earlier bibliography]). It is in the context of this major event that both Alkibiades' and the *polis'* sacrifice seem to have taken place according to the text.

[23] [Andoc.] 4.29.5–6: "ἐξηπάτησε καὶ ἀποδοῦναι οὐκ ἤθελε, βουλόμενος τῇ ὑστεραίᾳ πρότερος τῆς πόλεως χρήσασθαι τοῖς χρυσοῖς χερνίβοις καὶ θυμιατηρίοις". The general term for the ritual objects (κανᾶ, χερνίβια, θυμιατήρια, etc.) carried in the processions was πομπεῖα. In Athens a specially erected building called Πομπεῖον (Pompeion) would house processional equipment (at least from the beginning of the fourth century).

ranged and conducted towards the same goal. Directing and directed towards the same destination, these groupings and more precisely these escortings were set on the move, forming the *prosodos* to the altar.

The indicative examples mentioned above seem to support the grammatical structure and use of the terms πέμπω and πομπή. The semantic aspect "conduct, escort" that is encapsulated in the term *pompe* does not seem to be neutralized when the term is used in a more "focused" or marked way. The "technical" usage of the term seems to presuppose and to develop on the basis of the central significance of the word. The procedure by which the term came to be gradually used in specific ritual contexts may be difficult to detect historically, and the surviving literary sources may not be always helpful. Ancient Greeks themselves seem to have been more puzzled about the establishment and development of the phenomenon of processions (rather than its linguistic denotation). Herodotos conjectured foreign influences (2.58), while others adduced remote origins and mythical beginnings connected with Crete: Didymos Chalcenteros in particular seems to have attributed the introduction of the custom to the mythical king Melisseus (according to Lactant. *Div. Inst.* I 22.19). The antiquity of the ritual in the Greek world is beyond any doubt (according to historical/archaeological sources),[24] and this situation may be reflected in mythical conjectural patterns and accounts such as that of Didymos. However, no substantial evidence seems to emerge from such scattered views; what they do indicate, nonetheless, is the Greek attempt to associate the mythical and

the exotic with the historical, contemporary experience and phenomena. A privileged "place" in which such associations could be made was certainly poetry. Aetiological myths constituted a basic feature in early poetic compositions and although no myth about *pompai* (in their generalized form and application) seems to have survived directly, Didymos' reference to Melisseus' myth was included in his commentary on the poetic compositions of Pindar ("in libris ἐξηγήσεως Πινδαρικῆς", according to Lactantius *l.c.*; also Didymos Chalcenteros II.5.14 Schmidt). In Classical times more particularly, tragedy seems to have been a primary forum for mythical narration and explanation; it thus offered ample room for the accommodation and reinterpretation of ritual phenomena which are presented therein (as it has often been observed) in *statu nascendi,* originating in the mythical past but foreboding developments familiar to the play's contemporary audience. In such a context in which word and action combine for the rearticulation and reinterpretation of mythical (or mythicized) events, meanings and terms are explored and even recreated. Language seems to be tested anew in the context of action, so that the multiple levels of significance are better illuminated, re-associated and reworked.

A most eloquent example of a multivalent usage of the terms πέμπω and πομπή that can be used as a test case and can illuminate the discussion is provided by the end of Aischylos' *Eumenides*: an end which constitutes the magnificent finale of the whole *Oresteia* trilogy and seems to function as an aetiological act for the celebration of the Semnai and even of Athens more broadly.

It is well known that the exodos of Aischylos' *Eumenides* takes the form of a sacred procession played out in full on stage (1003–1047). The goddess Athena, who presided over the juridical procedures earlier in the play (566–777), now organizes and supervises the ceremonial part, so that the Erinyes/Semnai are

---

[24] Neolithic evidence points towards phallic processions (Burkert 1985, 52), while in Minoan-Mycenaean iconography, processions are extensively portrayed (see e.g. Marinatos 1986, 25–27, 32–35; *eadem* 1993, 31–36 and 51–75). Note also the linguistic traces on Linear B tablets: *θρονοελκτήρια PY Fr 1222, θεοφόρια KN Ga 1058.

solemnly conducted and accompanied to their newly-prescribed sacred abodes at the foot of the Athenian Acropolis and close to the Areopagos (805, 855, 1004–05, 1023).[25] Under Athena's instructions, torches (1005), sacrificial victims (1006), temple servants (1024) and officials (1011) move solemnly with hymns across the scenic space, sealing the trilogy with a grand finale which seems to echo the civic ceremonial of fifth-century Athens.[26] Nonetheless, the very *physical* participation in the procession of divine figures such as Athena and the Erinyes (transformed into *Semnai,* explicitly called so at 1041)[27] distinguishes the theatrical occasion from those of "real life" and transfers it to the mythical past. Rituals, however, create links between past and present, and so the enacted processional event may be suggestive (in implicit or explicit ways) of a broader ritual frame familiar to a contemporary audience, thereby complicating rigid distinctions and categorizations. In this particular case the suggestiveness is most successfully brought forward, as the dramatic text is particularly evocative of the performative dimension of the action, which seems to create an inseparable link between language (referring and attributed to a mythical past) and stage event (watched by a contemporary audience and echoing contemporary ritual practice). This performative dimension can be better accounted for through performance analysis which may illuminate both the stage action and the key terms πέμπω and

πομπή, which are used in self-referential statements by the central agents of the scene, i.e. by Athena and the choral group singing.[28]

Instead of accommodating some implicit and covered signals or allusions to stage action (as is usual in tragic texts), the last part of the *Eumenides* seems to be organized as a full account of stage directions.[29] The role of the director in this case, however, does not belong to the poet or the *didaskalos*, but is attributed to the goddess Athena, whose utterances abound in *deictic markers* which bridge the gap between word and action: copious use of demonstrative pronouns (τῶνδε προσώπων 990, τοῖσδε πολίταις 991, τῶνδε προπομπῶν 1006, τῶνδε σφαγίων 1007, ταῖσδε μετοίκοις 1011, etc.), second person imperatives (ἴτε 1007, ἡγεῖσθε 1010, τιμᾶτε 1029, etc.) and other imperatives (e.g. ἀπέχειν, πέμπειν 1009, 1010, ὁρμάσθω 1029), references to movement and walking (στείχειν 1004, ἴτε 1007, σύμεναι 1008, etc.), self-referential statements and performative futures (ἐμέ 1003, αἰνῶ 1021, πέμψω 1022). Through this emphatically performative language Athena prescribes the

---

25 The main evidence for the location of the precinct of the Semnai is Paus. 1.28.6.

26 Cultic personnel, representatives of various social groups, sacrificial animals and offerings, musical accompaniment (choir singing and/or instrumental music), as well as symbols, sacrificial instruments and insignia were constituent parts of the processional ceremonies during public feasts. For modern reconstructions and discussions of relevant cultic material, see the notes at the beginning of this work.

27 But also perhaps in the corrupt passage after 1027; see Sommerstein 1989 *ad loc.* and *ad* 1041–1042.

---

28 It should be noted that this part of the tragedy has a basically choral structure. In this respect the Aischylean text confirms that the performative aspect is significant in choral contexts and "invites" performance analysis, as is made evident by relevant studies applied to poetic texts within and outside drama: see indicatively Prins 1991; Calame 1999; Bierl 2001 (and now Bierl 2009); the contributions in Felson 2004; some relevant material in the recent volume Athanassaki & Bowie 2011.

29 This does not mean that staging arrangements are now clear to us who are simple readers and not spectators of the original performance (where all deictic markers for example would be directly deciphered). The arrangement of the exodos of the *Eum.* is still debated today; it remains contested for example who the *propompoi* (1006) are, if they are to be identified with the Jurors (1011–1012) or the *prospoloi* (1024), whether the *prospoloi* are present or not, who the singers of the last choral ode are and who responds antiphonically (especially with *ololyge*). For relevant discussions, see *exempli gratia* Taplin 1977, 230–238, 410–411; Sommerstein 1989 *ad* 1021–1047; Podlecki 1989 *ad* 1032–1047; West 1990, 294; Collard 2002, 112 and *passim.*

organization of an event which evokes historical ritual processions familiar to the contemporary audience: prescribed movement towards a sacred place (θαλάμους 1004, τόπους 1023), participation of particular religious and social groups (such as the priestesses of Athena and official statesmen 1010, 1024), positions, roles and arrangement (προτέραν 1003, προπομποί 1006), and most importantly sacrificial offerings (σφάγια 1007), symbols (φῶς ἱερόν 1005, λαμπάδων 1022), and external insignia such as the φοινικόβαπτα ἐσθήματα (1028); all these explicit indications recall analogous patterns and schemata familiar from historical processional examples and recognizable by a contemporary (to the play) audience well-versed in the public ceremonial of the Greek *polis*.[30]

What is particularly interesting here is that despite all these evocative signs which recall basic festive features, the Aischylean example does not seem to identify with a *particular* festive occasion: the emphasis on the honour of the Semnai Theai and the chthonic element in the arrangement (through the use of torches[31] and the choice of the term σφάγια for the sacrificial animals[32]) may point to rituals associated with the chthonic realm and may thus recall indirectly celebrations in honour of the Semnai and more particularly the splendid procession of the historical feast for these goddesses.[33] At the same time, however, the scene seems to evoke the atmosphere of panegyric public festivals like the Panathenaia, a connection that can

hardly be avoided.[34] The all-inclusive character of the procession (in which all Athenian social groups seem to be represented, with Erinyes following as metics) and the presence of Athena and her priestess (1024) are probably the closest reminiscences of the Panathenaic celebration. It is true that in a "real life" Panathenaic procession the goddess Athena would not be present at the head of the procession as in the Aischylean version. Her presence, however, might be symbolically invoked through the presence of her cultic personnel, since it was customary in Greece to have priests and priestesses enact the part of the deity on festive occasions.[35] Thus, the presence of the goddess in the procession might not have been so remote from contemporary assumptions. In the tragic world of the theatre—where earthly restrictions do not apply—Athena's presence and leading role are clearly emphasized and are brought forward through the self-referential form πέμψω ("I shall lead/escort" 1022). Πέμψω is an emphatic first person form of performative future which manages to bridge language and action and which helps make manifest the intimate link between the mythical and the ritual level (as regards the use of πέμπω in the scene): Athena

---

30 See references in notes 2, 4 & 5 above.
31 A frequent and well-known attribute of chthonic figures such as Persephone or Hades.
32 For the chthonic associations of the term σφάγια, see Stengel 1910, 92–97.
33 As Parker 1996, 299 recognizes too. The main source for the feast is the ancient scholion to S. *OC* 489 (referring to Polemon's testimony). The feast seems to bear some chthonic characteristics such as the prescription for silence (ἡσυχία), the wineless offerings, and the exclusion of some social groups ("Eupatrids"; see Parker 1996, 323–324).

34 It has been repeatedly made by scholars especially since the time of the publication of Headlam's article (1906) which stressed the association between the φοινικόβαπτα ἐσθήματα in the text and the metics at the Panathenaic procession. This association is insufficient, however, to support a *strictly* "Panathenaic" interpretation, since apart from Photius (referred to by Headlam), all other surviving sources connect the *phoinikoun* colour of garments either with processions in general or with Dionysiac processions in particular; see Harp. s.v. σκαφηφόροι; Poll. 3.55; *Suda* s.v. ἀσκοφορεῖν. Hence, there is nothing intrinsically Panathenaic in the φοινικόβαπτα ἐσθήματα.
35 See Connelly 2007, 105–115. Vase-paintings seem to "play out" this blurring of roles between divinity and priesthood in various ways; e.g., on a band cup associated with the Panathenaia (Shapiro 1989, 29, pl. 9a–b), goddess and priestess stand on one side of the altar receiving the long sacrificial procession coming from the other side.

announces and concurrently performs the leading (πέμψω) of a large group of participants at a mythical ceremony; at the same time this ceremony bears all the generic features of a *ritual* πέμπειν, of a solemn πομπή. From the point of view of the audience attending and watching at the theatre, the mythical and the ritual act of conduct overlap in this case.

At the same time, the play seems to attempt to create bridges from other directions too. As the goddess hastens to make clear after having announced her leading role (πέμψω 1022), she will not do the *pempein,* the act of conducting, by herself, but ξὺν προσπόλοις αἵτε φρουροῦσι βρέτας τοὐμόν (1024). This prepositional phrase qualifies Athena's πέμψω and introduces into the picture Athena's cultic personnel who are explicitly said to take part in the act of *pempein.* In this way a link seems to be formed between the mythical instance and the historical cases of celebration in which the cultic personnel would have a leading role. This link seems to be further encouraged in the text, as the reference to the *prospoloi* is particularly interestingly formulated. The *prospoloi* may indeed be present and should perhaps be identified with the *propompoi.*[36] In this particular instance (1024), however, the reference to them is not accompanied by a demonstrative (which would narrow down the picture to the particular); it is, thus, opened up to future time and to possible future celebrations (with the generalizing plural assisting this aspect). Noticeably, it is exactly this reference to the *prospoloi* (with its generalized, future-evoking character) that is followed by the disputed and probably corrupt passage (1025–1028) which foresees παῖδες, γυναῖκες and στόλος πρεσβυτίδων and which may also suggest future, recurrent action and

periodic celebrations[37] in which the contemporary audience would also be included.

Athena's strong performative πέμψω signals the completion of the gathering and ordering of people and objects as well as the setting off of the procession. As the long array of people and offerings starts moving, their rhythmical pace—that one can imagine on the basis of the surviving text—would unite with the melody of a choral song that probably the group of the *propompoi* (or a part of it) begins to sing, thus giving the tone to the whole moving spectacle which in its turn acquires both a visual and an acoustic aspect. The song (1032–1047) is basically a *prosodion* (in the literal sense of the word), a song accompanying a literal *pros-odos,* i.e. a pro-cession, a movement forward; aptly, each of its two strophes opens up with an imperative suggesting movement (βᾶτε, "move on, proceed", ἴτε, "go", "make your way"), a feature which manages to account for and manifest at the same time the spatial dimension of the performance.

At the same time the song seems to reveal even more explicitly the mythico-ritual character of the whole arrangement, as the ritual terms used therein multiply: τιμαῖς (1037), θυσίαις (1037), σπονδαί (1044), μολπαῖς (1043, 1047), εὐφαμεῖτε (1035, 1038), ὀλολύξατε (1043, 1047). The whole song seems to be structured in a speech act mode,[38] effecting every action through its explicit and repeated announcement in words. More importantly, throughout the song the chorus seems to address (or at least to include in its address) not only the internal audience but even the extradramatic one, by using such general terms as the vocative χωρῖται ("inhabitants", "men of this country", 1035,

---

[36] As some have suggested; see Sommerstein 1989 *ad* 1021–1047; also West 1990, 293–294.

[37] As most editors and commentators have noted; see comprehensively Sommerstein 1989 *ad loc.*

[38] The term comes from Austin's theory (Austin 1962) but has been repeatedly used more broadly in the analysis of literary texts. It also proves useful for performance analysis in tragedy; see for example Prins 1991.

1038) and the all-inclusive πανδαμεί ("in the whole city", 1038). The repeated use of second person imperatives inciting ritual action (εὐφαμεῖτε, ὀλολύξατε) and addressed to the wider audience achieves a unique blending of the dramatic and the performative level to the extent that the dramatic register tends to be subsumed under the performative one.

Magnetized by an imposing spectacle and invited almost explicitly to attend the moving procession and to participate through *euphemia* or even *ololyge* (familiar and customary reactions to a processional ceremony), the audience is energetically implicated in a spectacle that has all the basic characteristics of a solemn procession and which is even labelled by the chorus in explicit terms: βᾶτε ὑπ' εὔφρονι πομπᾷ (1034). The term πομπή, structured here in a prepositional phrase and used in the poetic Doric form πομπά, seems somehow remote from the "technical" Attic usage of πομπή and could simply imply "under a kindly escort". However, in such an intense ritual moment that activates a strong audience participation, the ritual connotations of the term πομπά can hardly be obliterated. In communicative terms the *pompe,* organized and proclaimed on stage, proves to be both the procession (*prosodos*), moving solemnly before the eyes of the audience, and at the same time the escort, offered by all those present on stage. In this case *pompe* as "escort" seems to denote the *action* ("escorting", "conducting", "attending and proceeding") as well as the *content* of the action, i.e. the group of people, who have gathered in response to a call and offer themselves to act, to serve, to make manifest and to proclaim, showing their goodwill (εὔφρονι 1034) towards the divine and expecting reciprocal benefits (as the adjectives ἵλαοι and εὐθύφρονες, referring to the Semnai, 1040, suggest; cf. εὔφρονας εὔφρονες 992).

In this respect the *pompe* seems to be a concrete manifestation of community and at the same time an open call to all, both mortals and immortals, for communication and interaction, mutual acceptance and exchange. Linguistically, this call is expressed as a form of wish, of desire or request, hence the repeated imperatives (ἴτε, βᾶτε) and optatives (τύχοιτε 1037). It is not, however, an indiscriminately open wish: all the linguistic markers that surround it have a speech act quality, i.e. they activate and *effect* action, focusing on the particular, present instance; hence the use of the aorist root for the verbal forms (βᾶτε, τύχοιτε, ὀλολύξατε), a feature which implies "in this particular moment, at this instant".[39] In this light the *pompe* functions as the frame for an attempt at an instant fulfilment of this wish or request. At the same time, the periodic re-ordering and re-conducting of the *pompe* also seems to be hinted at in the text (as analyzed above) and it could, thus, be seen as a conscious effort to regain this sense of the immediate and the particular, in an attempt to achieve through verbal and ritual repetition this wished-for unity of "now and forever",[40] so persistently pursued in ritual as well as in tragedy.

The Aischylean scene seems to be poised between the mythical and the ritual, between the particular and the recurrent (or periodic). In this scene πέμπω and πομπή are used with their full, "literal" sense (of "escort", conduct, etc.). Nonetheless, they are applied to a context in which there are strong ritual, performative markers which are actually activated so that the—play's contemporary—audience is invited to be involved and implicated as in "actual" ceremonial procedures. In this ingenious way the general significance and the "ritual" significance of the terms are made to interact and interlace so that both are directly communicated to the audience.

---

[39]   See Smyth 1956, 429–430 (especially §1927). Εὐφαμεῖτε in the present is a standard ritual cry; see also, for example, Ar. *Ach.* 237, 241.

[40]   For a sensitive and penetrating discussion of this theme see Easterling 2004.

The Aischylean picture complements and corroborates the evidence that the grammatical forms and structure as well as the historical usages also suggested. The basic semantic aspect of the terms πέμπω and πομπή is active even in the ritual (marked) uses of the terms, and no *rigid* distinction and separation can hold. In their ritual application *pompai* seem to suggest and connote not simply the movement but also the body of people moving, the assemblage and community leading and being led to a common goal. As such the *pompe* seems to establish contacts and encourage interaction with the divine on both an immediate and a recurrent basis, so that mutual relations can be re-established and hopefully sustained.[41]

Sketching some consequences

The perception of the *pompe* not only as movement but also as conducting or escort, i.e. as a concrete instance of community and co-direction opening up ways for future (and fuller perhaps) interaction, can help us better appreciate the basic fact that, for the Greeks, processions (*prosodoi, pompai*) were on a par with sacrifices, often mentioned together in the texts as signs of *eusebeia* (Dem. 18. 86, Isoc. 5.32). Both processions and sacrifices could be "most sacred" (ἱερώταται πρόσοδοι, Ar. *Nub.* 308), and the promise of future processions seems to have been such an appealing gift to the gods that it could even be used as a "bribe" along with sacrifices in Aristophanic comedy (Ar. *Pax* 396–399[42]). This popular perception seems to

find its theoretical expression in the Platonic corpus in which both *pompai* and sacrifices are explicitly defined as δῶρα (δωρεῖσθαι, "making a present") to the gods.[43]

This ancient attitude towards *prosodoi* or *pompai* does not seem to have been taken seriously by earlier students of Greek religion who found little sense of religion in manifestation rituals such as processions.[44] This stance may conceal an association of "religiousness" with morality and consciousness rather than action.[45] In current theoretical assumptions, however, Greek religion is "practical", manifestation-oriented and embedded in society.[46] Seen from this perspective and under the weight of the analysis above, processions may seem particularly eligible to function as a potent gift: in their function as *pompai*, i.e. as concrete assemblages of people set on the way opened up by the deity, acting for and ready to lead and be led by the deity, processions might seem to present to the divine not only material goods and offerings but most importantly the community itself in a symbolic and representative form. The collective body, in other words, might seem to dedicate itself somehow through the *pompe*.[47]

---

[41] The wider implications of such cosmotheoretical "statements" articulated in tragedy (in a dramatic context) are important, since as Sourvinou-Inwood has strongly argued, tragedy played a crucial role in the articulation of the religious discourse of the *polis* (Sourvinou-Inwood 2003, 1–14, 50–53, 149–154 and *passim*).

[42] Ar. *Pax* 396–399: "καὶ σε θυσίαισιν ἱεραῖσι προσόδοις τε μεγά-/λαισι διὰ παντὸς ὦ δέσποτα ἀγαλοῦμεν ἡμεῖς ἀεί".

[43] [Pl.] *Alc.* ii.148e: "ἀνθ' ὅτου ποτὲ … πομπάς τε πολυτελεστάτας καὶ σεμνοτάτας ἐδωρούμεθα τοῖς θεοῖς ἀν' ἕκαστον ἔτος"; Pl. *Euthphr.* 14c: "τὸ θύειν δωρεῖσθαί ἐστι τοῖς θεοῖς".

[44] Some indicative views: Wilamowitz-Moellendorff 1932, 2. 353: "von wirklicher Religion kann da keine Rede sein"; Nilsson 1951, 169: "die Religion aber im öden Prunk erstickte"; Bömer 1952, 1894: "man darf die Panathenaia als die grosse politische, die *Pompe* nach Eleusis als die grosse religiöse und (…) die Dionysia als die beim Volke beliebteste Pompe bezeichnen".

[45] Cf. also Konaris in this volume.

[46] See for example Parker 1996, 265–266, 265–273; Sourvinou-Inwood 1990 and 1988a; Bremmer 1994, 1–10; Gould 2001, 203–234.

[47] A fact which may be echoed by the use of the processional motif on votive reliefs; see Edelmann 1999, *passim*. In her extended discussion of votive reliefs of the Classical period (36–180) Edelmann shows that the processional motif persists on votive reliefs throughout the fifth and fourth century (despite con-

As a kind of ἀνάθημα, the *pompe* might appear to have the potential not only to open up the cycle of *charis* between humans and immortals but even to aim at a long-term *charis*-relationship (by analogy perhaps to the votive offerings fixed at sanctuaries).

Divine favour, however, can never be guaranteed. *Pompai* had to be arranged and re-arranged every year in an effort to sustain the flow of *charis*, since the prosperity of the community necessitated (according to Greek perceptions) the attraction of divine favour. This major social and religious goal was served by the *pompai* which were performed and re-performed every year *in favour* of the community, as is explicitly acknowledged not only in the dramatic but also in the surviving inscriptional sources: πέμπηται ἡ πομπὴ παρεσκευασμένη ὡς ἄριστα τῇ Ἀθηνᾷ καθ' ἕκαστον τὸν ἐνιαυτὸν ὑπὲρ τοῦ δήμου τῶν Ἀθηναίων (*LSCG* 33 B. 3–5).

ATHENA KAVOULAKI
Department of Philology
University of Crete
kavoulaki@phl.uoc.gr

Bibliography

Athanassaki & Bowie 2011 — *Archaic and Classical choral song: Performance, politics & dissemination*, eds. L. Athanassaki & E.L. Bowie, Berlin 2011.

Austin 1962 — J.L. Austin, *How to do things with words: The William James lectures delivered at Harvard University in 1955*, ed. J.O. Urmson, Oxford 1962.

Bell 1992 — C. Bell, *Ritual theory, ritual practice*, Oxford 1992.

Bierl 2001 — A. Bierl, *Der Chor in der Alten Komödie: Ritual und Performativität*, München & Leipzig 2001. (English translation: *Ritual and Performativity: the Chorus in Old Comedy*, Cambridge, Mass. 2009.)

Bömer 1952 — F. Bömer, 'Pompa', *RE* 21.2, 1878–1972.

Bowie 1993 — A.M. Bowie, 'Religion and politics in Aeschylus' *Oresteia*', *CQ* 43, 1993, 10–31.

Bremmer 1994 — J. Bremmer, *Greek religion* (G&R New surveys in Classics, 24), Oxford 1994.

Burkert 1979 — W. Burkert, *Structure and history in Greek mythology and ritual*, Berkeley 1979.

Burkert 1985 — W. Burkert, *Greek religion: Archaic and Classical*, Oxford 1985.

Calame 1999 — C. Calame, 'Performative aspects of the choral voice in Greek tragedy: civic identity in performance', in *Performance culture and Athenian democracy*, eds. S. Goldhill & R. Osborne, Cambridge 1999, 125–153.

Chantraine 1968 — P. Chantraine, *Dictionnaire étymologique de la langue grecque: histoire des mots*, Paris 1968.

Collard 2002 — C. Collard, *Aeschylus: Oresteia*, Oxford 2002.

Connelly 2007 — J. Connelly, *Portrait of a priestess: Women and ritual in Ancient Greece*, Princeton 2007.

Easterling 2004 — P.E. Easterling, 'Now and for ever in Greek drama and ritual', in *Greek ritual poetics*, eds. D. Yatromanolakis & P. Roilos, Cambridge, Mass. & London 2004, 149–160.

---

trary trends on vases of the fourth century). Lehnstaedt (1970, 137–140) also discusses the "Weihecharakter" of processional representations on vases.

Edelmann 1999   M. Edelmann, *Menschen auf griechischen Weihreliefs*, München 1999.

Felson 2004   N. Felson, *The poetics of deixis in Alcman, Pindar and other lyric* (= *Arethusa* 37:3, special issue) 2004, 253–266.

Frisk 1973   J. Frisk, *Griechisches etymologisches Wörterbuch*, Heidelberg 1973.

Gould 2001   J. Gould, *Myth, ritual, memory and exchange: Essays in Greek literature and culture*, Oxford 2001.

Graf 1996   F. Graf, 'Pompai in Greece: Some considerations about space and ritual in the Greek polis', in *The role of religion in the early Greek Polis. Proceedings of the third international seminar on ancient Greek cult, organized by the Swedish Institute at Athens, 16–18 October 1992* (ActaAth-8°, 14), ed. R. Hägg, Stockholm 1996, 55–65.

Grimes 1982   R. Grimes, *Beginnings in ritual studies*, Washington 1982.

Headlam 1906   W. Headlam, 'The last scene of the *Eumenides*', *JHS* 26, 1906, 268–77.

Herda 2006   A. Herda, *Der Apollon-Delphinios-Kult in Milet und die Neujahrsprozession nach Didyma. Ein neuer Kommentar der sog. Molpoi-Satzung* (Milesische Forschungen, 4), Mainz 2006.

Kavoulaki 1997   Α. Καβουλάκη, 'Η γαμήλια πομπή στην αρχαία ελληνική τραγική σκηνή', in *Acta: First panhellenic and international conference on ancient Greek literature*, ed. J.-Th. Papademetriou, Athens 1997, 351–371.

Kavoulaki 1999   A. Kavoulaki, 'Processional performance and the democratic polis', in *Performance culture and Athenian democracy*, eds. S. Goldhill & R. Osborne, Cambridge 1999, 293–320.

Kavoulaki 2005   A. Kavoulaki, 'Crossing communal space: The Classical ekphora, "public" and "private"', in *Ἰδίᾳ καὶ δημοσίᾳ: Les cadres "privés" et "publics" de la religion grecque antique* (Kernos, Suppl. 15), eds. V. Dasen & M. Piérart, Liège 2005, 129–145.

Kirshenblatt-Gimblett & McNamara 1985   B. Kirshenblatt-Gimblett & B. McNamara, 'Processional performance', *The Drama Review* 29 (3), 1985, 1–5.

Lehnstaedt 1970   K. Lehnstaedt, *Prozessionsdarstellungen auf attischen Vasen*, diss., München 1970.

Marinatos 1986   N. Marinatos, *Minoan sacrificial ritual: Cult practice and symbolism*, Stockholm 1986.

Marinatos 1993   N. Marinatos, *Minoan religion*, New York 1993.

Miller 2003   S. Miller, 'The organization and functioning of the Olympic games', in *Sport and festival in the ancient Greek world*, eds. D.J. Phillips & D. Pritchard, Swansea 2003, 1–40.

Nightingale 2005   A. Nightingale, 'The philosopher at the festival: Plato's transformation of traditional Theoria', in *Pilgrimage in Graeco-Roman and early Christian Antiquity: Seeing the gods*, eds. J. Elsner & I. Rutherford, Oxford 2005, 151–180.

Nilsson 1951 M.P. Nilsson, 'Die Prozessions-typen im griechischen Kult', in *Opuscula selecta ad historiam religionis Graecae* 1, Lund 1951, 166–214.

Pache 2001 C.O. Pache, 'Barbarian bond: Thracian Bendis among the Athenians', in *Between magic and religion: Interdisciplinary studies in ancient Mediterranean religion and society*, eds. S.R. Asirvatham, C.O. Pache & J. Watrous, Lanham, Md 2001, 3–11.

Parker 1996 R. Parker, *Athenian religion: A history*, Oxford 1996.

Parker 2005 R. Parker, *Polytheism and society at Athens*, Oxford 2005.

Parkin 1992 D. Parkin, 'Ritual as spatial direction and bodily division', in *Understanding rituals*, ed. D. de Coppet, London & New York 1992, 11–25.

Pfuhl 1900 E. Pfuhl, *De Atheniensium pompis sacris*, Berlin 1900.

Podlecki 1989 A.J. Podlecki, *Aeschylus: Eumenides*, Warminster 1989.

Prins 1991 Y. Prins, 'The power of the speech act: Aeschylus' Furies and their Binding song', *Arethusa* 24.2, 1991, 177–195.

Risch 1974 E. Risch, *Wortbildung der homerischen Sprache*, Berlin & New York 1974.

Schechner 1988 R. Schechner, *Performance theory*, London & New York 1988.

Schwyzer 1959 E. Schwyzer, *Griechische Grammatik* I, München 1959.

Seaford 1994 R. Seaford, *Reciprocity and ritual: Homer and tragedy in the developing city-state*, Oxford 1994.

Seaford 1996 R. Seaford, 'Processions', in *Oxford Classical Dictionary: third edition*, eds. S. Hornblower & A. Spawforth, Oxford 1996, 1250.

Shapiro 1989 A. Shapiro, *Art and cult under the tyrants in Athens*, Mainz 1989.

Smith 1982 J.Z. Smith, *Imagining religion: From Babylon to Jonestown*, Chicago 1982.

Smyth 1956 H.W. Smyth, *Greek grammar* (revised by G.M. Messing), Cambridge, Mass. 1956.

Sommerstein 1989 A.H. Sommerstein, *Aeschylus: Eumenides*, Cambridge 1989.

Sourvinou-Inwood 1988a C. Sourvinou-Inwood, 'Further aspects of *polis* religion', *AION* 10, 1988, 259–74. (Reprint in *Oxford Readings in Greek Religion*, ed. R. Buxton, Oxford 2000, 38–55.)

Sourvinou-Inwood 1990 C. Sourvinou-Inwood, 'What is *Polis* religion?' in *The Greek city from Homer to Alexander*, eds. O. Murray & S. Price, Oxford 1990, 295–322. (Reprint in *Oxford Readings in Greek Religion*, ed. R. Buxton, Oxford 2000, 13–37.)

Sourvinou-Inwood 2003 C. Sourvinou-Inwood, *Tragedy and Athenian religion*, Lanham, Md 2003.

Stengel 1910 P. Stengel, *Opferbräuche der Griechen*, Leipzig & Berlin 1910.

Taplin 1977 O.P. Taplin, *The stagecraft of Aeschylus: The dramatic use of exits and entrances in Greek tragedy*, Oxford 1977.

True *et al.* 2005   M. True *et al.*, 'Greek processions', in *ThesCRA* I, ed. J. Boardman *et al.*, Los Angeles 2005, 1–20.

Turnbull 1985   C. Turnbull, 'Processional ritual among the Mbuti pygmies', *The Drama Review* 29.3, 1985, 6–17.

West 1990   M.L. West, *Studies in Aeschylus* (Beiträge zur Altertumskunde, 1), Stuttgart 1990.

Wilamowitz-Moellendorff 1932   U. von Wilamowitz-Moellendorff, *Der Glaube der Hellenen* 1–2, Berlin 1931–1932.

OLIVER PILZ

The performative aspect of Greek ritual
THE CASE OF THE ATHENIAN OSCHOPHORIA

Abstract*

Although concepts of performance theory were successfully applied to the study of rituals in the social sciences, research on ancient Greek ritual practice was not affected by such approaches to any significant degree. To a large extent, this might be due to the fragmentary character of the available evidence, consisting mainly of material remains of ritual activities in the archaeological record, and representations of rituals in art. In the absence of detailed descriptions of ritual practice in literary sources, it is therefore difficult to reconstruct whole ritual sequences, which would greatly facilitate their interpretation as performative acts. Criticizing a view of ritual as primarily non-verbal and action orientated, this paper emphasizes the role of speech in Greek rituals and examines some of the evidence for mimetic and narrative ritual performances. Drawing on the example of the Athenian Oschophoria, the performative aspect of a specific ritual is investigated. In addition, the simplified interpretation of the Oschophoria as an "ephebes' rite" is dismissed in favour of a more balanced reading that adequately considers not only the eminent agricultural aspect of the festival but also the different groups of participants.

"Ritual studies" is a relatively new field of research involving several disciplines of the social sciences and humanities, including anthropology, sociology, psychology, communication studies, history, linguistics and religious studies.[1] As a category in its own right, ritual indeed deserves a distinct interdisciplinary approach. However, the emergence of ritual studies as an independent discipline has contributed to the considerable expansion that the meaning of the term "ritual" has undergone over the last few decades. Originally confined to the religious sphere, the concept has subsequently been extended to include secular ceremonies and even daily routine behaviour. It is here, however, that the risk of a complete dissolution of the concept lies. If ritual is reduced to its repetitive aspect, then even brushing one's teeth could be considered a ritual activity. Since it is obvious that the notion loses all analytical value and becomes meaningless in this sense, more precise criteria are needed to discern ritual from everyday behaviour. A performative approach, emphasizing the staged aspect rather than the formalized and rigid character of ritual action, has proven useful in the attempt to establish these criteria.

* I would like to thank Athena Kavoulaki and Renaud Gagné for their comments during the conference as well as Chikako Sugawara for information about the *san-san-kudo* ritual. Furthermore, I am grateful to Uta Kron and Klaus Junker for reading and commenting on earlier drafts of this paper. All errors, of course, remain my own. I owe particular thanks to Caitlin D. Verfenstein and Lisa Yager for correcting and improving my English text.

[1] For the historical development of the term "ritual", see Bremmer 1998, 14–24.

It was actually the field of cultural anthropology that first contributed to the theoretical understanding of ritual. Ritual theories proposed by Victor Turner and Clifford Geertz have been extremely influential even beyond the limits of their own discipline.[2] Both scholars emphasized the transformative power of ritual, which is produced by a symbolic representation of cultural and social values. In the mid 1950s, the anthropologist Milton Singer proposed the concept of "cultural performance" as a unit of reference for events such as plays, concerts, prayers, rituals and festivals.[3] According to Singer, in cultural performances, the beliefs and values central to a culture are displayed through the use of various media such as acting, dancing and singing. Furthermore, Singer assumed that cultural performances reveal such values and beliefs more explicitly than other, non-performative contexts within that same culture. Elaborating on Singer's ideas, scholars such as the sociologist Erving Goffman, the cultural anthropologist Victor Turner and the theatre director Richard Schechner gradually expanded the concept into what is known today as performance theory.[4]

Victor Turner, in particular, applied the performative approach to the study of ritual. According to Turner, ritual is a "… transformative performance revealing major classifications, categories and contradictions of cultural processes".[5] In this definition, the two essential aspects of Turner's theory—the transformative power of ritual as well as the concept of ritual as staged performance—are combined. The latter is, furthermore, clearly inherent in the drama analogy frequently used by Turner with regard to ritual. Although Turner recognized, especially in his later writings, the aspect of enactment and role-playing in ritual activity, his theory of ritual revolves around the symbolic structure of ritual action. Considering ritual an instrument that channels and mediates endemic social conflicts, Turner primarily focused on decoding the symbolic meaning of ritual sequences.

In the philosophy of language and linguistics, particularly within the framework of speech act theory, the term "performance" has a limited meaning. In speech act theory, "performance", in a general sense, refers to the act of producing an utterance. A more significant application of the term, however, is comprised in the notion "performative utterance", introduced by John Austin in his famous 1955 Harvard lecture series, subsequently published under the title *How to do things with words*.[6] In contrast to utterances that describe or state something, Austin defined performative utterances as acts of doing something by saying something. Austin's example *par excellence* for a performative utterance is the case of a minister who joins two people in marriage by saying, "I now pronounce you husband and wife". Subsequently, John Searle described the relation between these two meanings as follows, "Though every utterance is indeed a *performance*, only a very restricted class are *performatives*".[7] With regard to ritual action, Stanley Tambiah rightly noticed that ritual can be regarded as performative in three distinct senses: in the Austinian sense of doing some conventional act by saying something; in the quite different sense of a staged performance, and in the third sense of the indexical values the actors attach to, or derive from, the performance.[8]

Theories current in cultural anthropology have rarely affected the interpretation of the meaning and function of ancient Greek rituals to any significant degree. One of the reasons

---

2   Turner 1969; Geertz 1973.
3   Singer 1955.
4   Cf. Fischer-Lichte 2003, esp. 37–41; Grimes 2006.
5   Turner 1986, 75.

6   Austin 1962. Cf. Searle 1969.
7   Searle 1989, 536.
8   Tambiah 1979, 119.

for this might be due to the dissimilar character of the available evidence. Since direct observation of rituals is a privilege of the empirical social sciences, the best that Classical scholars can do is to study the preserved regulations for, and descriptions of, rituals in literary sources as well as their physical remains in the archaeological record.[9] All previous scholarship suggests to me that the way in which Classical scholars conceptualize ritual is frequently shaped by the notably fragmentary nature of the available evidence in their specialized area of study. In a recent lecture, Walter Burkert illustrated his conception of ritual with an interesting example from personal observation. Since this passage very clearly reveals Burkert's perspective on ritual, I will present a full quotation here from the English translation of his lecture published in the volume *Ritual and communication in the Graeco-Roman World*:

> "When, as I was recently able to observe at a wedding in a temple in Japan, a festively dressed maiden quite carefully pours liquid out of a pitcher into a cup, three times, alternately for the bride and the groom, and these latter then equally carefully and pointedly drink, each twice, from this cup, then that is a ritual, a schematised action meant as a message. I have mentioned this example because it shows how rituals are recognisable independently of any language: I know absolutely no Japanese, but I do believe that I have understood the ceremony to some extent."[10]

Burkert explicitly conceives of ritual as a sequence of formalized bodily actions performed in order to transmit a message. In a social context, he therefore considers ritual to be a means of non-verbal communication that is, at least partially, analogous to language.[11] To prevent any misunderstanding, Burkert is careful not to deny the existence of speech in ritual, but he seems to conceive of verbal utterances and bodily movements as two largely independent and unrelated facets of ritual action. Admittedly, Burkert has chosen an example that fits extremely well with his vision. The "message" of the *san-san-kudo* ritual, a rite of the Shinto wedding ceremony, seems obvious: the couple is now married. Since speech is absent from this pouring and drinking ritual, understanding the "message" does not depend on language, nor does it have to do with the specific actions performed in the rite. In fact, it could be argued that Burkert was able to "... have understood the ceremony to some extent ..." because of a rather simple analogy to Western culture. A ritual centred on a young couple would probably have been recognizable as a wedding to a Japanese observer in Europe as well.

Despite the limitation on the bodily aspect of ritual activity, Burkert's view has been quite influential among Classical scholars. Katharina Waldner, for instance, equally stresses the "Sprachlosigkeit" of rituals, defining them as purely physical activity.[12] Describing *polis* religion as a system that consists of both mythological discourse and ritual action,[13] Waldner assigns speech to the discursive part, eliminating it from ritual action. In this context, she refers not only to Burkert but also to the late Catherine Bell's practice theory approach to ritual. According to Bell, the avoidance of explicit speech and narrative is a distinctive characteristic of ritualization.[14] Moreover, Bell

---

[9]   In a broader sense, the latter category also includes the preserved representations of rituals in art.
[10] Burkert 2006, 23.

[11] Cf. Burkert 1983, 150.
[12] Waldner 2000, 23f.
[13] Waldner 2000, 21: "... ein System von sprachlichen Diskursen einerseits und kultischen Handlungen andererseits ...".
[14] Bell 1992, 94–98, 111. Cf. Bell 1997, 82: "The most subtle and central quality of those actions we tend to call ritual is the primacy of the body." Bell is using "ritual" and "ritualization" as broadly interchangeable terms.

argues that the main purpose of ritual (or ritualization) is to produce what she calls a ritualized body.[15] Ritualization is defined as "… a strategy for the construction of a limited and limiting power relationship".[16] The strategies of ritualization aim to establish these power relationships by inscribing symbolically meaningful schemes of formalized actions on the body. Since these pre-existing schemes are "impressed" on the body,[17] the ritual actor himself assumes a merely passive role. The intentions and strategies of those who perform rituals are therefore largely neglected in Bell's approach. Ronald Grimes has rightly criticized her general tendency to ascribe an agency to the ritual process (or to the strategies of ritualization) rather than to the ritual actors themselves.[18]

In Classical studies, the claim of a dichotomy of bodily action and speech seems rooted in the differentiation between λεγόμενον ("that which is said") and δρώμενον ("that which is done"), used by Jane Harrison to contrast Greek myth and ritual.[19] Referring to Harrison's terminology, Albert Henrichs recently argued that ritual "… hugely favors the *dromena* over the *legomena* …", describing rituals such as sacrifice and libation as "… predominately nonverbal and action orientated …".[20] However, since sacrificial rites were usually accompanied by invocations, prayers and screams (*ololyge*),[21] they should not be characterized as being predominately without speech. Moreover, speech acts that are uttered, for instance in the context of an oath ritual, represent explicit performa-

tive utterances in the Austinian sense.[22] It is, in fact, the illocutionary force of these utterances that constitutes the binding character of the oath. It seems that the tendency to downplay the role of speech in Greek ritual is caused more by our fragmentary knowledge of the *legomena* than by their actual importance in the ritual action. A dualistic view of mind-orientated mythological discourse and body-orientated ritual action, as proposed by Waldner, does not match the reality of ancient Greek ritual or most other forms of ritual activity.

The fact that there is evidence for the ritual enactment of myths sheds a somewhat different light on the aforementioned interrelation between myth and ritual. Diodoros affirms that the sacred marriage of Zeus and Hera was ritually enacted in a sanctuary near Knossos that has not yet been located.[23] Using the verb ἀπομιμέομαι ("to imitate"), Diodoros clearly stresses the mimetic character of this representation. Even though the source does not give any further description, there is no obvious reason to assume that speech has been omitted in the enactment of the myth. In her recent book, *Cultic theatres and ritual drama*, Inge Nielsen seems to have overlooked the aforementioned literary evidence, which would have fit in very well with what she calls "ritual drama". Nielsen defines the concept of ritual drama as follows, "… a dramatic performance with a plot taken from the myth of the god in whose honour it was enacted as a ritual during the festive liturgy".[24] According to Nielsen, ritual drama "combines" myth and ritual. However, as she rightly states in her definition, it falls under the

---

15   Bell 1992, 93, 98, 107.
16   Bell 1992, 8.
17   Bell 1992, 98f.
18   Grimes 2004, 134f.
19   Harrison 1927, 328f.
20   Henrichs 2000, 176. See also the critical remarks by Mylonopoulos 2006, 92, n. 97.
21   Animal sacrifice: Burkert 1985, 56. For libation and prayer, see *ibid.* 71. Cf. Ar. *Pax* 435: σπένδοντες ἐχώμεσθα.

22   For Greek oath rituals, see e.g. Saladino 1998.
23   Diod. 5.72.4: "λέγουσι δὲ καὶ τοὺς γάμους τοῦ τε Διὸς καὶ τῆς Ἥρας ἐν τῇ Κνωσίων χώρᾳ γενέσθαι κατά τινα τόπον πλησίον τοῦ Θήρηνος ποταμοῦ, καθ᾽ ὃν νῦν ἱερόν ἐστιν, ἐν ᾧ θυσίας κατ᾽ ἐνιαυτὸν ἁγίους ὑπὸ τῶν ἐγχωρίων συντελεῖσθαι, καὶ τοὺς γάμους ἀπομιμεῖσθαι, καθάπερ ἐξ ἀρχῆς γενέσθαι παρεδόθησαν."
24   Nielsen 2002, 12.

category of ritual action. Several Greek sanctuaries are provided with theatres or stairways, which might have accommodated the spectators of such cultic plays.[25] Particularly in the context of mystery cults, forms of ritual drama and cultic play could have been used to communicate messages to the initiates. Since these rites were kept secret, it is difficult to determine what specific role speech might have played in these ritual performances. With regard to the Eleusinian mysteries, ancient writers usually emphasize the *seeing* of sacred objects during the celebration in the Telesterion.[26] Nevertheless, it would be unwise to assume that the absence of speech was a recurrent pattern in rituals performed in the context of mystery cults.

Even though there are specific forms of ritual that might lack explicit speech, for instance cultic dance,[27] the absence of speech is by no means a general characteristic of ritual action. On the contrary, speech plays an essential role in various rituals. As Ulrich Demmer has recently shown, basing his arguments on the healing and death rituals of the Jēnu Kuṟumba in South India, rituals can actually take the shape of discursive performances in which issues are *verbally* negotiated between the participants.[28] Therefore, a comprehensive view must take into account the fact that verbal utterances and bodily movements in ritual activity are often mutually dependent and deeply interrelated.

In Classical studies, performance theory approaches have been applied less frequently to the analysis of ritual than to the study of dramatic and rhetoric performances.[29] Two studies

on processional performance by Athena Kavoulaki can be noted as exceptions.[30] Kavoulaki convincingly demonstrates the ritual character of Greek *pompai*, which had occasionally been questioned in previous research.[31] Every procession strictly followed fixed rules and regulations regarding not only the route but also the dress and other possible attributes of the participants in addition to the arrangement of different groups of participants within the procession.[32] The formalization extended even to the manner of walking, which was to have been more pointed and stylized than one's everyday stride.[33]

One of the fundamental ideas of performance theory is that actions are carried out to be seen, and things are said to be heard. At first glance, this seems to imply a clear differentiation between ritual actors and observers. Such delineation, however, might be misleading.[34] Taking into account, for instance, the usual sequence of procession and animal sacrifice in Greek cult practice, it becomes clear that the majority of the participants in the procession assumed a passive role during the sacrificial rite, which was usually performed by only a few cult officials and assistants. The situation would then, once again, be inverted during the subsequent sacrificial meal generally involving the whole cultic community. Thus, the distinction between ritual actors and observers is rather blurred when the view is extended to the entire ritual sequence of a Greek festival. Roy Rappaport's clear distinction between ritual, which he defines as having only actively engaged participants, and drama, which he defines as having both actors *and* audience, therefore seems,

---

[25]   Nielsen 2002, 86–148; Becker 2003, 217–259. See also Mylonopoulos 2006, 94–99.

[26]   Cf. Clinton 1992, 87.

[27]   On dance as a form of non-verbal communication, see Naerebout 1997, 375–406. Yet, cultic dance may be accompanied by music and song.

[28]   Demmer 2006, esp. 32–67, with further references.

[29]   See e.g. the papers collected in Goldhill & Osborne 1999.

[30]   Kavoulaki 1999; *eadem* 2000.

[31]   *RE* XXI.2 (1952), 1886, s.v. Pompa (F. Bömer).

[32]   Kavoulaki 1999, 295; *eadem* 2000, 145.

[33]   Polyaenus *Strat.* 5.5.2: νόμῳ πομπῆς βαδίζοντες. Kavoulaki 1999, 294; *eadem* 2000, 154.

[34]   See Kavoulaki 2000, 146 on the perception of processions as spectacles. For spectators (*theatai*) watching processions: Xen. *Eq. mag.* 3.2; Ar. *Ach.* 262.

at least in relation to ancient Greece, inappropriate.[35]

By drawing on the example of the Athenian Oschophoria, I shall now focus more explicitly on the performative aspect of a specific ritual. The festival of the Oschophoria was celebrated in autumn, probably on Pyanopsion 7.[36] A naked youth carrying vine branches with grape clusters (ὄσχοι), depicted on the calendar frieze of Hagios Eleutherios (*Fig. 1*), has been convincingly associated with this festival.[37] The main literary sources concerning the Oschophoria (Proclus' treatment of "oschophoric songs" and Plutarch's *Life of Theseus*) aetiologically link the festival with Theseus'

Cretan adventure.[38] Although the sources are fragmentary and partly contradictory, it is widely agreed that the Oschophoria included a procession from a Dionysiac sanctuary in Athens to the shrine of Athena Skiras in Phaleron, a sacrifice followed by a libation and a footrace of ephebes from each tribe.[39] This sequence of procession, animal sacrifice and athletic contest, is a recurrent pattern in Greek religion and it can safely be assumed that these events were performed in the same order at the Oschophoria.[40] Since the procession led to the precinct of Athena Skiras at Phaleron, it is furthermore very likely that both the sacrifice and race took place there as well.

Fig. 1. Calendar frieze, Pyanopsion. Athens, Little Metropolis. Neg. D-DAI-ATH-Athen Varia 1282.

[35] Rappaport 1999, 39–43.
[36] Cf. Parker 1996, 315f., n. 85.
[37] Deubner 1932, 146, n. 7, 250, pl. 35; Simon 1983, 90, pl. 3:1; Palagia 2008, 220, fig. 3. For a Hadrianic/Antonine dating of the frieze, see Palagia 2008, 233f.

[38] Procl. *Chrestomathia* ap. Phot. *Bibl.* 322a.13–30; Plut. *Thes.* 22.2–4; 23.2–5 (= Demon *FGrH* 327 F 6).
[39] For the reconstruction of the festival, see Deubner 1932, 142–146; Parke 1977, 77–81; Waldner 2000, 101–116; Parker 2005, 211–214.
[40] Calame 1990, 148; Waldner 2000, 114f.

Additional information on the festival is provided by an inscription first published in 1938.[41] The text, an arbitration of a conflict between two factions of the Salaminioi, reveals the important role this *genos* played in the organization of the Oschophoria. Since the inscription was issued under the archonship of Charakleides (363/62 BC), it firmly attests that the festival was celebrated in the first half of the fourth century BC. The earliest trace of the Oschophoria, however, is provided by the fact that Pindar composed an "oschophoric song" for an unknown Athenian.[42] As Robert Parker rightly noted, Pindar's *oschophorikon* was probably not a victory ode in the strict sense, because a song performed during a festival, unless improvised, could hardly refer to a victory in the footrace at the very same occasion.[43] Moreover, Proclus treats the oschophoric songs in connection with other processional songs such as *daphnephorika* and *tripodephorika*. It is therefore more likely that the *oschophorika* were performed during the procession.[44]

Plutarch discusses the aetiological connection of the Oschophoria with the Theseus legend in two different passages. In the first passage, two characteristic elements of the festival are associated with the ambiguous emotional situation at the moment of Theseus' arrival from Crete when the joy at the hero's glorious return is heavily overshadowed by the grief over the death of his father Aigeus.[45] The first element involves the fact that it is not the herald, but the herald's staff, that is crowned. The second deals with the characteristic exclamation during the libation (*eleleu, iou, iou*), which ex-

presses, according to Plutarch, both hope and desperation.[46]

At the end of the second passage that is relevant to the Oschophoria, Plutarch explicitly refers to his sources, the fourth-century BC Atthidographer Demon (= *FGrH* 327 F 6):

"ἐπεὶ δ' ἐπανῆλθεν, αὐτόν τε πομπεῦσαι καὶ τοὺς νεανίσκους, οὕτως ἀμπεχομένους ὡς νῦν ἀμπέχονται τοὺς ὠσχοὺς φέροντες. φέρουσι δὲ Διονύσῳ καὶ Ἀριάδνῃ χαριζόμενοι διὰ τὸν μῦθον, ἢ μᾶλλον ὅτι συγκομιζομένης ὀπώρας ἐπανῆλθον. αἱ δὲ δειπνοφόροι παραλαμβάνονται καὶ κοινωνοῦσι τῆς θυσίας, ἀπομιμούμεναι τὰς μητέρας ἐκείνων τῶν λαχόντων· ἐπεφοίτων γὰρ αὐτοῖς ὄψα καὶ σιτία κομίζουσαι· καὶ μῦθοι λέγονται διὰ τὸ κἀκείνας εὐθυμίας ἕνεκα καὶ παρηγορίας μύθους διεξιέναι τοῖς παισί. ταῦτα μὲν οὖν καὶ Δήμων ἱστόρηκεν."[47]

"And when he came back, he himself and these two young men led a procession, dressed as those are now dressed who carry the vine branches. They carry these in honour of Dionysos and Ariadne on account of the legend; or rather because they came back at the time of the vintage. The *deipnophoroi* take part and share in the sacrifice, and imitate the mothers of those on whom the lot fell, for these kept coming to them with meat and bread. And tales are told because those mothers recounted tales to comfort and encourage their children. These details are also to be found in the history of Demon."

Both Proclus and Plutarch agree that the procession was led by two youths who were dressed as girls and held vine branches with bunches of grapes (ὄσχοι). The two *oschophoroi* were chosen by the already known herald, a priestess (of Athena Skiras?), and an archon, who was ap-

[41] Ferguson 1938; *LSS* 19; *SEG* 21, 527; Lambert 1997.
[42] Rutherford & Irvine 1988, on *P Oxy* 2451 B fr. 17.
[43] Parker 2005, 212.
[44] Kavoulaki 2000, 153.
[45] Plut. *Thes.* 22.2–4.
[46] Plut. *Thes.* 22.4: "ὅθεν καὶ νῦν ἐν τοῖς Ὠσχοφορίοις στεφανοῦσθαι μὲν οὐ τὸν κήρυκα λέγουσιν, ἀλλὰ τὸ κηρύκειον, ἐπιφωνεῖν δ' ἐν ταῖς σπονδαῖς 'ἐλελεῦ ἰοὺ ἰού' τοὺς παρόντας, ὧν τὸ μὲν σπένδοντες ἀναφωνεῖν καὶ παιωνίζοντες εἰώθασι, τὸ δ' ἐκπλήξεως καὶ ταραχῆς ἐστι."
[47] Plut. *Thes.* 23.3–5.

pointed by lot alternately from both factions of the Salaminioi.[48] Independently, we learn that the two boys came from wealthy and noble families.[49] According to Plutarch, the *oschophoroi* carried vine branches in honour of Dionysos and Ariadne or because Theseus *returned* from Crete during the vintage season. Immediately afterwards, however, Plutarch refers to a second tradition which apparently linked the procession to Theseus' *departure* from Athens. As Waldner has convincingly shown, here Plutarch unsuccessfully tried to reconcile different versions of the atthidographic tradition.[50] According to Proclus, the *oschophoroi* were followed by a chorus chanting oschophoric songs.[51] What remains unclear is whether this chorus was male, female or mixed. There is no obvious reason to postulate, as is generally done, that it was a male chorus.[52] Given the close aetiological connection with Theseus' Cretan adventure, it might in fact be more reasonable to assume that it was a mixed chorus made up of both boys and girls.[53] An exclusively male or female chorus would not have fit the myth, which clearly speaks of seven youths and seven maidens accompanying the hero to Crete. At any rate, it would be unwise to use the composition of the chorus, which as we have seen remains uncertain, as an argument for the interpretation of the festival.

Supposedly, already in the course of the procession, women called δειπνοφόροι ("dinner-carriers") acted as the mothers of the twice seven chosen to accompany Theseus to Crete.

Interestingly, the verb ἀπομιμέομαι is again used to emphasize the staged aspect of the performance. To comfort and encourage their "children", the *deipnophoroi* not only offered them food, but also told them stories (μῦθοι). Unfortunately, it is not entirely clear exactly where and when in the course of the various festival events that this ritual meal and storytelling took place. According to the aetiological tradition, the seven youths and seven maidens were held in seclusion during the days before their departure for Crete, but their mothers continued to bring them food.[54] In connection with the fact that Hesychios mentions a place called the *oschophorion* situated near the temple of Athena Skiras at Phaleron,[55] scholars generally believe that the meal was consumed there.[56]

Even though Plutarch does not allude to the ephebic race mentioned by Proclus and others, the association with the Oschophoria is supported by the fact that a competition (ἄμιλλος) is mentioned in the Salaminioi inscription.[57] Edward Kadletz postulated a race run from a temple of Dionysos in Athens to the precinct of Athena Skiras in Phaleron,[58] but Deubner had already shown that both the account of Aristodemos and that of the scholiast to Nicander are most likely the products of a confusion between the race and procession at the Oschophoria.[59] The winner of the race drank from a vessel called the πενταπλόα, which contained a mixture of olive oil, wine, honey, cheese and barley.[60] Pierre Vidal-Naquet has recognized close parallels between the race at the Oschophoria and the race of the *staphylodromoi* ("grape cluster runners") during the

---

[48]   *LSS* 19, ll. 47–50.
[49]   Istros *FGrH* 334 F 8; cf. Hsch. s.v. Ὀσχοφόρια: παῖδες εὐγενεῖς; Phot. *Lex.* s.v. ὀσχοφορεῖν: εὐγενὴς παῖς.
[50]   Waldner 2000, 110.
[51]   Procl. *Chrestomathia* ap. Phot. *Bibl.* 322a. 26–27.
[52]   See e.g. Parker 2005 (217) who argues for a male chorus to strengthen his interpretation of the Oschophoria as an "ephebes' rite".
[53]   Calame 1990, 335, 338; Calame 2001, 127f. Without out a justified reason, Waldner says the chorus is female, Waldner 2000, 115f., 141.

[54]   Philoch. *FGrH* 328 F 183.
[55]   Hsch. s.v. Ὀσχοφόριον· τόπος Ἀθήνησι Φαληροῖ, ἔνθα τὸ τῆς Ἀθηνᾶς ἱερόν.
[56]   See e.g. Waldner 2000, 163.
[57]   *LSS* 19, l. 61.
[58]   Kadletz 1980, esp. 370.
[59]   Deubner 1932, 145 on Aristodemos *FGrH* 383 F 9 and Schol. Nic. *Alex.* 109a. Cf. Parker 2005, 213f.
[60]   Procl. *Chrestomathia* ap. Phot. *Bibl.* 322a.28–30.

Spartan Karneia held in honour of Apollo Karneios.[61] The Karneia, an annual festival of the
phratriai, was celebrated in the summer month
of Karneios.[62] The ancient tradition emphasizes the military aspect of the festival, describing
it as an imitation of soldier life.[63] In each of the
nine temporarily erected tent-like constructions (σκιάδες), nine men ate together. There
is strong evidence that musical competitions
took place at the Karneia, and choral dances by
youths and maidens may have been performed
during the festival.[64] What seems to be the most
important ritual during the festival was the
race of the *staphylodromoi*. In this race, a man
wrapped up in woollen fillets (στέμματα) was
chased by youths (νέοι) called *staphylodromoi*.
The *staphylodromoi* were chosen by lot among
the *karneatai*, unmarried (ἄγαμοι) men who
were in charge of the organization of the festival.[65] To catch the fillet-draped runner meant
good luck for the city. Interestingly, the sources
do not explicitly mention that the *staphylodromoi* carried bunches of grapes as in the case of
the *oschophoroi*, and perhaps the *staphylodromoi* were merely wreathed with grapevine.[66]

Sam Wide has emphasized the agricultural
aspect of the Karneia ("Weinlesefest") and
explained the *staphylodromia* as an expiation
rite.[67] However, since the Karneia was held

in midsummer rather than in autumn, a close
connection with the grape vintage remains
doubtful. It was Henri Jeanmaire who first suggested an interpretation of the festival as a rite
of passage for male adolescents on the threshold of nubile age.[68] This interpretation has wide
acceptance but the specific character of the
staphylodromia as a pursuit race is not easy to
reconcile with any initiatory interpretation. It
has long been noted that the man draped with
the *stemmata* resembles a sacrificial animal,
probably a ram.[69] Moreover, in contrast to the
oschophoroi leading the procession, the runners in the race at the Oschophoria most likely
did not carry grape clusters or vine branches.[70]
As will be shown later on, the *oschophoroi* belonged to a somewhat younger age group than
the ephebic runners in the races at the Oschophoria and Karneia. Thus, the alleged parallels
between the *oschophoroi* and the *staphylodromoi* seem rather superficial.

Despite the fact that the Oschophoria are
clearly associated with both Athena Skiras and
Dionysos in the textual sources, a long-standing
debate arose about which deity was chiefly honoured at the festival. Whereas Deubner, Simon,
and more recently Hedreen, argued for a festival
of Dionysos,[71] the Oschophoria were primarily linked to Athena by Ferguson, Ziehen and
Parke.[72] Lately scholars have tried to resolve the
issue by attributing the festival to both gods.[73]
Even though the Oschophoria are, according
to present day knowledge, the only case of a
shared cult of Athena and Dionysos, it would

---

61 Vidal-Naquet 1986, 116, 126, n. 51. For the Karneia, see Wide 1893, 73–87; Burkert 1985, 234–236;
Pettersson 1992, 57–72.
62 According to Plut. *Nic.* 28.2, the Spartan month
of Karneios corresponds to the Attic month of Meta-
geitnion (August/September).
63 Ath. 4.141e–f.
64 Musical competitions: Ath. 14.635e–f (= Hellanikos *FGrH* 4 F 85a). Choral dances: Burkert 1985, 234,
440, n. 6. Cf. Calame 2001, 203, n. 349.
65 Anecd. Bekk. I, 305.25; Hsch. s.v. καρνεᾶται,
σταφυλοδρόμοι.
66 *Pace* Wide 1893, 76: "... Staphylodromen, welche
wahrscheinlich Traubenzweige in den Händen hielten ... ".
For the scarce evidence of grapevine wreaths, see Blech
1982, 211.
67 Wide 1893, 75–83.

68 Jeanmaire 1939, 524–526. Cf. Pettersson 1992, 71f.
69 Wide 1893, 78f. and Burkert 1985, 235 on Theoc.
Id. 5.83 and Hsch. s.v. κάρνος. For the adornment of
sacrificial animals with *stemmata*, see Blech 1982, 303f.
70 Cf. above n. 59.
71 Deubner 1932, 143f.; Simon 1983, 90, 91f.; Hedreen 1992, 84, n. 132.
72 Ferguson 1938, 38–41; Ziehen 1942, 1541f.; Parke
1977, 79.
73 Deacy 1997, 160; Waldner 2000, 145–150, 159–
163; Calame 2001, 125, 137; Parker 2005, 215.

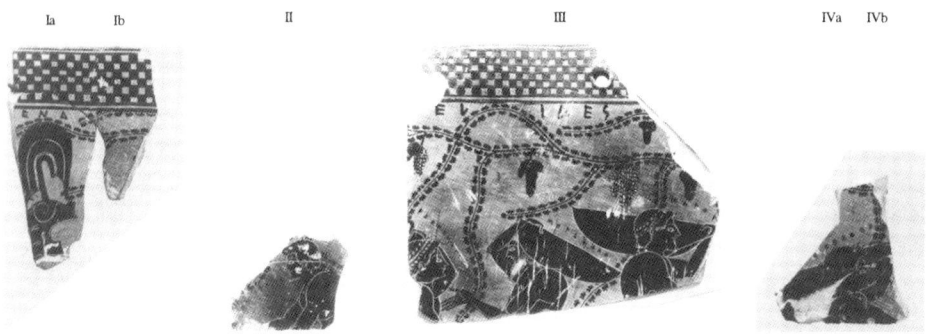

Fig. 2. Attic pinax (inv. no. 15124). Athens, National Museum. After Fritzilas 2000, pl. 3:1.

in fact be unwise to deny that both gods played a similarly important role in the festival. Several Attic black-figured vases showing Athena and Dionysos engaged in conversation might be seen as a glimpse into their cultic community at the Oschophoria. Interestingly, all these vases date to a rather short period covering the late sixth and early fifth centuries BC.[74]

Less surprisingly, the interpretation of the festival itself has been similarly controversial.[75] Since the Oschophoria are clearly related to the grape harvest, various scholars have, in the tradition of Wilhelm Mannhardt, interpreted the festival as a thanksgiving.[76] Claude Calame substantially modified this "agricultural" interpretation focusing on the symbolic value of the grape clusters carried by the *oschophoroi*, the *pentaploa* with its five ingredients and the food (ὄψα καὶ σιτία) brought by the *deipnophoroi*. He interpreted the sequence of these rites as a symbolic representation of human dietary development from raw fruit, closely linked to

Dionysos, to a cooked "nourriture civilisée" associated with Athena.[77]

While Dionysos is intimately connected with winegrowing, Athena's link with fertility is much less straightforward. However, there is some scattered evidence that associates the goddess with affairs of this kind.[78] A fragmentary Attic black-figured pinax from the Athenian Acropolis (*Fig. 2*) shows Athena—only her helmet is preserved on the left edge—watching the harvest of grapes carried out by youthful and bearded men.[79] Since all these figures are wreathed and apparently naked, a religious connotation is obvious, and the representation should therefore not be regarded as a genre scene.[80] Given the prominent role of Athena at the Oschophoria, a festival closely linked with the grape harvest, one wonders if the painter might have had this specific occasion in mind. In the Salaminioi inscription, the sacrifice of a pregnant sheep to Athena Skiras is attested.[81] This sacrifice, however, did not take place at the Oschophoria but in the following month of Maimakterion. In addition, a possible case of a pregnant sacrificial victim for Athena is attest-

---

[74] *LIMC* II (1984), 1000 s.v. Athena, nos. 486–488, pl. 755 (P. Demargne); *LIMC* III (1986), 466 s.v. Dionysos, nos. 500–504, pl. 357 (C. Gasparri).
[75] Cf. Waldner's (2000, 134–138) remarks on the previous research.
[76] Mannhardt 1877, 253–256; Deubner 1932, 146; Ferguson 1938, 40; Parke 1977, 160f.; Simon 1983, 90.

[77] Calame 1990, 324–327, 338f.
[78] Cf. Parker 2005, 418.
[79] Fritzilas 2000.
[80] *Pace* Fritzilas 2000, 40: "reale Weinleseszene".
[81] *LSS* 19, l. 92. Cf. Ferguson 1938, 28, 40.

ed iconographically. A fragmentary votive relief found at the Athenian Acropolis and dated to ca 490 BC shows a man, a woman and three children (two boys and a girl) appearing before the goddess.[82] In the foreground, an apparently pregnant sow, the family's offering to Athena, is depicted. It is widely agreed that pregnant sacrificial victims are associated with fertility goddesses.[83] Emphasizing the abnormal and allegedly negative character of such sacrifices, Jan Bremmer has recently contradicted this view.[84] Bremmer argues that a "negative" sacrifice would fit the "abnormal" transitional period between youth and adulthood. Be this as it may, in the specific case of the votive relief it seems somewhat daring to deduce a direct link between the sacrifice of a (possibly) pregnant animal and a boy's rites of passage.[85] Given the general proximity of the concept of fertility and the maturation of children and adolescents, the connection is more likely an indirect one. At any rate, it has become clear that Athena, in particular Athena Skiras, might have been involved to some extent with fertility.

In more recent research, the "agricultural" interpretation of the festival has been pushed aside in favour of a different interpretative approach focusing on the reputed initiatory character of the rite.[86] Expressing some reservation about terms such as "rite of passage" and "initiation", Robert Parker has recently proposed a reading of the Oschophoria as an "ephebes' rite". His interpretation, however, falls generally in line with the traditional initiatory approach.[87] According to this view, the cross-

dressing of the two boys carrying vine branches is a clear indication of the rite's initiatory character. Furthermore, it is generally assumed that the two *oschophoroi* stand for their entire age class.[88] In this line of reasoning, however, scholars seem to neglect the fact that the *oschophoroi* and the ephebes competing in the tribal race almost certainly did not represent the same age group. Only Waldner rightly emphasized that the literary sources describe the *oschophoroi* as παῖδες, νεανίσκοι or νεανίαι, whereas the runners are usually referred to as ἔφηβοι or ἠίθεοι.[89] It is therefore probable that the *oschophoroi*, and perhaps also the members of the chorus following them, were not identical to the male adolescents competing in the tribal race but may have represented a younger age group. The aforementioned calendar frieze of Hagios Eleutherios possibly illustrates this age difference. Next to the naked youth holding a grapevine is depicted a little boy with a large branch on his shoulder (*Fig. 1*). The branch is commonly interpreted as the *eiresione*, an olive or laurel branch wound with woollen ribbons and decorated with various kinds of fruits. In all likelihood, the figure alludes to the Pyanopsia, a festival of Apollo which was celebrated on Pyanopsion 7, as were most likely the Oschophoria.[90] The official procession at the Pyanopsia was led by a boy with "both parents alive" (παῖς ἀμφιθαλής) carrying the *eiresione*.[91] Based on epigraphical evidence, Noel Robertson was able to establish an age of about seven years for two such boys.[92] Regarding the much older male adolescent representing the Oschophoria (*Fig. 1*), various interpretations have been sug-

---

[82] van Straten 1995, 77, 289, R58, fig. 79.
[83] Nilsson 1967, 151f.; Scullion 1994, 86; Parker 2005, 416.
[84] Bremmer 2005.
[85] Cf. Bremmer 2005, 162. For an interpretation as an offering on the occasion of the Apatouria, see Palagia 1995.
[86] Jeanmaire 1939, 344–358; Vidal-Naquet 1986, 116f.; Leitao 1995, 133, 148f.
[87] Parker 2005, 216f.

[88] Bremmer 1999, 190f.; Parker 2005, 217.
[89] Waldner 2000, 114, n. 49f.
[90] For the Pyanopsia, see Deubner 1932, 198–201; Parke 1977, 75–77; Parker 2005, 204–206.
[91] With regard to the Oschophoria, a single source (Schol. Nic. *Alex.* 109a), probably confusing the race with the procession, speaks of the runners as παῖδες ἀμφιθαλεῖς; cf. above n. 59.
[92] Robertson 1984, 389f.

gested. Whereas Erika Simon believed that Dionysos himself is depicted, Kadletz argued that it was the winner in the ephebic race.[93] Be this as it may, the *oschophoroi*, whose age could have approximately corresponded to that of the boy carrying the *eiresione* at the Pyanopsia, almost certainly belonged to a somewhat younger age group than the adolescents participating in the race at the Oschophoria.

It is evident that a complex festival such as the Oschophoria cannot be interpreted simply in terms of either its agricultural *or* initiatory aspect. A comprehensive approach must take account of both aspects and must also properly consider the specific role of each group of participants. As we have seen, along with the ephebes competing in the tribal race, children (*oschophoroi*), adult women (*deipnophoroi*) and, most likely, male and female adolescents (chorus members) also took part in the rites. Moreover, it can be assumed that other groups not explicitly mentioned by Plutarch and Proclus participated in both the procession to, and the sacrificial rites at, Phaleron.[94] The conventional initiatory approach, though, not only exclusively focuses on the male adolescents competing in the race and the allegedly ephebic *oschophoroi*, but also tends to interpret the role of all other participants in relation to both of these groups. The transvestism of the *oschophoroi* is usually seen as a way of dramatizing the moment of transition from girlish boy to mature man,[95] yet cross-dressing is not necessarily connected with initiation, since the phenomenon occurs in a wide range of instances including wedding rites and Dionysiac status reversal

rituals.[96] Calame, in fact, explicitly rejected an initiatory interpretation and described the festival as an example of "bouleversement des catégories sociales", typical for rituals associated with Dionysos.[97] Given the diversity of the participating groups, a mere initiatory approach or a label such as "ephebes' rite" seems inadequately reductive, since these interpretations cannot provide a comprehensive explanation of the festival.[98] Even though the aspect of socialization of male, and possibly also female, children and adolescents clearly plays an important role, the Oschophoria should not be seen as either a rite of passage for a specific male age group or as a "survival" of a tribal rite of initiation.

Elaborating on the earlier interpretative approaches, Waldner recently proposed a more balanced reading of the Oschophoria.[99] Despite her practice theory approach to ritual already criticized above, Waldner's interpretation has several points of contact with a genuine performative perspective. Particularly with regard to the procession, the display of wealth and social status is acknowledged as an essential element.[100] Waldner furthermore recognized the importance of the personal experience of the ritual actors, but her perception of this experience was largely determined by the view that the rituals at the Oschophoria reflect *polis* ideology. This view is ultimately rooted in the Durkheimian concept of ritual as replicating and reinforcing social structure. Performing the rites at the Oschophoria, the participants indeed experienced *polis* religion as a norma-

---

[93]   Simon 1983, 90; Kadletz 1980, 368.

[94]   Women called κώπαι ("handles") are mentioned in the Salaminioi inscription (*LSS* 19, l. 46; cf. Ferguson 1938, 46f.; Parker 2005, 215, n. 101) and probably played a role in the festival.

[95]   Vidal-Naquet 1986, 116. Cf. Leitao 1995, 146 for the case of the Ekdysia at Phaistos.

[96]   For a recent general discussion of cross-dressing in ancient Greece, see Miller 1999, 241–246 with references. On Dionysiac transvestism, see Csapo 1997, 262–264.

[97]   Calame 1990, 334–337, 339.

[98]   For a general criticism of the application of the initiation scheme, see Versnel 1993, 48–60, 56f. (Oschophoria).

[99]   Waldner 2000, 138–175 (brief summary in *Der neue Pauly* IX [2000], 81f. s.v. Oschophorien).

[100]   Waldner 2000, 139.

tive system. Yet, what is largely neglected in this approach is the participant's *individual* experience of the rite, which is obviously much more difficult to grasp. It is important to note that the transformative capacity of ritual lies precisely in the personal experience of the single individual rather than in the "external" aspect of, for instance, a status change which is moreover often wrongly ascribed to the respective rites.[101]

On a basic level of interpretation, several parts of the Oschophoria could be seen as a ritual re-enactment of Theseus' Cretan adventure.[102] Since the plot is not taken from the myth of the gods in whose honour the festival is celebrated, this re-enactment would not exactly correspond to the definition for ritual drama given by Nielsen, but it should definitely be described as a form of cultic play.[103] With regard to the ritual actors, the mimetic character of the ritual performance implies intensively experienced role-playing through a temporally framed identification with the mythical protagonists. Here, the case of the women serving as *deipnophoroi* is of particular interest. By acting as "dinner-carriers", these women directly experience the feelings and emotions of mothers whose children's lives are at stake. This experience might have strengthened their ability to face similar situations in their own lives. The fact that the women tell stories (μῦθοι) testifies to the essential role that speech played in this specific ritual performance. We do not learn what these stories were about, but they probably functioned within the framework of the mythical plot, that is, the mothers told the *mythoi* in order to encourage and comfort their "children". Obviously, the stories told by the *deipnophoroi* do not constitute performative utterances in the Austinian sense, but narratives. As we are impeded from any analysis of their

pragmatics and formal structure, it can only be very generally noted that storytelling is frequently used as an instrument by which social identities are constructed and negotiated.[104] No matter whether the stories were derived from the Theseus myth or not, the Oschophoria might have thus provided a public forum for the negotiation of personal and collective identities by means of ritualized narrative performances. Regarding the personal experience of the ritual actors, a similar point can be made for the *oschophoroi* which were, as already pointed out, chosen from wealthy and noble families. Leading the procession, the boys did not merely display the high social status of their families but *experienced* this status personally. By trying to properly "play" their roles as *oschophoroi*, the boys aimed, in the first place, to fulfil an obligation toward their families. Nevertheless, this experience would certainly have helped them become aware of the elevated position of their families in Athenian society.

In an interesting case study of the ceremony concluding the Hindu funeral of V.S. Naipaul's sister Sati, celebrated in Trinidad in 1985, Tomas Gerholm demonstrated that there was no coherent perspective on this ritual which would have been shared by all participants.[105] Gerholm's analysis was based on the description of the ceremony the West Indian author gave in an autobiographical novel published two years after his sister's death.[106] Aside from Naipaul himself and the ritual expert performing the rite, Sati's widowed husband and her adolescent son were present. Gerholm detected a plurality of different attitudes to the ritual that depended not only on the religious knowledge and devotion but also on the level of emotional involvement of the individual participants. These different attitudes were

---

[101] See Grimes 2004, esp. 116, 122 for a sceptical view of the transformative properties of ritual.
[102] Nielsen 2002, 115.
[103] Cf. above n. 24.

[104] Bauman 1986, 113.
[105] Gerholm 1988.
[106] Naipaul 1987, 343–354.

likely to have caused a considerable diversity in the individual experience of the ritual. The implications of this insight are far-reaching: there is no coherent meaning of a given ritual that would have been conceived by all participants in the same way. The fact that the individual experiences of the participants substantially differ from each other results instead in a fragmentation of meaning. Considering the case of the Oschophoria, there could be reasons to assume that Gerholm's perceptions are valid not only for our culturally fragmented modern world but, at least partly, also for the supposedly more coherent cultural system of ancient Greece.

DR OLIVER PILZ
Institut für Klassische Archäologie
Johannes Gutenberg-Universität
opilz@uni-mainz.de

Bibliography

Austin 1962   J.L. Austin, *How to do things with words*, Cambridge, Mass. 1962.

Bauman 1986   R. Bauman, *Story, performance, and event: Contextual studies of oral narratives*, Cambridge 1986.

Becker 2003   T. Becker, *Griechische Stufenanlagen. Untersuchungen zur Architektur, Entwicklungsgeschichte, Funktion und Repräsentation*, Münster 2003.

Bell 1992   C. Bell, *Ritual theory, ritual practice*, New York & Oxford 1992.

Bell 1997   C. Bell, *Ritual: Perspective and dimensions*, Oxford & New York 1997.

Blech 1982   M. Blech, *Studien zum Kranz bei den Griechen* (Religionsgeschichtliche Versuche und Vorarbeiten, 38), Berlin & New York 1982.

Bremmer 1998   J.N. Bremmer, '"Religion", "ritual" and the opposition "sacred" vs. "profane"', in *Ansichten griechischer Rituale. Geburtstagssymposion für Walter Burkert, Castelen bei Basel, 15. bis 18. März 1996*, ed. F. Graf, Stuttgart & Leipzig 1998, 9–32.

Bremmer 1999   J.N. Bremmer, 'Transvestite Dionysos', in *Rites of passage in ancient Greece: Literature, religion, society* (= Bucknell Review 43, 1999), ed. M.W. Padilla, Lewisburg 1999, 183–200.

Bremmer 2005   J.N. Bremmer, 'The sacrifices of pregnant animals', in *Greek sacrificial ritual, Olympian and chthonian. Proceedings of the sixth international seminar on ancient Greek cult organized by the Department of Classical Archaeology and Ancient History, Göteborg University, 25–27 April 1997* (ActaAth-8°, 18), eds. R. Hägg & B. Alroth, Stockholm 2005, 155–165.

Burkert 1983   W. Burkert, 'The problem of ritual killing', in *Violent origins: Walter Burkert, René Girard, and Jonathan Z. Smith on ritual killing and cultural formation*, ed. R.G. Hamerton-Kelly, Stanford 1983, 149–176.

Burkert 1985   W. Burkert, *Greek religion: Archaic and Classical*, Cambridge, Mass. 1985.

Burkert 2006   W. Burkert, 'Ritual between ethnology and Post-modern aspects: Philological-historical notes', in *Ritual and communication in the Graeco-Roman world* (Kernos, Suppl. 16), ed. E. Stavrianopoulou, Liège 2006, 23–35.

Calame 1990   C. Calame, *Thésée et l'imaginaire athénien: légende et culte en Grèce antique*, Lausanne 1990.

Calame 2001   C. Calame, *Choruses of young women in ancient Greece*, Lanham 2001.

Clinton 1992   K. Clinton, *Myth and cult: The iconography of the Eleusinian Mysteries* (ActaAth-8°, 11), Stockholm 1992.

Csapo 1997   E. Csapo, 'Riding the phallus for Dionysus: Iconology, ritual and gender-role de/construction', *Phoenix* 51, 1997, 253–295.

Deacy 1997   S. Deacy, 'Athena and the Amazons: Mortal and immortal femininity in Greek myth', in *What is a god? Studies in the nature of Greek divinity*, ed. A.B. Lloyd, London 1997, 153–168.

Demmer 2006   U. Demmer, *Rhetorik, Poetik, Performanz. Das Ritual und seine Dynamik bei den Jēnu Kurumba (Südindien)*, Münster 2006.

Deubner 1932   L. Deubner, *Attische Feste*, Berlin 1932.

Ferguson 1938   W.S. Ferguson, 'The Salaminoi of Heptaphyloi and Sounion', *Hesperia* 7, 1938, 1–74.

Fischer-Lichte 2003   E. Fischer-Lichte, 'Performance, Inszenierung, Ritual: Zur Klärung kulturwissenschaftli-cher Schlüsselbegriffe', in *Geschichtswissenschaft und "performative turn". Ritual, Inszenierung und Performanz vom Mittelalter bis zur Neuzeit*, eds. J. Martschukat & S. Patzold, Köln, Weimar & Berlin 2003, 33–54.

Fritzilas 2000   S.A. Fritzilas, 'Athena beim Weinlesefest. Eine Votivtafel des Rycroft-Malers', *Hefte des Archäologischen Seminars der Universität Bern* 17, 2000, 15–19.

Geertz 1973   C. Geertz, *The interpretation of cultures: Selected essays*, New York 1973.

Gerholm 1988   T. Gerholm, 'On ritual: A postmodernist view', *Ethnos: Journal of Anthropology* 53, 1988, 190–203.

Goldhill & Osborne 1999   *Performance culture and Athenian democracy*, eds. S. Goldhill & R. Osborne, Cambridge 1999.

Grimes 2004   R.L. Grimes, 'Performance theory and the study of ritual', in *New approaches to the study of religion* II: *Textual, comparative, sociological, and cognitive approaches*, eds. P. Antes, A.W. Geertz & R.R. Warne, Berlin & New York 2004, 109–138.

Grimes 2006   R.L. Grimes, 'Performance', in *Theorizing rituals: Issues, topics, approaches, concepts*, eds. J. Kreinath, J. Snoek & M. Stausberg, Leiden & Boston 2006, 379–394.

Harrison 1927   J.E. Harrison, *Themis: A study in the social origins of Greek religion*, Cambridge 1927².

Hedreen 1992 G.M. Hedreen, *Silens in Attic black-figure vase painting: Myth and performance*, Ann Arbor 1992.

Henrichs 2000 A. Henrichs, 'Drama and dromena: Bloodshed, violence, and sacrificial metaphor in Euripides', *HSCP* 100, 2000, 173–188.

Jeanmaire 1939 H. Jeanmaire, *Couroi et Courètes: essai sur l'éducation spartiate et sur les rites d'adolescence dans l'antiquité hellénique*, Lille 1939.

Kadletz 1980 E. Kadletz, 'The race and procession of the Oscophoria', *GRBS* 21, 1980, 363–371.

Kavoulaki 1999 A. Kavoulaki, 'Processional performance and the democratic polis', in *Performance culture and Athenian democracy*, eds. S. Goldhill & R. Osborne, Cambridge 1999, 293–320.

Kavoulaki 2000 A. Kavoulaki, 'The ritual performance of a pompê: Aspects and perspectives', in Δώρημα. *A tribute to the A. G. Leventis Foundation on the occasion of its 20th anniversary*, ed. A. Serghidou, Nicosia 2000, 145–158.

Lambert 1997 S.D. Lambert, 'The Attic genos Salaminioi and the island of Salamis', *ZPE* 119, 1997, 85–106.

Leitao 1995 D.D. Leitao, 'The perils of Leukippos: Initiatory transvestism and male gender ideology in the Ekdusia at Phaistos', *ClAnt* 14, 1995, 130–163.

Mannhardt 1877 W. Mannhardt, *Wald- und Feldkulte* II. *Antike Wald- und Feldkulte*, Berlin 1877.

Miller 1999 M.C. Miller, 'Re-examining transvestism in Archaic and Classical Athens: The Zewadski stamnos', *AJA* 103, 1999, 223–258.

Mylonopoulos 2006 J. Mylonopoulos, 'Greek sanctuaries as places of communication through ritual', in *Ritual and communication in the Graeco-Roman world* (Kernos, Suppl. 16), ed. E. Stavrianopoulou, Liège 2006, 69–109.

Naerebout 1997 F.G. Naerebout, *Attractive performances. Ancient Greek dance: Three preliminary studies*, Amsterdam 1997.

Naipaul 1987 V.S. Naipaul, *The enigma of arrival*, New York 1987.

Nielsen 2002 I. Nielsen, *Cultic theatres and ritual drama: A study in regional development and religious interchange between East and West in antiquity*, Aarhus 2002.

Nilsson 1967 M.P. Nilsson, *Geschichte der griechischen Religion* I, München 1967[3].

Palagia 1995 O. Palagia, 'Akropolis Museum 581: A family at the Apaturia', *Hesperia* 64, 1995, 493–501.

Palagia 2008 O. Palagia, 'The date and iconography of the Calendar Frieze on the Little Metropolis, Athens', *JdI* 123, 2008, 215–237.

Parke 1977 H.W. Parke, *Festivals of the Athenians*, London 1977.

Parker 1996 R. Parker, *Athenian religion: A history*, Oxford 1996.

Parker 2005 R. Parker, *Polytheism and society at Athens*, Oxford & New York 2005.

Pettersson 1992   M. Pettersson, *Cults of Apollo at Sparta: The Hyakinthia, the Gymnopaidiai and the Karneia* (ActaAth-8°,12), Stockholm 1992.

Rappaport 1999   R. Rappaport, *Ritual and religion in the making of humanity*, Cambridge 1999.

Robertson 1984   N. Robertson, 'The ritual background of the Erysichthon story', *AJP* 105, 1984, 369–408.

Rutherford & Irvine 1988   I.C. Rutherford & J.A.D. Irvine, 'The race in the Athenian Oschophoria and an Oschophoricon by Pindar', *ZPE* 72, 1988, 43–51.

Saladino 1998   V. Saladino, 'Aspetti rituali del giuramento greco', in *Seminari di storia e di diritto antico* II. *Studi sul giuramento nel mondo antico*, ed. A. Calore, Milano 1998, 87–106.

Scullion 1994   S. Scullion, 'Olympian and Chthonian', *ClAnt* 13, 1994, 75–119.

Searle 1969   J.R. Searle, *Speech acts: An essay in the philosophy of language*, London 1969.

Searle 1989   J.R. Searle, 'How performatives work', *Linguistics and Philosophy* 12, 1989, 535–558.

Simon 1983   E. Simon, *Festivals of Attica: An archaeological commentary*, Madison 1983.

Singer 1955   M. Singer, 'The cultural pattern of Indian civilization: A preliminary report of a methodological field study', *Far Eastern Quarterly* 15, 1955, 23–35.

van Straten 1995   F.T. van Straten, *Hierà kalá: Images of animal sacrifice in Archaic and Classical Greece* (Religions in the Graeco-Roman World, 127), Leiden, New York & Köln 1995.

Stavrianopoulou 2006   *Ritual and communication in the Graeco-Roman world* (Kernos, Suppl. 16), ed. E. Stavrianopoulou, Liège 2006.

Tambiah 1979   S.J. Tambiah, 'A performative approach to ritual', *Proceedings of the British Academy* 65, 1979, 113–169.

Turner 1969   V. Turner, *The ritual process: Structure and anti-structure*, London 1969.

Turner 1986   V. Turner, *The anthropology of performance*, New York 1986.

Versnel 1993   H.S. Versnel, *Inconsistencies in Greek and Roman religion* II. *Transition and reversal in myth and ritual*, Leiden, New York & Köln 1993.

Vidal-Naquet 1986   P. Vidal-Naquet, 'The Black Hunter and the origin of the Athenian *ephebia*', in P. Vidal-Naquet, *The Black hunter: Forms of thought and forms of society in the Greek world*, Baltimore 1986, 106–128.

Waldner 2000   K. Waldner, *Geburt und Hochzeit des Kriegers. Geschlechterdifferenz und Initiation in Mythos und Ritual der griechischen Polis* (Religionsgeschichtliche Versuche und Vorarbeiten, 46), Berlin & New York 2000.

Wide 1893   S. Wide, *Lakonische Kulte*, Leipzig 1893.

Ziehen 1942   L. Ziehen, *RE* XVIII.2 (1942), 1537–1543, s.v. Oschophoria.

KATERINA KOLOTOUROU

Musical rhythms from the cradle to the grave

Abstract*

Musical performance was a powerful and integral element of Greek religious ritual that helped worshippers to partake in the divine essence. In this paper I examine the religious significance of percussive music in the historical period. I argue that the *drōmenon* of percussive performance conveys concepts that are essential to the ritual, and which stem from the origins and effects of mundane percussive actions and from the biological value of rhythmically structured behaviour. The analysis of selected examples of percussive performance in Greek ritual reveals the inherent potential of percussive enactment to imitate the nature of the divine through sequences of metaphorical associations. The morphology, musical potential and playing method of different types of percussion all have a role in ritual dramatization. Rattles and clappers in particular are shown to take on the values of *rhythmos* as a notion complementary to *harmonia* for the realization of natural and social order. The agency of these percussive practices in ritual enactment is also reflected in myth, such as Herakles' use of *krotalon* (clapper) and *platage* (rattle) in his vanquishing of the Stymphalian birds. Art, literature and material remains provide a multifaceted picture where complementary religious concepts and social practices are reconciled via the performance of percussive music.

---

* I would like to thank Andrew Barker, Keith Rutter and Ellen van Keer for their fruitful discussion and comments on earlier versions of this paper, as well as the editors for their diligence with the manuscript. Any remaining mistakes or omissions are my own responsibility.

Sound and drōmenon

> "... ἥ τε μουσικὴ περὶ τε ὄρχησίν οὖσα καὶ ῥυθμὸν καὶ μέλος ἡδονῇ τε ἅμα καὶ καλλιτεχνίᾳ πρὸς τὸ θεῖον ἡμᾶς συνάπτει ..." (Strab. 10.3.9)

> "... music, which includes dancing as well as rhythm and melody, at the same time, by the delight it affords and by its artistic beauty, brings us in touch with the divine ..." (trans. H.L. Jones).

Strabo's contention in the tenth book of the *Geography* that through the delight and artistry of *choreia*, rhythm and melody we are brought in contact with the divine, encapsulates deep-rooted ways of thinking about the elevating and enlightening powers that music has upon the celebrants of a religious rite. Connection with the gods entails a degree of participation in the divine nature that mortals are able to realize mainly by way of imitation. Strabo goes on to declare that experiencing the happiness (*eudaimonia*) which derives from celebrating festivals, pursuing philosophy and engaging in music is the optimum way of imitating the god. What guarantees music's effectiveness as a decisive mimetic avenue is the earnest belief that all forms of music are of divine origin, promulgating the order of the universe which is καθ' ἁρμονίαν (in accordance with harmony), a concept that is much elaborated within the

Pythagorean and Platonic schools of thought.[1] With its god-given credentials, the practice of *mousikē*, defined as the unified continuum of poetry-song, instrumental music and co-ordinated physical movement, was central to Greek religion and worship from earliest times.

The intricate correlation between music and religion is an absorbing question. My contribution focuses on the signification of percussive performance, which is viewed in a rather deceptive way in the majority of Greek musical studies. Percussion instruments are customarily described as exotic noisy paraphernalia of eastern origin that may offer handy rhythmical accompaniment for the dances, but nevertheless remain peripheral to authentic Greek musicianship.[2] Moreover, since the repetitive

sounds of percussion are generally unsuitable for producing melody or supporting it harmonically, existing scholarship tends to regard them as musically unrewarding and devoid of aesthetic or symbolic value by default.[3]

Influenced very much by western harmony-based evaluations of music, this reductive approach derives also from the neglect of percussion in the philosophical and musical-theoretical treatises of antiquity where, by contrast, the harmony and ethos of stringed and wind instruments is a recurrent theme, often discussed in connection with the universal "harmony of the spheres". While these writings vividly substantiate categorizations of stringed and wind instruments in Greek musical thought and practice, percussion receives very little mention as a distinct instrumental class. In the middle of a lengthy account of various stringed instruments, the second-century AD writer Athenaios makes a brief reference to instruments "such as *krembala*" that "merely produce a noise" (ψόφου μόνον ποιητικά), which

---

[1] Cf. Strab. 10.3.10: "Καὶ διὰ τοῦτο μουσικὴν ἐκάλεσε Πλάτων καὶ ἔτι πρότερον οἱ Πυθαγόρειοι τὴν φιλοσοφίαν, καὶ καθ'ἁρμονίαν τὸν κόσμον συνεστάναι φασί, πᾶν τὸ μουσικὸν εἶδος θεῶν ἔργον ὑπολαμβάνοντες." For Strabo, the heavenly derivation of music justifies sufficiently the principle that music has curative powers on the mind, which is precisely the reason why music has supreme educational importance (see comments in Hardie 2004, 14–15). A similar line of reasoning is conveyed in Ath. 14.632B–C; Pl. *Ti.* 32c, 35b–36d, 37a, 41b; Resp. 616b–617c; Plut. [*De Mus.*] 1138b–1139f, 1147a (see Barker 1984, 227–230, 248f. n. 261). On the analogy between musical harmony and universal harmony and cosmology, see Kartomi 1990, 115–117; Lippman 1963, esp. 3–25; Kinkeldey 1948, 30f. The Indo-Iranian ancestry for the cosmological significance of the concept of harmony has been argued by Curtis-Franklin 2002, 7–10.

[2] I am using the term "percussion" to indicate as a whole the types of instruments that are classified in the Hornbostel-Sachs system as idiophones and membranophones. The difference lies in the nature of the vibrating body. Idiophones produce sounds as the sound device itself vibrates, while membranophones resonate by way of a vibrating membrane (Hornbostel & Sachs 1961, 14). Rattles, *seistra*, clappers, cymbals, bells and gongs belong to the former category, whereas drums and tambourines to the latter. Idiophones are further distinguished according to the method of excitation (striking, shaking, scraping etc.). Greek membranophones are usually beaten with the palms and fingers, while other forms of beater are far less common. In my discussion I shall also be using the term "percussive" to

refer collectively to these methods of sound production.

[3] Cf. Comotti 1989, 74–75, "Among the Greeks, *unlike other ancient peoples*, percussion instruments were never widespread nor particularly important. Their use was generally *restricted* to the rituals of the cults of Dionysos and Kybele, and were always perceived as *exotic instruments not connected with the most ancient and genuine traditions of the Greeks*" (my italics). Prominent scholars of ancient music have espoused analogous views; among others, see Aign 1963, 128–129; Landels 1999, 81; West 1992, 122, 126; Winnington-Ingram 1980, 663. Notably contrasting, however, is Mathiesen's musical appraisal of percussion. He remarks on the ability of idiophones and membranophones to articulate the rhythmic and metric patterns of music and also "to sound multiple simultaneous patterns, such as the contrast between the rhythmic and metric patterns that frequently appears in the musical fragments" (Mathiesen 1999, 162f.; with expanded rhythmic pattern analysis in 1985, 169–179). Recent accounts of Bronze Age musical practice have drawn attention to the value of the Minoan *seistron* for rhythm-keeping in performance and in music instruction (Younger 1998, 8f.; Mikrakis 2000, 164).

he sets apart from instruments that are "blown into" (ἐμφυσωμένων) and from those "divided up by strings" (χορδαῖς διειλημμένων).[4] Clearly, Athenaios' aim was to exhibit a *tour de force* of scholarly connoisseurship by recapitulating the Aristoxenian tripartite classification system of strings, wind and percussion that was already in existence in the fourth century BC. Aristoxenos' taxomony introduces percussion as a type of instrument that resounds when held and touched upon (καθαπτά).[5] His wording emphasizes the playing action, whereby the surfaces of such instruments are struck or made to collide.[6] Although Aristoxenos rated strings and percussion above wind instruments, his admission of percussion as a separate instrument category did not stimulate further aesthetic or scientific discussion of its music. He neverthe-

less validated the sounding action of beating that positively reflected the nature of the resulting sound.[7]

The general absence of percussion from theorizing is nevertheless counteracted by the richness of textual, epigraphic and iconographic sources that principally present percussive music in tandem with religious activity, and particularly, although not exclusively, in association with mystery-related and initiation rituals.[8] It therefore creates a considerable paradox to underestimate percussive music as performatively insignificant on the grounds of its predominantly unmelodic, rhythmical and "noisy" character, especially when we consider the amply documented apotropaic, protective and purificatory qualities that were attributed to *krotos*.[9] Faith in the latter's magical superpow-

---

[4]   Ath. 14.636d: "ἦν γὰρ δή τινα καὶ χωρὶς τῶν ἐμφυσωμένων καὶ χορδαῖς διειλημμένων ψόφου μόνον ποιητικά, ὡς τὰ κρέμβαλα [...]." The term *krembala* is generally understood as an alternative for *krotala*, indicating clappers and castanets. According to Barker, on occasion it may have denoted instruments with a ringing metallic timbre such as cymbals or *seistra* (Barker 1984, 297f. nn. 193–194).

[5]   Cf. Wehrli 1967, fr. 95: "ὁ μέντοι Ἀριστόξενος προκρίνει τὰ ἐντατὰ καὶ καθαπτὰ τῶν ὀργάνων τῶν ἐμπνευστῶν, ῥᾴω εἶναι φάσκων τὰ ἐμπνευστά." The Aristoxenian tripartite system of string, wind and percussion revised an older bipartite schema which remained in use until Late Antiquity and distinguished mainly between wind and strings (cf. Aristid. Quint. 2.16, 2.18; see DiGiglio 2000, 182–183, T3–4). While Aristoxenos' classification system demonstrates preoccupation with playing action in conjunction with the nature of the vibrating body, the bipartite schema reflects the rudimentary distinction between resonating air versus resonating matter. This may explain how strings and percussion became assimilated in the bipartite taxonomy of Pollux consisting of "beaten" (κρουόμενα) and "blown" (ἐμπνεόμενα) instruments (*Onom.* 4.58–87). For the two systems, see Kartomi 1990, 108–121; Di Giglio 2000, 99–107; Mathiesen 1999, 162.

[6]   Aristoxenos' emphasis on sound production by impact echoes earlier experimentations of Lasos of Hermione and the Pythagorean Hypassos of Metapontion, who investigated pitch by striking metal discs of different thickness and vessels part-filled with liquid; see West 1992, 128, 234.

[7]   Percussion instruments are also referred to as κρουστά (beaten), πληττόμενα and ἐπιπληττόμενα (struck), ἁπτικά (sensitive to touch), or ἔνηχα (resounding), most terms stemming from the playing action that caused the sound; for relevant ancient excerpts see DiGiglio 2000, 106.

[8]   Percussive performance is attested in connection with Dionysos, Kybele, Demeter, Artemis, Mother of the Gods, Korybantes, Sabazios, Apollo Amyklaios, Pan, Aphrodite, Hera and Athena; the list of evidence is extensive and cannot be exhaustively cited here. Textual, epigraphic and archaeological testimonia are amply collected in *ThesCRA* 2, 348f., 351, 353, 363, 383–390 and *ThesCRA* 5, 376–384; see also Mathiesen 1999, 162–176. Literary references: West 1992, 122–128; Schatkin 1978, 151, 160–164; Barker 1984, 59–60, no. 29 and nn. 23–24, p. 74, no. 63 and n. 77, p. 76, nos. 69–71 and nn. 89–90 and 93, 296–298. Material and textual evidence relating percussion with Artemis, Aphrodite, Dionysos, Kybele and Pan: Zschätzsch 2002, 66, 73f., 84, 121–123, 124 respectively; Vendries 2001 for Roman Kybele; Castaldo 1995, especially for cymbals. Percussion in mystery cult and Dionysian scenes: Hardie 2004, 16 nn. 29 and 31; Bélis 1988, 13–20; Villing 2002, 285–289; Guizzi & Staiti 1992–1995, esp. 51–70.

[9]   *ThesCRA* 5, 376. For the apotropaic sound of beating bronze in particular, see Schatkin 1978, 150, 156–160; Cook 1902, 14–25; Constantinidou 1992, esp. 153–159; Villing 2002, 278–282, 289–294, with bibliography and remarks on bronze bells. Bérard 1974, 75–87, 166 connects the noisy sound devices with the Lévi-Straussian "instruments of darkness" (Lévi-Strauss

ers was without doubt one of the grounds that automatically lent percussion a special significance in cult. An integrated approach, however, requires that we assess percussive music as an integral component of the practice of *mousikē* and an element of performance which, by means of its acoustic, visual and kinetic outcome, generates appropriate psychological-affective, aesthetic and cognate responses within ritual.

When incorporated into the ritual sequence, musical performance becomes a paradigm of action by means of which the participants are acculturated and instructed. The edifying quality of *mousikē* in imparting religious and social knowledge has been recently demonstrated both in relation to mystery cults and within the broader context of communal festivals.[10] This is not to say that music stands as a symbolic manifestation of religious concepts, but that the act itself of "making music" engenders elements of the required knowledge.[11] In other words, the musical act employed in the ritual action reinforces the concepts of social and cosmic order endorsed by the ritual. In this respect, the form and constituents of the act ought to be pertinent to that knowledge in order to promote the right messages. It is thus only appropriate that essential elements of the ritual "truth" should be embedded in the *drōmenon* of percussive performance, since the context of the ritual reserves no space for actions that have little or nothing to do with the *nomizomena*.

Percussion and ritual

It is important for our purposes to consider at this point the mechanisms that render percussion a vital tool in religious ritual. The roots of this connection between percussion and ritual lie precisely in the oldest mundane percussive actions. The repetitive and rhythmical sound of beaten, scraped or shaken objects was among man's most primitive performative experiences, one that occurred repeatedly in the process of tool making, food processing, hunting and fighting. Such enterprises, the successful accomplishment of which not only secured subsistence and survival but also supported the creation of social hierarchy and organization, relied heavily on carrying out audible percussive actions. The auditory incidents were thus perceived in a more or less tight causal relationship between the sound actions and their effects, being an integral part of man's most essential self-maintaining activities. On this premise, orchestrated percussive expressions could be distinguished from casual noise into meaningful sound with sensory effects that could inform ritual behaviour.

Analogous acoustic effects normally accompany mystifying natural phenomena such as the clap of thunder or the trickle of rain. Such incidents inevitably lie beyond human control, yet they decisively affect human survival and cognitive ability. They would be experienced as powerful extra-human manifestations, with the effect that they could be naturally assimilated with principal conceptual configurations that explicate the workings of the universe and endorse human life and endurance.[12]

"Percussive results" deriving from both human and non-human agency, such as artefact making, rain and crop growth, the killing of an-

1973, 359–421) that possess both disruptive and constructive qualities according to the context of action.

[10] Hardie 2004, esp. 21–29 expounded the analogy between partaking in choric *mousikē* and in mystic doctrine. Similarly, Kowalzig 2004 argued that choral performance served as a medium for ethical-religious collective education that promoted the shaping of social behaviour; her ideas are developed further in Kowalzig 2008.

[11] See Bell 1992, 41–46 on performance as "meaningful action"; Rappaport 1999, 104–138.

[12] See Rault 2000, 12 for impressions of the natural soundscape upon early man; in connection with percussion, see Blades 1984, 33–36.

imals and so on, have important social implications for the emergence, preservation or adaption of community structures. It is therefore a viable option for particular social strategies to promote the establishment of conceptual links between percussive sounds or experiences and socially valuable attributes such as the potency for cultivation, creation, nature control, animal/foe subjugation, protection, coming of age or the acquisition of status, and so on. Incorporated in a chain of metaphorical associations, a percussive act "links different social categories via strong sensory experience", working itself as a metaphor that motivates transformation from one category to another.[13] It acquires indexical and symbolic value that refers to features both of the social hierarchy and of the cosmic order.[14]

Of special relevance with regard to the ritualization[15] of percussion is the repetitive character of percussive actions and sounds. This factor accentuates the experience of rhythmical sequences and directs the focus onto changes in tempo and dynamism. Rhythm is the spinal column underlying our motor and vocal behaviour. The connection between patterned (hence rhythmical) action with conceptual thought was initially theorized by Blacking, who speculated on the evolutionary role of "proto-dance" and "proto-music".[16] His ideas were followed up and are now supported by research in the area of biomusicology and evolutionary musicology, investigating the ways in which rhythmic and melodic biological faculties structure human cognition, behaviour and communication at a primal level. These findings substantiate the importance of rhythmic arrangement in biological and social processes such as successful courtship and procreation, or the development of communication and learning skills, leading up to the creation of language and the inception of artefact manufacture and its techniques.[17] They further demonstrate that group integration and interaction, which are shown to be vital for the aforementioned processes, are largely achieved by adherence to repeated temporal patterns that allow synchronization, and to which humans respond cognitively and emotionally in order to confirm unity and affiliation. Thus, by conditioning motor and vocal communication, rhythmically structured behaviour effectively enhances group participation and bonding.[18]

The biological dimension of rhythmicality is particularly instructive for our understanding of ritual as patterned, interactive behaviour that essentially forges group identity and bonding, what Blacking coined as "conceptual synchronism".[19] Under this principle, the repetitive and formulaic patterns that govern effective communication as well as combat, subsistence and preservation strategies would also appear to be mechanisms that bring about ritual behaviour. I have already stressed that in the course of these strategies recur repetitive,

---

[13] Knauft 1979, 189; Fernandez 1974. For metaphor as a process that governs understanding, see Tilley 1999.

[14] Following Peirce's distinctions of sign, indexicality describes a relation with the object that brings about (re)action. Within ritual, it concerns what the performers do with, in and through their performance; see Peirce 1932, 303–308; Kreinath 2005, 104. Symbols, on the other hand, are characterized by arbitrariness as they represent their object interpretatively without physical or contextual associations.

[15] By ritualization I refer to the process of distinguishing an action in comparison with other, more quotidian activities of similar nature; see Bell 1992, 88–93.

[16] Blacking 1976, 6, 11; Blacking 1973.

[17] See essays collected in Wallin *et al.* 2000; Morley 2003, 77–21 for more recent assessment with further bibliography. Compare Fitton 1973, 270 on the biological value of rhythm which endorses dexterity essential in dance and war.

[18] See in particular Wallin *et al.* 2000, 301–328 and 389–424 (contributions by Richman, Merker, Dissanayake and Freeman).

[19] Cf. Blacking 1976, 9; Maróthy 1993–1994, 425. Compare Rudhardt 1992, 146 and Lonsdale 1993, 92f., 99–107 on dance (musico-kinetic synchronism) as metaphor of *communitas*.

rhythmical percussive actions accompanied by sounds of percussive nature. The essential patterning of these movements and sounds translates into rhythmically articulated audio-kinetic expressions, which can further manifest themselves audibly and visually with the aid of actual sound devices. It is a viable hypothesis that the initial employment of percussive devices may have actually occurred in the process of ritualization of originally mundane percussive actions. Ethnomusicologists, on the other hand, have long speculated that the origin of intentionally produced sound tools may rest in rhythmical sound-movements such as body-slapping and foot-stamping.[20] In his recent cultural analysis of percussive behaviour Mowitt explores the concept of the (body) skin as a surface possessing interiority which becomes expressed through the act of striking. The percussive process therefore administers a point of contact between the internal and the external.[21] This interplay between the "internal entity" of the individual and the external world is intrinsic in ritual, for the latter serves both to separate and to unify these two spheres.

Metaphor and mimesis

It should be clear now that percussion, being in itself a means of accentuating rhythm and also a metaphorical reflection of significant natural and social conditions, is inherently relevant to ritual enactment. Simple in concept and easy to fashion from everyday objects, percussion instruments mimic, evoke and musically elaborate on acoustic prototypes which are connected with man's most ancient perceptions, concerns and patterns of action. Ritual enactment largely depends on the associative aspects

of the actions and sounds involved. In this respect, percussion is widely diversified in terms of timbre, colour, volume and sustainability of the sound-output: it can easily range from an overpowering or deafening volume to a subtle suggestive hum that is just about audible. As a result, the emotive impact of percussive music can be substantially different and tailored to the specific requirements of a rite. The implications of such multiple possibilities have not been considered previously in the context of Greek musical practice, and cannot be dealt with thoroughly here. For now it suffices to say that, although the most common descriptions of Greek percussion are as shrill, thunderous or fear-inducing,[22] alternative impressions were also available: for instance, the syncopated clacking of wooden or metal clappers, the continuous echoing of the bronze cauldrons at Dodona,[23] or the soft rustling that terracotta rattles would have emitted when shaken.[24] It is

---

[20] Cf. Sachs 1940, 25; Marcuse 1975, 3, 16; Blades 1984, 33.

[21] Mowitt 2005, 16–21.

[22] Daemonic and chthonian sound of *tympana*, *krotala* and cymbals: *Mir. Ausc.* 838b.33; Strab. 10.3.16; Aesch. *Ἠδωνοί* fr. 57 (Radt 1985); Plut. *Mor.* 590c–f.

[23] A line of overlapping cauldrons encircled the Dodona precinct yielding sympathetic reverberations when one of them was struck; Callim. *Del.* 286; Steph. Byz. s.v. Δωδώνη; *Suda* s.v. Δωδωναῖον χαλκεῖον. The unstoppable sound of the instrument had become proverbial. Cook 1902, 3–13, quotes all references in full and also discusses a later version (Κερκυραίων μάστιξ) where the wind caused a chain set above a single cauldron to strike it perpetually; Suhr 1971, 224f; Nicol 1958, 139f.

[24] Terracotta rattles deposited in graves: Athens, Late Geometric (*Kerameikos* V, 29, 38f., pl. 118; comparanda in Buchholz 1987, 101–102, pl. IV:c, d); Eleusis, Late Geometric (Skias 1898, 112, figs. 30, 31); Ritsona and Halai, Archaic (Burrows & Ure 1907–1908, 256, 280, pl. XIIc; Goldman & Jones 1942, 382, nos. 1, 2; Brocato & Buda 1996, 75, nos. 8, 25); Thera, Archaic (Andrikou *et al.* 2003, 184, no. 74); Tanagra, Boeotia and Ialysos (Kephalidou 2001, 214, nos. 11–12, 215f. 15, 4, 5); the Polyandrion at Thespiai, 424 BC (Brocato & Buda 1996, 75, nos. 21–24). Other deposits: Athens Agora Hedgehog Well, fourth century BC (Thompson 1954, 79–82, 87, no. 11, pl. 19:11). There are numerous Cypriote clay rattles from burials and other deposits dated from the Middle Cypriote to the Roman period: see Kolotourou 2005, 186f. with references.

reasonable to envisage that the acoustic versatility gained by different kinds of instruments would inform ritual experience, even if qualitative evaluations of the various effects remain, unfortunately, mostly unattested.

Ritual performance is largely orchestrated by way of metaphorical associations in which mimesis can play an important role. At Krannon in Thessaly, in time of drought, the ritual entailed prayers accompanied by the shaking of a bronze chariot in imitation of thunder.[25] In other words, it included a sort of percussive performance that mediated the transformation from the existing to the desired condition. The specific percussive method has no inherent relation to the imitated phenomenon, but it is devised in connection with an unambiguous status symbol, the chariot, a fact that may suggest the ritual's innate preoccupation with the establishment of leadership. At the sanctuary of Zeus at Dodona, however, the thunderous rumble is alluded to in a very different way, by the ceaseless metallic reverberations of a row of cauldrons known as *chalkeion* (see n. 23). Here the performance implicates a powerful symbol of the hearth and of prowess, and a ritual medium of divine truth. In the context of the oracular sanctuary of Zeus, the percussive sound would thus double as the god's voice from the sky, setting off the mantic process.[26] In contrast with the Thessalian practice at Krannon, the choice of percussive device at Dodona strongly reflects the sanctuary's preoccupation with the ritual appropriation of the god's utterance.

More widely attested in ritual dramatization is beating the earth with mallet-like implements, batons, whips or even hands and feet in order to induce the epiphany of chthonic deities from the ground by means of the powerful impact and its ensuing sound.[27] The imitative character of this physical provocation is manifold. Without necessarily discounting the simulation of early agricultural practices, Bérard argued that gestural mimesis may be translated from realistic to mythical codes. He therefore proposed that the ritual beating bore allusions to Hephaistos' mythical forging of Pandora.[28] This polysemous act encapsulates the notion of archetypal creation that challenges once and for all the prerogative of parthenogenesis. Forging is nevertheless a dynamic process. It entails strategic destruction and immanent restoration in a new state or form. As such, it places the concept of creation in constant interplay with its binary opposite, death. In ritual, the percussive action and performance may thus enact in a physical manner the fierceness that impels the dynamic transition from one state to the other, in the same way that the mythical dismember-

---

[25] Antig. Car. 15; Frazer 1949, 77. The mimetic evocation of thunder is reflected in the myth of Salmoneus, son of the Thessalian king Aiolos and founder of Salmone in Elis. Salmoneus emulated Zeus and his thunder by driving his chariot on a brass bridge and trailing behind him clanging bronze cauldrons and dried skins; Apollod. *Bibl.* 1.9.7; Hyg. *Fab.* 60–61; Verg. *Aen.* 6, 585.

[26] For the mantic nature of the instrument at Dodona, see Cook 1902, 20–22; for thunder as the god's voice see Frazer 1949, 159; Nicol 1958, 140; Suhr 1971, 225. For the tripod cauldron as a medium of truth and intelligence, see Papalexandrou 2005, 9–63.

[27] Bérard 1974, 75–87. Whips or flywhisks beating the air rather than the earth are seen together with harps, seistra and menats in the context of the Hathoric cult in Egypt (Manniche 1991, 64, 115). On whips and their apotropaic character see Cook 1902, 24–25. A bronze figurine of Min-Amos with a whip was dedicated to the Heraion at Samos (Jantzen 1972, 23, B1446, pl. 26). In Near Eastern iconography we often find a seated figure (deity or ruler) in front of a table with offerings approached by a figure usually interpreted as a priestess, who beats the air with a whisk-like object (Dentzer 1982, figs. 32, 37, 45). A similar object features in a fragmentary bronze bowl from the Idaian Cave in Crete (Markoe 1985, 163f., 167, Cr. 11), which also shows parts of a musical procession. It is noteworthy that on a comparable bronze bowl from Idalion (Markoe 1985, 171, Cy. 3) the priestess holds or shakes a rattle-like object instead.

[28] Bérard 1974, 77–78 with reference to earlier scholarship on the agricultural connection.

ment of Dionysos conveys the message of de-struction and restoration in a narrative form.

Among the iconographic representations of the divine *anodos* collected by Bérard, there is a scene on a black-figure crater where the deities are invoked not through direct beating of the earth, but with dancing accompanied by the sound of clappers (*krotala*).[29] Central in the panel are the gigantic heads of Dionysos and Kore as they spring from the earth; these are flanked by female dancers wearing wreaths of vine-leaves and playing the clappers, followed by participating satyrs. We witness in this scene the replacement of the original percussive metaphor with another rhythmically structured musico-kinetic sequence, where the "beating" is confined to the clashing of the prongs of the musical instrument. The percussive act is further distilled in the Eleusinian ritual, where its content is transferred onto the formalized beating of a bronze gong known as *echeion* or *bronteion*, the subterranean sound of which summoned Persephone from the underworld.[30] The Eleusinian *echeion* should be regarded as a ritual piece of equipment with intensified agency in comparison with other percussion instruments such as tambourines, clappers, and so on. We could nevertheless envisage that percussive alternatives in general would easily take on the metaphorical substitution of the original mimetic action, at least within the unifying framework of the Mysteries and their accompanying music. The analogy of earth-beating must have retained its prominence in the case of tambourines (*tympana*) in particular, as a

brief reference in the context of epistemological discourse compares the shape of the earth with the broad flat surface of the *tympanon*, suggesting that the instrument provides a suitable synecdoche for earth.[31]

From the conceptual and performative schema of the divine *anodos* it is evident that percussive music has the potency to establish communion with the gods and to channel divine presence. At the oracular sanctuary of Zeus at Dodona the permanent sound of the *chalkeion* may have been intended to perpetuate the presence of the divinity but, otherwise, direct interaction between gods and mortals is afforded only at designated times in one's communal and private life-cycle. The statement by Strabo quoted at the beginning articulates the prominence of music in inducing communion with the divine, which is particularly exemplified in the context of the Mysteries. He speaks of music being "the work of gods" (see n. 1), a notion that recurs again and again with the mythical and artistic representations of the gods themselves as musical performers (a point to which I shall return later in this section).

If gods themselves make music, as they are presumed to, then the practice of *mousikē* can be understood as a ritualistic mimesis of the divine nature.[32] Percussive music is not to be excluded from this equation. Through their musical performance the participants in ritual aspire to connect with the divine powers which

---

[29] *CVA* Louvre 2/III, He pl. 5.1 (France 2); Bérard 1974, 63f., 72f., 145, pl. 5:16.
[30] Poll. *Onom.* 4.130. Ancient references cited in full in Cook 1902, 14 n. 1, 15. Boyancé 1937, 53, n. 3 suggested that the sound of the instrument would rhythmically regulate the call. We have no information regarding the form of the Eleusinian instrument. It may have comprised a metal disc like a gong, or a cauldron-shaped device similar to the instrument at Dodona. See discussion in Bérard 1974, 84f.

[31] Arist. *Cael.* 293b.32. The connection between the two is further illustrated by a reference to the personified Earth withholding the winds being represented as a statue of a female holding a *tympanon* (*Suda* s.v. Γῆς ἄγαλμα and Ἑστία). Varro also interprets the tambourine of the Great Mother as a symbol of the earth (August. *De civ. D.* 7. 24); see Vendries 2001, 212. According to Blades (1984, 49) the connection of the drum with the earth derives from the primitive practice of stretching the hide with pegs over a hole that forms a natural resonator.
[32] Previous analysis of *choreia* as a mimetic representation of the qualities embodied by the divine is pertinent here; see Lonsdale 1993, 40–110.

have the ability to reconcile death with birth, elimination with growth, peril with existence, and ultimately chaos with order. There is no more explicit manifestation of the communion with the divine than that of divine possession, which is an integral part of the rituals of mystery cults. The importance of music and dance in reaching the state of *enthousiasmos*, whereby the worshippers are possessed by the divine spirit, is well known. In Plato's account of telestic *mania* it is maintained that through the disorder of their ecstatic dancing the ritual participants will be "healed" and re-establish their union with the cosmos, which is ultimately orderly and harmonious.[33]

Orgiastic dancing leading to possession in a state of trance is a specific context where we find percussion depicted in performance.[34] The ample attestation of percussion in Bacchic scenes, in connection with the lack of theoretical and philosophical treatment of percussive music discussed earlier, has led to the fallacy that the intensity and rhythmicality of percussive sounds were factors aesthetically delimiting but essentially appropriate in stirring excitement for the telestic *mania*.[35] While the rhythmic element is of course essential for the emotive effects that dance has upon dancers and spectators, the view that percussion *per se* generates a state of possession is forcefully disputed by Rouget in his seminal study on music and trance. Rouget demonstrates that

the agency of music and the sort of sound that triggers trance are determined by social convention, in the same way that conceptual links between instruments, rhythms, melodies and social, emotional or mental conditions are culturally constructed. He is right to point out that Plato, in his exposition of telestic *mania*, does not link trance with percussive music and its sound intensity, nor with the frenzied aspect of rhythm that may well have characterized orgiastic music.[36]

What we can infer from Rouget's compelling analysis is that the religious significance of Greek percussion must be sought not simply in the physiological effects of its performance, which could indeed culminate in trance within the cults that required it, but in the culturally constructed metaphors that assimilate percussion with the nature of the divine. When imaging divine musical performance, it is usually earth goddesses such as Kybele, her variants Mother of the Gods and Rhea with the associated Kouretes, as well as Aphrodite-Astarte, that take on percussion.[37] Similarly, Aphrodite brings on her *tympana* and cymbals to entertain the distressed Demeter in a passage from Euripides' *Helen* (1338–1352), while a scene on a red-figure volute crater of the Dinos

---

[33] Pl. *Leg.* 790d–791b; Dodds 1951, 78–80, 99; Rouget 1985, 201–213; Lonsdale 1993, 78f.

[34] Along with shaking *thyrsoi*, which could also be taken as a form of percussion, the Dionysian *thiasos* commonly plays clappers, tambourines and cymbals together with *auloi*; occasionally the participants may tinkle bells, blow horns and twirl bullroarers. See Bélis 1988, 9–21; Bremmer 1984, 278f. A similar array of percussion and wind instruments characterizes the imagery of Kybele (Vendries 2001, 203–208).

[35] Cf. for instance Fitton 1973, 263 for the Korybantic dance inducing possession and trance "by the all pervading rhythm"; similar reasoning appears regularly in existing literature.

[36] Rouget 1985, 169–176, 213f.

[37] For representations of Kybele with a tambourine see *LIMC* VIII (1997), s.v. Kybele nos. 17–20, 32–40, 42, 47 (E. Simon) and *LIMC* III (1986), s.v. Attis nos. 389, 397 (M.J. Vermaseren). Kybele is often depicted enthroned holding the instrument, an imagery also appropriated by a Cypriote terracotta from Idalion that may represent Aphrodite-Astarte (Kolotourou 2005, 189f., pl. 23.2). The Cypriote figure from Idalion holds the tambourine in front of her abdomen area, an arrangement that is not unusual in Cypriote and Levantine coroplastic. This motif is also taken up by a couple of late seventh-century BC Cretan mould-made female terracotta plaques (Higgins 1967, 28, pl. 10A; Matz 1970, 97 no. D11, pl. 42d). These may well feature Rhea or Mother of the Gods, both closely comparable with the divine personas of Kybele and Aphrodite-Astarte. Kouretes clashing shields and *krotala*: Schol. Soph. *Aj.* 699e.4.

Painter shows Demeter or Ariadne clashing the cymbals next to Dionysos as they attend the return of Hephaistos accompanied by the dancing thiasos.[38] No doubt, these renderings of divine percussionists emanate from the established cultic contexts where the instruments were played. But the idea of a divine precedent for percussive activity, on which mortals would model their own performances, is a mythological analogue to an ingrained belief in the powers of such actions to generate life and thus to reinstate cosmic order, as the performative example of the *anodos* clearly demonstrates. Order and disorder as well as destruction and creation are periodically alternating states, the temporal patterning of which structures the natural as well as the human cycle. The Hesiodic religious model presents a world where order results from strife and it designates divine powers to be as much destructive as they are restoring. This duality similarly characterizes percussive actions that encode man's earliest experiences of generation and elimination, as discussed above ("Percussion and ritual"). Percussive enactment, therefore, can be understood as a means to imitate ritually the divine, realizing through human agency the link between the polar opposites of creation and destruction.

In order to appreciate further how percussive music embodies elements of the divine, we must turn to depictions of the Muses rendered as a clapper playing chorus. On a late sixth-century black-figure amphora from Vulci, the Muses sing and clash their clappers (*krotala*) in the presence of Hermes.[39] Another amphora of the same period is even more telling; it depicts Hermes leading Apollo and four Muses in a musical procession to be received by the seated figure of Zeus.[40] Apollo plays his *kithara* and the Muses follow, with their clappers protruding from their palms in a bi-fork rendition. The schema presenting the Muses as percussionists is of particular significance, for it introduces percussion in an elevated sphere of musicianship, removed from the usual context of Dionysian revelry. We may compare it to the performance of the Delian chorus, described in the *Homeric Hymn to Apollo* (162–4) as capable of imitating the voice and *krembaliastun* of all peoples in the setting of the Panhellenic festival. Many scholars have associated the term *krembaliastun* with the mousiko-poetic rhythms of different ethnic groups alluding to the ethos and artistry of their music.[41] The term would thus ascribe great importance to the rhythmical expressiveness that characterizes *choreia*. This feature is also typical of percussive music in general, but the sound of clappers in particular was said to match the verbal articulacy of the human voice.[42] We can surmise that the Delian chorus would have aspired to emulate the divine chorus of Apollo. In the scene from Vulci, such a chorus is playing the clappers together with the highbrow stringed instrument of Apollo in a solemn and dainty performance for the supreme leader of the Olympian pantheon. Apollo *Kitharōdos* is the emblem of divine harmony and of the music which is emitted by a perfectly tuned cosmos. His choral entourage, the Muses, confer knowledge through artistic eloquence as patrons of the arts and education. We are thus witnessing a performance that ought to be perfect by definition, given the identities of the performers,

---

[38] Bologna, Museo Civico Archeologico P283, 450–400 BC; Castaldo 1995, 42f., no. 4, fig. 4.
[39] München, Antikensammlungen 1490; Boardman 1991, fig. 218.

[40] *CVA* Copenhagen 3, pl. 102 (2b) (Denmark 3); Paquette 1984, P3.
[41] Webster 1970, 55; Barker 1984, 40 n. 4; Mathiesen 1999, 84, n. 120. See also n. 4 above.
[42] The connection between the sound of clappers and the human voice is attested in *Suda*: "τῶν φωνὴν διηρθρωμένος, καθάπερ τὰ κρόταλα, ἀντὶ τοῦ εὔγλωττος, εὔστομος."

and which is expressed in a musical form that combines the harmonic structure of the *kithara* with the rhythmical flow of the *krotala*. In the hands of the Muses, percussion clearly conveys the indispensability of rhythm in artistic creation and expression.[43] But in addition to this, it also underlines the necessity for structure in all intellectual spheres that fall under the control of the Muses, including *logos* and *paideia* as well as poetry and music.[44] Considered in this context, the role of rhythmic patterning acquires a far greater significance, pertaining to the structuring of elements that harmonize not only the natural cycle but also human life.

Rhythmos, order and hero

The Greek conception of *rhythmos* is crucial at this point in our discussion for recognizing further links between percussive performance and the concepts of structure and order that define all existence. In a strictly musical context, especially from the end of the fifth century BC onwards, the term denotes musical rhythm, the measured structuring of melody, words and body movement.[45] But in Greek thought the words *rhythmos* and *rhythmizein* describe the general concept of structuring matter, giv-

ing shape or form.[46] This notion prevails even in purely musical works such as the Aristoxenian *Elementa Rhythmica* where "temporal forms—expressed as rhythmic proportions—are treated much like geometric forms".[47] Musical rhythm thus shapes time that was previously undifferentiated and pertains to the concepts of order, measure and proportion that govern Greek thought in general, from aesthetics to political and philosophical theories. Aristides Quintilianus informs us of three natures of rhythm that embrace most aspects of human perception: one for motionless bodies (for example, a eurhythmic statue), one for things that move, and one in a musical sense for the particular divisions of sound.[48] In essence, the three types of rhythm describe two overlapping dimensions, the temporal and the spatial, with good order being the underlying key to the discourse. Movement is the physical state that best reflects both temporal and spatial organization, and this is precisely how musical rhythm is understood: as the shaping and orderly arrangement of movement in time.[49] Movement, however, is not reflected only in intervals of time perceived by the senses through dance, song and emotive response (ethos); it is also reflected in intervals of pitch (*harmonia*) that

---

[43] Ancient music theoreticians and philosophers recognized the bond between melody and rhythm. Aristides Quintilianus remarks that it is the elements of rhythm that make clear the character of the melody, whereas notes alone, without any differentiation in their movement, are inactive and insufficient to represent the melody clearly (Aristid. Quint. 31.10–13; Barker 1989, 434). For references to the negative and unpleasant effects of a musical performance that failed to keep the rhythm, see West 1992, 130, n. 4.

[44] See Murray 2004, esp. 366–373. For Plato (*Ti.* 47b–d) rhythm was a gift from the Muses to help correct the irregular and graceless ways of mankind.

[45] Mathiesen 1985, 160–169; musical rhythm as element of form and order: Barker 1984, 130, n. 18, 141, 143, 179.

[46] Cf. Barker 1984, 225 n. 131; Aesch. *Pers.* 747; Hdt. 5.58. See especially Benveniste 1951 for this meaning of *rhythmos*. I wish to thank Andrew Barker for bringing this article to my attention.

[47] Cf. Rowell 1979, 67; see Mathiesen 1999, 337f., n. 99 for the plausible connection of the Aristoxenian "shaping of time" with the Platonic theory of forms; most recent analysis of Aristoxenos' theory of rhythm in Gibson 2005, 77–98.

[48] Aristid. Quint. 1.13; Mathiesen 1999, 336 n. 98.

[49] Cf. Pl. *Leg.* 665a: "The name for order in movement is 'rhythm', and order of the voice where high and low are mixed together at once, is given the name 'harmonia', while the combination of the two is called 'choreia'" (trans. Barker 1984, 149); Rowell 1979, 68. From the etymological connection of *rhythmos* with the meaning of "flow" Fitton suggested that the original flow of body movement was subsequently translated into metric (Fitton 1973, 270).

"move" from low to high and vice versa. In this sense, *rhythmos* is closely akin to *harmonia* as the philosophical description of orderly movement within the cosmos, based on or expressed by mathematical arrangements of ratios and intervals.[50] The coupling of Apollo *Kitharōdos* with the *krotalizousai* Muses on the amphora from Vulci illustrates explicitly the coupling of harmony and rhythm, the orderly movement in space and time that moulds the cosmos under the sanction of the supreme divine ruler. Like mortal versions of Apollo and the Muses, worshippers would grasp the essence of the universal harmony through their musical performance, which is realized in rhythm as well as in melody.

Order is considered as a feature of nature that, from an empirical point of view, manifests itself most evidently in rhythm which structures movement. Percussive performance is relevant here as the rhythmic device *par excellence* that facilitates patterned movement. In the Pseudo-Aristotelian *Problems* it is maintained that: "We enjoy different styles of melody because of their moral character, but rhythm because it is characterized by a recognisable and orderly number, and moves us in an orderly way. Orderly movement is in its nature more closely akin to us than disorderly, and so is more natural".[51] As a natural condition, patterned movement gives shape and regulates the whole of nature and mankind. Plato remarks that good rhythm (*eurythmia*) and good attunement (*euarmostia*) are mandatory in the lives of men.[52] The need for a well-paced, structured life and for a well-articulated ethos necessary for an orderly community is thus in accordance with nature. The notion of *eurythmia* is already introduced to small children in the domestic context as they are soothed with rattling play-things from the moment of their birth. According to Aristotle, learning rhythmic communication by playing the *platage*, in all probability a kind of rattle or clapper, was the first step for children's musical and social interaction.[53] In this sense, percussion becomes a paradigmatic educational tool that not only instructs them on rhythm and ethos but also marks the shaping of their otherwise unstructured life pattern.

The atomistic view that the elements of the cosmos collide whilst in constant motion may further elucidate percussion as a paradigm of the natural condition. A reference in Plutarch, which nevertheless conflates positions from natural and platonic philosophy, is of interest here. While discussing the therapeutic and regenerating aspects of the Egyptian cult of Isis and Osiris, Plutarch refers to the playing of the *seistron*, an elaborate kind of rattle, as indicative of the ways that the universe functions: "The sistrum also makes it clear that all things in existence need to be shaken, or rattled about, and never to cease from motion but, as it were, to be waked up and agitated when they grow drowsy and torpid. They say that they [the Egyptians] avert and repel Typhon by means of sistrums,

---

[50] For the Pythagoreans, as for Plato and the philosophers and theorists who echo their words, the cosmos is created on the basis of "musical fitting together" (*harmonia*) and the application of harmonic analysis can explain the ordering of nature, for all regular motion produces sound. Cf. Plut. *De Mus.* 1147a: "... the motion of that which is, and the movement of the stars, come about and have their constitution through the influence of music: everything, they [the school of Pythagoras, Archytas and Plato] say, was constructed by God on the basis of *harmonia*" (trans. Barker 1984, 248–249 and n. 261).

[51] Arist. [*Pr.*] 19.38 (trans. Barker 1984, 199–200). For Plato, order is an inherent natural condition that rests within disorder and eventually replaces it; see Pl. *Ti.* 48.a.

[52] Pl. *Prt.* 326.b.5–6: "πᾶς γὰρ ὁ βίος τοῦ ἀνθρώπου εὐρυθμίας τε καὶ εὐαρμοστίας δεῖται." See also Seebass 1991, 12 n. 2.

[53] Arist. *Pol.* 1340.b.26ff. In this passage Aristotle is concerned with musical education in general and maintains that engagement in musical activities at a young age is the best method of teaching youth to recognize what kinds of behaviour and morals are accepted by the communal consensus and what are not; see also Ford 2004.

indicating thereby that when destruction constricts and checks Nature, generation releases and arouses it by means of motion".[54] Plutarch's theoretical explication of the ritual enactment amalgamates aspects of earlier Greek thought and practice. His remarks on the regenerating effect of rattling, whereby the discs of the *seistron* collide with shaking, bring to mind the analogous result of the striking metaphor in the context of *anodoi* discussed in the previous section. He further transposes onto the shaking of the rattle a rather simplified paradigm of movement that has the potency to bring nature in good shape and restore order.

Plutarch' s comments are particularly intriguing considering that rattles and *seistra* are the earliest percussion instruments for which we have evidence of ritual use in the Aegean from the Bronze Age. In the well known representation of a public agricultural rite on the Harvester Vase from Agia Triada in Crete, dated to the 16th/15th centuries BC, the ceremonial procession and its leading singers are conducted by the sounds of a *seistron*. Similarly, a rhyton from Kalavarda in Rhodes, dated to the 14th/13th centuries BC, depicts amidst birds and flowers a ritual masqueraded pageant of wild boars, one of which shakes a spherical rattle by its handle.[55] Rattles are thus clearly entrenched in earlier stages of religious practice. From the two scenes we may infer rituals of a regenerating character and we can surmise that the playing of the instruments would have conveyed relevant meaning. The demonstrable ancestry of rattling and its apparent importance in ritual enactment may account for the

fact that percussion instruments with colliding surfaces are also presented as beneficial tools of divine or heroic manufacture in Greek myth.

The myth in question is Herakles' sixth labour, taking place in Arcadia, where Lake Stymphalis was infested by mighty flocks of monstrous birds spreading death in the area. Herakles' dangerous task of clearing the lake from the Stymphalian birds is told by various ancient authors with minor variations. In some versions the hero drives the birds away by making a terrible noise with a rattle or a clapper; in others, after scaring the birds with the noise he finally kills them off with his weapons. In some accounts the instrument is fashioned by Hephaistos and bestowed by Athena, while in others Herakles devises it on his own.[56] With the help of percussive tools, Herakles restores the natural order in a situation where it has gone off balance. He tames nature as a proper culture hero and renders the area safe for habitation by shaking the rattle or the clapper. The act may be taken as a symbolic re-shaking of the cosmos, as Plutarch would have it, which expels destruction and brings back the desired state of generation. It is likely, though, that Herakles' rattling originates from agricultural and hunting practices and that the percussive device refers us back to the world of mundane actions. Sachs has noted the similarity between Egyptian Bronze Age curved or sickle-shaped clappers and concussion sticks with bent sticks that were aptly used as missiles by Egyptian hunters who "approached the papyrus thickets on the

---

[54] Plut. *De Is. et Os.* 376c–e (trans. F.C. Babbitt). Typhon is the destructive power that in the Egyptian myth dismembers the body of Osiris so that Isis will reassemble it.

[55] For the Harvester Vase, see Forsdyke 1954; Younger 1998, 6–9, cat. 53, pls. 1.1, 2; for the Kalavarda rhyton, see Vermeule & Karageorghis 1982, 154–155; Karantzali 1998, 97, figs. 9–10.

[56] Myth featuring *krotalon* (clapper): Apollod. *Bibl.* 2.6.1–12; Paus. 8.22.5; featuring *platage* (rattle): Diod. 4.13.2.1–12, Ap. Rhod. *Argon.* 2.1052–7; Schol. Ap. Rhod. *Argon.* 203.14–204.4; Hellanikos, *FGrH* 4 fr. 104; Pherekydes, *FGrH* 3 fr. 72. Clappers and rattles are morphologically different instruments. For reasons that I will not present here as they require textual scrutiny, I believe that these terms are used leniently to indicate percussion instruments of that sort in general. To my knowledge, the sound device does not feature in any of the representations of the myth.

Nile banks, clapped their missiles together to scare up the water birds and then hurled them after the soaring game".[57] We thus have a precedent where the form of the percussive device is conflated with that of an agricultural implement or a hunting weapon and may have metaphorically replaced it. Another mythical battle between Pygmies and Cranes, modelled along lines similar to the Stymphalian myth, explicitly mentions *krotala* being used in battle both as bird-scarers and as actual weapons.[58] These tales may reflect problems encountered by the Greek farmers in their attempt to protect their crops from cranes and other birds, especially in locations where aquatic birds would have been prolific and a threat to the harvest, or where they would be hunted as a source of food. By fashioning a sound device that results in the chasing and killing of the birds in a manner that mirrors existing hunting and agricultural practices, Athena, Hephaistos and Herakles act as agents of civilization, protectors of the hunt and sponsors of successful cultivation of the land. Divine protection, commonly required for a successful hunt or growing crops, endows the practical knowledge and experience with divine grace, which is passed thereafter onto the instrument and its performance. Just like Amphion, who built the walls of Thebes with the sound of his lyre, Herakles employs sound with supernatural powers, in this case an unmelodic, frightening and loud din, rhythmically repeated until the terrifying birds are vanquished and order is restored.

Herakles' hunting activity takes place in the marshes forming the realm of Artemis, where Pausanias informs us that there was also a temple dedicated to the goddess, decorated with sculptures of young maidens with bird's legs (Paus. 8.22.7). The practical knowledge of using percussive methods in the hunt takes on a different spin in connection with a deity that presides over the chase not only between human and animal, but also between male and female. If we consider Sergent's identification of the Stymphalian birds with young girls that have undergone metamorphosis in the course of their rite of passage, then Herakles' labour may equally denote a stage in his own rites of passage, whereupon he combines his successful hunt with the subjugation of the terrible female.[59] In the metaphorical context of the sexual hunt, percussion facilitates the capture of the hunted, thus paving the way for and promoting the natural order of (pro)creation.

I have argued that the biological and conceptual dimensions of mundane percussive actions establish metaphorical associations that endorse the performance of percussion in Greek ritual. When transposing the percussive effect in social terms, we have found that percussive sounds mark the natural rhythm of human life as they regulate one's orderly movement from one stage to the next. During childhood, rattles, like the *platage* of Archytas, entertain and educate children in the notion of rhythm. Rattling instruments accompany their stages of maturation and initiation, as well as their bridal dances.[60] Eventually they get buried with them and are silenced forever in death (see n. 24). It is not unlikely that percussion was somehow employed in the burial rites or their aftermath, as the scenes of the so called Rattle-Group or

---

[57] Sachs 1940, 88; *NGDMI i*, s.v. Clappers 387; Lexová 2000, fig. 61.
[58] Hekataios, *FGrH* 1 fr. 328a–b. Representations of the battle portray club-like sticks; see Sparkes 2000, fig. 5.3.

[59] Sergent 1996, 23–26; *idem* 1993, 102–105; Twele 1977.
[60] Clapper playing at initiation dances at Brauron: Lonsdale 1993, 187 with references; at a wedding context (wedding of Hektor and Andromache): Sappho fr. 44.25 (Lobel & Page 1955). Rattles dedicated to the deity along with other games/symbols of youth: *Anth. Pal.* 6, 280; see also Brocato & Buda 1996 for *phormiskos*-shaped rattles from South Italian female burials, which they interpret as instruments related to the initiation of virgin maidens, marking their wedding age.

depictions of *phormiskoi* may suggest.[61] Although it is not certain that percussion instruments were played in the course of the funeral, we should not overlook the fact that a pair of bronze anthropomorphic rattles were mounted on the burial chariot which carried an eminent deceased to his final destination, in the royal Tomb 79 in Salamis, Cyprus.[62] Does the final interment of percussion proclaim that this is the natural order of things? Or is it the means to exorcize the miasma of death and combat the fate of ultimate destruction? Perhaps the answer lies somewhere in the middle. After all, chthonic monsters such as the Sirens also sing along to lyres, auloi and *krotala* and thus perpetuate, by means of their threatening sounds, the harmony of the universe.

KATERINA KOLOTOUROU
Department of Classics
University of Edinburgh
k.kolotourou@ed.ac.uk

---

[61] The rattle-and-lyre performance depicted on the Attic Late Geometric scenes of the Rattle-Group is considered funerary by most scholars; see Rystedt 1992 for the most comprehensive account, with earlier bibliography. Compare with funerary imagery on lekythoi where a *phormiskos*-shaped object that may be interpreted as rattle is associated with the deceased: Brocato & Buda 1996, 82 fig. 3.5, 86f. On *phormiskoi* and *phormiskos*-shaped rattles from burial contexts see Brocato & Buda 1996, Kephalidou 2001 and Andrikou *et al.* 2003, 184, no. 74. According to Brocato & Buda (1996, 75) the rattle from the Polyandreion at Thespiai was used during the ceremony of the burial, as it was found near the levels of the pyre.

[62] Karageorghis *et al.* 1973–1974, 19, 24, 80f. fig. 10, pls. G, CI–CV, CCLIV, CCLVII.

Bibliography

Aign 1963   B. Aign, *Die Geschichte der Musikinstrumente des Ägäischen Raumes bis um 700 v. Chr.*, diss. J.W. Goethe Universität, Frankfurt am Main 1963.

Andrikou *et al.* 2003   Ε. Ανδρίκου, Α. Γουλάκη-Βουτυρά, Χ. Λαναρά, Ζ. Παπαδοπούλου, *Μουσών δώρα. Μουσικοί και χορευτικοί απόηχοι από την αρχαία Ελλάδα*, Athens 2003.

Barker 1984   A. Barker, *Greek musical writings* I. *The musician and his art*, Cambridge 1984.

Barker 1989   A. Barker, *Greek musical writings* II. *Harmonic and acoustic theory*, Cambridge 1989.

Bell 1992   C. Bell, *Ritual theory, ritual practice*, Oxford 1992.

Bélis 1988   A. Bélis, 'Musique et transe dans le cortège Dionysiaque', in *Transe et théâtre. Actes de la table ronde internationale, Montpellier 3–5 Mars* (Cahiers du GITA, 4), Montpellier 1988, 9–29.

Benveniste 1951   E. Benveniste, 'La notion de "rhythme" dans son expression linguistique', *Journal de Psychologie* 44, 1951, 401–410.

Bérard 1974   C. Bérard, *Anodoi. Essai sur l'imagerie des passages chthoniens*, Roma 1974.

Blacking 1973   J. Blacking, *How musical is man?*, London 1973.

Blacking 1976   J. Blacking, 'Dance, conceptual thought and production in the archaeological record', in *Problems in economic and social archaeology*, eds. G. De G. Sieveking, I.H. Longworth & K.E. Wilson, London 1976, 3–13.

Blades 1984 J. Blades, *Percussion instruments and their history*, London & Boston, 1984².

Boardman 1991 J. Boardman, *Athenian black figure vases: A handbook*, London 1991².

Boyancé 1937 P. Boyancé, *Les cultes des muses chez les philosophes grecs*, Paris 1937.

Bremmer 1984 J.N. Bremmer, 'Greek maenadism reconsidered', *ZPE* 55, 1984, 267–86.

Brocato & Buda 1996 B. Brocato & C.Z. Buda, 'Phormiskos o platagè? Crepundia? Studio sulla funzione di un oggetto fittile in ambito greco, etrusco e latino', *AION* 3, 1996, 73–90.

Buchholz 1987 H-G. Buchholz, 'Rasseln und Schellen, Reifen, Wippen und Schaukeln', in *Sport und Spiel* (ArchHom, 3), ed. S. Laser, Göttingen 1987, 100–116.

Burrows & Ure 1907–1908 R.M. Burrows & P.N. Ure, 'Excavations at Rhitsóna in Boeotia', *BSA* 14, 1907–1908, 226–319.

Castaldo 1995 D. Castaldo, 'Rapresentazioni dei kymbala nella ceramica attica', *RidIM/RCMI Newsletter* XX/2, 1995, 39–48.

Comotti 1989 G. Comotti, *Music in Greek and Roman culture*, Baltimore 1989.

Constantinidou 1992 S. Constantinidou, 'The importance of bronze in early Greek religion', *Dodone* 21, 1992, 137–164.

Cook 1902 A.B. Cook, 'The gong at Dodona', *JHS* 22, 1902, 5–28.

Curtis-Franklin 2002 J. Curtis-Franklin, 'Harmony in Greek and Indo-Iranian cosmology', *Journal of Indo-European Studies* 30:1/2, 2002, 1–25.

Dentzer 1982 J-M. Dentzer, *Le motif du banquet couché dans le proche orient et le monde Grec du VIIe au IVe siècle avant J.-C.* (Bibliothèque des Écoles françaises d'Athènes et de Rome, 246), Roma 1982.

Dodds 1951 E.R. Dodds, *The Greeks and the irrational*, Berkeley 1951.

DiGiglio 2000 A. DiGiglio, *Strumenti delle muse*, Bari 2000.

Fernandez 1974 J. Fernandez, 'The mission of metaphor in expressive culture', *CurrAnthr* 15:2, 1974, 119–145.

Fitton 1973 J.W. Fitton, 'Greek dance', *CQ* 23:2, 1973, 254–274.

Forsdyke 1954 J. Forsdyke, 'The Harvester Vase of Agia Triada', *Journal of the Warburg and Courtauld Institutes* 17, 1954, 1–9.

Ford 2004 A. Ford, 'Catharsis: The power of music in Aristotle's Politics', in Murray & Wilson 2004, 309–336.

Frazer 1949 J.G. Frazer, *The golden bough*, London 1949.

Gibson 2005 S. Gibson, *Aristoxenus of Tarentum and the birth of musicology*, New York & London 2005.

Giuzzi & Staiti 1992 F. Guizzi & N. Staiti, 'Mania e musica nella pittura vascolare apula', *Imago Musicae* IX/XII, 1992–1995, 43–90.

Goldman & Jones 1942 H. Goldman & F. Jones, 'Terracottas from the Necropolis of Halae', *Hesperia* 11, 1942, 365–421.

Hardie 2004   A. Hardie, 'Muses and mysteries', in Murray & Wilson 2004, 11–37.

Higgins 1967   R.A. Higgins, *Greek terracottas*, London 1967.

Hornbostel & Sachs 1961   E.M. Hornbostel & C. Sachs, 'Classification of musical instruments', *Galpin Society Journal* XIV, 1961, 3–29. (Translated by A. Baines and K.P. Wachsmann from the original text 'Systematik der Musikinstrumente. Ein Versuch', *ZfE* 46, 1914, 553–590.)

Jantzen 1972   U. Jantzen, *Samos* VIII. *Ägyptische und orientalische Bronzen aus dem Heraion von Samos*, Bonn 1972.

Karageorghis et al. 1973–1974   V. Karageorghis *et al.*, *Excavations in the Necropolis of Salamis* III (Salamis, 5), Nicosia 1973–1974.

Karantzali 1998   E. Karantzali, 'A new Mycenaean pictorial Rhyton from Rhodes', in *Eastern Mediterranean: Cyprus-Dodecanese-Crete 16th–6th cent. B.C.*, eds. V. Karageorghis & N.C. Stampolidis, Athens 1998, 87–103.

Kartomi 1990   M.J. Kartomi, *On concepts and classifications of musical instruments*, Chicago & London 1990.

Kephalidou 2001   E. Kephalidou, 'Polychrome pottery from Aiani', *Hesperia* 70, 2001, 183–219.

Kerameikos V   K. Kübler, *Kerameikos. Ergebnisse der Ausgrabungen* V. *Die Nekropole des 10. bis 8. Jahrhunderts*, Berlin 1954.

Kinkeldey 1948   O. Kinkeldey, 'The music of the spheres', *Bulletin of the American Musicological Society* 11/12/13, 1948, 30–32.

Knauft 1979   B.M. Knauft, 'On percussion and metaphor', *CurrAnthr* 20:1, 1979, 189–191.

Kolotourou 2005   K. Kolotourou, 'Music and cult: The significance of percussion and the Cypriote connection', in *Cyprus: Religion and society. From the Late Bronze Age to the end of the Archaic period*, eds. V. Karageorghis, H. Matthäus & S. Rogge, Erlangen 2005, 183–204.

Kowalzig 2004   B. Kowalzig, 'Changing choral worlds: Song-dance and society in Athens and beyond', in Murray & Wilson 2004, 39–66.

Kowalzig 2008   B. Kowalzig, *Singing for the gods*, Oxford 2008.

Kreinath 2005   J. Kreinath, 'Ritual: Theoretical issues in the study of religion', *Revista de Estudos da Religião* 4, 2005, 100–107.

Landels 1999   J.G. Landels, *Music in ancient Greece and Rome*, London 1999.

Lévi-Strauss 1973   C. Lévi-Strauss, *From honey to ashes*, London 1973.

Lexová 2000   I. Lexová, *Ancient Egyptian dances*, New York 2000.

Lippman 1963   E.A. Lippman, 'Hellenic conceptions of harmony', *Journal of the American Musicological Society* 16:1, 1963, 3–35.

Lobel & Page 1955   E. Lobel & D.L. Page, *Poetarum Lesbiorum Fragmenta*, Oxford 1955.

Lonsdale 1993   S.H. Lonsdale, *Dance and ritual play in Greek religion*, Baltimore & London 1993.

Manniche 1991   L. Manniche, *Music in ancient Egypt*, London 1991.

Marcuse 1975   S. Marcuse, *A survey of musical instruments*, New York 1975.

Markoe 1985   G. Markoe, *Phoenician bronze and silver bowls from Cyprus and the Mediterranean*, Berkeley 1985.

Maróthy 1993–1994   J. Maróthy, 'Rite and rhythm. From behaviour patterns to musical structures', *Studia Musicologica Academiae Scientiarum Hungaricae*, T. 35:4, 1993–1994, 421–433.

Mathiesen 1985   T. Mathiesen, 'Rhythm and meter in ancient Greek music', *Music Theory Spectrum* 7, 1985, 159–80.

Mathiesen 1999   T. Mathiesen, *Apollo's lyre: Greek music and music theory in antiquity and the Middle Ages*, Nebraska 1999.

Matz 1970   F. Matz, *Dädalische Kunst auf Kreta im 7. Jahrhundert v. Chr.* Mainz am Rhein 1970.

Mikrakis 2000   Μ. Μικράκης, 'Μουσική στην Κρήτη και την Αίγυπτο. Ένα ιδιαίτερο πεδίο ανάπτυξης πολιτισμικών δεσμών', in *Κρήτη Αίγυπτος. Πολιτισμικοί δεσμοί τριών χιλιετιών. Μελέτες*, eds. Α. Καρέτσου, Μ. Ανδρεαδάκη-Βλαζάκη & Μ. Παπαδάκης, Athens 2000, 162–169.

Morley 2003   I. Morley, *The evolutionary origins and archaeology of music. An investigation into the prehistory of human musical capacities and behaviour*, diss. University of Cambridge, Cambridge 2003.

Mowitt 2005   J. Mowitt, *Percussion: Drumming, beating, striking*, Durham & London 2005.

Murray 2004   P. Murray, 'The muses and their arts', in Murray & Wilson 2004, 365–389.

Murray & Wilson 2004   *Music and the muses. The culture of 'mousikē' in the Classical Athenian city*, eds. P. Murray & P. Wilson, Oxford 2004.

NGDMI   *The New Grove Dictionary of Musical Instruments* vols. i–iii, ed. S. Sadie, London 1984.

Nicol 1958   D.M. Nicol, 'The oracle of Dodona', *GaR* 5:2, 1958, 128–143.

Papalexandrou 2005   N. Papalexandrou, *The visual poetics of power. Warriors, youths, and tripods in early Greece*, Lanham, Md 2005.

Paquette 1984   D. Paquette, *L'instrument de musique dans la céramique de la Grèce antique*, Paris 1984.

Peirce 1932   C.S. Peirce, *Collected papers*, eds. C. Hartshorne & P. Weiss, Cambridge, Mass. 1932.

Rappaport 1999   R.A. Rappaport, *Ritual and religion in the making of humanity*, Cambridge 1999.

Radt 1985   S. Radt, *Tragicorum Graecorum Fragmenta* vol. 3, Aeschylus. Göttingen 1985.

Rault 2000   L. Rault, *Musical instruments. A worldwide survey of traditional music-making*, London 2000.

Rouget 1985   G. Rouget, *Music and trance*, Chicago 1985².

Rowell 1979   L. Rowell, 'Aristoxenus on rhythm', *Journal of Music Theory* 23:1, 1979, 63–79.

Rudhardt 1992   J. Rudhardt, *Notions fondamentales de la pensée religieuse et actes constitutifs du culte dans la Grèce classique*, Paris 1992².

Rystedt 1992   E. Rystedt, 'Notes on the rattle scenes on Attic Geometric pottery', *OpAth* 19, 1992, 125–133.

Sachs 1940   C. Sachs, *The history of musical instruments*, New York 1940.

Schatkin 1978   M.A. Schatkin, 'Idiophones of the ancient world', *JAC* 21, 1978, 147–172.

Seebass 1991   T. Seebass, 'The power of music in Greek vase painting: Reflections on the visualisation of *rhythmos* (order) and *epaoidē* (enchanting song)', *Imago Musicae* 8, 1991, 11–38.

Sergent 1993   B. Sergent, 'Les traveaux de Brian', *Ollodagos* 5, 1993, 69–129.

Sergent 1996   B. Sergent, 'Ces demoiselles de Stymphale', in *Héraklès. Les femmes et le feminin*, eds. C. Jourdain-Annequin & C. Bonnet, Bruxelles & Roma 1996, 20–34.

Skias 1898   Α.Ν. Σκιάς, 'Πανάρχαια 'Ελευσινιακή Νεκρόπολις', *ArchEph* 1898, 29–122.

Sparkes 2000   B. Sparkes, 'Small world: Pygmies and co.', in *Word and image in ancient Greece*, eds. K. Rutter & B. Sparkes, Edinburgh 2000, 79–98.

Suhr 1971   E.G. Suhr, 'The tripod', *Folklore* 82:3, 1971, 216–232.

Tilley 1999   C. Tilley, *Metaphor and material culture*, Oxford 1999.

Thompson 1954   D.B. Thompson, 'Three centuries of Hellenistic terracottas', *Hesperia* 23, 1954, 72–107.

Twele 1977   J.R.A. Twele, 'Artemis and Herakles on a Geometric oinochoe in Copenhagen', *AJA* 81, 1977, 103–107.

Vendries 2001   C. Vendries, 'Pour les oreilles de Cybèle: images plurielles de la musique sur les autels tauroboliques de la Gaule romaine', in *Chanter les dieux. musique et religion dans l' antiquité*, eds. P. Brulé & C. Vendries, Rennes 2001, 197–218.

Vermeule & Karageorghis 1982   E. Vermeule & V. Karageorghis, *Mycenaean pictorial vase painting*, Cambridge, Mass. 1982.

Villing 2002   A. Villing, 'For whom did the bell toll in ancient Greece? Archaic and Classical Greek bells at Sparta and beyond', *BSA* 97, 2002, 223–295.

Wallin, Merker & Brown 2000   *The origins of music*, eds. N.L. Wallin, B. Merker & S. Brown, Cambridge, Mass. 2000.

Webster 1970   T.B.L. Webster, *The Greek chorus*, London 1970.

Wehrli 1967   F. Wehrli, *Die Schule des Aristoteles* vol. 2. *Aristoxenos*, Basel & Stuttgart 1967[2].

West 1992   M.L. West, *Ancient Greek music*, Oxford 1992.

Winnington-Ingram 1980   R.P. Winnington-Ingram, 'Greece, ancient', in *The new Grove dictionary of music and musicians* vol. 7, ed. S. Sadie, London 1980, 657–672.

Younger 1998   J.G. Younger, *Music in the Aegean Bronze Age*, Jonsered 1998.

Zschätzsch 2002   A. Zschätzsch, *Verwendung und Bedeutung griechischer Musikinstrumente in Mythos und Kult* (Series Internationale Archäologie, 73), Rahden 2002.

CHRISTINA MITSOPOULOU

The Eleusinian processional cult vessel

ICONOGRAPHIC EVIDENCE AND INTERPRETATION

Abstract*

During the Classical and Hellenistic periods a specific vase shape was developed in Attica in relation to the Sanctuary of Demeter and Kore at Eleusis. It has since long been identified with vase-names relevant to the Eleusinian Mysteries, like the πλημοχόη or the κέρνος. Despite a long period of discussions and varied attempts to sum up the available data, major questions related to their definite and complete understanding still remain open: their exact destination of use, their moment(s) of use during the Mysteries, product(s) contained within and consumed from them, their ancient name(s), the chronological range of production, and the reason for their iconographic use as a symbol of the Eleusinian Mysteries. The vessels may now be closer interpreted through rare iconographic evidence, contemporary with their original period of use. The contribution of the famous red-figured votive tablet of Ninnion towards a definite interpretation of the vases is questioned, and another pair of images are added to the discussion. The aim of this paper is to propose new arguments towards the understanding of the use, as well as the choice, of the vessel as an official symbol of the Eleusinian Mysteries.

Eleusinian cult vessels compose a very specific category of vases, produced in Athens or Attica, probably from the fifth century BC, and at least until the second century BC.[1] The shape

Eleusinian vessel on the Pyxis lid from the BMFA Acc. No. 03.877 is her achievement, which inaugurated this whole research programme. I am indebted to Professor Kevin Clinton for extensive discussions. I owe gratitude to the Boston Museum of Fine Arts and the National Archaeological Museum of Athens for permitting use of the new images, and especially to Mrs E. Stasinopoulou, Curator of the Collections of Vases and Jewellery in Athens, for permission to study and republish the golden bands from the Stathatos collection. Gratitude is expressed to Dr J. Stroszeck for permission to study the material from the Kerameikos, and for encouragement and significant help during the study period; to Professor Michalis Tiverios for help concerning research in—and about—Eleusis, and also to K. Papangeli for permissions and excellent support in the Eleusis Museum. Sincere thanks must be expressed to painter Katerina Mavraganis for realizing the original drawing of the golden strip bands from the Stathatos collection, and also to A. Gounaris and N. Zachou for preparing the drawing of the new scene of the Boston pyxis. The editors of this volume contributed to the improvement of the English text. For corrections and comments I thank I. Leventi, P. Valavanis and V. Mitsopoulos-Leon, and V. Sabetai for inspiring discussions. All further errors remain mine. The relevant research has been carried out within the framework of the European Union Herakleitos Program, no. 70/3/7233, and an early version of this work was presented in my doctoral thesis, Mitsopoulou 2007 (unpublished). The augmented interest which the two new and hitherto unpublished images provide for the interpretation of the Eleusinian cult vessels is the reason for their presentation in this congress. The following abbreviations are used: a) Bibliography: *ΑΕΘΣΕ = Αρχαιολογικό Έργο Θεσσαλίας και Στερεάς Ελλάδας; EEKM = Επετηρίδα Εταιρείας Κυκλαδικών*

* This article would never have been conceived without the valuable help and guidance of Assoc. Professor Iphigeneia Leventi, who firstly awakened my interest in Eleusinian iconography. The identification of the

is of specialized destination and use and it was produced in clay, bronze, gilded clay or marble.[2] It has little in common with other vase-shapes, widely attested and of large chronological range, which have been discussed by modern scholarship in relation to the ancient term *kernos*.[3] Almost exclusively found in Athens and Eleusis, the shape appears in direct relation to the Eleusinian cult.[4] The only other area in Attica from which it has been systematically reported is Laureion–Thorikos, mostly from the mining areas and houses or private shrines in proximity to the former.[5] Only the still unpublished vases from the Doric building in Thorikos might belong to a more official cult area.[6] Eleusinian vases outside Attica remain of utmost rarity: besides the few vases from Hellenistic Alexandria,[7] a few sherds have been identified amidst the votive material from a sanctuary of Demeter on the acropolis of Kythnos in the Cyclades.[8]

Edmond Beulé was the first to extensively discuss these peculiar vessels in 1858, in his attempt to interpret the vases depicted on some Athenian coins.[9] He was led to propose an Eleusinian interpretation due to the leafy branches decorating the handles, which he thought to be ears of corn. He hesitated between the three vessels mentioned by texts in relation to the ancient Greek Mysteries: κοτυλίσκος, πλημοχόη, and κέρνος.[10] As the term *kernos* did not convince him right from the beginning as being specifically linked to the Eleusinian Mysteries, he proposed to adopt the

---

Μελετών; F&R = Furtwängler & Reichhold 1905.
b) Museums: BMFA: Boston, Museum of Fine Arts; MMNY: New York, Metropolitan Museum; NMA: National Archaeological Museum of Athens; ArchCollThess: Archaeological Collection of Thessaloniki University; CCVASU: Iris & B. Gerald Cantor Centre for Visual Arts at Stanford University; MHTU: Museum of Historical Treasures of Ukraine (Kiev).

[1] For this time range the use of the vases can be traced through the archaeological record, even if the main bulk of material should be dated from the early fourth century to the third century BC. See Pollitt 1979, 211–222, 226, with revised dating from *c.* 400–390 to the second half of the second century BC by M. Miles: *Agora* XXXI, 97–98. A few representations of the vases date to the Roman era: architectural reliefs, probably from the City Eleusinion in Athens (*Agora* XXXI, 95, pls. 22, 23b) or on the *kiste* carried by the marble Karyatids of the Lesser Propylaia at Eleusis (Mylonas 1961, fig. 56; Papangeli 2002, 48–49, 117–119), even if not very faithful to the Classical Greek shape. It remains unknown, however, if real vases were still produced and used in the Roman period.
[2] For the various materials, see Bakalakis 1991, 109–110. Clay is evidently the most common material for the category. Bronze vases have been reported from Eleusis and Thorikos, but have not yet been published: see Philios 1884, 64–65, n. 2; Rubensohn 1898, 283.
[3] A good introduction to the issue is to be found in Bignasca 2000, 1–3, n. 2–11; 2005, 250–251. The term "kernos" for all the categories, Eleusinian and other, was used by Schauroth Upson 1944, 190 (*non vidi*). See now the synthesis in Mitsopoulou 2010b.
[4] For the Athenian Agora, see Pollitt 1979 and *Agora* XXXI, 95–103. For the Kerameikos, see *Kerameikos* XVII, 96–97; earlier Willemsen 1977, 137–138 and n. 73, pl. 57:I. A catalogue of the Eleusinian vases from the site is in preparation by the author (unpublished). For Eleusis, see Bakalakis 1991, with full references. For finds from a deposit near the *Hiera Hodos*, see most recently Tsirigoti-Drakotou 2009, 316; *Ελευθεροτυπία*

30.03.2007; for a potter's kiln with Eleusinian vases in the Kerameikos area, see *ArchDelt* 1994, Chron. B´1, 35, pl. 20c; Orfanou 2000, 382, n. 439–442. A volume with various contributions presenting new find places and vases from Attica is under preparation by the author.
[5] Ellis-Jones 1982; Tsaimou & Oikonomakou 1998, with multiple sites and references.
[6] This important information was published by Tsaimou & Oikonomakou 1998, 213. For the excavation, see *Ergon* 1996, 19–23 and further, n. 84.
[7] One from the necropolis of Sciatbi: Breccia 1912, no. 248. For stray finds: Pagenstecher 1913, 12, fig. 18 (recently located in the collection of Antiquities, Albertinum, Dresden: Inv. ZV 2600 G 488). See also n. 116.
[8] Mitsopoulou 2005, 325–331, 357, fig. 22, 2–9; *eadem* 2010, 153–154 and n. 50.
[9] Beulé 1858, 155–158.
[10] See *ThesCRA* V, 2005: for *kernos*, Bignasca 2005, nos. 616–622; Ath. 11. 478c–d; for *plemochoe*: Krauskopf 2005, nos. 641–643; Ath. 11. 496a; Poll. *Onom.* 10.74; Hsch. s.v. πλημοχόη.

Fig. 1. Drawing of the Ninnion tablet by Gilliéron. Reproduced from ArchEph *1987, 394, Fig. 7.*

term *plemochoe* and thus to associate the shape with the homonymous finishing ritual of the Eleusinian Mysteries. Beulé's thoughts antedated the discovery of the first real vases in Eleusis by almost three decades.

The coins discussed by Beulé later turned out to belong to the New Style Coinage, introduced in Athens during the second century BC.[11] However, Eleusinian vases do appear on Athenian coins (Eleusinian festival coinage and tokens)[12] from the 330s onwards, first as a discrete adjacent symbol,[13] and later, towards the third century, as an independent type of the obverse.[14] All these fourth- to third-century coins or tokens are of Eleusinian character, and the Eleusinian vase appears amidst other cult paraphernalia. The first seem to be minted in

---

[11] Thompson 1961.

[12] For tokens, see Engel 1884, 1–21, nos. 17, 187, 189–191; Svoronos 1926, nos. 37–39, pl. 102.

[13] In Group 39 of Kroll, *Agora* XXVI, 30, 41 (Svoronos 1926, pl. 103:33–37). Unfortunately this group is not precisely dated, ranging from early to mid-330s BC. For the first systematic effort at dealing with Eleusinian coinage, see Thompson 1942; Kroll 1992, 355–356; *Agora* XXXI, 96 and n. 4.

[14] From Kroll Group 61 onwards, Period B, third century BC, undated, *Agora* XXVI, 28, 47 (Svoronos 1926, pl. 103:29–32). This group remains mainly undated within the third century BC; it is an isolated emission of limited mintage.

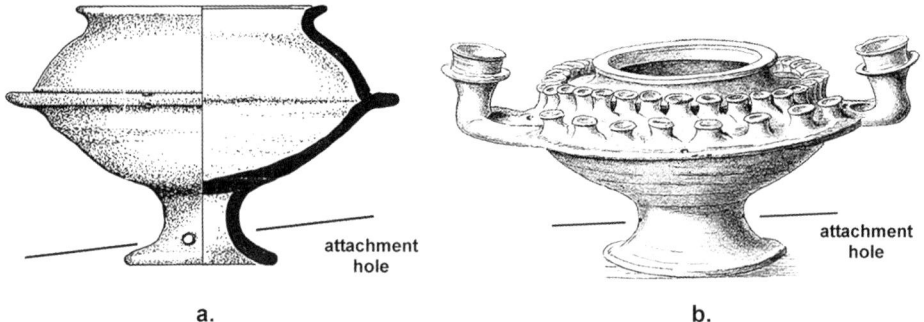

Fig. 2. Simple and complex variants of Eleusinian vessels: a. Plain type (ASP 54, from Ellis Jones 1982, 193, fig. 1), b. Type with schematic kotyliskoi (from Philios 1885, pl. 9:5).

a period of transition, from the Classical *polis* towards the Macedonian era, initiating probably around the years of Lykourgos.[15] With these issues the official Athenian state decided to systematically project the Eleusinian cult onto coin iconography, using the widely recognizable equipment or offerings of the initiate besides the Eleusinian deities.[16] These repeated representations of the cult vase on Athenian coins are doubtless much more current than the scarce testimonies from earlier iconographic sources. They may indicate an important

official change in the use of images within the Eleusinian administration of cult.[17]

After Beulé, the vessels were soon projected into the centre of interest of archaeological Eleusinian studies during the first systematic excavations of the Eleusinian sanctuary.[18] Real specimens of the shape appeared in 1882, in clay, metal and marble, verifying the Eleusinian interpretation previously proposed. Soon after, in 1895, the same excavations brought to light the red-figured votive tablet of Ninnion, on which these vases are depicted in the moment of transportation, attached to the heads of walking or dancing women (*Fig. 1*).[19] Ever since, research has been divided between attempts to either support or to question the interpretation of the depicted scene as a possible *kernophoria*.[20] The special features of the

---

[15] Homer Thompson had suggested that the *kernos*-finds from the City Eleusinion might be connected with a revival of interest in the cult during the regime of Lykourgos, see Mitchel 1973, 198, 207; Pollitt 1979, 226, n. 17; Hintzen-Bohlen 1997, 133 and n. 311. This suggestion now seems to be strengthened by chronological indications. Thompson 1942, 218–219 had already tried to establish a link between the money with Eleusinian devices and the Greater Eleusinia festival. She proposed to date the start of Eleusinian coinage issues to the era of Lykourgos (338–326 BC), the festival year 335 BC. Such an exact dating does not result from Kroll's aforementioned dating. The period of the monetary financial reform and the simplification of the vessels' form, both seem to be close to his era.
[16] Such as the myrtle wreath, the piglet, the mystery myrtle staff (*bakchos*), the Eleusis ring and the vase. See Svoronos 1926, nos. 1–53, pls. 103–104.

[17] The period is close in date to a revival and important change of the ancestral custom concerning the offering of the *aparchai* to the Eleusinian Sanctuary, see *IG* II² 1672 = Clinton 2005, no. 177; Clinton 2010. Earlier, Hintzen-Bohlen 1997, 124 and nn. 252–253.
[18] Philios 1882, 89, n. 2; Philios 1884, 64–65, n. 2; Philios 1885, 171–174.
[19] First presentation by Skias 1901, 1–39. Most recently, Tiverios 2008, 129–131 and 150–151, no. 66 (K. Papangeli) with further references.
[20] The words κερνοφόρος, ἐκιρνοφόρησα do appear in ancient texts (see Bignasca 2005, 251, nos. 616, 619, 620), hardly however in clear connection with the Attic Eleusinian Mysteries, but rather with Rhea and Kybele.

vessels, and their obvious link to the Eleusinian sanctuary, highlighted by their almost complete absence from other contexts, revitalized the discussion concerning their interpretation: was it the *kernos*, the *kerchnos*, or the *plemochoe*? Tullia Linders put a definite end to the confusion with the word *kerchnos*,[21] and today scholars hesitate between *kernos* and *plemochoe*.[22]

On the red-figured tablet the woman or women are represented carrying the vases on their heads, obviously attached by strings (*Fig. 1*). The certainty that the vessels were systematically destined for transportation in this manner is revealed by the almost constant presence of attachment-holes on the shoulder rim,[23] as well as on the stem of the clay vases (*Figs. 2a–b, 19*).[24] Even miniature and obviously votive specimens often maintain this feature (*Fig. 3a–b*), revealing the importance of the act of transportation.[25] If a kind of Eleusinian *kernophoria* was depicted on the tablet, then the definition of the *kernos* by Athenaios would provide the ingredients contained in the vessels depicted

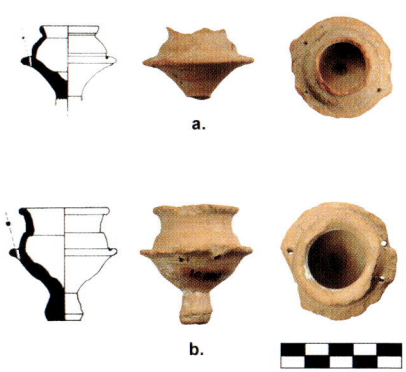

Fig. 3a–b. Kerameikos: two miniature plemochoai conserving four attachment holes on the antyx (a: KER. 10.780, b: KER. 10.778). Drawing C. Mitsopoulou, © DAI Athen.

here. The presence of wine (*oinos*) and broad beans (*kyamoi*) in the recipe—both products reported to have been banned from the Eleusinian Mysteries—should however have aroused objection much earlier than the voice of Karl Kerényi,[26] which hardly influenced subsequent scholarship.[27]

The interpretation which is most widely accepted today is rooted in F. Brommer's thesis of 1980: the simple vessels without plastic decoration may be identified with the *plemochoe* (*Fig. 2a*), whereas the complex specimens may still be called *kernoi* (*Fig. 2b*). This view has been mostly followed since, without the examination of

---

This uncertainty had already been pointed out by Beulé 1858, 155 and n. 3.

[21]   Linders 1988, 229–230.

[22]   Brommer 1980, 544–549. Followed by Miles, *Agora* XXXI, 95–103; Krauskopf 2005, 252–255; Bignasca 2005, 250–251; Clinton 2007, 351; Tiverios 2008, 130–131; Clinton, 2009; Mitsopoulou 2010a, 47–51; *eadem* 2010b, 149–154.

[23]   We will not further discuss the opinion that the holes were intended for positioning of myrtle branches. The vases are most often depicted with branches near their handles, but the use of attachment strings is confirmed by the Ninnion tablet. Decoration may have been their secondary use.

[24]   Philios 1885, pl. 9:5, 7 published vases which belong to the complex type, whereas the vase published by Ellis-Jones 1982, 193, fig. 1, no. ASP 54 belongs to the plain type. However, they both have a hole in their stem, showing that both shape varieties were destined to be transported in the same way, at least partly attached to the heads of initiates.

[25]   The observation is based upon material from the German excavations in the Kerameikos (specifically on the miniature vases cat. nos. KER 5008, KER 10780 and KER 10778), now studied for publication.

[26]   On the interdiction of broad beans (*kyamoi*) for initiates of the Eleusinian Mysteries, see Paus. 1.37. 4–5. On incompatibility of wine, following the *Hymn. Hom. Cer.*, 206–208, Kerényi 1967, 177–186 and esp. 184. However, wine is mentioned amidst products used at the Thesmophoria in Cholargos (*IG* II² 1184 = *SEG* 35 239, 334/3 BC), see Schwenk 1985, 138–139, no. 26 and Clinton 1996, 121, no. 4. On wine mentioned in a sacred law from the Eleusinion, dated *c.* 510–480 BC (*IG* I³ 232.B, l. 59–66), see Clinton 1996, 124, n. 34.

[27]   The definition of the *kernos* by Athenaios continues to be reproduced or referred to in studies arguing in favour of the Eleusinian character of the vase: Pollitt 1979, 205; Brommer 1980, 548; Bakalakis 1991, 105; Bignasca 2005, 251, nos. 617–618 (*contra* Bignasca 2000, 1–2); most recently Clinton 2009, 240, 243.

new archaeological data or a re-examination of the available unpublished material.[28] Recently, this division has been developed further by K. Clinton.[29] He proposes that the simple variety, the *plemochoe*, may be related to the Eleusinian Mysteries, whereas the complex vases relate to the *kernos* and the Thesmophoria. Leaving this question aside, we will focus on the simple, plain variety of Eleusinian vases.[30]

The Ninnion tablet was produced probably as a commission of the initiate signing with the name of Ninnion.[31] The varied attempts at interpretation have proposed a unitary reading of the upper and lower register of the scene,[32]

or a differentiated one, proposing either different moments of the Eleusinian Mysteries (first and last days at Eleusis),[33] or different festivals (Lesser Mysteries of Agra and Mysteries of Eleusis).[34] E. Simon proposed repeatedly that not the Mysteries, but some other festival of Demeter was narrated (the *Haloa*),[35] denying simultaneously the similarity between the depicted vessels—which she interpreted as thuribles—and the clay vessels excavated in Eleusis.[36] Most recently M. Tiverios argued that the principal scene depicts the arrival of initiates at the great Eleusinian sanctuary, however not necessarily for the Great Mysteries, and distinguished three families arriving in procession.[37]

It is obvious that the Ninnion tablet will not succeed in providing a clear interpretation for the vessels and their use, as long as the precise identification of the moment and the place of the procession are not understood. However, a possible independently rooted comprehension of the destination of the vessels might put an end to the controversial readings of the private votive tablet. For a long period, this tablet was considered to be the only iconographic testimony for the vessels during use.

---

[28]   *Agora* XXXI, 94 and n. 2; Krauskopf 2005, 252–255; Bignasca 2005, 250; Clinton 1992, 74, n. 59.
[29]   Clinton 2009, 245–246.
[30]   This suggestion has been discussed elsewhere: briefly Mitsopoulou 2010a, 50–51; *eadem* 2010b, 153, 163. Here we also avoid extended discussion concerning the eventual use of the vases as incense burners (von Fritze 1897, 165; Simon 1966, 88 and n. 96; *Agora* XXIX, 211 and n. 41; Tiverios 2008, 13) or containers for lamps. No secure archaeological evidence has ever proved their direct use as fire recipients; the old discussion is based on their often perforated lids and a vague indication by Philios 1885, 173 that some vases were found in Eleusis containing ash and charcoal traces. As vividly pointed out by Kourouniotes 1898, 24–25 and n. 12, these external traces are due to contamination by burnt soil within the deposit. Rubensohn 1898, 286–287 also states that none of the vessels in the Eleusis Museum showed traces of burning. Flames are in fact depicted in the broad large vessel which is positioned in the centre of the scene on the Regina Vasorum (Hermitage Museum, St Petersburg, St. 525 (B–1659). It often has been identified as an Eleusinian *plemochoe*: Clinton 1992, 80, 134 with ref. no. 5, 170, fig. 18; followed by Leventi 2007, 118–119, n. 46, fig. 9 and n. 56. However, this open bowl-shaped vessel is definitely not an Eleusinian *plemochoe*, but a large shallow thurible (*thymiaterion* or *escharion*), see Zaccanigno 1998, 162, Variant I², RT 458, tav. 2; for a close clay example, see Papangeli 2002, 26.
[31]   A new interpretation has been proposed by Tiverios 2008, 131: the tablet might have been sold ready-made. Only later was it appropriated by Ninnion, through her votive inscription, as it was incised after firing.
[32]   Tiverios 2008, 131, 150, no. 66 with bibliography (K. Papangeli). He reads the whole principal represen-

---

tation as scenes of devotees at the moment of their arrival at the sanctuary of Eleusis. Previous synthesis of opinions in Simon 1966, 86–91; Peschlow-Bindokat 1972, 105–107, 146–147.
[33]   Clinton 1992, 73–75 and n. 58; 84–85 argues that the two scenes show the beginning and the end of the Mysteries at Eleusis (the procession of Iakchos and the final rite of the *Plemochoai*); also, Clinton 2007, 351, 353. Previously in this sense, Nilsson 1935, 560–561; Metzger 1965, 31–32; Peschlow-Bindokat 1972, 107.
[34]   Svoronos 1901, 233–263; Mylonas 1960, 81–88.
[35]   Simon 1966, 91, n. 114; 1983, 36.
[36]   Simon 1966, 88 and n. 95–96. She supported the distinction between *kernoi* with cuplets and the simple shape, which she interprets as a thurible. When later informed about the *realia* from the Agora and Eleusis, she maintained this opinion, while proposing as a compromise simultaneous *kernophoria* and use as thuribles: Simon 1983, 36–37, n. 77.
[37]   Tiverios 2008, 129–131, esp. 131.

At this point we enrich the discussion with two further artefacts contributing towards the interpretation of the Eleusinian vessels. The first, a pair of golden strip bands from the Helene Stathatos Collection in the National Museum of Athens, is not entirely absent from former scholarship. It has been reintegrated recently into the discussion concerning the Eleusinian cult vessel, though without a complete description.[38] Here it will be re-examined, and detailed new images are used in order to minutely observe and update the precious data provided by this unique—for our topic—artefact.[39] The second, a fragmentary red-figured pyxis lid from Athens, now in the Museum of Fine Arts in Boston, was partly known since 1905. But only recently it was comprehensively discussed, allowing a new examination of the rare iconography.[40]

The Stathatos headband

Two identical thin narrow oblong golden strip bands[41] are reported to have been found in Demetrias in Thessaly during the 1920s, but their precise provenience is unknown (*Figs. 4a–b, 5a–b*).[42] They are not exactly rectangu-

lar, as both tend to show a slight curving of the extremities towards the top. They were sewn upon a supporting structure, cloth or leather, as indicated by the numerous small holes in proximity to the upper and lower margins,[43] and were probably united through a joining element.[44] They may be associated with the category of strip diadems.[45] Both bear an identical scene in hammered embossed relief, produced by the same matrix. They have been dated to *c.* 300 BC, based on stylistic features.[46] Their

---

[38] Krauskopf 2005, 254, 652. Formerly, Möbius 1955, 36–40.
[39] See also Mitsopoulou 2010b, 168–172.
[40] Leventi 2007, 121–122, n. 56, fig. 12; Mitsopoulou 2007, Part III, 769–819, pl. 7.1–7.11; Mitsopoulou 2010b, 166–168, fig. 7.
[41] NMA, Stathatos Collection no. St. 342a–b; dimensions: length: 0.25 m.; width: 0.0215 m.; thickness: 0.0025 m.; diam. hole: 0.035 m. Each band has a corroded silver ring at one extremity (left and right respectively), and a rectangular cutting at the other. The surface is quite damaged and the borders torn, but the bands were never folded. The objects were used and conserved as open strips.
[42] Unfortunately, the exact provenience of these finds, as the whole of the so-called Demetrias Treasure, remains unknown. Information available to Amandry 1953, 85 did not allow the determination of a precise location. The treasure was said to come from Deme-

trias, and to have been bought in 1931 by H. Stathatos. No other information has ever been published. Scholars have mostly discussed possible proveniences (Demetrias or Halmyros in Thessaly, Lianokladi-Lamia or Domokos in Phthiotis, Karpenissi in Eurytania) of the second, so-called Karpenissi treasure, bought in 1929 partly by H. Stathatos (now in the NMA) and the Benaki Museum. Parts of the latter were also bought by Princeton University; Segall 1938, 31; Segall 1945, 3 and more specifically Kambanis 1934, 101–102; Amandry 1953, 89–90; Miller 1979, 2; Kostoglou-Despoini 1996, 30. We note that all the proposed proveniences are located in Central Greece.
[43] No series of holes are visible on the diadem from Kertsch (see below n. 44). However, similar sewing holes are observed on the upper frame of two golden diadems from Scythia, Ukraine, fourth century BC: Bunjatjan 1995, 79 (from Kurgan 1) and nos. 48 and 75, no. 41 (from Kurgan 17). Holes are denser in the lower part, but also present on the top border.
[44] As demonstrated by another funeral diadem with Eleusinian iconography, the rape of Kore, from Kertsch (Pantikapaion), mid-fourth century BC: Lindner 1984, 39, 131, n. 168, pl. 16. Here the two identical golden bands are symmetrically arranged by a central retaining jewel, in the shape of a Herakles knot. The bands may have been assembled during their second use, as the scenes are violently interrupted and damaged by the binding with the connecting jewel.
[45] Treister 2001, 181–182. Strip diadems are a type of Hellenistic diadem; they may also be called "diadems of a constant width", in opposition to pedimental diadems.
[46] Amandry 1953, 87: end of fourth century BC. Möbius 1955, 39: the lot might come from a single grave, dated to the third century BC; Krauskopf 2005, 254: third century BC; Leventi 2007, 122: late fourth or third century BC. See n. 55, 67.

Fig. 4a–b. Pair of golden strip bands (NMA St. 342a–b): Eleusinian scene, photo by the author, permission NMA.

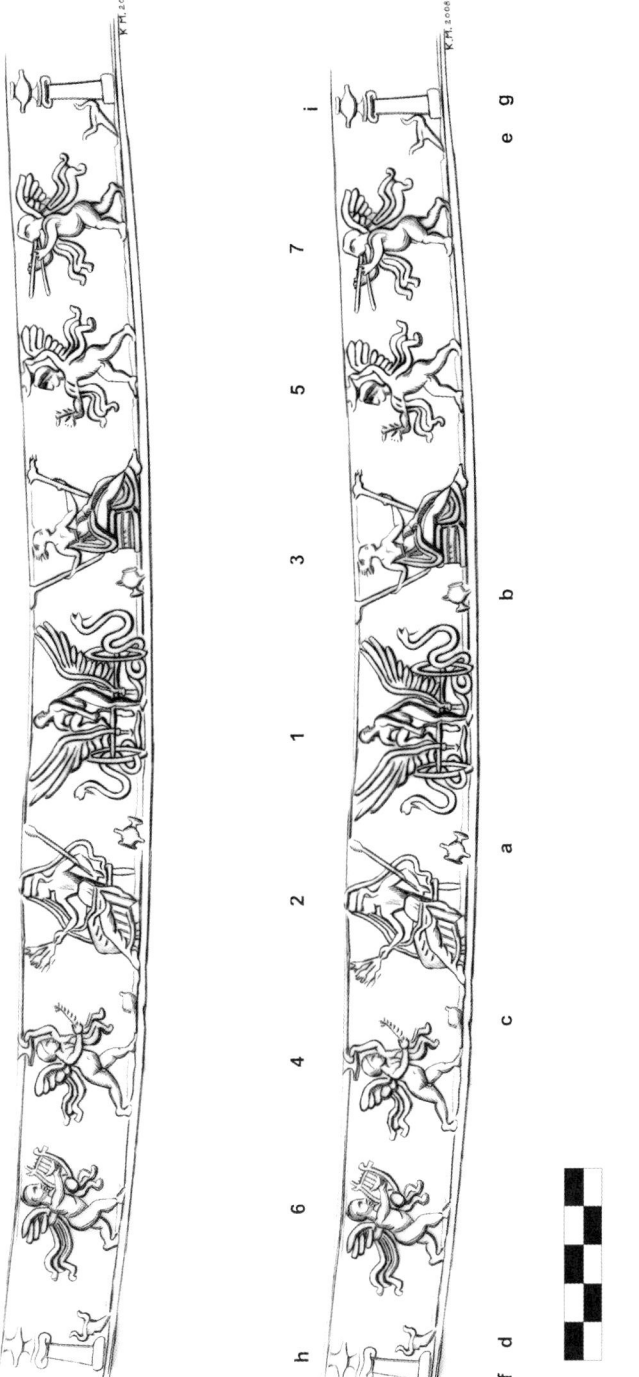

*Fig. 5a–b.
NMA, golden
strip band with
Eleusinian scene
(NMA St. 342),
drawing by
K. Mavraganis,
adapted from
both bands.*

destination was most probably funeral,[47] but they show no important typological differences from real diadems worn by Hellenistic kings during their lifetime.[48] We cannot tell at this stage whether they might previously have served as *stemmata* during an Eleusinian initiation,[49] due to the lack of identified relevant finds and the uniqueness of the scene.[50]

These strips were first published by Amandry,[51] unfortunately with depictions of low clarity and without drawings.[52] Some of the detailed peculiarities of the scene were not recognized and as a consequence the sheets failed to impose upon later scholarship.

The complex Eleusinian scene is identical on both bands: seven figures are depicted in a single frieze and a column frames the scene at either extremity. The centre is occupied by the winged chariot, shown in frontal view, with two bearded snakes projecting symmetrically towards left and right. Triptolemos is rendered in a rare gesture and position borrowed from contemporary sculptural types, in a convention indicating preparation for departure (*Fig. 5b:1; Fig. 6*). His body is slightly bent forward. He is reposing on his left leg, while the toes of his right foot are positioned on the axis of the chariot; the arms are touching his ankle, where he is obviously binding his sandal laces, preparing for departure. His head is turned to his left, as if disturbed by some noise. He is almost nude; a *himation* hangs from his shoulders, falling towards the ground, behind the axis of the chariot. The central scene obviously indicates the completion of the Eleusinian

---

[47]   Examples of golden funeral diadems with Eleusinian iconography are known from the Black Sea area and Euboia: the aforementioned golden headband from Kertsch, Lindner 1984, 38–39, no. 27, pl. 16, and a funeral golden strip diadem from Eretria, late third–early second century BC; see Kuruniotes (*sic*) 1913, 319–324, fig. 11; Treister 2001, 182 and n. 122–123 (fig. 92, missing). Depicted is a complex scene with Demeter and Kore in the centre, and two repeated scenes with Aphrodite in a chariot driven by rams and led by Hermes, Eros nearby, approaching the enthroned Zeus and Demeter or Hades and Persephone.

[48]   To compare with the narrow strip diadem worn by Demetrios I Poliorketes on the portraiture attributed to him. Most representative is the smaller than lifesize marble head in the Louvre, inv. no. MA 3293; Frel 1994, 77, figs. 63–64; on royal diadems, Smith 1988, 34–38; on Demetrios, Smith 1988, 64–66, 156, cat. no. 4. Discord is however expressed in relation to the material of real royal diadems worn during a king's lifetime. The white bands are considered to have been manufactured of cloth, see Ritter 1965, 12, no. 4: ταινία λευκὴ περὶ τῷ μετώπῳ (Lucian *Navigium* 39); Smith 1988, 34 and n. 26; Virgilio 2006, 41, n. 88 and fig. 6. Most characteristic are the fringed ends of the cloth falling down the neck. However, golden diadems existed (Ath. 5.201d); diadems were also known to coexist with golden wreaths in royal burials, as reported for Alexander's burial, Ritter 1965, 74–78. He further notes that golden funeral wreaths and headbands may not have been reserved for kings, but simply for very privileged individuals (p. 74, n. 4). On insignia and diadems of Hellenistic kings, see Trehuedic 2008 (*non vidi*). Papapostolou (1990, 83) insists on the funeral destination of thin bands, in opposition to objects used during an individual's lifetime. However, he maintains some doubts concerning the exclusive use of golden strips as diadems; Papapostolou 1990, 92 and n. 42. For golden diadems of Classical date also, see Kostoglou-Despoini 1996, 65–68.

[49]   See Parker 2005, 361 and n. 151; Mylonas 1961, 238–239; Riedweg 1987, 125–127.

[50]   No parallel finds have been reported from Thessaly or elsewhere. The rarity of identical headbands has been

pointed out by Treister 2001, 177. Funeral diadems with Eleusinian scenes are rare, see nn. 43–44. Thessaly however has a tradition in inscribed funeral Orphic, Bacchic or Demetrian gold leaves, and especially for those with "long" texts, see Parker & Stamatopoulou 2007, 15–16, 18. Six such artefacts are known, dating approximately from the middle of the fourth century BC to the first quarter of the third century; the figured bands are contemporary with the tradition of inscribed funeral leaves.

[51]   Amandry 1953, 86–88, no. 230/231, pl. 34.

[52]   A complete depiction of the complex scenes is hardly possible by photography. Möbius 1955, 36 regrets that the older generations of archaeological draughtsmen had died out: "Bedauern kann man nur, dass die Antikenzeichner der früheren Zeit ausgestorben sind, denn für die Verdeutlichung mancher technischer Details und einzelner Figuren auf den Goldbändern Nr. 230/231 wären anspruchslose, aber genaue Zeichnungen willkommen gewesen".

Mysteries on the last day, when the departure of the agrarian god for his Eleusinian mission is known to have taken place.[53] This peculiar iconography of Triptolemos did attract immediate attention once observed,[54] but it did not enter the synthetic iconographic studies on his behalf, as slightly postdating the Classical period.[55] The obvious reflection of the Lysippic "Sandalenbinder" type has led to the dating of the artefacts to the end of the fourth century BC or later.[56]

Möbius was the first to make the important observation, which was reintroduced recently

Fig. 6. Detail of Eleusinian scene, NMA St. 342: Triptolemos binding his sandal, winged chariot, two plemochoai.

into the Eleusinian discussion by Krauskopf:[57] at either side of Triptolemos' winged chariot is depicted a small inclined stemmed vase with handles (*Fig. 5b:a–b, Fig. 6*). A thorough observation of these miniature objects reveals a minute rendering of the precise Eleusinian shape we here examine (*Figs. 2a and 19*). The disposition of the vases in proximity to the final closing episode of the Eleusinian Mysteries appears to be a unique and precious fourth- or third-century illustration of the rite of the *Plemochoai*, as described by Athenaios (Ath. 11.495–6): "Plemochoe is an earthen dish shaped like a top, but firm on its base ... They use it at Eleusis on the last day of the Mysteries, a day which they call from it Plemochoai; on that day they fill two plemochoai, and they invert them (standing up and facing the east in the one case, the west in the other), reciting a mystical formula over them." (trans. C.B. Gulick, *Loeb Classical Library*, 2004).[58]

---

[53] Mission of Triptolemos: Dugas 1960, 123–139. The mission is adopted in Athens between 510 and 480 BC, see Raubitschek & Raubitschek 1982, 111, n. 15; Matheson 1994, 362. Sophocles presented his tragedy (or satyr play) *Triptolemos* in 469/8 BC, see Matheson 1994, 347–348, nn. 8–10.

[54] Amandry 1953, 87; Möbius 1955, 39. The echo of the Lysippean "Sandalenbinder" type was immediately pointed out, but not further discussed. For the serious attribution of the original of the "Sandalenbinder" type, to the oeuvre of Lysippos or his school, see Vierneisel-Schlörb 1979, 457–468, no. 42, figs. 227–232; Moreno 1995, 230–231; earlier Ridgway 1964 (selected references).

[55] The golden bands are not included in recent synthetic discussions of the iconography of Triptolemos, such as Schwarz 1987; *LIMC* VIII.1 (1997), 56–68, s.v. Triptolemos (G. Schwarz); Hayashi 1992. On this topic, see discussion in Mitsopoulou, forthcoming b.

[56] In three dimensions, the homonymous statue attributed to Lysippos is the first artefact of the type. For the Lysippean posture, see the early study by Lange 1879. In the art of two-dimensional relief the sandalizing position can be followed back to the mid-fifth century BC: on the west side of the Parthenon frieze, youth no. 29, Brommer 1977, 21–22, pls. 44–45, W XV; Vierneisel-Schlörb 1979, 459, n. 22. In Classical art it is often Eros or winged Hermes with the attribute of the *caduceus* who is represented in this posture: winged Hermes on the bezel of a fifth-century golden ring from Kertsch, Reeder 1999, 186–187, no. 74 (MHTU, inv. no. AZS 1692); Eros on the red-figured Attic *chous* from New York (MMNY, inv. no. 25.190), Schmidt 2005, 191–192, fig. 98, *c.* 360 BC. The position of Triptolemos amidst the enormous wings of his dragon-wheeled chariot gives the visual impression that the figure is winged, in similarity to the two former images.

[57] Möbius 1955, 39; Krauskopf 2005, 254, no. 652. The first to remark on the brief comment by Möbius was Ochsenschlager 1968, 58, 61. However, he rejected the identification of the pair of vases framing Triptolemos' chariot with the *plemochoai*, and proposed that here was depicted some offering of seeds relevant to the departure of Triptolemos. The left *plemochoe*, behind Demeter, is also depicted in *LIMC* IV, 2, pl. 589, no. 382, but was neither observed nor commented upon.

[58] "Πλημοχόη σκεῦος κεραμεοῦν βεμβικῶδες ἑδραῖον ἡσυχῇ, ὃ κοτυλίσκον ἔνιοι προσαγορεύουσιν, ὥς φησι Πάμφιλος. χρῶνται δὲ αὐτῷ ἐν Ἐλευσῖνι τῇ τελευταίᾳ τῶν μυστηρίων ἡμέρᾳ, ἣν καὶ ἀπ᾽αὐτοῦ προσαγορεύουσι Πλημοχόας. ἐν ᾗ δύο πλημοχόας πληρώσαντες τὴν

So far, the Stathatos headband has provided a strong new iconographic argument reinforcing the identification of the vessels with the *plemochoe* and the rite of the last day of the Mysteries. Furthermore, it suggests through iconography the immediate relation of this rite with the departure of Triptolemos.[59] The hint that this libation may be closely linked to the departure of Triptolemos, as a ritual irrigation, a tide of liquids,—πλήμη—for the seeds just sown during his instruction by Demeter, and as a conceqence for the imminent ploughings and sowings to follow during his mission of agrarian instruction, adds a new—more agrarian and Eleusinian instead of chtonian—aspect to the *plemochoe* ritual.[60]

The obvious and definite conclusion that the Eleusinian vessels are the ritual vases for the final rite of the Eleusinian Mysteries remains, however, somewhat weakened by the Ninnion tablet, as it still remains in need of a convinc-

ing identification of the exact moment(s) of the depicted scene(s), with the woman (women) proceeding with the Eleusinian vase attached to her (their) head(s). The problem is that they again transfer the simple *plemochoe*-variety, even if no obvious indication can link the entire scene to the final rites of the Mysteries.[61] Obliged by the contradiction between the literary evidence and the iconography of the votive tablet, Krauskopf stated that a varied use of the vessels may be possible and that "this image (Ninnion Tablet) is not sufficient as an argument against the secure identification of the cult-vase with the Plemochoe".[62]

However, the scene on the Ninnion tablet does not necessarily contradict the scenes on the headband, as it may simply be complementary. To date, scholars have been severely confused in their attempts to define the single and unique interpretation of the vessels. But what if the latter had not one, but two distinct destinations of use within the same Eleusinian cult?[63]

Triptolemos excepted, the other figures of the scene are symmetrically duplicated in a mir-

---

μὲν πρὸς ἀνατολάς, τὴν δὲ πρὸς δύσιν ἀνιστάμενοι ἀνατρέπουσιν, ἐπιλέγοντες ῥῆσιν μυστικήν."

[59] The libations of the *Plemochoai* rite have mostly been interpreted by modern scholarship as chthonic libations, eventually rooted in older ancestral rites for the dead: Mylonas 1961, 279; Pollitt 1979, 230–231; *Agora* XXXI, 100–101; follows Bignasca 2005, 250: "... le plemochoai nella libagione chtonia per Plutone". These affirmations were founded on Ath. 11.496b: "μνημονεύει αὐτῶν καὶ ὁ τὸν Πειρίθουν γράψας, εἴτε Κριτίας ἐστὶν ὁ τύραννος ἢ Εὐριπίδης, λέγων οὕτως ἵνα πλημοχόας τάσδ᾽ εἰς χθόνιον χάσμ᾽ εὐφήμως προχέωμεν"(Krauskopf 2005, no. 641). Ochsenschlager 1970, 323 had already questioned this conclusion, due to lack of further testimonies in favour of the chthonic character. Different view, Lambrinoudakis 2001, 10 and fig. 5; see now Lambrinoudakis 2008, 93. For earlier comments on libation scenes by Triptolemos, preceding his departure, see Dugas 1960, 126; Raubitschek & Raubitschek 1982, 112–113.

[60] I retain the intriguing comment of N. Papalexandrou during the discussion of the Symposium that the proximity of the vessels to the heads/mouths of the snakes pulling the chariot might be of some further significance. Would the snakes satisfy their thirst from the ritual tide, before departure? Would the beverage strengthen the motor force of the chariot?

[61] Some scholars have proposed that the upper register of the main scene depicts the end of the Mysteries (Clinton 1992, 74), but nobody has ever proposed that the entire scene is narrating the rite of the *Plemochoai*. The obvious arrival from faraway of the initiates at the lower level does not allow such an argument. And why would initiates transport the vases on their heads during their arrival from Athens (and be depicted doing this), if the vases were only meant to be used two days later, at the end of the rites? This does not seem convincing. However, see Tiverios 2008, 131: "... we may presume that the three plemochoai depicted on the Ninnion pinax contained the unknown preparation with which the initiates performed the libation on the concluding day of the Mysteries".

[62] Krauskopf 2005, 253.

[63] Krauskopf 2005, 253 proposed that the shape might be the recipient for the *kykeon*, as Kerényi had already proposed, but she affirms that there are no proofs for this supposition. Tiverios (2008, 131) also suggested that the Eleusinian vessels might have more than one use.

Fig. 7. Detail of Eleusinian scene, NMA St. 342: Demeter seated on wellhead, with sceptre and ears of corn.

Fig. 8. Detail of Eleusinian scene, NMA St. 342: Kore seated on kiste, *holding two torches.*

ror image.[64] Positioned on either half of the diadem, they are slightly differentiated in their details. The chariot is framed by the two seated Eleusinian goddesses, looking in opposite directions: Demeter is seated on a wellhead, turned towards the left (*Fig. 5b:2, Fig. 7*).[65] Her head is covered by a veil; she wears a *chiton* and a girdled *peplos* falling over her lower limbs, while holding a sceptre in her left arm and two or three ears of corn in her right hand.[66] Kore is turned towards the right. She is seated on a somewhat higher *kiste*, wearing a girdled *peplos* and *himation*, holding two torches (*Fig. 5b:3, Fig. 8*). Each goddess receives a pair of winged running baby Erotes, proceeding towards the centre (*Fig. 5b:4–7, Figs. 9–10*).[67] They are naked, their male sex is slightly visible (on the drawing), and from their shoulder hangs a *himation*, excited

by the movement. The two leading Erotes are holding a little leafy branch, probably myrtle,[68] whereas the following Erotes are musicians,[69] the left one playing a *lyra* or *kithara*[70] and the right one the double flute (*diaulos*). The Erotes could be interpreted as the personification of the procession of the initiates[71] on the fifth or

---

[64] On dating criteria of mirror images, balance and symmetry, see Jackson 2006, 55.

[65] For the discussion concerning Demeter seated on a wellhead, see Leventi 2007, 118–124.

[66] Demeter echoes a well-known iconographic type, formerly known from Hellenistic silver tetradrachms from Paros (second century BC); Ruhland 1901, 102, n. 2, fig. 8; Head 1959, 76, no. 26, pl. 43; Beschi 1988, 859, no. 133; Sheedy 2006, 94 and n. 661.

[67] A multiplicity of Erotes, as their transformation into chubby babies, is characteristic of early Hellenistic art, late fourth or early third century BC, see Jackson 2006, 53. These Erotes provide a *terminus post quem* dating criterion for the headband, in combination with the Lysippic echo in the figure of Triptolemos.

[68] Amandry 1953, 87 called it a palm branch. Möbius 1955 proposed myrtle branch for the left, the "bakchos" for the right Eros.

[69] On the iconography of Erotes as musicians in Attic Archaic and Classical vase-painting and literary sources, see Vergara Cerqueira, forthcoming. Musical instruments are current attributes of Eros, especially the *aulos* and the *lyra*. The most common environment for these earlier scenes is the world of women and the marital context, rarely with the presence of men.

[70] For music in processions of Archaic and Classical periods, see Nordquist 1992; for the use of the *aulos* in Classical Athens, see Wilson 1999; music in Hellenistic processions was common, as revealed by the splendid procession of Ptolemy II Philadelphos in Alexandria, in the early third century BC, reported by Kallixeinos of Rhodes (Ath. 5, 197c–202b; *FGrH* 627 F 2); see Tsochos 2002, 207–208; Rice 1983, 57–58, 113–115, and esp. 114 on κιθαρισταί: 300 *kitharistai* accompany the procession; Ath. 5, 201f. On the concept of *pompe*, see also Kavoulaki, this volume.

[71] For the personification of ΠΟΜΠΗ, the procession, see the red-figured *chous* from New York, *supra* n. 56. In this case the procession is obviously of Dionysiac character, with the presence of Dionysos and the sandalizing Eros ready for departure, in proximity to the female personification rendered in the iconography of Aphrodite. In the case of the headband the four winged running Erotes have replaced the figure of ΠΟΜΠΗ,

Fig. 9. Detail of Eleusinian scene, NMA St. 342: couple of running Erotes, proceeding towards Demeter.

Fig. 10. Detail of Eleusinian scene, NMA St. 342: couple of running Erotes, proceeding towards Kore.

sixth day of the Mysteries,[72] the arrival of *Iakchos* or *Pompe*.[73]

Further observation of the twin scenes reveals more important details: the pair of forerunning Erotes seems to support with their left free hands an Eleusinian vase positioned on the head (*Fig. 5b:4–5, Figs. 9–10*).[74] This second pair of vases is identified here for the first time.[75] Eleusinian cult vessels are thus depicted during two different phases of use on the head-

Fig. 11. Detail of Eleusinian scene, NMA St. 342: Pillar with ionic capital, bucranion *and* plemochoe, left end of scene.

band: once during the arrival of the initiates' procession at Eleusis—as on the Ninnion tablet—and once during the finishing rite, meaning the first *and* the last days of the Eleusinian part of the festivities. Even if—following Clinton's reading—the procession indicates the beginning of the rite of the *Plemochoai*,[76] and not of the Mysteries *per se*, we again have a double use of the vases, a) during arrival/procession (for which they bear attachment holes), and b) inclined for liquid libation.

We finally observe that a further, third pair of vases frames the extremities of either scene (*Fig. 5b:h–i, Figs. 11–13*): each vase is

---

standing for the group of proceeding initiates. However, the rendering of initiates as Erotes may be a choice reflecting and alluding to the strong Dionysiac character of the merry Iakchos procession: Robertson 1998, 559–560 and n. 37.

[72] On problems concerning the exact day of the procession, see Graf 1996; Robertson 1998.

[73] I am indebted to K. Clinton for extensive discussion of this scene, after the oral presentation of my paper. See now Clinton 2009, 242–243. He suggests that the procession would not have to stand for the arrival of the initiates at Eleusis, but could rather refer to a procession in the Telesterion during the rite of the *Plemochoai*, at the end of the Mysteries. He prefers to read the whole scene as a unified depiction of this specific rite, and tends to reject a double narration of two distinct phases of the Mysteries on the headband. This interpretation would lead to different conclusions for the entire scene. See n. 126.

[74] The drawing was created by artist Katerina Mavraganis in 2008.

[75] Amandry (1953, 87) had called them "flat and round objects", whereas Möbius (1955, 39) also called them "flache Schalen mit Deckeln", flat bowls with lids, and already compared them with the "kernos" on the Ninnion tablet. It was a paradox that, having in fact correctly observed them, he did not appreciate the obvious similarity between the inclined vases on the floor and those transported on the heads. Krauskopf 2005, 254,

no. 652 described them as not precisely identifiable objects ("bowl with lid?"), following Möbius.

[76] Following Clinton's suggestion, see n. 73. This view would have an important impact on the reading of the scene on the headband, and on the products contained in the vases (liquids for pouring only, or also products brought to Eleusis on arrival from Athens), but would not question their second use as processional vases. An important argument towards this reading is that the seated Demeter is depicted as holding the ears of corn, which will then be offered to Triptolemos during instruction and before departure.

Fig. 12. Detail of Eleusinian scene, NMA St. 342: Pillar with ionic capital, bucranion and plemochoe, *right end of scene.*

Fig. 13. Detail of Eleusinian scene, NMA St. 342: Pillar with ionic capital and plemochoe, *detail (right).*

positioned upon a heavy Ionic column or pillar, obviously monumental and votive, further highlighting their importance within the Eleusinian cult. The *bucranion* deposited on the ground near each column may allude to a previous sacrifice, and clearly defines them as votive. They might be associated with the sacrifice of bovines attested in inscriptions and Eleusinian iconography.[77]

A few marble vessels are known from Eleusis and the City Eleusinion[78] and one bears an explicit votive inscription to Demeter and Kore:[79]

[- - - -]άτης
[Δήμη]τρι καὶ Κόρει
ἀνέθηκε

The observation above allows us to suggest that these marble vessels may have actually been used as decorations in the area of the sanctuary, for the celebration of the *Plemochoai*, or may have been offered in gratitude for successful completion of initiation. Could the initiated deceased anonymous owner of the headband have been in some way related to the actual offering of such monumental marble votives?

The scene on the golden headband is an explicit allusion to the completion of the Eleusinian experience. We do not know if the *Plemochoai* rite was accessible to all initiates, or only to the *epoptai* who remained at the end.[80] The importance of the experience manifested here rather suggests the latter. The central scene on the Stathatos headband poses the question concerning the initial conception of the iconography of the *Plemochoai* rite. The iconography of the Classical period (fifth and early fourth century BC), the period of the main expansion of the Eleusinian cult, never produced—to our knowledge—any depiction of

---

[77] The *Aparchai* Decree *IG* I³ 78 = Clinton 2005, 38, no. 28, l. 40 mentions bovines with gilded horns (βον χρυσόκερον) to be offered to the Eleusinian deities and Athena. Simon (1997, 102 and 107, n. 43) tried to interpret gilded bucrania in Eleusinian iconography as an echo of this fifth-century decree. An example would be the lekane lid from Tübingen (Clinton 1992, 178, fig. 30). The idea is based on Leskien 1994 (*non vidi*), published by Simon 1997, 102, n. 43. Two thousand bulls with gilded horns were mentioned in Kallixeinos of Rhodes' account of Ptolemy II Philadelphos in Alexandria (Ath. 5.202a).
[78] Two are published from Eleusis, Papangeli 2002, 23; many more were actually found, as noted by G. Bakalakis (in his as yet unpublished archive). Only one is known from the Eleusinion: M. Miles (*Agora XXXI*, 100, no. A2410, fig. 13, pl. 40, cat. III, 17) first identified and published the monumental marble *plemochoe*, which is conserved to a height of 0.405 m., but may originally have reached 0.62 m. The cut flat rear part indicates its positioning against a wall. It is not freestanding like the smaller marble votive vessels from Eleusis: Kourouniotes 1898, 25, n. 13; Bakalakis 1991, 109, 112. Recent colour photographs in Papangeli 2002, 23.
[79] Clinton 2005, 113, no. 121 (= *SEG* 41 22), with further bibliography; Krauskopf 2005, 254, nr, 647a; dated to the fourth/third century BC, it appears to be close in date to the headband.

[80] For grades of initiation at the Eleusinian Mysteries and the separation of *mystai* and *epoptai* at the end, see Dowden 1980, 425–427; on Eleusinian initiation, Clinton 2003, 50–60. The fundamental passage for the study of initiation grades and required time span is Plut. *Dem.* 26.1–3.

this rite. Could the late creation of the specific iconography be due to the personal ambition of an individual initiate of the early Hellenistic period? Doubtless this anonymous individual was not a simple initiate, but a person of influence, capable of creating or adapting new iconography on his behalf.[81]

If the vases are correctly observed to have been used during two different moments of ritual (as processional vessels at the arrival of the procession, as on the Ninnion tablet, and as vessels for liquid libations during the final rites of the Mysteries), and if we have enough written sources that can help us understand the meaning, and the name of the final rite of the *Plemochoai*, we unfortunately lack any written source mentioning the use of the vases during the procession and upon arrival at Eleusis. The testimony that Lykourgos renewed *kosmoi* (adornment) for Demeter and Kore,[82] when his provision of gold and silver processional vessels (*pompeia*) for Athena is elsewhere explicitly mentioned,[83] is not sufficient evidence for the use of processional vessels within Eleusinian processions.[84] Our only source of information

remains iconography. The new observation of processional vases on the headband might perfectly contribute towards a more comprehensive reading of the Ninnion tablet: the mortals arriving towards the Eleusinian deities, obviously after having travelled from quite far (as indicated by a stick, a bag etc.) are the initiates, having behind them the procession on the *Hiera Hodos*, on the fifth or sixth day of the Mysteries, the *Iakchos* or *Pompe* on the 19th or 20th of Boedromion.[85] Scholars now tend to agree upon this point. But what did the initiates transport in their vases, if these are to be recognized as the *plemochoe*?

The Boston pyxis lid

The fragments of a red-figured pyxis lid from Athens,[86] kept in the Museum of Fine Arts, Boston (*Figs. 14–15*),[87] were recently re-examined by I. Leventi.[88] The lid had long been attributed to the Marsyas painter,[89] the most

---

[81] See Mitsopoulou forthcoming b, for further discussion. The scene probably reflects lost large-scale votives, as it is rather unlikely that the goldsmith would create new iconographic types.

[82] Lykourgos was known to have invested much in the embellishment of cult paraphernalia, and the revival of cult activities: the *kosmoi* for Demeter and Kore are mentioned in *IG* I² 333, l. 28–29: [τοὺς κό]σ[μους ἱεροὺς τῆι Δήμητρ[ι] καὶ τῆι Κόρηι μείζο[νας καὶ καλλίονας ἢ ἐῶντι ὥσπερ νῦν ἔ]χει. See Mitchel 1973, 197–198, 205; Pollitt 1979, 226, n. 17; Schwenk 1985, 239, 108–126 and no. 21; Hintzen-Bohlen 1997, 119–120, n. 221.

[83] In Plut. *Mor.* 841D he offers Athena gold and silver processional vessels (πομπεῖά τε χρυσᾶ καὶ ἄργυρα τῆ πόλει κατεσκεύασε). *Pompeia* are also mentioned in *IG* II² 333, l. 7, see above.

[84] Some clay vases from Eleusis were originally gilded: Philios 1884, 64–65, n. 2; 1885, 171–172; Skias 1894a, 200–201, n. 1; 1894b, 66; Rubensohn 1898, 283, 297–298; Bakalakis 1991, 111. One is displayed in the Eleusis Museum. A significant number of bronze vessels remain unpublished in Eleusis. Bronze vases may originally have shone like gold, as appropriate for proces-

sional vases. One bronze Eleusinian vase has also been reported from Thorikos: Tsaimou & Oikonomakou 1998, 213. For the excavation, see *Ergon* 1996, 19–23. On the topic of the processional vessels see Mitsopoulou forthcoming a.

[85] See n. 72.

[86] The vase was purchased in Athens by E.P. Warren in March 1903, with the Francis Bartlett fund (information from the museum catalogue card no. AP 532, a, b, c, d, e, f, kindly provided by the BMFA). Metzger 1965, 35, n. 1 underlines that very few vases of Eleusinian iconography were found in Athens.

[87] BMFA acc. no. 03.877.

[88] Leventi 2007, 121–122 and n. 56, fig. 12, discussing the iconography of Demeter seated on the wellhead.

[89] First attribution, by Hodge-Hill 1903, 72, no. 66; First attribution, and depiction with permission of E. Robinson, by *F&R*, 53, fig. 24 (here *Fig. 15*); Schefold 1934, 4, no. 5, 159, but expresses doubts on p. 124. Beazley (*ARV²*, 1474–1476) did not include it in the painter's list; see Valavanis 1991, 269 and n. 594. On the identification of the later phases of the Marsyas Painter with the so-called Eleusinian Painter, see Valavanis 1991, 282–286. Recently, also Kogioumtzi 2006, 103, 182, no. L 127. Contra, with some scepticism, Esch-

prominent Athenian painter of the Kertsch Style of the first half of the fourth century BC. The Eleusinian character of the scene had been previously proposed[90] and then rejected.[91]

The lid belongs to a pyxis (*Fig. 14*);[92] it has a broad flat rim decorated by myrtle leaves, whereas the dome is covered by figured groups, three of which are partly preserved. The preservation is fragmentary. Only two scenes can be securely identified.

First, three figures on the left seem to compose a well-known Eleusinian episode (*Fig. 14, Fig. 17d–f*): the female figure depicted while growing out of the ground, without feet, may be recognized as Kore in ascension, her *Anodos* (f).[93] Hermes is seated to her right (e), identified by his *petasos*.[94] He is reposing, which

means that his positive intervention on behalf of the return of Kore is completed. The fragmentary female figure near Hermes, with the torch(es) is consistent with Hekate (d). In lines 438–440 of the *Homeric Hymn to Demeter* the role of Hekate as the chief attendant during Kore's return is emphasized.[95] This artistic rendering of the episode is not faithful to the exact narration of the *Homeric Hymn*, but is canonized in Eleusinian iconography.[96]

The second scene, following to the right, may also be read without too much controversy (*Figs. 14, 17g–h*): a standing man is turned towards the left and obviously holds a myrtle mystery staff, a so-called *bakchos*, with the characteristic rings (h).[97] The seated goddess

---

bach 1995, 462. Robertson (2000, 244) agrees with the conclusions expressed by Valavanis, concerning the earlier period of production for the Marsyas Painter.

[90] *F&R*, 53 and n. 2, fig. 24; Eleusinian identification on behalf of the seated Demeter on the wellhead (?), by Bielefeld 1951–1952, 8, no. 23. Metzger 1965, 40, no. 34. Brief reference, Bérard 1985, 22 and n. 42–43. He mentions a forthcoming study of the vase (not published, to my knowledge). Beschi 1988, 877, no. 401 and pl. 592; Metzger 1992, 176–177; Leventi 2007, 121.

[91] Clinton 1992, 27, n. 62; see further n. 96.

[92] It may belong to a late specimen of Type C pyxides, a type dated as a shape from *c.* 430 to 350 BC, Roberts 1978, 143–145, pl. 85. However, a profile drawing of the lid should still be established, in order to identify the exact type. I owe this remark to Dr Oliver Pilz.

[93] This figure has been recognized as Kore, see Leventi 2007, 122, n. 56; for Kore in *Anodos*, see the lost lekane lid from Tübingen E 183 (1666); Hayashi 1992, 169, no. 152 with bibliography; the fragment is not discussed in Bérard 1974, 129–139. Bérard 1985, 22 and n. 43 questioned the *Anodos* of Kore on this lid, as he considered some episodes, like the return of Persephone, to be incompatible with the depiction of the "bakchos" scenes.

[94] Hermes is the best-preserved figure of the scene, and a beautiful specimen of Attic fourth-century vase painting. The obvious quality in the positioning and rendering of the figure has led to the identification of the hand with the so-called Marsyas Painter. See Hodge-Hill 1903, 72, no. 66, who described Hermes as "a seated man, who wears a *petasos* like that of Hermes in the pelike from Kertsch with scenes from the Eleu-

sinian Cycle". Then *F&R* (p. 53 and n. 2) draw a direct comparison between the Hermes on the second side of the Eleusinian Pelike Leningrad (former St. 1792, now Pelike inv. no. Pav. 8, see Simon 1966, pl. 18, 19:2) and the Hermes on the Boston pyxis lid, suggesting the same painter.

[95] On Hekate in the Eleusinian narration, see *Hymn. Hom. Cer.* 438–440; Simon 1985, 278, n. 43, 279; Clinton 1992, 117–120.

[96] On artistic representation as a complementary source of knowledge for the Eleusinian cultic events, see Clinton 2007, 344, 353. Hermes in the *Hymn. Hom. Cer.* 334–385, brings Kore up on his chariot; there is no description of an *Anodos*. For a fifth-century representation of Hermes and Hekate assisting the *Anodos* of Kore, see the red-figured crater MMNY, inv. no. 28.57.23; Bérard 1985, pl. 15, fig. 50. A once again non-canonical representation of Hermes, assisting the abduction of Kore, is preserved on the fresco from the "Tomb of Persephone" in Vergina; Andronikos 1994, 74, 105, fig. 28. The abduction is not part of the Eleusinian drama, it was presupposed, Clinton 2007, 353. On the abduction and return of Kore/Persephone, see Bérard 1987, 132–133.

[97] Hodge-Hill 1903, 72 already saw a mystic staff or wand ("bakchos") in the object held by the standing man ("a man with a bakchos stands before a seated woman"), and as a consequence the drawing accompanying the publication by *F&R* (fig. 24) clearly shows the characteristic rings. The rings are rendered in the common convention, with parallel lines, and pointed spiky myrtle leaves projecting at intervals. Also in favour of the identification of the mystic staff is Metzger 1992, 31, n. 78. However, the existence of these rings

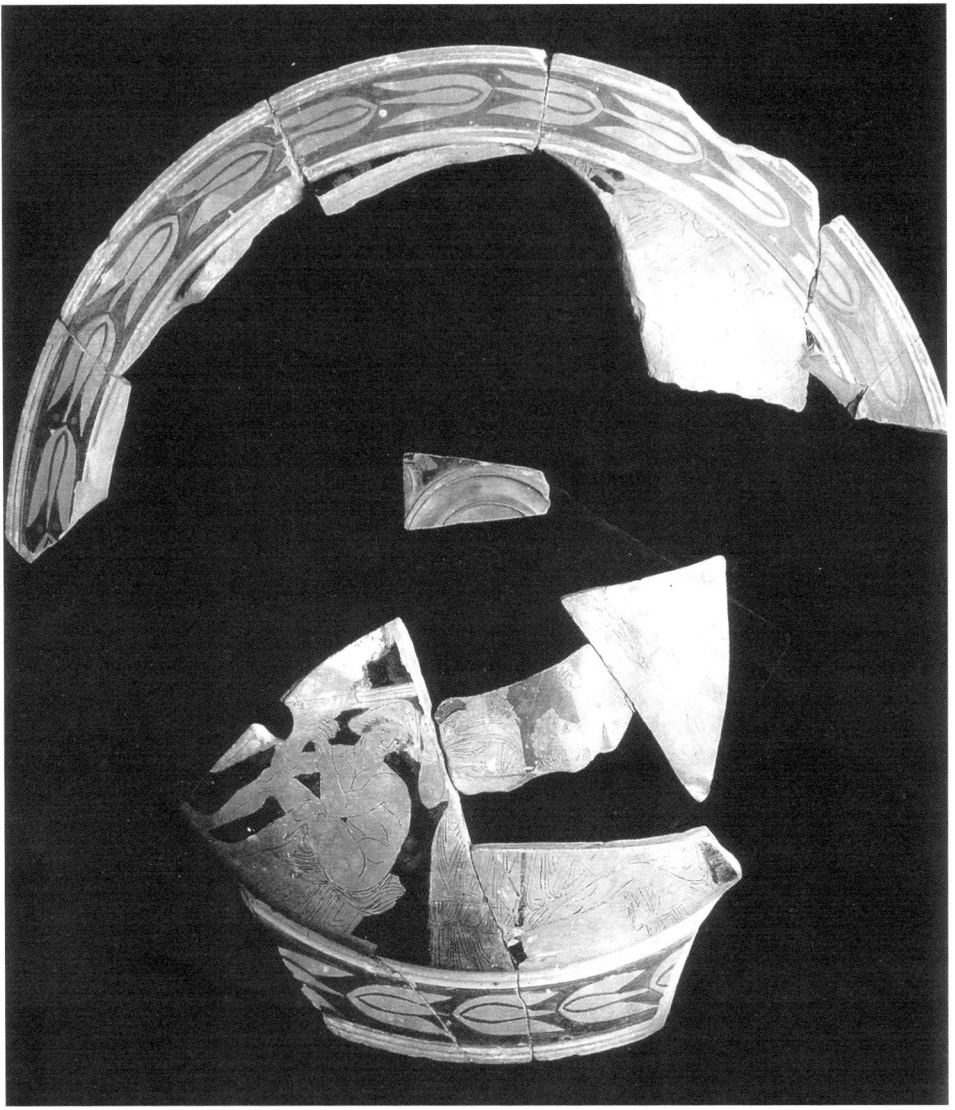

Fig. 14. BMFA, Francis Bartlett Donation of 1900, no. 03.877a–c, pyxis lid. Neg. BC9640, Photograph © (2009) Museum of Fine Arts, Boston.

Fig. 15. BMFA no. 03.877a, pyxis lid: Hekate, Hermes, Kore, Demeter and initiate (Herakles?) with myrtle staff. Reproduced from Furtwängler & Reichold 1905, fig. 24.

was rejected by Clinton (1992, 27 and n. 62), as the then available photograph (published in *LIMC* IV.1, 877, no. 401, s.v. Demeter, pl. 592, detail with initiate) does not allow clear observation of the area. He was aware of the earlier drawing, but questioned the interpretation by Furtwängler. As a consequence he rejected the Eleusinian character of the whole fragmentary scene. Our new observations oblige us to re-discuss this point, and to accept the older reading proposed by Furtwängler, see n. 89. On myrtle in Eleusinian cult, see Kunze-Götte 2006, 90–91. The name "bakchos rings" was proposed by Beazley 1941, 1–7; the more appropriate name "Eleusinian rings" was recently proposed by Kroll (*Agora* XXVI, 28, n. 23–24), following Clinton 1992, 27, n. 62 and Bérard 1985; Bérard 1987, 131.

he faces is consistent with the iconography of Demeter on the wellhead (g).[98] We propose to recognize here the arrival of a first-initiate, *(proto)mystes*, before Demeter at Eleusis. The male initiate may be identified with Herakles, or one of the Dioskouroi.[99] The second scene has to be positioned later in the narration of

[98]   Probably the Kallichoron/Parthenion well of Eleusis? For the long discussion concerning Demeter seated on the wellhead, see Clinton 1986, 44 and recently Leventi 2007, 118–124, with further bibliography.
[99]   The choice depends on the missing scenes. As we have only the single figure, Herakles might be the most appropriate identification.

Fig. 16. BMFA, Francis Bartlett Donation of 1900, no. 03.877a–c (detail), pyxis lid. Neg. C10451, Photograph © (2009) Museum of Fine Arts, Boston.

the mythological episodes, as the arrival of an initiate presupposes the successful return of Kore, and the former instauration of the Mysteries, with the instruction and mission of Triptolemos. It should be the final scene of the depicted narration, providing us with one useful fixed point. The scenes may therefore have been developed anticlockwise, from right to left.

The new photograph of the entire fragmentary lid reveals, however, that two further parts

of the lid are preserved in addition to the main part (*Figs. 14, 17*).[100] One group of fragments partly preserves a third figured scene, to be placed somewhere to the right of the initiate. If the narration is anticlockwise, the new third

---

[100] Sent by the BMFA in 2005: no. 03.877a–c, neg. BC9640; Leventi 2007, fig. 12; Mitsopoulou 2010b, 167 and n. 117, fig. 7.

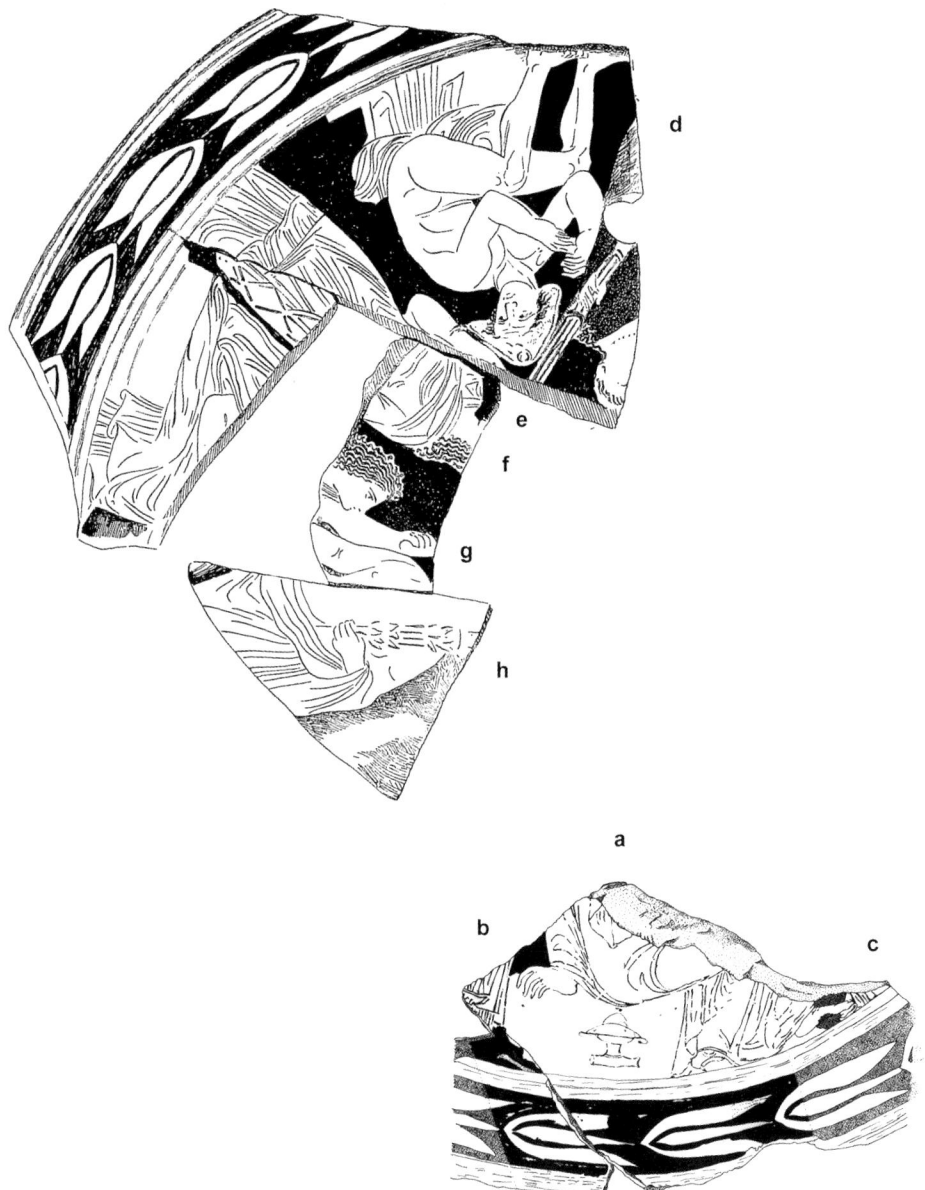

Fig. 17. BMFA, Francis Bartlett Donation of 1900, no. 03.877a–c, pyxis lid. Combination of drawings. Drawing of new scene from neg. C10451. By N. Zachou.

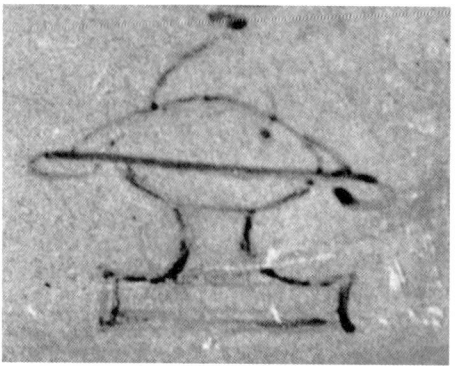

Fig. 18. BMFA, Francis Bartlett Donation of 1900, no. 03.877a–c (detail), pyxis lid. Neg. C10451, crop, Photograph © (2009) Museum of Fine Arts, Boston.

Fig. 19. Eleusinian plemochoe *from Alexandria, Sciatbi. Reproduced from Breccia 1912, pl. 58:131.*

scene has to be sought in narration well before the ascension of Kore and the final instauration of the Eleusinian Mysteries. The number of missing scenes is however too significant to allow a more precise location of the scene within the sequence of narration of the Eleusinian drama.

The lower part of a female figure (*Fig. 17a*) is preserved: she is turned towards the right, seated upon an irregular projection, probably a rock; her right hand rests on the rock, behind her back, the body is covered by a long draped *chiton* and *peplos*, underneath which project her feet. Two more standing figures were framing her, one at either side, identified by minimal parts of their drapery (*Fig. 17b–c*).

I. Leventi succeeded in remarking a further and hitherto unnoticed detail on the overexposed part of the photograph (*Fig. 14*): was there a vessel underneath the seated figure, and more specifically an Eleusinian one?[101] What first appeared an attractive probability, proved to be the reality. The new detailed im-

age depicts the fragments in utmost clarity.[102] It allows the safe recognition of the characteristic Attic Eleusinian vessel (*Fig. 16, Fig. 18*). The painter has added the lidded vessel in clear lines, deposited on the floor underneath the rocky seat of the female figure. It has a steady base, a stem, the characteristic carinated body

---

[101] Together we tried to further evaluate and decide whether near the seated female figure was depicted a vessel resembling the Eleusinian type we here examine.

[102] BMFA acc. no. 03.877, neg. C10451. This unpublished fragment must however have been available to Clinton 1992, 27, n. 62, as he comments: "In fact, if the scene is Eleusinian, it is unlike any other; and the photograph of another fragment (apparently not available to Furtwängler or Schefold; not shown or mentioned in *LIMC*, Demeter, 401), which shows the lower half of a seated figure, adds to the difficulty of taking it as Eleusinian". The fragment described is obviously the fragment here depicted in our *Figs. 14, 16–18*. Clinton did not comment on the Eleusinian vase beneath the seated woman, which would have duplicated the arguments in favour of the scene's Eleusinian character. See previously Leventi 2007, 122. The *bakchos* is however affirmed in Schwarz 1988b, 45, no. 15, and by Bérard 1985, 22.

Fig. 20a–b (above and right). Plemochoe *on a "West Slope" Pyxis lid (detail), Agora inv. no. P 22962. Photograph © American School of Classical Studies at Athens: Agora Excavations.*

shape with the perimetric horizontal *antyx* and handles, and it is covered by a high domed lid ending in a knob at the top. The comparison with clay examples allows hardly any doubt concerning the similarity of the shapes and the accuracy of the rendering (*Figs. 2a, 19*).

We hence have at our disposal *five* representations of the Eleusinian vessel in Athenian vase painting: only three are found in figured (red-figured) vases,[103] whereas two more can be added from the non-iconographic, purely decorative category of the slightly later West Slope Ware (*Fig. 20a–c*).[104] The red-figured scenes are earlier, dated to the second quarter of the fourth century BC, a period well known for the

Fig. 20c. Plemochoe *on a "West Slope" Pyxis lid, inverted drawing. By N. Zachou.*

renewed interest in the Eleusinian Mysteries it displayed.[105]

Despite the clarity of the depicted vessel, the Boston lid is so fragmentary that it cannot easily lead towards a persuasive interpretation. In opposition to the Ninnion tablet, which remains unparalleled in its private conception and human-based iconographic narration, the new scene in question seems to belong to the

---

[103] In addition to the two discussed here, a red-figured sherd depicting the Eleusinian vase has been identified by J. Stroszeck in the Kerameikos. It will appear in the final publication of the Tritopatreion, in preparation; on this sanctuary, see Stroszeck 2010.

[104] One unpublished, from the Kerameikos, and one on a pyxis lid, published by S. Rotroff: *Agora* XXIX, 188–189, 360, no. 1215 (P 22962), pl. 90: it is represented with latticed lid, myrtle sprouts projecting from the handle holes and again positioned on the ground, upon a slight projection. It is slightly later than the two previous scenes, dated towards the end of the fourth century BC.

---

[105] Clinton 1994a, 169–170; Tiverios 1997, 170–172.

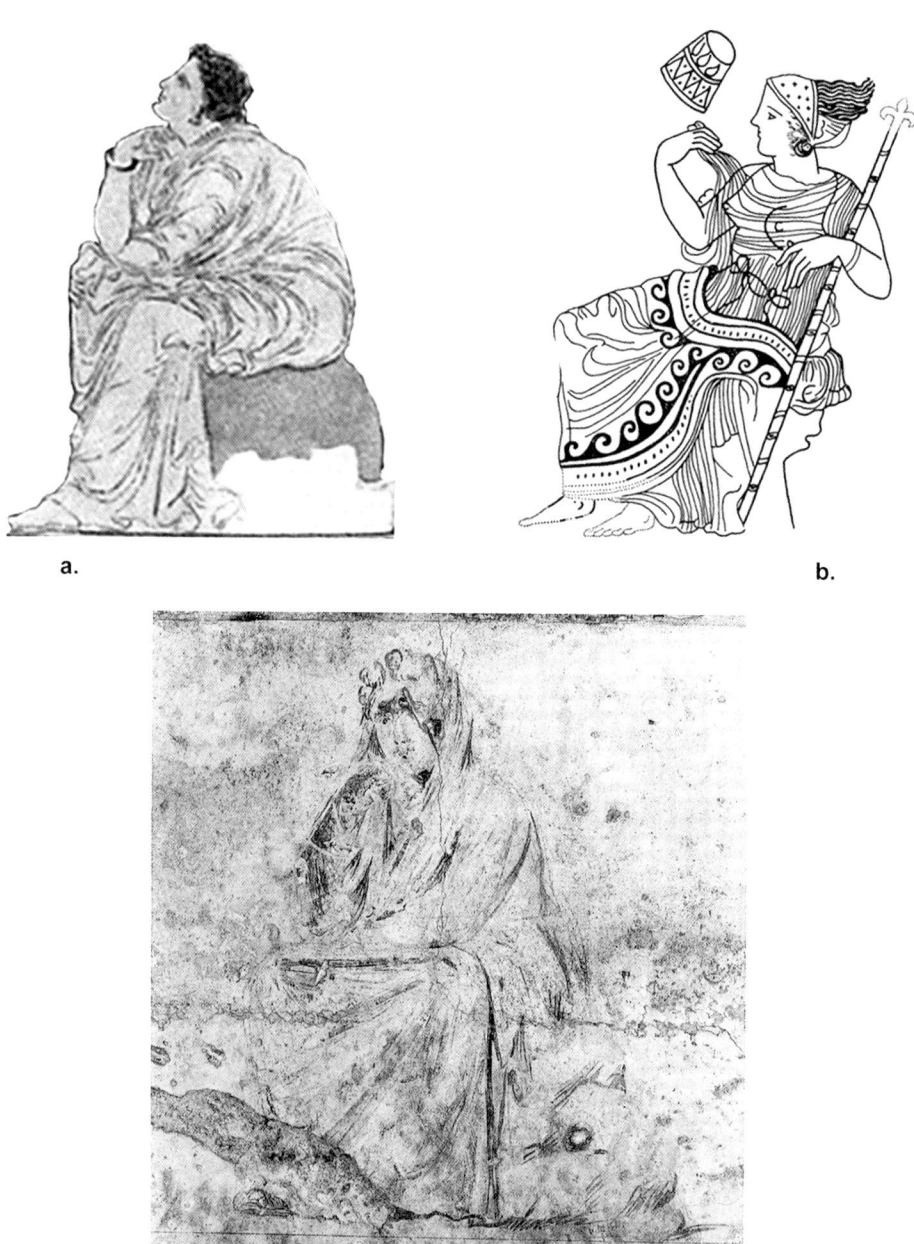

a.

b.

c.

Fig. 21a–c. Representations of Demeter on the mirthless rock, Agelastos Petra: *a. "Eleusinian" Pelike, St Petersburg, Hermitage, St. 1972 (detail from Simon 1997, fig. 14); b. Skyphos from Olynthos, no. 34.161 (detail from Yiouri 1972, 8, fig. b); c. Vergina, "Tomb of Persephone": fresco of the rape of Kore, from east wall (detail from Andronikos 1994, 74, fig. 28).*

original and official Athenian iconographic Eleusinian circle. Scenes may be influenced by the episodes of the *Homeric Hymn*, without accurate rendering, however, or they may depict otherwise canonized episodes of the Eleusinian drama.

The questions which now appear concern the identity of the fragmentary female figure, and whether the fragmentary scene with the seated woman may be related to a known episode from the *Homeric Hymn*. As Demeter is already depicted once on the lid (*Fig. 17a*), she is not an obvious point of departure for this hypothesis. However, and in spite of the missing upper part of the woman, we have observed that this figure is seated upon a rocky projection (*Fig. 16*). In Eleusinian iconography, female figures—often in a mourning position—tend to be identified with Demeter. The rocky formation may be identified with the *Agelastos Petra* ("Mirthless Rock"), one of the common seats of the goddess in iconography.[106] A glimpse at available parallels reveals four examples, three of which are securely identified with Demeter (*Fig. 21a–c*).[107] The figure on the Eleusinian Pelike Leningrad 1792 (*Fig. 21a*) has received controversial interpretations, varying from Demeter again, to other female goddesses or personifications.[108]

Here we touch a very delicate point in the discussion, since the possible double representation of the goddess in iconography, which would imply a narrative depiction of successive and independent episodes and scenes, is not fully accepted. Some scholars prefer to interpret these doublet cases as complementary figures of large arrays in a closed composition.[109] Others, however, defend the idea of the repeated representation in (Eleusinian) iconography,[110] within a narrative cycle of deeds. At this point, we choose to follow the possibility of recognizing Demeter on the fragment for a second time (*Figs. 16, 17a*).[111] If we recognize Demeter here in a new episode of the narration, we might get a little closer to the decipherment of the allusion intended by the rare depiction of the cult vessel near the goddess.

The painter who added the cult vase to the scene obviously did this on his own initiative, as this case remains an absolute exception within the known range of Eleusinian iconography and Attic vase painting of the fourth century BC. It is evident that only an important painter, a master, might be in a position to add personal details to an already canonized official iconographic narration. The figured lid has since early times been attributed to the

---

[106] However the *agelastos petra* is not mentioned in the *Homeric Hymn*, see Clinton 1992, 80; Clinton 2007, 346–347 for literary sources.

[107] 1: The seated woman on the east wall of the "Tomb of Persephone", mural painting, Vergina: Andronikos 1994, 73–79, fig. 27–29 (here *Fig. 21c*). 2: Red-figured skyphos from Olynthos, no. 34.161 (ArchCollThess): Yiouri 1972, 6–8, no. 1, fig. A–B (here *Fig. 21b*); extensively Mitsopoulou 2007, 965–992. 3: Stanford volute crater by the Kleophon painter, CCVASU: no. 1970.12; Raubitschek & Raubitschek 1982, 115 and n. 40, pl. 15b (securely identified by an inscription, according to the authors).

[108] Eleusinian Pelike, Hermitage, St Petersburg, St. 1792: Metzger 1965; Simon 1966; Clinton 1992; Tiverios 1997; Simon 1997.

[109] Simon 1966, 72–73 and n. 6–8 on the Eleusinian Pelike with former references; Simon 1997, 106; Tiverios 1997, 169, n. 32 on the Regina Vasorum and 170, n. 60 on the Eleusinian Pelike, interpreting both figures as personifications of Eleusis.

[110] Nilsson 1935, 93, on double depiction of Demeter on the Ninnion tablet; Clinton 1992, 78–82 on the Regina Vasorum and the Eleusinian Pelike, especially 82 and n. 106–107 on behalf of narrative style of repetition of the same figure on vases; Bérard 1985, 22; Bérard 1987; Clinton 1992, 82; *idem* 2007, 352; Valavanis 1990, 345–348 (passage entitled "L'expression de la continuité temporelle dans les représentations des amphores panathénaïques"); Leventi 2007, 127–129, and nn. 71–73 for opposing opinions.

[111] Even though the alternative of a relevant female personification would not be incompatible with the arrangement with the "talking/speak symbol" of the Eleusinian Mysteries.

Marsyas Painter.[112] Now that the scene is more complete, it may re-attract scholarly attention. The Marsyas Painter, probably to be identified also with the Eleusinian Painter at an advanced stage of his life, has created a series of prime examples of Eleusinian iconography.[113] He is the leading hand of an important ceramic workshop, having functioned under strong state influence, as it also produced several successive series of Panathenaic amphorae in the black-figure technique.[114] It is highly probable that he had personal knowledge and experience of the Eleusinian Mysteries. At least, he is the major representative of this iconography in a period when the official Athenian state seems strongly preoccupied by Eleusinian subjects.[115] It seems that the painter added the vase as a "speak symbol" near the seated figure, inspired by a common use of the vessel in his day. Contemporary archaeological finds support this idea, as the shape strongly resembles original clay specimens found in Eleusis or elsewhere (*Figs. 2a, 19*).[116]

We may further examine the painter's choice: Kerényi had tentatively proposed in 1967 a relation between the peculiar Eleusinian vessels and the cult beverage of the Eleusinian Mysteries, the *kykeon*.[117] The episode where Demeter demands and consumes the ritual beverage is described in lines 198–211 of the *Homeric Hymn to Demeter*:[118]

δηρὸν δ᾽ ἄφθογγος τετιημένη ἧστ᾽ ἐπὶ δίφρου,
οὐδέ τιν᾽ οὔτ᾽ ἔπεϊ προσπτύσσετο οὔτε τι ἔργῳ,
ἀλλ᾽ ἀγέλαστος ἄπαστος ἐδητύος ἠδὲ ποτῆτος   200
ἧστο πόθῳ μινύθουσα βαθυζώνοιο θυγατρός,
πρίν γ᾽ ὅτε δὴ χλεύῃς μιν Ἰάμβη κέδν᾽ εἰδυῖα
πολλὰ παρὰ σκώπτουσ᾽ ἐτρέψατο πότνιαν ἁγνὴν
μειδῆσαι γελάσαι τε καὶ ἵλαον σχεῖν θυμόν·
ἣ δή οἱ καὶ ἔπειτα μεθύστερον εὔαδεν ὀργαῖς.   205
τῇ δὲ δέπας Μετάνειρα δίδου μελιηδέος οἴνου
πλήσασ᾽, ἣ δ᾽ ἀνένευσ᾽· οὐ γὰρ θεμιτόν οἱ ἔφασκε
πίνειν οἶνον ἐρυθρόν, ἄνωγε δ᾽ ἄρ᾽ ἄλφι καὶ ὕδωρ
δοῦναι μίξασαν πιέμεν γλήχωνι τερείνῃ.
ἣ δὲ κυκεῶ τεύξασα θεᾷ πόρεν ὡς ἐκέλευε·   210
δεξαμένη δ᾽ ὁσίης ἕνεκεν πολυπότνια Δηὼ

R. Parker has previously underlined the extent to which this specific "section can be held for the aetiological core of the poem, rich in allusion to the preliminary ritual of the Mysteries …".[119] In the hymn, mourning Demeter seeks shelter at Eleusis and is received by Metaneira in the Palace. Upon the offering of wine, which she rejects for the sake of the rite, she asks for a drink prepared of barley, water and soft mint:

---

[112] See n. 89 and Mitsopoulou 2010b, 166.

[113] Schefold 1934, 127–131; Valavanis 1991, 268–286; Robertson 1992, 280–289; Robertson 2000, 244. Scepticism is expressed by Eschbach 1995, 462.

[114] According to Valavanis, he might even be identified with one of the two owners of the workshop, Bakchios or Kittos. Their work ceases around 330 BC, when the funerary epigram testifies the death of Bakchios, see Valavanis 1997, 90 and n. 54.

[115] The introduction of Triptolemos on the columns of the Panathenaic amphorae in the year of the archon Polyzelos 367/6 BC, by the hand of the Marsyas Painter, is only one example of the case: the earliest vase attributed to the Marsyas Painter is the Panathenaic amphora Brussels A 1703 from 367/6 BC, see Eschbach 1986, 30–31, no. 17; Valavanis 1991, 279, 250, n. 549; Valavanis 2011.

[116] Kerényi 1967, 183, fig. 61; Rubensohn 1898, pl. 13:4. However, the closest parallel for the shape, combined with a high lid with knob, is an Eleusinian vase found in the necropolis of Sciatbi, Alexandria: Breccia 1912, no. 248, pl. 58:131. It was first correctly identified as Eleusinian by Pagenstecher 1913, 11–12, fig. 17; introduced into Athenian bibliography by Thompson 1934 (1987), 150, n. 2. The identification was rejected

by Rotroff (*Agora* XXIX, 211 and n. 41), who interpreted the vase from Sciatbi as a *thymiaterion* (thurible).

[117] Kerényi 1967, 177–186. See also Dugas 1960, 126–128. However, we point out that K. Clinton has argued that the specific hymn was unlikely to reflect the official cult-legend of Eleusis, and neither are the rites mentioned within. See Clinton 1986, 44, on the assumption that initiates drank the *kykeon*, like Demeter. The use of the *kykeon* might be questioned for the Eleusinian Mysteries.

[118] The text reproduced here is from Foley 1994, 13.

[119] Parker 1991, 8.

the *kykeon*. Kerényi had pointed out[120] that lines 208–209 of the hymn are followed by a lacuna, for which he proposed a relevant completion borrowed from the *Orphic Hymn to Demeter* (Clem. Al. Protr. 2.18, here after Kerényi): δέξατο δ᾽ αἰόλον ἄγγος, ἐν ὧι κυκεὼν ἐνέκειτο (she received the glittering vessel which contained the *kykeon*).

He therefore proposed the insertion of line 211a, as following:

δεξαμένη δ᾽ ὁσίης εἵνεκεν πολυπότνια Δηὼ   211
ἔκπιεν αἰόλον ἄγγος ἐν ὧι κυκεὼ ἐνέκειτο   211a

Had the proposal by Kerényi appeared somewhat daring and difficult to prove, and had it been mostly ignored by later scholarship on Eleusinian vases due to the growing acceptance of Brommer's thesis in favour of the *plemochoe*, this newly identified vase fragment might now invite us to reconsider it. The lid is dated to the second quarter of the fourth century BC; it is an original artefact testimony from the Classical Athenian world. The image might well represent mourning Demeter at Eleusis, having just received the ritual drink in the lidded cult vessel.[121] The rocky seat alludes to Eleusinian topography, as to the unsmiling—ἀγέλαστος—mood of Demeter (*Homeric Hymn to Demeter*, l. 200). This scene might for the first time provide an original material argument and allusion towards the correlation of the Eleusinian vessels with the Eleusinian beverage *kykeon*, known so far only from texts. When R. Parker underlined that "Demeter's consumption of the *kykeon* for the sake of the rite can be interpreted as a link for the reliving of the exact experience of grieving Demeter by the initiates", he was most probably right.[122] The numerous clay vessels found in Eleusinian contexts of Attica would therefore be the material link and testimony to the ritual re-enactment of *kykeon* consumption by the initiates, in reminiscence of Demeter's fasting. Even more, the famous *synthema* reported by Clement of Alexandria, "ἐνήστευσα, ἔπιον τὸν κυκεῶνα", "I fasted; I drank the draught (*kykeon*)" (Clem. Al. *Protr.* 2.18), would now acquire a valuable original Attic-Eleusinian archaeological-iconographic parallel, from the mid-fourth century BC.[123]

This interpretation would also apply well towards the understanding of the iconography of the Ninnion tablet. We propose to read the lower section of the scene as the arrival scene of initiates at the sanctuary, while transferring the *kykeon* on their heads for immediate consumption during the rites to follow.[124] The *kykeon* is known to have been prepared in Athens, during the day of the Epidauria festival, before the

---

[120] Kerényi 1967, 181 and n. 1.

[121] On the Stanford crater, Demeter is receiving a libation from the trefoil oinochoe held by a maiden standing in front of her, labelled "Parthenos": Raubitschek & Raubitschek 1982, 116, pl. 15a. The authors supposed that she was holding a phiale. On the Ninnion tablet, the male initiate behind the woman with the *plemochoe* on the upper register is also holding an oinochoe. Tiverios (2008, 130–131) proposed that this vase, identified with the *kothon*, would be more appropriate for use as a drinking cup, instead of the *plemochoe* itself. On the earlier Stanford crater it is however of intermediate function, used only for pouring. We therefore need an initial container for the liquid, before served, the pouring vessel (*kothon* or *oinochoe*) and a final recipient for drinking (a phiale?).

[122] Parker 1991, 8; Rosen 1987, 419, n. 15; Richardson 1974, 211–217.

[123] For a sixth-century relation of the *kykeon* with the Eleusinian Mysteries, as given by Hipponax, fr. 48 DG, see Rosen 1987, 418–426. In general regarding the *kykeon*, see Delatte 1955. Also, for cult vessels and special beverages within cults, see Bookidis 2003, 255, n. 75; relevant is Rosen 1987, 422, n. 27.

[124] After the *nesteia*. Against the suitability of the vases as drinking cups for the *kykeon* is Tiverios 2008, 130–131. M. Miles informs me that she tested drinking from original vessels, with negative results (personal communication). However, the need for safe transportation of the ingredients might have prevailed onto the act of consumption, which may in turn have been achieved by the use of other auxiliary vessels.

Bookidis 2003   N. Bookidis, 'The sanctuaries at Corinth', in *Corinth XX*, 247–259.

Breccia 1912   E. Breccia, *La Necropoli di Sciatbi*, Cairo 1912.

Brommer 1977   F. Brommer, *Der Parthenonfries: Katalog und Untersuchung*, Mainz am Rhein 1977.

Brommer 1979   F. Brommer, *Konkordanzlisten zu alter Vasenliteratur*, Marburg 1979.

Brommer 1980   F. Brommer, 'Plemochoe', *AA* 1980, 544–549.

Bunjatjan 1995   E.P. Bunjatjan, 'Gli Sciti', in *Dal Mille al Mille. Tesori e popoli del Mar Nero*, Milano 1995, 39–95.

Burkert 2004   W. Burkert, 'Initiation', *ThesCRA* II, 3.c. (2004), 91–124.

Clinton 1986   K. Clinton, 'The author of the Homeric hymn to Demeter', *OpAth* 16, 1986, 43–50.

Clinton 1988   K. Clinton, 'Sacrifice at the Eleusinian Mysteries', in *Early Greek cult practice. Proceedings of the fifth international symposium at the Swedish Institute at Athens, 26–29 June 1986* (ActaAth-4°, 38), eds. R. Hägg, N. Marinatos & G. Nordquist, Stockholm 1988, 69–79.

Clinton 1992   K. Clinton, *Myth and cult. The iconography of the Eleusinian Mysteries. The Martin P. Nilsson lectures on Greek religion delivered 19–21 November 1990 at the Swedish Institute at Athens* (ActaAth-8°, 11), Stockholm 1992.

Clinton 1994a   K. Clinton, 'The Eleusinian Mysteries and Panhellenism in democratic Athens', in *The archaeology of Athens and Attica under the democracy* (Oxbow Monograph, 37), eds. W.D.E. Coulson, O. Palagia, T.L. Shear Jr., H.A. Shapiro & F.J. Frost, Oxford 1994, 161–172.

Clinton 1994b   K. Clinton, 'The Epidauria and the arrival of Asclepius in Athens', in *Ancient Greek cult practice from the epigraphical evidence. Proceedings of the second international seminar on ancient Greek cult organized by the Swedish Institute at Athens, 22–24 November 1991*, ed. R. Hägg (ActaAth-8°, 15) Stockholm 1994, 17–34.

Clinton 1996   K. Clinton, 'The Thesmophorion in central Athens and the celebration of the Thesmophoria in Attica', in Hägg 1996, 111–125.

Clinton 2003   K. Clinton, 'Stages of initiation in the Eleusinian and Samothracian Mysteries', in *Greek Mysteries: The archaeology and ritual of ancient Greek secret cults*, ed. M.B. Cosmopoulos, London & New York 2003, 50–78.

Clinton 2005   K. Clinton, *Eleusis. The inscriptions on stone. Documents of the sanctuary of the two goddesses and public documents of the deme* vol.1, Athens 2005.

Clinton 2007   K. Clinton, 'The Mysteries of Demeter and Kore', in *A companion to Greek Religion*, ed. D. Ogden, Malden, Mass. 2007, 342–356.

Clinton 2009   K. Clinton, 'Donors of Kernoi at the Eleusinian Sanctuary of the Two Goddesses', in *Le donateur, l'offrande et la déesse. Système(s) votif(s) dans les sanctuaires de divinités féminines en Grèce et en Asie Mineure, HALMA-IPEL, XXXIe Symposium International, Lille 13–14–15 décembre 2007*, (Kernos, Suppl. 23), ed. C. Prêtre, Lille & Liège 2009, 239–246.

Clinton 2010   K. Clinton, 'The Eleusinian *aparche* in practice: 329/8 B.C.', in *Ιερά και λατρείες της Δήμητρας στον αρχαίο ελληνικό κόσμο, Πρακτικά Επιστημονικού Συμποσίου, Πανεπιστήμιο Θεσσαλίας, Βόλος 4–5 Ιουνίου 2005*, eds. I. Λεβέντη & Χ. Μητσοπούλου, Volos 2010, 1–15.

Corinth XX   *Corinth, The centenary 1896–1996* (Corinth, 20), eds. C.K. Williams II & N. Bookidis, Princeton 2003.

Delatte 1955   A. Delatte, *Le Cycéon. Breuvage rituel des mystères d'Éleusis*, Paris 1955.

Dugas 1960   C. Dugas, 'La mission du Triptolème d'après l'imagerie Athénienne', in *Recueil Charles Dugas* (Publications de la Bibliothèque Salomon Reinach, 1) Paris 1960, 125–139.

Dowden 1980   K. Dowden, 'Grades in the Eleusinian Mysteries', *RHR* 197, 1980, 409–427.

Ellis Jones 1982   J. Ellis Jones, 'Another Eleusinian kernos from Laureion', *BSA* 77, 1982, 191–199.

Engel 1884   A. Engel, 'Choix de tessères grecques en plomb. Tirées des collections athéniennes', *BCH* 8, 1884, 1–21.

Eschbach 1986   N. Eschbach, *Statuen auf Panathenäischen Preisamphoren des 4. Jhs. v. Chr.*, Mainz am Rhein 1986.

Eschbach 1995   N. Eschbach, 'Πάνος Δ. Βαλαβάνης: Παναθηναϊκοί Αμφορείς από την Ερέτρια. Συμβολή στην Αττική Αγγειογραφία του 4ου αι. π.Χ. αι. στην Αθήνα: Αρχαιολογική Εταιρεία 1991', *Gnomon* 67, 1995, 455–463.

von Fritze 1897   H. von Fritze, 'Συμβολή εις το τυπικόν της εν Ελευσίνι λατρείας', *ArchEph* 1897, 163–174.

Foley 1994   *The Homeric Hymn to Demeter. Translation, commentary and interpretive essays*, ed. H. Foley, Princeton, N.J. 1994.

Frel 1994   J. Frel, 'The portraits of Demetrios Poliorketes by Lysippos and Teisikrates', in *J. Frel, Studia Varia*, Roma 1994, 70–91.

Furtwängler & Reichhold 1905   A. Furtwängler & K. Reichhold, *Griechische Vasenmalerei* II, München 1905.

Graf 1996   F. Graf, 'Pompai in Greece. Some considerations about space and ritual in the Greek *polis*', in Hägg 1996, 55–65.

Hägg 1996   *The role of religion in the early Greek polis. Proceedings of the third international seminar on ancient Greek cult, Athens, 16–18 October 1992*, (ActaAth-8°, 14), ed. R. Hägg, Stockholm 1996.

Hayashi 1992   T. Hayashi, *Bedeutung und Wandel des Triptolemosbildes vom 6.–4. Jh. V. Chr.* (Beiträge zur Archäologie, 20), Würzburg 1992.

Head 1959 Barclay V. Head, *A guide to the principal coins of the Greeks from circ. 700 B.C. to A.D. 270 based on the work of Barclay V. Head, British Museum, Dept. of Coins & Medals*, London 1959.

Hintzen-Bohlen 1997 H.B. Hintzen-Bohlen, *Die Kulturpolitik des Eubulos und des Lykurg. Denkmäler- und Bauprojekte in Athen zwischen 355 und 322 v. Chr.*, Berlin 1997.

Hodge-Hill 1903 B. Hodge Hill, 'Report of the curator of Classical antiquities', BMFA, *Twenty-Eighth Annual Report for the Year* 1903.

Jackson 2006 M.M. Jackson, *Hellenistic gold Eros jewellery: Technique, style and chronology* (BAR, 1510), Oxford 2006.

Kambanis 1934 M.L. Kambanis, 'Notes sur le classement chronologique des monnaies d'Athènes', *BCH* 58, 1934, 101–102.

Karoglou 2010 K. Karoglou, *Attic pinakes. Votive images in clay*, Oxford 2010.

Kerameikos XVII U. Knigge, *Kerameikos* XVII. *Der Bau Z*, München 2005.

Kerényi 1967 C. Kerényi, *Eleusis. Archetypal image of mother and daughter*, Princeton 1967.

Kogioumtzi 2006 D. Kogioumtzi, *Untersuchungen zur attisch-rotfigurigen Keramikproduktion des 4. Jhs. v. Chr.: die sog. Kertscher Vasen*, Berlin 2006.

Kostoglou-Despoini 1996 Α. Κώστογλου-Δεσποίνη, *Ελληνική τέχνη: αρχαία χρυσά κοσμήματα*, Athens 1996.

Kourouniotes 1898 Κ. Κουρουνιώτης, 'ΚΕΡΝΟΙ', *ArchEph* 1898, 21–28.

Krauskopf 2005 I. Krauskopf, 'Plemochoe', *ThesCRA* V, 2b (2005), 252–255.

Kroll 1992 J.H. Kroll, 'Athenian bronze coinage and the propagation of the Eleusinian Mysteries', *AJA* 95, 1992, 355–356.

Kunze-Götte 2006 E. Kunze-Götte, *Myrte als Attribut und Ornament auf attischen Vasen*, Kilchberg 2006.

Kuruniotis 1913 K. Kuruniotis, 'Goldschmuck aus Eretria', *AM* 38, 1913, 289–328.

Lambrinoudakis 2001 Β.Κ. Λαμπρινουδάκης, 'Το αρχαίο ιερό του Γύρουλα στο Σαγκρί της Νάξου', in *Το αρχαίο ιερό του Γύρουλα στο Σαγκρί*, ed. Ε. Σημαντώνη Μπουρνιά, Athens 2001, 7–13.

Lambrinoudakis 2008 V. Lambrinoudakis, 'Apollon and Demeter: Could they have a common cult?', in *Demetra: la divinità, i santuari, il culto, la leggenda. Atti del I Congresso internazionale, Enna, 1–4 luglio 2004* (Biblioteca di Sicilia antiqua, 2), ed. C.A. Di Stefano, Pisa & Roma 2008.

Lawton 1995 C.L. Lawton, *Attic document reliefs. Art and politics in ancient Athens*, Oxford 1995.

Lange 1879 K. Lange, *Das Motif des aufgestützten Fusses in der antiken Kunst und dessen statuarische Verwendung durch Lysippos*, diss., Leipzig 1879.

Leskien 1994 H. Leskien, *Tierschädel und Gehörne auf attisch rotfigurigen Vasen*, M.A. thesis, Würzburg 1994.

Leventi 2007 I.K. Leventi, 'The Mondragone relief revisited. Eleusinian cult iconography in Campania', *Hesperia* 76, 2007, 107–141.

Leventi & Mitsopoulou 2010 — *Ιερά και λατρείες της Δήμητρας στον αρχαίο ελληνικό κόσμο, Πρακτικά Επιστημονικού Συμποσίου, Πανεπιστήμιο Θεσσαλίας, Βόλος 4–5 Ιουνίου 2005*, eds. Ι. Λεβέντη & Χ. Μητσοπούλου, Volos 2010.

Linders 1988 — T. Linders, 'Kerchnos and kerchnion, not kernos but granulation', *OpAth* 17, 1988, 229–230.

Lindner 1984 — R. Lindner, *Der Raub der Persephone in der antiken Kunst*, Würzburg 1984.

Matheson 1994 — S.B. Matheson, 'The mission of Triptolemos and the politics of Athens', *GRBS* 35, 1994, 345–75.

Metzger 1965 — H. Metzger, *Recherches sur l'imagerie athénienne*, Paris 1965.

Metzger 1992 — *La région nord du Létôon* (Fouilles de Xanthos, 9), eds. A. Bourgarel, H. Metzger & G. Siebert, Paris 1992.

Miller 1979 — S.G. Miller, *Two groups of Thessalian gold* (Classical Studies, 18), Berkeley & Los Angeles 1979.

Mitchel 1973 — W. Mitchel, 'Lykourgan Athens: 338–322', in *University of Cincinnati Classical Studies* II. *Lectures in memory of Louise Taft Semple* II, Norman 1973, 163–214.

Mitsopoulou 2005 — Χ. Μητσοπούλου, 'Βρυόκαστρο Κύθνου: Κεραμεική, Λύχνοι και Ειδώλια από την αρχαία πόλη και το ιερό της Ακρόπολης. Πρώτα στοιχεία από την Επιφανειακή Έρευνα', in *Πρακτικά Β΄ Κυκλαδολογικού Συνεδρίου,*

Θήρα 31 Αυγούστου–3 Σεπτεμβρίου 1995, Μέρος Β΄ (ΕΕΚΜ 18), Athens 2002–2003 (2005), 293–358.

Mitsopoulou 2007 — Χ. Μητσοπούλου, *Το ιερό της Δήμητρας στην Κύθνο και το αττικό ελευσινιακό σκεύος* Ι–ΙΙΙ, diss. University of Athens, Athens 2007.

Mitsopoulou 2010a — Χ. Μητσοπούλου, 'Το ιερό της Δήμητρας στην Κύθνο και η μίσθωση του ελευσινιακού τεμένους', in Leventi & Mitsopoulou 2010, 43–90.

Mitsopoulou 2010b — C. Mitsopoulou, 'De nouveaux Kernoi pour Kernos... Réévaluation et mise à jour de la recherche sur les vases de culte éleusiniens', *Kernos* 23, 2010, 145–178.

Mitsopoulou forthcoming a — Χ. Μητσοπούλου, 'Ο Αλκιβιάδης και η πομπή των Μεγάλων Ελευσινίων του 408/7 π.Χ.', in *The world as a stage: the spectacle in antiquity. International Conference, University of Thessaly, Feb. 2–4, 2007*, ed. Ι. Βαραλής, Volos forthcoming.

Mitsopoulou forthcoming b — Χ. Μητσοπούλου, 'Η ελευσινιακή μύηση του Δημητρίου Πολιορκητή: εικονογραφικές παρατηρήσεις με αφορμή ένα χρυσό διάδημα από την αρχαία Δημητριάδα', in *3ο ΑΕΘΣΕ, Βόλος, 12–15 Μαρτίου 2009* (ΑΕΘΣΕ, 3), forthcoming.

Möbius 1955 — H. Möbius, 'Pierre Amandry: Collection Hélène Stathatos. *Les bijoux antiques*, Strasbourg 1953', *Gnomon* 27, 1955, 36–40.

Moreno 1995 — P. Moreno, *Lisippo. L'arte e la fortuna*, Milano 1995.

Mylonas 1960
G.E. Mylonas, Ἐλευσίς καὶ Διό-νυσος, *ArchEph* 1960, 68–118.

Mylonas 1961
G.E. Mylonas, *Eleusis and the Eleusinian Mysteries*, Princeton 1961.

Mylonas 1987
G.E. Mylonas, 'Eleusis and the Eleusinian Mysteries', *ArchEph* 126, 1987, 385–396.

Nicolet-Pierre & Kroll 1990
H. Nicolet-Pierre & J.H. Kroll, 'Athenian tetradrachm coinage of the third century B.C.', *AJN* ser. 2, 2, 1990, 1–35.

Nilsson 1935
M.P. Nilsson, 'Die Eleusinischen Gottheiten', *ArchRW* 32, 1935, 79–141.

Nordquist 1992
G.C. Nordquist, 'Instrumental music in Greek cult representations', in *The iconography of Greek cult in the Archaic and Classical periods. Proceedings of the first international seminar on ancient Greek cult, organized by the Swedish Institute at Athens and the European Cultural Centre of Delphi, Delphi, 16–18 November 1990* (Kernos, Suppl. 1), ed. R. Hägg, Athens & Liège 1992, 144–168.

Ochsenschlager 1968
E.L. Ochsenschlager, 'The plemochoe, a vessel from Thmuis', *JARCE* 7, 1968, 55–71.

Ochsenschlager 1970
E.L. Ochsenschlager, 'The cosmic significance of the plemochoe', *History of Religions* 9, 1970, 316–336.

Orfanou 2000
V. Orfanou, 'Kerameikos Station: From the refuse deposit of a workshop', in *The city beneath the city: antiquities from the Metropolitan Railway excavations*, eds. L. Parlama & N.C. Stampolidis, Athens 2000, 382.

Pagenstecher 1913
R. Pagenstecher, *Die Griechisch-Ägyptische Sammlung Ernst von Sieglitz* Bd II, Teil 3, Leipzig 1913.

Pakkanen 1996
P. Pakkanen, *Interpreting early Hellenistic religion. A study based on the mystery cult of Demeter and the cult of Isis*, Helsinki 1996.

Papangeli 2002
Π. Παπαγγελή, *Ελευσίνα. Ο Αρχαιολογικός Χώρος και το Μουσείο*, Athens 2002.

Papapostolou 1990
Ι.Α. Παπαποστόλου, 'Κοσμήματα Πατρών και Δύμης. Παρατηρήσεις σε τύπους κοσμημάτων του 4ου αι. π.Χ. και της ελληνιστικής εποχής', *ArchEph* 1990, 83–139.

Parker 1991
R. Parker, 'The Hymn to Demeter and the Homeric Hymns', *GaR* 38, 1, 1991, 1–17.

Parker 2005
R. Parker, *Polytheism and society at Athens*, Oxford 2005.

Parker & Stamatopoulou 2007
R. Parker & R.M. Stamatopoulou, 'A new funerary gold leaf from Pherai', *ArchEph* 143, 2004 (2007), 1–32.

Peschlow-Bindokat 1972
A. Peschlow-Bindokat, 'Demeter und Persephone in der attischen Kunst des 6. bis 4. Jahrhunderts', *JdI* 87, 1972, 60–157.

Philios 1882
Δ. Φίλιος, 'Ἔκθεσις περὶ τῶν ἐν Ἐλευσῖνι ἀνασκαφῶν', *Prakt* 1882, 84–103.

Philios 1884
Δ. Φίλιος, 'Ἔκθεσις περὶ τῶν ἐν Ἐλευσῖνι ἀνασκαφῶν', *Prakt* 1884, 64–87.

Philios 1885
Δ. Φίλιος, 'Ἀρχαιολογικὰ εὑρήματα τῶν ἐν Ἐλευσῖνι ἀνασκαφῶν', *ArchEph* 1885, 170–184.

Pollitt 1979 — J.J. Pollitt, 'Kernoi from the Athenian Agora', *Hesperia* 48, 1979, 205–233.

Raubitschek & Raubitschek 1982 — I.K. Raubitschek & A.E. & Raubitschek, 'The mission of Triptolemos', in *Studies in Athenian architecture, sculpture and topography, presented to Homer A. Thompson* (Hesperia, Suppl. 20), 1982, 109–117.

Reeder 1999 — *Scythian gold: Treasures from ancient Ukraine, New York: Harry N. Abrams in association with the Walters Art Gallery and the San Antonio Museum of Art*, ed. E.D. Reeder, New York 1999.

Rice 1983 — E.E. Rice, *The grand procession of Ptolemy Philadelphus*, Oxford 1983.

Richardson 1974 — N.J. Richardson, *The Homeric hymn to Demeter*, Oxford 1974.

Riedweg 1987 — C. Riedweg, *Mysterienterminologie bei Platon, Philon und Klemens von Alexandrien*, New York 1987.

Ridgway 1964 — B.S. Ridgway, 'The date of the so-called Lysippean Jason', *AJA* 68, 1964, 113–128.

Ritter 1965 — H.W. Ritter, *Diadem und Königsherrschaft: Untersuchungen zu Zeremonien und Rechtsgrundlagen des Herrschaftsantritts bei den Persern, bei Alexander dem Grossen und im Hellenismus*, München 1965.

Roberts 1978 — S.R. Roberts, *The Attic pyxis*, Chicago 1978.

Robertson 1992 — M. Robertson, *The art of vase-painting in Classical Athens*, Cambridge 1992.

Robertson 1998 — N.D. Robertson, 'The two processions to Eleusis and the program of the Mysteries', *AJPh* 119, 1998, 547–575.

Robertson 2000 — M. Robertson, 'Thoughts on the Marsyas Painter and his Panathenaics', in *Periplous. Papers on Classical art and archaeology presented to Sir John Boardman*, eds. G.R. Tsetskhladze, A.J.N.W. Prag & A.M. Snodgrass, London 2000.

Rosen 1987 — R.M. Rosen, 'Hipponax Fr. 48 Dg. and the Eleusinian *Kykeon*', *AJPh* 108, 1987, 416–426.

Rubensohn 1898 — O. Rubensohn, 'Kerchnos', *AM* 23, 1898, 271–306.

Ruhland 1901 — M. Ruhland, *Die eleusinischen Göttinnen: Entwicklung ihrer Typen in der attischen Plastik*, Strasbourg 1901.

Samons 2000 — L.J. Samons II, *Empire of the owl. Athenian imperial finance*, Stuttgart 2000.

Schauber 2005 — H. Schauber, 'Bakchos. Der eleusinische Kultstab', *ThesCRA* V, 2b, 2005, 385–389.

Schauroth Upson 1944 — F. Schauroth Upson, *The kernos in ancient cult*, 1942, diss., abstract in *AJA* 48, 1944, 190.

Schefold 1934 — K. Schefold, *Untersuchungen zu den Kertscher Vasen*, Berlin 1934.

Schmidt 2005 — S. Schmidt, *Rhetorische Bilder auf attischen Vasen. Visuelle Kommunikation im 5. Jahrhundert v. Chr.*, Berlin 2005.

Schwarz 1987 — G. Schwarz, *Triptolemos: Ikonographie einer Agrar- und Mysteriengottheit*, Horn 1987.

Schwarz 1988a G. Schwarz, 'Athen und Eleusis im Lichte der Vasenmalerei', in *Proceedings of the 3rd symposium on ancient Greek and related pottery in Copenhagen 1987*, eds. J. Christiansen & T. Melander, København 1988, 578–584.

Schwarz 1988b G. Schwarz, 'Eubouleus', *LIMC* IV, I, 1988, 43–46.

Schwarz 1997 G. Schwarz, 'Triptolemos', *LIMC* VIII.1, 1997, 56–68.

Schwenk 1985 C.J. Schwenk, *Athens in the age of Alexander. The dated laws and decrees of the "Lykourgan Era" 338–322 B.C.*, Chicago 1985.

Segall 1938 B. Segall, *Goldarbeiten im Benaki Museum, Athen*, Athens 1938.

Segall 1945 B. Segall, 'Two Hellenistic gold medallions from Thessaly', *Record of the Museum of Historic Art, Princeton University* 4, 1945, 3–11.

Sheedy 2006 K.A. Sheedy, *The Archaic and early Classical coinage of the Cyclades* (Royal Numismatic Society. Special Publications, 40), London 2006.

Simon 1966 E. Simon, 'Neue Deutungen zweier eleusinischer Denkmäler des 4ten Jh. v. Chr.', *AntK* 9, 1966, 72–90.

Simon 1983 E. Simon, *Festivals of Attica: An archaeological commentary*, Madison, Wis. 1983.

Simon 1985 E. Simon, 'Hekate in Athen', *AM* 100, 1985, 271–284.

Simon 1997 E. Simon, 'Eleusis in Athenian vase-painting: New literature and some suggestions', in *Athenian potters and painters. The conference proceedings*, eds. H. Oakley, W.D.E. Coulson & O. Palagia, Oxford 1997, 97–108.

Skias 1894a Α. Σκιάς, 'Ἐπιγραφαὶ Ἐλευσῖνος', *ArchEph* 1894, 199–201.

Skias 1894b Α. Σκιάς, 'Περὶ των εν Ελευσίνι ανασκαφών', *Prakt* 1894, 14–17.

Skias 1895 Α. Σκιάς, 'Περὶ της εν Ελευσίνι ανασκαφής', *Prakt* 1895, 159–193.

Skias 1901 Α. Σκιάς, 'Ελευσινιακαὶ κεραμογραφίαι', *ArchEph* 1901, 1–39.

Smith 1988 R.R.R. Smith, *Hellenistic royal portraits*, Oxford 1988.

Stavropoullos 1938 Φ.Δ. Σταυρόπουλλος, 'Ιερατικὴ οικία εν Ζωστῆρι Αττικῆς', *ArchEph* 1938, 1–31.

Stroszeck 2010 J. Stroszeck, 'Das Heiligtum der Tritopatores im Kerameikos von Athen', in *Neue Forschungen zu griechischen Städten und Heiligtümern. Festschrift für Burkhardt Wesenberg zum 65. Geburtstag*, eds. H. Frielinghaus & J. Stroszeck, Möhnesee 2010, 55–83.

Svoronos 1901 J.N. Svoronos, 'Ερμηνεία του εξ Ελευσίνος μυστηριακού πίνακος της Νιννίου. Μέρος δεύτερον: Ερμηνεία των παραστάσεων του πίνακος', *JIAN* 4, 1901, 233–263.

Svoronos 1926 J.N. Svoronos, *Les monnaies d'Athènes*, München 1923–1926.

Thompson 1942 M. Thompson, 'Coins for the Eleusinia', *Hesperia* 11, 1942, 213–229.

Thompson 1961 M. Thompson, *The new style silver coinage of Athens*, New York 1961.

Tiverios
1997

M. Tiverios, 'Eleusinian iconography', in *Greek offerings. Essays on Greek art in honour of
John Boardman*, ed. O. Palagia,
Oxford 1997, 167–175.

Tiverios
2008

M. Tiverios, 'Women of Athens in the worship of Demeter:
Iconographic evidence from
Archaic and Classical times',
in *Worshipping women. Ritual
and reality in Classical Athens*,
eds. N. Kaltsas & A. Shapiro,
New York 2008, 124–135.

Trehuedic
2008

K. Trehuedic, *Insignes et mar-
queurs du pouvoir hellénistique.
Traditions et stratégies dans la
royauté d' Alexandre et dans
l'Orient hellénisé*, diss. Univer-
sité Paris 12, Créteil 2008.

Treister 2001

M.Y. Treister, *Hammering
techniques in Greek and Roman
jewellery and toreutics* (Col-
loquia Pontica, 8), Leiden,
Boston & Köln 2001.

Tsaimou &
Oikonoma-
kou 1998

Κ.Γ. Τσάϊμου & Μ. Οικονομάκου,
'Κέρνοι στη Λαυρεωτική', in
*Ζ΄ Επιστημονική Συνάντηση
Νοτιοανατολικής Αττικής,
Κορωπί 19–22 Οκτωβρίου 1995*,
eds. Σ. Κόλλιας & Δ. Πρόφης,
Koropi 1998, 210–222.

Tsirigoti-
Drakotou
2009

Ι. Τσιριγώτη-Δρακωτού, 'Η ιερά
οδός των ρωμαϊκών χρόνων', in
*Η Αθήνα κατά κατά τη ρωμαϊκή
εποχή. Πρόσφατες ανακαλύψεις –
νέες έρευνες, Πρακτικά του Διεθ-
νούς Επιστημονικού Συμποσίου,
Αθήνα 19–21 Οκτωβρίου 2006*,
ed. Σ. Βλίζος, Athens 2009.

Tsochos
2002

C. Tsochos, *Pompás pémpein:
Prozessionen von der minoischen
bis zur klassischen Zeit in Griechenland*, Thessaloniki 2002.

Valavanis
1990

P. Valavanis, 'La proclamation
des vainqueurs aux Panathé-
nées. À propos d'amphores
panathénaïques de Praisos',
BCH 114, 1990, 325–359.

Valavanis
1991

Π.Δ. Βαλαβάνης, *Παναθηναϊκοί
αμφορείς από την Ερέτρια. Συμβολή
στην αττική αγγειογραφία του
4ου π.Χ. αι.*, Athens 1991.

Valavanis
1997

Π.Δ. Βαλαβάνης, 'Βάκχιος,
Κίττος και παναθηναϊκοί
αμφορείς. Σκέψεις για τη δομή
των αττικών κεραμικών εργα-
στηρίων του 4ου αι. π.Χ.', in
*Athenian potters and painters.
The conference proceedings*, eds.
J.H. Oakley, W.D.E. Coulson
& O. Palagia, Oxford 1997,
85–95.

Valavanis
2011

Π. Βαλαβάνης, 'Addenda et
corrigenda σε παναθηναϊκούς
αμφορείς και σε ζωγράφους του
4ου π.Χ. αιώνα', in *Ταξιδεύοντας
στην Κλασική Ελλάδα. Τόμος
προς τιμήν του καθηγητή Πέτρου
Θέμελη*, ed. Π. Βαλαβάνης,
Athens 2011 (in print).

Vergara
Cerqueira
forthcoming

F. Vergara Cerqueira, 'Iconographical representation of
Eros—the god—depicted in
musical scenes or with musical
instruments in hand', in *An
international conference on Eros
in ancient Greece, University
College London & the Institute
of Classical Studies, London,
Saturday 28–Tuesday 31 March
2009*, eds. E. Sanders, C. Thu-
miger, C. Carey & N. Lowe,
forthcoming.

Vierneisel-
Schlörb
1979

B. Vierneisel-Schlörb, *Klassi-
sche Skulpturen des 5. und 4.
Jahrhunderts v. Chr.*,
München 1979.

Virgilio 2003   B. Virgilio, *Lancia, Diadema e porpora. Il re e la regalita ellenistica*, Pisa 2003.

Willemsen 1977   F. Willemsen, 'Zu den Lakedämoniergräbern im Kerameikos', *AM* 92, 1977, 117–157.

Wilson 1999   P. Wilson, 'The aulos in Athens', in *Performance culture and Athenian democracy*, eds. S. Goldhill & R. Osborne, Cambridge 1999, 58–95.

Yiouri 1972   Ε. Γιούρη, Ἡ κεραμεική της Χαλκιδικής στον 4ο αιώνα π.Χ., in *ΚΕΡΝΟΣ. Τιμητική προσφορά στον καθηγητή Γεώργιο Μπακαλάκη*, Thessaloniki 1972, 6–14.

Zaccagnino 1998   C. Zaccagnino, *Il thymiaterion nel mondo greco: analisi delle fonti tipologia*, Roma 1998.

Zervoudaki 2000   Η. Ζερβουδάκη, *Εθνικό Αρχαιολογικό Μουσείο: Συλλογή Σταθάτου*, Athens 2000.

CLARISSE PRÊTRE

Les mots et les choses

DE L'OFFRANDE D'UN BOUCLIER CRÉTOIS A DÉLOS

Abstract

For too long, we have forgotten to tackle religion by what is its spirit: the offerings. The dedication in Delos of a θυρεὸς κρητικὸς περιχρύσους ἔχων ἐπίσημον σκορπέρωτα, a Cretan shield with a *skorperota* as *episema*, opens first of all the problem of the semantic interpretation of what is recorded in the inventories. Nevertheless, only one lexical study would not be satisfactory and we must strengthen it with a research into the *realia* so that we can understand not only the votive object but the motives of its dedication and then to put them into the perspective of the dedicatory system of the Delian sanctuary.

Thus, through the study of a term and of its possible archaeological parallels, we will endeavour to show the very useful alliance of several fields of knowledge, such as philology, archaeology and iconography, in order to think about religion more complementary, and while giving a concrete fundamental correspondant to the theoretical reflexions on the votive practices.

À Délos, comme dans les autres sanctuaires à inventaires dans une moindre mesure, la difficulté de compréhension des offrandes enregistrées dans les catalogues peut se situer à divers niveaux:

• au niveau du terme lui-même désignant l'objet dédié. C'est ainsi que les administrateurs ont souvent eu recours à des hapax[1] qu'il nous est difficile de décrypter en l'absence de toute comparaison. Et même quand le terme n'est pas un hapax, il a pu être employé à Délos dans un sens nouveau. La polysémie est en effet une des caractéristiques majeures des inventaires déliens.

• au niveau du contexte de présentation: on peut citer par exemple l'offrande de "coquillages sur colonnettes en bois", ὄστρεῖα ἐπὶ κιονίων ξυλίνων[2] qui paraît absurde si on ne remet pas cette dédicace en perspective avec les parallèles archéologiques. On sait qu'à Délos on a trouvé des coquillages offerts en ex-voto sans doute par des pêcheurs: dans l'établissement des Poseidoniastes, on a ainsi des exemplaires dédiés vraisemblablement à Poséidon et Aphrodite Astarté.[3] Cependant si grands fussent-ils, ces coquillages ne pouvaient être présentés sur des colonnettes sous peine de ruiner la mise en scène votive. Selon toute vraisemblance, il faut plutôt songer à des reproductions de conques en métal qui servaient souvent de bassins à laver ou encore à des vases ainsi dénommés parce qu'affectant la forme stylisée d'un coquillage.[4]

---

[1]   Prêtre 2004, 85–101.

[2]   *ID* 1403B, fr. Bb, col. II, l. 17.
[3]   Picard 1920, 132, n. 2. Agathé Tyché par ailleurs reçoit deux coquilles marines avec des extrémités en bois doré enfermées dans un coffret en bois (κόγχους δύο θαλαττίους ἐν θήκαις τὰ ἄκρα ἔχοντας ξύλινα καὶ περικεχρυσωμένα), cf. Roussel 1916, 246.
[4]   Vases très en vogue à Rome également. Martial parle d'un vase en or ayant la forme d'un murex (3.82.27).

Les conques étaient de taille moyenne, marquées de côtes et souvent plaquées d'or ou d'argent.[5] Elles nécessitaient donc un présentoir en rapport avec leur ornementation et leur forme. C'est ici un exemple de difficulté de compréhension provenant du contexte de présentation ou parfois d'enregistrement.

• enfin, l'objet lui-même peut poser un problème d'interprétation, évidemment, car bon nombre d'offrandes décrites dans les inventaires déliens n'ont jamais eu de parallèle archéologique convaincant; c'est le cas d'ἐνώίδια χρυσᾶ θάσια, "boucles d'oreilles thasiennes", alors qu'à Thasos, aucun bijou ne possède de caractéristique locale,[6] et c'est aussi le cas des βουβάλια dans l'offrande d'une paire de bracelets, comportant de petits Eros sur du bois et ces énigmatiques *boubalia*.[7] En fait, ce terme désigne une variété de concombres sauvages, et même si le parallèle archéologique est introuvable, il s'agit vraisemblablement d'une perle de forme allongée.

On voit donc que les strates d'incompréhension des dédicaces déliennes sont nombreuses et peuvent se combiner et s'ajouter les unes aux autres. L'offrande présentée dans cet article comporte d'ailleurs les trois niveaux de problèmes évoqués et son étude démontre encore—si besoin en est—l'intérêt de l'alliance entre des recherches lexicales et archéologiques.

Il s'agit d'un "bouclier crétois doré avec un *skorperota* en épisème", θυρεὸς κρητικὸς περιχρύσους ἔχων ἐπίσημον σκορπέρωτα. L'offrande de ce bouclier est mentionnée dans deux inventaires[8] concernant l'ancien temple d'Apollon, le *Porinos Naos* et son premier enregistrement conservé date des années 160 av. J.-C. La lecture est claire sur la pierre, même si nous n'avons qu'une attestation avérée du

terme σκορπέρωτα, la première occurrence étant restituée: la formule la plus complète est donc [ἄλλον κρητικὸν περίχρυσον ἔχοντα ἐπίσημ]ον σκορπέρωτα. Rien ne permet d'affirmer que ce bouclier était réellement doré, la restitution ayant été faite par déduction, en se fondant sur les autres θυρεοί le précédant. Il était en tout cas en bois, car il fait partie d'une série de boucliers recensés sous l'appellation générique ξύλινα.

On aura compris que le terme qui pose problème est σκορπέρωτα ou *σκορπέρως si on admet qu'il s'agit d'un accusatif singulier en analogie au mot simple ἔρωτα. Avant cependant de tenter de comprendre la signification de cet hapax, il est nécessaire de remettre rapidement en contexte l'offrande toute entière.

A Délos, les inventaires enregistrent trois principaux types de boucliers dédiés, qui recouvrent les trois grands types connus, l'ἀσπίς, la πέλτη et le θυρεός. L'ἀσπίς est le bouclier le plus usité dans l'Antiquité grecque. Il correspond au *clipeus* latin. Mentionné d'abord chez Hésiode, il est de forme circulaire et porte souvent un omphalos en son centre, sorte de partie bombée sur laquelle les flèches rebondissent en étant déviées: Homère évoque les ἀσπίδες ὀμφαλόεσσαι.[9] De nature défensive, l'ἀσπίς aurait été inventé à Argos, d'où sa fréquente dénomination ἀσπίς ἀργολική, et se distingue de l'ἀσπίς béotien par les échancrures que ce dernier comporte sur les bords, réminiscence peut-être des boucliers du Dipylon. L'ἀσπίς en général, comporte une âme de bois encastrée dans un disque de métal.

Le θυρεός en revanche possède une armature de bois ou d'osier simplement recouverte de métal guilloché ou même de peau à l'origine, mais non encastrée dans un disque de métal. Plus ancien, il doit son nom à sa forme souvent rectangulaire et allongée, qui évoque une porte θυρά. Alors que l'ἀσπίς perdure pendant toute l'Antiquité, rapidement le θυρεός n'est plus uti-

---

5   *ID* 442B, l. 179, pour un κόγχος ἀργυροῦς.
6   Prêtre 2009.
7   *IG* XI 2 161B, l. 118.
8   *ID* 1403B, fr. b, col. I, l. 88 et *ID*1414, fr. a, col. I, l. 17.

9   Hom. *Il.* 4.448.

lisé et disparaît presque complètement après le VIIème s., sauf en Achaïe où il se maintient jusqu'au IIIème s., selon les dires de Pausanias :

"φοροῦντας γὰρ μικρὰ δοράτια καὶ ἐπιμηκέστερα ὅπλα κατὰ τοὺς Κελτικοὺς θυρεοὺς ἢ τὰ γέρρα τὰ Περσῶν, ἔπεισε θώρακάς τε ἐνδύεσθαι καὶ ἐπιτίθεσθαι κνημίδας, πρὸς δὲ ἀσπίσιν Ἀργολικαῖς χρῆσθαι καὶ τοῖς δόρασι μεγάλοις"

"[l'infanterie] avait en effet de petites lances et de grands boucliers semblables à ceux des Gaulois et des Perses; [Philopoimen] leur fit prendre des cuirasses ainsi que des armures pour les jambes, et les engagea à se servir de boucliers argiens et de longues piques."[10]

La πέλτη, rarement recensée dans les offrandes déliennes est d'interprétation plus délicate tant les descriptions antiques diffèrent. Selon toute vraisemblance, il s'agit d'un bouclier léger, fait d'une âme d'osier recouverte de peau de chèvre,[11] dont les bords étaient échancrés, à la manière de l'ἀσπίς béotien.

Ces deux types de boucliers étaient sans doute peu maniables: parfois de grande taille puisque certains boucliers couvraient presque tout le corps,[12] ils offraient le moyen de protection le plus efficace contre les armes de jet, notamment lorsqu'ils étaient employés en formation fermée, afin de protéger également l'arrière du combattant. C'est ainsi qu'on explique l'usage apparu très tôt des épisèmes qui étaient avant tout des signes distinctifs servant à reconnaître au premier coup d'œil qui se trouvait en face, ami ou ennemi.

G.H. Chase distingue un certain nombre de types d'emblèmes sur boucliers, classés selon les motivations intrinsèques ou externes qu'ils comportent: à côté des motifs se référant au caractère personnel du possesseur de l'arme (appartenance à une famille, fortune, nationalité, culte à une divinité précise), il y avait bien sûr les emblèmes à vertu apotropaïque et d'intimidation; les images représentées servaient à la fois à éloigner le mauvais œil et à faire peur à l'ennemi: subjugué par la représentation d'un animal fabuleux ou de la Gorgone terrifiante, l'ennemi en perdait ses moyens et devenait ainsi vulnérable.[13] On peut évoquer ici l'anecdote du Spartiate qui avait représenté une mouche de grandeur nature sur son bouclier: accusé de couardise, il répondit que cela forcerait l'ennemi à s'approcher très près pour comprendre le symbole et qu'il pourrait alors l'occire sur le champ de bataille.[14] C'est à la suite de cela, qu'on instaura à Sparte l'usage d'un blason unique, en l'occurrence le lambda.

Outre les différentes catégories d'emblèmes qu'on figurait sur les boucliers, on pouvait en effet y placer également la première lettre du nom de la cité, comme indice d'une appartenance à une nation: l'individu comme entité guerrière disparaissait au nom de la défense de tout son peuple, et les Messéniens comme les Sicyoniens adoptèrent le même système que Sparte. Pausanias raconte d'ailleurs la ruse utilisée par les Messéniens pour tromper Elide et rentrer en ses murs en arborant des boucliers à la lettre des Lacédémoniens alors alliés des Eléens: τῶν δὲ Μεσσηνίων λογάδες χίλιοι φθάνουσιν ἀφικόμενοι

---

10   Paus. 8.50.1.
11   Aristote: "ἢν δὲ ἡ πέλτη ἀσπὶς ἴτυν οὐκ ἔχουσα (οὐδ') ἐπίχαλκος (οὐδὲ βοὸς ἀλλ') αἰγὸς (ἢ οἰὸς) δέρματι περιτεταμένη", cf. Rose 1886, n° 498, l. 6.
12   Du moins dans les écrits homériques puisque nous n'avons pas retrouvé d'exemplaires de grande taille et que sur les monuments figurés, les boucliers sont toujours plus petits afin d'être soulevés aisément jusqu'à la tête. Sans doute les boucliers de taille humaine décrits dans l'*Iliade* étaient-ils destinés à souligner la force des combattants.

13   Chase 1902, 78.
14   Plut. *Mor.* 234c: "Λάκων ἐπὶ τῆς ἀσπίδος μυῖαν ἔχων ἐπίσημον καὶ ταύτην οὐ μείζω τῆς ἀληθινῆς, ὡς καταγελῶντές τινες ἔλεγον <ὅτι> ὑπὲρ τοῦ λανθάνειν τοῦτο πεποιήκει, 'ἵνα μὲν οὖν' εἶπε 'φανερὸς ὦ· οὕτω γὰρ τοῖς πολεμίοις πλησίον προσέρχομαι, ὥστε τὸ ἐπίσημον ἡλίκον ἐστὶν ὑπ'αὐτῶν ὁρᾶσθαι.'"

πρὸς τὴν Ἦλιν, σημεῖα ἐπὶ ταῖς ἀσπίσι Λακωνικὰ ἔχοντες.[15] De toute évidence, le motif ornant le bouclier délien qui nous intéresse ici se réfère à un élément personnel ou possède une vertu apotropaïque, mais il reste à déterminer le sens de cet emblème.

A Délos, les offrandes recensées dans les inventaires reflètent clairement les grandes catégories de boucliers ainsi que les variations ornementales attendues. Il faut également préciser qu'au fur et à mesure des décennies, les consécrations y deviennent plus importantes, en nombre, en prix et en renom. Cette évolution dans la mentalité des donateurs se note particulièrement bien dans le cas des boucliers.

Ainsi, les exemplaires d'ἀσπίδες offerts au IVème s. sont assez frustes: on relève sept ἀσπίδια ξύλινα[16] qui se trouvaient dans le Néôrion ou l'Aphrodision mais on ne trouve plus d'offrandes nouvelles de boucliers en bois à partir du IIIème s. A l'instar des armes véritables, les dédicaces déliennes d'ἀσπίδες sont dorénavant en métal ou tout du moins, avec une apparence métallique même si l'âme reste en bois. Certains boucliers sont recouverts de bronze: 29 ἀσπίδας ἐπιχάλκους[17] sont recensés dans la Chalcothèque, et on les trouve encore mentionnés plus de 70 ans après leur première occurrence. La variante ἀσπίδες κεχαλκωμέναι[18] désigne le même processus. Il ne s'agit pas de boucliers en bronze mais de boucliers plaqués de bronze. Les participes parfaits passifs à valeur d'état sont très souvent utilisés pour décrire les offrandes recevant un traitement métallique particulier sans être forcément en métal massif.[19]

Dans un inventaire des années 220, on relève un ἀσπίδιον ἀργυροῦν.[20] C'est ici la première occurrence d'un bouclier en argent dans les catalogues, au milieu d'une énumération d'objets hétéroclites (phiales, plaques votives, statuettes ou encore lampes). En 179 un Romain en offre un autre: ἀσπὶς ἀργυρᾶ, Τίτου Ῥωμ[αίου ἀνάθεμα].[21] Plus on avance dans le temps, plus la matière d'ornementation (et non de confection) des boucliers devient riche. Ainsi dans les années 155, les dédicaces de boucliers plaqués d'or sont fréquentes: ἀσπίδας ἐπιχρύσους γραφὰς ἐχούσας ἑξήκοντα.[22] On en vient même à garder des fragments, sans doute de métal précieux, tombés des boucliers: λεπίδ<α>ς ἀσπίδων.[23]

Les mentions de θυρεός sont moins fréquentes dans les inventaires déliens. Lors de l'Indépendance de l'île, on ne compte qu'une seule offrande d'un bouclier de ce type, θυρεὸν ἐπάργυρον, "recouvert d'argent", dédié par Antiochos en 240.[24] Le reste des dédicaces est répertorié lors de la seconde domination athénienne de l'île après 160. On relève alors un θυρεὸν ἱππικὸν ἐμ πλαισίωι περιχρύσουν,[25] "bouclier hippique doré dans un cadre", ainsi que θυρεοὺς πεζικοὺς τρεῖς ἐμ πλαισίοις ἐπιχρύσους,[26] "trois boucliers de fantassin dorés dans des cadres"; enfin, le dernier exemplaire recensé dans les inventaires déliens est en bois doré et porte des roues et un bouclier comme épisème:

---

15 Paus. 4.28.5.
16 *ID* 104(26)B, l. 19. La forme suffixée en -ιον implique une idée de miniature ici puisqu'elle est associée à une matière qui suggère plutôt un caractère votif que réellement défensif, mais ce n'est pas systématique. Cf. Prêtre 1997, 673–680. Sont laissées de côté les mentions d'ἀσπιδίσκη qui n'est pas un bouclier mais un petit disque d'ornementation. Un seul cas délien est ambigu car son rangement parmi des armes fait plutôt songer à un véritable bouclier qu'à un bijou.
17 *IG* XI 2 161C, ll. 106–107.
18 *ID* 372B, l. 31.

19 Chantraine 1927, 55. A Délos, on relève par exemple κεχρυσμένος, (*ID* 101), περιηργυρωμένος (*ID* 310), μεμολυβδωμένος (*ID* 421) ou encore ὑποσεσιδηρωμένος (*ID* 399).
20 *ID* 346B, l. 7.
21 *ID* 442B, l. 178.
22 *ID* 1417A, col. I, l. 149.
23 *ID* 1417B, col. I, l. 102.
24 *ID* 298A, l. 122.
25 *ID* 1403B, fr. b, l. 40.
26 *ID* 1403B fr. b, col. I, l. 54.

[ἄλλον περί]χρυσ[ον ἔχοντα] ἐπίσημον θυρεὸν καὶ τρόχους.[27] Au vu de l'ornementation et de la matière il s'agit ici de toute évidence d'un bouclier votif, comme sans doute le θυρεὸς κρητικὸς περιχρύσους ἔχων ἐπίσημον σκορπέρωτα auquel est consacré cette étude.

A côté des *aspides* et des *thureoi*, on recense une seule consécration de πέλτη à Délos : πέλτη ἐπίχαλκος offerte dans les années 280.[28] Là encore on peut penser que la πέλτη enregistrée ici a une vocation purement dédicatoire : dans la réalité, les *peltai* recouvertes de métal sont extrêmement rares car il s'agissait d'une structure en osier recouverte de peau, destinée à être légère.

Comme vont le confirmer les *realia* ensuite, il semble donc à Délos que le θυρεός soit moins fréquemment offert que l'ἀσπίς; passé ce premier constat, il est encore plus surprenant de signaler l'absence totale de θυρεοί dans les inventaires des autres cités : que ce soit en Attique ou à Didymes, aucun catalogue d'offrandes ne recense de θυρεός dédié. En revanche, l'ἀσπίς constitue une offrande fréquente dans les inventaires attiques et du Péloponnèse : on a ainsi ἀσπ[ὶς ἐπίχρυσος ηυπόχσυλος],[29] "bouclier recouvert d'or avec une âme en bois", ἀσπὶς λευκὲ μία, "un bouclier blanc",[30] [ἀσπίδες] ἐπίχρυσο[ι λεῖαι δύο], "deux boucliers recouverts d'or, sans motif",[31] ἀσπίδες λακωνικαί, "boucliers laconiens",[32] ἀσπίδια πομπικά, "boucliers de procession",[33] ἀσπίδες λευκαὶ κατ[τιτέριν]αι, "boucliers blancs en étain",[34] pour ne citer que les plus significatifs. Les inventaires de Délos, une fois encore, se démarquent de leurs homologues par la richesse du lexique qui reflète bien la variété des offrandes : à côté des inventaires attiques où les ἀσπίδες sont quasiment le seul type de bouclier dédié, à Délos, on recense les trois variétés de cette arme défensive.

Avant d'évoquer les épisèmes, il reste encore deux points à examiner en ce qui concerne le θυρεὸς κρητικὸς περιχρύσους ἔχων ἐπίσημον σκορπέρωτα délien : la mention de κρητικός comme adjectif qualificatif de provenance et le mode de dénomination de la matière.

En ce qui concerne l'adjectif κρητικός, il s'agit de tenter de comprendre comment cette qualification était immédiatement perceptible aux administrateurs qui ont enregistré cette offrande.[35] Quand on compulse les autres inventaires d'offrandes en cherchant des spécificités crétoises, on constate que les dédicaces d'objets crétois appartiennent souvent au domaine de l'armement.

Des Κρη[τικαὶ ἀκίδες], "pointes de javelot crétoises"[36] sont recensées dans le Parthénon ainsi que τόξα Κρητικὰ δύο, "deux flèches crétoises", dans le temple d'Apollon délien.[37] Les Crétois étaient réputés pour leurs archers et outre les inventaires, on retrouve cette réputation dans les sources textuelles : on évoque ainsi les ἀκίδες Κρηταί chez Athénée,[38] un Κρητικὸ βέλος chez Plutarque[39] et une scholie à l'Iliade explique pourquoi les flèches crétoises sont si redoutables : τὰ Κρητικὰ βέλη ἐμπήσσεσθαι μὲν τῇ σαρκὶ ἀκωλύτως, ἐξέρχεσθαι δὲ δυσχερῶς διὰ τὰς ἀπαγκιστρώσεις, "les flèches crétoises

---

[27] *ID* 1403B, fr. b, col. I, l. 87.
[28] *IG* XI 2 161C, l. 108.
[29] *IG* I³ 344, l. 32.
[30] *IG* IV² 787, l. 20.
[31] *IG* II–III² 1421, col. II, l.31.
[32] *IG* II–III² 1425B, col. I, l.397.
[33] *IG* II–III² 1425B, col. I, l.401.
[34] *IG* II–III² 1469B, col. I, l. 70.

[35] On exclut l'idée d'une offrande ainsi nommée parce que déposée par un Crétois : non que le phénomène soit impossible mais parce que le nom et l'origine du donateur auraient alors été indiqués. Rappelons en outre la remarque de Lerat 1980, 102: "Les offrandes d'armes dans un sanctuaire sont faites non par des peuples qui les ont en usage mais par leurs adversaires victorieux."
[36] *IG* II–III² 1416, l. 12.
[37] *IG* XI 2 161B, l. 100.
[38] Ath. 10.421c: au milieu d'une énumération d'armes diverses, c'est le seul adjectif de provenance mentionné.
[39] Plut. *Pyrrh.* 29.8.4.

transpercent complètement la peau, et il est difficile de les retirer en raison de leurs pointes recourbées".[40] Diodore de Sicile évoque l'origine crétoise de l'archerie initiée par Apollon en personne, εὑρετὴν δὲ καὶ τοῦ τόξου γενόμενον διδάξαι τοὺς ἐγχωρίους τὰ περὶ τὴν τοξείαν, ἀφ᾽ ἧς αἰτίας μάλιστα παρὰ τοῖς Κρησὶν ἐζηλῶσθαι τὴν τοξικὴν καὶ τὸ τόξον Κρητικὸν ὀνομασθῆναι, "c'est à lui aussi que les Crétois doivent l'arc et la manière d'en tirer. Ils donnent à cette arme le nom de crétois et elle fait un des exercices où ils se piquent le plus de réussir".[41] Les inventaires attiques recensent en outre une série d'armes enregistrées sous le terme générique Κρητικὰ, comprenant des pointes de lances (στυράκια) et des boucliers (ἀσπίδες) à épisèmes.[42]

Enfin, un passage de Pollux énumère les différentes origines artisanales des armes les plus réputées: εὐδόκιμα δὲ θώραξ Ἀττικουργής, κράνος Βοιωτουργές, πῖλος καὶ ἐγχειρίδιον Λακωνικά, ἀσπὶς Ἀργολική, τόξον Κρητικόν "la cuirasse est attique, le casque de facture béotienne, le *pilos* et le poignard laconiens, le bouclier argien et l'arc crétois". On constate donc que c'est essentiellement l'archerie crétoise qui est réputée mais non pas les boucliers. Il a été prouvé que dans les inventaires déliens, l'usage des épithètes géographiques est mal systématisé et souvent très arbitraire. Rien n'interdirait alors de penser que Κρητικός ne souligne plus depuis longtemps la particularité ethnique du bouclier. Cela irait dans le sens de l'étude de Ph. Bruneau sur le problème des épithètes géographiques; il avait d'abord cherché les trois raisons d'une telle nomenclature : était-ce une indication de l'origine réelle d'un objet, une information sur l'origine du type, ou une épithète purement descriptive? Au terme de sa démonstration, il admettait que l'épithète géographique est "souvent moins le reflet de

l'origine historique des produits ainsi désignés qu'un mode de dénomination typologique ».[43] Si l'on applique la thèse de Bruneau au bouclier offert à Délos, il ne serait donc pas sûr que les administrateurs déliens aient encore pu distinguer *ex abrupto* un θυρεός crétois d'un ἀσπίς argien au IIe s. av. J.-C. On en serait alors à faire de cette épithète une qualification figée qui ne reflètait plus vraiment une réalité.

Est-il toutefois possible d'imaginer qu'il ait subsisté une spécificité que les administrateurs reconnaissaient immédiatement à l'instar des boucliers béotiens par exemple, qui affectaient une forme caractéristique? Plutarque pour sa part, faisait référence à des Κρητικαὶ πέλται, donc une autre variété de boucliers.[44] En ce qui concerne le bouclier crétois recensé à Délos, en dépit de la description assez longue, rien n'indique une marque crétoise dans la forme.

On connaît cependant par les fouilles un type de bouclier dit crétois, parce que les premiers exemplaires ont été retrouvés dans l'antre de l'Ida en Crète.[45] Identifiable immédiatement, il possède en son centre un disque à protomé léonine parfois remplacée par toute la partie antérieure du lion. L. Lerat,[46] à propos des deux exemplaires retrouvés à Delphes dans la région NE du sanctuaire déclare que "l'un, comme c'est la règle en Crète, avait été travaillé à partir d'une seule pièce de bronze". On réunit là deux caractéristiques propres à une facture crétoise et que les administrateurs du sanctuaire délien pouvaient identifier immédiatement. La plupart des boucliers crétois datent toutefois des IX-VIIIème s. et l'offrande délienne en question a été faite dans les années 160 av. J.-C.[47] On devra donc songer à une sorte

---

[40] Erbse 1969, XXI, 474a, ligne de scholie 5.
[41] Diod. 5.74.
[42] *IG* II–III² 2 1425B, col. I, l. 388.

[43] Bruneau 1976, 15–45 et particulièrement 36 *sqq.* pour un dépouillement des épithètes géographiques.
[44] Plut. *Aem.* 32.6.
[45] Voir notamment Kunze 1931, 61–68, nos. 2–25.
[46] Lerat 1980, 104.
[47] Pour les débats sur la question de la datation, la discussion a été amorcée notamment par Hencken 1950, 297.

de terminologie figée et calquée sur un modèle ancien, en rejoignant un peu la définition de Bruneau; plutôt cependant que d'imaginer que l'appellation θυρεός κρητικός ne reflétait plus qu'une origine lointaine non déterminée, on peut supposer qu'un bouclier à protomé animale évoquait une facture crétoise originelle dans l'esprit des administrateurs athéniens du sanctuaire de Délos au IIème s. Cela explique également pourquoi cette protomé n'était pas mentionnée dans la description du bouclier puisqu'elle constituait l'essence même du modèle crétois: l'adjectif κρητικός seul impliquait qu'il y ait eu ce motif. Et cela explique aussi que le seul élément signalé soit l'épisème.[48]

A Délos, hormis le fameux σκορπέρωτα, il y a assez peu de mentions détaillées d'autres épisèmes sur boucliers, ce qui ajoute encore de l'intérêt à cette précision. On a le θυρεός déjà évoqué précédemment, qui porte lui-même un autre θυρεός et des roues en guise d'emblème: ἄλλον περίχρυσον ἔχοντα ἐπίσημον θυρεὸν καὶ τρόχους.[49] L'idée de reproduire une arme sur les boucliers est apparemment quelque chose de fréquent puisque les inventaires déliens recensent également "deux boucliers plaqués d'or, dont un porte une miniature de bouclier et une lance, et l'autre une proue de bateau », ἀσπίδας ἐπιχρύσους δύο, ὧν τὴμ μὲν ἀσπίδιον [ἔχουσαν καὶ δο]ράτιον, τὴν δὲ ἀκροστόλιον.[50] Peu d'animaux fabuleux ou de personnages mythologiques en revanche à Délos, étonnamment, et on peut juste signaler un ἀσπίς qui porte le Triton, ἔχον ἐπίσημον Τρίτωνα.[51] Les autres boucliers, s'ils ont des emblèmes, sont juste parfois signalés comme ἀσπίδες γραφὰς ou ἐπιγραφὰς ἔχουσαι.[52]

Les inventaires attiques recensent quant à eux des animaux — fabuleux en règle générale comme le dragon —, ἀσπίδες ἐπίσημοι δράκο[ν] τα ἔχουσαι,[53] et les sources textuelles nous en fournissent des parallèles: c'est le cas du bouclier d'Alcméon au serpent-dragon bigarré[54] qui rappelle sa dynastie familiale, ou celui d'Epaminondas à Mantinée, car il appartenait selon Pausanias, à ceux qui sont nés des dents du dragon.[55]

En Attique, la Gorgone demeure un épisème fréquent: ἀσπὶς ἐπίχρυσος γοργόνειον ἔχοσα[56] et on retrouve le même emblème sur des boucliers de personnages connus: le célèbre passage sur le bouclier d'Agamemnon dans l'Iliade décrit une image de Gorgone: ἂν δ᾽ ἕλετ᾽ ἀμφιβρότην πολυδαίδαλον ἀσπίδα θοῦριν καλήν, ἣν πέρι μὲν κύκλοι δέκα χάλκεοι ἦσαν, ἐν δέ οἱ ὀμφαλοὶ ἦσαν ἐείκοσι κασσιτέροιο λευκοί, ἐν δὲ μέσοισιν ἔην μέλανος κυάνοιο. τῇ δ᾽ ἐπὶ μὲν Γοργὼ βλοσυρῶπις ἐστεφάνωτο δεινὸν δερκομένη "Agamemnon prend en main son vaste et impénétrable bouclier, dont la solide épaisseur est formée de dix cercles de cuivre enlacés, sur lesquels brillent vingt clous d'étain; le centre est d'un noir acier; on y voit une Gorgone à l'œil louche, couronnée de serpents".[57]

Enfin, dernier exemple de Gorgone, le bouclier d'un Crétois dans l'Anthologie Palatine, qui représente une Gorgone et le motif appelé triskèle, à trois jambes pour inciter l'ennemi à s'enfuir rapidement:[58] Σᾶμα τόδ᾽ οὐχὶ μάταιον ἐπ᾽ ἀσπίδι παῖς ὁ Πολύττου Ὕλλος ἀπὸ Κρήτας θοῦρος ἀνὴρ ἔθετο, Γοργόνα τὰν λιθοεργὸν ὁμοῦ καὶ τριπλόα γοῦνα γραψάμενος· δήϊος τοῦτο δ᾽ ἔοικε λέγειν. "Ἀσπίδος ὦ κατ᾽ ἐμὰς πάλλων δόρυ, μὴ κατίδῃς με, ἢ φεῦγε τρισσοῖς τὸν ταχὺν ἄνδρα ποσίν." "Sur son bouclier le fils de Polyttos, Hyl-

---

[48] Pour une étude du mot lui-même, voir Lacroix 1955, 89–115.
[49] *ID* 1403B, fr. b, col. I, l. 87.
[50] *ID* 1403B, fr. b, col. I, l. 39.
[51] *ID* 1426A, col. I, l. 6.
[52] *ID* 1412, fr. a, l. 23; *ID* 1414, a, I, l. 13.

[53] *IG* II–III² 2 1455, fr. c, col. III, l. 61.
[54] Pind. *Pyth.* 8, v. 45.
[55] Paus. 8.11.8.
[56] *IG* II–III² 2 1424a, col. I, l. 81.
[57] Hom. *Il.* 11.32–37.
[58] *Anth. Pal.* 6.126.

los, le brave guerrier de Crète, n'a pas mis un emblème insignifiant, en y faisant représenter la Gorgone qui pétrifie et en même temps trois jambes. Trouves-tu le sens de cet emblème? Cela veut probablement dire: 'O toi qui lances un javelot contre mon bouclier, ne me regarde pas, et fuis l'homme rapide aux trois jambes.'"

Point en revanche de mentions de *σκορπέρως, évidemment, mais pas plus de scorpions. La fin de cet hapax faisant logiquement songer à ἔρως, on peut cependant évoquer alors l'épisème du bouclier d'Alcibiade. Il descendait de deux grandes familles athéniennes mais avait choisi de représenter un Eros au foudre sur son blason plutôt qu'un élément rappelant sa généalogie: l'intention d'intimidation était plus forte que le sens de la dynastie.[59] Et c'est peut-être cette idée d'intimidation qu'il faut voir dans l'épisème représentant un *σκορπέρως.

Le phénomène de composition nominale par juxtaposition, le *dvandva*,[60] est très courant pour les noms d'animaux comme λεόπαρδος, "le léopard" par exemple, mais surtout pour les animaux fabuleux : ἱππαλεκτρύων, "cheval-coq", γρυπαίετος, "griffon-aigle", γυπαλέκτωρ, "vautour-coq", λυκάνθρωπος, "lycanthrope", ou encore τραγέλαφος "bouc-cerf", autre hapax délien apparaissant sur le chaton d'une bague.[61] Alors que l'union de certains de ces termes se laisse facilement interpréter, le *σκορπέρως offre plus de difficultés de compréhension. S'il s'agit d'un néologisme procédant du même mode de création par juxtaposition, on peut alors poser: σκορπίος + Ἔρως > *σκορπέρως qui adopte naturellement la déclinaison de Ἔρως et qui donne σκορπέρωτα à l'accusatif, seule forme attestée. Quel est alors le symbole qu'on a voulu attribuer à cette créature hybride, si symbole il y a?

Ecartons d'emblée une interprétation zodiacale; certes les monstres dimorphes étaient présents dans les constellations et les signes qui leur correspondaient: le sagittaire comme le capricorne—mi-chèvre mi-poisson—étaient déjà bien connus à l'époque de la dédicace du bouclier crétois à l'épisème étrange.[62] Le scorpion était aussi associé à Arès dans les grands traités astrologiques au début de notre ère.[63] "Foudroyant ou non, le scorpion ne pouvait guère avoir de clients paisibles. Il suscite les batailleurs, les ravageurs, les gladiateurs, maîtres d'armes et autres espèces de la gent querelleuse" écrivait Manilius.[64] Serait-il alors possible de voir dans l'épisème crétois une réminiscence du monstre mi-scorpion mi-homme des légendes cosmogoniques?[65] Chez les Grecs en tout cas, le scorpion mythologique était celui qu'Artémis avait envoyé piquer le vaniteux et trop empressé Orion. C'est ainsi qu'on expliquait que dans le ciel, la constellation d'Orion disparaissait quand se levait celle du Scorpion. Il est possible qu'il y ait eu une allusion indirecte voire inconsciente au caractère perfide et agressif du scorpion zodiacal dans la construction de cette créature hybride mais rien ne permet de l'affirmer.

Dès l'origine, de toute façon, le scorpion n'est pas considéré comme un insecte bienfaisant. On sait que les attaques d'insectes pouvaient avoir une grande influence sur le cours d'un combat,[66] si on se réfère au récit d'Elien sur les insectes venimeux d'Inde.[67] Certains passages bibliques suggèrent même qu'il y

---

[59] Plut. *Alc.* 16.
[60] Pour les *dvandva*, cf. Masson 1988, 171–177.
[61] *IG* XI 2 161B, l. 48.

[62] Voir Alexis le Comique, *PGC*, 2. 263, qui évoque au IVème s. déjà un plat figurant l'hémisphère avec la constellation du poisson et du scorpion.
[63] Chez Manilius notamment, dans ses *Astronomica*.
[64] Manilius, *Astronomica,* 4. 217–229.
[65] La légende chaldéenne du héros Gilgamès le présente attaqué par l'homme-scorpion qui gardait le soleil. Les Grecs connaissaient ce mythe dès le IVe s. av. J.C. Cf. Bouché-Leclercq 1899, 142–143.
[66] Cf. Mayor 2003, *passim*.
[67] Ael. *NA* 6.20, 23; 8.13.

avait des tactiques militaires axées sur les insectes.[68] Il s'agissait essentiellement d'insectes volants, évidemment, comme les guêpes, parfois confondues avec les abeilles. Enée le Tacticien recommandait de garder des guêpes et des abeilles dans les souterrains sous la forteresse pour les lâcher sur l'ennemi en cas de danger.[69] Onze sortes de scorpions étaient connues dans l'Antiquité. Elien racontait que le désert d'Hatra était rempli de scorpions se cachant derrière chaque pierre. Il y en avait tant que pour faire l'expédition de Suze jusqu'en Médie, les rois perses organisaient des chasses avec récompenses.[70] Pline[71] donne aussi une description effroyable des scorpions et des effets de leurs piqûres et donc en règle générale, le scorpion était vu comme un animal nuisible, symbole de ruse.[72]

La représentation d'un dard de scorpion sur un bouclier constituait sans doute alors une image redoutable: sur une amphore d'Andokidès, le scorpion arme un guerrier soutenu par Hermès face à l'adversaire champion d'Athéna.[73] Au Ier s. ap. J.-C. d'ailleurs, le scorpion est adopté comme emblème officiel du bouclier de la Garde Prétorienne à Rome.

Mais le terme *scorpios* désigne aussi une sorte de catapulte à balancier, par analogie à la queue recourbée de l'insecte. Ainsi, dans un passage d'Hérodien qui évoque une attaque avec des pots d'argile remplis de *scorpioi*, certains commentateurs modernes y voient davantage

l'usage complexe d'un engin de guerre que des insectes.[74] Il est aussi intéressant de constater qu'une représentation sur une gemme met en scène une catapulte de ce genre actionnée par un Eros.[75] Néanmoins, il semble que la formation du mot-même dans les inventaires déliens interdise de songer à ce genre de figuration sur un bouclier. Si on prend comme référence syntaxique les enregistrements de sceaux et d'intailles qui obéissent au même modèle descriptif que les boucliers dans les inventaires — déliens ou attiques, on constate que rarement les personnages sont mis en scène: pour les divinités par exemple, on a aussi bien δακτύλιος σημεῖ[ον Ἀθηνᾶς πρόσω[πον ἔχον[76] que plus précisément δακτύλιος χρυσοῦς Ἀθηνᾶς κράνος ἔχων,[77] mais la formulation habituelle est simple, δακτύλιον χρυσοῦν σάρδιον ἔχοντα ἐπίσημον Ἀπόλλωνα[78] alors que les sceaux de Délos offrent pourtant des représentations d'Apollon en action: en train de décocher une flèche, tenant un instrument de musique, etc.[79] On peut légitimement supposer que l'effigie d'un Eros en train d'actionner une catapulte n'aurait pas donné lieu à la création d'un hapax ainsi construit. Tout au plus aurait-on eu une formule comme "Eros avec scorpion-catapulte".

Sur le bouclier délien, il s'agit bien plutôt d'une évocation de l'animal qui hantait l'imagerie commune. On objectera peut-être que l'association de cet insecte redoutable à une image comme celle d'Eros est pour le moins étrange. Le bouclier d'Alcibiade cité plus haut aide cependant à comprendre l'intention de cette association car il procède déjà d'un principe connu dans la constitution des épisèmes: pour compenser le sens positif qu'aurait eu un

---

68   Cf. Neufeld 1980, 30–57.
69   Aen. Tact. 37.4.1:" Ἤδη δέ τινες καὶ σφῆκας καὶ μελίσσας εἰς τὸ διόρυγμα ἀφέντες ἐλυμήναντο τοὺς ἐν τῷ ὀρύγματι ὄντας."
70   Ael. *NA* 15.26: "ὑπὸ παντὶ γὰρ λίθῳ καὶ βώλῳ πάσῃ σκορπίος ἐστί."
71   Plin. *HN* 11.30.1–5.
72   Pour une synthèse sur les différents types de scorpions mais aussi sur le sens en mécanique militaire du mot, voir Montbrun 2003, spécialement 148–157.
73   Pour un dessin de cette amphore du Louvre, voir la reproduction claire bien que vieillie dans Norton 1896, 8 = *CVA* Ic 25/2a. Pour d'autres représentations sur vase, voir la liste de Chase 1902, 119, n° CCXXIV.

74   Hdn. 3.9.3–8.
75   Reproduite dans *DAGR*, s.v. Tormentum, 370, fig. 7024.
76   *IG* XI 2 164A, l. 73.
77   *IG* XI 2 203B, l. 69.
78   *ID* 380, l. 3.
79   Boussac 1992, s.v. Apollon.

Les quelques épisèmes de boucliers retrouvés lors des fouilles n'ont bien sûr pas conservé une telle représentation, pas plus que les boucliers figurés sur vases. Nous avons cependant à Délos justement une source iconographique incomparable, des cachets de sceaux datés des IIème et Ier s. av. J.-C. et donc contemporains de l'offrande enregistrée dans les inventaires. Sur plusieurs d'entre eux, figure le parallèle iconographique de l'hapax des inventaires (*Fig. 1* et *2*).[80] Peu importe ici de savoir si c'est l'épisème de bouclier qui a inspiré le sceau ou le contraire. Il est tout à fait probable cependant de voir dans la représentation sur un sceau un reflet d'une réalité guerrière. Les figurations sur vases tout comme les descriptions par les auteurs contemporains, poètes ou non, semblaient

Fig. 1. Sceau de Délos avec Skorperos, être mi-scorpion, mi-Eros. Stampolidis 1992, pl. XLVIII. Photo: © EfA/ Ph. Collet.

simple Eros, on l'avait justement représenté brandissant un foudre. Et c'est bien là la même construction symbolique sur cet épisème délien; quand on sait que tout était bon pour intimider l'adversaire, on discerne mieux l'intention: d'abord apaiser l'ennemi en lui présentant une image d'Eros, à connotation pacifique; puis lorsque sa méfiance est retombée, mieux le dérouter en lui montrant la seconde partie du corps, qui se termine par une queue de scorpion. La dualité de cet être hybride est très symbolique ici: endormir l'attention de l'adversaire pour mieux le tuer ensuite. Nul doute que l'ennemi qui regardait cette figure, en supposant qu'il commençait bien par le haut, était pétrifié par la signification qu'elle revêtait: c'est la ruse par excellence, redoublée encore par le symbole du scorpion, représentant déjà en soi la ruse dans l'opinion populaire des Grecs anciens.

Fig. 1. Sceau de Délos avec Skorperos, être mi-scorpion, mi-Eros. Stampolidis 1992, pl. XLVIII. Photo: © EfA/ Ph. Collet.

---

80 Stampolidis 1992, pl. XLVIII.

s'inspirer directement des motifs qu'on voyait alors sur les boucliers.[81] On constate alors qu'à cette époque, il existe bien dans l'imagerie grecque—ou tout du moins délienne—un être fabuleux, mi-Eros, mi-scorpion, destiné sans doute à intimider l'adversaire en le surprenant par son aspect hybride. Présent sur plusieurs cachets déliens, il témoigne clairement de la connaissance par les rédacteurs des inventaires de cette créature dimorphe pour laquelle ils ont créé un hapax. Si la forme du bouclier évoque un type crétois, la représentation figurée semble quant à elle proprement délienne.

Lorsqu'on unit donc des recherches sur des domaines aussi cloisonnés que l'épigraphie (et ici la sémantique) et l'archéologie, on atteint une fine compréhension des offrandes recensées dans les sanctuaires; l'utilité de cette alliance est ici pleinement prouvée par la correspondance entre le mot et l'objet.

CLARISSE PRÊTRE
CNRS, UMR 8164 "HALMA-IPEL"
clarisse.pretre@free.fr

Bibliographie

Bouché-Leclercq 1899 A. Bouché-Leclercq, *L'astrologie grecque*, Paris 1899.

Boussac 1992 M.-Fr. Boussac, *Les sceaux de Délos* 1. *Sceaux publics*, Paris 1992.

Bruneau 1976 Ph. Bruneau, 'D'un *Lacedaemonius orbis* à l'*aes Deliacum*', in *Recueil Plassart: études sur l'antiquité grecque offertes à André Plassart par ses collègues de la Sorbonne,* ed. A. Plassart, Paris 1976.

Chantraine 1927 P. Chantraine, *Histoire du parfait grec*, Paris 1927.

Chase 1902 G.H. Chase, 'The Shield Devices of the Greeks', *HSCP* 13, 1902, 61–127.

DAGR Ch. Daremberg & E. Saglio, *Dictionnaire des antiquités grecques et romaines*, Paris 1877.

Erbse 1969 H. Erbse, *Scholia graeca in Homeri Iliadem (Scholia vetera)*, Berlin 1969–1988.

Hencken 1950 H. Hencken, 'Herzsprung shields and Greek trade', *AJA* 54:4, 1950, 295–309.

Kunze 1931 E. Kunze, *Kretische Bronzereliefs*, Stuttgart 1931.

Lacroix 1955 L. Lacroix, 'Les "blasons" des villes grecques', *Etudes d'Archéologie classique* 1, 1955, 89–115.

Lerat 1980 L. Lerat, 'Trois boucliers archaïques de Delphes', *BCH* 104:1, 1980, 93–114.

Masson 1988 O. Masson, 'Noms grecs du type Ἀρκολέων "ours-lion"', in *Ediston logodeipnon, Logopédies: mélanges de philologie et de linguistique grecques offerts à Jean Taillardat*, Paris 1988.

Mayor 2003 A. Mayor, *Greek fire, poison arrows, and scorpion bombs*, New York 2003.

Montbrun 2003 Ph. Montbrun, 'Apollon, le scorpion et le frêne à Claros', *Kernos* 16, 2003, 143–170.

Neufeld 1980 E. Neufeld, 'Insects as warfare agents in the ancient Near East', *Orientalia* 49, 1980, 30–57.

Norton 1896 R. Norton, 'Andokides', *AJA* 11, 1896, 1–48.

PCG *Poetae Comici Graeci* vol. 2, *Agathenor-Aristonymos*, eds. R. Kassel & C. Austin, Berlin & New York 1991.

---

[81] C'est en tout cas l'idée de Chase 1902, 79.

Picard 1920 — Ch. Picard, *L'établissement des Poseidoniastes de Bérytos* (EAD, 6), Paris 1920–1921.

Prêtre 1997 — C. Prêtre, 'Imitation et miniature: étude de quelques suffixes dans le vocabulaire délien de la parure', *BCH* 121:2, 1997, 673–680.

Prêtre 2004 — C. Prêtre, '"Erreurs" de graphie involontaires et volontaires dans les inventaires déliens: de la création d'hapax à l'usurpation d'identité', *Tekmeria* 8, 2004, 85–101.

Prêtre 2009 — C. Prêtre, 'Thasos-Délos: un aller-retour paradoxal dans le matériel votif', *Revue de l'Histoire des Religions* 227:4, 2010 [sous presse].

Rose 1886 — V. Rose, *Fragmenta varia*, Leipzig 1886.

Roussel 1916 — P. Roussel, *Délos, colonie athénienne*, Paris 1916.

Stampolidis 1992 — N. Stampolidis *Les sceaux de Délos* 2. *O erotikos kuklos*, Paris 1992.

MICHAEL SCOTT

Displaying lists of what is (not) on display

THE USES OF INVENTORIES IN GREEK SANCTUARIES

Abstract*

Scholarship on Greek religion has recently been criticized for its focus both on a particular model of activity (that of *polis* religion) and on particular kinds of evidence for it (literary and historical sources). In contrast, this paper seeks to investigate a set of inscriptional sources from a variety of different places and time periods, the temple inventories from the Acropolis and Asklepieion at Athens, the Sanctuary of Apollo on Delos and the Sanctuary of Athena Lindia on Rhodes, in order to think about the ways in which these inscriptions, both as texts and as physical monuments within the landscape, reflected and articulated visitors' responses to, and understandings of, the places and things around them. This paper argues that these inventories were key not just in forming a visitor's impression of what was (and what was not) on display in the sanctuary itself, but also in demonstrating how that particular sanctuary related itself, its visitors and the listed objects both to one another and to the wider religious and political frameworks of the Greek world.

Introduction

Scholarship on the inventory lists found in numerous Greek sanctuaries has often been separated from wider discussions of Greek religion and has instead been published within volumes dedicated to ancient Greek accounting/list-making; within volumes focusing on the objects listed in the inventories rather than on the lists themselves, or, more recently, within stand-alone monographs focusing on the inventory material from a particular site.[1] In this article, in contrast, I attempt to do three things. First, to focus on the lists as lists rather than simply on the objects contained with them. Second, to compare and contrast the form, style and content of some of the inventory lists from different sanctuaries and time periods, in order to investigate what unites the range of uses to which inventories could be put and, in so doing, to sketch the historical and political development of those uses. Third, rather than separating inventories from discussions of Greek religion, I argue that such an understanding of the range and development

*   My thanks go to Matthew Haysom and Jenny Wallensten for organizing the conference "Current Approaches to Greek Religion", April 2008, held in the British School at Athens and the Swedish Institute at Athens, and for inviting me to speak. My thanks go also to the participants in the conference who offered many helpful comments, and to my students in Cambridge for discussions on inventories during supervision. For comments on the written version, my thanks go to Prof. Robin Osborne and to the anonymous reader for The Editorial Committee of the Swedish Institutes at Athens and Rome. All remaining errors are of course my own.

[1]   Separated from Greek religion: Davies 1994; D. Harris 1994; Lewis 1988. Accounting volumes: de Ste-Croix 1956. Focus on objects contained within the lists: Lewis 1986. Stand-alone monographs: Hamilton 2000; D. Harris 1995; Higbie 2003.

of inventory use offers a potentially important way for us to improve our understanding, not just of the inventories themselves, but of the wider context of Greek religion in which they were situated.

The argument will unfold as follows. In the first part of this paper, I look briefly at the different reasons for inscribing these lists outlined in previous scholarship, and give a sense of where we find them and when. In the second part, I examine four specific case studies from different sanctuaries and time periods. Finally, in the third part, I argue that the case studies show how inventories created a series of important relationships between object and viewer, temple and *polis*, sanctuary and sanctuary, *polis* and *polis*, which in turn constructed an interwoven political, historical and religious landscape which was crucial to the articulation of Greek religious practice, and which offers us today a useful way into thinking about the development and operation of Greek religion.

What, where and why?

Inventory lists are much more common than we might at first imagine. Large numbers have been found on the Acropolis and in the Asklepieion at Athens, but also smaller numbers at Brauron, at the temple of Aphaia on Aigina, and at Isthmia. Further afield, large numbers have been found at Delos and a sizeable collection at Didyma, with some single lists at Samos, Miletos, Ilion, Halikarnassos, and on Rhodes.[2] They range in date from the fifth cen-

tury BC to the second century AD. They are all different in their style, layout, focus and policies of inclusion.

The inventories found at Athens have, however, often paved the way for descriptions of an inventory's general purpose. The accounts at Athens detail the *paradosis*, the handover from one set of Treasurers of Athena to the next, at which a stock-check of sacred objects under their control was made to ensure nothing was amiss. These lists, placed in public view, thus acted as end of year accounts and were part of the fiduciary transparency of the city, their appearance in the fifth century BC often linked (as with the advent of all published documentation in Athens) to the advent of democracy.[3]

Yet cracks have appeared in this theory, not least given the sheer un-readability of these stelai measuring sometimes two metres in height, inscribed with over 400 lines of text. Objects disappear and reappear from one year to the next and there is little standardization in the layout, description and punctuation. In 2000, Hamilton argued that "scholars have agreed these written lists serve no practical purpose, because they are neither comparable with each other nor easily compared with the actual objects in the temple".[4] Instead of ascribing a functional value, scholars have spoken mainly of their symbolic use, as statements of wealth, piety, power, the principle of accountability and civic worth.[5] This split between functional

---

[2]   Acropolis: D. Harris 1994; *idem* 1995; Lewis 1986; *idem* 1988. Asklepieion: Aleshire 1989; Davies 1994; Sickinger 1999. Brauronia (on Acropolis and at Brauron): Linders 1972; Peppas-Delmousou 1988. Aigina: *IG* IV 39. Isthmia: *IG* IV 203. Delos: Hamilton 2000; Linders 1988; Tréheux 1988b. Didyma: Dignas 2002. Lindos on Rhodes: Higbie 2003. Miletos: Günther 1988. For other singles lists: Dignas 2002; Sickinger 1999.

[3]   Davies 1994, 205; Hansen 1991, 11; D. Harris 1994, 214; Hedrick 1994; Pébarthe 2006, 244–260.

[4]   Hamilton 2000, 1. "They are monuments of actions performed, not records to be consulted": D. Harris 1994, 213. They are not bookkeeping but rather the actions and oral communications of magistrates: Linders 1992. They protect and confirm the values of the city: Thomas 1992, 128. They make visible the riches of the deity and the city and prove the good management of the treasurers: Pébarthe 2006, 278.

[5]   How much was inscribing on stone "a functional act rather than one driven by ornamental or ritual or symbolic reasons?": Davies 1994, 202.

and symbolic roles is, however, flawed, since there is little clear difference between the two. The symbolic potential of these lists rests upon their grounding in functional reality—they must have some usable information to provide (or at least the potential to do so) if they are also (to continue) to be a symbolic marker of power.[6]

I argue that a way forward from this impasse of functionality vs. symbolism is to think in terms of the ways in which the inventories create relationships between different entities.[7] As many scholars have argued, inscriptions tell a story, encourage a form of behaviour, and situate the reader. The inventory lists are no exception. By listing a series of sacred objects, these inventories place the treasures of the gods into a framework of associations. Objects are placed in a series of transactions between bodies of citizens, between citizens and their *polis* or sanctuary and ultimately between those *poleis*/sanctuaries and the gods. These relationships are, through their description on the stelai, put on display to be read by the visitor to the sanctuary, which both cements those relationships in the public eye and draws the viewer into thinking about them.[8]

---

[6] The inventories were erected "more as symbols than as records": Linders 1992, 31. They were dedications in their own right: Linders 1992, 36. In favour of their use as functional records, however, particular details of the full accounts appear to have been actively chosen to be inscribed on stone: it is an active process: Pébarthe 2006, 268; Samons 2000, 312–317. For their use (and authority) as archives (as opposed to being simply partial copies of the archives): Linders 1992; Pébarthe 2006, 269–270. The inventories as both texts and monuments: D. Harris 1994, 213. Their functional importance as evidenced by later corrections made to the stelai: Samons 2000, 315. Their accountability factor as but one of their uses: D. Harris 1994, 216. The inventory for 346/5 BC from the Temple of Hera on Samos (Michel 1900, n. 832, 1, ll. 38–40) details how inspectors should check the inventory with the rolled seal for items missing. This inscription is used as evidence both for the functionality and symbolic importance of these inscriptions, as part of a wider set of consultable records including temporary archive records and oral memory: Pébarthe 2006, 271–272. Similarly, *IG* II² 1440 (349/8 BC) from the Athenian Asklepieion makes reference to the use of these stelai as important reference points: Pébarthe 2006, 272–273. *IG* II² 120 (353/2 BC) outlines a procedure for the complex checking of the stele inventory by many layers of bureaucracy and underlines the use of the stele as a viable form of reference, with the temporary archive to be brought out only as a last resort: Pébarthe 2006, 274–275. The very functional use of these inventories is also recorded in the literary sources: Demosthenes, in *Against Androtion,* focuses on how Androtion wrongly persuaded the people to melt down gold crowns stored in the Parthenon (the process of *kathairesis*) and subsequently oversaw the melting process (and inscribing of the process in the lists) without a tax official present (358–355 BC). He also had the temerity to re-inscribe the newly formed gold crowns with his own name rather than the original dedicatory inscription: Dem. 22.70–73; D. Harris 1995, 32–33.

[7] Cf. D. Harris 1995, 241–245.

[8] Cf. Pausanias, who records the way in which lists of people who have benefited from Asklepios' healing powers at Epidauros are studied by sanctuary visitors (Paus. 2.27.3). We do not know for sure whether the temple inventory lists were read out in public at the time of their creation. If they were, the lists create another particular relationship with their viewers and listeners, who are involved in authenticating their contents and by consequence the job done by the sacred treasurers and list compilers. The community reiterates its faith in itself through the performance of reading, cf. Osborne 1999. The Lindos chronicle begins by outlining the decree passed in the assembly to form the list (A1–13), and the list was checked because there is a fine detailed for non-performance of the job of preparing it (A11), but we can not say if it was actually read out. In Athens, it has been argued that the document was first prepared on whiteboards and then copied over to the stone, possibly with a verifying stage: D. Harris 1994, 220. In Delos, Linders has argued that the lists seem to have been prepared directly in front of the objects, but the lists give little information about the co-operation of the temple staff: Linders 1988, 41, 45. In the early Acropolis lists, there is a clear visual concern for presentation and legibility (e.g. *IG* I³ 317–324): Pébarthe 2006, 278. On the question of whether people were able to read the stelai for themselves, that is on the issue of general literacy in this period: see Camp 2001, 157–159, 166, 168; W.V. Harris 1989, 62–63, 79–80, 102, 104; Harvey 1966; Hedrick 1994, 174; Murray 1980, 96; Ober 1989, 156–191; Pébarthe 2006, 282–283; Rhodes 2001; Thomas 1992; Whitley 1997, 644–645.

In the second section of this paper, I want to expand this way of looking at inventories by examining four case studies: the inventories of the Athenian Acropolis, the Athenian Asklepieion, the Sanctuary of Apollo at Delos, and the Sanctuary of Athena at Lindos on Rhodes. These case studies have been chosen because of the good deal of recent scholarship on their inscriptions, making them far more accessible than those at other sites. In conclusion, I will return to sum up how this approach helps us to understand the many uses to which these inventories could be put, the historical development of those uses, and the role of inventories in Greek religious practice.

Inventories at Athens, Delos and Lindos

The inventory lists for the Acropolis at Athens, and particularly for the Parthenon, are extensive, surviving from *c.* 434 BC to the end of the fourth century BC.[9] The objects are described by their number, material, function, weight and origin. Such details immediately create a series of relationships for the objects and for the city that now owns them. Their weight was expressed in a financial value—drachmai: for example a silver drinking cup weighing 66 dr in *IG* I[3] 303, lines 48–9 (423/2 BC), which ensured a clear and direct appreciation of the wealth stored in the city and its temples. Details of their origin (Milesian couches for example in *IG* I[3] 343, line 13 (434/3 BC)) added cultural connotations to the viewer's visual image of the object (their image of what made a couch particularly Milesian), but also underlined both the breadth of Athens' hold over far-flung parts of the world, and its dynamic reputation, by its ability to acquire such gifts.[10]

At the same time, the objects are divided up on the list by their location in the Parthenon (and indeed the Erechtheion and the "Opisthodomos"—thought to be the old Temple of Athena). For the first forty years of the inventories, separate stelai were used for each of the main three rooms of the Parthenon (*pronaos* (front part), *hekatompedon* (middle part) and *parthenon* (back room)), before being consolidated into one single massive stele.[11] This meant that the lists actually provided the viewer with a visual image of the spatial layout and contents of parts of the inside of the Parthenon which they could rarely see, and as a result encouraged them to imagine and expect certain forms of behaviour within each space.[12] Phialai were the main objects held in the pronaos according to the lists, reflecting and ensuring the pronaos' role as the place for libation pouring. In fact, *IG* I[3] 292, lines 6–7 (434/3 BC) makes this particularly clear: "a gold phiale from which lustrations are made" is recorded in the inventories.

The hekatompedon had much more gold (gold leaves and gold crowns).[13] The parthenon room in contrast was a strange miscellany, with gold, crowns, phialai, armour, furniture, lyres and jewellery.[14] The three different areas of the Parthenon could thus be visualized through reading their inventory lists (even if the visual impression created was that of a jumbled mess). These lists collapsed the distance between the inside and outside of the temple, allowing what had to be kept sacred and off limits in honour of the goddess also to be fully part of the public discourse in the world outside.

---

[9]   For debate over why they began at this date, and their association with the Kallias decree: Samons 1996.

[10]   Lewis 1986.
[11]   Lewis 1986, 72.
[12]   Such a virtual spatial layout is also created for the treasures in the Erechtheion: D. Harris 1994.
[13]   D. Harris 1995, 104.
[14]   Lewis 1986, 74–76.

Yet these lists, as they gathered side by side over the years, also enunciated the changing relationship between Athens, its people and the outside world. As Athens expanded its reach, so the numbers of more exotic objects increased.[15] As the Peloponnesian war dragged on, the lists become shorter and more objects are recorded as being melted down. By the end of the war eight of the nine golden *nikai* have been melted down and the pronaos is recorded as only having one crown in it (*IG* I[3] 316 (407/6 BC)). Yet the confiscated property of the Thirty Tyrants was recorded as being turned into twenty silver *hydriai* for the Parthenon.[16] The fourth century saw a steady accretion of objects commissioned, dedicated and received, and a systematic operation to melt down damaged and small objects to create larger ones.[17] Lykourgos' influence is also clear: he had the lists put on bronze rather than marble stelai and reformed the nature of their recording, increasing the stock used for the Panathenaic processions.[18] When democracy was restored in 307/6 BC, there was a great degree of activity recorded, with twenty-nine new crowns entering the lists to accompany the thirty-three already there.[19] And even the end of the lists is recorded under Demetrios Poliorketes in 304/3 BC, when the list pointedly highlights that the objects were *not* handed over to next years' treasurers.[20]

The inventories at Athens thus establish a series of relationships through the description of the objects, through their arrangement on the lists, and through the changing contents of the lists over time between the Athenians, their

gods, the world around them, the objects and the viewers in the sanctuary. The lists create a way of engaging with and defining what makes Athens "Athens" by bringing objects into play which would otherwise have been out of sight and out of mind except for the few days a year when they were used in religious processions.

The lists at the Sanctuary of Asklepios on the south side of the Acropolis offer a slightly different picture. These inventories cover almost the entire sanctuary's life, 400 BC to AD 250–300. The lists do not cover every dedication received by the sanctuary, in fact probably less than half of those received each year.[21] The element of choice in what was written up would have been very visible to users of the sanctuary, since, in contrast to the Parthenon inventories, many of the offerings mentioned would have been on full view. Thus these lists do not create images of the objects, but rather reinforce the presence of particular items. The lists divide into three sections, depending on type of offering: body part ex-votos; coins and typoi. By far the largest group are the body part ex-votos, which have the clearest link between the dedicator, the god and the reason for the offering (since they visualize the affected body area). Thus a pair of gold eyes placed on a tablet are dedicated by Lysis in 339/8 BC following, we presume, his healthy recovery from an eye problem.[22] Each object listed testifies to a successful interaction between the god and an individual, and the combined lists testify to the popularity of the god within the local community. Coins take up about one sixth of the dedications (many of which are in Aleshire's inventory VI) and *typoi* about one fifth (many of them in Aleshire's inventory V). In listing these different types of offerings, the inventories represent a broad range of activity within the sanc-

---

15 Lewis 1986, 78.
16 D. Harris 1995, 29; Lewis 1986, 75; Walbank 1982, 97–98.
17 Lewis 1986, 72.
18 Lewis 1988, 298. Lykourgos seems also to be responsible for increasing the number of stelai on which the accounts are written, thus increasing (once again) their visibility and legibility: Pébarthe 2006, 278.
19 Lewis 1988, 303.
20 *IG* II[2] 1477. Dignas 2002, 242; Lewis 1988, 304.

21 Aleshire 1989.
22 *IG* II[2] 1533, ll. 22–23; Aleshire 1989, 137 (Inventory III.122).

tuary, confronting newcomers to the sanctuary with proof of the god's power, but also drawing the users into particular ways of relating to the god and, in turn, encouraging them to thank the god in similar ways.

Investigation of these inventories has also revealed particular patterns of display in the identity of the dedicators; first and foremost, the strong tendency to name them. Harris points out that there are 908 named dedicators in the Asklepieion lists, which is far higher than in the Acropolis lists.[23] It seems that the sanctuary was keen to ensure the very visible presence of people in the lists as much as of the objects they brought with them, perhaps in order to increase the image of the sanctuary's popularity.[24] In addition, the crowd was overwhelmingly local, with very few foreigners listed, once again underlining the strong link between the sanctuary and its surrounding community.[25] The lists also reveal a particular set of gender balances. In terms of the type of dedications, women offered ex-votos more frequently than men, and men offered coins more frequently than women and were also more likely to offer crowns and cult equipment.[26] In terms of sheer numbers, outside of Aleshire's inventory V, women make more dedications than men (54.96% of the dedications, with men responsible for 42.55%, the remaining 2.49% of unknown gender). In inventory V, the balance between men and women dedicating is more equal, yet this disguises heavy fluctuations from year to year with a high of 80.00%

and a low of 33.33%.[27] Women are thus much more apparent in these inventories than they are in the Acropolis inventories, which one would perhaps expect given the more personal nature of the interaction recorded. As a result, a particular kind of community is created and displayed for the sanctuary, different from the articulation of other communities around it (for example in the theatre or on top of the Acropolis).

Special inventories commissioned for particular reasons found at the Asklepieion also attest to its constant upkeep by that community. In the third century BC, a list is made of all the items in the store room, along with notes on their state of repair.[28] In the second century BC, three *bouleutai* are chosen to replace part of the tholos and to make a list of equipment kept there.[29] Equally, at the end of the second century, a priest makes a careful recording of worn out objects which are to be repaired.[30] These special one-off inventories, alongside the regular inventories of dedications, are thus utilized to put forward a very visible picture of strong local attachment to a popular sanctuary fully embedded in the local culture.

The Delian inventories are notoriously complex, not least because of their sheer un-readability today (stelai in the 360s BC are 2m high, with lines of text 5mm high, which is reduced further down the stele to fit more in). Here, I only want to concentrate on one facet of the inventories: the changes seen between the inventories produced during the period of Athenian control over the island and the period of independence, and their repercussions for how these inventories created relationships between the island and its controllers. The independence period is dated from 314 BC to 166 BC. During this time, one of the most notable changes

---

[23] D. Harris 1995, 228.
[24] At the end of the Peloponnesian war, however, the number of names mentioned in the Acropolis lists increases significantly, perhaps because of Athens' need to visibly thank more people: Pébarthe 2006, 278.
[25] Rather than this being in contrast to the Acropolis, it is a distinctly similar picture: relatively few foreigners are recorded in the Acropolis lists, the major exception being the catalogue of wreaths dedicated by Athenian allies: D. Harris 1995, 241.
[26] Aleshire 1989, 46.

[27] Aleshire 1989, 45.
[28] Sickinger 1999, 123.
[29] Sickinger 1999, 122.
[30] *IG* II² 840, ll. 18–28.

is that the Delians replace the Athenian archon periods with their own as the standard dating reference.[31] The Delians' insistence on stamping their authority onto the inventories was further strengthened by their re-arrangement of the layout. Instead of listing new dedications in each year as a separate category, the Delians integrated the new additions with the existing items within one single category.[32]

Yet this system did not remain unchanged throughout the period of independence. The inventories fall into two groups, the first dated 314—end of third century BC, and the second end of third century—166 BC. In the first group, the offerings listed are almost exclusively of gold and silver, and the different groups of objects are listed according to their topographical location, with damaged parts of offerings collected and listed separately.[33] In consecutive years (279 and 278 BC for example—*ID* 161 and 162) the objects are listed in approximately the same order, but the description is lengthened for some objects and shortened for others. The list for 276 BC (*ID* 164) differs to an even greater extent. Thus, while each provides a decent visual treasure map "snap shot" of the sanctuary, each inventory is also a separate document, not intended to provide a method for following the history of an object over a period of years.

In contrast, the second group of inventories is remarkably uniform, showing a concerted effort for all dedications to be placed in the temple of Apollo rather than Artemis.[34] The *paradosis* formula—the text explaining the point of these inventories as a list made at the time of handover between priests—is also now used in the body of the text rather than simply as a prescript, often to introduce each new entry.[35]

This unique constant repetition of the *paradosis* to introduce individual items—an expensive decision as it dramatically extends the amount of carving required—focuses our attentions on the actors involved rather than on the objects and, even more specifically, it focuses our attentions on the actors' scrupulous actions at each stage of the process.[36]

The flavour of the accounts from the period of independence is that the Delians immediately moved to distance themselves from Athenian models and methods, using the inventories as a motor for proclaiming and showing off Delos' ability to do as it pleased. In time, this changed to a highly expensive focus on showing that the sacred duty was duly being performed. The Delians used the inventories to underline their relationships (or rather non-relationship) with the Athenians, with their own treasures and crucially it seems with the gods through their expensive documentation of (their) scrupulous religious observance.[37] The contrast after the re-imposition of Athenian power could not have been stronger. The Athenians re-imposed their own secretaries and officials, re-imposed their system of separating old and new objects, and dramatically increased the coverage of the lists, entering many objects not previously seen (27 treasuries were recorded in the Athenian period—more than double that previously).[38] The same imposition of Athenian power through the imposition of a particular type of inventory layout and style can be seen much earlier in the Brauronion inventories, which may also reveal instances of Athens borrowing money from the sanctuary to fund other events, money which was transported to be stored on the Acropolis.[39] The Delian inventories thus display how

---

[31] Hamilton 2000, 7.
[32] Hamilton 2000, 4–5.
[33] Tréheux 1988b.
[34] Linders 1988, 41.
[35] Linders 1988, 42–44.

[36] Expense: Hamilton 2000, 2.
[37] "The Athenian lists are fundamentally fiscal whereas the Delian lists are solely religious": Hamilton 2000, 348.
[38] Hamilton 2000, 4, 11.
[39] Peppas-Delmousou 1988, 338; Tréheux 1988a. The lists at the Temple of Aphaia on Aigina are simi-

the nature of lists of objects could be manipulated to display a sense of ownership—not only over the objects, but over the system and society in which they existed.

The inventory of objects dedicated at the Sanctuary of Athena at Lindos on Rhodes is our final example and in many ways the most interesting. Crucial here is what is announced in the first lines of the inventory: the offerings themselves have all been lost in fire destruction and so this list is to provide the only evidence for their existence and for the "visible presence of the goddess" (lines A3–9 in Higbie). This inventory is thus unique—not a *paradosis* of objects handed over, or even objects out of sight, but of objects which no longer exist. The list recreates the history of the sanctuary through a chronological inventory of the objects that once adorned it.

Yet, although it is an inventory of objects, it is not the objects that take pride of place. First in each entry is not a description of the object, but of the dedicator. The people are more important than the things. Through a chronological list of the people who came to Lindos, the inventory is able to insert Lindos into the crucial times and periods of Greek history and more importantly myth. Panhellenic heroes like Kadmos (BIII), Minos (BIV) and Herakles (BV) are said to have dedicated, alongside heroes of the Trojan war (BX) all the way through to Alexander the Great (CXXXVIII). Evidence for all of these dedicators and dedications is posited with the entry in the form of literary corroborations for their existence (e.g. BXIV, in which Teucer's quiver is corroborated by Xenagoras' *Annalistic Account*, as well as by Gorgon in his book *About Rhodes* and by Theotimos in *Against Aielouros*). The list builds a case for Lindos' importance by creating relationships between Lindos and dedicators

from all parts and time periods of the Greek world, relationships which are themselves corroborated through a network of related literary works.[40]

The list also reinforces Lindos' constant place in these relationships through its physical layout. Early mythical and Trojan war dedicators are placed in a single separated section (B) first on the stone, with dedicators from the Archaic, Classical and Hellenistic periods (in section C) following on, which are in turn followed by a series of epiphanies to the goddess (section D), themselves in chronological order to reinforce the sense of continuity of the sanctuary through time.

The list was written in 99 BC, when Lindos needed to promote itself to a Roman audience and create for itself a history which the Romans could engage with on their grand tours. To that end, it is crucial that no dedications later than the early Hellenistic period are mentioned (in contrast to the Delian inventories e.g. *ID* 442B (179 BC)).[41] The sanctuary suspends itself in history, denying its relationship to the current state of the world, and thus protecting its status as part of the golden age of Greece, rather than as connected to its current subjected state of enslavement. The list is for the Romans, but it is most definitely not relating Lindos to Greece under Roman rule.

Conclusion

The Lindos list has been described as a document "in the twilight between material culture and literary text".[42] It demonstrates just how diverse the use of an inventory can be. In this paper, we have seen how inventories could be used to facilitate some kind of accountability

---

larly stamped with Athenian control by being written in Athenian dialect (*IG* IV 39).

[40] Higbie 2003, 290.
[41] Higbie 2003, 168.
[42] D. Harris 1994, 213.

between officials handing over from one year to the next or provide some kind of check list at times of clean-up, repair or emergency stock-take.[43] This seems to be the general impetus behind the initial creation of inventories, as witnessed by the series of single one-time lists which were created in different sanctuaries in response to these types of particular needs.[44]

But that relational accountability is only the beginning of a series of relationships created by these texts. First and foremost, they reinforce the sense of the continuing relationship between the people and the divine, both through highlighting the fact that objects are being dedicated and through their own presence as documents which highlight the people's continual care for those objects. Second, these lists create particular relationships between the people and what they perceive as their most sacred and important objects: in some places this is gold and silver jewellery, in others clothes are the focus of the inventories (such as in Miletos), and in others, like Brauron, it is on the utensils of cult.[45] Third, these lists articulate relationships between the sanctuary and particular kinds of community around them, like at the Asklepieion which articulated its very local and women-orientated community.[46] Fourth, these lists create relationships between the *polis*/sanctuary in which they stand and other places within the world. Those relationships can either be mutual cultural links (such as those created between Lindos and Macedon), or they can be expressions of the extension of power (like those created at Athens with the statements of items from across the Aegean held in the Parthenon), or they can be statements of ownership (like those created both by the Athenians and the Delians through the inventories at Delos).[47]

---

[43] In some cases these lists are extremely accurate, particularly when documenting the *kathairesis*, or melting down of worn out or small objects to make bigger ones. Lewis argues that from the extant lists, you can even calculate the percentage cut given to the workmen carrying out the job: Lewis 1986, 79.

[44] It is worth noting that only sacred treasures and accounts are ever inventoried. Annual accounts of money kept on the Acropolis were not inventoried in the same way: D. Harris 1994, 216. Davies argues that, in Athens at least, inventories of sacred objects were sparked off by a "curatorial need" formed in response to the first Kallias decree (*IG* I³ 52) in 434 BC: Davies 1994, 208. For this see also Dignas 2002, 240; Samons 1996. They may even have served to prepare Athens financially for the Peloponnesian war: Davies 1994, 209. Putting Athens' financial machinery in order: Dignas 2002, 241; Lewis 1986, 72. Inventories needed to protect growing numbers of valuables in the city: Aleshire 1989, 202; Davies 1994, 202–204. Testifying to the honesty of officials: D. Harris 1995, 224. Individuals also erected lists of their dedications on their grave stele: Richter 1961, no. 53. Whatever the reason for their initial creation, those that became regular series of inventories seem to have gathered additional roles. Dignas argues that the habit of recording inventories probably established a further, subconscious interest in detail without any particular motive: Dignas 2002, 235. There were many kinds of lists published on stone in ancient Greece besides inventories: tribute lists, magistrate lists, athletic victor lists, sales of public contracts, confiscation of goods, lists of war dead. Each served to tell a particular story and reflect and construct the community in particular ways: Osborne 2011.

[45] Günther 1988, 220; Peppas-Delmousou 1988, 336. In the lists on the Acropolis, jewellery is described in an unusually high degree of detail: D. Harris 1995, 95; Lewis 1986, 75.

[46] A peculiar set of inventory lists here might be those listing the phialai dedicated by slaves on being granted their freedom, lists kept in Athens for circa two decades in the third quarter of the fourth century BC. Here the objects are secondary to the people who are dedicating them. These lists establish a particular relationship between the city, the household freeing the slave and newly freed members of the city's community, highlighting the individuals' (and community's) piety to the god but also the community's benevolence to its slaves and its continuing growth and flexibility as a community. For the lists: Lewis 1959; 1968.

[47] One particularly clear enunciation of a relationship is *IDidyma* 424 in 288/7 BC. Apollo was given dedications by Seleukos I, who sent a letter to the council of Miletos with an appendix listing the offerings he was planning to make. The whole letter was subsequently copied onto stone, with a prescript placed above it as if it was an inventory list. The letter highlights the strong relationships between the council at Miletos and the

At the same time, the lists also create a sense of history. To a certain extent, they create a history of the objects themselves, particularly in those lists which record damage done to objects and their subsequent melting down and reforming, which at the same time stresses the strong degree of attachment to these objects and piety to the gods displayed by their owners.[48] But more importantly, the lists create histories of people and places.[49] This history can either be one of the particular city or sanctuary created through the chronological evolution generated within a particular list (like at Lindos), or it can be the changing history of a city or sanctuary over time produced through the changing relationships perceived between different sets of lists placed near to one another (such as in Athens).

Yet, in each case, in each particular set of inventories which catalogue and express these relationships in different ways, the inventories, by their very presence as texts and monuments, can also play a crucial part in enunciating what makes each city or sanctuary different from one another. The lists at Didyma, for instance, are much more akin to those at Lindos in as far as they focus on the names of dedicators rather than the objects, while the lists at Samos follow a much more Athenian model of recording objects in their topographical locations.[50] The style, layout and policy of inclusion of the list itself tie its surroundings into a larger set of relationships and power structures within the Greek world.

More, however, than simply tying its surroundings into a general power structure, the very presence and structure of these lists demonstrate the spread of a very particular power within the Greek world. It has often been noted that the earliest examples of inventories come from Athens, and it is from Athens that we see the use of inventories spread out chronologically and geographically across the Aegean (for example to Delos when inventories are introduced during the first period of Athenian control or to Aigina when under Athenian conquest). Their appearance in Samos may well be due equally to its close working relationship with Athens, and its adoption of the Athenian inventory style supports the sense that Samos adopted something which might be considered, to some extent, an Athenian cultural product. In setting up inventory lists within their sanctuaries, different sanctuaries and cities were making a statement, not just about their similarity and difference with other cities, but very particularly about their close relationship with Athens and its political and religious system.[51] The historical development of the use of inventories is thus also a story of the spread

---

King, as well as the power of the Sanctuary of Apollo in attracting such offerings. The form of the inscription, as a letter, reinforces the sense of exchange and relationship between the different parties. Cf. Dignas 2002, 242–243.

[48] In Delos, damaged items are listed, and broken parts of objects are also listed separately (at least in the first set of Independence inventories): e.g. inventory *ID* 161B 33 (279 BC): Linders 1988, 40. In Samos in the fourth century, explicitly missing items from each room in the Temple are listed: Dignas 2002, 239. At the Acropolis in Athens in the fourth century, there seems to be a systematic melting down of damaged objects: Lewis 1986, 72. At the Asklepieion, catalogues are kept of objects which are melted down and decrees are inscribed recording the need to create lists of damaged objects and outline the repairs needed e.g. *IG* II² 840, ll. 18–28; Sickinger 1999, 122–127.

[49] We may compare the function of lists in Homeric epic, like the catalogue of ships in *Iliad* book two, which create a history of people and places by grouping them together in a common cause and creating links between them.

---

[50] Dignas 2002, 242–244.
[51] Equally, in the absence of inventories, we can also see the articulation of a distance from Athens and its political system. Inventories, for instance, are rarely produced within oligarchic systems. They must be considered, to some extent, an Athenian cultural, religious and political product: Pébarthe 2006, 272. On the other hand, the sheer price of these "dedications" may preclude some sanctuaries and cities from buying into them, even if they had wanted to: Pébarthe 2006, 271.

of Athenian dominance, its resistance and re-imposition.

But it is in the relationships these lists create between the viewer and the objects in question that these documents are perhaps at their most powerful and interesting. They create normative patterns of dedicatory behaviour, encouraging people to behave and to dedicate in the model of previous visitors. They allow objects, hidden out of sight, to have a second life and play an active role in the city's discourse by making them visible once again, inscribed on stone and located within a virtual spatial image of the temple or treasury in which they are contained. They create a new imagined 3D world in which the objects can be harnessed, through the lists in which they are placed, to support a multitude of different assertions. And in the case of the Lindian lists, they allow objects, once lost, to be present again in order to reassert and indeed create a history for the sanctuary. They inform a way of viewing on the visitor, both of viewing the dedications and of viewing the sanctuary, its history and its current place in the world.

Inventory lists, perhaps often themselves considered as elaborate dedications to the god in their own right,[52] provoke a series of relationships between the viewer and the object, the sanctuary, the *polis*, the wider Greek world and the divine. They make, structure and re-adjust memories of objects, traditions, processions, events, people and power. Far from being unusable and unreadable documents, they offered what the visitor could not so easily see at first glance: a representation of the sanctuary and city's projection of itself. It is in this sense that inventories can be so useful to our developing understanding of Greek religion and religious ritual. In a very direct way, these inventories represent the important link between a particular community and the divine, and the regular performance of that community's sacred duty towards the divinity. More than that, however, they represent how a *polis* or sanctuary thought about its relationships with the divine *and* with the human world. As such, they are useful representations to think with in three key areas of current debate over the nature of Greek religion.

Firstly, the study of Greek religion has recently been dominated by Sourvinou-Inwood's *polis*-religion model, in which the *polis* is considered as the principal unit through which religion is articulated.[53] In response, these inventories offer an excellent example not only of how the *polis* was implicated at the centre of religious worship, but also of how Greek religious practice offered the potential for the articulation of different communities within, and distinct from, that of the *polis*. Inventories mark the importance of communities other than that of the *polis* in the articulation of religious practice. In addition, they underline the constant interplay of religious and political forces behind ritual practice and ritual change. In doing so, they offer us a way in which to both validate and extend the *polis*-religion model to cover the real complexities of Greek religious behaviour, in which multiple types of communities, both overlapping with and differing from that of the *polis*, are engaging in religious activity motivated by a wider spectrum of political, social, economic, cultural and religious factors.

Secondly, current scholarship in Greek religion has often been blind to the importance of the religious landscape—where the focus is not simply on activity within a particular sanctuary but more importantly on the potential for the perception of similarity and difference

---

[52] Cf. D. Harris 1995, 17. Compare also Plato, who argued that the Athenians were masters at the art of trading with the gods: Pl. *Euthphr.* 14e.

[53] Sourvinou-Inwood 1990; *eadem* 2000. For a recent critique of this approach: Kindt 2009.

across the Greek world. Here too, inventories, because of the way in which they provoke both political and religious relationships between different individuals, *poleis* and sanctuaries, offer us a particular way into mapping and interpreting that wider landscape. They allow us to think about the way in which the inscribed presentation of objects associated with Greek religious ritual both offered a communality of experience and identity at the same time as distinguishing difference. They allow us to develop a more nuanced perspective on the Greeks' perception of the variety of their own religious landscape.

Finally, these inventories help us illuminate the interplay between Greek religious practice and the ancient economy. Irrespective of their legibility and degree of functionality, these inventories give Greek piety an economic value. They, alongside other types of financial and accounting documents to be found in Greek sanctuaries like the building accounts for the Parthenon and other temples, translate the Greeks' relationship with the divine into a tangible product, illuminating a series of assets which have to be maintained and managed as part of the sanctuary's and *polis*' economic value and activity. Inventories highlight, once again, the interconnectedness of Greek religion to every part of Greek society and livelihood. By their presence as monuments, as well as by their text, inventories promote the series of relationships in which they, and their surroundings, are involved. They are inscribed performances of the centrality, fluidity and interconnectedness of religion in the Greek world.

MICHAEL SCOTT
Darwin College
Cambridge University
michaelcscott@gmail.com

Bibliography

Aleshire 1989 — S.B. Aleshire, *The Athenian Asklepieion: The people, their dedications and the inventories*, Amsterdam 1989.

Camp 2001 — J. Camp, *The archaeology of Athens*, New Haven 2001.

Davies 1994 — J.K. Davies, 'Accounts and accountability in Classical Athens', in Osborne & Hornblower 1994, 201–212.

Dignas 2002 — B. Dignas, '"Inventories" or "offering lists"? Assessing the wealth of Apollo Didymaeus', *ZPE* 138, 2002, 235–244.

Günther 1988 — W. Günther, '"Vieux et inutilisable" dans un inventaire inédit de Milet', in Knoepfler 1988, 215–237.

Hamilton 2000 — R. Hamilton, *Treasure map: A guide to the Delian inventories*, Michigan 2000.

Hansen 1991 — M. Hansen, *Athenian democracy in the age of Demosthenes*, London 1991.

D. Harris 1994 — D. Harris, 'Freedom of information and accountability: The inventory lists of the Parthenon', in Osborne & Hornblower 1994, 213–225.

D. Harris 1995 — D. Harris, *The treasures of the Parthenon and the Erechtheion*, Oxford 1995.

W.V. Harris 1989 — W.V. Harris, *Ancient literacy*, Cambridge, Mass. 1989.

Harvey 1966 — F.D. Harvey, 'Literacy in the Athenian democracy', *RÉG* 79, 1966, 585–635.

Hedrick 1994
C.W. Hedrick, 'Writing, reading and democracy', in Osborne & Hornblower 1994, 157–174.

Higbie 2003
C. Higbie, *The Lindean chronicle and the Greek creation of their past*, Oxford 2003.

Kindt 2009
J. Kindt, 'Polis religion – a critical appreciation', *Kernos* 22, 2009, 9–34.

Knoepfler 1988
Comptes et inventoires dans la cité grecque, ed. D. Knoepfler, Neuchâtel 1988.

Lewis 1959
D. Lewis, 'Attic manumissions', *Hesperia* 28, 1959, 208–238.

Lewis 1968
D. Lewis, 'Dedications of phialai at Athens', *Hesperia* 37, 1968, 368–380.

Lewis 1986
D. Lewis, 'Temple inventories in ancient Greece', in *Pots and pans. A colloquium on precious metals and ceramics*, ed. M.J. Vickers, Oxford 1986, 71–82.

Lewis 1988
D. Lewis, 'The last inventories of the Treasurers of Athena', in Knoepfler 1988, 297–308.

Linders 1972
T. Linders, *Studies in the treasure records of Artemis Brauronia found in Athens*, Athens 1972.

Linders 1988
T. Linders, 'The purpose of inventories: A close reading of the Delian inventories of the Independence', in Knoepfler 1988, 37–48.

Linders 1992
T. Linders, 'Inscriptions and orality', *Symbolae Osloenses* 67, 1992, 27–40.

Michel 1900
C. Michel, *Recueil d'inscriptions Grecques*, Paris 1900.

Murray 1980
O. Murray, *Early Greece*, Brighton 1980.

Ober 1989
J. Ober, *Mass and elite in democratic Athens*, Princeton 1989.

Osborne 1999
R. Osborne, 'Inscribing performance', in *Performance culture and Athenian democracy*, eds. R. Osborne & S. Goldhill, Cambridge 1999, 341–358.

Osborne 2011
R. Osborne, 'Greek inscriptions as historical writing', in *The Oxford History of historical writing* vol. 1, eds. A. Feldherr & G. Hardy, Oxford, 2011, 97–121.

Osborne & Hornblower 1994
Ritual, finance, politics, eds. R. Osborne & S. Hornblower, Oxford 1994.

Pébarthe 2006
C. Pébarthe, *Cité, démocratie et écriture. Histoire de l'alphabétisation d'Athènes à l'époque classique*, Paris 2006.

Peppas-Delmousou 1988
D. Peppas-Delmousou, 'Autour des inventaires de Brauron', in Knoepfler 1988, 323–346.

Rhodes 2001
P.J. Rhodes, 'Public documents in the Greek states: Archives and inscriptions: Part I and II', *GaR* 48, 2001, 33–44, 136–153.

Richter 1961
G.M. Richter, *The Archaic gravestones of Attica*, London 1961.

Samons 1996
L. Samons, 'The "Kallias Decrees" and the inventories of Athena's treasure in the Parthenon', *CQ* 46, 1996, 91–102.

Samons 2000
L. Samons, *Empire of the owl: Athenian imperial finance*, Stuttgart 2000.

Sickinger 1999
J. P. Sickinger, *Public records and archives in Classical Athens*, Chapel Hill 1999.

Sourvinou-Inwood 1990   C. Sourvinou-Inwood, 'What is *polis* religion?', in *The Greek city from Homer to Alexander*, eds. O. Murray & S.R.F. Price, Oxford 1990, 295–322. (Reprint in *Oxford readings in Greek religion*, ed. R. Buxton, Oxford 2000, 13–37.)

Sourvinou-Inwood 2000   C. Sourvinou-Inwood, 'Further aspects of *polis* religion', in *Oxford readings in Greek religion*, ed. R. Buxton, Oxford 2000, 38–55.

de Ste-Croix 1956   G. de Ste-Croix, 'Greek and Roman accounting', in *Studies in the history of accounting*, eds. A.C. Littleton & B.S. Yamey, London 1956, 14–74.

Thomas 1992   R. Thomas, *Literacy and orality in ancient Greece*, Cambridge 1992.

Tréheux 1988a   J. Tréheux, 'Observations sur les inventaires du Brauronian de l'Acropole d'Athènes', in Knoepfler 1988, 347–355.

Tréheux 1988b   J. Tréheux, 'Une nouvelle lecture des inventaires d'Apollon à Délos', in Knoepfler 1988, 27–35.

Walbank 1982   M.B. Walbank, 'The confiscation and sale of the Poletai in 402/1BC of the property of the Thirty Tyrants', *Hesperia* 51, 1982, 74–98.

Whitley 1997   J. Whitley, 'Cretan laws and Cretan literacy', *AJA* 101, 1997, 635–661.

NASSOS PAPALEXANDROU

Vision and visuality in the study of Early Greek religion

Memory of Eun-Su Lee, 1971–2009

Abstract

A fruitful, but insufficiently explored, domain of Greek religious practice has to do with vision in the nexus of religious experiences. Drawing on recent studies on the theory and anthropology of vision and visual culture, this paper is based on the premise that vision is a culturally conditioned category of human behaviour. The exploration of the cognitive and psychological dimensions of active vision and its objects involves the consideration of the multiple ways of seeing and being seen. The Homeric corpus, for example, points to the complexity of phenomena of vision in a period of intensive contacts and dialogues with the cultures of the Near East. Moreover, the importance of material culture in this inquiry can not be emphasized enough. It is of primary importance to ask how material objects were meant to be seen, by whom, under what circumstances, and to what ends.

Introduction

What is the role of vision in Early Greek religion? What modes of viewing were attendant to the special circumstances of religious practice? The formulation of these questions is possible as long as we provide the qualification from the very beginning that vision was inseparable from the other senses in the actuality of religious experience in ancient Greece.[1] From the very beginning, Greek worship was predicated on "multisensory" *dromena*, the aural, gustatory, olfactory, tactile and visual components of which effected communication among humans and between humans and gods.[2] Isolating vision, therefore, as an object of inquiry is only a heuristic step, albeit a necessary one for reconstituting an important component of a hitherto elusive aspect of life in Early Greece. In this paper I start by delineating certain theoretical and methodological considerations that pertain to my analysis of the problem of vision in Early Greek culture. In particular, I begin by situating the study of vision in current discussions regarding the global intellectual and social history of the five senses; then I foreground the concept of visuality as a fundamental tool for addressing the role of visual culture in the shaping of religious environments; and finally I conclude by looking closely at textual and material sources and what they have to offer to this inquiry. Throughout I will explore the idea that

---

[1] This study is the result of my preoccupation with two projects, titled "Art as a means of communication in preliterate societies", and "Monsters, Fear, and the Uncanny in Early Greek Visual Culture". I would like to thank the organizers and Maria Mili for the invitation to present my work and for a very stimulating scholarly event in Athens.

[2] The concerted multisensoriality of Greek religion has not been subjected to rigorous scholarly analysis. Numerous studies treat various aspects of it. See, for example, Burkert 1983 and Parisinou 2000.

Early Greek sanctuaries functioned by default as crucibles for the negotiation, institutionalization, and control of special *viewing attitudes* towards the formidable objects that shaped their otherworldly sacred ambience.

Vision is not a universal category

First and foremost I would like to stress that vision is not a universal category of human experience. It is important to clarify that humans have not always looked at the world with the same, unchanging eyes. The practices and attitudes constituting seeing as action, conscious or unconscious, are conditioned by cultural norms and the degree to which groups or individuals subscribe to or resist the maintenance of these cultural norms. As Robert Nelson has aptly put it "... visuality is similar to sexuality. Both pertain to natural and universal human acts, but both are also learned, socially controlled, and organized, and therefore domesticated".[3] Recent anthropological work, both theoretical and applied, has emphasized the historical contingency of vision and the other senses.[4] As far as the Early Greek world is concerned, even a cursory look at Raymond Prier's important study *Thauma Idesthai. The phenomenology of sight and appearance in Archaic Greek* establishes the cultural specificity of vision in early Greece.[5] Prier has focused on the semantic connotations of Early Greek terms for vision, seeing, and its objects. His insights on the multiple ways of seeing in the Greek epic and lyric reveal a diverse and wide array of physical and cognitive action involved in looking and viewing.

McLuhan's/Ong's binary model and critique thereof

Second, it is important to point out that any discussion of Early Greek vision needs to take into account the most influential model regarding the cognitive role of the senses in past societies. We owe this model to the work of Marshall McLuhan and Walter Ong, who predicated a fundamental cultural shift in the invention and dissemination of typography from the Renaissance onwards.[6] This is essentially a binary model that opposes the dominance of sound and hearing in the pre-Renaissance period to the increasing primacy of vision and its printed objects as cognitive tools from the Renaissance until the twentieth century. Ong's insights were formed as oral-formulaic theory established itself as the primary explanation for the composition of the Early Greek and other epic traditions. It was partly on the work of Adam Perry and Alfred Lord that Walter Ong based his delineation of what he called "the cognitive psychodynamics of orality" (in his *Orality and literacy*)—essentially how the self constitutes its cognitive relationship with itself and the cosmos in contexts of primary orality.[7]

The importance of this binary model in the hermeneutic endeavours of the humanities and the social sciences in the last generation cannot be overemphasized. However, scholars have recently been critical of this model, especially regarding its reductionist character, its rigidity, and its oversight of various facets of the sensorium in history, both before and after the Renaissance.[8] The disequilibrium of this binary approach is most salient when it neglects the active agency of visual culture, in periods before the Renaissance. This is partly the result

---

[3] Nelson 2000, 8–9.
[4] This is a primary tenet of the so-called "anthropology of the senses". See Howes 2003, 29–58.
[5] Prier 1989.

[6] McLuhan 1962; Ong 1982.
[7] Ong 1982, 31–77.
[8] Smith 2007, 1–19; Howes 1991; Howes 2003, 3–28.

of the fact that scholarship has been slow to ask precisely *how the artworks and images were meant to function as means of communication or media for the storage and dissemination of information*. Even the very idea that art has semantic functions other than aesthetic has been met with resistance. In view of this situation the following questions are in order: what was the cognitive value of images or other visual materials in antiquity? Is it possible to assess the viewing subjects' reactions on the basis of textual sources and archaeological evidence? Provided that vision is culturally constructed, as I proposed above, what were the specifically Greek ways of looking at things? And finally, what is the formative role of vision in the religious experience of early Greeks?

Visuality

In response to these questions I propose to build upon the notion of *visuality*, an analytical tool that, to my knowledge, has not been put to work in the study of Early Greek culture. My understanding of "visuality" encompasses the culturally conditioned modes of seeing, or being seen, as *active practices*, which are regulated, on the one hand, by social norms, and, on the other, by the status and availability of the visual domain in a certain cultural environment.[9] Both practices of seeing and the status of the visual are interdependent and they cannot be examined in relationships of cause and effect. They are two facets of the same coin, continuously shaping each other in the actuality of social life. First I will discuss the active practices

of seeing and then I will proceed to address the status and availability of the visual.

ACTIVE SEEING

The active practices of seeing should be understood as learned behaviours of response such as the viewing subjects' attentive gazing, their proximity to the objects of vision (proxemics), strategies of decodement, attendant bodily gestures or movement (kinesics), and oral or other physical or mental responses. A good example of this is the reaction of audiences, intended and unintended, to the synaesthetic effect of the shield of Achilles in the *Iliad*. The thunderous (*anevrache*) effect of the divinely crafted weapons signals the overwhelming effect of both their figural content and their technological complexity. It causes fear and trepidation among the Myrmidons, who avoid visual contact with them precisely as they would before actual divine beings. It is easy to dismiss this as evidence of response in a religious setting. However, there is no doubt that the type and the imagery of the intricately crafted round shield reflects the well-known category of hammered shields that became current in Cretan and other sanctuaries from the late ninth century BC.[10] It is perhaps not by accident that the foundational myth and ritual in the Idaian cave, the find spot *par excellence* of the Cretan shields, features complex synaesthetic phenomena that resonate with the aurality of Achilles' weapons.

---

[9] On visuality, see Nelson 2000; Mirzoeff 1999; Heywood & Sandywell 1999. For systematic applications of the concept in Classical studies, see Clarke 2003; Zanker 2004; Elsner 2007. An important component of this inquiry has to do with ongoing research in the neurophysiology of vision. See, for example, Zeki 1999.

[10] Kunze 1933; Matthäus 2005.

... the goddess laid the armor down at Achilles' feet

And the gear clashed out in all its blazoned glory (*anevrache daidala panta*)

A tremor ran through all (*hele tromos*)

the Myrmidon ranks ... none dared

To look straight at the glare, each fighter shrank away (*anten eisideein ... etresan*)

Not Achilles. The more he gazed, the deeper his anger went,

(*hôs eid', ws min mallon edu cholos*)

His eyes flashing under his eyelids, fierce as fire ... (*...osse deinon...hôs eis selas exephaathen*)

Exulting, holding the god's shining gifts in his hands (*en cheiressin echôn*)

At once he'd thrilled his heart with looking hard at the armor's well-wrought beauty ...

(*... tetarpeto daidala leussôn ...*)

(*Iliad*, book 19, ll. 15–27, transl. Robert Fagles)

Notwithstanding the enhancing and distancing effect of epic rhetoric, the importance of the narrative here cannot be overemphasized. This sensitive moment associates a range of sentiments with the effect of a divinely crafted visual work. In doing so, I would argue that here the epic prescribes a multiplicity of attitudes towards the prototypical figurative work in the Greek epic. On the one hand, we see the Myrmidons averting their gaze with trepidation because of the aural and visual power of the shield; on the other hand, Achilles is modelled as an ideal viewer whose gaze shines with the intensity of *selas* as he experiences an uncanny mixture of intense aesthetic delight (*tetarpeto*) and *cholos*. It is important to stress the synergy of other senses here: Achilles' *cholos* (gall) references his anger (*mênis*), but the very same word evokes the bitter taste of *cholos*. Likewise the action of vision has a tactile component: Achilles looks while he explicitly handles (*en*

cheiressin) the divine artefacts. Conversely, the Myrmidons turn away, they instinctively distance themselves under the force of the shield's radiance and monstrous appearance.

This association of vision and the visual object with ambivalent sentiments and divergent attitudes appears elsewhere in early Greek sources.[11] I would argue that it derives from the uncertain status of the visually endowed artefacts precisely when the Greek world experiences a shock under the influx of new media and techniques of representation. The epic ideology reserves aesthetic delight for Achilles, the ideal viewer, and by extension, to the elites of the period that model themselves after the best of the Achaians.

The ambivalent response to the epic shield is also of interest because it highlights the active efficacy of the artwork itself. Anthropologist Alfred Gell has emphasized that artefacts (works of art, visually endowed objects) exercise their own active agency not only towards viewers but all around their surrounding environments.[12] That is, they shape their perceptual environments no less than the responses they make possible by means of their physical attributes. I have elsewhere discussed the ambient space of artefacts as a "performance arena"—to be understood as the space in which responses to the artefact are dramatized and ritualized in the form of enactments that substantiate the *kleos* of the artefact as social and religious value.[13] This status is evident in the earliest verbal testimonies on dedicatory objects. I mention, for example, the Boiotian Mantiklos statuette in Boston (MFA 03.997), the inscription of which endows it with its own "subjective" voice (*Mantiklos m' anetheken*) that sets it in a one-to-one dialogue with Apollo, the recipient

---

11 Constantinidou 1994, 11–15.
12 Gell 1998.
13 Papalexandrou 2005, 2–3.

of the dedication (*Fig. 1*).[14] I will have more to say on this later on, but right now I would like to emphasize the function of the inscription as a visual trope that attracts the scrutinizing, decoding gaze of both mortal and immortal viewers. The multisensory effect of the combination of inscription (meant to be performed out loud), sculpture (meant to be seen and to cast its gaze) and attendant sanctuary circumstances can only be imagined today.

Status of the visual

My discussion so far has established that an account of the religious aspects of Early Greek visuality encompasses the mutual relationships between viewers and objects in the context of Early Greek sanctuaries and sacred space. The exact nature of these relationships is interdependent with the *status of the visual* in Early Greek culture and society. That is to say, there is a dialectic relationship between the visual practices at large and the special modes of viewing at work in the context of sacred space and practice.

The status of the visual pertains to the availability of the visual media and to the varying degrees that visual or special artefacts are experienced in the actuality of social life. Although rigid in its implications, Marshal McLuhan's concept of the "ratio of sensory perception" is useful in our attempts to reflect upon the intensity and quality of Early Greek visual cultures.[15] As I discussed above, McLuhan posited that cultures are cognitively determined by the varying degrees to which certain technologies

of communication privilege one sense or another. In other words, the dominance of one sensory faculty over another is predicated on the prevalence of media that function as extensions of the human senses. In Greece, for example, McLuhan would have a good reason to argue that in the pre-alphabetic Iron Age, the dominant technology of communication was speech and all its mnemotechnic inflections, whereas the dominant sense was hearing, with sight, vision, and its objects standing at a much lower level in the hierarchy of the human sensorium. Similarly McLuhan argued that in the post World War II period, western culture witnessed a resuscitation of orality/aurality mainly because of the dominance of media such as radio, television, film, and photography.

Using this "ratio of sensory perception" as a tool of analysis in comparison with the archaeological evidence regarding the quality and nature of visual media, I would argue that the earlier part of the Early Iron Age was a period of extremely restricted visuality. Even if we reckon with materials that do not survive in the archaeological record, we are left with a material and visual deficit, the most striking symptom of which is the extreme scarcity and conscious avoidance of figuration—a complicated phenomenon for which at the moment no single explanation has been met with consensus.[16] It is as if the dominant sense in the period was not *vision* but *hearing* and the fact that it is precisely during this period that the oral tradition of epic was gradually forged as the authoritative medium *par excellence* would seem to corroborate this. Would this mean, then, that the cognitive input of vision in religious experience was of no consequence during this period? The answer to this question cannot be negative, if we take into account the nuanced lexicon of vi-

---

[14] See Papalexandrou 2005, 84–86, where the argument is put forward that this bronze was originally attached to a tripod cauldron. On the performativity of the inscription, see Day 1994. See Papalexandrou 2005, for a systematic exploration of the performativity of dedications before the introduction of writing.
[15] McLuhan 1962; McLuhan 1964.

[16] See, for example, Kopcke 1977; Rystedt 1999; Lemos 2000; Rystedt & Wells 2006.

sion preserved in the Homeric epic.[17] Until the eighth century BC the crux of cultic life and experiences evolved around performative events, such as dances, prayers, processions, sacrifices and other enactments, which are not easily recognizable in the archaeological record. As Walter Burkert has aptly put it "... the seriousness, the gravity, and the solemnity of religion is bound not to tales about gods but to the institutions of ritual, which are mainly, sacrifice, libation, and prayers".[18] Active involvement of participants in these ritual events entailed the synergy of the entire sensorium, with hearing perhaps more attuned to the cadences, pitch, and tempo of religious song and utterances, whereas vision would have been more alert to the observance and registration of significant gestures, textures, colours, and patterns of movement.

Now, if we switch our attention to the period starting in the late ninth century onwards, we have to seriously consider the gradual and systematic emphasis on material culture appearing with the explosive force of a big-bang in various contexts of life, but more emphatically so in the context of Greek sanctuaries. If we are to think once more in terms of McLuhan's "ratio of sensory perception", then we have to concede that in the Greek sanctuaries, at least, there was much more to stimulate the senses, and that material culture, in its most exquisite forms, contributed a great deal to the elaboration of new religious experiences and sentiments. What was the role of vision in this age of radical reorientation, experiments, and social change? In the remainder of this paper I will focus on certain dimensions of this new visuality. First, I address the issue of accessibility, both physical and cognitive, of the sanctuaries and their wondrous contents in the eighth

and seventh centuries BC. Second, I will consider the cultural registration of a new aesthetic that was predicated on the category of *daidalon*, a notion which encapsulates visual, social, and religious values. This will lead my discussion to the visual action entailed by the experience of *daidalon*, epitomized in the formulaic expression of *thauma idesthai* ("a wonder to behold"). Finally, I will focus on material evidence for clues that point to the new visuality also involving new conceptions and actions of vision, namely evidence from the representation of vision in the visual arts and the emphasis on the monstrous and monstrosity in Greek art from the eighth century onwards.

Accessibility/visibility versus invisibility. Who looks?

To begin with, it is important to establish whether the developments of the eighth century overturned the condition of *restricted visuality* I described above as a quintessential cultural condition in the first centuries of the first millennium. At first sight, it would seem that in the eighth century the plethora of new technologies such as figuration, and the wondrous artefacts found in numerous sanctuaries, would point to an expanded, easily available, and widely shared visuality. However, there are reasons to argue that this was not necessarily the case. Scholars, such as James Whitley, have effectively argued for the rigorous application of rationing in Early Iron Age societies—certain groups impose restrictions on the usage of certain categories of material culture or expressive media as means of social differentiation.[19] It is possible that similar restrictions apply to special spaces or to the physical or cognitive accessibility of certain aspects of material culture—I am thinking again of the sanctuar-

17   Prier 1989.
18   Burkert 1991, 84. Same article is reprinted in Burkert 2001.

19   Whitley 1991, 192–194.

Fig. 1. The dedication of Mantiklos. Museum of Fine Arts, Boston, 03.997, H. 20.3 cm, Francis Bartlett Donation of 1900. Photograph © 2003 Museum of Fine Arts.

ies and their contents. Moreover, our scholarly practices may occlude the true dimensions of ancient visualities. The accumulation of visual objects between the covers of publications or in museum displays creates new experiences that efface the ancient contexts, intensity, frequency and duration of seeing and being seen.[20] It is therefore legitimate to ask: Who looks, or rather, who is allowed to look, and how, and for how long, and when? One thinks, for example, of the wondrous tripods of Hephaistos in *Iliad* 18.376–377. These are made to move out to the visibility of the divine performative space (*agon*) only for a short while and then they move back to the mystique and secrecy of an interior space (*doma*). This passage from invisibility to visibility and vice versa alludes to the manipulation of vision and its cognitive objects in the Early Greek sanctuaries.[21] Who is present when these objects are visible, or who is allowed to get close to them when they form the material focus of performative events? The same questions are prompted by the explicit mention of all the Delphic riches in an interior space at Delphi (*Il.* 9.381: *lainos oudos entos eergei*). The threshold of stone stands metonymically for a barrier that protects but it can equally be understood as a device that conceals and hides magnificent sacred objects that are not for everybody to see. Religious establishments are often opaque, secretive, and strict in controlling information about and knowledge of their extraordinary or sacred objects, traditions, and enactments. In this way they establish a buffer zone between the cultic focus and viewing or perceiving subjects; that is, they cre-

ate "distance" or "resistance," all inflections of which (e.g. physical or psychological) enhance their ambience of supernatural otherness.[22] In their effort to enhance their prestige and otherworldly aura, the Greek sanctuaries would have instituted mechanisms of controlling the sensory and cognitive accessibility to their magnificent possessions and the enactments that gave them religious and social meaning. I suspect, for example, that a specific instantiation of this phenomenon is presented by the well-known, yet poorly understood as functional objects or as objects of vision, orientalizing cauldrons.[23] Excavations have produced numerous specimens of them in many sanctuaries of the Greek world, yet we have extremely few representations in art and only a single mention in the available textual sources.[24] This discrepancy becomes all the more striking if we consider the rival objects, the numerous tripod cauldrons, about which there are numerous mentions in texts, an abundance of iconographic sources from the eighth century onwards, and a well-documented range of important religious values.[25]

Daidalon/nature of the art work

At this point, it is useful to switch our focus to exactly how the early Greeks conceptualized the extraordinary objects of vision in their sacred spaces. In particular, I would like to call

---

[20]   This is not meant to downplay the hard work of those involved in the scholarly reproduction of material culture. My aim is to stress the arbitrariness of our own cognitive media, which can obscure as much as they enlighten, especially when it comes to the question of meaning. See discussion in Shanks & Tilley 1992, 68–100.
[21]   Papalexandrou 2005, 30–33, 65–67.

[22]   Gilsenan 2000, 77–78; for a specific example of this phenomenon, see Papalexandrou 2008a.
[23]   Papalexandrou, forthcoming.
[24]   See the list of representations of Orientalizing cauldrons in Sakowski 1998, 61–70; Papalexandrou (forthcoming) undertakes a systematic analysis of the nature of these representations.
[25]   Papalexandrou 2005; *idem* 2008b. On representations of tripod cauldrons in a variety of media, see Sakowski 1997.

attention to the seminal role of the category *daidalon* in this discussion—a term that only very partially approximates to the dominant definition of "art" in Western culture from the Renaissance onwards. The Greeks and their neighbours instead favoured functional objects that were intricately crafted, in exotic and expensive materials of rare and enchanting technical, formal, and sensory qualities such as metallic shine and resonance, colour, size, shape, figurative content and a mind-boggling number of ornaments.[26] All these qualities were understood or at least they were presented as divine in quality and origin. These objects were otherworldly and extremely valuable, and their fame, enshrined in oral poetry, was programmed to circulate far and wide along with the fame of their distinguished divine and mortal owners. It would not be excessive to state that these *daidala* were meant as much to be seen in the exclusive circumstances of the sanctuaries as to circulate widely in the elaborate oral media of the time. As the Homeric *ekphrasis* of the shield of Achilles shows, the performativity of the artwork/*daidalon* was a quality inherent to its nature, social life, and reception. It constituted a religious value no less than the other outstanding qualities of the object.

Ways of seeing/*thauma idesthai*

A deeper understanding of the sacred character of the *daidalon* is possible, if we pause for a moment to consider attentively the kind of visual action warranted by the nature of the *daidalon*. The language of epic contains a nuanced vocabulary for the expression of attentive looking at extraordinary objects. For example, we saw Achilles experiencing delight from

handling the divine armour while looking at it with radiant eyes. In this instance, the lexical economy of the epic employs the verb *leussein*, the semantic connotations of which have to do with the intense experience of objects that emit light.[27] An even more intense sentiment is communicated by verbs denoting wonder, stupefaction, or marvel at visual experiences (*theaesthai/theesthai/thaumazein*). To look attentively at *daidala* is tantamount to wonder, that is, you stop dead in your tracks and you surrender all your senses to a protracted experience of the extraordinary.[28] The formulaic expression of this aesthetic of wondrous experience is epitomized in the phrase *thauma idesthai* ("a wonder to behold"), which always accompanies the description of magnificent, otherworldly artefacts, such as the automatic tripods of Hephaistos or Aphrodite's shiny garments in the *Iliad*. This is, of course, the vocabulary of a specialized poetic language. Nevertheless, I would argue that it was precisely in the performative contexts of Greek religion that this vocabulary was forged to express an authoritative ideology and morality of material culture. Its usage in the epic can be understood as an idealized projection of attitudes and behaviours that were exclusive to those who had access to the Greek sanctuaries and their formidable contents.

Figures see: Vision represented

This new visuality and its inflections may account for the radically new emphasis on the very organ of vision, which appears in the representational arts from the second half of the eighth century BC onwards. To repeat the old descriptive trope, it is as if all of a sud-

---

[26] On the category "daidalon" see discussions in Morris 1992; Himmelmann 1998; Papalexandrou 2005.

[27] Prier 1989, 68–71.
[28] Hunzinger 2002; Prier 1989, 81–108; Himmelmann 1998.

den likenesses of humans and animals opened their eyes to the world and started looking attentively, if not aggressively, at their surroundings. This is manifest in artefacts found in both graves and sanctuaries, as the illustrated examples make clear (*Fig. 1*: Mantiklos bronze in MFA, Boston; *Fig. 2*: Ivory goddess from Dipylon; *Fig. 3*: the eyes of bronze griffins from Olympia). These phenomena have been explained as symptomatic of the formal surrender of the abstract art of Greece to naturalistic influences from the Near East. This interpretive line, however, turns out to be narrow in scope, if we consider the pragmatic functions of these visual objects, that is, their interactive character in the actuality of ritual practice. They look at you so that you, divine or mortal, look back at them only to become emotionally and cognitively enchanted by them. As Irene Winter has recently shown, these functions are exemplary of a millennia-old tradition of mutual communication between figures and their divine or mortal onlookers in various regions of the Near East.[29] In view of this cultic pedigree, the appearance of the same practice in the Greek world cannot be the result only of artistic influence—artists or patrons making choices out of a new pool of models. An entire system of seeing and being seen must have been infused into the Greek world, and the critical question is not whether foreigners or their products are to account for this new visuality. Rather, we should ask, what kind of interactions, exchanges, negotiations, and strategies were at work when divergent visualities

Fig. 2. Dipylon Ivory Goddess, Athens NM 776. Photograph: Hermann Wagner, D-DAI-ATH-NM 3282A, Neg. All rights reserved. Courtesy DAI Athen.

---

[29]   Winter 2000. See Papalexandrou 2010 for a discussion of Early Greek visuality as a product of hybrid contacts and interactions.

Fig. 3. Bronze Griffin from Olympia, detail. Photo: author.

converged or met each other? A good example in this discussion is once again the Mantiklos statuette in the Museum of Fine Arts at Boston (*Fig. 1*).[30] Its type and iconography place it in the old Geometric tradition of the warrior statuettes of the ninth and eighth centuries BC. In formal terms, however, this figure has abandoned the iconic, hieroglyphic (formulaic) function of the old type. This is especially evident in the rendering of the head. Instead of the abstract simplicity of the Late Geometric idiom, it featured extraordinarily penetrating eyes, probably in a precious material that animated the bronze figure.[31] These eyes, I submit, thematized vision as a quintessential aspect of the figure and its religious "content." In doing so they attracted attention to themselves, to the gaze they cast, and to the visuality inherent in the dialogic experience of the figure.

---

[30] Papalexandrou 2005, 84–86.

[31] The now lost eyes were most probably of glass or stone. See Kozloff & Mitten 1988, 53. Bone or semi-precious stones cannot be excluded, however.

Fig. 4. Idaian Cave Shield, line drawing (the so-called "hunt" shield), Herakleion Museum 7.

Monsters and vision: Monsters attract vision

Similar questions are in order regarding the appearance of monstrosity, which makes itself manifest in the Greek arts from the late eighth century onwards.[32] My examples this time are from the visual arts of Crete, an island with plenty of evidence for mixed populations and intercultural contact from the ninth to the seventh centuries BC. Here, the most striking example of iconographic, stylistic, and technical novelty is provided by the famous votive shields

from the Idaian Cave, Zeus' famous birthplace, on Mount Ida (*Fig. 4*). Scholars have been able to detect iconographic and stylistic elements of North Syrian and Neo-Assyrian art in these shields, whereas elements of content, syntax, and decoration have been labelled as Greek.[33] What state of visuality does this hybridity point to? At this point, it is important to stress the unprecedented emphasis on the visual *as special religious experience* that these objects demonstrate. More specifically, the context of cult suggests a framework of rare and wondrous experiences: certain iconographic elements dis-

---

[32]   Padgett 2003.

[33]   Kunze 1933; Matthäus 2005; Hoffman 2005.

close the *epiphany of divinities*, a cultic element with deep roots in the Bronze Age cultures of Crete but also current in the art and rituals of many Near Eastern contexts.[34] Other elements are construed to invite scrutiny and close attention. Pride of place among these is emphasis on detailed and visual narratives, but also the frequent appendage of lion protomes in the middle of the visual field of the shields (*Fig. 4*). Ferocious and merciless, with their predatory gazes and thunderous roars, these monsters hark back to the ubiquitous monsters of Near Eastern daemonology and, like all monsters in art, they have been viewed as apotropaic in nature, that is, guardian figures against human or numinous enemies. This may be true to a large extent. Yet, I would argue that the monstrous, by means of its idiosyncratic visual nature, was meant to call attention to the very act of close viewing and scrutiny as appropriate modes of interaction with extraordinary objects. The same response must have been elicited by the crispness of incision and the tactile vivacity of the shallow repoussé work. This engagement was predicated on the performative circumstances that framed the visibility and accessibility of these special objects. Like the shield of Achilles, the Orientalizing shields of Greece caused terror even as they opened new unexplored vistas for the cognitive initiation and delectation of their mixed viewers.

Conclusion

In conclusion, I have tried above to explore the input of vision and its objects to the religious experiences of early Greeks. I repeat again that vision is only part of a complex synergy of sensory experiences whose affective qualities in-

formed what one experienced in sacred space. Throughout my discussion I emphasized that the extraordinary objects that contributed to the ambience of sacred spaces were inseparable from their "performative software", in brief, the performative events that established their values. The Early Greek lexicon still preserves the special ways of looking and interaction that were part and parcel of how one was supposed to interact with the material culture deposited in the sanctuaries. Objects were an essential component of the extraordinary ambience of sacred space as objects of admiration and attentive looking, as carriers of memories, and as containers of the *kleos* of humans and gods.

NASSOS PAPALEXANDROU
Department of Art and Art History
The University of Texas at Austin
papalex@mail.utexas.edu

Bibliography

Burkert 1997 — W. Burkert, 'From epiphany to cult statue: Early Greek *Theos*', in *What is a God? Studies in the nature of Greek divinity*, London 1997, 15–34.

Burkert 1991 — W. Burkert, 'Homer's anthropomorphism: Narrative and ritual', in *New perspectives in Early Greek art*, ed. D. Buitron Oliver, Washington DC 1991, 81–91. (Reprinted in Walter Burkert, *Kleine Schriften* I. *Homerica*, ed. C. Riedweg, Göttingen 2001, 80–94.)

Burkert 1983 — W. Burkert, *Homo Necans: The anthropology of Greek sacrificial ritual and myth*, Berkeley 1983.

---

[34]   The bibliography on epiphany is extensive. See Burkert 1987; *idem* 1997; on the epiphanic nature of Idaian cave bronzes, see Gehrig 2004, 168–171.

Clarke 2003   J. Clarke, *Art in the lives of ordinary Romans: Visual representation and non-elite viewers in Italy, 100 B.C.–A.D. 315*, Berkeley 2003.

Constantin-idou 1994   S. Constantinidou, 'The vision of Homer: The eyes of heroes and gods', *Antichthon* 28, 1994, 1–16.

Day 1994   J. Day, 'Interactive offerings: Early Greek dedications and ritual', *HSCP* 96, 1994, 37–94.

Elsner 2007   J. Elsner, *Roman eyes: Visuality and subjectivity in art and text*, Princeton 2007.

Gehrig 2004   U. Gehrig, *Die Greifenprotomen aus dem Heraion von Samos* (Samos, 9), Bonn 2004.

Gell 1998   A. Gell, *Art and agency: An anthropological theory*, Oxford 1998.

Gilsenan 2000   M. Gilsenan, *Recognizing Islam: Religion and society in the modern Middle East*, New York 2000.

Heywood & Sandywell 1999   *Interpreting visual culture: Explorations in the hermeneutics of the visual*, eds. I. Heywood & B. Sandywell, London 1999.

Himmel-mann 1998   N. Himmelmann, 'The plastic arts in Homeric society', in *Reading Greek art: Essays by Nikolaus Himmelmann*, ed. W.A.P. Childs, Princeton 1998, 25–66.

Hoffman 2005   G. Hoffman, 'Defining identities: Greek artistic interaction with the Near East', in *Crafts and images in contact: Studies on Eastern Mediterranean art of the first millennium BCE*, eds. C.E. Suter & C. Uehlinger, Göttingen 2005, 351–388.

Howes 2003   D. Howes, *Sensual relations: Engaging the senses in culture and social history*, Ann Arbor 2003.

Howes 1991   D. Howes, 'To summon all the senses', in *The varieties of sensory experience: A sourcebook in the anthropology of the senses*, ed. D. Howes, Toronto 1991, 3–21.

Hunzinger 2005   C. Hunzinger, 'La perception du merveilleux: θαυμάζω et θηέομαι', in *Études sur la vision dans l' Antiquité classique*, ed. L. Villard, Rouen 2005, 29–38.

Kopcke 1977   G. Kopcke, 'Figures in pot-painting before, during, and after the Dark Ages', in *Symposium on the Dark Ages of Greece*, ed. E.N. Davies, New York 1977, 32–50.

Kozloff & Mitten 1988   A. Kozloff & D.G. Mitten, *The gods delight: The human figure in Classical Bronze*, Cleveland 1988.

Kunze 1933   E. Kunze, *Kretische Bronzereliefs*, Stuttgart 1931.

Lemos 2000   I. Lemos, 'Songs for heroes: The lack of images in early Greece', in *Word and image in ancient Greece*, eds. N.K. Rutter & B.A. Sparkes, Edinburgh 2000, 11–21.

Matthäus 2005   H. Matthäus, 'Toreutik und Vasenmalerei im früheisenzeitlichen Kreta: Minoisches Erbe, locale Traditonen und Fremdeinflüsse', in *Crafts and images in contact: Studies on Eastern Mediterranean art of the first millennium BCE*, eds. C.E. Suter & C. Uehlinger, Göttingen 2005, 291–350.

McLuhan 1962   M. McLuhan, *The Gutenberg galaxy*, Toronto 1962.

McLuhan 1964 — M. McLuhan, *Understanding media*, New York 1964.

Mirzoeff 1999 — N. Mirzoeff, *An introduction to visual culture*, London 1999.

Morris 1992 — S. Morris, *Daidalos and the origins of Greek art*, Princeton 1992.

Nelson 2000 — R.S. Nelson, 'Introduction: Descartes's cow and other domestications of the visual', in *Visuality before and beyond the Renaissance: Seeing as others saw*, ed. R.S. Nelson, Cambridge 2000, 1–23.

Ong 1982 — W.J. Ong, *Orality and literacy: The technologizing of the word*, London & New York 1982.

Padgett 2003 — J.M. Padgett, *The centaur's smile: The human animal in early Greek art*, Princeton 2003.

Papalexandrou 2005 — N. Papalexandrou, *Warriors, youths, and tripods: The visual poetics of power in early Greece*, Lanham, Md 2005.

Papalexandrou 2008a — N. Papalexandrou, 'Hala Sultan Tekke, Cyprus: An elusive landscape of sacredness in a liminal context', *JMGS* 26, 2008, 251–282.

Papalexandrou 2008b — N. Papalexandrou, 'Boiotian Tripods: The tenacity of a Pan-hellenic symbol in a regional context', *Hesperia* 77, 2008, 251–282.

Papalexandrou 2010 — N. Papalexandrou, 'Are there hybridic visual cultures? Reflections on the Orientalizing phenomena in the Mediterranean of the early first millennium B.C.E.', *Ars Orientalis* 38, 2010, 31–48.

Papalexandrou forthcoming — N. Papalexandrou, *Monsters, fear, and the uncanny in Early Greek culture*, forthcoming.

Parisinou 2000 — E. Parisinou, *The light of the gods: The role of light in Archaic and Classical Greek cult*, London 2000.

Prier 1989 — R.A. Prier, *Thauma idesthai: The phenomenology of sight and appearance in Archaic Greek*, Tallahassee 1989.

Rystedt 1999 — E. Rystedt, 'No words, only pictures: Iconography in transition between the Bronze Age and the Iron Age in Greece', *OpAth* 24, 1999, 89–98.

Rystedt & Wells 2006 — *Pictorial pursuits: Figurative painting on Mycenaean and Geometric Pottery. Papers from two seminars at the Swedish Institute at Athens in 1999 and 2001* (ActaAth-4°, 53), eds. E. Rystedt & B. Wells, Stockholm 2006.

Sakowski 1998 — A. Sakowski 'Darstellungen von Greifenkesseln', *BaBesch* 73, 1998, 61–82.

Sakowski 1997 — A. Sakowski, *Darstellungen von Dreifußkesseln in der griechischen Kunst bis zum Beginn der Klassischen Zeit*, Frankfurt am Main 1997.

Shanks & Tilley 1992 — M. Shanks & C. Tilley, *Reconstructing archaeology: Theory and practice*, London & New York 1992.

Smith 2007 — M.M. Smith, *Sensing the past: Seeing, hearing, smelling, tasting and touching in history*, Berkeley & Los Angeles 2007.

Versnel 1987 — H. Versnel, 'What did ancient man see when he saw a god? Some reflections on Greco-

Roman epiphany', in *Effigies Dei: Essays on the history of religions*, ed. D. van der Plas, Leiden 1987, 42–55.

Winter 2000   I.J. Winter, 'The eyes have it: Votive statuary, Gilgamesh's axe, and cathected viewing in the ancient Near East', in *Visuality before and beyond the Renaissance: Seeing as others saw*, ed. R.S. Nelson, Cambridge 2000, 22–44.

Zanker 2004   G. Zanker, *Modes of viewing in Hellenistic poetry and art*, Madison 2004.

Zeki 1999   S. Zeki, *Inner vision: An exploration of art and the brain*, Oxford 1999.

JOANNIS MYLONOPOULOS

Divine images behind bars

THE SEMANTICS OF BARRIERS IN GREEK TEMPLES

Abstract*

In some Greek temples there is a very challenging archi-tectural feature, a barrier of wood, metal or stone before the cult statue. A combination of archaeological data, inscriptions, and literary sources reveals that more tem-ples had a barrier in their cella than scholarship tends to believe. From a terminological point of view, epi-graphic evidence suggests that terms such as ἡ κιγκλίς and ὁ τρύφακτος/δρύφακτος were used to designate a barrier. Pausanias uses a third term, τὸ ἔρυμα, to de-scribe the stone screen wall around the statue of Zeus in Olympia. Among other places, remains of barriers have been archaeologically identified in temples in Aigina, Athens, Kleonai, Lindos, Lykosoura, Olympia, Priene, and Sounion. Scholarly interpretations have viewed barriers in Greek temples either as an aesthetic element for the museum-like presentation of cult images or as an important physical regulator of official and private ritual activity inside the temple. This paper argues that a barrier in a Greek temple was a boundary and at the

same time a sign of the partial accessibility of the cult building on a regular, even daily basis, while the area around the cult statue remained inviolable.

In the late seventh and even more the sixth cen-tury BC, monumental temple architecture and impressive dedications acquired great signifi-cance among Greek cities in their competition for prestige. In the second half of the fifth cen-tury, a new medium made its appearance: the monumental cult statue. Especially after the erection of the chryselephantine masterpieces by Pheidias in Athens and Olympia, divine im-ages entered the arsenal of symbolic weapons, as it were, a "war of monuments". Nearly every Greek community sought to acquire statues that would secure its position in the arena of Panhellenic competition.[1] Cult statues thus be-came more and more necessary to the physical expression of prestige without, however, losing their meaning and function in daily religious life.

In the Greco-Roman world, images in gen-eral and divine images in particular represented a medium of communication on many differ-ent levels. New precious cult statues made by renowned masters such as Pheidias, Praxite-les, or Damophon, and placed in appropriate

* Earlier versions of this paper were presented at the University of Durham (2007), the University of Cali-fornia at Berkeley, and the Free University of Berlin (2008). I would like to thank the audiences in these three places for their constructive remarks. I am also thankful to Jenny Wallensten and Matthew Haysom for the invitation to the conference "Current Approaches to Religion in Ancient Greece", which gave me the opportunity to share my thoughts with friends and colleagues interested in and puzzled by similar prob-lems. Bibliography appearing after January 2009 could not be fully considered. I am very grateful to Dr Irina Oryshkevich for improving my English. All translations are those of the author except where otherwise noted.

---

1 For a somewhat polemic view on "Panhellenism", see Scott 2010, 250–273, esp. 256–260.

architectural settings, served as symbolic but quite explicit indicators of prosperity. At the same time, age-old images equally underscored a city's claim to an authoritative religious position. Nevertheless, the main function of cult statues was not to generate competition, but to offer mediation: while the altar remained the centre of ritual activity, cult images were the main visual point of reference in the communication between mortals and gods.

In ancient Greece, access to ritual communication was relatively open. This openness had a direct impact on the way divine images were presented and displayed in temples. Cult statues were visible, in many cases even touchable, and not hidden behind high, windowless walls. Despite written cult regulations (rather misleadingly called *leges sacrae*), which placed the interaction with the divine under limitations and control,[2] the architectural design of Greek temples leaves no doubt that visual contact between the community and the divinity was of great importance in the performance of rituals. The contrast with temples in different cultural and religious contexts is quite instructive, especially in the case of Egyptian temples. When the latter are compared to the Greek concept of the "house of a god", they demonstrate how a dissimilar religious system was translated into architecture and the differences in the particularities of the interrelationship between physical context (temple) and cult statue.[3] One of the best-known examples is the temple of Amun at Luxor;[4] after the establishment of the last court under Ramses II, over 250 metres stretched between the cult statue and the entrance to the sanctuary. The location of the statue chamber behind the shrine for the Amun barque, as well as a colonnaded room without any direct axial connection between them, prevented anyone but priests and the pharaoh from even stealing a glance at the cult statue.[5] The only opportunity for visual contact between the religious community and its gods were major festivals, when cult statues were transported outside their temples for processions.[6]

Interaction with divine images in ancient Greece was definitely not exclusive.[7] Nonetheless, there is a very challenging architectural feature in some Greek temples, a barrier of wood, metal or stone in front of the cult statue, which could be interpreted as a physical boundary between the worshipper and the object of his or her veneration.[8] At first sight, these barriers seem to serve a purpose similar to that of the architectural layout of Egyptian temples: the creation of a boundary, rooted in theological concepts and ritual practices. In many respects though, the situation in Greece is more complex.

---

[2]   See in general Lupu 2005, 9–33, 54–79. See also the critical remarks on the use of the term "sacred law" in Parker 2004.

[3]   Arnold 1992, 13: "die Kultbilder führten im Tempel ein geheimnisvoll elitäres, von dem sie verehrenden Ägyptervolk völlig abgeschirmtes Dasein". On the contrary, Metzler (1995, 61–65) assumed that like Greek cult edifices, the architecture of Egyptian temples also functioned as a visual axis that guided light towards the cult statue. He thus overemphasized the superficial formal resemblances between Greek and Egyptian temples.

[4]   Arnold 1992, 127–132.

[5]   For the architecture of Egyptian temples as an intellectual and religious reflection of a divine kosmos, see Assmann 1991, 35–50.

[6]   For such a festival in Abydos, see Kucharek 2006.

[7]   On the aspect of religious exclusivity in cultic participation in Greece, see Krauter 2004, 53–113.

[8]   It is noteworthy that modern scholarship tends to neglect the importance of interior arrangements in Greek temples. Most recently, Knell 2007 has discussed the visual and conceptual interconnections between divine images and temples as if the latter were completely empty spaces.

Barriers in Greek temples: Archaeological and textual evidence

One should stress from the beginning that archaeological evidence does not reveal that every temple featured a barrier before its cult image. To some extent this may be due to insufficient or problematic architectural documentation or to the poor state of preservation of the respective monuments. Whenever inscriptions and literary sources complement the archaeological material, they reveal that more temples had a barrier in their cella than archaeological evidence would have us believe. From a terminological point of view, epigraphic evidence—mainly the Delian inventories of the second century BC—suggests that terms, such as ἡ κιγκλίς and ὁ τρύφακτος/δρύφακτος were used to designate a barrier. While *kigklis* is usually interpreted as a movable wooden barrier, *tryfaktos/dryfaktos* was most probably a parapet wall of some sort.[9] An inventory from the sanctuary of Amphiaraos at Oropos dated to the late third or early second century BC, for example, records dedicated *phialai*, placed apparently on the wooden *tryfaktos* of the temple (ἐπὶ τοῦ τρυφάκτου).[10] Architectural evidence has proven the existence of such parapet walls between the columns in the cella of the temple.[11] There is no archaeological evidence, however, for the existence of a barrier in front of the cult statue. Thus, *tryfaktos* in the Amphiareion of Oropos most probably refers to the screen walls in the intercolumniations that prevented an all too direct spatial communication between the aisles of the temple building.

Is then *kigklis* the ancient term for the feature that is the focus of this study? This cannot be the case, since both the archaeological and the literary evidence confirm the existence of parapet walls, not just movable wooden barriers, before cult images. More importantly, the term *kigklis* as a designation of a wooden barrier is epigraphically attested only on Delos. Pausanias uses a third term, τὸ ἔρυμα, to describe the stone screen wall around the statue of Zeus in Olympia.[12] But this term never appears in inscriptions in this type of context. All ancient Greek terms seem too generic in their use to be connected exclusively to a specific form of barrier in sacred buildings.

Despite such terminological ambiguities, traces of barriers in front of cult statues have been more or less securely identified in several Greek temples during excavations[13] or with the help of epigraphic evidence.

In Olympia, at the west end of the so-called Kronos hill and between the Nymphaeum of Herodes Atticus and the treasury of the Sikyonians, lie the remains of a small *naiskos* dating to the Archaic period, which is probably the oldest archaeologically attested example of a temple with a barrier in front of its cult statue (*Fig. 1*). In the better preserved west wall, two holes are still visible; another appears in the east wall.[14] Their shape, as well as the lack of any kind of traces on the floor, implies that the holes were almost certainly used for wooden beams that functioned as a barrier between the entrance and the cult statue, the base of which is still *in situ*. Neither the appearance, nor the material of the cult statue, nor the divine owner of the shrine are known.

---

9   Orlandos 1986, 152 s.v. κιγκλίς, 85 s.v. δρύφακτος; Ginouvès 1992, 19.
10   *IOropos* 325 l. 4–5.
11   Petrakos 1968, 106.

12   Paus. 5.11.4. Pausanias seems to be aware of the generic use of the term τὸ ἔρυμα, since he explicitly adds that the barriers were made like walls: ἐρύματα τρόπον τοίχων πεποιημένα τὰ ἀπείργοντά ἐστι.
13   With the exception of Priene, Mattern 2007, 141–153 discusses the same archaeological evidence as this paper.
14   Dörpfeld 1935, 109–111.

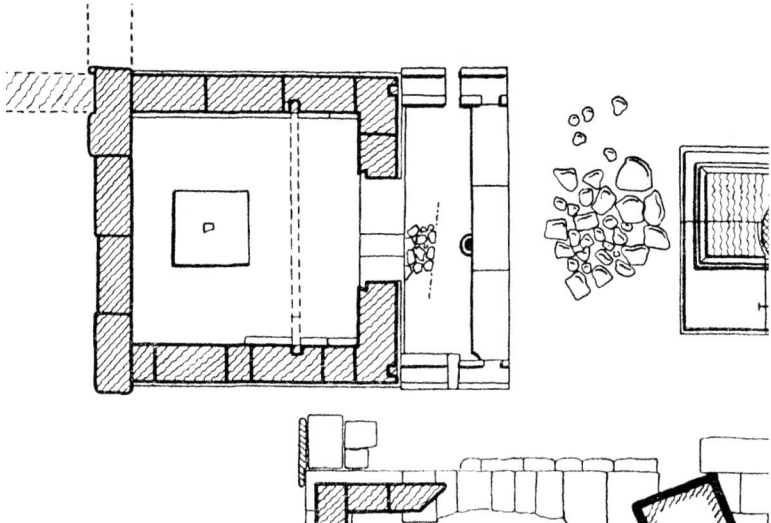

Fig. 1. Olympia. Naiskos on the Kronos Hill. After Dörpfeld 1935, pl. 7 (detail).

The late Archaic temple of Aphaia on Aigina, dated to around 500 to 480 BC, belongs to the earliest cult buildings that featured a barrier not just in front of but all around the cult statue. Four mortises around the traces of the base of the pseudo-chryselephantine statue (a gilded acrolith) of Aphaia point to the existence of wooden barriers (*Fig. 2*).[15] Based on G. Welter's assumption, G. Gruben suggested that barriers already surrounded the cult statue of Aphaia in the temple of the early sixth century, and that this spatial arrangement was copied in the late Archaic edifice.[16] Compared to other later examples, these barriers stand much closer to the cult statue. An inscription from the last third of the fifth century BC found in the sanctuary refers to ἴκρια περὶ τὸ ἕδος (barriers around the cult statue), and thus confirms the archaeological evidence.[17] The term *ikria* usually indicates some kind of wooden scaffolding, and, especially in Attica, a wooden construction that accommodates seating. In the case of

the temple of Aphaia, however, it must refer to the barriers around the cult image.

In addition, in the early fifth-century temple of Athena at Sounion, the intercolumniation of the two columns before the cult statue's base as well as the space between the columns and the cella walls were closed with a parapet wall or metal barriers (*Fig. 3*).[18] Nothing is known with certainty about the statue of Athena Sounias that could help explain the existence of the barrier in front of it. It should be stressed that in the temple of Poseidon on top of the promontory no barrier is reported to have existed in the cella.[19]

Notably, one of the most prominent examples of a barrier in a Greek temple is at the same time one of the most debated ones. Soon after the first studies of the Parthenon's architecture, two cuttings were observed running to the plinth of the pedestal of Athena's chryselephantine statue, but not continuing beneath it. A

---

15 Fiechter 1906, 43, pl. 31, 32.
16 Gruben 2007, 142–145.
17 *IG* I³ 1456 (*c.* 450–400 BC).

18 Stais 1900, 127, pl. 8. 9 (detail); Goette 2000, 37–38, pl. 41, fig. 78.
19 This could be due to the state of preservation of the rear part of the cella, see Dörpfeld 1884, 327–328; Orlandos 1917, 213–224.

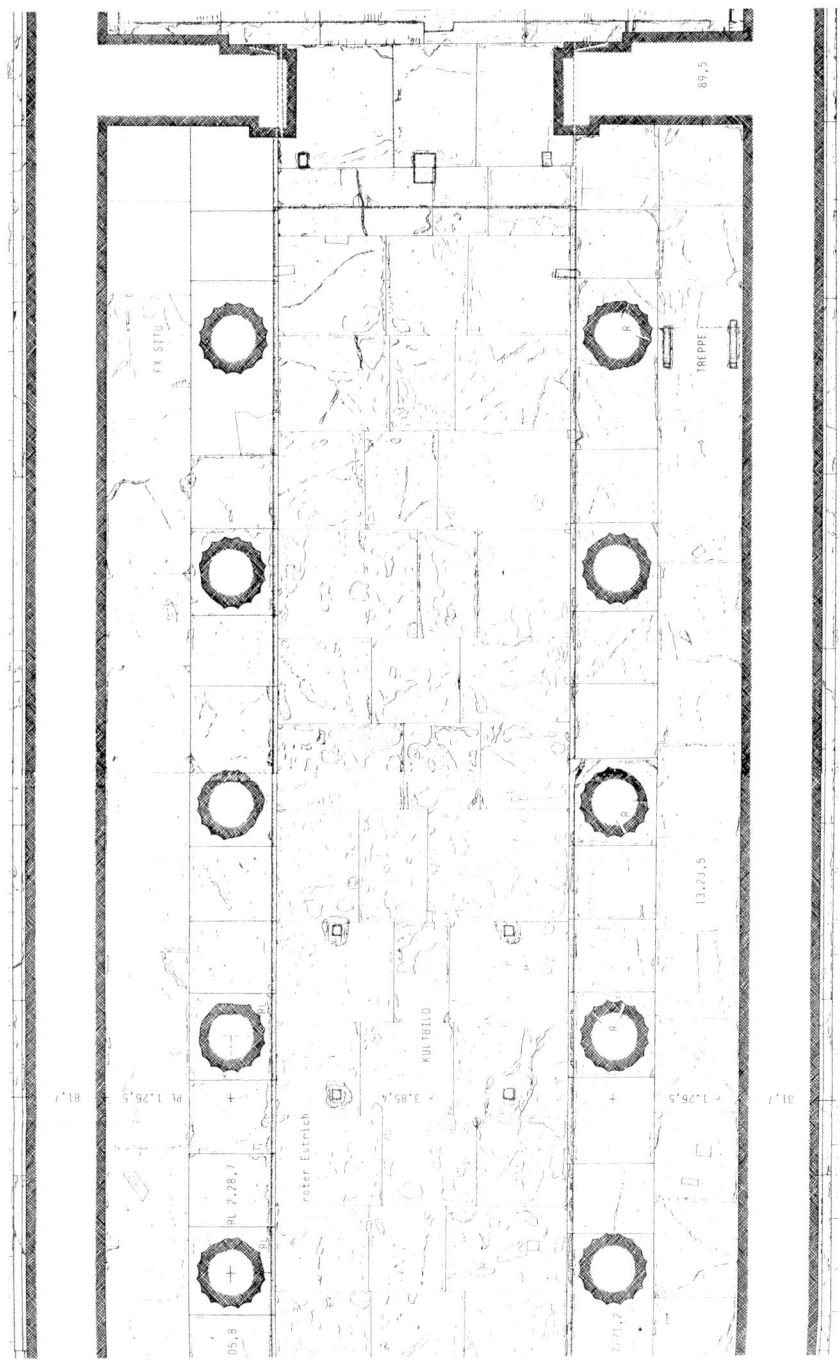

Fig. 2. Aegina. The cult statue area in the Aphaia temple. After Fiechter 1906, pl. 31 (detail).

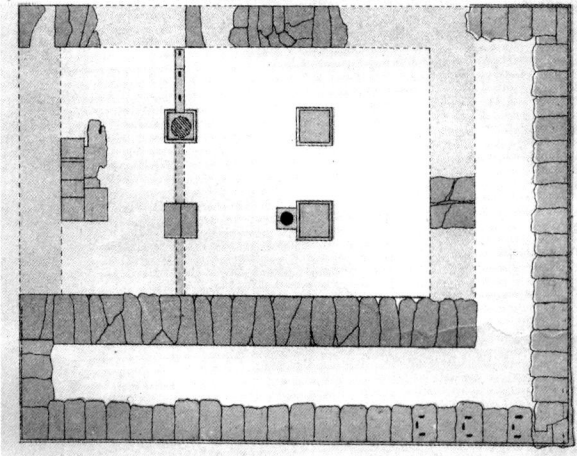

Fig. 3. Sounion. The temple of Athena Sounias. After Stais 1900, pl. 8 (detail).

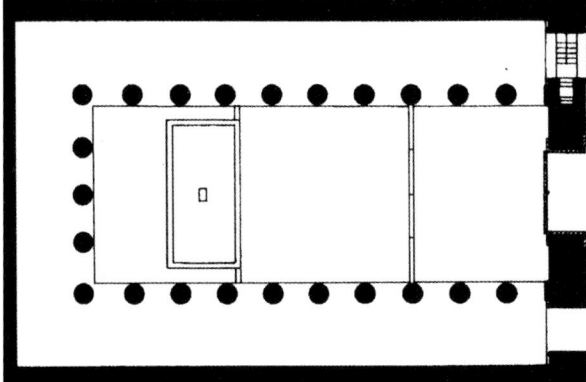

Fig. 4. Athens. The cult statue area in the Parthenon. After Neils 2001, 29, fig. 23.

similar cutting exists nearly in the middle of the cella, in the area close to the third column from the east of the south interior colonnade. An iron dowel was found near this cutting. Initial interpretations described these three cuttings and the dowel as evidence of a protective barrier for the precious cult statue,[20] but as early as 1955 G.P. Stevens argued convincingly against this hypothesis, suggesting instead that the cuttings were part of the rim of the water basin before the Athena Parthenos statue.[21]

According to Pausanias, this water basin was a protective measure for the statue and especially its wooden core and ivory parts against the dry climate.[22] Stevens' suggestion was widely accepted despite the fact that the exact connection between the dowel and the rim could not be satisfactorily explained. It seems more probable that the dowel was associated with a screen wall before the shallow water basin. The only certainty about this architectural detail in the

---

[20] Michaelis 1871, 25.
[21] Stevens 1955, 267–270. In his monumental monograph on the Parthenon, Orlandos 1977–1978, 387–389 follows Stevens' suggestion.

[22] Paus. 5.11.10–11. The impressive aesthetic impact of this water basin in front of the Athena Parthenos statue can be adequately visualized by comparison with the mirror image of the Lincoln Memorial in the reflecting pool in Washington DC.

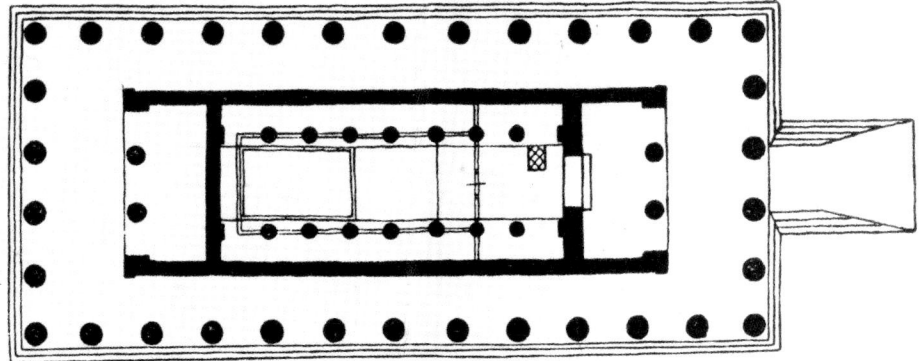

Fig. 5. Olympia. The temple of Zeus. After Dörpfeld 1935, pl. 3 (detail).

cella is that it postdates the statue, but archaeological data do not allow us to date the erection
of the screen walls and the creation of the shallow basin with any certainty (*Fig. 4*). Nevertheless, the analogous case of the temple of Zeus
at Olympia suggests that the refurbishment of
this area in front of the statue took place shortly after the statue's completion.

In the temple of Zeus at Olympia, the floor
before the statue was covered with black stones
with a raised rim of Parian marble. According
to Pausanias, the raised rim helped contain not
water but the olive oil used for the care of the
ivory parts of the chryselephantine statue in
this area.[23] This entire zone was protected by
parapet walls in the respective intercolumniations as well as by a screen wall between the second columns from the east (*Fig. 5*). Pausanias
also describes the panels of the parapet wall as
being decorated with mythological paintings
by Panainos.[24] Both side aisles were also closed
from the second columns backwards. German
excavations have suggested that these measures
were not part of the original plan, but were tied
to the erection of the chryselephantine statue

in the cella after 430 BC.[25] In a later, perhaps
Hellenistic, phase of refurbishment the last
remaining intercolumniations along the base
of the statue were also closed, but not with
parapet walls.[26] Holes in the side faces of the
columns demonstrate that this was probably a
wooden construction with simple beams.

Only epigraphic evidence exists for the barrier in front of the chryselephantine statue of
Asklepios in his temple at Epidauros built in
390/80 BC. A long and very detailed inscription documents construction campaigns in the
sanctuary, the persons in charge, their wages,
and the expenses for building materials. In this
inscription, the term τὸ μάκελλον is used to
designate the barrier or parapet wall in front
of the cult statue.[27] The archaeologically at-

---

[23] Paus. 5.11.10.
[24] Paus. 5.11.5–6. For the figural decoration of these
panels, see Völcker-Janssen 1987.

[25] Dörpfeld 1935, 235–239.
[26] Dörpfeld 1935, 236, 247.
[27] *IG* IV2 1 102 (c. 370 BC), l. 107–108: μ[ακ]έλλω
ἐργασίας [Πα]/σιθέμι HHH ⸗⸗⦂⦂⦂· (To Pasithemis for
constructing the metal fence, 349 drachmas); l. 296:
παρδείχματος μακέλλο Ἀπολ[λ]οδώρωι - ⦂⦂ (To Apollodoros for the model of the metal fence, 15 drachmas); l.
298: σιδάρο ποὶ τὸ μάκελλον Φρίκωνι ⸗ (To Phrikon, for
the iron for the fence, 20 drachmas); l. 301: δακτυλίων
καὶ ἐπιούρων ἐς τὸ μάκελλον Ἀντιφάνει ⸗⸗⸗⦂⦂⦂⦂ (To An-
tiphanes, for rings and bolts for the fence, 68 drachmas). Burford 1969 offers a mainly economic interpretation and understanding of the large Epidaurian
inscription. However, a new study of the inscription

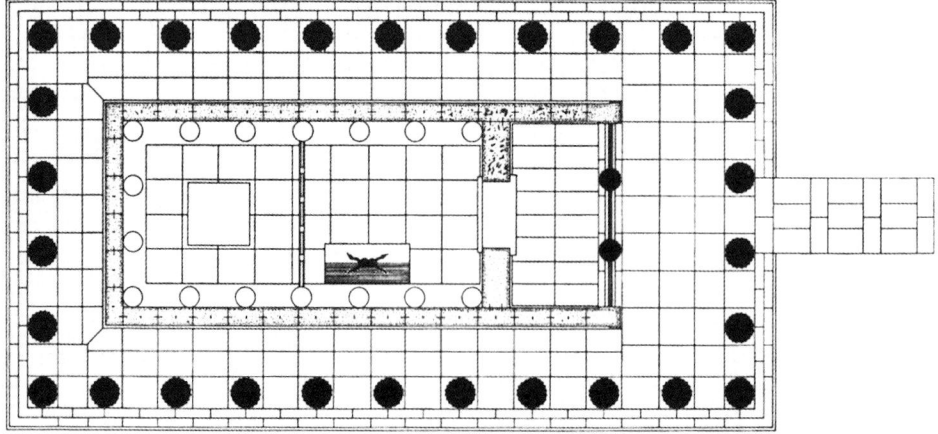

Fig. 6. Epidauros. The temple of Asklepios. After Riethmüller 2005, vol. I, 296, fig. 43.

tested artificial cavity in the front part of the cella, which may have been used as a treasury, permits a reconstruction of the barrier only between the inner, probably Corinthian, columns in the very centre of the cella (*Fig. 6*).[28] It is worth mentioning at this point that the chryselephantine statue of Asklepios, a work of the Parian Thrasymedes, adopted the iconography of Zeus at Olympia.

Danish excavations likewise uncovered traces of a barrier in the Hellenistic temple built around 300 BC at the sanctuary of Athena on the acropolis of Lindos. Sockets in the walls and floor of the cella suggest the presence of a barrier related to a large podium identified by E. Dyggve as an altar (*Fig. 7*).[29] It seems more plausible, however, that this was a monumental *trapeza* (offering table) near the cult statue. A small part of its base was unearthed in the rear part of the cella. The cult statue is not preserved and the literary sources are not particularly

helpful. On the basis of terracotta figurines found in the sanctuary, the cult statue has been reconstructed as a standing Athena analogous to the Athenian Parthenos, but wearing a tall polos instead of a helmet. The famous Lindian *anagraphe* reports that the statue was fastened to the back wall of the cella.[30] In the eleventh century AD, the Byzantine author Georgios Kedrinos referred to "the statue of Athena Lindia four cubits [about 1.80 m] high and made of green stone, a work by the sculptors Scyllis and Dipoenus, which Sesostris [which, due to the well-known Herodoteian passage,[31] should be understood as Amasis], the ruler of Egypt, once sent as a gift to Cleobulus, ruler of Lindos".[32] The late date of Kedrinos' account clearly makes this information unreliable.

Recent archaeological research at the small extra-urban sanctuary of Herakles at Kleonai has demonstrated the existence of a barrier in front of the cult statue there (*Fig. 8*).[33] The temple dates to the first half of the second cen-

---

from an architectural point of view will reveal invaluable insights into the design and layout of a temple's interior. The author of this paper is currently working on such a study.
[28] Riethmüller 2005, vol. I, 306.
[29] Dyggve 1960, 85–87, pl. IV A–B.

[30] Bettinetti 2001, 142, n. 19.
[31] Hdt. 2.182.
[32] *Compendium historiarum*, vol. 1, 564, ll. 7–10.
[33] Mattern 2002, 6.

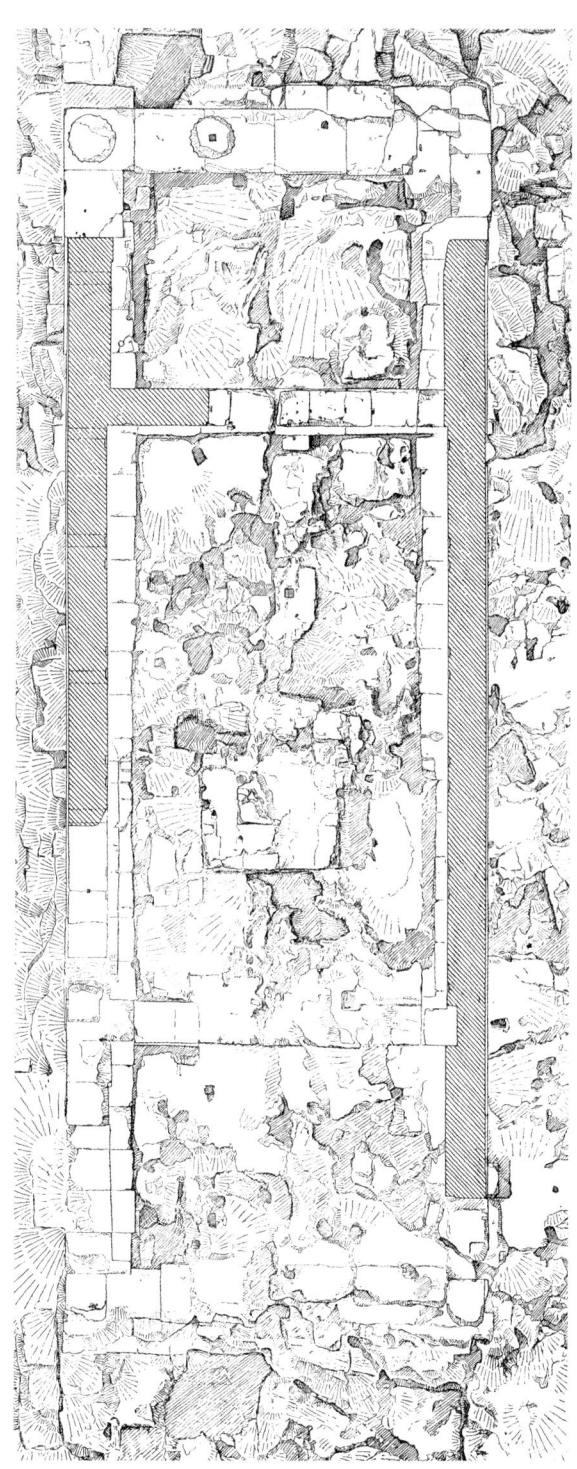

Fig. 7. Lindos. The temple of Athena. Situation after the excavation. After Dyggve 1960, 134 pl. IV A.

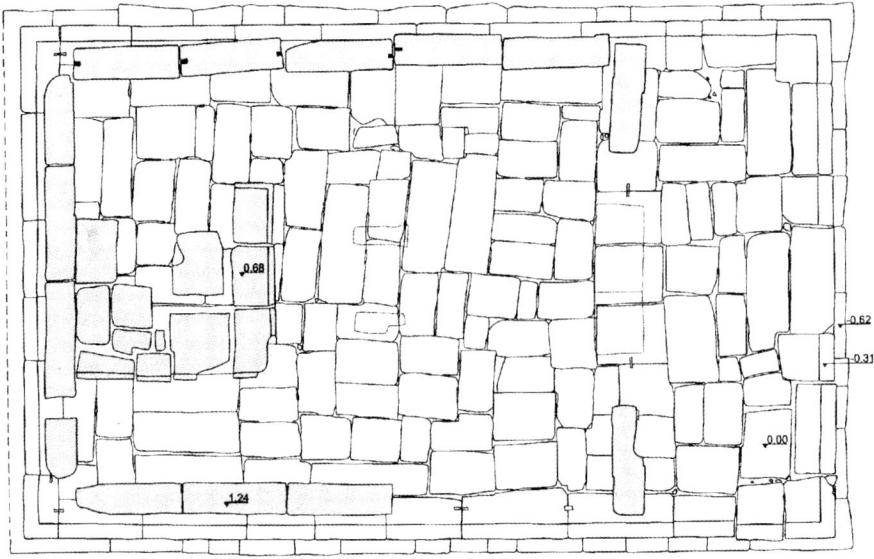

Fig. 8. Kleonai. The temple of Herakles. After Mattern 2002, 4, fig. 4.

tury BC. A *trapeza*, of which only traces of the stand on the floor have survived, stood in the middle of the cella. Just behind it a barrier prevented worshippers from approaching the cult statue. The fact that there are no traces of mortises in the floor, but only sockets in the orthostates of the temple walls, clearly points to the former existence of a relatively simple barrier rather than a parapet wall. The interconnection between the *trapeza* and the barrier recalls the situation in the temple of Athena at Lindos. The cult statue made of local grey marble has been identified as a seated Herakles.[34]

The best-preserved remains of a barrier in a Greek temple were excavated in the cella of the famous temple of Despoina at Lykosoura in Arcadia, which dates to the second century BC.[35] Here, the base of a nearly complete parapet wall was unearthed between the cult statue group, made by the Messenian Damophon, and the mosaic decorating the front portion

of the cella (*Fig. 9*). A row of relatively narrow stones (with a width of about 30 cm) with mortises marks the position of the barrier. Since no remains of the panels were found, it is unknown whether they bore relief decoration or paintings such as those in the temple of Zeus in Olympia.[36]

Numerous second-century BC inscriptions from Delos document the existence of wooden barriers or stone parapet walls in at least ten different Delian temples and shrines. None of these, however, have been verified archaeologically. In addition, it is unclear whether the epigraphic evidence always refers to such installa-

---

[34] Damaskos 1999, 19–22.
[35] Leonardos 1896, 111.

[36] Stewart (1990, fig. 788) reconstructs the barrier in the form of a single beam placed on a row of low posts. I suggest a more elaborate screen wall, however, perhaps decorated with paintings. Such a screen wall would correspond to the strikingly embellished interior of the relatively small temple. The fact that Pausanias does not mention the existence of a screen wall is of no consequence, since he solely describes the cult statue group (with no reference to the mosaic or the temple's side entrance).

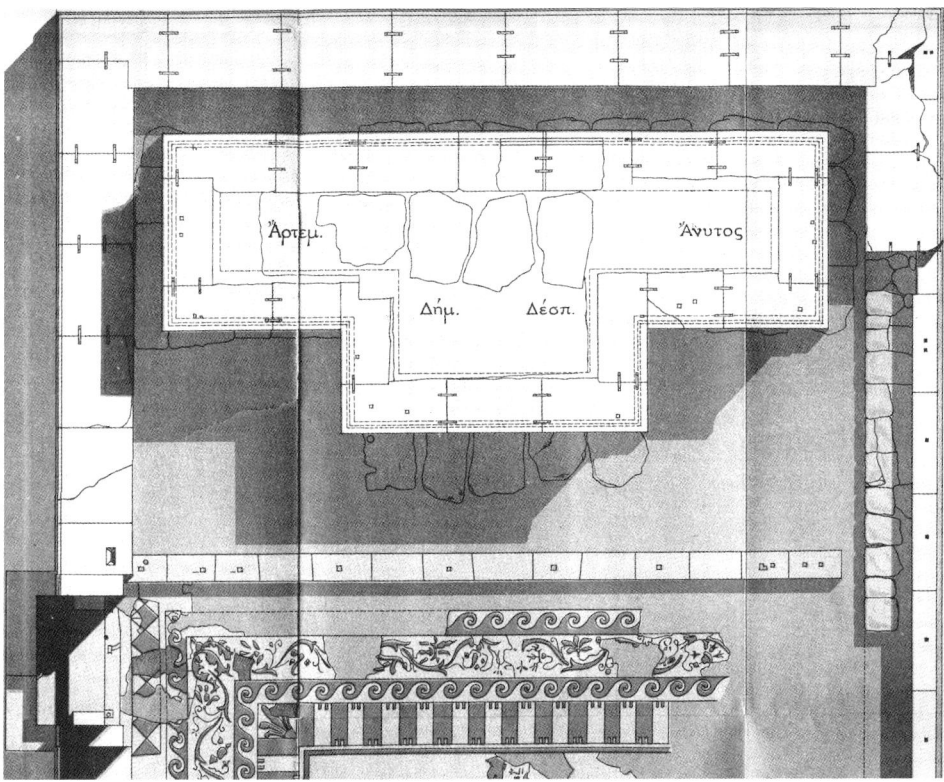

Fig. 9. Lykosoura. The cult statue area in the temple of Despoina. After Leonardos 1896, pl. 2 (detail).

tions inside the cella in front of the cult statues or to constructions already blocking the entrance in the area of the *pronaos*.[37] For example, in the case of the Delian *porinos naos* the same inscription refers to both a barrier of unspecified material in the *prodomos* and to a wooden one in the *naos*. The author of the inscription makes no terminological distinction and uses the word τρύφακτος for both barrier forms.[38] In any case, the Delian inventories clearly show that there were barriers in Greek temples that can no longer be detected by archaeological means.

An incompletely excavated sanctuary of the second century BC in the Arcadian city of Pheneos reveals a possible variation on how a boundary between worshippers and divine image could be created. The south cult room of the double temple was dedicated to Asklepios and Hygieia. The north cult room features an elevated floor level in the cella's rear part where the base for the bronze cult statues still stands. The transition point to the higher level is clearly marked by a low marble *trapeza* on the axis of the entrance and the statues' base (*Fig. 10*). The floor in the two parts of the temple was also different: in the rear it consists of reddish soil with remains of plaster, while at the front there was almost certainly a wooden floor.[39]

---

[37] Hellmann 1992, 210–212.
[38] *ID* 1403B, fr b, col. I l. 80 and ll. 95–96.

[39] Protonotariou-Deilaki 1961–1962, 59–60, pl. 65a; Riethmüller 2005, vol. II, 219–224.

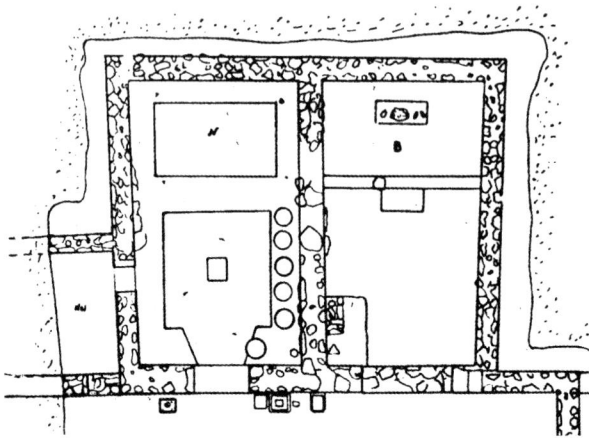

Fig. 10. Pheneos. The excavated part of the Asklepieion. After Riethmüller 2005, vol. II, 220, fig. 119.

Perhaps crossbeams at the edge of the elevation separated the area of the cult images from the rest of the cult building.[40] The positioning of the *trapeza* at the edge of the elevation reminds us of the arrangement of the offering table and the barrier in the temples of Herakles at Kleonai and of Athena at Lindos.

Finally, the most problematic case from an archaeological point of view seems to be the barrier in the temple of Athena Polias at Priene. The cuttings—dowel holes with pour channels—which fastened the base of a screen wall, as well as the cella floor, have disappeared due to the temple's pillage. Their existence is known solely thanks to a more or less detailed drawing in the notebooks of R.P. Pullan, the first explorer of the site (*Fig. 11*).[41] This drawing also documents the existence of two cuttings—one large and one small—in each of the north and south walls of cella, which were certainly related to the screen. The statue pedestal behind the screen also has a problematic history in scholarly research. The base was dated to the mid-second century BC on the basis of six or

seven silver coins of Olophernes of Cappadocia found in its core, not during regular excavations, but by a British merchant on a picnic at the site in 1870.[42] On the other hand, relying on a thorough stylistic analysis, W. Königs and especially F. Rumscheid date both the base and its crowning mouldings to the late fourth or early third century and suggest a renovation of the base in the mid-second century, when elements of the earlier structure were reused.[43] The fragments of the acrolithic cult image, an adaptation of the statue of Athena Parthenos by Pheidias on the Athenian Acropolis, should be dated to this later construction campaign in the cella. It is not known to which phase the screen wall belongs. In Roman Imperial times the area behind the screen was further modified, when portraits of the Julio-Claudian dynasty were arranged in a semicircle around the cult statue of Athena.[44] It is possible therefore that the screen was not erected until the second half of the first century AD. Finally, the physical appearance of the screen wall is also a matter of debate; usually, a small door is reconstructed in the middle of the screen, and two sets of four small holes are interpreted as a means to

---

[40]   Mattern (2006, 175) suggests that there was no barrier in the form of a wooden beam or screen wall. According to Mattern, it was the elevation that functioned as a barrier.

[41]   Carter 1983, 229–231, fig. 24.

[42]   Carter 1983, 231–235.

[43]   Koenigs 1983, 160–161; Rumscheid 1994, vol. I, 43.

[44]   Steuernagel 2010, 248–250.

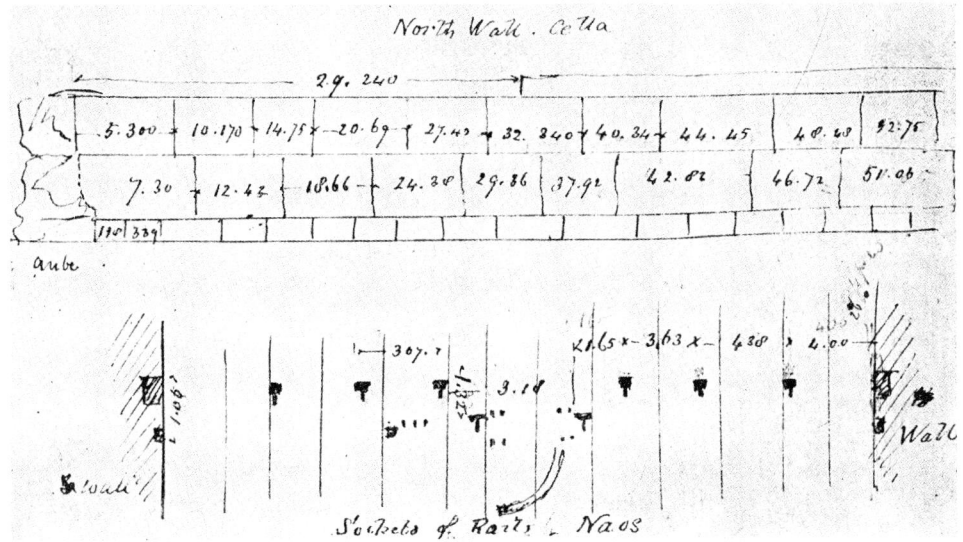

Fig. 11. Priene. Drawing of the cuttings for the barrier in the temple of Athena. After Carter 1983, 229, fig. 24.

fasten the sill. A *trapeza*, however, is a probable alternative that finds support in archaeological evidence from the temples in Pheneos, Lindos, and Kleonai.

Barriers in Greek temples: An interpretation

In a volume dedicated to churches from Late Antiquity to the Middle Ages, the editor, S. Gerstel, addressed briefly but precisely the methodological problems associated with the scholarly examination of barriers in such structures. Her observation applies equally to the situation regarding the study of barriers in Greek temples: "Finally, one should acknowledge the difficulty of the topic. Although the demarcation of the sacred is one of the defining elements of religious architecture and ritual, the ubiquity of barriers in sacred spaces has often been the very cause of their neglect by authors of historical, theological, and liturgical [one should definitely add, "archaeological" and "art historical"] sources. The near absence

of contemporary notice and the problematic and contested nature of the surviving evidence make the study of sacred screens particularly challenging to modern scholars".[45]

Consequently, a fundamental question must be raised before addressing possible interpretations for the existence of barriers in Greek temples: Are we dealing with a very specific and limited phenomenon that needs to be explained separately in every single case or should we presuppose the existence of barriers in front of cult statues in all Greek temples? Furthermore, is the bad state of preservation simply distorting our understanding of a widespread phenomenon? Needless to say, there is no secure definite answer to these questions, but for methodological reasons we should keep them in mind.

Adequate comprehension of barriers and their significance in Greek temples depends largely on the presupposition that a barrier has an enormous impact on the physical and intel-

---

[45] Gerstel 2006, 4.

lectual organisation of any given space since it grants meaning to the different parts of the spatial entity it actually divides. A. Rapoport has stressed the importance of both fixed and semi-fixed elements in the process of perceiving an architecturally defined space, pointing out that a "site could be read on the basis of its fixed-feature elements, although this was greatly helped by semifixed-feature elements".[46] The interior of a temple could easily be recognised as such based on fixed architectural elements, but the existence of a barrier, a semi-fixed element, could help visitors understand details of symbolic meaning that differentiate a specific temple building with a barrier from one without a structure that separates the area of the cult statue from the surrounding architecture. Furthermore, low accessibility to the area of the cult statue as defined by a barrier would translate immediately into an understanding of the difference in use and significance of different parts of the same temple.

If barriers have an inherent meaning, then one should ask whether this meaning is fixed and transcends all barriers in Greek temples. It is important to ask whether there are any common features in the temples presented thus far that could possibly explain the construction of barriers in a cella (*Table 1*). Four such features come to mind, but none of them can explain all the cases in which barriers existed in a temple:

The material value of the statue: Included among those that display this first possible common feature is a group of statues made of precious material, namely the chryselephantine statues in the Parthenon, the temple of Zeus at Olympia, and the temple of Asklepios at Epidauros, as well as the gilded acrolithic statue in the temple of Aphaia on Aigina, and perhaps the Athena of green stone in Lindos. Literary sources, however, provide information on more than fifty chryselephantine (cult) statues that

apparently stood in temples without a barrier.[47] In addition, the existence of a barrier in the temples at Kleonai and Priene cannot be justified by the preciousness of the material used for their cult statues.

The fame of the cult statue's sculptor: The prominence of the sculptor cannot be regarded as a significant parameter for the erection of a barrier in front of a cult statue. Pheidias and Damophon were certainly famous, but Thrasymedes, the sculptor of the cult statue of Asklepios in Epidauros, is known solely for this work. In most cases, such as Aigina, Kleonai, Lindos or Sounion, we do not even have the name of the sculptors. If barriers were constructed for the protection of works produced by famous masters, then why were the cult statues in the temple of Asklepios at Messene, also made by Damophon, not protected by a barrier?[48]

Rituals, i.e., the existence of a cult table for offerings: An interesting common feature of the temples in Kleonai, Lindos, Pheneos, and perhaps Priene lies in the coexistence of the barrier with a table of offerings.[49] But these cases, along with at least two further examples in the temple of Zeus Labraundos and the Athenian Parthenon—both only epigraphically attested[50]—are the only known examples of such an

---

[46]   Rapoport 1990, 91.

[47]   See the Appendix I in Lapatin 2001, 193–197.
[48]   Orlandos 1971, 168–171; Themelis 1989, 64–69.
[49]   On the typology and significance in cult of tables of offerings, see in general Gill 1991.
[50]   Several inscriptions from the Athenian Acropolis refer to the existence of a *trapeza* (sometimes explicitly characterizing it as chryselephantine) in the Parthenon, see Mansfield 1985, 232. Orlandos (1977–1978, 371) suggests that this table was used during the ceremony of the crowning of the Panathenaic victors in a way comparable to the chryselephantine table in the Heraion at Olympia (Paus. 5.20.1–2). *ILabraunda* 60 (second century AD): the decree prevents visitors from trespassing upon the "tryfaktos between the silver incense altar and the table of offerings (*trapeza*) of the god" in the temple of Zeus. J. Crampa, the editor of the inscription, suggests that the "bar separated the sacred part of the shrine from the profane" (Crampa 1972, 121). This is not the place to discuss the important semantic

Table 1. Barriers in Greek temples (selection).

Place	Date (all BC)	Divinity	Material/technique of the cult statue		Sculptor	trapeza	Ancient term
Aigina	early 5th cent.	Aphaia	Gilded acrolithic		?	–	τὰ ἴκρια
Athens	second half 5th cent.	Athena (Parthenos)	Chryselephantine		Pheidias	x	?
Delos	3rd/2nd cent.	Agathe Tyche, Aphrodite, Apollo, Artemis, Hera, Isis, Poseidon, Sarapis	Various (mainly marble; e.g. the statue of Agathe Tyche was gilded)		?	?	ἡ κιγκλὶς ὁ τρύφακτος
Epidauros	early 4th cent.	Asklepios	Chryselephantine		Thrasy-medes	–	τὸ μάκελλον
Kleonai	first half 2nd cent.	Herakles	Local marble		?	x	?
Labraunda	first half 4th cent.	Zeus	?		?	x	ὁ τρύφακτος
Lindos	early 3rd cent.	Athana (Lindia)	?		?	x	?
			According to Kedrinos				
			"Green stone"	Scyllis and Dipoenus			
Lykosoura	2nd cent.	Despoina	Local marble		Damophon	–	?
Olympia	6th cent.	?	Local stone (?)		?	–	?
Olympia	2nd half 5th cent.	Zeus	Chryselephantine		Pheidias	–	τὸ ἔρυμα
Pheneos	2nd cent.	?	Bronze		?	x	?
Priene	mid-2nd cent.	Athena (Polias)	Acrolithic		?	x (?)	?
Sounion	early 5th cent.	Athena (Sounias)	?		?	–	?

assemblage in a temple cella. They can therefore not be used to explain all the other barriers. It must also be stressed that there are numerous tables of offerings in Greek temples that are not combined with a barrier. For example, in the temple of Amphiaraos at Oropos the bases of both the cult statue and a stone *trapeza* were unearthed without any physical evidence of a barrier between them.[51] Another prominent example for the existence of a *trapeza* in front of a cult statue without a barrier is the temple of Nemesis in Rhamnous.[52]

---

[51] Petrakos 1968, 99–107.

[52] Travlos 1988, 389, fig. 495. Miles (1989, 215), on the contrary, suggests that the channels found on the pavement of the cella could indicate the existence of a screen instead of a cult table. Petrakos (1991, 28, fig. 18) restores both a *trapeza* and a barrier before the cult

---

problems associated with the dichotomy between the "sacred" and the "profane" within a cult building.

Aesthetic trends of a particular period: Finally, the erection of barriers is not a chronologically limited phenomenon that can be explained as a temporary fashion within the context of an aesthetic museum-like enhancement of the divine image.[53] Indeed, most examples belong to the fifth and fourth centuries, even though the earliest example in Olympia dates to the sixth century BC, and the temples at Kleonai, Pheneos, and Lykosoura belong to the second. Thus, barriers cannot be associated with a specific period and its visual expectations for the presentation of divine images in the architectural context of a temple.

If barriers in Greek temples were not protecting precious and costly cult images, if they were not preventing indiscrete worshippers from approaching the masterpieces of famous sculptors, if they were not seen as an appropriate supplement to the offering tables, and if they were not merely a temporary fashion attested only in cult buildings of a very specific period, then how can we explain their existence in temples that differ so widely in terms of architecture, cultural landscape, and time?

Two main lines of interpretation remain: the first views barriers in Greek temples as an aesthetic element for the museum-like presentation of cult images across time; the second regards them as an important physical regulator of ritual activity inside the temple.

The aesthetic model may work in relation to monumental temples with impressive cult images, as in the case of the Parthenon or the temple of Zeus at Olympia.[54] It makes hardly

any sense when it comes to the barriers in the temple of Aphaia on Aigina, or in the small edifice in the Olympian sanctuary. The barriers in these temples are so close to the respective statues that they could never have seriously contributed to an aesthetically elevated presentation of the divine image. However, there can be no doubt about the importance of the visually dramatized presentation of cult images in temples. For example, Antiochos IV dedicated to the temple at Olympia a precious veil for "hiding" the cult statue. According to Pausanias, ropes were used to cast the veil down to the ground before the Pheidian statue.[55] One can only imagine the visual impact of such a revelation to visitors entering the temple, whenever the veil was lifted. It must have been almost equivalent to a divine apparition. Barriers can hardly have served such a function. Aesthetic reasons certainly played an important role in the material form of a barrier. While the barrier in Kleonai, for example, remained a simple beam separating the area of the cult statue from the front part of the temple with the *trapeza*, the screen wall in the temple of Zeus at Olympia became an integral part of the mythological narratives that surrounded both decoratively and contextually the Pheidian Zeus. Aesthetics were a significant parameter for the form of a barrier (wooden beam, screen wall with or without decoration, bronze fence) and its exact positioning within a temple, but not for the initial decision as to whether or not a barrier was to become part of the interior arrangement of a temple.

Therefore, the most plausible model of interpretation is that emphasizing the rituals that were performed inside the temples. It is well

---

statue. Mattern (2007, 153) seems to accept this reconstruction.

[53] Cain (1995, 124) considers barriers in Greek temples in the context of Hellenistic aesthetic trends.

[54] Cain 1995, 124 (in respect to Lykosoura and the Pergamene shrine of Dionysos Kathegemon, where a bronze barrier was placed at the entrance); Zinserling (1957, 24–30) argues that the barriers in the temple of Aphaia on Aigina and in the temple of Zeus at Olympia served practical purposes, but those in the Parthenon

aimed exclusively at the aesthetic enhancement of the Athena Parthenos statue.

[55] Paus. 5.12.4. In this context, Pausanias refers to a similar veil in the Artemision of Ephesos that was raised to reveal the cult statue just like a theatrical curtain at the beginning of a performance.

known that official religious practices included intensive interaction with divine images that took the form of washing, dressing, adorning, or carrying them through a city in processions. Ancient sources report on private expressions of religiosity that entailed a great deal of physical interaction, such as kissing, touching, or embracing the divine image. Numerous authors also refer to cases of mutilation, deprivation, or sexual harassment, and even rape of cult images—the latter certainly being part of the *agalmatophilia* against which Apollonius preached.[56]

The few scholars, such as T. Mattern, who have discussed barriers in Greek temples—mainly in connection with ritual practices—ascribe great significance to the distinction between official and private religious practices related to cult statues.[57] According to their interpretation, the barriers were a means of physically expressing this differentiation. In the context of official cults, no barriers existed for priests and priestesses. In the context of private cult practice, on the other hand, barriers explicitly created limits between the accessible and inaccessible parts of a temple, while simultaneously expressing differentiation between the ritual expert and the worshipper in cultic functions.

In this respect, one could draw a parallel—at least phenomenologically—between a barrier in an ancient Greek temple and the iconostasis in Orthodox churches. The Orthodox iconostasis, as we know it today, has a very long tradition. It originated in a simple parapet wall around the altar in Early Christian churches,[58]

reminiscent of the barriers around the cult statue in the temple of Aphaia on Aigina. Evidence from Egypt and Syria demonstrates that marble, wood, and even glass were used for the construction and decoration of such parapet walls. The earliest surviving example lies in the fourth-century AD church of Kellis in the Dakhleh oasis in Egypt. In the north basilica of Khirbat al Filusiyya on the Mediterranean coast of the Sinai Peninsula there is another illustrative example of an early parapet wall from the early sixth century.[59] The tall iconostasis was probably developed in Russia after the conquest of Constantinople.[60] Such an iconostasis, a "wall" full of images, creates a very sophisticated system of inclusion and exclusion based on its three doors, which are closed or open depending on the stage of the liturgy and the grade of ritual secrecy. The iconostasis thus functions as a means of both separation and mediation between the community and the priest who performs the ritual, since only the priest and his ministrants can enter the holy area behind the barrier.

Such an explanation, based on the ritual activity inside the cella, certainly provides a plausible answer to the general question about the function of a barrier in a temple, but it leaves unanswered the important issue of the reasons for erecting a barrier in one temple and doing without in another. Although the distinction between official and private expressions of religiosity played an important role in the decision of whether or not to add a barrier to the architectural concept of a temple, there was in my view a far more crucial aspect at play, namely the temple's regular accessibility. In a scene in the *Iliad*, in which Hekabe and other Trojan women go to the temple of Athena to pray to the goddess, the temple is not accessible to

---

56 Corso 2007, 172.
57 Mattern 2006, 175–176. Mattern (2007, 153–159) argues that barriers served primarily cultic purposes, but had protective and aesthetic value as well.
58 Yasin (2009) does refer to chancel barriers in churches but rather emphasizes the importance of the main entrance to the building as the boundary of ecclesiastical space. More significant appears her observation that saints were often depicted on or near chancel barri-

ers (278–280). It seems that saints visually marked the boundaries between lay and clerical spheres.
59 Bolman 2006, 73–89, esp. 76–79.
60 Belting 2000, 266–278.

the religious community, but must be opened by the priestess Theano.[61] It is well known that the key is the main iconographic attribute of a priestess.[62]

A great number of cult regulations specify that some temples were supposed to be open only on the day of festivals, while others were open on a daily basis. The best-documented example of a temple with regulated and quite restricted accessibility is the temple of Apollo at Delphi. Only those visitors who sought to consult the oracle and had already paid for the preliminary sacrifice were allowed to enter the temple, but even they could only do so once a month, between spring and autumn.[63] Pausanias stresses that at the sanctuary of Aphrodite at Sikyon visitors had to view the chryselephantine statue—a work of Kanachos—and pray while standing at the entrance.[64] A decree of Pergamon, related to the ceremony for the erection of an inscription that commemorated the alliance between Pergamon and Rome, stipulates that on that day all priests and priestesses had to open all the temples of the gods.[65] This means, of course, that not every Pergamene temple was open on a daily basis. On the other hand, the sacred regulation concerning the duties of the priest of Asklepios in Chalkedon, obliges him to open the temple each day.[66] This explicit clause makes sense only if this was not the case

in all priesthoods and all temples. Another engrossing inscription from Teos refers to the daily opening and closing of the temple of Dionysos and the accompanying ritual practices.[67]

Many scholars assume that Greek temples were commonly open only on special days, but such generalisations create scientific axioms that distort our understanding of ancient Greek culture.[68] Whether or not a temple was open on a daily basis depended on the nature of the cult (*e.g.*, oracle, healing deity, or mystery cult), on its location (within the city or at a distance), or on the importance of the cult to a community. The fourth mimiambos of Herodas picked the visit of two women to the sanctuary of Asklepios at Kos as a central theme. After they had sacrificed a rooster to the god, they admired the dedicated statues before entering the temple, since the door was open and the veil drawn to the side. The temple was apparently open and the women could enter without being controlled.[69] Athenaios tells the story of how Tyrrhenian pirates even stole the old cult image of the Samian Hera with great

---

[61] Hom. *Il.* 6.293–304.

[62] Mantis 1990, 28–65; Georgoudi 2005, 80–81; Connelly 2007, 92–104.

[63] Bowden 2005, 17.

[64] Paus. 2.10.4: Τοῖς δὲ ἄλλοις καθέστηκεν ὁρᾶν ἀπὸ τῆς ἐσόδου τὴν θεὸν καὶ αὐτόθεν προσεύχεσθαι (All others [except for the female neokoros and the annually appointed virgin priestess] are required to gaze at the goddess [Aphrodite] from the entrance, and to pray from there).

[65] *LSAM* 15, ll. 42–43 (129 BC): [ἀνοίξα]ντας τοὺς ναοὺς | [τῶν θ]εῶν (after they have opened [all] the temples of the gods).

[66] *LSAM* 5, ll. 24–25 (first century BC/AD): ἀνοί|γε]ν δὲ τὸν ἱερῆ τὸν ναὸν κατ᾽ ἀμέ[ραν] (The priest has to open the temple every day).

[67] *LSAM* 28, ll. 7–14 (first century AD): ὕμνους [ᾄδεσθαι | καθ᾽ ἑκά]στην ἡμέραν τοῦ προκαθηγεμ[όνος τῆς | πόλεω]ς θεοῦ Διονύσου ἐν τῇ ἀνοίξει τ[οῦ νεὼ ὑπὸ | τῶν ἐ]φήβων καὶ τοῦ ἱερέως τῶν παί[δων· ἐπὶ | δὲ τῇ] ς ἀνοίξεως καὶ κλείσεως τοῦ νε[ὼ τοῦ θεοῦ | ὑπὸ] τοῦ ἱερέως Τιβερίου Καίσαρος σ[πένδεσ|θαι] καὶ θυμιᾶσθαι καὶ λυχναπτεῖσθαι ἐ[κ τῶν ἱε|ρ]ῶν τοῦ Διονύσου πόρων (The ephebes and the priest of the boys shall sing hymns for the god Dionysos, the patron of the city, every day, as soon as the temple is opened. When the temple of the god is opened and closed by the priest of Tiberius Caesar, libations should be offered, and incense should be burned, and lamps should be lit from the sacred revenues of Dionysos [rather than: when the temple of the god is opened and closed, libations should be offered, and incense should be burned, and lamps should be lit by the priest of Tiberius Caesar from the sacred revenues of Dionysos]).

[68] Corbett (1970, 151) refers only briefly to the assumption that some temples were freely accessible, at least in Pausanias' times and perhaps even before that.

[69] Herod. 4.55: Αὕτη σύ, μείνον. ἡ θύρη γὰρ ὤικται κἀνεῖθ᾽ ὁ παστός (You, stay here! The door is open and the veil is drawn).

ease, since the temple did not have a door in early times.[70] In Kaphyai in the Peloponnese, in turn, a story was told to Pausanias of children who strangled Artemis. Playing near the temple they found a piece of rope, put it around the neck of the cult statue, and started spreading the news that the goddess has been strangled.[71] Obviously, the temple of Artemis, the most important temple in this small Arcadian town, was open to the public without the need for any official religious act to be performed, for, otherwise, the playing children would not have had the opportunity to "strangle" the goddess. In addition, a fragmentary sacred regulation from Epidauros monitors the daily service at the sanctuary.[72] As noted, this was also the case in Chalkedon. In the sanctuary of another healing god, Amphiaraos in Oropos, however, the priest was not obliged to come to the sanctuary in the winter; during the rest of the year he was allowed to be absent, though not for more than three days in a row, and he had to be there for at least ten days each month.[73] Another sacred

law from Kos regarding the duties of a priestess obliges her to open the temple at sunrise on the days when religious custom permits sanctuaries to be open.[74] The rest of the time, the temple must have remained closed.

Barriers naturally make sense in the case of temples which were regularly accessible.[75] Conversely, had a temple been usually closed and opened only on special occasions for public festivals or sacrifices, and in the presence of the temple personnel that controlled entrants, then the existence of barriers separating a specific part of the building would not have been justifiable, unless it is assumed that in all temples with a barrier before the cult statue the area defined by it was an *abaton*. Such an assumption leads to more unanswered questions, such as why did a barrier exist in the temple of Zeus at Olympia and not in that of Hera, why in at least ten temples on Delos but not in the three for Apollo?[76] This is why I am inclined to

---

[70] Ath. 15.672c: Ἀθύρου δὲ ὄντος τότε τοῦ νεὼ ταχέως ἀνελέσθαι τὸ βρέτας καὶ διακομίσαντας ἐπὶ θάλασσαν εἰς τὸ σκάφος ἐμβαλέσθαι (Because the temple had no door at that time, they [the Tyrrhenian pirates] soon picked up the image and after carrying it to the sea, they placed it in their ship).

[71] Paus. 8.23.6: Παιδία περὶ τὸ ἱερὸν παίζοντα – ἀριθμὸν δὲ αὐτῶν οὐ μνημονεύουσιν – ἐπέτυχε καλῳδίῳ, δήσαντα δὲ τὸ καλῴδιον τοῦ ἀγάλματος περὶ τὸν τράχηλον ἐπέλεγεν ὡς ἀπάγχοιτο ἡ Ἄρτεμις (Some children, the number of whom is not remembered, while playing in the sanctuary found a rope, and tying it round the neck of the image said that Artemis was being strangled).

[72] *LSS* 25 (second/third century AD): The fragmentary inscription starts with the "title" ἡμερείσια [ἱερὰ] (daily services).

[73] *LSCG* 69, ll. 2–6 (fourth century BC): Τὸν ἱερέα τοῦ Ἀμφιαράου φοιτᾶν εἰς τὸ ἱερό|ν, ἐπειδὰν χειμὼν παρέλθει, μέχρι ἀρότου ὥρης, μὴ πλέον διαλείποντα ἢ τρεῖς ἡμέρας καὶ | μένειν ἐν τοῖ ἱεροῖ μὴ ἔλαττον ἢ δέκα ἡμέρα|ς τοῦ μηνὸς ἑκά[σ]του (After the end of the winter, the priest of Amphiaraos should attend the sanctuary (every day) until the season of ploughing, and he should not stay away for more than three days and he should stay in the sanctuary for no less than ten days each month).

[74] *ICos* ED 236, ll. 8–10 (first century BC): ἁ ἱέρεια ἑκάσ|[τας] ἁμέρας ἃς ὅσιόν ἐστιν ἀνοίγειν τὰ ἱερὰ παρεχέτω τὸ[ν | ναὸν ἀ]νεῳ[γ]μένον ἅμα ἁλίωι ἀντέλλοντι (On each one of the days on which it is permitted by religious custom to open the sanctuaries, the priestess shall make sure that the temple opens at sunrise).

[75] An overall discussion of every kind of barrier within the broader context of a sanctuary is certainly beyond the scope of the present paper. There can be no doubt that a Greek sanctuary represented a very sophisticated spatial system of inclusion and exclusion. For some worshippers, the visit to a sanctuary already ended, for ethnic or gender reasons, at the entrance to the *temenos*. Others would be allowed to enter the sanctuary, but would be excluded from entering specific parts of it. Others would be permitted to enter even the temple, and in such cases the existence of a barrier would prevent them from approaching the cult statue. Even within the architectural context of a temple the existence of screen walls in the pronaos and/or in the ptera and/or in the cella would create an intricate system of differentiated levels of accessibility. Lattices, usually between the front columns of some temples, were probably meant as additional protection overnight.

[76] The existence of a shrine within a temple housing a normally small cult statue, as, for example, in the Erechtheion, cannot be adequately compared to a barrier, since a closed shrine would have completely prevented

explain barriers before cult statues as a physical, symbolic, and religious boundary between the divine image and the worshipper in temples that were open on a more or less regular basis.

The majority of temples without barriers were probably closed most of the time and opened only under the supervision of the responsible priest or *neokoros*, so that a barrier before the cult image was not necessary. In these cases the boundary was normally the closed doorway of the temple. Temples in which barriers existed were doubtless more numerous than those in which barriers have left detectable material evidence. The Delian inventories clearly demonstrate this. They refer to at least ten temples with barriers in which such a construction cannot be verified by archaeological remains. According to my interpretation, a barrier in a Greek temple was a boundary and at the same time a sign of the partial accessibility of the cult building on a regular, even daily basis, while the area around the cult statue remained inviolable. In accordance with Rapoport's model, barriers in a temple organized *space* (the physical separation of the cult statue area from those spaces used by worshippers), *time* (the visual designation of a temple open on a regular basis), *communication* (the definition of levels of interaction with the divine image), and *meaning* (with the low or no accessibility designating the most ceremonial spaces within a temple).[77]

The psychological impact of such a barrier in an open temple cannot be gleaned from sources, but it certainly played a significant role. Interpretations of dreams, for example, were an important way to channel and form attitudes, and thus the violation of a temple in a dream was considered an omen of bad luck, as explained in Artemidoros' *Onirocritica*.[78] Even today, no pious person dares to enter the area behind the iconostasis in an Orthodox church or to ignore the low barrier in a Turkish mosque, even when no religious authority is present. I suspect that barriers had the same effect in a Greek temple. For the impious violators of a temple, boundaries either in the form of a closed doorway or a barrier inside the cella, were merely an unimportant physical obstacle that had to be overcome. Only those who accepted their symbolic meaning respected boundaries of any form.

JOANNIS MYLONOPOULOS
Department of Art History and Archaeology
Columbia University
jm3193@columbia.edu

Bibliography

Arnold 1992   D. Arnold, *Die Tempel Ägyptens. Götterwohnungen, Kultstätten, Baudenkmäler*, Zürich 1992.

Assmann 1991   J. Assmann, *Ägypten. Theologie und Frömmigkeit einer frühen Hochkultur*, Stuttgart 1991[2].

Belting 2000   H. Belting, *Bild und Kult. Eine Geschichte des Bildes vor dem Zeitalter der Kunst*, München 2000[5].

Bettinetti 2001   S. Bettinetti, *La statua di culto nella pratica rituale greca*, Bari 2001.

---

visual communication between the worshipper and his object of veneration. On the contrary, a barrier prohibits physical approach to the cult statue, while offering at the same time an almost unhindered view of the divine image.

[77]   Rapoport 1990, 179–183.

[78]   Artem. 3.3.2: "breaking into a temple or stealing the votive offerings of the gods indicates bad luck for everyone, except for priests and prophets. This is because tradition allows them to take the offerings to the gods and thus, in a certain sense, they are supported by them".

Bolman 2006   E.S. Bolman, 'Veiling sanctity in Christian Egypt: Visual and spatial solutions', in *Thresholds of the sacred: Architectural, art historical, liturgical, and theological perspectives on religious screens, East and West*, ed. S.E.J. Gerstel, Washington 2006, 73–89.

Bowden 2005   H. Bowden, *Classical Athens and the Delphic oracle. Divination and democracy*, Cambridge 2005.

Burford 1969   A. Burford, *The Greek temple builders at Epidauros*, Liverpool 1969.

Cain 1995   H.-U. Cain, 'Hellenistische Kultbilder. Religiöse Präsenz und museale Präsentation der Götter im Heiligtum und beim Fest', in *Stadtbild und Bürgerbild im Hellenismus*, eds. M. Wörrle & P. Zanker, München 1995, 115–130.

Carter 1983   J.C. Carter, *The sculpture of the sanctuary of Athena Polias at Priene*, London 1983.

Connelly 2007   J.B. Connelly, *Portrait of a priestess. Women and ritual in ancient Greece*, Princeton 2007.

Corbett 1970   P.E. Corbett, 'Greek temples and Greek worshippers: The literary and archaeological evidence', *BICS* 17, 1970, 149–158.

Corso 2007   A. Corso, *The art of Praxiteles* II. *The mature years*, Roma 2007.

Crampa 1972   J. Crampa, *The Greek inscriptions* (Labraunda, III.2), Lund 1972.

Damaskos 1999   D. Damaskos, *Untersuchungen zu hellenistischen Kultbildern*, Stuttgart 1999.

Dörpfeld 1884   W. Dörpfeld, 'Der Tempel von Sunion', *AM* 9, 1884, 324–337.

Dörpfeld 1935   W. Dörpfeld, *Alt-Olympia. Untersuchungen und Ausgrabungen zur Geschichte des ältesten Heiligtums von Olympia und der älteren griechischen Kunst*, Berlin 1935.

Dyggve 1960   E. Dyggve, *Le sanctuaire d'Athana Lindia et l'architecture lindienne* (Lindos, III.1), Berlin 1960.

Fiechter 1906   E.R. Fiechter, 'Beschreibung des Tempels', in *Aegina. Das Heiligtum der Aphaia*, ed. A. Furtwängler, München 1906, 21–68.

Georgoudi 2005   S. Georgoudi, 'Athanatous therapeuein. Réflexions sur les femmes au service des dieux', in *Les cadres "privés" et "publics" de la religion grecque* (Kernos, Suppl. 15), eds. V. Dasen & M. Piérart, Liège 2005, 69–82.

Gerstel 2006   S.E.J. Gerstel, 'Introduction', in *Thresholds of the sacred: architectural, art historical, liturgical, and theological perspectives on religious screens, East and West*, ed. S.E.J. Gerstel, Washington 2006, 1–5.

Gill 1991   D. Gill, *Greek cult tables*, New York 1991.

Ginouvès 1992   R. Ginouvès, *Dictionnaire méthodique de l'architecture grecque et romaine* II, Paris 1992.

Goette 2000   H.-R. Goette, ʹΟ ἀξιόλογος δῆμος Σούνιον. *Landeskundliche Studien in Südost-Attika*, Rahden 2000.

Gruben 2007   G. Gruben, *Klassische Bauforschung*, München 2007.

Hellmann 1992   M.-C. Hellmann, *Recherches sur le vocabulaire de l'architecture grecque, d'après les inscriptions de Délos*, Paris 1992.

Knell 2007   H. Knell, 'Raum und Rahmen des Götterbildes in griechischen Tempeln archaischer und klassischer Zeit', in *Mouseion. Beiträge zur antiken Plastik. Festschrift Peter C. Bol*, eds. H. Steuben, G. Lahusen & H. Kotsidu, Möhnesee 2007, 187–197.

Koenigs 1983   W. Koenigs, 'Der Athenatempel von Priene. Bericht über die 1977–82 durchgeführten Untersuchungen', *IstMitt* 33, 1983, 134–175.

Krauter 2004   S. Krauter, *Bürgerrecht und Kultteilnahme. Politische und kultische Rechte und Pflichten in griechischen Poleis, Rom und antikem Judentum*, Berlin 2004.

Kucharek 2006   A. Kucharek, 'Die Prozession des Osiris in Abydos', in *Archäologie und Ritual. Auf der Suche nach der rituellen Handlung in den Kulturen Ägyptens und Griechenlands*, eds. J. Mylonopoulos & H. Roeder, Wien 2006, 53–61.

Lapatin 2001   K.D.S. Lapatin, *Chryselephantine statuary in the ancient Mediterranean world*, Oxford 2001.

Leonardos 1896   V. Leonardos, Ἀνασκαφαὶ τοῦ ἐν Λυκοσούρᾳ ἱεροῦ τῆς Δεσποίνης', *Prakt* 1896, 93–126.

LSAM   F. Sokolowski, *Lois sacrées de l'Asie Mineure*, Paris 1955.

LSCG   F. Sokolowski, *Lois sacrées des cités grecques*, Paris 1969.

LSS   F. Sokolowski, *Lois sacrées des cités grecques. Supplément*, Paris 1962.

Lupu 2005   E. Lupu, *Greek sacred law. A collection of new documents* (Religions in the Graeco-Roman World, 152), Leiden 2005.

Mansfield 1985   J.M. Mansfield, *The robe of Athena and the Panathenaic peplos*, diss. UC Berkeley, Berkeley 1985.

Mantis 1990   A.G. Mantis, *Προβλήματα της εικονογραφίας των ιερειών και των ιερέων στην αρχαία ελληνική τέχνη*, Athens 1990.

Mattern 2002   T. Mattern, 'Kleonai 2000–2001. Vorbericht über die Arbeiten im Herakleion', *AA* 2002.2, 1–8.

Mattern 2006   T. Mattern, 'Architektur und Ritual. Architektur als funktionaler Rahmen antiker Kultpraxis', in *Archäologie und Ritual. Auf der Suche nach der rituellen Handlung in den Kulturen Ägyptens und Griechenlands*, eds. J. Mylonopoulos & H. Roeder, Wien 2006, 167–183.

Mattern 2007   T. Mattern, 'Griechische Kultbildschranken', *AM* 122, 2007 (2008), 139–159.

Metzler 1995   D. Metzler, 'Abstandsbetonung. Zur Entwicklung des Innenraumes griechischer Tempel in der Epoche der frühen Polis', *Hephaistos* 13, 1995, 57–71.

Michaelis 1871   A. Michaelis, *Der Parthenon*, Leipzig 1871.

Miles 1989   M.M. Miles, 'A reconstruction of the temple of Nemesis at Rhamnous', *Hesperia* 58, 1989, 133–249.

Neils 2001   J. Neils, *The Parthenon frieze*, Cambridge 2001.

Orlandos 1917   A.K. Orlandos, Ἴοῦ ἐν Σουνίῳ ναοῦ τοῦ Ποσειδῶνος τοῖχοι καὶ ὀροφή, *ArchEph* 1917, 213–226.

Orlandos 1971   A.K. Orlandos, Ἀνασκαφὴ Μεσσήνης, *Prakt* 1971, 157–171.

Orlandos 1977–1978   A.K. Orlandos, Ἡ ἀρχιτεκτονικὴ τοῦ Παρθενῶνος, Athens 1977–1978.

Orlandos 1986   A.K. Orlandos, Λεξικὸν ἀρχαίων ἀρχιτεκτονικῶν ὅρων, Athens 1986.

Parker 2004   R. Parker, 'What are sacred laws?', in *The law and the courts in ancient Greece*, eds. E.M. Harris & L. Rubinstein, London 2004.

Petrakos 1968   V.C. Petrakos, Ὁ Ὠρωπὸς καὶ τὸ ἱερὸν τοῦ Ἀμφιαράου, Athens 1968.

Petrakos 1991   V.C. Petrakos, *Rhamnous*, Athens 1991.

Protonotariou-Deilaki 1961/1962   E. Protonotariou-Deilaki, Ἀνασκαφὴ Φενεοῦ, *ArchDelt* 17, 1961/62, *Chron.*, 57–61.

Rapoport 1990   A. Rapoport, *The meaning of built environment. A nonverbal communication approach*, Tucson 1990².

Riethmüller 2005   J. Riethmüller, *Asklepios. Heiligtümer und Kulte* vol. I–II, Heidelberg 2005.

Rumscheid 1994   F. Rumscheid, *Untersuchungen zur kleinasiatischen Bauornamentik des Hellenismus* vol. I. *Text*, Mainz 1994.

Scott 2010   M. Scott, *Delphi and Olympia. The spatial politics of Panhellenism in the Archaic and Classical periods*, Cambridge 2010.

Stais 1900   V. Stais, Ἀνασκαφαὶ ἐν Σουνίῳ, *ArchEph* 1900, 113–150.

Steuernagel 2010   D. Steuernagel, 'Synnaos theos. Images of Roman emperors in Greek temples', in *Divine images and human imaginations in ancient Greece and Rome* (Religions in the Graeco-Roman World, 170), ed. J. Mylonopoulos, Leiden 2010, 241–255.

Stewart 1990   A. Stewart, *Greek sculpture. An exploration*, New Haven 1990.

Stevens 1955   G.P. Stevens, 'Remarks upon the colossal chryselephantine statue of Athena in the Parthenon', *Hesperia* 24, 1955, 240–276.

Themelis 1989   P. Themelis, Ἀνασκαφὴ Μεσσήνης, *Prakt* 1989, 63–122.

Travlos 1988   J. Travlos, *Bildlexikon zur Topographie des antiken Attika*, Tübingen 1988.

Völcker-Janssen 1987   W. Völcker-Janssen, 'Klassische Paradeigmata. Die Gemälde des Panainos im Zeus-Tempel von Olympia', *Boreas* 10, 1987, 11–31.

Yasin 2009   A.M. Yasin, *Saints and church spaces in the Late Antique Mediterranean. Architecture, cult, and community*, Cambridge 2009.

Zinserling 1957   G. Zinserling, 'Kultbild–Innenraum–Fassade', *Das Altertum* 3, 1957, 18–34.

Index of ancient sources

ANCIENT AUTHORS AND EPIGRAPHICAL EVIDENCE

Ancient sources

Epigraphical evidence

Index of geographical names

General index

SKRIFTER UTGIVNA AV DE SVENSKA INSTITUTEN I ATHEN OCH ROM
ACTA INSTITUTI ATHENIENSIS ATQUE INSTITUTI ROMANI REGNI SUECIAE

SERIES PRIMA IN 4°
ActaAth-4°

Vol. 45. Fasc. 2. A. Ingvarsson-Sundström, *Children lost and found. A bioarchaeological study of Middle Helladic children in Asine with a comparison to Lerna* (*Asine* III. Supplementary studies on the Swedish excavations 1922–1930). 153 pp. with 27 figs, 2 pls and 14 tables, 2008. SEK 600.

Vol. 54. *Mastos in the Berbati Valley. An intensive archaeological survey*, eds M. Lindblom & B. Wells.
189 pp. with 128 figs, 7 tables and 2 fold-outs, 2011. SEK 600.

ActaRom-4°

Vol. 26:5. Fasc 2. I. Pohl, *Excavations and finds. The Borgo. The Etruscan habitation quarter on the North-west slope. Stratigraphy and materials* (*San Giovenale. Results of excavations conducted by the Swedish Institute of Classical Studies at Rome and the Soprintendenza alle Antichità dell'Etruria Meridionale*).
262 pp., with 15 figs, and 114 pls (one fold-out), 2009. SEK 600.

Vol. 59. *Unexpected voices. The graffiti from the cryptoporticus of the Horti Sallustiani, and papers from a conference on graffiti at the Swedish Institute in Rome, 7 March 2003*, ed. O. Brandt. 188 pp. with 171 figs, of which 26 in colour, 2008. SEK 600.

Vol. 60. *Via Tiburtina. Space, movement & artefacts in the urban landscape*, eds H. Bjur & B. Santillo Frizell.
239 pp. with 140 figs in colour, 2009. SEK 600.

SERIES ALTERA IN 8°
ActaAth-8°

Vol. 20. *Encounters with Mycenaean figures and figurines. Papers presented at a seminar at the Swedish Institute at Athens, 27–29 April 2001*, ed. A.-L. Schallin in collaboration with P. Pakkanen.
192 pp. with 97 figs, 12 tables, 2009. SEK 600.

Vol. 21. *Current approaches to religion in ancient Greece. Papers presented at a symposium at the Swedish Institute at Athens, 17–19 April 2008*, eds M. Haysom & J. Wallensten.
314 pp. with 50 figs, 2011. SEK 600.

PERIODICALS

Opuscula Atheniensia. Annual of the Swedish Institute at Athens

Vol. 31–32, 2006–2007. 262 pp. with 202 figs., of which 16 in colour, 11 tables, 2008. SEK 600.

Contents: *K. Demakopoulou, N. Divari-Valakou, M. Nilsson & A.-L. Schallin*, Excavations in Midea 2005; *B. Wells, A. Penttinen, J. Hjohlman with contributions by K. Göransson, A. Karivieri & M.D. Trifirò*, The Kalaureia Excavation Project: the 2004 and 2005 seasons; *M. Johnson*, Early farming in the land of springs: settlement patterns and agriculture in Neolithic Greece; *M. Georgiadis & Ch. Gallou*, The cemeteries of the Argolid and the South-eastern Aegean during the Mycenaean period: a landscape and waterscape assessment; *H. Whittaker*, Burnt animal sacrifice in Mycenaean cult: a review of the evidence; *D.S. Reese*, Organic imports from Late Bronze Age Cyprus (with special reference to Hala Sultan Tekke); *H. Mangou, M. Petropoulos, A. Gasparatos, E. Tsakmakis & P.V. Ioannou*, The temple of Artemis (F)aontia, at Rakita, Achaia, Greece: chemical composition of metal and glass votives; *L. Sjögren*, The Eteocretans: ancient traditions and modern constructions of an ethnic identity; *J. Blid*, New research on Carian Labraunda in Late Antiquity; Book reviews; Books received.

Opuscula Romana. Annual of the Swedish Institute in Rome

Vol. 31–32, 2006–2007, 222 pp. with 181 figs., of which 11 in colour, 2008. SEK 600.

Contents: *J.R. Bengtsson*, Late Bronze Age handles from the Apennine settlement at Luni sul Mignone: some chronological observations; *I.M.B. Wiman & Y. Backe-Forsberg*, Surfacing deities in later Etruscan art and the sacellum at San Giovenale; *A. Klynne*, The Villa Selvasecca revisited; *J.W. Hayes*, Villa Selvasecca: the pottery finds; *E. Engström & R. Hedlund*, Villa Selvasecca: the coins; *D. Ingemark*, Villa Selvasecca: the glass; *A.-M. Leander Touati*, Interim report of the Swedish Pompeii Project: work 2000–2004/2005 in *Insula* V 1. Introduction; *M. Staub Gierow*, The House of the Greek Epigrams V 1,18.11–12: preliminary report 2000–2004; *A. Karivieri & R. Forsell*, The House of Caecilius Iucundus, V 1,22-27: a preliminary report; *H. Boman & M. Nilsson*, The commercial establishments V 1,13; V 1,14–16; V 1,20-21: preliminary report 2001–2004; *M. Robinson*, Evidence for garden cultivation and the use of bedding-out plants in the peristyle garden of the House of the Greek Epigrams (V 1,18i) at Pompeii; *H. Boman & M. Nilsson*, The early street and prehistoric finds in Vicolo delle Nozze d'Argento, Pompeii; *J. Lang*, Exempla römischen Wohnluxus': zu einigen löwenköpfigen Tischfüßen in der Antikengaleri Gustav III. in Stockholm; *O. Brandt*, Osservazioni sul battistero paleocristiano di Nocera Superiore; *A. Holst Blennow*, A puzzle from medieval Rome. Reconstruction of an inscription from the medieval church of S. Adriano in the Roman Forum; Book reviews. Books received.

Opuscula. Annual of the Swedish Institutes at Athens and Rome

Vol. 1, 2008, 198 pp. with 178 figs. SEK 800.

Contents: *K. Demakopoulou, N. Divari-Valakou, M. Nilsson & A.-L. Schallin with an appendix by K. Nikita*, Excavations in Midea 2006; *J.K. Papadopoulos*, The Archaic wall of Athens: reality or myth?; *A. Bonnier*, Epineia kai limenes: the relationship between harbours and cities in ancient Greek texts; *F. Vistoli*, Una nuova acquisizione di ceramica "white-on red" dall'ager Veientanus; *O. Wikander*, The religio-social message of the gold tablets from Pyrgi; *M. Gaifmann*, Visualized rituals and dedicatory inscriptions on votive offerings to the Nymphs; *G. Barbieri*, Materiali inediti da Sovana. Alcuni corredi funerari dalla necropoli di San Sebastiano; *M.G. Scapaticci*, Nuovi dati sul popolamento nella pianura di Tarquinia durante la romanizzazione. Il caso della località "Il Giglio"; *P. Roos*, A forgotten tomb at Hippokome and its neighbours; *H. Gerding*, Reconsidering the tomb of Aulus Hirtius; *O. Brandt*, I muri trasversali di Santa Croce in Gerusalemme e la sinagoga di Ostia; *C. Marcks*, Die Büste eines Afrikaners aus der Sammlung Piranesi in Stockholm; In memoriam: Paul Åström (*P.M. Fischer*); Paul Åström (*A.-L. Schallin*); Tullia Linders (*G. Nordquist*); Book reviews; Books received.

Vol. 2, 2009, 232 pp., 223 figs. SEK 800.
Contents: *K. Demakopoulou, N. Divari-Valakou, M. Nilsson & A.-L. Schallin*, Excavations in Midea 2007; *S. Voutsaki, S. Dietz & A.J. Nijboer*, Radiocarbon analysis and the history of the East Cemetery, Asine; *L. Karlsson*, Labraunda 2008. A preliminary report on the Swedish excavations with contributions by Jesper Blid and Olivier Henry; *A. Penttinen & B. Wells with contributions by Dimitra Mylona, Petra Pakkanen, Jari Pakkanen, Arja Karivieri, Anne Hooton and Emanuel Savini*, Report on the excavations in the years 2007 and 2008 southeast of the Temple of Poseidon at Kalaureia; Appendix: *T. Theodoropoulou*, The sea-shells from the excavations in Area H; *B. Wells*, A smiting-god-figurine found in the Sanctuary of Poseidon at Kalaureia; Appendix: *A. Karydas*, *In situ* analysis of a bronze figurine in the Poros Archaeological Museum; *J. Wallensten & J. Pakkanen*, A new inscribed statue base from the Sanctuary of Poseidon at Kalaureia; *J. Pakkanen*, A tale of three drums: An unfinished Archaic votive column in the Sanctuary of Poseidon at Kalaureia; *D. Grassinger*, Zersägte Köpfe. Die Transformation antiker Porträts zu monumentalen Gemmenbildern im 18. Jahrhundert; *Y. Backe-Forsberg*, The Brygos painter at San Giovenale; *T. Staub*, Decorative effects and room functions. The evidence of thresholds studied in the residential quarters of insula V I, Pompeii; In memoriam: Berit Wells (*A.-L. Schallin*); Book reviews; Books received.

Vol. 3, 2010, 225 pp. with 272 figs. SEK 800.
Contents: *K. Demakopoulou, N. Divari-Valakou, M. Lowe Fri, M. Miller, M. Nilsson & A.-L. Schallin*, Excavations in Midea 2008–2009; *J.K. Papadopoulos*, The bronze headbands of Prehistoric Lofkënd and their Aegean and Balkan connections; *L. Karlsson*, Labraunda 2009. A preliminary report on the Swedish excavations with contributions by Jesper Blid and Olivier Henry; *J. Habetzeder*, Marsyas in the garden? Small-scale sculptures referring to the Marsyas in the forum; *A.-M. Leander Touati*, *The Swedish Pompeii project*, Water, well-being and social complexity in insula V I; *M.G. Scapaticci*, Un inedito lastrone a scala da Tarquinia presso l'Antiquarum di Monte Romano; *E. Weiberg*, Pictures and people. Seals, figurines and Peloponnesian imagery; *F. Gilotta*, Chiusi e il Clusium Group. Un nuovo documento dagli scavi di Orvieto; Book reviews; Books received.

Distributor:

eddy.se ab, Box 1310, SE-621 24 Visby, Sweden

Contact information:

www.ecsi.se
Orders are placed at http://ecsi.bokorder.se